China's Economic Zones: Design, Implementation and Impact

Chief Editors: Tao Yitao & Lu Zhiguo

Paths International Ltd

社会科学文献出版社
SOCIAL SCIENCES ACADEMIC PRESS (CHINA)

China's Economic Zones: Design, Implementation and Impact

Chief Editors: Tao Yitao & Lu Zhiguo

Paths International Ltd

社会科学文献出版社
SOCIAL SCIENCES ACADEMIC PRESS (CHINA)

Preface

Special Economic Zones and the Chinese Road

This book, *China's Economic Zones: Design, Implementation and Impact,* is revised and condensed on the basis of 《中国经济特区史论》 with the main idea unchanged.

The publication of the bookmarked the 30th anniversary of China's reform and opening up to the outside world. Therefore, we are well aware of the publication's significance, as the book is indeed a chronicle of China's structural transition during its transformation. However, the praise and affirmation the book received after publication still exceeded our expectations. In 2008, the year it was published, the Publicity Department of the Communist Party of China (PDCPC) designated the book as one of "the 35 books recording China's reform and opening up" for nationwide recommended. In 2010, the National Planning Office of Philosophy and Social Science (NPOPSS) included the book in the "Translation Program for Chinese Academic Works" to be introduced worldwide. In 2011, the Guangdong Provincial Government awarded the book the first prize of "Excellent Works of Philosophy and Social Science." Meanwhile, Chinese and overseas scholars also thought highly of the book. We were grateful and proud of these achievements and, more importantly, inspired us to continue our intellectual journey.

The Chinese Road

China's structural transition centered on the establishment of the market economy embodies the difficult, as well as remarkable, development path of the Special Economic Zones (SEZs). The SEZs, typically Shen Zhen, have implemented the policy of reform and opening up, overcoming difficulties and achieving great results. The experiences of China's SEZs have pointed out the path, characteristics and the future trend of the unique "Chinese road" towards modernization. Also, their correct choice and great achievements have vigorously promoted the sinicization and modernization of Marxism.

By "Chinese road," I mean the road of SEZs that China has followed in order to realize structural transition and economic development. More precisely, it is a road followed by a large country, whose planned economy, favored by the traditional ideology, had already been established for 30 years. It is a road whose breakthrough point was to rely on the establishment of SEZs to realize structural transition. It is a road which will gradually guide China to transform from a planned economy to a comprehensive market economy and it is a road at the end of which China will truly become a country with a well-developed structure, a sound legal system, and a prosperous socialist market economy.

China's modernization is not only a topic that has captured the attention of many Chinese scholars, but is also a dream that generations of Chinese statesmen and people with lofty ideals have been fighting for all their lives. We have once faced the harsh reality that we can only "learn from the enemies so as to defeat them." We have also been embarrassed by our craze to "overtake the West." But the roads we chose to realize these goals led us to the exact opposite, and the Chinese people, dreaded by grinding poverty, had to rethink whether their choice was correct.

Some Chinese scholars have compared the modernization process that some major countries underwent in the 19th century with the modernization that some other major countries underwent in the 20th century. They point out that the capitalist modernization in the 19th century combined private property rights with market competition, which was formed naturally after several hundreds of years of development. Such a modernization process was characterized by private ownership, market orientation and gradual transformation. However, in the 20th century, the backward countries established socialism though radical political revolution and coercive industrialization, as described by Chinese scholars, "from top to bottom." These countries attempted to achieve rapid modernization by following the Soviet Union model, relying on national planning and radical reforms on the basis of pure public ownership. But after a temporary success, this model soon suffered a crisis.

Chinese scholars generally agree that it was not until the 1990s that China found the correct modernization road. Just as Deng Xiaoping planned, with the goal of reform and opening up, China would follow the socialist modernization road with Chinese characteristics through the establishment of SEZs.

The "Chinese road" should be a modernization road with Chinese characteristics. The "Chinese characteristics" indicate the national, historical and international features of the road, and are not a negation of the essence and the inherent value of modernization. Therefore, the characteristics are only embodied in the process of modernization, not in modernization itself. They represent the Chinese recognition of the universal values of human kind, not the denial of the international common practice. In fact, the Shenzhen SEZ is more than a city. Rather, it is a unique model that an entire nation chooses to march towards modernization, as recorded in the chronicle of China's reform and opening up.

Scientific Development

In a broader sense, compared with the traditional structure and development mode during the planned economy period, the establishment of SEZs was a crucial choice for China to realize scientific development. The success of the Shenzhen SEZ is indeed a process of adjusting development strategy by trial and error, optimizing the industrial mix, shifting the development mode and exploring how to change from a growth-oriented society to a welfare-oriented society with all-around development. The concept of scientific development spreads "the development concept" from the economic sphere to the social sphere. Shenzhen explains the meaning of the "Chinese road" by its own development path.

China's transition from a planned economy to a market economy is the transition of its development strategy. China no longer promotes development with the irrational aim of overtaking the west. Rather, China allows its different regions to attain different speeds of development. During the planned economy period, some people in select regions had a one-sided understanding of the correct judgment, "development is the absolute principle" and adopted a "blind concept of development" which justified development at the price of the environment and people's welfare.

To correct such misunderstandings, China developed the Scientific Outlook on Development, which undoubtedly determined that China would follow the development road of sustainable growth. The Scientific Outlook on Development is both a total negation of the ultra-leftist thinking that "man can conquer nature" and a complete correction of the blind development concept that "we should promote development at all costs." More importantly, the judgment "development is the absolute principle" was thereby thoroughly understood and was established as a correct development concept which embodied the major motive and goal of living of all humanity. The essence of the Scientific Outlook on Development is development, which is not in contradiction with the judgment "development is the absolute principle." It emphasizes the scientific and correct choice of the development mode and methods and does not have any dispute about whether to develop or not.

We firmly believe that it is only because of the adoption of the scientific development concept that China has set up SEZs, that hundreds of millions of people are pursuing universal wealth, and that China has made remarkable achievements during the past three decades.

Shenzhen SEZ

The Beginning

The growth of Shenzhen SEZ is indeed a process of adjusting development strategy by trial and error, optimizing the industrial mix, shifting the development mode and exploring how to change from a growth-oriented society to a welfare-oriented society with all-around development.

The Shenzhen SEZ started to develop by relying on "three processing and one compensation" (processing with materials, samples and parts supplied by the clients and compensation trade). Such a development mode was determined by the factor endowment at that time. In the initial stage of reform and opening up, Shenzhen was a little known fishing village with a weak planned local economy. Among factors of production, Shenzhen only had cheap labor and land with relative advantage, but it lacked capital, technology and management. But it was at the time when Hong Kong was upgrading its industries and restructuring its economy and Shenzhen was in urgent need of a manufacturing industry. Therefore, with the guidance of the opening up policy, labor intensive industries centered on processing industry timely and suitably settled in Shenzhen. Meanwhile, as Hong Kong transferred industries, capital, technology, management and modern enterprise system were all gradually transferred to the growing Shenzhen.

As countries and regions with a developed market economy upgraded their industries, Shenzhen was able to lower the cost of development in the initial stage, as well as the cost of learning from the market economies, thereby forming its characteristic as an export-oriented economy. Meanwhile, the derived demand from the "imported" processing and manufacturing industries led to the emergence and development of the tertiary industry. In 1993, net export of the three types of foreign-funded enterprises (Sino-foreign equity joint venture, Sino-foreign contractual joint venture, and wholly foreign owned enterprises) and charged fees of "three processing and one compensation" accounted for 87% of Shenzhen's foreign trade. The tertiary industry accounted for 46% of Shenzhen's GDP and absorbed 32.2% of Shenzhen's labor forces.

Adjusting the Development Mode

As Shenzhen's development accelerated, the deficiency of lacking natural resources was quickly revealed, which drew the policy-makers' attention. Lack of natural resources meant that, under the law of scarcity, people would have to pay a higher cost for the growth pattern built on consumption of natural resources. That is to say, the price of economic development would be higher due to the rising cost of wealth creation. However, as Shenzhen took the lead in establishing a market economy in China, it could not repeat the old development mode of traditional industries. It had the responsibility to explore a new development mode so as to set an example for the whole country.

Independent Innovation

Just as the Chinese old saying goes, "a man should become independent at the age of 30." Today, the 30-year-old Shenzhen SEZ has become mature and entered a period of steady growth. Shenzhen has maintained a growth rate of over 15% for many years, and its GDP has risen from 196 million yuan when it was just established as an SEZ, to 820.123 billion yuan in 2009. Its per capita GDP has increased from 606 yuan in 1979 to 93,000 yuan in 2009.

It is by following the track of high speed growth that Shenzhen has brought wealth to its hard-working people. Nevertheless, GDP is the material base, but not the ultimate goal, of social development. Without the simultaneous increase of social happiness, the growth of GDP and per capita GDP is only material growth, which lacks character.

Friedrich Nietzsche said, "nothing is rarer among philosophers than intellectual integrity." Progress of human society not only calls for diligence and passion, but also reflection and reason.

The Need for Reform of the Political Structure

The aim of reform is to liberate productive forces so that human agents, the principal actors in the economy and society, "have the substantive capabilities to lead the lives they have reason to value." As the economic value of human agents rises, China will enter a realm of new and better opportunities, to then the government should no longer dominate over the economy and society by its own will. Instead, it should respect the role of the market, as well as create a favorable institutional climate so as to provide public goods and build the social welfare system. Development is the result of reform, as well as the material condition to deepen reform. However, development cannot replace reform. Without reforms of the political structure that accommodate the economic structure, the reforms of the economic structure cannot achieve real success. As a result, on the unique "Chinese road" towards modernization and a civic society governed by the rule of law, Shenzhen, as the first city to achieve rapid development, must also shoulder the responsibilities for future development.

Determined by the immaterialness of human capital, its survival and growth call for institutional environments. Human capital creates wealth for society, so it demands institutional safeguards from the society. It not only promotes economic growth, but also the growth of its own economic value, which in turn, will further encourage the institutional environment to become more conducive for the development of human capital.

A favorable institutional environment of society not only benefits the formation and recreation of human capital, but also helps to increase the rate of return of investment in human capital. Meanwhile, the institutional changes that occur in response to the rising economic value of the human agent call for a new economic model and a new growth pattern. In this sense, the real force contributing to the change of the economic growth pattern is not subjective wishes, but the increase of the economic value of human agents that are part of the internal mechanisms of the economy and the society.

Substantive Freedom

Amartya Sen pointed out in his book *Development as Freedom* that "Development can be seen, it is argued here, as a process of expanding the real freedoms that people enjoy. Focusing on human freedoms contrasts with narrower views of development, such as identifying development with the growth of GDP, or with the rise in personal incomes, or with industrialization, or with technological advance, or with social modernization.... But freedoms depend also on other determinants, such as social and economic arrangements (for example, facilities for education and health care) as well as political and civil rights (for example, the liberty to participate in public discussion and scrutiny).... Development requires the removal of major sources of unfreedom: poverty as well as tyranny, poor economic opportunities as well as systemic social deprivation, neglect of public facilities as well as intolerance or over activity of repressive states."

Amartya Sen answers the question, "What is the aim of human society development?" with a scholar's conscience, humanity and wisdom: development of human society should be people-oriented, and the ultimate aim and evaluation criterion is freedom. Admittedly, wealth, income, technological progress and social modernization, etc are aims that people pursue, but in the final analysis, they are only the instruments used to promote human development and welfare.

There is an internal connection between the market and people's basic freedom. It will be partial if market mechanism is only praised on account of its efficiency. Market failure may become an important reason for people to repel the market. However, market failure is actually not a denial of market mechanism, but its defense —the market can only do what it can do. It is the government's responsibility to do what the market do or cannot do well.

Admittedly, the role of government power is indispensable in the process of coercive system transformation, which is characterized authorization from top to bottom. However, a dominant government will damage market mechanism, rather than correct market failures if it ever predominates over market rules. The government cannot lead economic and social development by its own will. Instead, it should respect the role of market and create a favorable institutional environment in order to provide public goods and to build the social welfare system.

China's reform started from economic reform, which was undoubtedly its best choice. But this choice quickened the exposure of China's inherent deficiencies, such as inconsistency of the social environment and lack of effective institutional support. These deficiencies constitute the institutional bottlenecks for deepening reform.

Institutions are always embedded in the institutional environment, without the support of which real institutional transition cannot be accomplished. Similarly, without the reform of the political structure that accommodates reform of the economic structure, reform of the economic structure cannot achieve real success. In essence, the existence of many social problems today is the result of lagging reform in the political structure.

For a transition society, the process of establishing a new social operation mechanism is both a process of weakening, or even removal, of the government officials' power and vested interests, and a process of the formation, cultivation and growth of a service government. In a system where only the government can take the government power away, good behavior and great vision of the government is of the utmost importance to the performance of the social institutions.

Tao Yitao
Shenzhen University
November 8, 2011

Acknowledgements

The book was completed as a collaborative effort with great team spirit. Those who participated in writing this book are all young doctors, full of intellectual enthusiasm and innovative spirit. Some joined our research group as soon as they joined the College of Economics of Shenzhen University, so they actually began to know the college and their colleagues by being a member of the group. The group was both a platform for their academic discussion and a spiritual home for people who share the same ambitions.

Chapter 1 to Chapter 6 of Section 1, "The History of Shenzhen Special Economic Zone," was written and revised by Dr. Wu Fenglan. Dr. Wu was a diligent PhD student of mine. She is a master of economic theories and has great potential for more achievements. Meanwhile, she is amiable, dedicated and good at cooperating with others. When the book's first edition was published, she passed her PhD dissertation defense with a remarkable performance. When the revision of the second edition was completed, she had developed from a PhD student to an associate professor. Such coincidences, I believe, may have special significance for her entire academic career, or even the rest of her life.

Chapter 7 of Section 1 was written and revised by Professor Lu Zhiguo. Professor Lu has good intellectual skill and research abilities. He is an excellent academic who has undertaken and completed many provincial and ministerial research projects. He is also quite reliable, precise and respectable. His made a special contribution to the book by independently taking on the time-consuming and difficult task of compiling the book and arranging it according to stylistic rules and layout. With his scrupulousness and friendliness, he painstakingly proofread the drafts, and patiently exchanged ideas with the authors so that the book was finally ready for publication.

Section 2, "The History of Zhuhai Special Economic Zone," was written and revised by Professor Yan Yanfeng. He is an associate professor and received his doctoral degree at the University of Hong Kong. With a low profile, he is quite a scholarly academic who is conscientious in both character and conduct.

Section 3, "The History of Shantou Special Economic Zone," was written and revised by Dr. Wang Xiaoling. Shantou is Dr. Wang's hometown, and this fact makes research convenient for her to carry out since she has good knowledge of the city and can speak its dialect. A gentle scholar with strong will, Dr. Wang continued her writing diligently, even during her pregnancy. After the book finished revision, her daughter was born in this beautiful SEZ as the 30th anniversary of the establishment of the SEZ slowly approached, providing the book with a special feeling of warmth.

Section 4, "The History of Xiamen Special Economic Zone," was written and revised by Dr. Zhang Jihai. Dr. Zhang received his doctoral degree at Shandong University. With a lively mind, he enjoys academic discussions and is an innovative, enterprising young academic. He is also straightforward and practical. He is an important member of our faculty who actively engages in direct classroom teaching. While writing the book, he continued to undertake a great amount of undergraduate teaching assignments in specialized basic courses, such as Western Economics. As the book finished revision, he was promoted to associated professor.

Section 5, "The History of Hainan Special Economic Zone," was written and revised by Professor Liu Weili. She is an associate professor and received her doctoral degree at Dongbei University of Finance and Economics. She is an ambitious and enthusiastic young academic with unwavering perseverance, as is seen in her academic research. She has made use of many of her holidays to visit Hainan, collecting historical data and attending various seminars on Hainan SEZ. Such efforts add to the reliability of the book's historical data. As the book completed, Professor Liu successfully began her research journey in the postdoctoral program of the Graduate School of Peking University. As the second edition finished revision, she also gained the happiness of love.

Section 6, "The History of Pudong New Area of Shanghai," was written and revised by Dr. Wang Saide. Dr. Wang received his doctoral degree at Shanghai University of Finance and Economics. Not only is he well trained in elementary economic theories, but he is also exceptional at English and mathematics, which have been instrumental, as well as a methodological help, for his research. Like Dr. Zhang, Dr. Wang is also an excellent teacher, actively engaged in classroom teaching. During his writing of the book, he has also led a happy life.

We sincerely appreciate the input of Social Sciences Academic Press's president Xie Shouguang and Zhou Li, Li Yanling, Zhao Shixiong, Lu Bei at Social Sciences Academic Press served as editors and support staff. They have done much work in arranging the preparation of the English version. We also sincerely appreciate the hard work of translators WANG Yu and MA Yating, as well as the final reader and editor, Rachel Frattarola and Eric Levy. Without their diligent work this English version would not exist. Finally, we especially appreciate the guidance and support of National Planning Office of Philosophy and Social Science in its support in the publication of this book.

We hope our work can give an objective record and reflection of the development of China's SEZs. We hope our work can provide scholars who are interested in SEZ studies with valuable historical data, and we hope that our work can leave something useful for the history of China's reform and opening up. I also believe that our work will lead to continued research and improvements in the future.

Tao Yitao
Shenzhen University
November 8, 2011

CONTENTS

1 The History of Shenzhen Special Economic Zone

"The development and experience of Shenzhen testified the correctness to the policy of establishing the economic zone in Shenzhen."

——by Deng Xiaoping

In every great historic period of China's territory, there were one or two glorious metropolises where thousands of successful businessmen gathered. Such metropolises exhibited the politics, economy, culture and society of the era, as well as the advances and hopes of the time. The remote borderland of Shenzhen established its historical position by opening the gate towards China's modernization, which occurred at the instigation of Deng Xiaoping, the great man of the time.

East of Mirs Bay, west of Zhujiang Entrance, south of New Territories and north of the city of Dongguan and Huizhou, Shenzhen was formed by the landscapes of hilly countries, terraces and plains along the Shenzhen Bay. Shenzhen was regarded, for many years, as having soil suitable for agriculture, farming, fishing and herding, while Hong Kong, the city divided from Shenzhen by a thin river, had already become the prosperous international shipping and financial center as well as the emergent manufacturing base as early as 1970s~1980s.

The policy-makers in the Central Committee had foreseen the gap between the two cities and the geographical advantage of Shenzhen. Their foresight brought great opportunity for Shenzhen's development. The Shenzhen Special Economic Zone was established in August 1980. As a trial city for reform and opening-up policy, the initial goal of Shenzhen SEZ was to explore the development of market economy, to break the shackles of the old planning economy system and to seek the new platform for exchanges between China and foreign industrial resources and other economic factors.

Shenzhen SEZ both developed in and aroused great debate. The debates were mainly focused on issues such as the adoption of socialism or capitalism, on the persistence of specialization, on the mass's concern about the city's further development, and on the selection of the leading industry. The influence the debates bore on the belief of the Chinese and the direction of its development aroused wide public concern. Seeking truth and staying pragmatic was the methodology the constructor of Shenzhen adopted. In retrospect, Shenzhen witnessed confusions in development process, gained its right ideology in debates and harvested experience in practices. In 30 years, time brought great changes to Shenzhen and finally made it a modern metropolis standing by the South China Sea.

The achievements gained by Shenzhen SEZ and the city have been witnessed by all. The industry system, based on information technology, spanned the process of industrialization and urbanization. Reforms in state-owned enterprises made excellent examples all around the nation. The capital market was gradually established, and law and regulations constantly perfected. Population in Shenzhen continuously expanded and living standards greatly improved. The expansion and renovation of the city created an early model of a regional central city with international characteristics.

The success of the establishment of Shenzhen SEZ was not only attributed to the initial trial of the opening-up policy in Shenzhen, but also the indispensable historical opportunity of the twice-international industry transfers. Under the humanistic environment of advocating absorption and imitation, as well as inheritance and innovation, Shenzhen opened and broadened its mind and rapidly integrated into the international industrial division system to complete the two most difficult stages in its development—capital accumulation and industry upgrading. Looking into the future while regarding the past, the struggling pioneer image has always been regarded as a sign of the entrepreneurial spirit of Shenzhen, and which has deeply planted into the minds of Shenzhen's new generation.

At the time when the development strategy of the country was focused on Shanghai Pudong area and the underdeveloped western regions, Shenzhen achieved a sustained development thanks to the trend of integration of Shenzhen and Hong Kong after the latter's return. Shenzhen, under the policy of constructing a comprehensive reform-pilot zone, once again seized a new opportunity to test the accuracy of its development strategy. Rising up in frustration and improving in practice, Shenzhen Special Economic Zone was on the path towards taking on a heavier historical responsibility.

1.1 On the Eve of the Establishment of Shenzhen SEZ

When Vice Premier Gu Mu visited Shenzhen, he commented on the phenomenon of Hong Kong influx. He said, "Under current situations, a lot of people are immigrating to Hong Kong, but I believe in the future the trend will definitely be reversed. Let's try our best to make it happen."

In fact, Gu was already aware that immigration location depended on the attraction of the destination. The most fundamental approach for stopping illegal emigration was to develop productivity and authentically enhance living standards. It was futile to talk about "the superiority of socialism" to people who were living in hunger.

1.1.1 Social Economic Conditions

Named from the Shenzhen River, Shenzhen was developed from a county known as Bao'an. The history before establishment of Shenzhen Special Economic Zone was actually traced back to the history of Bao'an County.

1.1.1.1 Population Distribution

After the liberation in 1949, 19 townships, with a total number of 310 administrative villages, were established in Bao'an, bringing the population to 184,700. In the movement to establish communes in 1958, 41 production management areas and six communes were set up in Bao'an County, namely the Shenzhen commune, Nantou, Songgang, Guangming, Guanlan and Buji. These were further adjusted into an administrative division in 1961, developing into 22 communes and seven agricultural (forest) fields under the jurisdiction of five major areas, namely the Nantou, Songgang, Buji, Henggang, and Kuiyong. In accordance with the first census result in 1953, the county had a residential population of 190,012, of whom 91,078 were males and 98,934 were females. By the second census in 1964, the county's population increased to 262,228, of whom 121,262 were males and 140,966 were female were. In 1979, Bao'an developed into a city with the permanent population of 314.1 thousand, of which 142.6 thousand were men, and 170 thousand women, and a household population of 312.6 thousand and 1.5 thousand temporary residents.

During the 30 years before the establishment of the SAR, population slowly grew at an average annual growth rate of 2.34%. Affected by immigration to Hong Kong, the absolute population in Bao'an County experienced declines in 1961 and 1979. In the construction of the total population, agricultural population accounted for the majority. In 1953, agricultural population made up 94.5% of the total and remained around 91.72% in 1979. Therefore, before the establishment of the SAR, the Bao'an area remained a typical agricultural society.

1.1.1.2 Economy Development

From the 1950s to 1970s, Bao'an County made several changes in its administrative role. In 1949, Bao'an was under the jurisdiction of Dongjiang Commission, in 1952 under the Yuezhong Administration Commission, and later under the jurisdiction of the Huiyang area and Foshan area, and under the jurisdiction of Huiyang from 1963 to 1979. Economic development relied primarily on agriculture. For 30 years, its self-sustained and semi-self-sustaining economy experienced transformation, restructure, consolidation and disintegration after the liberation of the nation.

In the early 1950s, completing the socialist transformation in agricultural and commercial industries, the Bao'an County rapidly resumed recovery and development. By 1955, agricultural output reached 30.08 million RMB, area of grain to 775,666 acres with total output of 77038.15 kg (average production of 206.5 kg per mu), a 24.6% increase from 1952. Total output of rice reached 71460.4 kg with average production of 109.5 kg per mu. The county planted 8,550 acres of lychee with the annual production of 3250 kg. Since 1967, Bao'an County turned over 50 million kg of grain to the state each year with over 200 kg per capita, higher than any other county in the Pearl River Delta area. By that time, it was becoming an important grain production base in eastern Guangdong. Main crops produced included rice, peanut, soybean, vegetables, oyster, and lychee, among others. In 1979, productions of major agricultural products were as follows: 127,559 tons of rice, 4,285 tons of potatoes, 6,877 tons of peanuts, 8,639 tons of vegetables, 2,401 tons of fruit, 25,633 cattle, and 116,900 pigs. Major seafood production: 6,068 tons of marine products and 971 tons of fresh water products.

Before the establishment of the SEZ, Bao'an County had a very fragile industrial basis. According to "Bao'an County Document," recorded in 1978, there were five industrial enterprises at provincial level, one at municipal level, 266 owned by the county, 60 by town, 185 by village, among which 242 belonged to the light industry, 30 to heavy industry, 27 owned by the whole people, and 245 of collective ownership. All of them were close-end backward factories in towns clattered with outdated equipment and technology. The majority were machinery plants, factories producing lime and brick, and other small factories producing nothing more than chemical fertilizers, small farm tools and other primary products essential to local agriculture. In 1979, major industrial products were at a mere 6.09 million kwh electricity generation and 21,500 tons of cement.

In 1979, GDP of Bao'an was only 19,638 RMB. Primary industry output value was 72.73 million yuan, secondary industry's output value was 40.17 million yuan, tertiary industry's output value was 83.48 million yuan, accounting for 37.04%, 20.46% and 42.51% of GDP. It was quite obvious that due to the geographical advantage of Bao'an to Hong Kong, the development of commercial trade became faster than the first and second industries, which differed greatly from the economic structure of Guangdong over the same period.

In 1979, the agricultural land in the county covered 532,100 mu with agricultural output value of 131.06 million RMB, of which planting industry took up 64.94 million yuan, accounting for 49.6%, forestry industry took up 850,000 yuan, accounting for 0.6%, livestock industry took up 15.98 million yuan, accounting for 12.2%, sideline industry took up 44.96 million yuan, accounting for 34.3%, and fishing industry took up 4.33 million yuan, accounting for 3.3%. Industrial output value came to 71.28 million yuan, of which light industry took up 52.40 million yuan, accounting for 73.51%, and heavy industry took up 8.21 million yuan, accounting for 26.49%. Retail sales reached 112.59 million RMB. Total imports and exports revenue reached 16.76 million USD. Contracted foreign capital utilization was 29.84 million USD. Local budget revenue reached 17.21 million RMB.

Judging from slow economic development, Bao'an area had a weak industrial and agricultural foundation. Total agricultural output value in 1978 increased by only 2.5 times than in 1950 and industrial output value by only 5.2 times than in 1952. By contrast, the national industrial output value at the same time increased by 32 times[1] due to the fact that the state did not put aside money for the construction of Bao'an, which played the role as a border city only a river width away from the capitalist world. From 1950 to 1955, total investment in the Bao'an County was 385,300 yuan, with 1.9843 million yuan of various loans. While in 1979, total capital investment reached 49.88 million yuan, of which 9.76 million yuan were invested in agriculture, forestry, animal husbandry and fishery, and 8.24 million yuan in manufacturing. In the three decades before the establishment of the SEZ, Bao'an County received little investment from the state, so its economic development was dependent on the natural growth of the industry. Its prior function as border defense, rather than economic development, led to long-term underdevelopment and poverty.

1.1.1.3 National Income

By the end of 1979, the amount of laborers in Bao'an County was 139,500, of which 33,700 worked for state-owned enterprises, 6,500 for collective enterprises, 4,100 self-employed in urban areas and 95,200 working in rural areas. Local fiscal revenue was 53 yuan per capita local and annual income of a rural residence was 152 yuan with 303 kg of rations. The average annual wage of an urban worker was 769 yuan, an average monthly wage at 64 yuan. The amount of urban and rural residents' savings amounted to 37.13 million yuan. Urban and rural incomes remained at a very low level, and at the time the

1 Edited by Shenzhen Museum: ***Shenzhen SEZ History***, People's Press, 1999, P16

average annual income of urban residents was 5 times more than rural residents, leading to severe inequality in income distribution. Throughout the 1970s, with revenue and expenditure under a unified financial system, the single source of income for urban residents depended on their wage, while rural residents were dependent on the work hours distributed by production teams. People were living in poverty, dependent on national supply to maintain production and livelihood.

1.1.1.4 Retrospect on Shenzhen

In 1953, the county government moved from the south into the town of Shenzhen, making it the political, economic, cultural and educational center of Bao'an County.

The town of Shenzhen is located on one side of the valley basin within Shenzhen Bay, lying north, with the Buji River and Nigang river running through towards the south into the Shenzhen River and finally into the Shenzhen Bay. In the middle of the Ming Dynasty, the Lohu area was located in the vicinity of the villages settled by several clans, such as villages of Hongkan (now Caiwuwei), Luohu, Getang (now Shuibei Village), Hubei, Xiangxi, Huangbeiling, Nantang and other villages. Clan members started fair trades, known as "Shenzhen Fair," on vacancies among different villages. These "fairs" further developed into "towns." By the end of the Ming Dynasty and beginning of the Qing Dynasty, Shenzhen Town had already developed into a well-known business city. In accordance with the descriptions in "Bao'an County Document," "Since the Opium War, Shenzhen became a Chinese border town adjacent to Hong Kong and Kowloon, the British leased land."

In 1979, the area of the old town was less than three square kilometers, while the area of buildings in the entire city was only 10 million square meters. With the urban population of 23,000, the city contained roads of about eight km and the highest building was only five stories. City businesses were operated in a mess. The old town was laid-out in a village scale: there were fields from the south part of the town to the end of Luohu bridge; waste hillocks and wasteland from the east part of the town ran to the Shenzhen Reservoir and from the north part of the town to Buji; farmland or wasteland from the west part of the town ran to Futian area; and waste hillocks were located near the Shangbu and Bagualing area.

Bao'an County did not receive outstanding achievements in economic development in the first three decades after liberation. Under the administrative jurisdiction of Huiyang, before the establishment of the SEZ, Bao'an had no other choice but the self-sufficient agricultural production pattern to maintain the survival of the local urban and rural residents. Prior to the institutional reform in separation of land ownership and managerial right, most of the population was affixed to the area where they were born due to the household registration and food supply system. During this period, economy grew slowly in urban and rural areas. People lived in poverty. With the core issue of land, the collapse of the planned economic system in Bao'an County, realized in exploration of market economy under the impetus of political power, adopted a unique economic organizing form (special economic zone instead of political), thus pushing forward the comprehensive reform of China.

1.1.2 Shenzhen on the Eve of Opening-up

Shenzhen was liberated on October 19, 1949. Because of the tense international relationship, Shenzhen started to seal its borders in 1951, which led to illegal emigration that spread constantly over and around the Shenzhen area. A succession of climaxes came in 1957, 1962, 1972 and 1978. 119,274 people planned to emigrate and 60,157 of them managed to do so.[2] During the following 30 years after 1949, illegal emigration was the main problem of this town.

On November 1, 1977, Deng Xiaoping inspected Guangzhou. At that time, Shenzhen, a small border town with less than 30,000 people, broke into Deng's view. Illegal immigration to Hong Kong from Shenzhen was an important part of the Guangzhou Provincial Government's report to the Central Committee. However, Deng Xiaoping keenly pointed out that the problem was rooted in the policy of China. Wu Nansheng, the party secretary of the Guangdong province, went through practical research after Deng's resignation. The phenomenon Guangdong discovered was quite provoking. There was one impoverished Luofang village in Shenzhen with the revenue per capita of 134 RMB and the other affluent Luofang village in the New Territory with the revenue per capita of 13,000 RMB on the opposite bank of Shenzhen. Ironically, there was no such village in the New Territory. All the residents there were immigrated from the impoverished Luofang village in Shenzhen. In early 1979, Yuan Geng, who was of Bao'an County descent, visited Shenzhen for the first time with plans to construct a new Shekou industrial zone. However, he drove back only to find an unpleasant sight of his hometown after the separation of two to three decades. On the street of Shenzhen, there were only one or two old buildings and rows of dilapidated, scattered tile-roofed houses. Yuan went back to his hometown, Dapeng Island, but failed to see any town fellow. The population of 20,000 villagers at the early

2 Edited by Huang Yeping: ***China Strategy Document(Part One)***, Guangming Daily Press, P180

period of the Liberation declined to 5,000 by the late 1970's. The majority immigrated to Hong Kong, while others were stranded in the UK, the U.S. and Holland.

In the April 1979, Shenzhen Municipal Committee issued "Notification on Stopping Illegal Immigration and Rectifying the Social Order." However, with inadequate result of the "Notification," the wave of illegal immigration still could not be contained. On May 14, 1979, Gu Mu, the Vice-Premier, visited Shenzhen. He commented on the phenomenon of Hong Kong influx, saying, "Under the current situation, a lot of people are immigrating to Hong Kong, but I believe in the future the trend will definitely be reversed. Let's try our best to make it happen."

In fact, Gu Mu was already aware that where to immigrate depended on the attraction of the destination. The most fundamental approach for stopping illegal emigration was to develop the productivity and genuinely enhance living standards. In the late 1970s, China was completely stricken by poverty. It further aroused a unique social phenomenon: "illegal emigration" from Shenzhen, known as a "remote frontier town." It cannot be judged simply as a lack of awareness of the people or the allurement from the enemies. The root cause of "illegal emigration" was poverty which had to be resolved before "illegal emigration" could be eradicated.

In the endless fight against "illegal emigration" and poverty, the eve of Reform and Opening-up quietly fell on Shenzhen.

1.2 Start-up Period of Shenzhen Special Economic Zone

Comrade Deng Xiaoping was closely watching the meeting of the Central Government. He already reached his own assumption of the characteristics of the area, which would be separated in Guangdong, so when it came to naming the region, he said, "We can call it Special Economic Zone. The Shan-Gan-Ning area is one aspect of the special economic zone." When Xi Zhongxun wanted to supply funds from Central Government, Comrade Xiaoping said, "The Central Government does not have the money. Rely on your own, and fight through the difficulties like a true champion."

1.2.1 The Establishment of Shenzhen Special Economic Zone

The establishment of Shenzhen Special Economic Zone as an opening-up window was a comprehensive test of the overall reform of Chinese economic construction model. After 30 years of being blocked and embargoed on the international stage, China was now trying out this model.

1.2.1.1 Background

1.2.1.1.1 International Background

1.2.1.1.1.1 Worldwide Division Structure after the 1970s

International division is the division of labor and specialization of production between countries in the international production system. A country's domestic division of economic industries goes beyond national boundaries, and forms the production supply chain in the international production market. This division system consists of the vertical division of labor, the mixed division and horizontal international division of labor.

Since the 18th century through the first Industrial Revolution, marked by the invention of steam engine and the second industrial revolution marked by the invention and use of electricity and electric motors, the western capitalist countries laid the basis for the international division system of the colonial era. It formed the international vertical division of labor production of industrial products from the advanced industrial countries and the supply of raw materials from underdeveloped agricultural countries. It strengthened along with the output of the international monopoly capital and imperialistic nations' territory and economy division. After World War II, the western colonial system collapsed. Through 50 years' economic recovery after the war, the international division structure underwent a profound change with the introduction of the computer, symbolizing the arrival of the third industrial revolution. Vertical division was still the focus, but it gradually transferred to horizontal division and mixed division. According to the forms of industrial organization, the horizontal division can be divided into intra-industry division and production division. Intra-industry division is a part of industry based on the decomposition of the industrial chain, placing different industrial elements at different countries and regions. In general, the developed countries engaged in high-value industries, controlling of the supply of core technology and key raw materials in the upstream link and business management skills, technical standards, the formulation of business rules, etc, grasping the value realization of industrial chain. Developing countries engaged in industrial chain processing, manufacturing and assembling to achieve functions of value production in the industry chain. Production division is the international production division based on production processes. In general, developed countries usually own high technical and high value added processing and the low added production processing usually is transferred to developing countries, taking advantage of cheaper human labor cost to complete manufacturing. In this process, multinational companies act as both the destroyer of the old international division structure and the builder of the new structure.

Since the 1970s, the hegemonic role of the United States, established by Bretton Woods, has been under major dispute. For the betterment of China, the U.S. forced the yen to appreciate, despite their own national troubles. However, the U.S. transferred the excess domestic production capacity through outputting products, technologies and capital, to stimulate domestic economic needs. Two decades after the war, the U.S. moved traditional heavy industries, including chemical fertilizer, textile, machinery and shipbuilding, to Japan and West Germany, by large-scale economic and military support. The United States itself forced the development of high extra value industries, like semiconductor industry, computer and communications and biomedical industry. The countries such as Japan and West Germany completed their industrialization process rapidly with tremendous monetary support.

Western countries, such as Japan, issued a series of policies designed to promote industrial upgrading in order to promote the industrial structure towards high-class development after completion of industrialization. They made many sectors, like large-scale integrated circuits, machinery, fine chemicals, household appliances, automobile manufacturing, aerospace aviation, optoelectronics and new materials, as pillar industries of the national economy for future nurturing. Labor-intensive industries, such as textile, leather and food manufacturing, were moved to southeastern Asia. Southeastern Asian countries and regions gradually supported and developed synthetic chemical, petro chemical, automobile, steel, machinery, household appliances and toys industries in the process of adopting international industries conversion, thus realizing the industry conversion from import substitution to export processing. Singapore, South Korea, Taiwan and Hong Kong, known as Asia's Four Little Dragons, became the newly emerging industrialized countries. The international division structure made East Asia and Southeast Asia join in a more advanced manufacturing industry chain due to the boom of Asia's Four Little Dragons.

In the late 1970s, the horizontal international division continued to deepen. Due to the increasing human capital and land cost, the labor-intensive industries in Southeast Asia suffered a decline in international competitiveness. They needed to find a cheaper area to relocate parts of industries or production processing, making room for the industrial structure adjustment and upgrading, in order to realize the re-configuration of the various industrial elements, including capital, labor, land and entrepreneurship. The international industrial division structure was ripe with new opportunities for change.

Concerning the historical starting point of China's opening-up, some scholars, later on, held on to the belief that the basic long term motivation for economic openness lied in the objective requirements of international division, open and globalized world economy. It is not a question of if a country is more or less developed.

1.2.1.1.1.2 Peace and Development Become Theme of the Times

In the late 1970s, eastern and western countries had more mutual communications and learning opportunities. On September 16, 1978, Deng Xiaoping, while listening to the work report from Jilin Provincial Party Committee of CPC, he said, "We are now to achieve the four modernizations. We have a lot of conditions now, which were not possible when Comrade Mao Zedong was still alive. Provided the Central Government does not dwell on problems and makes decisions under the current conditions, numerous problems can be avoided. For instance, when Mao was alive, we wanted to expand economic and technical exchanges between China and foreign countries, including the development of economic and trade relationships with some capitalist countries, and even the introduction of foreign investment, joint ventures, etc. But back then, we did not have the rights and others block us. Later on, The Gang of Four (Yao Wenyuan, Jiang Qing, Zhang Chunquiao, and Wang Hongwen) pasted the label of 'worship things foreign and fawn on foreign countries' and 'traitorous' on everything, which make us cut off from the world. Comrade Mao Zedong's strategic thinking about the three worlds opened the way for us. We consistently oppose imperialism, hegemony, colonialism and racism, maintain world peace and on the basis of the five principles of peaceful coexistence, actively develop international relations and boost economic and cultural exchanges with other countries. Through several years' efforts, today's international conditions are much better than before, which enables us to absorb the internationally advanced technology and management experience besides their capital." He also pointed out, "The world changes every day. New things and new problems keep popping up. Therefore, it is not feasible for us to close the national door, stay idle and lag behind." Deng had an acute knowledge of the international situation from late 1970s to early 1980s and held the belief that the superpower was in hegemonic expansion. But the peaceful forces were also growing in the world. He noted with great insight, "For the time being, the question is to race against time. What is there should be done at once. Large scale war is not going to happen. Do not be afraid, for there is no problem concerning the risk." By the mid-1980s, he briefly pointed out that "for this world the real big problem, the global strategic issues, is the peace issue, and another is economic or development issue." He made it clear that the present theme had been transferred to "peace and development" from "war and revolution."

"Peace and development" becoming the theme of the times marks a fundamental change toward understanding the Chinese Communist Party's international affairs. It is also the fundamental theory for the Chinese government to make domestic and foreign policies, seize the opportunity and accelerate the development.

1.2.1.1.2 Domestic Background

In the late 1970s, China was finally free from the 10 years of chaos known as the Cultural Revolution. When the Chinese settled down, they were surprised to find themselves far lagging behind the world. The Chinese had to begin reflecting on a new direction for China. The traditional system was clearly a dead end. The highly centralized planned economic system didn't bring about the "orderly development of the national economy." The form of ownership in "Big Commune" didn't link China to communism. Instead, it caused the loss of a positive initiative for producers. The egalitarian distribution didn't realize common wealth, but only let "common poverty" become more common. "Engaging in construction behind closed doors" appeared to protect China from "imperialism" exploitation, but China failed to catch up with the world's economic and technological development.

The third plenary session of the 11th Party Central Committee put a decisive end to the "take the class struggle as outline" slogan and shifted the work focus to economic construction. But at the beginning of reform process, people didn't have rational and profound understanding of the old system, therefore leading to the possibility of a flawed, new system model of the future. Any reform measure is an attempt, and the reforming process is like "crossing the river by feeling the stones." The reform that China carried out, as Deng Xiaoping said, "Marx didn't say before. Our predecessors have not tried yet and neither have the other socialist countries, so there is no real experience to learn from."

After third plenary session of the 11th Party Central Committee, the reform and opening up had finally become an irreversible trend. But the opening up was done with great caution. It was not to be done overnight. It was because, firstly, the "left" leaning trend of thought will not end with the Cultural Revolution and quit the stage of history easily. At the time, if a comprehensive and radical reform was performed, it was bound to encounter great obstacles and cause social unrest. Secondly, China has a vast territory, with geography, history and current conditions varying tremendously, so the reform and opening up at the same time could not be spread out across the country. Also, the reform and opening up was more sensitive than "revitalizing the domestic economy" reform. Moreover, China lacked the opening up experience and was not familiar with the rules of the international market. No one could predict what was waiting for China once the doors opened. In such a dilemma, the establishment of "special economic zone" as a breakthrough in reform and development process was, after all, a remarkable feat.

1.2.1.2 Birth of Shenzhen Special Economic Zone

1.2.1.2.1 Delegation Visit in Western and Hong Kong and Macao

In 1978, China's top leaders set off a wave of international tours. During this year, more than 13 Vice-Prime Ministers and the Vice-Chairmen successively visited 50 countries at least 20 times. Among these visits, Deng Xiaoping made four visits to eight countries alone, such as Japan, the United States, France, etc.[3] In April 1978, National Foreign Trade Ministry and the former National Development and Reform Commission organized a study group of economy and trade to inspect Hong Kong and Macao. In May, Vice Premier Gu Mu personally led a large mission to study foreign economy. They visited West Germany, Britain, France, Switzerland, Denmark, and Belgium, etc. The study group of economy and trade in Hong Kong and Macao submitted a "Report on Hong Kong and Macao's Economy and Trade," in which they expressed a strong intention to reform and open up. The report proposed a delimitation of Bao'an and Zhuhai, which were closed to Hong Kong and Macao as export bases, and strive to build them into an exterior production and processing base and a resort to attract Hong Kong's and Macao's guests in a projected three or five years.

From April 5 to 28, 1979, the Central Work Conference was held in Beijing. The first secretaries and all in charge of the economic work of each province, municipality and autonomous region, together with central party and political primary leaders were also supposed to attend the meeting. At the meeting, Xi Zhongxun, the first secretary of Guangdong Provincial Party Committee, clearly stated the "wish of more rights from the Central Government" and demanded to designate some areas for separate management in Shenzhen, Zhuhai and Shantou as the foreign investment places for the overseas Chinese, Hong Kong and Macao compatriots and foreign merchants in order to organize production in accordance with international market needs. This area was preliminarily entitled as "Trade Cooperation Zone." Comrade Deng Xiaoping had been closely watching the meeting of the Central Government. He had already gained his own consideration of the characteristics of the areas, which would be separated in Guangdong, so when it came to

---

3 Dong Bin, Gao Xiaolin: ***Breakthrough–Relevation of China's Special Economic Zones***, Wuhan University Press, p. 17.

naming this region, he said, "We can call it Special Economic Zone, and Shan-Gan-Ning area is one aspect of the Special Economic Zone."

1.2.1.2.2 The Birth of "Shekou Model"

Founded in 1872 by Li Hongzhang, China Merchants (Hong Kong) was a branch of China's first and largest shipping company, which later became a business establishment in Hong Kong under new China's Ministry of Communications as the connection to the outside world. As soon as the New Year's Day of 1979 passed, Yuan Geng, Vice Chairman of the Board of Directors of China Merchants (Hong Kong) of the Ministry of Communications, proposed to build docks and ports at Shekou, close to Hong Kong, in order to develop the trade between Hong Kong and China Merchants.

In the beginning, Yuan Geng exchanged views with the Guangdong Provincial Committee. At the time, Guangdong was in economic trouble. Despite Guangdong being at the same level with Jiangsu and Zhejiang and other provinces in the 1950s, their economy at the time fell far behind. Yuan Geng's proposal just came in time for a province that was eager to find a way out. The proposal was soon handed to the State Council by Guangdong Provincial Committee, along with the Ministry of Communications. Consequently, Hong Kong Merchants Shekou Industrial Zone was established in early 1979, under the direct instructions from Li Xiannian, sooner than Shenzhen Special Economic Zone. In the summer of 1979, the large-scale development of Shekou was in full swing, directed by China Merchants (Hong Kong).

The main contents of Shekou model are: streamlining the organization of industrial areas; eliminating duplication; nominating staff based on the job requirements; strictly applying responsibility to a system of managers; letting enterprises decide the jobs and fix costs and profits; no level among cadres and only the original position of recruits can be filed; only job requirements and recruits' ability are to be considered for re-employment; abolishing the life-long tenure of cadres and the stay of cadres of all levels must be decided once a year by the mass with their votes of confidence. If votes are not enough, the correspondent person will be eliminated, allowing the rational flow of talents and staff. Workers can be fired and can also resign. In addition, the reforms of wage and housing system and other aspects successfully advanced.

1.2.1.2.3 The Establishment of Shenzhen

In late January 1979, in order to strengthen the leadership of the production and construction in Bao'an district and establish export bases, the Guangdong Provincial

Committee decided to change Bao'an County into Shenzhen City, which was founded the City Committee, with dual leadership of the Guangdong Province and Huiyang region. Zhang Xunfu was appointed as the party secretary while Fang Bao was deputy secretary. The State Council required that Shenzhen be built into a relatively high level exporting base for both industrial and agricultural commodities in three to five years, a resort to attract tourists from Hong Kong and Macao and to act as a new border city. In February 1979, the State Council issued No.38 Document which stated a clearly defined goal for the next several years. Their goal was to develop Shenzhen into a high-level export base for industrial and agricultural commodities, to convert Shenzhen into an attractive tourist area of Hong Kong and Macao tourists, and meanwhile becoming a new border city. In March 1979, Central Government and Guangdong Provincial Committee decided to change Bao'an County into Shenzhen City, under dual leadership of Guangdong Provincial Committee and Huiyang region. In November, the Guangdong Provincial Committee decided to change Shenzhen into a provincial municipality be of the same level as region, directly under the provincial leadership.

1.2.1.2.4 Birth of Special Economic Zone

In April 1978, during the Central Work Conference, after listening to the Report of Responsible Comrades from Guangdong Province, Comrade Deng Xiaoping advised "to build a special zone." Meanwhile, Fujian Province also made the request to found "special zones." After this meeting, Vice Premier Gu Mu soon formed a work team with Duan Yun, Gan Ziyu, Deputy Director of State Planning Commission and Li Hao, Deputy General Secretary of the State Import and Export Commission, among others. They traveled to Guangdong and Fujian, launching investigations and studies. The work team then submitted a report to the Central Government. The Central Party Committee and the State Council studied this report and later issued the No.50 Document on July 15, 1979, which states the "CPC and State Council approve two reports about special policies implementation and flexible measures on foreign economic activities from Guangdong and Fujian provincial committee." Central Government decided to delimit parts in Shenzhen, Zhuhai, Shantou of Guangdong and Xiamen of Fujian as an "export zone" on a trial basis to attract foreign investment. The document also stressed that Shenzhen be given priority. The Central Government also decided to assign this work to Vice Premier Gu Mu to lead in person.

On December 11, 1979, the State Council held its first thematic briefing meeting for special zone preparation, Western Beijing meeting, at which the concept of "special economic zones" was first proposed. In May 1980, the Central Government and State Council issued No.41 Document, clearly identifying the need to build the special zone in an active and steady way. The name of "special export zone" was also officially changed to "special economic zone." Since then, the formal nature of Shenzhen Special Economic Zone has been the "special economic zone." Meanwhile, in order to strengthen the leadership of Shenzhen, Guangdong Provincial Committee decided to appoint comrade Wu Nansheng as the first Secretary of Shenzhen Municipal Committee. On August 26, the "Shenzhen Special Economic Zone Ordinance," which had been modified 13 times, came into public. Full autonomy was also bestowed upon the special economic zone, finally releasing them from the old system. The release of "regulations" symbolized the birth of "Shenzhen Special Economic Zone." Accordingly, August 26 has since become the birthday of Shenzhen Special Economic Zone.

1.2.2 Positioning of Shenzhen Special Economic Zone

In the year of 1547, Leghorn of Italy was declared to be a free port, and also recognized as the world's first Special Economic Zone. According to statistics, there are more than 1,000 Special Economic Zones in the world today. The natures and functions of the Special Economic Zones vary, but in general they can be divided into four categories: free port, free trade zones, export processing zones and science and technology industrial parks. Similarities also include a reduction of tariff and income tax, a preferential approach to attract foreign investment to develop the local economy. However, China's Special Economic Zones are far beyond the economic zones overseas in terms of both area and function. When speaking specifically of Shenzhen Special Economic Zone, how well does she play her functions?

1.2.2.1 Experimental Area for Economy Transformation

Comrade Deng Xiaoping once said, "The reform of economic system is our biggest test."[4] As the most important contribution of the "pacesetter," Shenzhen lay in the innovation of economic system. Early in May 1980, still in the preliminary phase, "Meeting Notes of Guangdong and Fujian" forwarded by the Central Committee of CPC had argued, "As to the management of Special Economic Zones, if it adhered to the four cardinal principles and there were no harm to the sovereignty, systems and policies which

4 ***Selected Works of Deng Xiaoping***, (the third volume), the People's Literature Publishing House, October 1993 1st edition, p. 130

are different from the mainland can be taken. It is the Market Regulation that is mainly implemented in Special Zones." That was 12 years before the formal establishment of "socialist market economy" as the goal of economic reform at 14th CPC National Congress. At that time, many people considered the market economy belonged to capitalism, and planned economy to socialism. But Shenzhen proved, by practice, that their country market regulation was not only feasible, but more efficient and beneficial for Shenzhen. In 1990, the 14th National Congress of CPC finally acknowledged that the objective of China's economic reform was to establish a socialist market economy. After 12 years of experimentation, this "market regulation" would be applied to the whole country.

"Market regulation" in Special Zones is undoubtedly the prelude of a national implementation of "market economy". Years of exploration in Shenzhen finally reveal a new world for the country's reform and opening up. In this "big test" for the establishment of a "socialist market economy system", Shenzhen took the lead as a model, and demonstrated a "vanguard" style.

1.2.2.2 Window of Opening Up

"Window function" of economic zones in China is a distinctive feature that differs from "free port," "Free Trade Zone", "export processing zones" and "Science and Technology Industrial Park" in foreign countries. For an open economic system, it is not necessary to open the "window" since it was not closed at all. Therefore, the main function of various foreign economic zones is to export in order to obtain foreign currency or to attract foreign investment. However, China has been closed to the outside since long before. The opening up process should be taken in small steps. Before China truly opened to the world, there were only a few "windows" like Shenzhen, Zhuhai, Shantou and Xiamen, which deepened the depth of reform and opening up. The opening of special zones to 14 coastal cities, then to the coastal area, and later to the opening along the river, along the border, and opening of the provincial capital city, formed a comprehensive, multi-level pattern of opening structure in just a dozen years. During this process, these firstly opening economic zones naturally acted as "windows."

Comrade Deng Xiaoping once stated, "Special zones are windows. They are windows of technology, of management, of knowledge, and windows of opening up. Special zones can bring in technology, give us access to knowledge and help us learn management, which is also knowledge. Special zones becoming an open base will not only benefit us in economic terms and training talents, but it will also enhance our influence."[5] Comrade Deng Xiaoping regarded the foreign "management" experience as a kind of knowledge, which can be learned, and is already a major breakthrough of the traditional theory. It is the "knowledge window" that closely follows "technology window" and "management window." Comrade Deng Xiaoping did not limit the scope of "knowledge," which objectively broadens the opening up space, so the special zones can experiment and learn from foreign countries about their policies and measures that can promote the development of productive forces.

1.2.2.3 Demonstration Base and Source of Influence

It cannot be denied that the Special Economic Zones play a huge role in promoting the development of the whole country, especially Shenzhen, whose function as a model, center of influence and leader for the inner land cannot be underestimated. In the 1980s, Shenzhen enhanced cooperation with 27 central ministries, 28 provinces and cities and autonomous regions, building 3,900 inland-associated enterprises in various forms. Those enterprises cannot only be viewed as funding from the inner land, because they are more like outposts from the inner land at the Shenzhen "open window". Through these enterprises, inner land can understand the operation of enterprises in economic zones, and feel the pulse of the international market. These companies in this free atmosphere have undertaken courageous exploration and are the first to break the oppression of a rigid inner land system. They boldly reform the employment system, wage system, enterprise management system, and initially establish a set of operation mechanism in line with the market economy and the international practice. These enterprises have more autonomy in operation, which weakens the reliance on inner land government. They have made important contributions for the economic prosperity in special zones, but the more influential significance is that these enterprises are bridges and links of the economic reform radiation from Shenzhen to inner land. Through this process they have accumulated the detailed first-hand information for the inner land economy reform. Taking Shenzhen as a "base", new ideas and thoughts adapted to market economy are spreading to the nation.

1.2.2.4 Promoting Hong Kong and Macao's Prosperity and Stability

Shenzhen, with the unique advantage of being adjacent to Hong Kong, plays more unparalleled roles than other "windows." Even in the era of being closed, people from

5 ***Selected Works of Deng Xiaoping***, (the third volume), the People's Literature Publishing House, October 1993 1st edition, p. 52.

Shenzhen can see Hong Kong's skyscrapers and perceive the exciting outside world. Through Shenzhen, our understanding of Hong Kong can be specific and in-depth. Hong Kong, as an important international financial center, holds a great deal of information on the world economy. It's another window through which we observe the world. With the deepening of opening up, people's understanding of Hong Kong and the abroad also constantly deepens. The outside world is far more than the buildings and the traffic one can see across the Shenzhen River. From this window, we have a better understanding of flows and the operation of international capital, the development of world science and technology, rules and skills of international trade and the management of multinational companies.

Four major functions of China's special economic zones have been brought into fuller play in Shenzhen. Indeed, people have had high hopes for Shenzhen Special Economic Zone since it was newly established. However, the actual achievements are far beyond initial expectations. Shenzhen gives full play to all the functions as a Special Economic Zone. No wonder Shenzhen has the title of "reform and opening up vanguard."

1.2.3 The Early Development Planning of Shenzhen Special Economic Zone

Right from the establishment to mid-1980s, Shenzhen developed three master plans to guide its development. Compared with the first planning, the second and third had greater improvements in many aspects, like city function localization, the scope of district planning, the configuration of municipal infrastructure system, city forestation, the construction of airport and harbor and so on.

1.2.3.1 The First City Plan——"Master Plan of Shenzhen Urban Construction"

In March 1979, the Central Government and Guangdong Provincial Committee decided to change the Bao'an County into Shenzhen, meanwhile forming the Shenzhen Municipal Committee. In July of the same year, the central authorities issued a document affirming the trial of "export zone." According to the central decision, Shenzhen would be built into a small city for work and home with an area of 10 square kilometers and a population of 100,000 people. For this reason, the Infrastructure Construction Committee was established to be responsible for urban construction and urban planning. Li Xinting was appointed as director of this committee.

In May 1980, the CPC Shenzhen Municipal Committee set up Shenzhen City Construction Committee, with Municipal Party Secretary Zhang Xunfu as the director and the Mayor of Shenzhen, Jia Huawei, as the deputy director. In the middle of May,

Guangdong province sent a city planning working group, led by Guangdong Provincial Construction Committee, Provincial Architectural Design Institute, Provincial Bureau of Surveying and Mapping, Geological Bureau and a number of units, to carry out the urban planning work in Shenzhen. In addition, municipalities planned and design units of fraternal provinces and cities. After working more than a month, the city planning office developed a general plot of "Master Plan of Urban Construction in Shenzhen," and plan and design for roads, bridges, water supply, drainage, flood control, landscape, power, telecommunications, gas, and ports and so on, based on the master plan The master plan was co-written by two engineers, Zhu Qihao and Zheng Shang from Guangdong Urban and Rural Planning and Design Institute.

The first city-planned area of Shenzhen was 50 square kilometers, with a population of 500,000 in 1990, and her development goal was mainly industry-based, meanwhile developing trade, agriculture, and tourism. With regards to road transportation, the main road width was as far as 50 meters in the planning and the road in Luohu District about the same, based on the alterations and expansion of the old city. Road in Shangbu new district was designed on a grid network. In terms of industry, the plans put forward the idea that focused on electronic industries, and planned two industrial areas: Shangbu Industrial Zone and Bagualing Industrial Zone. It also planned the clear river water storage area next to the Sungang cargo terminal. In the planning there were also detailed instructions about the residence building of in Luohu, Shangbu, Shenzhen reservoir and Wenjindu Bay. These residences functioned soundly, having a complete set of service facilities. On August 26, after careful studies, the Shenzhen Municipal Committee passed the master plan and used it to guide the early construction work of the Special Zones.[6]

1.2.3.2 The Second City Plan: "Socio-Economic Development Outline of Shenzhen Special Economic Zone"

In the end of May 1981, the State Council held the Economic Zones Conference of Shenzhen and Fujian Provinces in Beijing, which proposed that the work of building Special Economic Zones must be done well. The planning and construction of special zones had to be adapted to local conditions. Shenzhen Special Economic Zone should be built into an integrated zone, concurrent of industrial, commercial, agricultural, residential, tourism and other sectors. In August, Guangdong Province decided to give Shenzhen City

---

6 Shenzhen Chronicle Office, ***Establishment and Development of China's Special Economic Zones: Shenzhen***, CPC Party History Press, *1997, p83*

the same level of treatment as sub-provincial cities, just like Guangzhou City.

As new circumstances developed, the State Council put forward higher requirements for special zones. Shenzhen Municipal Party Committee and municipal government realized that the design goals and features of "Master Plan of Urban Construction in Shenzhen," which was made the year before, could not fulfill the development requirements. It was necessary to re-establish a socio-economic development framework of special zones, including city planning.

Shenzhen Municipal Committee and Government decided again to let Municipal Policy Research Team take the lead, with the Planning Bureau and other units participating, to survey the city's population and natural resources comprehensively and thoroughly, and make a prediction. Based on the original basis of urban planning, Dong Richen and Tang Ling from Shenzhen City Planning Board drafted an outline. Upon completing the draft, they made a detailed report to the Party. The Party Secretary Liang Xiang put forward further guidance to modify the draft. Early in 1982, the Party called all party cadres in Shenzhen above the level of county to discuss the draft and later various pertinent revisions were made. In April of the same year, the city government invited 73 various experts, professors, engineers and technicians in economy, planning, construction, foreign trade, agriculture, social sciences, and other areas of the country from Beijing, Shanghai, Guangzhou, assess the Shenzhen outline draft. In July, the city government invited prominent businessmen from Hong Kong to discuss the socio-economic development planning in Shenzhen. In mid-September, the government once again invited 32 experts and scholars to assess the revised outline. The Shenzhen Policy Research Office of the municipal government had modified the drafted outline eight times, and finally developed a more systematic and forward-thinking "Socio-Economic Development Outline in Shenzhen Special Economic Zone."

The "Outline" is divided into 12 chapters. The first chapter is about guiding principles of the planning. It proposes that Shenzhen should focus on electronic industries, and the products are mainly for the international market. As to agriculture and animal husbandry, they should "mainly provide services for special zones construction, as well as for export," meanwhile coordinating the development of commercial, residential, and tourism. The second chapter is on population planning. According to the population planning, the population of special zones would reach one million by the year 2000. The third chapter is about the land planning and function planning. It says that the land area, proper for construction, is 118.6 square kilometers, and it would be divided into East, the Middle, and West areas and 18 functional areas. The fourth chapter is about industry, aiming to build modern industry, requiring advanced technology, modern equipment, scientific management, and best economic efficiency. The fifth chapter is about agriculture. It proposes that by 2000, food-planning area would be reduced to 200,000 acres, and the output would reach the highest level of the country. The sixth chapter is about transportation, stating the planning is to use a grid layout for urban roads, mainly east-west, with north-south secondarily. The seventh chapter describes plans to build four large districts of warehouses with an area of 400 hectares, all connected with railway stations and roads. The eighth chapter details plans to build commercial, financial and administrative center in Futian new central area, including establishing commercial areas in Luohu, Nantou, and Shangbu. The ninth chapter states that the size of municipal utilities is planned according to 1 million people. The tenth chapter is about tourism, which, by 2000, was expected to receive over 1 million visitors per year. The eleventh chapter planned to popularize primary and secondary education to everyone. The twelfth chapter states the investment plan of Shenzhen in 20 years is about 22 billion RMB.[7]

Having established the "Outline," the Shenzhen Municipal Committee and Government never stopped revising it. In 1983, Party Secretary Liang Xiang visited Singapore with a delegation. Singapore's beautiful buildings and green urban landscape greatly impressed him. After returning to Shenzhen, he was determined to absorb the experience of Singapore's urban construction, expanding the area of urban green belt, and decided that all the housing area along main roads, which had not been built yet, would be set backward 30 meters from the red line, leaving space for the green belt. On the west side of the line from Shanghai Hotel to Shenda Telephone Company, an area with width of 800 meters for green belt (today's Central Park) should be reserved. His far-seeing vision left space for the future expansion and redecoration of Shenzhen.

1.2.3.3 Third City Plan: "Master Plan of Shenzhen Special Economic Zone"

As Shenzhen gradually became the forward city of China's reform and opening up, it attracts a large number of domestic workers into Shenzhen's construction. By 1984, the Shenzhen resident population reached 741,300, which was a 136% increase from the 1979 population of 427,200. The second development plan projected Shenzhen was to reach a population of 1 million by the year 2000. This projection was easily surpassed in 1986, reaching the size of a medium-sized city. At that time, Luohu, Shangbu and Shekou industrial zone, had formed the city size; however the Yantian, Shatoujiao, Futian and

7 Shenzhen Museum, ***History of Shenzhen Special Zone***, People's Publishing House, 1999. p 52-54.

Nantou were yet developed. Problems, such as how to layout industrial development, the location of the urban axis, how to arrange the supply systems of bus, electricity, water and gas, how to coordinate the topography of urban construction with other environmental factors, how to take the relationship between the short-term and long-term development into consideration, how to strengthen the link with Hong Kong in urban construction and so on were placed in front of Shenzhen decision makers. In accordance with the new conditions of domestic reform and opening up, the Central government further asked Shenzhen to play the role as window of technology, of management, of knowledge, of foreign policy, and the function of internal and external radiation. Shenzhen's role as a vanguard and pathfinder of reform and opening up further improved.

Despite the existence of the basic development idea of "Outline," the new situation required Shenzhen to establish a better and more scientific development plan. From 1984 to 1986, based on the original "Outline," the Shenzhen Municipal Government formulated the "Master Plan of Shenzhen Special Economic Zone," in which 122.5 square kilometers was set aside for urban land, which was approved by Guangdong Provincial People's Government. This master plan was regarded as the milestone in urban construction.

There were 190,000 words, 23 topics and 64 professional drawings in this Master Plan. It made a reasonable and flexible arrangement and design to the scale of urban development and urban construction layout. The plan standard was lower than Hong Kong's and higher than the standard of inner land. The city's building plan took Singapore and other developed countries as a reference. The Master Plan for Shenzhen's future development was divided into three stages: short-term (before 1990), mid-term (before 1995), and long-term (before 2000). In 1989, based on its development, Guangdong Provincial Government again made partial modifications.

"Master Plan of Shenzhen Special Economic Zone" exerted a profound impact on urban construction and development. It clearly defined the nature of "comprehensive industry-focused special economic zone" and made corresponding arrangements. Meanwhile, it confirmed the extent of development. Construction reached to 122.5 square kilometers in planning, with sufficient room reserved for future development. The population was expected to reach 1.1 million. Construction projected a "three horizontal and twelve vertical" road structure, 15 industrial zones, 179 residential areas, 22 municipal parks, nine tourist spots, one scenic area and road green belt of 140 km. At the same time, the city central area was being prepared with sufficient room for future development. The standard of Shenzhen construction was to be equivalent with the international advanced level.

1.3 Building the Foundation of Shenzhen Special Economic Zone (1980~1985)

On June 29, 1984, when Comrade Deng Xiaoping received foreign visitors, he spoke of the special economic zones again, saying "Shenzhen Special Economic Zone is a test for China. Now there are some issues remain unresolved. It took only three years for SEZ to start, and another three years will be needed to find solutions to all problems."[8]

1.3.1 Large-Scale Fundamental Urban Construction

1.3.1.1 Fundamental Construction Achievements

In 1979, before the establishment of Shenzhen Special Economic Zone, the area of Shenzhen was only 30,000 square kilometers with 20,000 to 30,000 urban citizens and a total building area of merely 290,000 square meters. Without any traffic control posts or traffic lights, streets were shabby and narrow, at the total length of only eight kilometers. With the highest building of only five-stories and the per capita living area of 2.74 square meters, the city was unfolding, shabby and old. Investment in infrastructure was less than 50 million yuan, and the completed housing area was merely 130,000 square meters. The infrastructure capacity of Shenzhen at that time was also very fragile, only one 500-employee construction company and a design team with only a dozen people.

In order to take on heavy responsibility on the SAR infrastructure, the Shenzhen Municipal Government adopted a flexible approach to open domestic and foreign construction market in Shenzhen. One masterpiece of this period was the achievement of the International Trade Building, hailed as "China's Highest Building," built by a Chinese construction company under the Third Construction Bureau. It stood at 160 meters high, with total of 53 floors and the total construction area of 100,000 square meters. Starting from October 1982 and completing in December 29, 1985, the project lasted for 37 months. On March 15, 1984, Xinhua Agency reported a new record in architectural history: one floor was created every three days on the Shenzhen International Trade Center. Since then, "three days for one floor" was known as a symbol of "Shenzhen speed."

1.3.1.2 Urban Development Mode of Attracting Investment and Making Money by Land

In the early period of constructing the SAR, money was the largest obstacle. The

8 Maomao, Denglin: ***My Father-Deng Xiaoping***, http://book.sina.com.cn/longbook/1092898767_dengxiaopin/77.shtml

Central Government provided policy support rather than monetary support. Therefore, how to raise funds for urban construction was a difficult issue for first few municipal leaders. Breakthrough lied in land management and utilization. Through continuous exploration, Shenzhen adopted an approach managing land resource and land assets. It took the lead in the implementation of paid transfer of land using rights so as to attract investment and make money by land.

In the early period of 1980s, as the main source of investment in city construction, the government established five companies: Housing Development Corporation (formerly known as Infrastructure Working Group), Industrial Development Services Company, Trust Investment Company, Guangdong Nuclear Power Service Corporation, and South Sea Petroleum Service Corporation. The first two were the major force of urban construction. Their development adopted the same approach that started with obtaining land authorized by government with no compensation and drew seed money from the bank to achieve continuous development by the exploitation of land.

Shangbu Industrial Zone, covering 120,000 square meters and developed by Industrial Development Services Company, was a key project in the construction of Shenzhen. Vast amounts of money were needed for land acquisition, demolition, and "seven-provided and one leveled" (including road conditions, electricity supply, water supply, sewage, communication, drainage system, gas and leveled field), and the construction of standard factory buildings. In 1982, the company first applied for a bank loan of 3 million yuan for land acquisition, demolition, and extensive publicity. When customers signed the contract to buy the plant, 40% of the purchase price was charged as the advance payment. Another 50% was charged when the third floor was built. The remaining 10% was paid in full after the factory was in normal use.[9] The Industrial Development Services Company set up a large number of standard factory buildings with 40 million loans and successfully achieved the goal of developing the industrial zone.

Established in January 1980, directly under the Real Estate Administration, Shenzhen Real Estate Company was responsible for the development, construction and operation of foreign real estate businesses. The company was set up on the transferred land from the government covering 3 square kilometers. The first project it joined with in Hong Kong was the East Lake Villa. When the project pre-design came out, Miao-Li Group started the pre-sales at a price of 2730 Hong Kong (HK) dollars per square meter. 266 suites were snapped up by more than 5,000 people. Necessary funds for construction were withdrawn

---

9 Edited by Shenzhen Museum: ***History of the Shenzhen SEZ***, People's Publish House, 1999, P62

in a very short time. Since then, the company, in collaboration with some HK companies, has developed three residential areas such as Hong Kong Bamboo Court and Lakeside Village by means of acquiring land from the real estate company and funding from the HK companies. From 1980 to the end of 1989, by means of cooperation, joint venture, sole-fund and self-running, 10 new residential villages were built up, with a completed construction area reaching 1.33 million square meters. 43 18+-story buildings, 415 multi-story residential buildings, and 321 villas, as well as hospitals, schools, kindergartens and other tourist facilities were completed.[10]

Figure 1-3-1 large-scale urban construction in late 1980[11]

By the mid 1980s, a mature management method of land paid leasing was being practiced in Shenzhen. In 1981, the Municipal Congress passed the "Shenzhen Special Economic Zone Interim Regulations on Land Management." In 1987, the "Land Management Regulations of Shenzhen Special Economic Zone" was formed on the revision of "Regulations on Land Management." It states that "the use rights of state-owned land should be monopolized and transferred at certain price decided by the government. Land transfer may take the following manner: (a) agreement; (b) tender; (c) public auction." Since 1988, Shenzhen cancelled the administrative allocation of land so all land would be supplied in the form of leasing in a certain period. According to related regulations, "land use right leasing price (hereinafter referred to as land price), land use and land use right leasing fee income shall be used as development fund under the management of the municipal government, for land development, protection, and shall not be misused." Land Development Fund was established and put into use. From 1988 to 2000, the

10 Edited by Shenzhen Museum: ***History of the Shenzhen SEZ***, People's Publish House, 1999, P76

11 http://www.5k5k.net/art/city/art_120. shtml

accumulated income of land development in Shenzhen reached over 40 billion yuan. 28,000 hectares of land were collected by using the fund to develop 19 industrial, residential and comprehensive areas of about 40 million square meters and the construction of about 50 major and minor roads, together with dozens of overpasses, which fundamentally realized the virtuous circle of urban construction. The novel urban construction pattern of attracting investment and making money by land source was rapidly replicated across the country, based on the success of Shenzhen.

1.3.2 Formation of the Industry Structure

In the initial five years of Shenzhen SEZ development, the biggest feature of its development was the large-scale investment and construction. Five years laid solid foundation for SEZ's rapid development in economy, culture and other social undertakings. By 1985, qualitative changes took place in Shenzhen's economy. In these five years, a healthy industry structure was set up. Proportions of three industries in GDP are shown as following:

Table 1-3-1 Proportions (%) of three industries in GDP (%)

Year	GDP	Primary Industry	Secondary Industry	Tertiary Industry
1979	100	37	20.5	42.5
1980	100	28.9	26	45.1
1981	100	26.9	32.3	40.8
1982	100	23	38.1	38.9
1983	100	17.2	42.6	40.2
1984	100	11.1	45.5	43.4
1985	100	6.7	41.9	51.4

Sources: ***Shenzhen Statistics Yearbook (Year 2000)***, P85

As can be seen from the table, in these five years, proportion of the primary industry was declining, the secondary industry was rising steadily, and the tertiary industry had little fluctuation. The ratio of the three remained stable in the next 15 years. By 1999, proportions of the primary, secondary and tertiary industries were 1.2%, 50.6% and 48.2% respectively, concluding that in the first five years of the establishment of Shenzhen Special Economic Zone, the prototype of the economic structure had been laid.

1.3.2.1 Breaking the Single Agriculture Industrial Structure

Shenzhen was formerly known as Bao'an County, a small border town, in a similar industrial structure and economic situation like many ordinary towns located in mainland China. Agriculture as main component of the economy was in dominant position, but industrial, transportation, construction, trade, service industry and science and education were quite weak. The industrial structure was basically a single agricultural one.

The industrial structure of Shenzhen SEZ underwent tremendous change from 1980 to 1985. While agriculture was in rapid development, its proportion in the entire national economy experienced rapid decline, while at the same time, the secondary and tertiary industries, such as the industrial and commercial services, developed rapidly. The previous exclusive agriculture structure was broken up, causing profound change in Shenzhen's industrial structures. In 1985, the primary industry was 261.11 million yuan, accounting for 6.7% of GDP, the secondary industry was 1.55477 billion yuan, accounting for 41.9%, and the tertiary industry was 15.0857 billion yuan, accounting for 51.4 %. It took seven decades for Shenzhen Special Economic Zone to take shape into a modern industrial city.

1.3.2.2 Changes in Traditional Agriculture to Earn Foreign Exchange

Since 1979, agricultural industry in Shenzhen, as in other cities, underwent a profound reform. However, its development had unique characteristics.

At this stage, agriculture development was characterized by its conversion from the traditional natural economy to commodity-oriented economy-from exclusive to integral. From 1979 to 1985, planting industry grew at an average annual rate of 10%. Compared with other industries, the growth speed was relatively slow due to the reduction of arable land in Shenzhen. During these five years, land usage for infrastructure led to the deduction of farming land to 40,000 mu, accounting for half of the cultivated area in SEZ. Cultivated land outside the SEZ reduced by over 10,000 mu due to the utilization of land for infrastructure construction and farmers' new adoption on husbandry, resulting in decrease in crop production. Agricultural growth mainly came from the aquaculture industry, animal husbandry and other sidelines. From the perspective of production value, agricultural output value took the largest share of the total agriculture output value, almost half in 1979, while the proportion of aquaculture industry and animal husbandry were comparatively low and forestry accounted for merely 3% of the total. In the following years, breeding and animal husbandry industries made significant development. The animal husbandry output value in 1985 took up one third of the agricultural output value. While the absolute agricultural output increased, its relative proportion dropped from one half of the total agricultural output value in 1979 to one third in 1985.

1.3.2.3 Rapid Development of the Secondary and Tertiary Industries

Shenzhen industrial development, particularly in the construction and electronics industries, was very rapid. Before the establishment of Shenzhen Special Economic Zone, industrial development in Bao'an County was quite slow and the industrial foundation was quite fragile under the guideline of "agriculture as the key link." In 1979, there were only 224 industrial enterprises to produce household goods and farming implements with a total output value of 60.61 million yuan. When SAR was established, industry grew rapidly and the industrial foundation quickly enhanced. In 1985, the number of industrial enterprises grew to 907, more than four times than in 1979. The industrial output value reached 2.674 billion yuan, 44 times than in 1979. By 1985, Shenzhen's industry covered metallurgical, electrical, chemical, machinery, building materials, food, textile, leather, paper, sewing and others. The proportion of secondary industry in Shenzhen rose from the third in 1979 to the first. Economic structure led by industry took shape.

In 1985, Shenzhen's GDP of tertiary industry was 1.50857 billion yuan, 18 times more than in 1979. The tertiary industry output value continued to rise from 42.5% in 1979 to 51.4% in 1985. In the tertiary industry, commercial development was quite appealing. In 1985, retail sales of social commodities soared from 127 million in 1979 to 2.646 billion, an increase of about 20 times.[12]

In the initial developing period, Shenzhen realized a fundamental reform in breaking its original production structure monopolized by agriculture. Although some aspects remained to be perfected in the internal structure of the various industries, a major breakthrough was created. Shenzhen laid a solid foundation for further development.

1.3.3 Setbacks

1.3.3.1 Where Shenzhen's Issues Lied

In 1984, Shenzhen became China's "Star City." Deng Xiaoping visited Shenzhen at the beginning of 1984, and left with the assertion that "Shenzhen's development and experience prove that our policy of establishing a SEZ was correct." Shenzhen was immersed in endless song of praise when, in May 1985, the Hong Kong *Wide Angle* magazine published, on its 152nd periodical, an article named "Where Shenzhen's Issue Lied." written by Dr. Chen Wenhong of the Asian Study Center of Hong Kong University. After a thorough investigation by Chen himself, he put forward his views on a series of

---

12 Zhang Minru: ***SEZ Econoly Course***, Guangdong Higher Education Press, p167

issues.[13] (Table 1-3-2). Firstly the pace of development of Shenzhen was a result of large investment in infrastructure. Secondly, since 1979, the total retail sales of large social and industrial commodities overwhelmed the total agricultural output value. In more recent years, a greater gap existed. This phenomenon reflected that Shenzhen's economic structure was based on trade, or in the sequencing of trade-industry-agriculture, rather than as the officially-reported on industry. Then, the article analyzed the development of the re-exports trade in Shenzhen, concluding that Shenzhen's economy was dependent on trade, mainly in re-exports trade to other domestic areas. Therefore, the Shenzhen Special Economic Zone did not meet the so-called "three-dominant" (foreign investment dominant, industry dominant and export-oriented dominant). In other words, SAR was making money from the pocket of other China areas.

Table 1-3-2 Statistics of Shenzhen Economy **Unit: 100 million HKD**

Index \ Year	1978	1979	1980	1981	1982	1983
Industrial and agricultural output value	1.7	1.6431	1.8924	3.4~3.7		8.7041
Gross industrial output value	0.6	0.6061	0.8444	2.4282	3.6212	7.2041
Gross agricultural output value	0.87009	0.8570	1.048		1.35/1.41	1.5
Infrastructure investment		0.4988	1.2487	2.7039	6.3265	8.8593
Actual foreign investment		1.2	2.5	5.9	8.8	11.3
Local fiscal revenue	0.2	0.35	0.55	1.18/1.3	1.63	2.96
Local foreign exchange earnings		0.28	0.4747	0.4~0.6	0.5638	0.67
Retail sales of social commodities	1.17	1.47	2.2	3.5	5.54	12.51

Table 1-3-3 Statistics of Shenzhen Economy

Index \ Year	1979	1980	1981	1982	1983
Industrial and agricultural output value:100 million RMB	1.7	1.87	3.41		
Gross industrial output value:100 million RMB	0.56	0.84	2.2499	3.741	6.73
Infrastructure investment:100 HKD			5.7~6.3	8.3	

Chen's persuasive article, detailed in data and thorough in analysis, was like a "wake-up call," shaking the Shenzhen people.

His opinions quickly aroused a fierce debate on the Shenzhen Special Economic Zone, both at home and abroad. Publications such as *Mirror*, *Economic Journal*, *South China Morning Post*, *Chinese Daily*, *The People* and even the American *China Daily News*

13 Dong Bin, Gao Xiaolin: ***Breakthrough—Apocalypse of China's SEZ***, Wuhan Publishing House, p230

published their evaluations on Shenzhen.

1.3.3.2 Time Limit of Three Years

The central government was long aware of Shenzhen's issues.

The Central Government attached great importance on issues in SEZ. On June 29, 1985, Comrade Deng Xiaoping said, when he met with a delegation of the Algerian National Liberation Front, that "Shenzhen Special Economic Zone is an experiment. We need time to see the rightness of this road. In short, it is a new socialist trial. It's our best wish to make it success. If not, it's still an experience for us."

On August 1, 1985, Comrade Deng Xiaoping met with the Japanese Komei Party delegation on their thirteenth visit to China. He made an important speech, saying "Now it's the initial period for Shenzhen's economy to develop outwardly. Any good products we are able to export are still limited. Time is needed to prove its capacity in healthy development. However, I heard that there has been some progresses." In December, when Comrade Deng Xiaoping meeting with foreign guests, he once again talked about the SEZ, saying "Shenzhen Special Economic Zone is a test for us. Now there are some issues remaining unresolved. However, the SEZ developed for only three years. Another three years will be enough to solve these problems."[14]

Deng, through his speech, timely clarified the attitude of the Central Government towards the SEZ. Many speculations and rumors proved unfounded. Meanwhile, Shenzhen shouldered a new task: to solve the existing issues in three years.

1.3.3.3 Grim Situation in 1985

In the early 1980s, the rapid economic development of Shenzhen made people ignore the many existing issues in the process. By 1985, these problems eventually became the focus of discussion. The Central Government finally decided on a complete overhaul of Shenzhen, which became much further and deeper than people expected, leading Shenzhen into a dilemma.

First of all, according to the state's unified plan, bank loans were in short supply. All of a sudden, 1 billion yuan was cut down from investment in Shenzhen's infrastructure. With the compression of infrastructure investment, the infrastructure team suffered a great reduction as well from 170,000 people to only 90,000 people. Construction was delayed on over 20 over 18+ story buildings.

---

14 ***Selected Works of Deng Xiaoping*** (third volume), People's Literature Press, first edition on October, 1993, p133

Secondly, many of the preferential policies were taken back. A new document stipulated a "comprehensively using permit system." Namely, all enterprises, no matter where its capital fund came from, should apply for and obtain a permit to conduct a contract. This permit could only be used once, thus called the "once valid permit."

Thirdly, the number of commodities produced in Shenzhen was strictly controlled by the state. In 1983, there were merely 129 kinds of commodities under the control of the provincial, ministry, and Central Government. By 1985, the number reached to 244, accounting for 80% of total exports, even more than before the Party's Third Meeting of the 11th Plenary Session. Exports, on the other hand, became a problem.

Thousands of companies were closed. Guests seldom visited restaurants and hotels, and the once bustling city became a backwater town overnight.

1.3.3.4 Change in Personnel Breaking New Ground for Future

The State Council approved Li Hao as the Mayor of Shenzhen on August 12, 1985. On August 29, the Guangdong Provincial Government removed Liang Xiang from the position of the Mayor of Shenzhen. On August 31, Xinhua Agency reported the news of Li Hao appointment as the Mayor of Shenzhen. At the same time, Li was also elected the Vice Governor of Guangdong Province on the fourth session of the Sixth Guangdong Province People's Congress and appointed as Vice Secretary of Shenzhen Municipal Party Committee. In May 1986, Li Hao replaced Liang Xiang as the Municipal Party Committee Secretary.

The new mayor gave an objective estimation of the situation, under which, Shenzhen began large-scale adjustments to meet the goals of "shifting from trade-dominant SEZ to export-oriented industrial-based economy, from the early stage of laying foundation and valuing input to upgrading production level and seeking production efficiency," [15] according to Li. The previous stage of development in Shenzhen ended, along with changes in personnel, and new development ideas were in preparation.[16]

1.4 The Developing Period for Shenzhen One (1986~1995)

On January 19, 1992, Mr. Deng Xiaoping met the fifth generation of the municipal officials of Shenzhen at Ying Bin Hotel in Shenzhen and delivered an important speech. He pointed out that "The most important experience of Shenzhen is daring to be the pioneer."

---

15 Dong Bin, Gao Xiaolin: ***Breakthrough—Apocalypse of China's SEZ***, Wuhan Publishing House, p254

16 Contents in the Chapter referring to ***Brief History of China SEZ***, edited by Su Dongbin, Guandong Economy Publisher, 2001

On January 23, Deng Xiaoping left Shenzhen. When his car arrived at Shekou Pier, he told Li Hao and other officials of Shenzhen, "You must be fast!"[17]

1.4.1 Early Opening Up (1986~1990)

1.4.1.1 Convening of the National Conference of Special Administrative Regions

From December 25 of 1985 to January 5 of 1986, the State Council held the National Conference of Special Administrative Regions. Head of 29 ministries of the State Consul, provincial leaders of Guangdong and Fujian and the officials of Shenzhen, Zhuhai, Shantou and Xiamen—the four Special Administrative Regions took part in the meeting. Vice-Premier Gu Mu hosted the meeting and gave important speeches.

It was agreed by the Conference that although the construction of the Special Administrative Regions was faced with some problems and difficulties, it was generally a success in the past five years. Under the policies of the Party Central and the State Council, the four SAR (Shenzhen, Zhuhai, Shantou and Xiamen) were developing fast and gained remarkable achievements. It started to play a role in the opening up and reforms of economic system in China and attracted the attentions at home and abroad. The practice of SAR showed that the policy of establishing SAR of the Central was correct. After five years' hard work, it laid a good foundation for future development. Its tasks were to combine the micro flexibility and the macro control, to change its main work from "set up the structure, build up the frame and lay the foundation" to "concentrate on product, upgrade the level and make profits" and to realize the goal of establishing an export-oriented economy. To realize this goal, big efforts were needed. On February 7, 1986, the State Council approved and carried out "Minutes for the Conference of SAR," which emphasized that during the period of the seventh Five-Year-Plan, the SAR should resolutely implement the instructions of the Central and the State Council, make good efforts on introductions abroad and the communication at home, set up an export-oriented economy based mainly on industry and the combination of industry and trading, fully play the role of the four windows and to promote the development in the mainland.

1.4.1.2 Major Reforms

1.4.1.2.1 Change the Functions for the Government

The question of how state-owned enterprises can get used to the market-oriented

---

17 ***Documentary for Deng Xiaoping's Visit in Shenzhen, Shenzhen*** SAR Daily, March 26th 1992.

economy kept being the focus for the economic academicians in China. As the laboratory for the market-oriented economy of China, Shenzhen had to be the first city to face this question. People in Shenzhen realized that the reform of state-owned enterprises was not separately an economic issue. The difficulty laid in its state-owned nature, not in the enterprise formation. Therefore, the idea to separate the enterprises from their government mother definitely became the idea to start the reforms.

Following this plan, Shenzhen carried out bold reforms of the governmental functions. In July 1987, one municipal Investment Management Center was established in Shenzhen, which, as a state-owned enterprise, took charge for the state-owned property in the enterprises and had four functions on management, supervision, investment and services. This reform was soon affirmed by the Central Government and promoted across the country. In 1988, the State Council established the state-owned Property Bureau as the independent representative of the state-owned property, which led the management over state-owned property to a brand new period.

1.4.1.2.2 Set up the First Foreign Exchange Rate Regulator

In the early 1980s, import and export trading developed fast in Shenzhen. During the first period, Shenzhen needed to import a large amount of machinery and equipment from abroad, but the products for export were few. This aroused a serious imbalance in the total volumes between import and export. (See the Table 1-4-1)

Table 1-4-1 Total Volume of Import and Export of Shenzhen from 1979~1985 Unit: 10,000USD

Year	Total Volume of Import and Export	Total Volume of Export	Total Volume of Import
1979	1676	930	746
1980	1751	1124	627
1981	2807	1745	1062
1982	2534	1597	937
1983	78642	6230	72412
1984	107247	26539	80708
1985	130632	56340	74292

Resource: ***Statistical Manual of Shenzhen 2000***, P91.

The explosion of import resulted to the vast shortage of foreign currency and made Chinese RMB faced with the heavy burden of devaluation. One journalist once investigated around the market of Shenzhen SAR, discovering the foreign exchange rate was 1:1 in mainland, but it was 1:13, even 1:15, in Shenzhen. However, under the single foreign currency management system, the official exchange rate between USD and RMB was fixed at 1: 3.2. The illegal trading of foreign currency was rampant.

On September 30, 1985, Mr. Li Hao formally issued the decision to establish the Foreign Exchange Regulator at the Conference of Municipal Government of Shenzhen. On November 9, the Municipal Government of Shenzhen officially issued No. 275 Article, entitled "Adjustment Approach on Foreign Exchange Rate of Shenzhen SAR." On March 10, 1988, the People's Bank of China issued No. 489 Article, entitled "Notice of Foreign Exchange Bureau on the Regulation of Foreign Exchange Rate Adjustment." Then, the Foreign Exchange Rate Regulator, born two years ago, got its legal identity.

1.4.1.2.3 The Birth of the Stock Exchange of Shenzhen

The Shenzhen Bao'an Joint Investment Company issued the first stock of China to the public on July 8th 1983. On July 25, Bao'an Joint Investment Company published the prospectus in *Shenzhen SAR Daily*: "Welcome the investment on the shares from the state-run collective units and the rural communities inside and outside Guangdong Province and individuals (including Chinese overseas, Hong Kong and Macau). Each single share costs 10RMB. People can invest and divest voluntarily. It guarantees the principal, pays the interests and shares the earning." When this news was spread, people from more than 20 provinces and cities bought the shares and some overseas Chinese and people from Hong Kong and Macau also became its shareholders. The county finance of Bao'an invested two million RMB as the state-controlled fund. Joint Investment finally raised 4.5 million RMB and was on its way up from then on.

At the start of Shenzhen stock market, there were only two or three business halls focusing on over-the-counter (OTC) business with few visitors. It held on and survived.

On November 15, 1989, the Municipal Government approved to prepare and establish the Stock Exchange. On December 1, it formally started its business.

1.4.1.2.4 Deepening the Reform on the Price Management System

Shenzhen started its Price Management System Reform in the early 1980s. At the end of 1984, the prices for daily commodities, including grains and oil, were totally open to the public. However, after the opening, price kept rising continuously and there was even double-digit inflation rate for several years. In 1985, the retail price index of Shenzhen is 123.2, increasing 18% from 1984. In 1988, the commodity price of China increased by 18.5%, but it increased by 30% in Shenzhen.

After research and studies, the Price Management Institute of Shenzhen carried out methods to control the inflation, which brought down the price index in Shenzen, while it rose across China. At the end of 1998, the retail price index started to negatively grow. The reform on the productive materials market gradually unfolded. In the same year, the Planning Bureau of Shenzhen proposed to establish a free market for productive materials under the macroinstruction of the socialist country, allowing any companies and individuals to operate business on productive materials and cancelled "two-track" system, whose price difference belonged to the municipal finance.

By 1990, the productive materials market in Shenzhen was almost open in all the fields, in which more than 90% of the productive materials were under the adjustment of the market. The opening of the price of productive materials not only avoided rent seeking under two-track system, but also paved the road for the establishment and improvement for the productive factors' market.

1.4.2 Tortuous Experience (1991~1992)

1.4.2.1 The Collapse in East Europe and Left-Leaning Thinking

At the end of 1980s and the start of 1990s, the International Society was suffering rapid changes, because of the radical changes of socialist countries in East Europe and the collapse of the first socialist country—the Soviet Union. The division of the Soviet Union broke the old structure of the world that stared its multi-polar development, but the new structure had not yet been established. After 1989, Western countries intensified the sanctions on China, which deteriorated the international environment for the economic development of China.

In China, "left–thinking" reactivated in 1990s. Some people were hesitant and confused about how to deepen the reform and were afraid that the opening up and reform might turn China to a capitalist country. Some questioned the new economic system, especially "the interior unite of plan and market" and "the government adjusts the market; the market guides the enterprises," which were issued by the 13th National People's Congress. Some critiqued the saying "the reform on the orientation of the market" and thought that to develop market economy was to develop capitalism. Many of the reforms in SAR aroused popular criticism. The discussion on the nature of the SAR—whether it was capitalist or socialist-was down after Deng Xiao Ping's visit to Shenzhen in 1984. However, at the beginning of 1992, it returned to the focus of debate.

The growth rate of the Chinese economy fell to its lowest point since the 3rd Session of National People's Congress, wandered around 5%. At the same time, the economy of neighboring countries around China quickly developed. Except Japan, the economy of the rest of the countries and regions of Asia grew at a high average rate of 6.2% by 1991. In

East Asia, not only East Asian Tigers (Hong Kong, Singapore, South Korea, and Taiwan) kept a fast developing economy, but also Malaysia, Thailand and others, which once fell behind, proved an active economic power.

Under this background, Deng Xiao Ping emphasized that development is an unyielding principle. From January to February of 1991, Deng Xiao Ping delivered encouraging speeches when he visited Shanghai. He hoped that people of Shanghai could "open their minds wider, take braver action and walk faster." He frequently mentioned SAR during his stay in Shanghai, saying "when the government affirmed the four SAR, we mainly considered the geographic situation. Shenzhen is next to Hong Kong; Zhuhai is close to Macau; Shantou has many Chaozhou people from Southeast Asia; many of the residents—Minnan people of Xiamen go abroad and do business. We didn't consider the human resource advantages in Shanghai." While seeing the once-largest industrial city fall behind Shenzhen and other SAR, Deng Xiao Ping stated, "if Shanghai started its development a few years ago like Shenzhen, it would be fine."

In February 1990, the State Council held the National Conference of SAR again in Shenzhen. Prime Minister Li Peng hosted the meeting and delivered important speeches. The conference assigned the tasks for the SAR for the following two to three years, emphasized to keep the special characteristics of the SAR, to deepen the reform of economic structure, adjust the industrial structure, upgrade the quality of the products and accelerate the economic development. In July, President Jiang Ze Min declared that Shenzhen "continue to develop Shenzhen Special Administrative Region and take efforts to explore the way for socialism with Chinese characteristics." On November 26, CPC Central Committee Secretary General and President Jiang Ze Min delivered speeches at a conference celebrating the 10th Anniversary of Shenzhen SAR and asked Shenzhen to "upgrade the level and increase the profit" and "constantly sum up experience and do not pause to put forward all aspects of work."

Faced with opportunities and challenges, Shenzhen had lost no time formulating a new development strategy. In December 1990, the Municipal Government issued a draft of the "Outline for the 8th Five-Year-Plan and the National Economic and Social Development Plan of Shenzhen." In October 1991, this outline was adopted on the Second Session of the First People's Congress of Shenzhen. It proposes that by 2000, the GDP of Shenzhen would arrive at 60 billion yuan, the Gross Industrial Output Value would reach 80 billion yuan, the total volume of the export would reach 13 billion yuan and financial income would reach 7.3 billion yuan. Then Shenzhen could reach or approach the mid-developed countries' level of the end of 1980s and become an "international outgoing and multi-functional metropolitan."

1.4.2.2 The Shock After Deng Xiao Ping's South Tour Speeches

At the beginning of 1990s, the pace for the national reform and opening up slowed down. Deng Xiao Ping, 88 –years old at the time, visited South China again. On February 28, the Central Committee issued No.2 (1992) Article and delivered Comrade Deng Xiao Ping's speech during his visit to South China, which was like blast that shocked the whole of China.

Figure 1-4-1 Deng Xiao Ping on the way to South China[18]

South Tour Speeches illustrated the nature of socialism: to liberate and develop productive forces and suggested taking the "Three Advantages" as the measure to check the result of reform and opening up. The speeches were actually the conclusion of the Third

18 http://cpc.people.com.cn/GB/64093/64387/5391918.html

Plenary Session of the 11th Central Committee, which answered many questions that fettered the people's thinking. The speeches were regarded as a new liberation of thinking after the discussion about the standard of truth in 1978. South Tour Speeches sounded the reform and development and China ushered in profound changes.

1.4.2.1.1 An Omni Bearing Structure of Opening up Across the Country

At the beginning of the reform and opening up, China cautiously established four special administrative zones in remote bordering towns. After their first success, Hainan Big SAR was set up and then the opening zones were enlarged to 14 cities along the coast, which made it a golden coast from south to north in East China. However, the opening up faced occasional standstills before 1992, which caused great hesitation.

Regarding South Tour Speeches of Comrade Deng Xiao Ping as an opportunity, in May 1992, the Central Committee drew up "Suggestions on Accelerating the Opening up, Enlarging the Reform and Striving to Promote Economy to a Higher Level" and delivered it as No. 4 Document of the Central Committee. The "Suggestions," following the spirit of "seizing the opportunity, speeding up the economic development, reform and opening up" of Deng Xiao Ping, issued a series of measures to enlarge the opening up. From then on, China enforced the reform, enlarged the scope and areas of opening up. The reform and opening up started at a high speed. There were many important measures of the opening up in 1990s, including the State Council's affirmation that Hainan can make use of foreign investment and explore and develop Yangpu Economic Zone 30 square kilometers in March 1992. Pudong new district of Shanghai was the focus of reform and opening up in the 1990s. In March 1992, the State Council affirmed Heihe, Suifenhe, Pichun and Manzhoulito be newly opened cities along the border. In the middle of March of the same year, the State Council approved Wenzhou as another new open city. At the end of April, China had opened 162 ports of aviation, marine and land transportation. Then, a comprehensive open structure of China, along the coast, the river, the border and the inland, from north to the south, from east to the west and in the middle of the country, was preliminarily formed.

1.4.2.1.2 Establishment of the Goal to Set up Socialist Market Economy

Based on the South Tour Speeches of Comrade Deng Xiao Ping, Market Economy got its legal identity in China, which had no need to be evasively used and started to live in the orthodox theory. On November 14, 1993, the 3rd Plenary of the 14th Central Committee of CPC approved "Decisions of Central Committee of CPC on Several Issues of Establishing

Socialist Market Economic System" which identified the goal and way of market economy reform. It oriented many fields of the reform, including functions of the government, the macroeconomic control, the enterprise system, and the price and the allocation mechanism, which planed the preliminary frame of socialist market economy.

Socialist market economy-oriented reforms promoted the most "special" nature of Shenzhen SAR to the whole country. Shenzhen, which had already been striving in the market economy for more than 10 years, announced that a socialist market economic frame had been basically established and grouped it into ten systems: ownership system with the public ownership as the mainstay, with various economic components fairly compete and develop; the state-owned property supervision, with a joined management and operation system with capital; the price system with market as the base; the market system with commodity market as base and factor market as pillar; the national economy and enterprise accounting system connected to international practice; the social supervision service system with intermediary organizations as mainstay; the social guarantee system with the combination of social solidarity relief and self-guarantee; the distribution system with distribution according to work, giving priority to efficiency with due consideration to fairness; the economic management and adjustment system with indirect means as mainstay facing to the whole society; and the law system adjusted to socialist market economy.

Shenzhen's conclusion on ten systems of socialist market economy became important reference for establishing socialist market economic system in China. Market economic system was a priceless treasure for Shenzhen. Its exploration was the greatest contribution from special administrative region to the reform and opening up of China.

1.4.3 Improvement and Development (1993~1995)

1.4.3.1 Adjustment on the Development Strategy

The South Tour of Deng Xiao Ping in 1992 aroused new high tide of reform and opening up throughout the country and brought with it new challenges to Shenzhen. Both in the theory and the practice, Shenzhen Special Administrative Zone suffered from unprecedented shocks. The 14th CPC National Congress established the goal for socialist market economy, which formed a comprehensive reform and opening structure around the country. With the generalization of reform and the overall promotion of opening up, the economic development in SAR acted as demonstration for inland areas. Many inland cities not only took similar reform measures, but in some fields they even implemented more flexible and more open polices than SAR. With policy convergence, mainland's institutional convergence with SAR was more profound. Market economy was no longer the patent for

SAR, so the question remained: was it necessary for SAR to keep their specificities?

Huge challenges made Shenzhen people aware that Shenzhen must upgrade its economic development level to keep its advantages and keep leading the trend of reform and opening up. The development of Shenzhen entered a period of upgrading.

On November 21, 1992, the first congress of CPC Committee of Shenzhen was held. The Municipal Party Secretary Li Hao, in terms of the Standing Committee of the Municipal Committee, delivered important report named "Fully Implement the 14th CPC Congress and Push the Reform and Opening Up of Shenzhen to a New Level," which got approved by the plenary session. In his report, the cross-century strategy of Shenzhen in the new period was firstly put forward and it disposed to accelerate the reform and opening up the modernization construction.

The cross-century strategic goal for Shenzhen in the new period was to establish Shenzhen an integrated modernized metropolitan with multiple functions and contribute to the realization of Guangdong Province to catch up with the Four Tigers of Asia, especially Singapore and Hong Kong.

From June 15 to 21, 1994, President Jiang Ze Min visited Guangdong and emphasized that the Central Committee would neither change its determination to develop SAR, nor change its basic policy in SAR or change SAR's position in the reform and opening up and modernization construction in China. These three stipulations greatly encouraged the people of Shenzhen.

1.4.3.2 Optimizing Industrial Structure

After the 5th Plenary Session of the 1st Central Committee of Shenzhen Municipal Government, especially the Seminar of Hi-tech & Industry of Pearl River Delta, the development of Shenzhen hi-tech industry went into a new period. To strive in the development of hi-tech industry became the drive of the whole society.

Following the establishment of Shenzhen Technology Industry Park, on May 13, 1994, the high-tech industrial village was set up in Shenzhen. In February 1995, the Municipal Government organized Municipal Hi-tech Park Leading Team to accelerate the development of high technological industry, which marked the united planned and managed period of Shenzhen's hi-tech district.

The third industry met its new opportunity. In 1992, the Central Committee and Municipal Government of Shenzhen issued and implemented "Guideline for the Development of the Third Industry of Shenzhen." The "Guideline" made detailed regulations for the focus, goal, strategy and measure for the third industry of Shenzhen, whose general idea was finance, security and information as head and trading, transportation and communication as mainstay to respond to the development of real estate and tourism. With its guide and the help from the Central Committee and Municipal Government of Shenzhen, the third industry developed fast. The employees of the third industry of Shenzhen took up 24.1% of the total number of the people with jobs in 1990. The number rose to 32.2% in 1995. With the fast development of the secondary industry, the third industry took up 46% of the GDP in 1995. Although it was lower than the proportion-49% of 1990- its absolute value differed greatly. The value of the third industry in 1990 was 8.77 billion RMB, but it was 36.58 billion in 1995.[19]

1.4.3.3 The Strategy of "Three Points in One Line"

On June 23, 1993, at the Working Conference, the present Secretary of Municipal Party Committee of Shenzhen pointed out that Shenzhen must seize the opportunity, make good use of the rich resources in mainland, its enormous potential and advanced technology and combine them with the advantages of SAR to develop various corporations and establish an economic structure of "three points in one line"—the international market, Shenzhen and the mainland. This strategy designated Shenzhen's horizontal association of economy.

The international market was the goal of the "three points in one line" strategy. With its instruction, the export industry of Shenzhen went to a higher level. In 1993, its total export volume was 8.33 billion USD, taking up 15% of the total export volume of the whole country. From 1993 to 1999, Shenzhen took first place in the export industry for seven years. Mainland was the other terminal of this strategy. With the fast development of foreign trade, Shenzhen enhanced the interior association. By the end of 1994, Shenzhen had about 10,000 enterprises connected with mainland. More than 6000 of them were established during 1993 to 1994. It was one and a half times as much as the total amount for the past 13 years. The gross industrial output value and the total export of the associated enterprises separately took up half of the corresponding index of Shenzhen and became one of the economic pillars of the city. More than 2000 enterprises of Shenzhen invested or set up their branches in more than 80 cities in mainland. The real invested capital reached 2 billion yuan, which equaled to the total amount invested from mainland to Shenzhen.[20]

---

19 Shenzhen Statistics Bureau: ***Shenzhen Statistics Annual of 2000***, China Statistic Press, 2000, P84

20 LIAO, Yuehui, History of Special Economic Region of China, Haitian Press, 1998.

1.5 The Developing Period for Shenzhen Two (1996~2000)

Li You Wei, the Secretary of Municipal Party Committee of Shenzhen, first proposed the slogan of the "Second Undertaking" on the 2nd CPC Congress of Shenzhen. It meant to start another 15-year undertaking on the first 15-year working base, strive to increase and create new advantages and to promote the SAR construction to a new level. That was to say, timeline for the Second Undertaking in practice was from 1996 to 2000, which matched the goal of the "9th Five-Year Plan" and the perspective of 2010 proposed by the 5th Plenary Session of the 14th CPC Congress.

1.5.1 The Proposal of the Second Undertaking

The year 1995 was one of the most important years in the history for the SAR development of Shenzhen. From April to May, the CPC Congress and the People's Congress were held in succession, which substantially modified the development goal for the year 2000, drafted in 1992. The Congresses planned that by 2000 Shenzhen needed to be a city with 165 billion yuan GDP, 28 billion yuan total export volume, 13 billion yuan financial income within domestic budget, with hi-tech industry output value taking up 35% of the total industrial output, 380,000 square kilometers urban area and a population of four million. They proposed that people needed to strive to build up Shenzhen as an "international city of socialist modernization," "a base for hi-tech industry, a regional center of finance, information, trading and transportation and a place of interest."

Li You Wei, the Secretary of Municipal Party Committee of Shenzhen, first proposed the slogan of the "Second Undertaking" on the 2nd CPC Congress of Shenzhen. It meant to start another 15-year undertaking on the first 15-year working base to promote the SAR construction to a new level. That was to say, timeline for the Second Undertaking in practice was from 1996 to 2000, which matched the goal of the "9th Five-Year Plan" and the perspective of 2010 proposed by the 5th Plenary Session of the 14th CPC Congress. The Second Undertaking was also Shenzhen's new strategy to adapt to the new situation and to realize its own new developing goal.

The Central soon approved the Second Undertaking. From December 5 to 7, 1995, before opening the curtain of the Second Undertaking, President Jiang Ze Min visited the people of Shenzhen again.

Secretary General Jiang Ze Min visited Zhonghua Bicycle Factory, Konka, Great Wall Computer, Changke International Electronics and Lianhuabei Village. He asked about the management of the enterprises, the development of the high technology and the life of the employee and the villagers. He was satisfied with the fast development of hi-tech and hoped it could develop faster. He pointed out that all throughout the world, where the economy was developing fast, high and new technology kept increasing.

In the evening of December 6, The Secretary General pushed for Shenzhen to "increase and create new advantages to promote Shenzhen to a new level." He said, "I said this last year, but this time I must repeat it. It is simple but clear, my mind." About its origin, the Secretary General Jiang revealed it at the meeting with the provincial delegate of the People's Congress. He said several years ago, he visited Shenzhen, Meizhou and other places. During that visit, he proposed to Guangdong and SAR that they should, again, create new advantages and advance themselves to a new level. He also exchanged ideas with Comrade XieFei. XieFei telephoned him that night saying that "create new advantages again" sounded like the original advantages were worth nothing, and if "increase and create" would be a better mantra, to which Secretary General Jiang agreed.

In April 1996, the State Council held the National Conference of Special Administrative Regions. The Second Undertaking became the hot topic of the meeting. Prime Minister Li Peng pointed out in his speech that "the SAR must change its thinking and working from mainly depending on the preferential policies to two fundamental changes. With the spirit of the Second Undertaking, they should make full use of the present, basic advantages and the policies to increase and create new advantages and promote the development to a new level. After this National Conference, the Second Undertaking issued by Shenzhen spread to every special administrative zone. With the leadership of Shenzhen, all the other SAR started to embark on a new developing strategy and the new round of undertaking began.

1.5.2 Hi-Tech Industry on its Way to Pillar Industry

1.5.2.1 Rise for the High and New Technological Industry

The high technological industry of Shenzhen started early and could be traced back to far-sighted series polices in 1980s. On November 28, 1986, Shenzhen carried out "Decisions on Enhancing Technological Work," which asked people to realize the importance of the technological work, make full use of the SAR advantages to accelerate the introduction and absorption of new technologies, strive to develop scientific, technological and product research, explore the technological market, reform the technological funds appropriation regulations, establish a qualified technological team and let the technicians play their full role in the production. On February 4, 1987, Shenzhen issued "Interim Provisions on Encouraging Technicians to Set up Private Technologies Enterprises," which stipulated that technicians could take the shares of the enterprises by cash, objects, private patent and trademark of proprietary technology and could get dividends and distributions.

In the 1980s, the high and new technology did not play an important role in the whole industrial structure. In 1988, the product output value of high and new technological industry was only 450 million yuan, taking up 4.5% of the gross industrial output value. In 1992, it reached 4.732 billion yuan and took up 12.25% of the gross industrial output value. On October 5,1995, Shenzhen issued "Decisions on Pushing the Scientific Technology to Make Progress." On February 9, 1998, "Provisions on Supporting High and New Technological Industry Development," which, on the basis of series of preferential policies, gave more powerful support to high and new technologies with preferential policies, human resources and materials. The municipal government firmly promoted the development of technology, which helped hi-tech bloom. From 1995 to 1999, the output value of high technological industry of Shenzhen increased from 14.6 billion to 106.464 billion yuan, increasing by 7.3 times. High-tech industry output value accounted for 15.2% of total industrial output value in 1992 and rose to 34.66% in 2000.[21] Among the high technological products, the products with independent intellectual property, accounted for 50.22% in 2000.[22]

When Shenzhen first proposed to develop hi-tech industry, many people questioned that Shenzhen was only a 20-year old city without famous universities or institutes. In their eyes, Shenzhen was only one city developing on the basis of "three plus one" industry (custom manufacturing with materials, designs or samples supplied and compensation trade) and the flood of cheap labor from the mainland were only a productive base for Hong Kong. The people questioned it could it be a city of technology. Then reality entered their sight. High and new technology became the pride of Shenzhen. In 1980s, when the municipal officials of Shenzhen met with foreign guests, they often proudly said that every one of four watches, at least, and every one of four bicycles were made in Shenzhen. The lens product volume of Shenzhen ranked the first all over the world. In 2000, when the situation of Shenzhen was asked, the officials preferred to tell them a series of figures: the product of magnetic head for the computer ranked the third of the world; the product of microelectronic computer accounted for 25% of the whole product of China; the product of private branch exchange took up 50% of China; the product of gene interferon accounted for 60% of the whole product in China. Shenzhen was also the biggest base in China for printers, hard drives and wireless telephones. Hi-tech industrial structure with five pillars

---

21 Figured out by relevant data from ***Shenzhen Statistic Annual of 2001***.

22 Shenzhen Statistics Bureau: ***Shenzhen Statistics Annual of 2007***, China Statistics Press, 2007, P317.

was formed in Shenzhen, including electronic information, biotechnology, new materials, optical, mechanic and electronic integration and lasers.

1.5.2.2 Performance Factors

The achievement of Shenzhen's high technology has become indisputable fact. What was its key to success?

1.5.2.1.1 Introduction of High Technologic Enterprises

Shenzhen tried its hardest to attract high technological enterprises and strived to make itself the prolific base for the industry of high technology. Lenovo came to Shenzhen in 1989. Shenzhen connected with Lenovo whose president, Liu Chuanzhi, visited Shenzhen three times. Finally, its South China headquarters and R&D center were moved back to Shenzhen. Liu Chuanzhi said, "Where there is good grass, where we are." The officials of Shenzhen said the government would like to grow the grass suitable for the enterprises. Like Lenovo, TCL did not start its business nor achieve its success in Shenzhen. However, it set up the R&D center, information base and one television-producing factory in Shenzhen. Skyworth also established their R&D center there.

The good environment for high technologic industry also attracted a lot of multinational enterprises. By 2000, the number of foreign technological companies increased and they became an important part of Shenzhen's hi-tech industry. In 2000, the magazine *Happy* listed that more than 70 of the top 500 companies in the world established branches in Shenzhen. Fifteen companies including IBM, Hitachi, Philips, DuPont, HP, Samsung and Toshiba invested in Shenzhen's high technological industry. There were also other well-known companies like Seagate, Uniden, Epson and Olympus.

The flood-like arrival of the famous domestic and foreign companies infused the high technological industry with infinite power. By 2000, 477 of the 521 research and development institutes were established by enterprises, accounting for 91%. 90% of the research and development staff stayed in enterprises and 90% of the investment came from enterprises, too.[23] High technological enterprises became an exclusive part of research and development, which brought Shenzhen to the front of scientific and technologic achievement and greatly upgraded the capability of Shenzhen's high technological industry in the international market. In order to catch up with the top technology of the world, more than ten companies of Shenzhen established research institutes or companies in Silicon Valley in the United States.

---

23 *Shenzhen High Technologic Industry Statistics Bulletin of 2000.*

1.5.2.1.2 The Success of "Hi-Tech Fair"

To pave the way for transforming high technological achievement into pragmatic productive power, the Standing Committee of Shenzhen Municipal Government made the decision that beginning in 1999, Shenzhen was to hold a high technological achievements fair every year. Prime Minister Zhu Rongji approved the report and the fair was named China (International) Hi-tech Fair. The first fair was held from October 5 to 10, 1999. Four ministries, 31 provinces, cities, autonomous regions, Hong Kong, Taiwan, Macau and 22 universities, including Tsinghua and Peking University, participated in the fair. 402 hi-tech enterprises, universities, institutes, financial and investment organizations from 26 countries, including the United States of America, Canada, Australia and Japan, gathered together. In total, 2856 enterprises with 4150 technologic achievements took part in the exhibition. 1459 of them went into transactions with a total volume of 6.494 billion USD.[24]

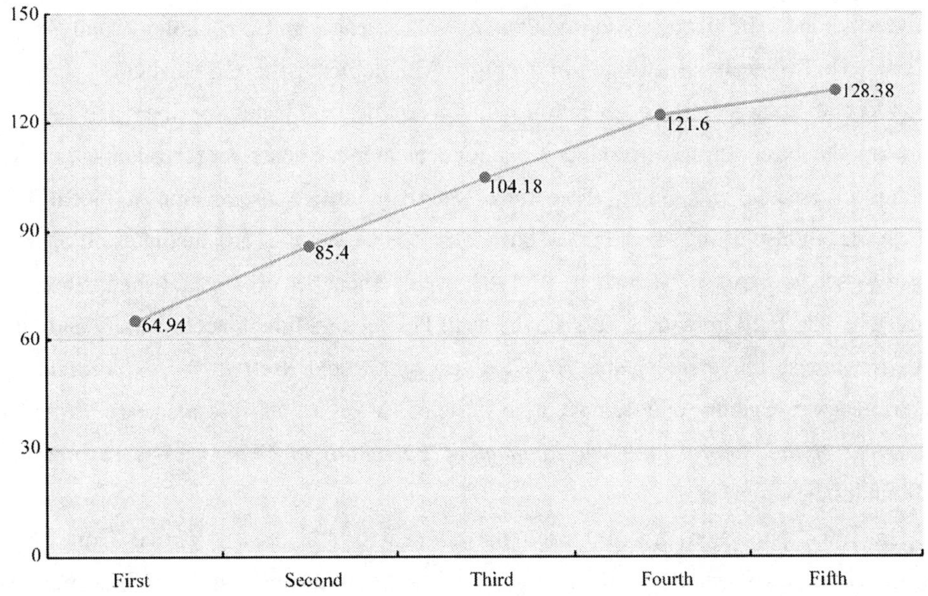

Figure 1-5-1 Turnover of the first five Hi-tech Fairs in Shenzhen (Unit: 100 million USD)[25]

Shenzhen started to hold the Lychee Festival in 1988 and stopped it in 1998. From 1999, the Hi-tech Fair started. This change demonstrated that Shenzhen, within 10 years, upgraded its industrial structure to a new level and the dominance of technologic industry

24 Shenzhen China (International) Hi-tech Fair, http://www.chtf.com/.

25 www.southcn.com/.../gjhxg/200410120618.htm

began to take shape.

1.5.2.1.3 Introduction of Intelligence Resources

Shenzhen realized early that if the intelligence of famous universities and institutes at home and abroad could not be made use of, the development of Shenzhen must lack in propulsion. Therefore, some of the companies in Shenzhen connected closely with the institutes established in universities of Shanghai, Beijing, Nanjing, Xi'an and Hefei, and the surrounding area. Famous universities at home and abroad aimed at its good market environment and capital advantages in Shenzhen to help realize the industrialization of the research achievements. Tsinghua University invested 1.9 billion yuan and established the information harbor of Tsinghua in Shenzhen, which is its biggest industrial base outside Beijing. Harbin Institute of Technology, Beijing Institute of Technology, Southwest Jiaotong University and other universities also located their industrial bases in Shenzhen. On August 16, 1999, Shenzhen Municipal Government signed the agreement with Peking University and The Hong Kong University of Science and Technology and set up PKU-HKUST Shenzhen Institution in the high technological park of Shenzhen.

Depending only on the cooperation with universities and institutes, Shenzhen could be, at most, the base for transforming technological achievements into products, but was lacking in creative capability. Therefore, Shenzhen strove to develop its local high education, but also trying its hardest to attract famous universities and institutes all over the world to set up bases in Shenzhen. In 1983, when Shenzhen was established, Shenzhen University was built up with the assistance from Peking and Tsinghua University and other famous Chinese universities. Shenzhen University devoted itself to the exploration and experiment on teaching and management systems. Many of its reforms were written in *Guideline of the Reform and Development of Education in China* and were promoted throughout the country.

In 1999, Shenzhen first proposed the concept of "Shenzhen Virtual University." Compared to newly establish universities, to implant famous universities in Shenzhen was more efficient, with less investment and higher start line. On September 10, 1999, Shenzhen Virtual University turned up with 22 famous universities, including Peking, Tsinghua, Nankai and University of Science and Technology of China, etc, gathering together in the high technology zone of Shenzhen. The Virtual University looked like an exhibition for famous universities of China. Its establishment acted as a new chapter for the cooperation between Shenzhen and the universities nationwide.

The establishment of the Virtual University was the milestone in the high education development history of Shenzhen. Shenzhen was not content with the solely the virtual university and planned to introduce real universities on this base. In July of 2000, the executive meeting of Shenzhen municipal government approved "General Program to Establish Shenzhen University Zone" (hereinafter referred to as "Program") in principle. It proposed that the basic idea to establish Shenzhen Universities Zone was "Unified planning, resource sharing, government guidance, independent schooling, diversity and openness, institutional innovation, convergence of advantages and striving for excellence" through "high standard introduction and multi-channel investment, brand-new system and the combination of research, study and production" to establish a high level universities zone which should be the stage for raising and gathering high quality human resources, the foundation for technological innovation and development for hi-tech industries, and the experimental field for openness of high education and the international cooperation.

1.5.2.1.4 Respect and Attraction for Talented Persons

The three major features of human resources are composed of the creativity and the ontology of human resources and the infinity of creativity. Its creativity and the infinity of creativity, especially the infinity and ontology of creativity, will inevitably result in another important feature—the freedom of human resources. Then freedom will inevitably lead to exclusive claim over ownership. That is to say the first economic claim of human resources is the recognition of their ownership.[26]

The recognition for the ownership of human resources was one of the tips of the success for Shenzhen's hi-tech industry. Through many channels, Shenzhen approved the ownership of human resources. The most successful experience was to allow the technology participating in the distribution as the factor of production, which realized the combination of the technologies and the capital. When Kaifa Technology Company was established in 1985, Chinese partner invested 2 million USD, accounting for 66% of the shares. Overseas Chinese Tan Wen Yan took up 34% of the shares by evaluating his technology and international trading networks. On September 23, 1997, not long after the 15th CPC Congress, there was shocking news about Shenzhen: Handsome Chemical and Coating Company were established with Dr. Shen Hao taking shares by technology. Handsome was composed of Shenzhen Constructional Materials Group, Shenzhen Investment Management Company and Dr. Shen Hao with 30 million yuan total investment. Shen Hao took up 17% of the shares with his technology, valued at 5.1 million yuan. By now, the technology

---

26 SU, Dongbin: ***Frontier Topics of SAR in China***, China Economics Press, 2000, P22.

shares were spread among the enterprises in Shenzhen. Backbone companies like Huawei and ZTE adopted this way.

The competition among hi-tech rooted in the competition among human resources. Shenzhen municipal government took effective measures to attract returned students to start undertakings in Shenzhen. In June of 2000, the municipal government issued "Provisions on Encouraging Returned Students to Start Undertaking in Shenzhen" as the policy guarantee for attracting the return people who studied abroad. With the leadership of the municipal government, Shenzhen Pioneer Park was established and the municipal and district breeding base for return people was gradually perfected. The return people from foreign countries devoting to research could get one start fee about 100,000 to 150,000 yuan. Shenzhen did highly effective work to introduce talented persons. In September of 1999, Academician of the Chinese Academy of Engineering, Niu Han Ben, together with his team of more than 20 people, settled in Shenzhen, which broke the nil record of Academician in Shenzhen. Shenzhen also set up 13 postdoctoral workstations with 30 people and gave them 50,000 yuan allowance every year. Post-doctoral could freely make use of the money.

1.5.3 Backward of the State-Owned Economy and Forward of the Private Economy

1.5.3.1 Deepening of the Reform over the State-Owned Enterprises

1.5.3.1.1 Promoting the Reform over State-Owned Enterprises

During the period of the 9th Five-Year Planning, Shenzhen implemented a modernization enterprises system pilot reform on 35 state-owned companies and carried out one set of practical reform program. The reform program proposed to improve the company legal person structure, reform the municipal level state-owned leader management system, deepen the reform on distribution system, try out operators' annual salary system and distribute shares with interior employees, enhance the interior democracy inside the enterprises, scientific policy-making system and encouraging, supervision and restrain system, set up a three-level management and operation system of state-owned companies, establish three capital operation companies in accordance with their industry natures and the capital scale, offer the identity of investor and authority to the capital operation company and formed state-owned capital management system with Shenzhen's characteristics. By 1998, the pilot reform obtained its primary success. These 35 enterprises offered precious experience for Shenzhen to promote modern enterprises system.

1.5.3.1.2 Implement Great Group Strategy

In the latter part of the 1990s, the historical environment of Shenzhen changed greatly. The policy advantages of Shenzhen gradually disappeared and the reform and opening up in mainland brought new market pressure. Shenzhen's export-oriented economy was faced with greater and greater pressure during the financial risk over Asia. Under the new situation, enterprises of Shenzhen revealed weakness. The total scale of the group was large, but the individual companies under the group were small and scattered, without clear major industry or products. The chain of the group was too long, with a wide range of management. Under this situation, Shenzhen Municipal Government carried out one "three batches" strategy in 1995. One of its cores was to develop one batch of big groups of enterprises during the period of the 9th Five-Year Plan and created one batch of famous brands. The implementation of big groups symbolized a new level of Shenzhen's development.

The big group strategy soon took effect. By 1997, these 32 enterprises' total property reached 163.711 billion yuan, increasing by 20.6% compared with 1996. The total income of sales was 80.542 billion yuan, increasing 23.26%. The total profit was 7.651 billion yuan, increasing 34.39%. The total capital, state-owned net capital, total sales and profit of 19 of these key enterprises on municipal level separately accounted for 61.5%, 62.37%, 53.65% and 70.26% of corresponding data of Shenzhen. In 1997, 18 of the municipal key enterprises of industrial group supported by the government's help took up 41.72% of the gross industry output of Shenzhen, the profit volume accounted for 58.63% of the individual accounting enterprises of the city and the export delivery value took up 36.32% of Shenzhen.[27]

1.5.3.1.3 Deepen the Opening up

In late 1990s, with the influence of Asia's financial risk and the devaluation of money in the neighboring countries, the export industry of China was confronted with great challenges. In 1998, the year of the most serious financial risk in Asia, the growth rate of Shenzhen's total volume of import and export reduced from 15.3% to 0.6%[28]. Under this kind of situation, Shenzhen figured out a series of policies and measures, encouraging and helping the enterprises adjust the product and market structures in many ways,

27 Figures resource: Shenzhen Municipal Commission ***Historical Tasks for the Crossing-century Development***, Guangdong Economics Press, P413.

28 Shenzhen Statistics Bureau: ***Shenzhen Statistical Annual of 2007***, China Statistics Press, 2007, P261.

implementing diverse strategies and strove for the exploration of the far overseas market. Shenzhen made use of the state policy of upgrading export tax refund and stimulated the development of export. In Shenzhen, the export tax refund rate of mechanical and electrical products, information products and clothing, shoes, watches, toys and other products reached or exceeded 13%. These measures achieved remarkable results. In 2000, the total volume of imports and exports in Shenzhen grew 15.4% from 1999.[29] During the difficult period of the late 1990s, large enterprises in Shenzhen showed great vitality. Numbers of enterprises with millions of turnover became the mainstay of exports in Shenzhen. By 2000, enterprises in Shenzhen who invested and set up factories abroad or developed overseas process trades. ZTE established a PBX assembly plant in Pakistan, a trade company and a research center in the United States. Huawei set up a PBX assembly plant in Russia. Konka Group established color TV assembly plant in India and technology research centers in the United States. Page set up a blanket factory in South Africa and Yihao Group built motorcycle assembly plant in Brazil.

By 2000, more than 100 multinational corporations and world-renowned large enterprises invested in Shenzhen with more than 180 investment projects. Among them, 76 of the top 500 corporations listed by the authoritative magazine *Happiness* of the United States settled down in Shenzhen, which was called The City of Large Fabulous Bird. By 2000, the number of the total approved foreign direct investment projects accumulated to 25,443 with 23.014 billion USD of foreign capital actually utilized.[30] Top 500 investment corporations utilized 2.132 billion USD of foreign capital, accounting for 10% of the total amount of the actual utilization of the foreign capital of Shenzhen during the past 20 years. Top 500 corporations invested in Shenzhen, mostly in the manufacturing industries, accounted for 63.2% of the total number of the enterprises. More than half of their investment were used in electronics and information industries, followed by the services sector, covering a wide range of industries, including retail, foreign trade, real estate, banking, and insurance. With large-scale investment and advanced technologies and management, multinational companies, which invested in Shenzhen, generally operated under good situation. In 1998, Seagate, Guangdong Nuclear Power, Kaifa Science and Technology, Huaqiang Sanyo and Epson, ranked in the annual "Top Ten Foreign Investing Corporations in China with High Export Volume."

---

29 Shenzhen Statistics Bureau: Shenzhen Statistical Annual of 2007, China Statistics Press, 2007, P284.

30 Figured by statistics of Shenzhen Statistics Bureau: Shenzhen Statistical Annual of 2007, China Statistics Press, 2007, P269 and 277.

After 20 years development, Shenzhen became a world-renowned place of interest for investment and its enterprises went abroad. Shenzhen involved itself deeper and deeper in the circle of world economy. Factors for production, like capital, information and talented persons, were freely allocated in Shenzhen. The openness of Shenzhen had arrived at an unprecedented height.

1.5.3.2 Fast Growth of Private Economy

In the last period of 1990s, the private economy of Shenzhen achieved unprecedented development. By 2000, non-public economy output value accounted for 85% of the gross economic output value of Shenzhen and became the backbone for the economy. By the end of 2000, Shenzhen had more than 43,000 private enterprises, nearly 13,000 foreign or Hong Kong, Macau and Taiwan investment companies, more than 8000 "three plus one" companies, many of which were the big tax payers and advanced enterprises with large operation scale and high quality.

The call for developing private economy in theory and the 20-year practice of market economic reform made people realize the role and function of private economy in China. At the beginning of 1999, the 2nd Session of the 9th National People's Congress carried out the Constitutional Amendments, approving "public ownership acts as mainstay with diverse forms of ownership developing together" as the fundamental economic system for China during its primary period of socialism and regarding private economy as "an important component of the socialist market economy of China." This was a remarkable breakthrough in theory, which cleared the way for the diversity and rationalization for ownership. Private economy finally got its identity in China.

At the same period when the Constitution re-judged the nature of private economy, the deepening of reform over state-owned companies also brought new opportunities for private economy. The 4th Plenary Session of the 15th CPC Congress proposed that by 2010, the tasks for strategic adjustment and reorganization should be primarily finished and the relatively perfected modern enterprises system should be established. In the strategic adjustment and reorganization, state owned enterprises took the idea of "go ahead with retreat and do some while giving up some."

The retreat of state owned economy demonstrated influence over the economic structure of China. It offered more space for private economy, but in addition, only with the fast development of private economy, could state-owned economy be refilled to guarantee the success of the strategy of the state-owned economy's retreat.

The fast development of private economy in Shenzhen happened under this kind of background, which not only offered powerful force for its own economic growth, but also cleared the way for the adjustment of the ownership structure all over the country.[31]

1.6 New Period for the Development of Shenzhen SAR (2001~2009)

1.6.1 Downturn and Adjustment from 2001 to 2003

1.6.1.1 Risks Aroused by the Suspended New Stocks

Securities market is a trading market for the financial resources allocation. Shanghai and Shenzhen Stock Exchanges are two national level securities trading stages. Since their establishment, they have been involved in a complex relationship of competing and cooperating at the same time. Although both of them are under the leadership of China Securities Regulatory Commission (CSRC), the competition for listing the stocks between them is obvious.

In 1997, CSRC made the decision that, on the issue of initial public offerings, enterprises could no longer choose to publish in Shanghai or Shenzhen Stock Exchange, but took the measure "one in Shanghai, one in Shenzhen." This, through administrative management, restrained Shenzhen with directly competing with Shanghai by a pragmatic and innovative system. In 1998, with the change of the leader of the State Council, the idea on the development of finance changed. Under the background of nationwide adjustment and control over financial industry, news for merging these two Exchanges could be heard from time to time, both in Shanghai and Beijing (certainly to merge Shenzhen Stock Exchange in to Shanghai's). The turnover of Shanghai exceeded Shenzhen in 1998. In 2000, following the model of promoting hi-tech industries in the USA by NASDAQ, to add GEM (Growth Enterprises Market) board in China became more and more popular. Finally, the State Council decided to add GEM board in Shenzhen Stock Exchange with the prerequisite of stopping the issue of new stocks on main board. Actually, the suspending of new shares in Shenzhen was carried out in September of 2000, but the proposal of GEM board had not yet been realized. The finance industry of Shenzhen fell into serious risks. Headquarters of many investment banks, funds and other finance organization moved to Shanghai.[32]

In fact, the suspending of new shares meant the financing function of Shenzhen Stock

---

31 Reference: SU, Dongbin: ***Brief History of SAR in China***, China Economics Press, 2001

32 ZHAO, Lingmin: ***Previous and Present Years of Shenzhen***—Talks with Dr. Zhu Wenhui (Commentator on Current Events of Fenghuang TV), ***South Wind***, Issue 5 of 2007.

was frozen. Its severity of impact was fully realized in the next two to three years. According to Dr. He Chengying's research,[33] since 1996, funds raised by Shenzhen A shares IPO accounted for more than 50% of the total funds raised in 1997 and 1999. In 1996 and 1998, the minimum amount was no less than 40% of the total. The suspending of new shares in 2000 significantly affected the total funds raised in Shenzhen. The proportion of A shares IPO accounting for the total dropped from more than 50% to 26.2%. In the subsequent 2001 and first ten months of 2002, this proportion fell to zero. Calculated by the ratio of 50%, in the following two years since the suspending for new shares in Shenzhen, funds raised by Shenzhen market had decreased 66.611 billion yuan, equaling to the total amount raised by A shares from 1998 to 2000. More seriously, the huge secondary market trading of funds losing due profits of IPO in Shenzhen transferred to the Shanghai market. It was estimated that in the following two years after the cessation of IPO, the losing funds of the secondary market in Shenzhen accumulated to 469.5 billion yuan with a monthly average loss of 18.78 billion yuan. Loss of secondary market trading funds directly led to the loss of the stamp duty on stock transactions. During these two years, the stamp duty averagely ran off 37.56 million yuan per month. The amount accumulated to 1 billion yuan, averagely 500 million yuan per year.[34]

For the securities businessmen, the transfer of funds from the primary market and secondary market meant to take away the fuel from the bottom of the boiling pot. According to the Shenzhen Securities Industry Association's statistics, in 2002, turnover of all the sales departments of Shenzhen Stock Exchange was 457.321 billion yuan. Compared with 875.219 billion yuan in 2001, the amount decreased by 48%, with two billion yuan lost averagely for each individual department. At the same time, the turnover of the stock market of the whole nation only decreased by 28.65%. Therefore, the market share of Shenzhen in the whole stock market of China fell from 10.71% in 2001 to 7.84% in 2002. Due to the sharp decline in transaction volume, commission income substantially reduced. In 2002, the brokerage business of securities industry in Shenzhen had 291 million yuan of loss. The average loss of each business department was 1.5581 million yuan. 146 of the business departments suffered from great losses. 126 of them lost more than the average amount of the whole city. The most serious loss for one of the business departments reached 115.3 million yuan. All throughout the city, only 53 business departments made

33 HE, Chengying: Seeking for Capital Investment Board—Analysis on Industrial View and Trend of Stock Market, Guidance for Securities, 1st Issue of 2004.

34 http://info.finance.hc360.com/2004/02/1310242448.shtml.

profits. This was the first industry-wide annual deficit since the start of the securities business in 1995.[35] The suspending of new shares not only impacted the securities industry, but also influenced relevant industries, like accounting and law services, securities trust business of the banks and investment funds, which were suffering from varying degrees of recession. The suspending of new shares aroused great recession over financial industry and crumbled the foundation of finance industry, which was one of the three pillar industries supporting the development of Shenzhen.

Later, two scholars of Peking University researched on the fluctuation spillover effect of the suspending of new shares by GARCH model. They believed that the suspending of new shares in Shenzhen decisively affected the relative positions in the securities market of China between the Shanghai and Shenzhen Stock Exchanges. It changed the direction of information transmission between the two exchanges. In the past, the last income fluctuation of Shenzhen greatly influenced the securities market of Shanghai, while the spillover effect from Shanghai to Shenzhen was not obvious, but later the spillover effects were reversed from Shanghai to Shenzhen unilaterally. In other words, the suspending of new shares in Shenzhen made Shanghai the dominance of information. Shanghai Exchange became the pioneer of the stock market of China. Shenzhen fell behind Shanghai in the fields of the amount of the listed companies, the turnover and daily average income rate of the large cap.[36]

1.6.1.2 2002: Shenzhen, Who Abandoned You?

In the history of the development in Shenzhen, it must be said it was a miracle that one article online could cause the strong concern from the mayor, down to the civilian population, which triggered a major controversy. In the afternoon of November 16, 2002, Development Forum of Xinhua Net and the Strong Country Forum of People's Net published "On the Edge of City One: Shenzhen, Who Abandoned You" written by a netizen named "Crazy for You." The article illustrated and analyzed on the development energy, finance industry, reform of state owned enterprises, efficiency of governmental departments, public order, urban environment, cooperation between Shenzhen and Hong Kong and other issues, which pained many readers. When the decline of Shenzhen's financial industry was mentioned, the author pointed out that "as the regional finance center in China, the conditions of Shenzhen could not compete with Guangzhou, if it seemed

35 http://www.cncapital.net/.

36 http://www.cenet.org.cn/cn/CEAC.

unnecessary to work with Hong Kong. If we looked at this through a boarder perspective, finance industry reflected the embarrassment of Shenzhen's economy—the geo-economic limitation. Shenzhen was sandwiched between Hong Kong, the window for China going to the world, Guangzhou, a gateway for Southern China and the center of Pearl River Delta. Although Shenzhen looked full of confidence under the SAR aura, when faced with the environment, Shenzhen felt confused, asking where it should go." This revealed the depression and confusion of Shenzhen people.

Two months after the article was published online, arranged by *NanfangDushi Daily*, a face to face talk between the author, Wo Zhongxiao, and the Mayor of Shenzhen, Yu Youjun, was held in Beijing Hall on the second floor of Guangdong Mansion in Dong Feng Street in Guangzhou. This was the first time that the governor responded to the talk of the town triggered by online articles.

This debate, met with widespread concern, finally achieved unified public opinion. As long as Shenzhen people did not abandon themselves, no one could do it. Actually, under the nationwide tide of industrial structure adjustment, the gap between Shenzhen and Shanghai was not narrowed, but widened day by day.

1.6.1.3 Reform of the Secondary Barrier

The second barrier in Shenzhen was started in June of 1982. The Central, Guangdong Province and Shenzhen invested one third of 138 million yuan—the total amount of the funds raised. In March of 1985, the project of the second barrier formally passed acceptance. At that time, although there were a lot of disputes on the project, it started in 1982 and finished in 1986. The second barrier artificially divided Shenzhen into two independent parts, but the reforms inside and outside it were in full swing. It played an important role to guarantee the substantial, fast and stable development of Shenzhen.

After the return of Hong Kong in 1997, more and more people questioned the existence of the second barrier. In 1998, CPPCC members of Shenzhen, Yu Wanjun and Chen Xitian, first submit proposals, suggesting reevaluating the necessity of the existence of the second barrier and recommending moving it back and deregulating in some aspects. In February 2000, the scholar Zhu Jianguo published an article online "When to Remove the Berlin Wall in Shenzhen," arousing attention of the majority of internet users and the members of CPPCC and CPC in Shenzhen. The call for removing the second barrier grew higher and higher. On June 25th of the same year, the "Shenzhen Second Barrier Moving Northward Investigate Group," led by the official of the SAR Department of the Reform Office from the State Council, arrived in Shenzhen. After a one week investigation and research, they thought that the political meaning for the second barrier was more important than its economic meaning. It could not be removed at present.

The second barrier was a historical product of the special administrative region. When would its meaning of existence last? It was difficult for the manager of the second barrier, governor of SAR and scholars to answer this question. When there was high discussion on the first and the second barriers, the corps and officers of Guangdong Boarder Defense adjusted and reformed the procedures, like issuing Prior Examine Certificate and Seven-Day Board Card and loosening the entrance for farming. However, these convenience measures could not catch up with the requests on the first and second barriers under the development situation. In May 2002, Guangdong Boarder Defense Corps Zhuhai and Shenzhen the First and Second Barrier Reform and Management team was established. After one-month research, "Shenzhen & Zhuhai the First and Second Barriers Management and Reform Plan" finally turned up. Huang Liman, Deputy Secretary of Guangdong Provincial Party Committee and Secretary of Shenzhen Municipal Party Committee, and Huang Longyun, standing committee of Guangdong Provincial Party Committee and Zhuhai Municipal Party Committee, supported the primary plan respectively. The plan also got approval and support from the Party Committee of Provincial Public Security Department and Provincial Politics and Law Committee. In October 2002, Guangdong Boarder Defense Corps submitted the deliberations on the reform plan from Provincial Standing Committee to the Public Security Ministry. In November, Reform Office and Hong Kong & Macau Affairs Office of the State Council and General Administration of Customs approved and agreed with the suggestions of reform from Guangdong Boarder Defense. On December 19, Finance Ministry, Public Security Ministry and National Development and Reform Commission jointly agree to cancel the charge for SAR entrance and exit for vehicles.

On April 11, 2003, the State Council and the Central Military Commission formally approved the important reform measure of Guangdong Boarder Defense. On May 28, 2003, Border Defense carried out reform on the Administrative Line, normally called the Second Barrier, and took nine measures for people's convenience. A faster and more effective customs and a harmonious boarder defense environment had a far-reaching impact on the development of Shenzhen.

1.6.2 Adjustment and Implementation of Important Policies from 2004 to 2009

1.6.2.1 Urbanization of Rural Areas

On October 30, 2003, Shenzhen held the General Assembly to speed up the urbanization of Bao'an and Longgang districts and formally launch the urbanization over these two districts. It decided to cancel the Town and Village Committee within the period from October 30, 2003 to December 2004, to set up neighborhood offices and community resident committees, to transfer rural residents to urban residential household, to change the ownership over land from collective-owned to state-owned and to maintain the fertility policy for rural residents for four years. This was the second time Shenzhen promoted urbanization, involving 18 towns, 218 administrative villages of more than 270,000 villagers in Bao'an and Longgang Districts. After urbanization, the original residents of Bao'an and Longgang districts who meet the standard of the age could enjoy pension and medical insurance in accordance with the standard of urban residents. After the transfer from agricultural residence households to non-agricultural households, residents could enjoy the guaranteed minimum living standards of the city. The original villagers, who met the application requests, could apply for employment within the city.

Urbanization was a major event in the history of Shenzhen and also a difficult task for its development. After the assembly for mobilization, according to the municipal government's schedule, Longhua Town in Bao'an District and Longgang Town in Longgang District were selected as the pilot of urbanization. At the end of June 2004, Shenzhen Municipal Government held a mobilization assembly again. After summing up the experience of the pilot, urbanization of Bao'an and Longgang districts was in full swing, with plans to complete the task of urbanization before the end of December 2004. Huang Liman, who was then the party secretary, pointed out in his speech that the pilot work of urbanization must be "in place at four aspects. That is, to ensure leadership is in place by strengthening leadership and organizing the work carefully, to ensure the is recognition in place by publicizing and uniting thinking, guarantee the policies in place by being realistic and matching the systems, and guarantee the effects by restructuring system and promoting development. She pointed out that to comprehensively promote urbanization of the Bao'an and Longgang Districts was another major historical turning point in the process of modernization and was a great progress that benefited the present and future generations. It was also a great issue concerning the immediate interests of hundreds of thousands of people and their long-term welfare with complex conflicts, varying interest, demands and uneven understanding. It was an important aspect of the urbanization of these two districts to unite people and cadres of the whole city, especially those of Bao'an and Longgang, and to promote them to do this work willingly. She also pointed out that urbanization of these two districts was not an ordinary concrete work, but was a great matter related to whether the development of Shenzhen's society and economy could be continued sustainably, whether Shenzhen could change comparative advantages into comprehensively competitive advantages, what kind of city could Shenzhen construct, what kind of home could Shenzhen people have, and a great matter concerning with the ruling capability and level of the Party and with the superiority of socialist system with Chinese characteristics playing full role.[37] After the conference, Shenzhen Municipal Government made great efforts, and by the end of 2004, they announced the completion of urbanization with 270,000 farmers transferring to urban residents. To ensure the employment of these new residents after urbanization, in March 2005, Shenzhen promulgated "Suggestions on Employment and Re-employment" after the acceleration of "Urbanization of Bao'an and Longgang," clarifying the specific responsibilities and tasks for district government, community commissions and other relevant departments of all levels on the issue of employment after the urbanization, implementing annual assessment, bringing shareholding corporations of the original and newly founded villages into unemployment insurance system by paying unemployment insurance as the means of solving the employment of rural residents in urban communities.

Focus of rural-urban transformation of Shenzhen was the land issue that was also the focus of various interests and conflicts in urbanization. On June 26, 2004, Shenzhen issued "Land Management Practices of the Urbanization of Bao'an and Longgang Districts of Shenzhen and three accessories—Compensation for the Transformation of Collective Land into State Owned of Bao'an and Longgang of Shenzhen, Provisions of Implement Procedures for Transformation of Collective Land into State Owned of Bao'an and Longgang of Shenzhen and Land Storage Management Provisions of Bao'an and Longgang of Shenzhen." In accordance with these provisions, the two district governments were asked to hand over their authorities of the land that was transferred into state-owned property to department of land management since the date of signing the compensation agreements or within 30 days after making decisions for compensation. Land management departments accepted the land in accordance with relevant materials. By the end of 2004, 956 square kilometers of collective land transferred into state owned land. The government compensated 265 square kilometers of it, most of which was farmland. 700 square kilometers of it did not get compensation mainly including more than 200 square kilometers of district that had been constructed and more than 300 square kilometers of

37 http://www.cenet.org.cn/cn/CEAC.

hills and forests. With concern for the ownership of the hill and forests, most of which were also undeveloped, the compensation issue was held in abeyance. The aforementioned more than 200 square kilometers of constructed area would be disposed in accordance with "Provisions of Disposals on Illegal Private Houses Left along History of Shenzhen Special Administrative Zone and Disposals on Illegal Productive Constructions Left along History of Shenzhen Special Administrative Zone."[38]

To take forceful measures of transformation, but not expropriation, from collective land into state owned in the urbanization reform of these two districts aroused many disputes in academic circles. Professor Wang Weiguo of China University of Political Science and Law believed that: "270,000 farmers entered into the city of Shenzhen. Their citizenship meant urbanization. In accordance with the provision of 'urban land is owned by the State' in the Constitution, their rural collective land should be handed over to the State." Chen Yin, Deputy Director of Law Institute of Chinese Academy of Social Sciences, thought that the basis for the land transformation in Shenzhen was the Fifth Article of the Second Item of *Enforcement Regulations of Land Management*, but this item itself was unreasonable. Urbanization was the result of economic development and would have certain legal consequences, such as agricultural households being transferred to citizens' households. However, China could not change the ownership of rural land. Under the Constitution, there was only one way to transfer land ownership in China that is the land acquisition system. Changes in household of farmers could not change the property relations. The nature of rural land ownership could not be directly changed without the following the land acquisition procedures simply because farmers became urban residents."[39] Han Jun, Minister of Development Research Center of Rural Economy of the State Council, believed that the collectively-owned land transformed into state-owned of Shenzhen was of great use for unifying the planning of the city, for the utilizing the urban environment and for reducing the land cost of the development of the city. However, rural land owned by the peasants collective was defined in the Law of China. According for the law, public ownership equals to private ownership while collective ownership equals to state owned ownership. Neither public authority could violate private right, nor could the state owned ownership violate the collective ownership. If it is thought that collective land

38 ***Requisition of Transformation: Land Issues behind the Urbanization of Shenzhen*** International Online: http://gb.cri.cn/1827/2004/09/27/1166@312226_1.htm.

39 Land Management Provisions: Article 2 Item 5, If all members of rural collective economic organization are transferred into urban residents, the land they hold must hand over to all the people of the country, that is to say it belongs to the Nation.

can be transferred by administrative compulsory measures without the agreement of the farmers, it will surely result in the violation from administrative rights to the collective property ownership and violation from the state ownership to rural collective ownership. No matter how they disputed in the academic circle, the completion of the urbanization reform in Shenzhen was an irrevocable fact. However, the reform over the rural area inside the city and the realization of harmonious development of urbanized rural communities still had a long way to go.

1.6.2.2 SEM Board Starts Its Performance

On June 25, 2004, the long awaited and remarkable Small and Medium Enterprises Board was listed in Shenzhen Stock Exchange, which experienced many ups and downs, and the new vista was finally seen. The first eight companies included Xin He Cheng (002001), Jiangsu QiongHua (002002), Weixing Shares (002003), Hua Bang Pharmacy (002004), Hao De Run Da (002005), Jing Gong Science and Technology (002006), HuaLan Biology (002007) and DaZu Laser (002008) with 2.287 billion yuan raised. By the end of May 2007, 134 companies were listed on SME Board. The raised IPO accumulated to 39.127 billion yuan with an average of 292 million yuan for each. IPO issues accumulated

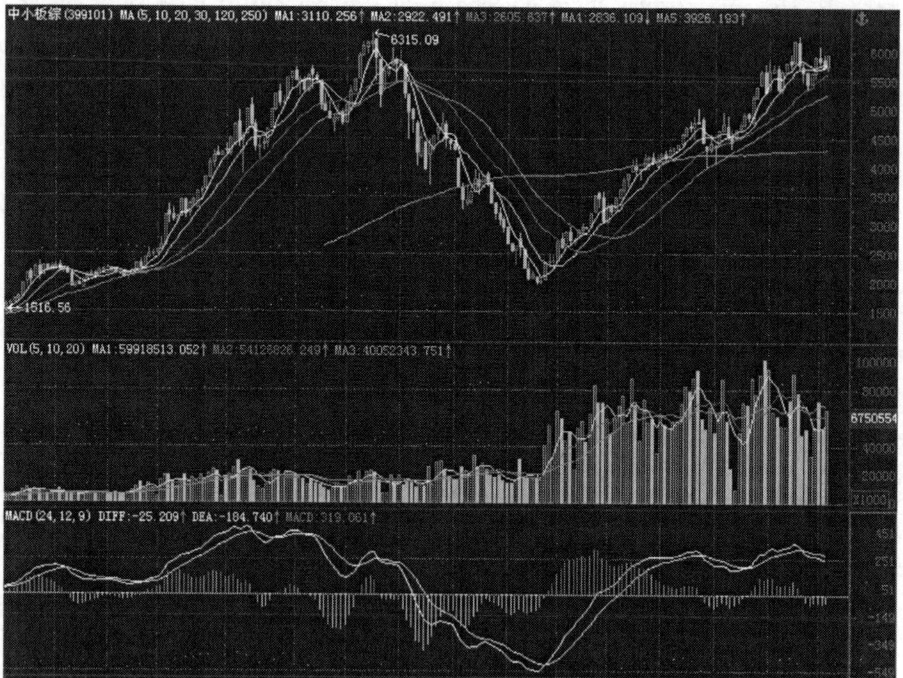

Figure 1-6-1 Shenzhen SME Board index weekly chart K (2006/04/07—2010/03/19)

to 4.619 billion shares with an average of 34.47 million shares for each. The average price per earning ratio was 17.2 times (compared with the capital stock before its issue) and 24.26 times (compared with the capital stock after its issue). The average growth rate was 91.3% on the first day of its issue.[40]

The beginning of SME Board resumed the capital raising capability of Shenzhen stock market and attracted many organizations and capital to Shenzhen. Investment banks of the local stock businessmen restarted their business deals. More importantly, SEM Board found one low-doorsill stage for the retreat of domestic risk investment and also offered one solution for the small and medium enterprises for raising the capital. It directly played a role in the revitalization of the stock market of Shenzhen and in the attraction of financial resources at home and abroad.

1.6.2.3 Implement of Closer Economic Partnership Arrangement (CEPA) and Following Policy Arrangement

June 29, 2003, *Closer Economic Partnership Arrangement* (CEPA) was officially signed in Hong Kong. On the basis of CEPA, from January 1, 2004, many goods could enter the mainland market duty-free and more than ten service industries could enjoy preferential policies.

CEPA was the inevitable outcome after China's induction to the World Trade Organization. After China entered the World Trade Organization, regional economic cooperation was immediately issued on the agenda. In November 2001, Hong Kong first proposed the "free-trade-alike zone" scenario and was responded by the mainland. After rounds of deliberation and consultation, the point of entrance of the proposal was evolved from region into relationship. That is to establish closer trade relations between tariff regions between mainland and Hong Kong. This would also partially resolve the conflicts between "one country two systems" and economic regionalization.

CEPA, under the great promotion of the government, was a new institutional arrangement and a new policy breakthrough. Its essence was institutional arrangement among governments and official systems taking place of free style regional cooperation with market as orientation, enterprises as mainstay and with comparative advantages and market selection as basis for industrial configuration. One of the inevitable intentions for CEPA was to "play with time difference." That was to take advantage of China fulfilling WTO obligations, to honor the commitments of the transition period and to relax the

40 http://finance.sina.com.cn/stock/mainmarket/20070525/00353627339.shtml.

restrictions of Hong Kong entering the mainland ahead of time. The existence of close regional relationship resulted in the "time difference will continue its effects."

CEPA would bring qualitative leaps for the economic cooperation between Mainland China, especially Southern China, and Hong Kong. The biggest opportunity it brought laid in Guangdong and Shenzhen, by virtue of its geographic advantages, becoming the most direct beneficiary. On the one hand, the cooperation between Shenzhen and Hong Kong during the previous 20 years emphasized traditional labor-intensive industries. The power of the market was fully released under the existing institutional arrangement and even the phenomenon of diminishing marginal utility turned up. For Hong Kong and Shenzhen, both their manufacturing and service industries required new business opportunities by the release of the new policy effect. On the other hand, policy effect of CEPA should be a long-term release process and would give birth to new market forces of the cooperation between Shenzhen and Hong Kong.

Some scholars[41] believe that countermeasures of Shenzhen under CEPA are as follows: Shenzhen should develop financial, logistics, tourism and other service industries to approach close to the developed countries as soon as possible; take advantage of the opportunities brought by CEPA to upgrade the high-tech industry level of development and further enhance the competitiveness of high-tech industry; speed up the pace of the full liberalization of the market and strive to improve the level of investment liberalization; establish government management system in accordance with international level; constantly learn advanced management experience from Hong Kong, an international cosmopolitan, and improve the market economy development level; Shenzhen as the geographical mediation between Hong Kong and the Pearl River Delta, Hong Kong and the mainland, Shenzhen should vigorously accelerate the building of infrastructure and information technology to make the communication between Hong Kong and the Mainland faster and more convenient.

1.6.2.4 The Start of GEM Board

On October 23, 2009, the opening ceremony for GEM Board was held in Wu Zhou Hall of Wu Zhou Guest House of Shenzhen. President Shang Fu Lin of China Securities Regulatory Commission (CSRC) participated in the ceremony and delivered an important speech. Elites from governmental departments and securities circle gathered

---

41 MENG, Jinghang: *Influence of CEPA on Pearl River Delta and the Policies of Shenzhen, Theory and Practice of SAR*, 12th Issue of 2003, p 20.

together to witness the historical event. GEM Board of China was the third greatest event of capital market, following the main board openness and reform of shares configuration.

Early in January of 1999, Shenzhen Stock Exchange officially submitted "Project Report on the Program Research of Starting the GEM Board" to CSRC and attached the implement program. In March 1999, CSRC, for the first time proposed that the hi-tech enterprises board could be considered to list on Shanghai and Shenzhen stock exchanges. In October 2000, Shenzhen Stock Exchange announced that the technological preparation for GEM Board had been finalized and its regulations (revised draft) were officially appealed online. On May 17, 2004, approved by the State Council, CSRC formally replied and affirmed the establishment for GEM Board in Shenzhen Stock Exchange, which symbolized that the step-by-step construction of GEM Board made substantial progress. On June 5, 2009, Shenzhen Stock Exchange officially published "GEM Board Listing Regulation of Shenzhen Stock Exchange" that would take effect starting on July 1st.

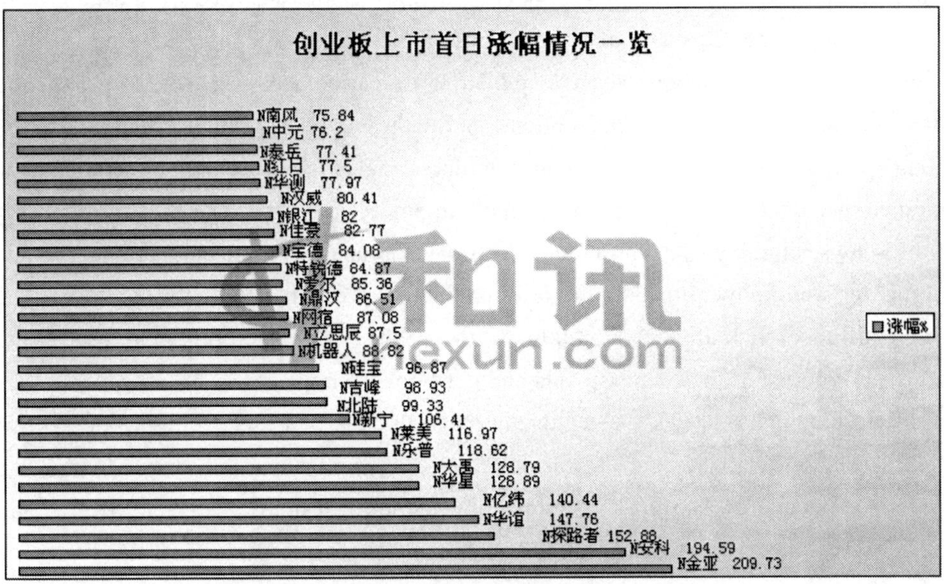

Figure 1-6-2 Increase of GEM Board at Its First Day

After 10 years' preparation, GEM Board of China was finally born. On October 30, 2009, the first 28 companies listed on GEM Board of Shenzhen Stock Exchange. As an important part of the multi-layer capital market of China, the birth of GEM Board enriched and perfected the functions of capital market, which was conducive to the adjustment of industrial structure of the whole nation and to the upgrading of the technological innovative capability of innovative enterprises by virtue of the financing stage. Especially for the private business, it meant to inject new blood and its function and influence would be great and far-reaching. At present, however, GEM Board was just born with a small market whose situation could not perfectly match with the constructive idea of the institutional frame and many regulations need to be improved.

1.6.3 Seeking for New Position

1.6.3.1 Shift for the Industries and Position of Regional Center City

After World War II, the international industry experienced three major waves of transfer. The first occurred in 1960s. The United States moved its iron, steel, textiles, shipbuilding and other traditional heavy industry to Japan, West Germany and other countries. The United States focused on the development of the semiconductor, computer, biomedical, telecommunications and other industries. Japan, West Germany and other countries relied on this to swiftly complete the post-war economic recovery and industrialization. Second international industrial transfer occurred from the 1970s to 1980s. Japan, West Germany and other countries moved the textile, clothing, leather, electronics and other labor-intensive industries or part of heavy chemical production processes to some countries and regions in Southeast Asia. South Korea, Singapore, Hong Kong and Taiwan gained strong manufacturing capabilities after undertaking the international industrial transfer (the Korean automobile, IT products in Taiwan, Hong Kong's toys, clothing and household electrical appliances of Singapore) and became origins for well-known brands in an international market. Their economy took off. The third shift occurred after the middle of the 1990s. Manufacturing and processing industries flooded from Southeast Asia and developed European and American countries to the developing countries, especially the coastal areas of China, bringing up a Pearl River Delta of small appliances, furniture, clothing and other industries. In the late 1990s, IT industry of Taiwan, communications equipment industry of South Korea and Japan were transferred to Shenzhen, Dongguan and Suzhou, creating the high-tech industries in Shenzhen and the computer, communication spare parts manufacturing of Dongguan and Suzhou. After entering the new century, the Japanese, European and American car manufacturers, iron and steel, nonferrous metals, petrochemical, shipbuilding and other heavy and chemical industries continued to transfer to Beijing, Tianjin, Tanggu, Yangtze River Delta and Pearl River Delta, building up the car manufacturing industry in Shanghai and Guangzhou.

Guangzhou, as the center city of Pearl River Delta in Guangdong Province, with a strong political, cultural, technological and economic strength supports, caught up with the historic opportunity of the third international industrial transfer, and quickly completed the adjustment of heavy-duty industries. In the space layout options of the industry, Guangzhou chose Nansha, at the mouth of Pearl River, as a gathering place for heavy-duty industry with more than 30 billion municipal fiscal invested in the development for Nansha. China Shipbuilding Group invested 4.5 billion in the construction of Nansha Shipbuilding Base there. Joint venture of Guangzhou Steel and Nippon Steel giant, JEF, produced hot galvanized steel for cars. In addition to Nansha, the heavy industry base of Guangzhou, Huadu District of Guangzhou was another heavy industrial base. Honda, Nissan, Toyota and other international auto giants gathered at Huadu. Nissan gathered its plant for major frame of cars, engine plant and R & D center in Huadu. Transferring process to heavy-duty industry made the industrial structure of Guangzhou rapidly enter into middle-late period of industrialization. Capital and technology-intense industries replaced labor-intense industries and topped the domain, while heavy industries led the industry of the whole city to rapidly develop. These laid Guangzhou ahead of the economic development in Pearl River Delta.

To review the economic development of Shenzhen during the past years, although dominated by industrial development inertia, the economy of Shenzhen constantly increased on a comparative high platform. After the middle of 1990s, gradually fading SAR policies made Shenzhen hesitate in the tide of industrial structural adjustment all through the nation and lose heavy-duty industry opportunity. While Shenzhen boasted about the glory of its hi-tech development, the hi-tech industry of mainland cities like Suzhou grew faster, with a lower cost. Structure of Shenzhen hi-tech industry, with electronic information industry as dominance, made its industrial ripple effect less powerful than the heavy-duty industry of Guangzhou. The problem of lacking subsequent power for the national economic development became obvious. Another pillar industry, finance, because of its suspending of new shares, led local small and medium enterprises, investment organizations and investment banks swallow years' worth of bitter fruit. Although logistics continuously developed, the narrow geographic layout limited its enlargement of radiation. As the natural economic center of Pearl River Delta, both the urban construction and the second, the third industrial development of Guangzhou surpassed the achievement of Shenzhen during the same period. The renaissance of Guangzhou laid tremendous pressure onto the perspective of Shenzhen that was positioned as the central city of the region.

1.6.3.2 Seeking for New Position: Establish Regional Internationalized City

The position of Shenzhen's development was an issue researched and discussed constantly in the academic circle and the governmental management level. Under the background of getting rid of preferential policies towards Shenzhen, awareness of unexpected situation that Shenzhen became a SAR without special characteristics ran though the policy agenda of the first generations of municipal government. The dispute of who abandoned Shenzhen started from 2002 was still being contested. The confusion over Shenzhen, which was once the experimental field and the bellwether of reform and opening up, aroused the attention from the Central Government. In 2003, not long after the establishment of the new government, the State Council dispatched a research group of seven people to Shenzhen, studying how Shenzhen could develop itself and how Shenzhen could play a unique role in maintaining prosperity of Hong Kong. The research group took materials of different aspects, which were provided by Shenzhen, but the Central Government did not declare on the issue concerning of the orientation and the position of the development of Shenzhen. This aroused discussions on the repositioning of Shenzhen in all social circles in 2003.[42]

From September 12 to 13, 2005, Prime Minister Wen JiaBao inspected Shenzhen and held the SAR Working Seminar. He commended the achievement of SAR and pointed out that in the new historical condition, the position and role of SAR could not be weakened nor disappeared. The Central Government reiterated that its decision on the development of SAR, the fundamental policies of SAR, the historical position and role of SAR in the reform and opening up and the modernization construction of the whole nation would not change. China would not only continue the development of SAR, but also strive to promote them to a better situation.

The dispute of whether SAR insisting on their special characteristics was completed by that time, but Shenzhen's proposals for new policies, larger scale and land areas and the position of municipality were not fulfilled by the Central Government. On March 26, 2006, the Third Plenary of the Second Session of the Fourth People's Congress of Shenzhen was held. The 11th Five-Year Plan of National Economy and Social Development of Shenzhen was overwhelmingly approved. During the 11th Five-Year Plan period and to the year of 2020, the strategic goal for the economic and social development of Shenzhen was, in the

---

42 *Weekend: Great Discussion on the Positioning of Shenzhen—where should you go?* http://news.sina.com.cn/c/2003-08-13/16391536583.shtml

Pacific Asia district, to establish an influential international hi-tech city, an international hub for logistics, an international financial and exhibition center, an international cultural and communicative center and an international tourist city and to establish Shenzhen an important regional internationalized city on the basis of realizing modernization of Socialism within 15 years.

The 11th Five Year Plan defined the position for Shenzhen to establish regional internationalized city and demonstrated that after years of confusion, Shenzhen found a definite and practical orientation.

1.6.3.3 National Experimental Zone for Comprehensive Reform

After 29 years of development, Shenzhen gained great achievements. In accordance with the statistics, in 2008, GDP of Shenzhen reached 780.654 billion yuan, with 89,800 yuan per capita, separately increasing by 3,974 times and 148 times that of 1978. Its GDP and GDP per capita ranked fourth and the first among the middle and big cities of the whole nation. Shenzhen became one example of the reform and opening up of China. However, the development of Shenzhen was also confronted with series of conflicts and problems, like over-population, tightening space and the unbalance between the areas inside and outside SAR. Shenzhen urgently needed to promote reform and opening up to a wider, deeper and higher level.

Before the Spring Festival of 2009, the State Council issued "Guidelines for the Reform and Development of the Pearl River Delta." The Municipal Government of Shenzhen, in order to thoroughly implement the spirit of the 17th Party Congress, to realize the "Guideline" *(2008~2020),* to continue the bellwether role of SAR in reform and opening up under the new situation and to promote the realization of scientific development of Shenzhen, carried out the "General Program of Comprehensive Reform of Shenzhen." On May 26, Shenzhen Municipal Government officially announced that the State Council approved the "General Program of Comprehensive Reform of Shenzhen" (hereinafter referred to the "General Program"). Thereafter, Shenzhen became the third national experimental zone for comprehensive reform, following Pudong District of Shanghai and Binhai District of Tianjin. In addition, Shenzhen and Hong Kong could complement functions between each other and promote the form of an international center of logistics, trading, innovation and cultural creation. Shenzhen, the window for reform and opening up of China, playing the role as a pioneer, changed from the first SAR of China to the national experimental zone of comprehensive reform. This undoubtedly boosted Shenzhen, then in its 30th year, and meant the acceleration of a new round of reform.

The basic idea of the comprehensive reform was to deepen the reform that was done in the past, to promote the reform that has been deployed by the Central Government and actively explore reform that matches the future development orientation. In accordance with the national strategic deployment of the reform, Shenzhen needed to pioneer in four aspects: the important measures for deepening the reform and enlarging the opening up; the institutional design meeting international practice and the orientation of the development of China in the future, which needed to be tested; the institutional innovation that had great impact on the economic and social development of Shenzhen and could play an important leading role of the whole nation; and the important issues to enhance the cooperation between the mainland and Hong Kong. Shenzhen must strive to gain breakthroughs in the fields and gain important relations, form institutional mechanism for scientific development all through the nation and create new experience for developing socialism with Chinese characteristics.

1.6.4 Returning to the Root of Government Affairs—Focusing on Livelihood Issues

1.6.4.1 Shenzhen of Harmony and Profits

In May 2005, the Fourth Party Congress of Shenzhen proposed to establish a harmonious and profitable Shenzhen and to realize the fundamental change of the development mode. In order to set up the harmonious society as a scientific practical procedure that can be operated, checked, assessed and controlled, Shenzhen researched and carried index for civilization, benefit and harmony.[43]

In April 2005, Shenzhen first introduced a civilization index evaluation system in the nation. Civilization index was composed of indexes of happiness, caring, humanities, security, credit, environment and probity. Happiness index measured the harmony between production and life, between GDP and life quality. Caring index measured disparity between the rich and the poor and the harmony among different groups of people. Civilization index measured the harmony between materials production and spiritual production. Security index measured the harmony between personal and property and the social environment. Credit index measured the harmony among market players and the harmony between market players and the government. Environment index measured the harmony between human beings and the nature. Probity index measured the harmony

43 WANG, Jingsheng: *Index, System and Soul of A Harmonious Shenzhen, Practice and Theory of SAR*, 6th Issue of 2006

between officials and common people. In accordance with the accounting of "Beneficial Shenzhen" index system, the integrated index of Shenzhen in 2006 was 114.08%, increasing 5.71 percentage points compared with 2005.

In September 2005, Shenzhen formally launched the Beneficial Shenzhen Evaluation System. Beneficial index was an important indicator for the real changes of the economic growth mode and developmental mode of Shenzhen. It became the principal scale, measuring the development quality and construction situation of a harmonious and beneficial Shenzhen. Beneficial index was composed of 21 individual indexes, including nine of economic benefits, four of social benefits, four of ecological benefits and three of human being development. With scientific development as guidance, with unit product replacing gross economic output and benefit taking place of the growth of GDP, this system emphasized on the quality and cost of the development, which symbolized the Shenzhen farewell to the "GDP Supreme Theory." Harmonious index was composed of six first level index (social development, fairness, social guarantee, social caring, security and ecological civilization) and 39 concrete indexes that were indicated with responsible departments concerning 19 governmental departments.

To establish a harmonious society, it needs, at least, four social foundations: the accumulation of social wealth; the establishment of fairness institution; the efficiency of moral basis; and the establishment of conflicts solution system. The future development of Shenzhen should emphasize balance, coordination and build up breakthrough in four aspects to form a harmonious society, such as the following: accelerate innovation of social institution to realize the coordination of economic and social development and the balance of ecology; set up new concepts for Shenzhen people and upgrade the home consciousness and urban recognition of all walks of life, including workers from places outside Shenzhen; adjust the disparity of social distribution and establish social fairness by market, government and society; enhance the coordination and unification of the plans, construction and management; and realize balance development inside and outside the SAR.[44]

1.6.4.2 Social Security for Migrant Workers

Migrant worker is one of the social groups that China should be most concerned with at the present, whose number has surpassed 110 million, while the Shenzhen absorbed about 10% of them. After nearly 30 years of construction and development, Shenzhen

44 YUE, Zheng: *Build up a Harmonious Shenzhen and Increase People's Welfare, Practice and Theory of SAR*, 6th Issue of 2006.

developed from a small border town into a thriving modern metropolis. In its nearly 30 year history, migrant workers have always been the main force in emerging sectors of the economy. They created the prerequisite primitive accumulation of capital for the urban economy and social development and promoted the reform of employment system. Floods of cheap labor promoted the adjustment of the industrial structure of Shenzhen. In addition, migrant workers in Shenzhen greatly contributed to the promotion of political civilization and the social development and the shaping of the spirit of Shenzhen.

The three major insurances of Shenzhen—pension, medical and work injury-have covered the non-resident households, with migrant workers as the main group. Pension of Shenzhen for migrant workers implemented private account system with two sources: individual paying 8% of his / her salary while the enterprises pay 5%. Both of these are transferred into a private account that can be transferred and withdrawn.

On March 1, 2005, "Shenzhen Experimental Measures for Migrant Workers" was officially implemented and first carried out a new medical insurance mode of "low charge, low guarantee" especially for migrant workers. It followed low level, wide coverage, high efficiency and step-by-step promotion and followed the principal of cash-based accounting for the cooperative medical funds and the principal of the balance between revenue and expenditure in one fiscal year. In order to connect migrant workers with medical insurance system of the urban residents, this institutional design broke through the limitation of "hospital insurance only" that was implemented in Shanghai, Beijing and Chengdu and it covered clinic and hospital in these two major parts. Hospital insurance was paid 90% by social fund and 10% by individual.[45]

In May 2009, Legal Office of the Municipal Government published "Amendment Decisions on Approach of Shenzhen Social and Medical Insurance" to seek for public comments. This was the amendment for "Approach of Shenzhen Social and Medical Insurance" that took effect beginning March 2008. One of the highlights of the amendment of the "Approach" was to enlarge the coverage of medical insurance. As long as having Residents Permit of Shenzhen, people could apply for Shenzhen Integrated Medical Insurance. Meanwhile, it enlarged the scope of maternity health insurance, allowing more non-resident workers to benefit, while the revenue and expenditure of the funds balanced by means of "low charge, wide coverage."

---

45 *Interpretation Shenzhen Non-Residents Workers Cooperative Medical Insurance Experimental Measures*, http://www.fsa.gov.cn/web_db/sdzg2006/MAP/EAL/zfcx059.htm

1.6.4.3 Net Welfare Index System of Livelihood

On December 30, 2006, the 5th Plenary of the 4th Municipal Committee Congress of Shenzhen first published "Net Welfare Index System of Livelihood," which was another local statistics system carried out on the basis of fulfilling the request of scientific development concept following "Beneficial Shenzhen Statistics Index System and Shenzhen Primary Realization of Modernization Index System."

"Net Welfare of Livelihood" originated from "Net Welfare of Economy" of economics. That is, all economic welfare brought by economic development minus compensation for consumption brought negative impact of economic development, meaning to change harmonious society into concrete measurable and operational objects. Materials and wealth growth are the fundamental basis for net welfare of livelihood with public goods and services served by the government as important conditions. To measure existence, livelihood and welfare conditions of people and the sharing achievements of social and economic development by statistics, checking the fiscal investment of government and its consequences is also new approach for the government to change its development mode.

Net Welfare of Livelihood System was composed of income distribution and fairness, security level, social guarantee level, public service level and the comprehensive development of the people with five major parts and 21 indexes. Income distribution and fairness mainly optioned growth rate of per capita disposable income and Geni Coefficient to show whether the economic growth of Shenzhen effectively changed into upgrading the income of the people and the fair distribution of income. Security Level index chose five major indexes, including over-proof of agricultural products' security check, days of class and air quality, and compliance rate of major drinking water resource, to reflect the security level of food, medicine, drinking water, air, traffic and personal security. Social guarantee level chose eight indicators, including urban registered unemployment rate, integrated insurance participating rate, and proportion of fiscal expenditure on social welfare in the total fiscal expenditure, to demonstrate the social guarantee level of employment, insurance, welfare, relief and donation. Public service level selected three major proportions of fiscal expenditure on science, education, cultural, sanitary and physics causes, environmental protection investment and public facilities in the whole fiscal expenditure. Level of people's comprehensive development mainly selected three indicators, average education period, occupational training hours of the staff and average number of books in the public library, to show education and training and other level of people's comprehensive development.

Net Welfare of Livelihood System has the effect and function of an indicating system. The basic starting point of establishing this system was to simplify the all complex relationship of the evaluation of the net welfare enjoyed by the Shenzhen citizens, to get more evaluation information by simplified indicators and to offer scientific basis for seizing and understanding the situation of the net welfare of Shenzhen people. In addition, this system had guidance on implementation function. The government must carry out relevant measures referring to the net welfare indicator system and make targeted policies. During its implement period, it will also promote the social management and public service functions of the government and guide and restrain the fiscal resources fully used to improve the livelihood and net welfare of Shenzhen people. That is to say people of Shenzhen will directly and indirectly benefit from Net Welfare of Livelihood System.

1.7 Achievements and Future Development of Shenzhen Special Economic Zone

Attributed to the support of national policy, the innovative spirit of pioneers and the geographical advantages of standing close to Hong Kong, Shenzhen, the pioneer of China's reform and opening up, has scored brilliant achievements over the past 30 years. It has created a miracle in modern urban development in leap and bounds, and also established a great many successful examples in the history of China's reform and opening up. Meanwhile, Shenzhen was also keenly aware of the future challenges, and realized that it has to preserve the reforming, innovative and pioneer spirit of the Special Economic Zone, continue to emancipate the mind, and actively take on the new historical mission of exploring the new way to construct a model city of socialism with Chinese characteristics.

1.7.1 Achievements of Shenzhen Special Economic Zone

Taking the lead in opening up and development, and resolving problems in the field of economic reform, Shenzhen Special Economic Zone explored a successful way for gradual reform, which not only developed a small fishing village off the edge of South China Sea into an internationally recognized city, but also greatly contributed to the cause of reform by providing valuable samples and experience in the field of deepening reform, expanding opening up, system innovation, industrial upgrading, and optimizing structure to the rest of China.

Figure 1-7-1 One of Shenzhen's urban landscapes

Source: Shenzhen Municipal Planning Bureau website, http://www.szplan.gov.cn/main/ghdt/tzgg/2005120506787.shtml

1.7.1.1 The Economic Achievements of Shenzhen Special Economic Zone

1.7.1.1.1 The Economy Developed in Leaps and Bounds

Shenzhen Special Economic Zone was founded with only less than a 3 million urban population and 1.9 billion yuan economic output. However, by the end of 2009, it developed into an economically prosperous, socially progressive, functionally completed and beautiful modern city with an 8.91 million resident population, out of 13 million actual management of population. The economy continuously developed to a new level. The city's gross domestic product (GDP) exceeded 200 billion yuan in four years, broke through 300 billion yuan in three years, surpassed 400 billion yuan within one year, reached 500 billion yuan within two years, and over 600 billion yuan, 700 billion yuan, 800 billion yuan with only 1 year respectively.

In 2009, the city's GDP was up to 820.12 billion yuan, ranked as the fourth largest in China's medium and large cities. The per capita GDP reached 92,045 yuan, took the first place in China's large and medium-sized cities' scorecard. The urban local financial revenue was 88.08 billion yuan, ranked the third among China's large and medium-sized cities, and the foreign trade volume achieved at 270.155 billion U.S. dollars, ranking second within China's large and medium-sized cities (see Figure 1-7-2~Figure 1-7-5).

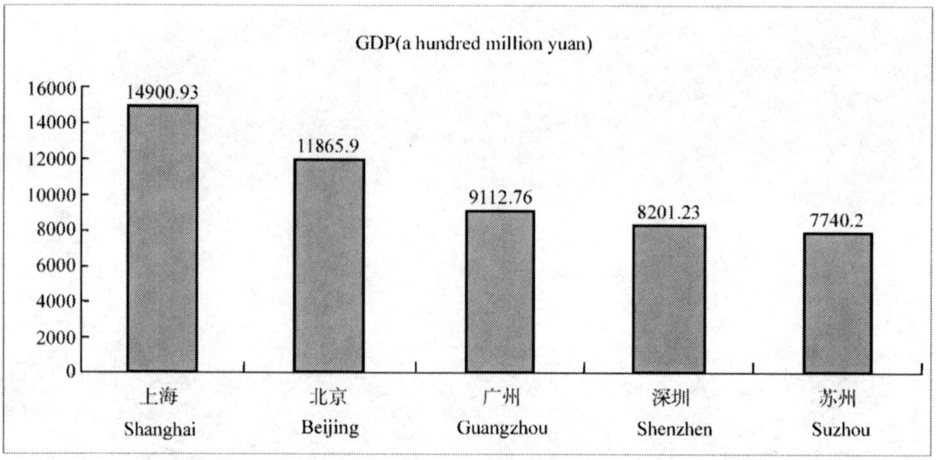

Figure 1-7-2 GDP of the five big cities in China, 2009

Source: the data of Shanghai, Beijing, Suzhou were respectively from the cities' statistical bulletin of economic and social development in 2009; the data of Shenzhen was from the Monthly Bulletin of Statistics published by Shenzhen Bureau in December 2009; the data of Guangzhou was from the macroeconomic database of Guangzhou Statistics Net.

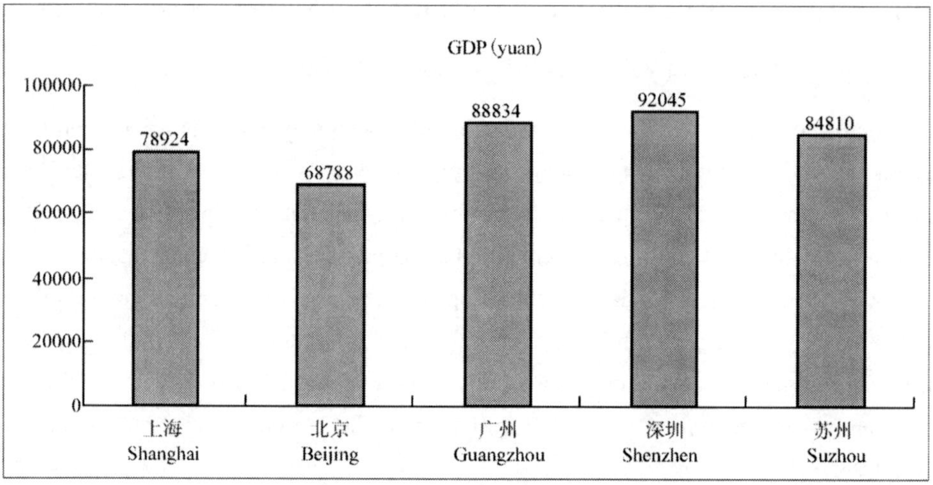

Figure 1-7-3 Per capita GDP of five major cities in China, 2009[46]

Source: the data of Shanghai, Beijing, Suzhou were respectively from the cities' statistical bulletin of economic and social development in 2009; the data of Shenzhen was from the Monthly Bulletin of Statistics published by Shenzhen Bureau in December 2009; the data of Guangzhou was from the macroeconomic database of Guangzhou Statistics Net.

46 The per capita GDP of Shenzhen was from GDP divided by the resident population.

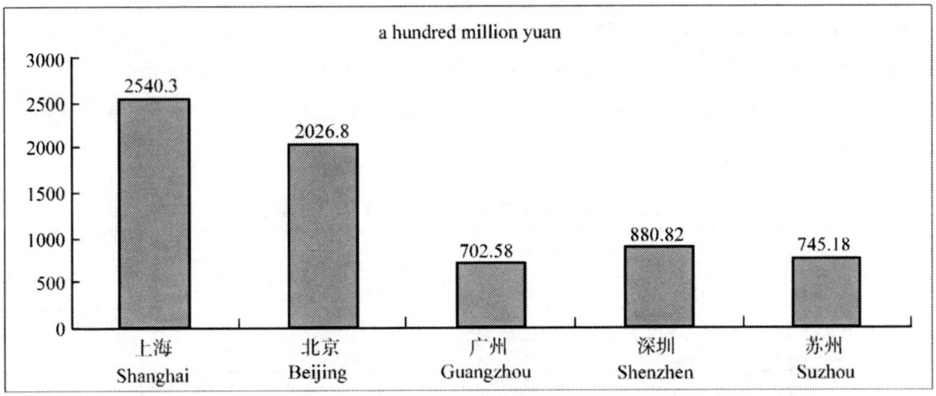

Figure 1-7-4 the local financial revenue of five big cities in China, 2009

Source: the data of Shanghai, Beijing, Suzhou were respectively from the cities' statistical bulletin of economic and social development in 2009; the data of Shenzhen was from the Monthly Bulletin of Statistics published by Shenzhen Bureau in December 2009; the data of Guangzhou was from the macroeconomic database of Guangzhou Statistics Net.

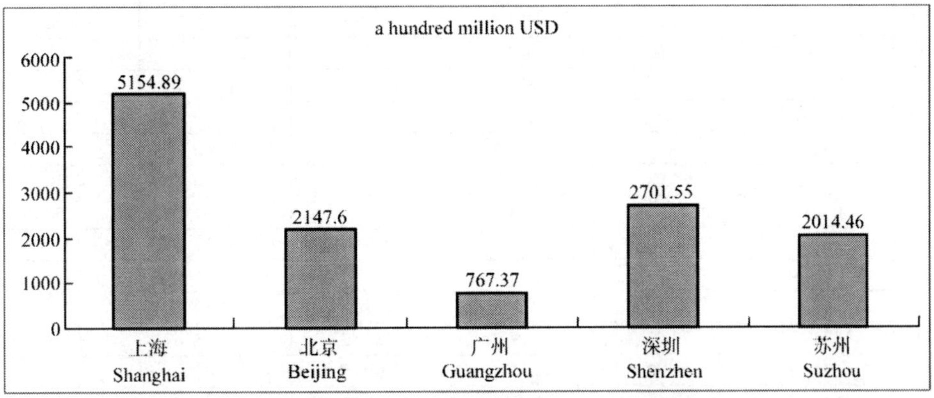

Figure 1-7-5 the foreign trade import and export volume of five big cities in China, 2009

Source: the data of Shanghai, Beijing, Suzhou were respectively from the cities' statistical bulletin of economic and social development in 2009; the data of Shenzhen was from the Monthly Bulletin of Statistics published by Shenzhen Bureau in December 2009; the data of Guangzhou was from the macroeconomic database of Guangzhou Statistics Net.

1.7.1.1.2 The Rapid Growth of Major Economic Indicators

Over the past 30 years, Shenzhen Special Economic Zone kept a sustained and rapid development; the major economic indicators growth by leaps and bounds.

1.7.1.1.2.1 The Unprecedented Economic Growth

From 1979 to 2009, the local GDP rose from 1.96 billion yuan to 820.12 billion yuan, calculated by the current prices, the average annual increase was up to 32.04%, more than 20% over the average growth rate of GDP in the same period, and, if calculated according to the constant prices of 1979, the average growth rate was still as high as 25.97%. The per capita GDP changed from 1979's 606 yuan to 2009's 92,045 yuan, 153 times increased. The growth rate was so exceptional in the world that it had already created a miracle of modern urban development (see Table 1-7-1).

Table 1-7-1 Shenzhen' GDP and growth rate from 1979 to 2009

Year	GDP (100 million, current year=100)	GDP growth rate (%, current year=100)	Per Capita GDP (Yuan, current year=100)	Local GDP (100 million Yuan, 1979=100)	GDP growth rate (%, 1979=100)	Per capita GDP (Yuan, 1979=100)
1979	1.96	-	606	1.96	-	606
1980	2.70	37.55	835	3.20	62.70	988
1981	4.96	83.53	1417	4.91	53.78	1405
1982	8.26	66.56	2023	7.78	58.43	1907
1983	13.12	58.90	2512	12.32	58.30	2359
1984	23.42	78.46	3504	19.70	59.89	2949
1985	39.02	66.65	4809	24.54	24.53	3025
1986	41.65	6.72	4584	25.20	2.70	2774
1987	55.90	34.23	5349	31.60	25.40	3024
1988	86.98	55.60	6477	42.94	35.90	3198
1989	115.66	32.97	6710	50.97	18.70	2957
1990	171.67	48.43	8724	67.54	32.50	3432
1991	236.66	37.86	11997	91.85	36.00	4170
1992	317.32	34.08	12827	122.34	33.20	4430
1993	453.14	42.80	15005	160.16	30.91	4750
1994	634.67	40.06	16954	209.69	30.93	5017
1995	842.48	32.74	19550	259.62	23.81	5396
1996	1048.44	24.45	22498	304.25	17.19	5847
1997	1297.42	23.75	25675	355.52	16.85	6302
1998	1534.73	18.29	27701	409.67	15.23	6623
1999	1804.02	17.55	29747	470.06	14.74	6942
2000	2187.45	21.25	32800	543.74	15.67	7303
2001	2482.49	13.49	34822	621.75	14.35	7812
2002	2969.52	19.62	40369	720.15	15.83	8769
2003	3585.72	20.75	47029	858.32	19.19	10083
2004	4282.14	19.42	54236	1006.73	17.29	11421
2005	4950.91	15.62	60801	1158.48	15.07	12744
2006	5813.56	17.42	69450	1350.23	16.55	14222
2007	6765.41	16.37	79221	1548.72	14.70	17976
2008	7806.53	15.39	89814	1735.61	12.07	19968
2009	8201.23	5.06	92045	1921.32	10.70	21564

Source: the data of GDP, per capita GDP of 1979 to 2008 calculated by the current prices was from the *Shenzhen Statistical Yearbook (2009)*; the data of GDP, per capita GDP of 1979 to 2008 calculated by the constant prices of 1979 were reckoned basing on the local GDP index of the corresponding year from the *Shenzhen Statistical Yearbook (2009)*; the GDP, per capita GDP of 2009 calculated by the current prices was reckoned basing on the related statistics of Shenzhen Statistics Web site (http://www.sztj.com/pub/sztjpublic/tjsj/tjyb/default.html); the data of 2009 GDP calculated by the constant prices of 1979 was from *Steady and healthy development of National economy, Shenzhen 2009*, released by the Shenzhen Development Committee and Shenzhen Bureau of Statistics.

The growth rate calculated by the constant prices of 1979 against Shenzhen's GDP from 1979 to 2009 is shown in Figure 1-7-6.

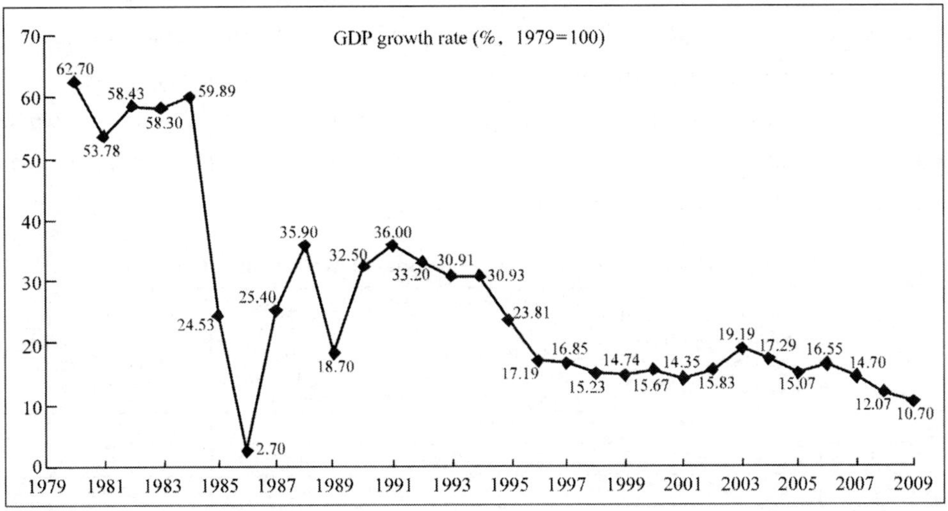

Figure 1-7-6 the growth rate calculated by the constant prices of 1979 against Shenzhen's GDP from 1979 to 2009

From Figure 1-7-6 we can see that in the 1980s, Shenzhen' economy developed at an unusually high-speed, but with great economic fluctuations. In the 1990s, although the growth rate was comparatively less, the economy developed more stable.

1.7.1.1.2.2 Arising Economic Efficiency Along with Rapid Economic Growth

While maintaining the rapid economic growth, Shenzhen has preliminarily established an economic development model with lower energy consumption, high output and efficiency. In 2009, the city's GDP was up to 820.123 billion yuan, the local financial revenue was 88.082 billion yuan, and the tax revenue amounted to 157.67 billion yuan.[47] In 2009, Shenzhen achieved the leading efficiency while maintaining its economic growth. By pre-research estimates, the GDP output per square kilometer was 4.2 billion yuan, increasing by 20 million yuan from 2008. Leading the other nationwide cities, its consumption on water and energy continued to decline. The overall effluent of Chemistry Oxygen met the target of annual emissions reduction, and the cumulative decline rate of

47 Data from the chief of Shenzhen taxation administration—Liujun's presentation in the briefing of "Shenzhen taxation progressed with Special Economic Zone"

sulfur dioxide emissions was full ahead of the "Eleventh Five-Year Plan" goals.[48]

The industrial added value of Shenzhen's industrial enterprises above designated size increased from 1990's 4.955 billion yuan to 2009's 342.99 billion yuan, growing by nearly 70 times at the current price of the year The total tax and profits amount against the industrial above designated size increased from 1990's 1.712 billion yuan to 2009's 115.721 billion yuan, growing by 66.8 times at the current price of the year. The whole social labor productivity rose from 1995's 43,125 yuan per capita to 2009's 128,044 yuan per capita, 196.91% growth at the current price of the year.

Table 1-7-2 The Economic Benefits Indicators in Main Years of Shenzhen

Year	The accomplished added value of large industrial enterprises, (100million the current year=100)	The total amount of large industrial enterprises' tax and profits (100 million, the current year=100)	The integrative index of industrial economic benefit (%)	the whole society productivity (Yuan per capita, the current year=100)
1990	49.55	17.12		
1995	286.97	82.18	142.73	43125
2000	815.22	286.93	182.50	70897
2005	2271.95	805.56	174.48	86556
2006	3086.56	960.09	172.50	92899
2007	3270.05	1157.21	189.80	103800
2008	3527.77	1261.25	188.30	117200
2009	3429.90	1160.94	179.30	128044

Source: the data of 1990, 1995, 2000, 2005, 2006, 2007, 2008 was from the annually *Statistical Yearbook of Shenzhen*; the data of 2009 was from the statistics generated on December 2009, Shenzhen Statistics Website (http://www.sztj.com/pub/sztjpublic/tjsj/tjyb/default.html).

1.7.1.1.2.3 Sustainable Growth in Financial Revenue

The financial revenue of Shenzhen increased from 1980's 30.43 million yuan to 2009's 88.082 billion yuan, increasing by 2895 times the current price of the year (see Table 1-7-3).

Table 1-7-3 The Financial Revenue in Main Years, Shenzhen

Year	1980	1985	1990	1995	2000	2005	2006	2007	2008	2009
Local Financial Revenue (100 million, the current year=100)	0.30	6.29	21.70	88.02	221.92	412.38	500.88	658.06	800.36	880.82

Source: data of 1980~2008 was from *The Statistical Yearbook of Shenzhen (2009)*; data of 2009 was from the *Statistics bulletin*, 2009 December, released by the Shenzhen Bureau of Statistics.

48 Data from the *analysis report on Shenzhen's steady and healthy development in 2009*, released by Shenzhen Development and Reform Commission and the Shenzhen Bureau of Statistics.

Since 2004, the local financial revenue of Shenzhen has annually increased: it exceeded 30 billion yuan by 2004; surpassed 40 billion yuan in 2005; reached 50 billion yuan in 2006; past 60 billion yuan in 2007; broke through 80 billion in 2008 and increased to 88 billion by 2009.

1.7.1.1.2.4 The Swift Development of Export-Oriented Economy

The export-oriented economy was one of the main strengths of Shenzhen's economic growth. From 1980 to 2009, the foreign trade volume and the actual use amount of foreign investment in Shenzhen grew swiftly. The main year's related data can be found in Table 1-7-4. Calculated by the constant price of 1979, from 1980 to 2009, the average growth of Shenzhen's foreign trade imports and exports volume was up to 34.47%.[49]

Table 1-7-4 the main year's correlation data of the foreign trade volume and the actual use amount of foreign investment in Shenzhen

Year	1980	1985	1990	1995	2000	2005	2006	2007	2008	2009
Foreign trade volume (100 Million $)	0.18	13.06	157.01	387.70	639.40	1828.17	2373.86	2875.33	2999.55	2701.55
Actual use amount of foreign investment (100 Million $)	0.33	3.29	5.19	17.35	29.68	29.69	32.69	36.62	40.30	41.60

Source: data of 1980 to 2008 was from the annually *Statistical Yearbook of Shenzhen*; data of 2009 was from *Shenzhen Monthly Statistics report*, December 2009, released by the Shenzhen Bureau of Statistics.

Affected by the global economic crisis in 2009, Shenzhen's total export volume dropped to 161.979 billion US dollars, accounting for 13.5% of the nation's total export, 45.1% of the entire province's total export, which still ranked first among the national large and medium-sized cities. In the total export, the amount of high-tech product was 85.048 million US dollars, accounting for 52.5%; the volume of mechanical and electrical products was 124.356 million US dollars, accounted for 76.7%.[50] Up to 2009, it was the 17th year

---

49 Shenzhen' total volume of imports and exports from 1980 to 2008 according to the constant price in 1979 was from the calculation on the annually total imports and exports volume and index from the annually *Statistical Yearbook of Shenzhen*; the total volume of imports and exports in 2009 was from *Shenzhen Monthly Statistics report*, December 2009, released by the Shenzhen Bureau of Statistics.

50 Data against 2005 to 2008 was from *Statistical Yearbook of Shenzhen (2009)*; the total export volume of China and Guangdong Province was from the *National Economic and Social Development Statistics Bulletin*; Shenzhen' 2009 data was from *Shenzhen Monthly Statistics report*, December 2009, released by the Shenzhen Bureau of Statistics.

for Shenzhen's gross export volume continually ranking the first among the nationwide large and medium-sized cities.

In 2009, the actual utilized foreign investment in Shenzhen was 4.160 million USD. By the end of 2009, 49,431 foreign direct investment projects had been approved, 51 billion USD foreign capital was actually utilized, and 148 Fortune 500 companies had invested in Shenzhen.[51]

1.7.1.1.2.5 The Resident's Income Steadily Increased

During 1980 to 2009, the resident's income increased steadily in Shenzhen (The main year's correlation data can be found in Table 1-7-5). The average annual money wages of the on-the-job staff and workers increased from 1980's 979 yuan to 44,220 yuan in 2009, a growth of 45 times the nominal monetary wage. Taking 1979 as the base period, from 1980 to 2009, the average annual money wages of the on-the-job staff and workers increased 14.60%, deducted the price factor, the average annual real wages of workers increased 7.2%.[52]

Table 1-7-5 The Main Year's Correlation Data of the Average Annual Money Wages of the On-the-job Staff and Workers, and the Per-capita Disposable Income of Urban Residents in Shenzhen

Year	1980	1985	1990	1995	2000	2005[53]	2006	2007	2008	2009
average annual money wages of the on-the-job staff and workers (Yuan)the current year=100	979	2418	4304	12276	23039	32476	35107	38798	43454	44220
the per-capita disposable income of urban residents (Yuan)the current year =100	-	1915	4127	12771	20906	21494	22567	24870	26729	29245
the Engel's coefficient(%)	-	47.5	47.2	39.9	29.4	33.4	33.3	32.5	36.0	35.0

Source: data of 1980~2008 was from *The Statistical Yearbook of Shenzhen (2009)*; the data of 2009 was from the *Statistics bulletin,* 2009 December, released by the Shenzhen Bureau of Statistics.

---

51 The total number of approved foreign direct investment projects and the cumulative amount of foreign capital in actual use in 2009 was sum up by the annually data of 1979~2009, of which the data of 1979 to 2008 was from *Statistical Yearbook of Shenzhen (2009)* and the data of 2009 was from *Shenzhen Monthly Statistics report.*

52 Calculated from the growth rate of the 1980~2009 average annual real wage of workers, the growth rate of the 2009 average annual money wages of workers and the inflation rate according to *Shenzhen's annual average growth rate of main indicators in 1980~2009,* (Shenzhen Statistics website, http://www.sztj.com/pub/sztjpublic/tjsj/tjnb/default.html)

53 From 2005, the sample households' number of Shenzhen raised to 600 (household + temporary) from 200, thus the average per capita of disposable income against 2005~2009 was not comparable with the one before 2005.

According to the data of Shenzhen's annual spot check of households, in 1985, the per-capita disposable income of urban residents averaged 1,915 yuan, and by the end of 2009, the figure soared to 29,245 yuan. The annual per capita expenses of urban residents reached 21,526 yuan; the Engel's coefficient was 35.0% (Table 1-7-6). At the end of the year, the per-capita living space of urban dwellers was 24.47 square meters, and the savings deposit reached 379,259 million yuan.[54]

1.7.1.1.2.6 High Growth in the Sector of Financial Services

As one of Shenzhen's pillar industries, the financial sector developed rapidly from 1980 to 2009. In 1980, the balance of the savings deposits of Shenzhen was only 203 million yuan, and the balance of loans was only 134 million yuan, and in 2009, the figure respectively increased to 1.693 million and 1.164 million. The total assets of financial sector reached as high as 2.8 trillion yuan, ranked the third among the national large and medium-sized cities. Calculated by the current year price, from 1980 to 2009, the balance of the savings deposits of Shenzhen increased by 8,344 times, the balance of loan increased by 8,691 times, and the annual average growth rate has respectively reached as high as 36.52% and 36.72%.

In 1980, the added value of Shenzhen's financial sector was 230 million yuan, and the contribution rate to GDP was 8.52%. In 2009, the added value of the financial sector increased to 114.814 million yuan, contribution rate to GDP was up to 13.9%. Especially in the past three years, the financial sector contributed more and more to Shenzhen's economic growth.

Up to 2009, Shenzhen had 17 securities companies with total assets of 470.107 million yuan, 58.55% growth compared to the last year's same period, ranked the first among nationwide cities; the fund scale of the 16 fund corporate was up to 807.128 million, and the net assets were 867.757 million yuan, approximately one-third of the national fund overall scale and total assets, second only to Shanghai; the accumulation proxy volume of trade for the 13 stock companies was estimated at 13.520 trillion yuan, 58.87% over last year's same period, representing about 10.36% among the nation. The insurance market in Shenzhen accumulatively achieved the original insurance premium income of 27.159 billion yuan, 12.78% increased than the same period last year.[55]

---

54 Data of 2009 was from *Shenzhen Monthly Statistics report*, December 2009, released by the Shenzhen Bureau of Statistics.

55 Data was from Shenzhen Government Online, http://www.sz.gov.cn/jrb/tjsj/zxtjxx/201002/t20100223_1466282.htm.

1.7.1.1.3 The Rapid Growing Private Economy Became the Main Force of Shenzhen's National Economy

The rapidly growing private economy was playing a more and more important role in Shenzhen's economic development. At present, there were nearly 300 thousand private enterprises in Shenzhen, accounting for more than 90% of all the enterprises in the city. The added value of the private economy reached 217.592 thousand yuan, representing 26.53% of the whole city's GDP. Restructuring and listing numerous private enterprises, as well as small and medium-sized enterprises, to market showed the sound and rapid development of Shenzhen's privately operated industry and trade, which definitely stimulated Shenzhen's economic growth.

In 2009, the privately operated industrial enterprise above designated size achieved sales revenue of 254.970 million yuan, growing by 12.60% from the same period last year, representing 16.5% of the whole city's sales revenue of industrial enterprises. Meanwhile, these enterprises kept a steady growth rate of more than 10%, which was higher than the aggregate level of the city. The processing trade imports and exports value of the private enterprises reached 3.980 million US dollars, 28.9% increase from the same period last year, of which export volume hit 2.560 million US dollars, import volume reached 1.932 million US dollars. The total sales of Shenzhen's privately operated wholesale and retail enterprises reached 169.060 million yuan, up by 19% over last year, accounting for 72.59% among the whole city's total sales of wholesale and retail enterprises. The 380 privately operated transportation as well as posts and telecommunications enterprises of the city achieved 1.057 million yuan revenue.

The private enterprise was the most active community of Shenzhen's independent innovation group. Currently, there were more than one thousand national and local high-tech enterprises, of which 60% are non-governmental enterprises. In 2009, nearly 42 thousand patents had been applied in Shenzhen, 20 thousand of which were applications for invention, and most applications were from the small and medium-sized or private enterprises. More than 40% of Shenzhen's R& D (research and development) people were gathered in the private enterprises, 64% private enterprises have their own intellectual property rights, and the total output value of derivative products accounted for 88% of Shenzhen's total output value of the products with independent intellectual property. Half of Shenzhen's national or provincial well-known trademarks were owned by the private enterprises. 91% of the software enterprises were privately operated, nearly all of which had their self-owned brands and core technologies with intellectual property rights, contributing to 98% to the total value of software industry and 99% of the profits.[56] After more than ten years development, the Shenzhen private enterprises were outstanding in the field of computer, communication, software, medical equipment, and new material, bioengineering and other high technology. A lot of large and strong private enterprises with core competitiveness emerged, such as Huawei, ZTE, Skyworth, BYD, Neptune, Tencent, Han's Laser, Kingdee, Mindray and so on.

Brand development of private enterprises achieved remarkable results. Relying on the innovation advantage and the support of China's thriving economy, a large number of backbone enterprises in Shenzhen showed their innovative vitality and strong resistance to the pressure. According to the statistics from World Intellectual Property Organization, in 2009, ZTE had 502 international public patented claims, increased by 52.58%, the increased range ranked the first in the world. At the end of 2008, Huawei ended Phillips' 10-year global supremacy, and ranked the second among worldwide companies in 2009. Substantial growth in international patent applications meant Shenzhen enterprises had more and more power in expanding the international market.[57]

The private enterprises significantly contributed to economic growth and financial revenue. In recent years, the tax revenue from privately operated and the small and medium-sized enterprises accounted for 50% of the total. In 2009, the privately operated and the small and medium-sized enterprise altogether paid the 87.797 million yuan tax (excluding tax from Customs, stamp duty on stock transfers and vehicles purchase tax), 2.5% increased from the same period last year, representing 52.4% of the whole city's enterprises tax revenue.[58]

1.7.1.1.4 Independent Innovation Drove Shenzhen's High Technology Developing Steady and Fast

In the early 1990s, facing the globally surging high technology revolution, Shenzhen Municipal Government made an assessment of the situation and decided it would devote major efforts to develop the high-tech industry, try to promote the city's overall competitiveness in the process and deepen innovation in science and technology.

Shenzhen's independent innovation had gone through the periods of start, grow and

---

56 *Why the private enterprise in Shenzhen* ***developed in adversity*****, Jing** *Bao*, July 27th, 2009.

57 *Shenzhen takes the first place in the International patent applications for the sixth consecutive year, Shenzhen Special Zone Daily, March 18th, 2010.*

58 *Private enterprises contributed thirty percent to Shenzhen' GDP and the recovery of most private enterprises in traditional industries, Shenzhen Special Zone Daily*, March 11th, 2010.

strengthen. During the "start period" from 1990s to 1995, Shenzhen issued "Decision on Promoting the Process of Science and Technology," which marked the beginning of Shenzhen's independent innovation. During the "growth period" from 1995 to 2000, Shenzhen put forward "Provisions on Further Supporting the Development of High Technology Industry," which led to a nationwide boom on hi-tech industrial development. Beginning in 2000, it entered the "strengthen period" in which the Shenzhen government promulgated Document No.1 "Decision on Improving the Regional Innovation System and Promoting the High-Tech Industry to Develop Steady and Fast" in 2004, and the renewed Document No.1 "Decision on the Implementation of Independent Innovation Strategy and Building the Innovation-Oriented City" in 2006, formally established independent innovation as the leading strategy of Shenzhen's urban development, aiming at built Shenzhen into a "national innovation-oriented city."

In April 2006, Shenzhen Municipal Government first applied to the National Development and Reform Commission on building the innovation-oriented city. In April 2007, Shenzhen signed the "Framework Agreement on Building a National Innovation-Oriented City" with the Ministry of Science and the Guangdong Provincial Government, proposing that Shenzhen be built into an important base of the high-tech research and development according to the national strategy. In October, Shenzhen signed the "Strategic Alliance Agreement on Promoting the Construction of a National Information Industry Model City with the Feature of Independent Innovation" with the Ministry of Information Industry, and the Guangdong Provincial Government. The document proposed that a number of state-level information industry zone and international demonstration zone for the talents in the field of information industry should be built up, and carries out the joint technological development in key technology and major projects of the state. In March 2008, Shenzhen Municipal Government resubmitted the "Request for Constructing Shenzhen into the State Innovation-Oriented City" to the Development and Reform Commission. In June 2008, the Development and Reform Commission issued a formal document on authorizing Shenzhen to become the pilot city of national innovation. This marked the construction of an innovative city in Shenzhen that had been incorporated into the national strategies, and its development of independent innovation entered a new phase.

1.7.1.1.4.1 Continuously Optimized Environment and Improved Independent Innovation Ability of Shenzhen

The independent innovation was an economic activity with strong externality, which means the innovation activity can hardly reach the most superior level of social needs by only depending on the market. There must be the government's guidance. Shenzhen did a great deal of work in building the policy environment for the independent innovation, according to incomplete statistics. Since the mid 1990's, Shenzhen has issued a total number of more than 50 important documents, local regulations and normative documents against science and technology. The five documents issued by municipal government, three local regulations and 48 normative documents had initially formed the policy making and legislation system of promoting the science and technology, as well as independent innovation process, which provided Shenzhen a sound policy and legislation environment in the process of independent innovation. Shenzhen's breakthrough in independent innovation policy was achieved mainly in the field of distribution system, the talent policy, the standardized strategy, the intellectual property rights protection, the promotion of the local enterprise's innovation development, the establishment and perfection of regional innovation system, the strategy transformation from industrial development to urban development and so on.

Shenzhen formed a good innovation culture. Shenzhen culture is a compatible culture based on the culture of immigration, and its resources superiority and the value mainly manifest in two aspects: (1) the cultural compatibility. Shenzhen culture had embraced the various domestic local culture and Western culture. Shenzhen was the most non-exclusive city in China, which made it the most favorite city to the talents.[59] (2) The young people and the immigrant as two chief cultural representatives, together with Shenzhen as the forefront of reform and opening up, the specific policy environment, and the spirit of risk, innovative and competition which contained in its culture.

The cultural environment in Shenzhen was diverse, open, inclusive, had respect for competition, dared to experiment and break new paths, but was also down to earth, tolerant in defeat, which altogether gradually formed the innovative culture atmosphere. In November 2005, the fourth Standing Committee of the National People's Congress deliberated the first domestic reform and innovation "Protection Art," so as to legislatively protect the innovation losers. Shenzhen was China's first pilot city of venture capital and, since 1994, started the exploration on building up the venture capital system, after more than a decade development. It had grown into an emerging investment and financing industry to a certain scale, and appeared the earliest and largest venture capital business partnership. At present, Shenzhen was not only leading in the number of business investment companies, especially the local institutions, but also in the scale of capital management, the investment of

59 Ni Heqin, *The challenges and missions of the cultural development in Shenzhen, Theory and practice of Special Economic Zone*, volume 6, 2002, Page 55~57.

the technological project and talents, etc. In April 2008, the four organizers of China Venture Capital & Private Equity Forum—the Central Committee of China National Democratic construction Association, the Ministry of Science and Technology, the People's Government of Guangdong Province and the Shenzhen Municipal Government-decided that, beginning in 2009, Shenzhen would be the permanent venue of the CVCF.

Since the 1990s, Shenzhen's independent innovation ability has enhanced continuously. The patented claim number increased from 261 in 1991 to 36,248 in 2008, grew 139 times in 17 years, the average annual increasing rate was 33.66% (Table 1-7-6). According to the information published by China Patent Protection Association, in 2009, two big enterprises of Shenzhen ranked the top two in the quantity of the nationwide patented claims, and among which the ZTE occupied the first place with 5,719 domestic patent applications, a more than 20% increase over the same period of last year. In addition, the overseas patent applications rose to 2,009, growing by more than 200% over the same period last year, the increasing rate ranked the first in the world.

Table 1-7-6 the major year patented claim quantity of Shenzhen

Year	1991	1995	2000	2005	2006	2007	2008
Quantity of patented claim	261	1104	4431	20940	29728	35808	36249

Source: data of 1991~2006 was from *The Statistical Yearbook of Shenzhen (2007)*; the data of 2007 was from the website of Shenzhen Bureau of Trade and Industry: http://www.szbti.gov.cn/newweb/mgdt/content.php?tmpid=0613200801220001; the data of 2008 was from Shenzhen Economic and Social development Statistics bulletin.

The independent innovation system with the enterprise remaining dominant has been gradually formed. First, it formed the "four above 90%" pattern, which means above 90% research and development institutions would be set up in the enterprises; above 90% research and development talents would be concentrated in the enterprises; above 90% research and development fund should be provided by the enterprises; above 90% service invention-creation should from the enterprises. Second, it formed a large-scale independent innovation enterprise group. By the end of 2008, there were 3,548 recognized high technology enterprises in Shenzhen. Third, it cultivated a batch of independent innovation leading enterprises, 620 high-tech enterprises' industrial production value has exceeded 100 million yuan, among which 84 enterprises exceeded one billion yuan, 48 exceeded two billion yuan, eight exceeded 10 billion yuan, and two exceeded 100 billion Yuan. The large, medium and small innovation enterprise echelon has already been built up.[60]

60 Data was from Shenzhen Small and Media Business web(http://www.szsmb.gov.cn/document/2008/4/details-47629.htm) and Shenzhen High-tech industrial Area web(http://www.chinahtp.com/ClassesHighTech.asp).

Shenzhen economy ranked the first in the contribution of advanced technology. With headquarters located in New York, the World Confederation of Productivity Science (WCPS) was an important international science confederation which gathered the world-renowned scientists and entrepreneurs. In December 2007, the World Confederation Productivity China Chapter held the "Seminar on the World Productivity and Scientific Development, also the 20th Anniversary of the Establishment of World Confederation Productivity China Chapter" in Shenzhen, and a new subdivision of the Chapter, Shenzhen Productivity Science Promoting Bureau was set up. From 2005, the proportion of Shenzhen's budgetary spending on research and development proportion has taken the lead in the country. The contribution rate of the science and technology in impelling the GDP development achieved between 60% and 70%, which marked Shenzhen as the fastest growing city by the propelling of science and technology. Shenzhen ranked the first in the field of "contribution rate of science and technology."[61]

1.7.1.1.4.2 High-Tech Industry Maintained a Good Momentum of Rapid Development

Shenzhen's high technology industry developed together with Shenzhen's independent innovation. Early in the 20th century, Shenzhen attached great importance to high technology, thus high technology industry had made considerable progress and became the key factor speeding up Shenzhen's economic growth. From 1999 to 2009, the output of Shenzhen's high-tech products reached an astonishing annual growth rate of 30.02%. As one of the four pillar industries in Shenzhen, the high technology industry contributed a great deal to the economic growth, especially the growth of industry, which guaranteed the sustainable growth of Shenzhen's economy. And among them, there was a raising ratio trend for the output of the high-tech products with independent intellectual property rights, accounting for the total output of the high-tech products (Table 1-7-7). From 1999 to 2008, the output of high-tech products with independent intellectual property rights achieved a 33.46% annual growth rate.

China High-Tech Fair (CHTF) was the largest and most influential exhibition on high technologies in China. Incorporating trade in hi-technologies, product exhibition, high-level forums, investment invitation and information exchange, CHTF is known as the top technology show in China. Since its foundation in 1999, the CHTF was annually held in October, and in 2009 celebrated its 11th anniversary. CHTF brought together a lot of

61 Material was from Shenzhen Trade and Industry Bureau Web, http://www.szbti.gov.cn/newweb/mgdt/content.php?tmpid=0613200711300002.

high-tech industries from both at home and abroad with an easy access to technology exchange and business cooperation, and achieved remarkable results. In 2009, Shenzhen Stock Exchange opened ChiNext, which aimed at boosting the financing development of high technology. This series of initiatives revitalized the development of Shenzhen's high-tech industry.

Table 1-7-7 Output of high-tech products with independent intellectual property rights in Shenzhen, 1999~2008

Year	1999	2000	2001	2002	2003	2004	2005	2006	2007	2008
Output of high-tech products with independent intellectual property rights(100 million Yuan, the current year=100)	383.36	534.54	745.63	954.48	1386.64	1853.09	2824.17	3653.29	4454.39	5148.17
Increasing rate according to the same period last year(%)	-	39.37	39.49	31.00	45.28	33.35	33.35	29.40	21.9	15.6
Ratio of the output of high-tech products(%)	46.76	50.22	53.67	55.82	55.85	56.73	57.81	57.90	58.62	59.1

Source: data of 1980~2008 was from The Statistical Yearbook of Shenzhen (2009)

As a major product of Shenzhen's industrial export productions, the high-tech product's exports accounted for a large share of Shenzhen's total industrial exports, holding the big share in the whole city industry export. In 2009, the total value of high-tech product exports was 85.048 million US dollars, 5.5% reduced from the last year, accounted for 52.51% of the total exports of the city.[62]

The overall output scale of high-tech industry in Shenzhen was further expanded, especially the products with independent intellectual property rights accounting for more than half of the total high-tech products, and the proportion was enhanced unceasingly, which reflected the continuously promotion in independent innovation of high-tech enterprises in Shenzhen.

1.7.1.1.5 Shenzhen Became One of China's Major Trade and Investment Promotion Centers

After 30 years development, Shenzhen cultivated a large number of enterprises with certain strengths and great wealth. It lead in the comprehensive economic strength among the Chinese big and media-sized cities and was an ever-growing economical influence.

62 Shenzhen Municipal Technology Industry and Information Commission web, http://www.szsitic.gov.cn/Index22/376.shtml.

However, because of the limit of objective condition, the issues on the "four difficulties" (land, resources, population and environment) starting to turn up. Due to the increasing operation cost, the industrial adjustment and promotion, as well as its pursue of further development and so on, large quantities of strong enterprises began to pay attention to the other cities across the nation. Relying on the advantage of technology, experience and funds formed by the superior development, as well as the geographical advantage to the investment and financing center, Hong Kong, Shenzhen became the investment target for more and more inland provinces. Promoting the outstanding investment environment and seeking the funds and the cooperative projects became a very important means for the economic development of provinces and cities. The statistics show that the Shenzhen investment accounted for about 80% of the total investment on inland provinces, thus Shenzhen became one of the most attractive investment centers of China.

1.7.1.2 The Achievements of Social Development in Shenzhen Special Economic Zone

From the social development perspective, Shenzhen has made tremendous achievements in the past 30 years.

1.7.1.2.1 All the Society Members Enjoy Relatively Fair Income Distribution

The Gini Coefficient, invented by the Italian statistician Corado Gini, calculating from the Lorenz curve, was the most often used indicator on reflecting whether or not distribution was fair in a given region or country. It was defined as a ration with values between zero and one that measured the degree of inequality in the distribution of income in a given society. The coefficient would register zero (0.0 = minimum inequality) for a society in which each member received exactly the same income and it would register a coefficient of one (1.0 = maximum inequality) if one member got all the income and the rest got nothing. About the Gini Coefficient, the stipulation of the world showed that: coefficient values lower than 0.2 mean the income distribution of the country was absolute equal; coefficient values between 0.2~0.3 mean average; coefficient values between 0.3~0.4 mean reasonable; coefficient values between 0.4~0.5 mean un-neglected gap; coefficient values over 0.5 mean polarizations.

Since the reform and opening up, China's economy has undergone tremendous and profound changes, while people's overall income significantly improved, the gap between rich and poor widened. According to the World Bank's statistics, the Gini Coefficient of China was 0.16 before the reform and opening up, but in 2003, the coefficient was already

0.458, exceeding the internationally recognized warning line of 0.4, and in 2004, the Gini Coefficient in China surpassed 0.465. It was 0.47[63] in 2005, 0.47 in 2006, and 0.48[64] in 2007, which already approached to 0.5.

Compared with the nation, Shenzhen's income distribution was relatively fair. Since 2000, the Gini Coefficient in Shenzhen remained at about 0.3, registering at 0.36 in 2005, which was lower than the nation's 0.47. It registered at 0.34 in 2006, a 0.02 decrease from 2005, and lower than the nation's 0.47. All of these showed that the income distribution in Shenzhen was relatively fair.

1.7.1.2.2 Broad Coverage of Social Security

Shenzhen was one of the cities in China that initially implemented the social security systems as a type of social insurance. The social security system in China was ideal, especially the construction of security system for the imported workers and the urbanized people.

The social security system in Shenzhen had already realized the entire coverage. On the one hand, the policy and method of the social security system in Shenzhen were unified. Shenzhen's social security system had unified the basic guarantee for institutions and enterprises, made them share the same endowment insurance, unemployment insurance, medical insurance, etc., basic insurance system, and on this basis, set up the supplementary insurance system. On the other hand, Shenzhen established the corresponding social security system for all city members, including the imported workers, basically carrying out the entire coverage. Shenzhen was the first to establish the medical insurance system for imported workers, and in June 2006, Shenzhen implemented China's first medical insurance practice for imported workers: "Interim Procedures for Medical Insurance of the Imported Workers in Shenzhen." According to the "Interim procedures," every month, the enterprise should hand over eight yuan while the individual pays four yuan, so people can be guaranteed both the outpatient service and hospital insurance. For the outpatient service, the reimbursement rate was 79%, and there were 1,200 types that could be found in the reimbursable drug list.[65]

The endowment insurance system realized the entire coverage in Shenzhen. The endowment insurance system in Shenzhen combined the mutual assistance programs with personal accounts, in which the mutual assistance programs practiced the model of

---

63 People, http://www.people.com.cn/GB/32306/33232/5544097.html.

64 Xinhua net, http://news.xinhuanet.com/fortune/2007-11/15/content_7079815.htm.

65 *Migrant workers would be fully covered with Medical insurance within two years*, *Guangzhou Daily*, March 26th, 2007.

pay-as-you-go (PAYG) system (DB type), while the individual accounts applied the payment predetermined fund system (DC). Up to December 31, 2009, the accumulative surplus of Shenzhen's basic endowment insurance was 68.224 million yuan, in which the accumulative surplus of the individual account was 51.199 million yuan, accounting for 75.05%. The individual account proceeded gradually.

The medical insurance in Shenzhen also realized the entire coverage. Shenzhen implemented the multi-level medical insurance system, which divided the medical insurance into two forms: the comprehensive medical insurance (including outpatient) and hospitalization medical insurance. The in-service workers of Shenzhen residence would enjoy the comprehensive medical insurance and those with temporary household registration and unemployed citizens would receive the hospitalization medical insurance. Shenzhen established a unified unemployment insurance system. All kinds of enterprises and institutions with enterprise style management registered in the Shenzhen economic special zone should pay the premium of unemployment insurance; and the state organizations, social organizations or institutions should also pay the unemployment insurance for their contractors. By the end of October 2009, there were 8,172,100 people getting the industrial injury insurance in Shenzhen, basically realizing the entire coverage.[66]

From March 3, 2008, Shenzhen started to issue the nationally used social security card, and also the social security cards with the features such as "multi-purpose" and "can be used throughout the country" within the city. Shenzhen planned to take three years to replacing all the Shenzhen labor security card or social security document to the social security card.[67]

Up to January 2010, Shenzhen was revising the "Scheme on Shenzhen Social Medical Insurance," which would include the non-registered permanent Shenzhen residence who possessed the resident certificate into the coverage of medical insurance. It was estimated that the basic medical insurance would cover the entire permanent residents by 2011.[68]

1.7.1.2.3 The Rapid Developed Culture and Strengthened Soft Power

With the rapid economic development, the cultural undertakings and industry made considerable progress. The new culture, which adapted with the construction of Special Economic Zone and the progress of reform and opening up, constantly grew. The urban

---

66 Shenzhen Social Security Fund Conservancy, http://www.szsi.gov.cn/sbjxxgk/tjsj/tj/200911/t20091113_2645.htm.

67 Shenzhen news, http://news.sznews.com/content/2008-03/04/content_1868755_2.htm.

68 Shenzhen Social Security Fund Conservancy, http://www.szsi.gov.cn/sbjxxgk/gzdt/201001/t20100113_2741.htm.

culture significantly enhanced, the cultural image increased, and the cultural atmosphere strengthened.

1.7.1.2.3.1 Fruitful in Cultural Development

A group of excellent programs and works were created, and since *the misfortune of a violin boy* and *Sentiment for the Chung Ying Street* won the national prize of "Five-One Project" in 1996, Shenzhen's Literary and artistic works continually received awards in the following six sessions, and until now, 34 works have received this honor. In September 2009, at the 11th session of "Five-One Project", 164 outstanding works received awards, and among them, the movie *Luminous*, the opera *I was born in 1978*, and the radio drama *The wild yak—Ba Lu* were made in Shenzhen.[69]

1.7.1.2.3.2 The Rapid Development of Cultural Industry

In recent years, culture has been stressed in Shenzhen, and as a result, the cultural industries were greatly strengthened. In the 11th session of the 3rd Shenzhen Municipal Committee Conference which was held in January 2005, the cultural industry, together with the high-tech, logistics, and finance industries were first proposed to jointly be the pillar of the harmonious and economic prospers Shenzhen. Prior to 2004, Shenzhen had already proposed the construction of "Capital of Creative Designing" and granted a series of generous support to the cultural and creative industries, including issuing "Several Opinions of the Supporting on the Development of Animation and Game Industry", the annual allocation of three billion special funds to support cultural industries by the government, the discount-interest loans and incentives granted to the creative industries, the three year exempted business income tax for the new cultural enterprises, annually held "Creative December" and brainstorming in the development of cultural and creative industry.

In recent years, the cultural and creative industries in Shenzhen developed rapidly. Up to 2009, Shenzhen built more than 30 creative industry parks, which started to achieve wide-scale effect and attracted the corporate grouped into a completed industrial chain in a short period of time, greatly facilitate the customer's seeking of the appropriate enterprise and at the same time showed the "cluster effect." The various creative industry parks in Shenzhen formed the differential patterns and respectively cultivated. Currently, there are nearly 60 film and television production sectors and more than 200 animation production

---

69 *Three of Shenzhen' artistic works on the list*, *Shenzhen Evening News*, September 29th, 2009.

sectors in Shenzhen. The industrial designs accounted for nearly half of the national market share, and there were more than 60,000 designers and over 6000 design enterprises in Shenzhen. Most of the top Chinese designers were gathered in Shenzhen. Ten of the 50 top international designers decided to develop their career in Shenzhen. John Hawkins, "the Father of Creative Industries" settled down in the capital of the creative industries park. The original animation by Yee King Animation Base successfully tapped into the Japanese market. Shenzhen's prosperous creative industry was attracting the world's attention.

Known as the "First Chinese Oil Painting Village" the Dafen Village in the Buji Town, Longgang District, was one of Shenzhen's most typical creative industry bases. It gathered more than 3,000 artists and painters, had over 300 galleries, exceeded 700 individual painting studios and workshops, and annually produced and sold more than 1 million oil paintings. 40% of the oil paintings in the world market were from the Dafen Village. Many overseas dealers chose to rent a house in the village and start their oil painting wholesale business.[70]

On December 7, 2008, Shenzhen was awarded the title of "Capital of Design" by the United Nations Educational, Scientific and Cultural Organization, becoming the sixth of the UNESCO Creative Cities, and also the first city in China to achieve this honor.

1.7.1.2.3.3 The Influential Cultural Brand

Founded in 1951 in Paris, the World Association of Graphic Designers was a prestigious authority which was organized by famous designers from across the world. Of the only six Chinese members, four were from Shenzhen. At present, Shenzhen's exhibition of the "Graphic Design in China" competition has become a resounding brand in China's design industry. After exploring the development environment of Shenzhen's creative industry, Kristian Keinänen, the former chairman of the Finnish Designers Association, believed that there were bright prospects for Shenzhen to develop the creative industries and turn it into an important support system for the city's economy.[71]

In June 2008, China Brand Research Institute released "China's Top Ten Capital of Brands," of which Shenzhen ranked the first.[72]

The International Cultural Industry Expo is a successful brand built by Shenzhen. The first Shenzhen International Cultural Industry Expo was held in November 2004, jointly

---

70 China Cultural Industries, http://www.cnci.gov.cn/news/Policy%5C20082l9/news_12975.htm.

71 Wu Dequn, *The innovative industries in Shenzhen received the new life and vigor of industrialization, Shenzhen Special Zone Daily*, May 18th, 2008

72 NF Daily, http://epaper.nfdaily.cn/html/2008-06/20/content_6665358.htm.

launched by the Cultural Industry Department of the Ministry of Culture, the Guangdong Provincial Department of Culture, Press and Publication Bureau of Guangdong Province, the Guangdong Provincial Radio, Film and Television Bureau and the Shenzhen Municipal People's Government. This expo was the first comprehensive international high-level cultural event of China. Approved by the Ministry of Culture, the expo would be held every two years in Shenzhen, which is the second state-level standing international exhibition following the "China International Hi-Tech Fair." In May 2006, the second International Cultural Industry Expo was upgraded, the full name turned changed to "China (Shenzhen) International Cultural Industry Fair" ("the Fair"). Adding "China" and "Fair" intended to indicate that the "Fair" was the unique state-level grant event which was jointly sponsored by the Ministry of Culture, State Administration of Radio Film and Television, General Administration of Press and Publication, Guangdong Provincial People's Government and Shenzhen Municipal People's Government, and undertaken by the Shenzhen Press Group, Shenzhen Media Group, Shenzhen Publish and Distribution group, Shenzhen International Cultural Industry Fair Co., Ltd. It would be held each May in Shenzhen. Until now, Shenzhen has successfully held six sessions and in May 2010, for the first time, all the 34 provinces, municipalities and autonomous regions attended the Fair. There were 1787 government groups, enterprises and institutions attending the Fair, and the sub-conference hall increased by 30 of the fifth session to 35, the ratio of leading enterprises attendance approached 51%, and the total turnover exceeded 100 billion.[73]

1.7.1.2.4 Remarkable Achievements in Eco-Environmental Protection

Since the reform and opening up, the ecological environment protection and eco-civilization construction in Shenzhen has made rapid progress. With the generally good environmental quality and remarkable achievements in environment protection, Shenzhen has been successively given the honor of the International "Garden City," "Global 500" of United Nations Environment protection, the "State-level Hygiene City," "National Environmental Protection Model City," "China Ozone Protection Contribution Award," the "National Model Ecological Garden City," "National Model City of Green," "National Excellent Tourism City," etc by domestic and international authorities.

Shenzhen Municipal Government has always attached great importance to the works of Eco-Environmental Protection. In 2003, Shenzhen had suggested building an ecological

73 Administration of Press and Publication of Guangdong Province web, http://www.xwcbj.gd.gov.cn/news/html/ztbd/2010/dljszwbhzt/

city and proposed to "build Shenzhen into China's most dynamic model eco-city" in the Eco-city planning.

In December 2006, the Shenzhen Municipal Government issued and implemented the "Eco-city Planning of Shenzhen." In January 2007, the Shenzhen Municipal Party Committee and the Shenzhen Municipal People's Government released "the decision for strengthen environmental protection and ecological city construction." These two documents marked the official beginning of Shenzhen's dedication in building a comprehensive eco-city and eco-civilization.

In 2009, the number of good air quality days in Shenzhen was up to 364 days, accounting for 99.5% of the total year. The main indicators of good air have attained the national standards for Grade II. The ratio of drinking water quality was 99.87%, except the Shiyan Reservoir (V class), the other reservoirs have reached the national standards for Grade 3 of surface water, and the river water quality of Shenzhen economic special zone has significantly improved.[74]

By the end of 2009, the total greenery area in Shenzhen was up to 97,598 hectares, of which park greenbelt was 14,527 hectares, and the per capita park greenbelt reached 16.3 square meters. A total of 653 parks took up an area of 20,452.46 hectares. The landscaping of the city's completed region was 36,609.4 hectares. The ratio of green coverage was 45.03%, whereas the ratio of green space was 39.14%. Nine garbage treatment plants (sites) were built, and the garbage treatment rate was 94.3%. All these indicators were in the forefront of the nation.

1.7.1.3 The City's Comprehensive Competitiveness Ranked the First Within Mainland Cities, Second Only to Hong Kong

Competition was the basic law of market economy, and the success or failure between cities depended on the strength of its competitiveness. Currently, the city's comprehensive competitiveness was most generally used in measuring the city's competitiveness. City's comprehensive competitiveness is reflected in the broad areas of urban development, which not only judged by the economic growth, but also including the developing and perfecting in the field of social, cultural and human beings. Dr. Ni Pengfei from the Institute of Finance and Trade, Chinese Academy of Social believed that urban competitiveness can be expressed as a city's ability to create wealth and value with greater, faster, better and more

74 Shenzhen environmental Monitoring Centre web, http://szems.szhec.gov.cn/hjzl/.

economical results than other cities during the development and competition.[75]

According to the China Urban Competitiveness Report No.5 and the China Urban Competitiveness Report No.7, which were respectively released by the Urban Competitiveness Project Group of the Institute of Finance and Trade, Chinese Academy of Social on 2007 and 2009, Shenzhen's urban competitiveness leaped from the fifth in 2005 to the second in 2006 (Hong Kong ranked first), and kept the score together with Hong Kong in 2007 and 2008. (Table 1-7-8 Table 1-7-9).

Table 1-7-8 Top ten in urban competitiveness of Chinese 294 cities in 2008

City	Overall Ranking	Ranking by growth	Ranking by Scale	Ranking by efficiency	Ranking by comprehensive development cost	Ranking by industrial level	Ranking by quality of life
HongKong	1	288	2	2	1	2	1
Shenzhen	2	81	4	7	58	3	4
Shanghai	3	233	1	14	66	4	2
Beijing	4	227	3	32	57	1	5
Taipei	5	291	7	1	6	5	6
Guangzhou	6	137	5	16	35	13	22
Qingdao	7	25	18	19	25	15	15
Tianjin	8	99	6	39	50	22	18
Suzhou	9	59	15	18	43	16	17
Kaohsiung	10	289	22	3	8	8	12

source: Ni Pengfei, editor in chief, China Urban Competitiveness Report NO.7, Social Sciences Academic Press, 2009 edition, page 1~2.

1.7.1.4 The Status of Region Key City Has Been Established

In 2009, the total economic output of Shenzhen was 820.123 billion yuan, accounting for 20.98% of Guangdong province's GDP with 3.908159 trillion yuan, continually ranked the fourth among China's large and medium-sized cities. Table 1-7-17 shows (take 2009 for example), Guangzhou and Shenzhen are still leading the economic development in the Pearl River Delta region and even in Guangdong Province, and by comparing the indicator of per capita GDP, total export-import volume, the local general budget revenue, disposable income of residents and etc., Shenzhen is superior to Guangzhou, and the overall competitiveness of Shenzhen is in the forefront of the province.

75 Ni Pengfei, editor in chief, *China urban competitiveness Report NO.7,* Social Sciences Academic Press (China), 2009 edition, Page 17.

Table 1-7-9 Contrast on the resident population and economic indicator of the 9 cities in Pearl River Delta, 2009[76]

City	Urban resident population (10, 000 people)	GDP (100 million Yuan)	Per Capita GDP (Yuan)	Total export-import volume (100 million USD)	Committed and paid-in foreign investment (100 million USD)	The local general budget revenue (100 million yuan)	Disposable income of residents (yuan)
Guangzhou	1018.2*	9112.76	88834	767.37	37.73	702.58	27609.59
Shenzhen	876.83*	8201.23	89814*	2701.55	41.60	880.82	29244.52
Zhuhai	148.11*	1037.69	69800	374.4	11.8	101.41	22859
Foshan	599.68	4814.5	80579	383.39	18.74	245.7	24578
Jiangmen	420.14	1355.26	32484	110.4	10.37	83.63	19004
Dongguan	635	3763.26	56591	551.69	25.94	231.16	33045
Zhongshan	251.74	1564.43	62225	244.7	6.86	100.12*[77]	23088
Huizhou	392.7*	1410.4	33077*	292.40	13.95	101.51	21278
Zhaoqing	388.83	846.34	22008	33.78	8.88	43.56*	15063
Whole Province[78]	9544*	39081.59	40748	6111.12	195.35	3649.19	21574.72

Source: besides the ones with marks, the rest data was respectively from the *2009 Statistical Bulletin of Economic and Social Development* and the *Monthly Statistics Bulletin* of Guangdong Province and related cities.

In 2002, basing on the demand of modernization, Guangdong Province started to implement a new round of the Regional Planning on Pearl River Delta. Three years later, in August 2005, the government issued the "Coordinated Urban Development Plan for the Pearl River Delta" (2004~2020) (hereinafter "Plan") which went into effect in November 2006. The "Plan" proposed that the development layout should consist of "two primary centers (Guangzhou and Shenzhen) plus one sub-center (Zhuhai)," indicating Shenzhen had grown into the central city of the Pearl River Delta region, on a par with Guangzhou. The main role of Shenzhen in the Pearl River Delta region was as an export-oriented, internationalized regional center and the most important external gateway city. The formulated "Plan" for implementation further illustrated that Shenzhen had already became a central city of the region.

In July 2008, the Guangdong Provincial Government discussed and adopted the "Urban Development Master Plan of Shenzhen" (2004~2020) through the executive

76 Due to insufficient information of 2009 on some city, data with * was of 2008.

77 Data from The Statistical Yearbook of Zhongshan (2009).

78 Data was from The Statistical Yearbook of Guangdong (2009).

meeting, and reported to the State Council for approval, thus solidifying the future of Shenzhen as an innovative, integrated economic zone, as an important center in southern China, and a cosmopolitan city, developed together with Hong Kong.[79]

According to the latest survey released by the government of City of London on March 12, 2010, against 75 financial centers of the world, for the first time London and New York shared the first place, followed up by Hong Kong, and the top-ranking city in China's mainland was Shenzhen in 9th place, Shanghai ranked as the 11th, and Beijing ranked as the 15th.[80]

1.7.2 Future Development of Shenzhen Special Economic Zone

In 30 years of rapid development, Shenzhen Special Economic Zone achieved many breakthroughs in the economic strength, scientific and technical innovation, regional influence capability, internationalization and so on, thus laying a good foundation for the new round of economic development. Growth, however, brought new problems and challenges. On one hand, it was severely restricted by the lack of development resources, but on the other hand, the previous distinctive policy owned by the Special Economic Zone will no longer exist, so Shenzhen must compete with the other mainland cities under the same system and policy environment. The changed circumstances required Shenzhen's intelligence in working out a proper and sensible plan for its future development, exploring the new driving force actively, upgrading its industrial by the opportunity of international economic changes and industrial restructuring, continuing to emancipate the mind, inspiring the wisdom, and striving to be the forerunner in China's reform again.

1.7.2.1 New Problems in the Economic Development

Shenzhen has made great achievements in economic development, but it still had to face and resolve some problems which threatened to constrain the sustainability of its future economic development.

1.7.2.1.1 The Widespread Preferential Policies

In 2005, China entered the post transitional period of World Trade Organization. In this period, the tariff concession was put into force, the opening of the service sector had almost been completed, and the protection on many industries had been canceled. The tariff

79 Sun Jin, *Shenzhen Special Zone Daily*, July 9th, 2008.

80 Chinanews, http://www.chinanews.com.cn/gj/gj-hqcz/news/2010/03-12/2165578.shtml.

level dropped from 43.2% in 1992 to 15.3% before joining WTO, and 9.9% after the first five years of joining WTO. In 2005, the dependence on foreign trade of China reached 63.89%. In honoring the commitments with WTO, China opened the financial, commercial, transport, tourism, and telecommunications sectors. In order to encourage the foreign merchants to invest in the western regions, the equity ratio and trade restrictions to the foreign investment had been relaxed. Some places offered more beneficial terms than the Special Economic Zone, which created competition among cities. In this sense, Shenzhen's former preferential policy on foreign investment has been widespread to some degree, thus the Special Economic Zone was no longer special. As a Special Economic Zone, while facing larger development space and more opportunities, Shenzhen also faced more fierce competition and serious challenges.

1.7.2.1.2 The Developmental Difficulties of Rising Cost and a Lack of Resources

Shenzhen was an area of scarce resources. It was short of land, freshwater, and energy as well as labor. In the past, it mainly attracted the mainland and foreign resources through its institutional superiority and tax preference. However, at a time of nationwide economic growth, there was an increasing demand of resources in every part of the country. Currently "the four difficulties in economic development"—land, resources, population and environment—made Shenzhen economic development difficult. According to Shenzhen's Urban Master Plan, by 2020, the amount of land used for urban construction should be controlled at 900 square kilometers. However, there are only less than 200 square kilometers available at present. Due to a lack of land resources, it was difficult to meet the land demand of manufacturing industries and the retail projects, especially the large projects.

At first, Shenzhen was less attractive to the foreign investors. At the beginning of reform and opening up, with the geographical and popularity advantages, Shenzhen Special Economic Zone attracted a large number of Hong Kong, Macao, Taiwan people as well as overseas Chinese to make investments and develop business in their hometown, which also played a very important role in leading the later influx of foreign investment. However, in the market economy, the instinct of capital was to seek maximizing profits, and the capital clearly would prefer the places with excellent economic returns. Investors had more choices in an increasingly open China. Judging from the recent years' foreign investment absorption report (Table 1-7-10), the growth of Shenzhen's foreign capital intake was slowing down, the gap between Suzhou and Tianjin was widening and much closer to Guangzhou, indicating that Shenzhen was facing fierce competition in absorbing investment.

Table 1-7-10 Comparison in the actual used foreign capital of Suzhou, Tianjin, Shenzhen and Guangzhou during 2004 to 2009

Year \ City	Suzhou		Tianjin		Shenzhen		Guangzhou	
	Absolute value ($100 million)	Growth rate (%)	Absolute value ($100 million)	Growth rate (%)	Absolute value ($100 million)	Growth rate (%)	Absolute value ($100 million)	Growth rate (%)
2004	50.33	-	24.72	51.4	23.50	10.4	24.01	64.4
2005	51.16	1.6	33.29	34.6	29.69	26.3	26.49	10.3
2006	61.05	19.3	41.31	24.1	32.69	10.1	29.23	10.4
2007	73.80	20.9	52.70	27.8	36.62	12.0	32.86	12.4
2008	81.30	10.2	74.20	40.8	40.30	10.0	36.23	10.3
2009	82.20	1.1	90.20	21.6	41.60	3.2	37.73	4.1

Source: data of 2004~2006 year was from *The development report of Shenzhen Economy (2008), edit by Le Zheng*, Social Sciences Academic Press, 2008, Page 11; data of 2007 ~2009 was respectively from each city's *Statistics Bulletin of the National Economic and Social Development*, of which the data of Shenzhen's actual used foreign investment in 2009 was from the *Monthly Bulletin of Statistics*, published by Shenzhen Bureau in December 2009.

Shenzhen's fresh water resource was also quite deficient. Shenzhen was one of the seven nationwide serious water scarcity cities, where the per capita share of fresh water was only 1/4 of the nation's resource, 1/5 of Guangdong Province's. Subject to the cost of desalination, currently there was no replacement for the fresh water. The lack of fresh water resources restricted the future development of Shenzhen's heavy industry.

With Shenzhen losing its appeal for both talent and common labor, labor costs were raising, therefore the human resources structure could not effectively support Shenzhen's upgrading industries.

Besides that, together with the pressure on land shortage and rising prices, the price of important means of production, like international oil, also kept fluctuating at a high level, all of which resulted in an increase of the enterprise production costs. Especially in 2009, due to the impact of global economic crisis, the continuous RMB appreciation, and the surging costs of various factors of production and labor etc., the operation costs went up and the sentiment indicator declined. The diseconomy on the various factors of production further weakened Shenzhen's competitiveness, which has also increased the pressure on Shenzhen's future economic development.

1.7.2.1.3 Hidden Troubles in the Economic Structure

1.7.2.1.3.1 Shenzhen's Secondary and Tertiary Industries

Manufacturing industry was always a leading force of Shenzhen's economic development. Over the past 30 years, the annual growth rate of Shenzhen manufacturing industry reached as high as 36%, much higher than the tertiary-industry's 26%. In 2009, the increasing volume of the second industry contributed 46.72% to the GDP, whereas the rate of tertiary industry reached 53.20%. As regards the development stage, when per capita GDP reached $6,500, the economy should reorient to high-value-added modern service sector, and all of the world major cities' economy was relying on the support of high value-added modern service industry. However, Shenzhen's current share of tertiary-industry was too low. With regards to resources, the second industry was still a great contributor to the GDP growth, which also owed much to the trouble of "the four difficulties in economic development."

In tertiary industry, the service industry developed insufficiently. In recent years, the financial industry was the fastest growing sector among Shenzhen's tertiary industry. In 2009, the added value of financial industry was 114.814 million yuan, up by 20.5% over 2008 and contributed 14% to the GDP.[81] But meanwhile, the internal sectors of Shenzhen tertiary industry showed unbalanced development. The information transmission, computer services and software, leasing and business services, scientific research, technical services, culture, sports and entertainment sectors only accounted for a strikingly low proportion of the tertiary industry.

1.7.2.1.3.2 The Risks of Single High-Tech Industrial Structure

During its continuous development, Shenzhen Industrial formed a unique industrial structure with the electronic information industry as its main body. From January to November 2009, the output value of Shenzhen high-tech industries accounted for 48.20% of the city's total output value. However, the electronic communications industries accounted for 90.50% of all the high-tech industry output value, whereas the biological pharmacy and new materials industries only accounted for 5.41%.[82]

It was difficult for such a single industrial structure to resist the risks brought by the macroeconomic regulation and international economic situation changes. In particular, one of the features of high-tech products was periodicity, with the gradually increasing investment in electronic information products and the continuing rise in raw material prices, the profit margins of electronic information products in Shenzhen became smaller and smaller. Since Shenzhen's high-tech industries was over-concentrated in electronic and

---

81 Shenzhen Statistics Bureau:*Smooth and healthy development of Shenzhen national economy*, 2009, http://www.sztj.com/main/xxgk/ywgz/tjfx/201002045300.shtml

82 Data from Shenzhen Statistic website, http://www.sztj.com/main/include/month/viewarticle.jsp?artid=4290

information, its further development would be restricted. Moreover, in the international division of labor, Shenzhen industry was at a relatively low level of the economic and technological development by mainly undertaking the production processing part of electronic information value chain, thus the added value of Shenzhen's electronic information industry was low and its competitiveness was relatively weak.

1.7.2.2 The Future Development of Shenzhen Economy

In accordance with the "National Medium and Long-Term Development Plan," by 2020, China would become one of the world's largest economies. This required the future China must to have a group of world-class cities, and Shenzhen's advantage in development naturally required it to undertake this arduous task.

1.7.2.2.1 Shenzhen Should Develop a Global Vision and Construct Itself into a City

In April 2009, an on-the-spot meeting of the Pearl River Delta (Shenzhen), Wang Yang, the Secretary of Guangdong Provincial Party Committee, clearly stated that all the cities of Pearl River Delta, and even the entire province, should "learn from Shenzhen." Shenzhen's sense of reform, innovations and development models, experience and practices should be provincially studied and shared. Meanwhile, he encouraged Shenzhen to never stop for pursuing excellence and continue to develop itself into an advanced world city in accordance with the spirit of "scientific development and pilot test."[83]

Planning the future with a global vision and constructing itself into an international city would be the inevitable choice of Shenzhen's historical development.

The renowned American scientist J. Friedman proposed that there should be seven criteria for an international city: the major financial centers, headquarters of multinational corporations, a body of international institutions with high growth service industries, main manufacturing centers, important world transportation hubs, and a certain amount of urban population.[84] By synthesizing the domestic and foreign related research, the formation of an international metropolis should have the following three conditions, which will also a main criterion for an international metropolis: (1) an economic hub. The core and essence of the urban economy internationalization represented as the urban economic development transferred from a territorial division of labor into the international division of labor, which meant it should enter the international economic cycle and have a higher participation and a

83 Shenzhen News website, http://www.sznews.com/zhuanti/content/2009-04/09/content_3684319.htm.

84 Friedman, J: *The World city Hypothesis, Development and Change*. International Journal of Urban and Regional Research, Vol.17, pp. 69~83, 1986.

stronger competitiveness in the global economy. Meanwhile, transfer its urban economy from the industrial economy to a service-oriented economy was an important factor in promoting the formation and development of an international city. Therefore, the international metropolises were usually also the world's major financial centers, trade centers, or the location of multinational corporations and international agencies. (2) The traffic information hub. With international ports and international airports, the international metropolis should be an important mode of the international transport network. At the same time, being a primary mode of the world information network and equipping with high-tech information technology and highly developed transportation and communication facilities would be a necessary material base for an international metropolis. (3) The cultural and technology exchange center. International metropolis should have an international standard of science and technology, culture, education facilities, research institutions and the corresponding talents. With a diverse cultural life, it should be strong in the power of culture radiant and appeal. It should be a place with countless new ideas and technology and, by virtue of these advantages, the city could carry out extensive and frequent exchanges in the field of international science, technology and cultural.[85]

Even though there was a big disparity for Shenzhen to catch up with the first-class international cities, it at least met the basic requirements of internationalization and had the potential to rival the more advanced world cities. In order to develop into an international city, Shenzhen still needed to make efforts in the following several aspects:

1.7.2.2.1.1 Continue to take the most advantage of the institutional innovation and speed up the docking with the international rules

Shenzhen needed to seek the support from Central Government and speed up its institutional innovation, continue to deepen reform of the economic system under the basic framework of the existing system, principles and policies, in order to upgrade itself from a Special Economic Zone to the Free Trade Economic Zone.

The efficient and convenient customs conditions, low-tax policies and free business environment made the Free trade Zone a major mode of Multinational Corporation's global layout. The establishment of the free trade zone would help complete the transaction of the foreign trade and economic development mode, promote the upgrading on service sectors, as well as further enhance the level and quality of opening up.

85 Kuai Dashen, *on culture essentials of the international metropolis*, enterprises development website, http://www.ccmedu.com/bbs12_251.html.

The free trade zone would feature "several parks within a district," "function division," "effective supervision" and "within the city yet outside of the customs" may first be set up in Shenzhen Shataukok Bonded Area, the Fukuda Bonded Area and the Yantiangang Bonded Area, then gradually expand the free-trade zone from three big bonded areas to the entire special economic zone. Specific legislation should be applied so as to make clear legal provision on the function type, central committee departments and supervision methods when processing the implementation on the Free Trade Zone system. This would push forward the nationalization of Shenzhen Special Economic Zone, and also gain more experience in direct docking with the international free-trade commitments for China in the process of economic globalization.

1.7.2.2.2 Optimize the industrial structure and accelerate the high-end transition of economic development

Along with the adjustment on the industrial structure, Shenzhen should also develop the manufacturing and service industries.

First, reasonable adjustment on industrial structure should be implemented, and more efforts should be put in the development of fine chemical, automotive, electronics, and other high-value added industries, so as to realize the high-end development. The development of the fine chemical and high-end automotive electronics needs the support of knowledge, technology, and funds, which Shenzhen could fully utilize its superiority.

Second, extend to the high-end segments of the industrial chains, and forge the World-class IT Production Base. The shape of the high-tech industrial revenue chain presented as "V." The profit margins of the upstream R & D and the downstream marketing services accounted about 20% to 25%, while the processing and manufacturing sector, which at the bottom of the curve of industrial chain was only 5%. This shows that only if taking the initiative to extend to the high-end segments of the industrial chain, the overall profits and self-reliance capacity could be enhanced, thus more value could be achieved. Shenzhen should try its best to develop into a new world-class IT industry base. Shenzhen's IT industry has great advantage on the gathering effectiveness and competitiveness in the high-tech industry group, which already met the requirements of industrial upgrading. Therefore, Shenzhen should further strengthen and accelerate its information industry upgrading, extend and prefect the electronic information industrial chain, construct a complete electronic information industry clusters, introduce the higher value-added chip manufacturing sector, strengthen the R & D and brand Marketing sectors, thus break an integrative manufacturing path from R & D to marketing and services, actively implement the technology leading strategy and technical norms strategy to promote the local high-tech enterprises transform to the Wintel Model from the current low-end competition model, and built Shenzhen into a world-class IT industry base with international competitiveness.

Third, Shenzhen should energetically expand the economic headquarters and achieve the high-end production stage. The so-called economic headquarters refers to region-specific resources to keep the R & D, testing, management, marketing and after-sales service in Shenzhen, but the layout of the manufacturing base to the mainland. Therefore, Shenzhen would become the center of R&D, administration, distribution and service, together with the external connection with Hong Kong and Macao to the world, integrated with the mainland regions, fully displays the advantage against information, fund, technical and talents, all of which would make Shenzhen a bright prospect in the space utilization.

Finally, Shenzhen should make full use of the superior connection to Hong Kong to speed up its development of modern service industry with the high-added value. Looking from the historic experience of the world metropolis, all of their development has experienced the economical center shift from industry to service. In terms of the industrial structure, the main global city tertiary industry accounted for over 80% of the GDP at present, whereas its employment figure represented over 70%. In the 1980s when the urban GDP per capita transitioned from 5000 US dollars to 8000 US dollars in Hong Kong and Singapore, the proportion of tertiary industry GDP had already surpassed 60%. At present, Shenzhen GDP per capita has amounted to 13,000 US dollars, but the proportion of the tertiary industry GDP was only 53%, which was obviously low. Shenzhen must try to attract more investments from the Hong Kong service industry, vigorously absorb the professional services in the area of Hong Kong's finance, logistics, accounting, legislation, business management and so on, make full use of Hong Kong's superiority in trade services, develop tertiary industry colony with Shenzhen characteristics, gradually enlarge the tertiary industry, especially the high added value modern service industry's proportion, to lead to high scale development. Shenzhen would be constructed into a center of modern business, logistics, service industry, regional finance and tourist attraction, carrying on its development inland.

1.7.2.2.3 Integrate the regional economies and build up the transport hub

Looking over the process of global urbanization, neighboring compliance is an important link in the regional economy development process. Shenzhen has the possibility to become an important mode in the Pan-Pearl River Delta in the consideration of economic cooperation scale, physical geographic position and the synthesis traffic conditions. Shenzhen, as a key city in Pan Pearl River Delta area, had the advantages of position, market and industry which other cities did not. At the same time, in the "one country two systems" principle, the role of inland special zone characterized Shenzhen from Hong Kong. Therefore, Shenzhen has the ability to fully play its core economic role and the cooperation mechanism emphasized in Pan-Pearl River Delta which took market impetus as primary and the administrative impetus as the auxiliary was also beneficial to Shenzhen's core function surmounting administration boundary, thus realizing mutual benefit with the Pearl River Delta in the broad cooperation. Shenzhen should strengthen its status of key city both in the Kowloon Railway and the Southeast Coast Rail Line, together with Hong Kong, to play the leading role in the region, strengthen its economical interaction and market radiation to Guangdong, Jiangxi and Fujian, effectively expand the economic development hinterland as an axis of Guangdong economic.

Shenzhen must build itself into a transport hub, speeding up the infrastructural facilities construction of the region transportation and increasing the input in the land, sea and airport construction. Shenzhen should gradually complete the global aviation hub construction through connecting economic vicinity internally and foreign market internationally; form the international shipping center by advancing the construction of international container hinge port, and construct city border track among Hong Kong, Shenzhen and Guangzhou. Shenzhen must enhance its links with the world cities by advanced, convenient and highly effective transport network, thus making Shenzhen move up in the global urban system and enhance its international status.

1.7.2.2.4 Further Deepening of the Cooperation Between Shenzhen and Hong Kong and Building Them Into a United World-Class Metropolis

Hong Kong factor was the first leverage in the economic development of Shenzhen, which was closely related to Shenzhen's initial success. Thanks to Hong Kong's traditional manufacturing industry shifts in large quantities, Shenzhen's manufacturing industry could develop at a high speed.

Starting in the early 1980s, the cooperation between Shenzhen and Hong Kong has experienced fast phases of development, relatively stagnate and comprehensive advancements, and has formed the industrial cooperation, the interstate infrastructural facilities and the service, the operational mechanism and the policy coordination three key cooperation contents.[86]

---

86 *Edit by Le Zheng, The development report of Shenzhen Economy (2008)*, Social Sciences Academic Press, 2008, Page 353.

For over ten years, the official interaction of cooperation between Shenzhen and Hong Kong has approximately experienced the process from "one hot, the other cold" to "both hot." In 1995, on the eve of Hong Kong's returning, after massive research, Shenzhen proposed a series of concept and theory frames of cooperation with Hong Kong. In 1998, at the meeting with Hong Kong chief executive Tung Chee-hwa, Shenzhen Municipal Party Committee Secretary Zhang Gaoli and Shenzhen Mayor Li Zibin suggested that Shenzhen and Hong Kong should build the "High-Tech Industry Corridor." In 1999, after Shenzhen had successfully held the first "China Hi-Tech Fair," Shenzhen's top officials expressed the willingness to hold the "China Hi-Tech Fair" together with Hong Kong for many years. In 2001, Shenzhen Mayor Yu Youjun proposed to construct "Shenzhen and Hong Kong economic cooperation zone." In 2003, Hong Kong industrialist Li Jiacheng proposed to construct the "tax-free industrial district" in the border between Shenzhen and Hong Kong, and in response, Shenzhen presented several alternative plans of developing "the Hetao area." In 2004, Shenzhen Mayor Li Hongzhong visited Shenzhen and officially proposed to the government of Hong Kong Special Administrative Region to develop "Hetao" together, and the HKSAR responded that they would "carefully considerate it." In 2004, Shenzhen proposed that the Chu Hong Kong-Macao Bridge would change from the shape of single Y to double Y. In March 2006, Shenzhen National People's Congress explicitly proposed to build "the Shenzhen and Hong Kong metropolis circle" in its Eleventh Five-year Plan; in July the same year, *Urban Development Strategy of Shenzhen in 2030* also explicitly indicated that Shenzhen's strategic position was as an "international metropolis jointly developed with Hong Kong." With regards to "the economic cooperation between Shenzhen and Hong Kong," over the past 10 years, Shenzhen has been acting truly and sincerely, while Hong Kong appeared uncooperative, due to more consideration on its own benefit, thus forming the phenomenon of "hot Shenzhen but cold Hong Kong." Therefore, the cooperation between Shenzhen and Hong Kong was merely discussed, but resulted in no action.

However, with the development of economic relationships between Shenzhen and Hong Kong, Hong Kong started to address the importance of cooperation with Shenzhen. In February 2007, Zeng Yinquan proposed explicitly in his campaign outline that Hong Kong would establish strategic partnership with Shenzhen, and jointly build a world-class international metropolis. On the tenth anniversary of reunification, the western channel, which connected Shenzhen and Hong Kong, was opened, and for the first time realized the entry pattern of "two inspections within one place," greatly reduced the waiting time and simplified the procedures. Afterwards, the two sides developed the border area and opened the new Fukuda port. On May 21, 2007, the signing ceremony was held at the Hong Kong Exhibition Center, which was a turning point for Hong Kong's initiation. On August 9th of the same year, Hong Kong Think Tank, which has won the name of "Royal Brain" of the HKSAR government, convened every media and trumpeted the "Research Report of Constructing 'Hong Kong and Shenzhen Metropolis.'" Hong Kong's release of the report, to a certain extent, reflected that Hong Kong had given "new hopes on the cooperation with Shenzhen."[87] In November 2008, the first corporation meeting between Shenzhen and Hong Kong was held in Shenzhen. Six mutual recognitions had been achieved: first, to establish the emergency mechanism to boost the prosperous development of the two sides under the financial Tsunami; second, promote the comprehensive financial cooperation; third, accelerate the contribution of Hong Kong and Shenzhen innovation circle; fourth, push forward the major infrastructure constructions; fifth, pay close attention to the development of Hong Kong enterprises under the financial Tsunami; and sixth, promote the cooperation between Shenzhen and Hong Kong comprehensively in multi-domains, such as in environmental protection, culture, as well as science and technology. After the meeting, Shenzhen and Hong Kong cooperation agreement was signed, marking the step forward of Shenzhen and Hong Kong's cooperation. The State Council officially approved the "Comprehensive Reform of Shenzhen Overall Program," which clearly stated that Shenzhen and Hong Kong would develop into the "global logistics center, trade center, innovation center and the international cultural creativity industry center," at the beginning of 2009. In June, 2009, Wang Rong, Secretary of CPC Shenzhen Municipal Committee as well as Shenzhen's Acting Mayor, paid a visit to Hong Kong on his tenth day in office, demonstrating the great attention attached to the cooperation with Hong Kong. His visit received positive response. After the meeting, the two sides decided to regularly discuss and make arrangements on significant items and accelerate the cooperation in the development of Hetao area, speed up the infrastructural facilities construction in Liantang / Heung Yuen Wai, Shenzhen and Hong Kong airport rail transportation contact lines, Guangzhou-Shenzhen-Hong Kong passenger transport line and so on.[88]

In April 2010, the "Cooperative Framework Agreement between Guangdong and Hong Kong" was signed, in which the key contents was cooperation between Shenzhen and Hong Kong, ranging from the cross-border infrastructure, modern finance service industry, the scientific innovation to the ecological construction, the environmental protection as

---

87 Sina website, http://news.sina.com.cn/c/2007-09-29/115314000709.shtml

88 People's government of Guangdong Province website, http://www.gd.gov.cn/govpub/zwdt/dfzw/200912/t20091231_110004.htm.

well as the key cooperation areas, including strives for cooperation in pilot to promote Hong Kong stock index fund in Shenzhen stock market, support the eligible enterprises in Shenzhen and Hong Kong growth enterprise market to be listed over-border, comprehensively advance the financial services such as credit, negotiable securities, insurance, stock, bond market and fund management. It may be said that the cooperation covered a wide range.

As the important international financial center in the Asia-Pacific area, becoming the service industry capital of Asia-Pacific area was the direction of Hong Kong's development. As an important economic center city in South China, Shenzhen was making great efforts to become a regional and international city. At present, Shenzhen and Hong Kong have completed the construction of the world leading global port facilities, the air harbor facility and transporting ability were first-class, and the advancement of both port facilities. Customs entry/exit ability kept its leading role for a long time, along with the gradually established land transport hub, all of which had greatly supported Shenzhen and Hong Kong jointly expanded their markets and growing space, as well as built the world-class metropolis. Today, both sides have realized that they have great homogeneity (both economies are close connected with international market), as well as obvious complementarities (complementary in manufacturing industry and service industry, international free port and huge domestic market), thus achieved a mutually beneficial cooperation. Cooperation between Shenzhen and Hong Kong was no longer the consideration of succeeding or failing in "a city or a place," but as an important part in the national development strategy. Generally speaking, Shenzhen and Hong Kong were both basically equipped with the infrastructures to construct the world-class metropolis.

In particular, Shenzhen must strengthen its cooperation with Hong Kong in the following areas:

First, strengthen the cooperation in the high-tech industry. Although due to the industrial shift, the manufacturing industry now took low proportion in Hong Kong GDP, and lacked foundation and motive power for the industrial upgrading, Hong Kong has the superiority in technical information, technical financing and testing equipments. The high technology industry has already become Shenzhen's pillar industry, which was also its future development direction. If combining with Hong Kong's technical superiority, carry on research on basic science and high-end technology in Hong Kong, while carrying on development and manufacture in Shenzhen as well as the Pearl River Delta, the original industrial level could be greatly enhanced, and Shenzhen could still maintained its leading role in the new industries such as bio-engineering, new technique, acme equipment manufacturing industry etc.

Second, strengthen the cooperation in the trade in services industry. The tertiary industry held a dominant position within Hong Kong's economic structure. Hong Kong's service trade level kept ahead in the world whereas Shenzhen's service trade level took the lead at home. Judging from the cooperation space and market prospective, Hong Kong could gradually shift its overseas' retailing center, planning centre and order center in Hong Kong to Shenzhen, which not only could greatly reduce the operating cost, but also expand their own development space by taking advantage of both city's strengths.

Third, strengthen the cooperation in the logistics industry. At present, Hong Kong was the largest marine and aerial harbor in the world. Shenzhen not only has the world's fourth largest container transport port, but also the nation's fourth largest aerial harbor, as well as developed railroad and the highway network connecting with the inland. The basic conditions were quite good. To cooperate in logistics industry, Shenzhen and Hong Kong first needed to strengthen their cooperation in information, and try to establish logistics administration center at both sides as soon as possible, therefore realizing the reasonable disposition and full usage of the logistic resources, avoiding waste and vacancy. Meanwhile, harbor cooperation was also quite important. Based on the great success achieved in the first and second phases of cooperative projects in Yantian harbor, both sides should further consider how to consolidate cooperation of both harbors from the perspective of economic integration so as to create better industrial development condition and larger industrial development space. In air transport, Shenzhen and Hong Kong, possessing advantages and disadvantages respectively, should strengthen their coordination and cooperation to achieve the goal of reinforcing each other's strength, co-sharing the resources, and communal development of aviation logistics.

Fourth, strengthen cooperation in the financial industry. As one of the most important international financial center cities in Asia, and in the world, Hong Kong has superior status as international financial center, good sources of fund, regular and mature capital market, as well as legal environment. While as one of the most important regional financial center cities at home, by the end of 2009, Shenzhen's total annual financial industry assets had amounted to 3.360 billion yuan, and the financial institutions of various kind reached 208. Shenzhen's financial institutions took a leading position in China, all of which had made it become one of the most important national multi-level capital market centers. The financial cooperation space for Shenzhen and Hong Kong was huge. At present, Shenzhen was actively striving for national support, attempting to permit electronic currency intercommunication between Hong Kong and Shenzhen in order to promote the segment transaction in both stock markets, accelerate the integration of capital market, as well as attract more Hong Kong financial institutions operation headquarters to settle in Shenzhen. Shenzhen also gradually expanded the cooperation in insurance market and jointly built the insurance company as well as auxiliary financial service organizations. Through the cooperation in financial industry, Shenzhen and Hong Kong would build the global financial center together.

1.7.2.2.5 Vigorously push ahead the cultural city strategy and completely promote Shenzhen's cultural soft power

Along with Shenzhen's rapid economic and social development, the cultural undertakings and industry had made encouraging progress, the civic culture strength grew significantly, initially had the profound culture for the construction of cosmopolitan city and the modern central city. Meanwhile, compared with the advanced world standard, Shenzhen's culture level of development still had a very big gap to the requirement of cosmopolitan city construction. Clearly realizing the current status, Shenzhen Municipal government formulated many policies to promote the culture development. Since 2005, the municipal government has issued many key documents such as "Certain Economic Policies on Speeding up Culture Industrial development, Outline of Shenzhen culture development: 2005~2010" to promote Shenzhen's cultural development.

In June 2008, "Certain Opinions on the Chinese Communist Party Shenzhen Municipal Party Committee and Shenzhen People's Government about to Construct the Demonstration City with Chinese Characteristics through Insisting Reform and Opening-up policy and Impetus Scientific Progress," which had been passed through in the four session of the tenth plenary meeting of Communist Party Committee of Shenzhen, elaborating Shenzhen culture development strategy by the great length, proposed to enhance the city's humanity level, further promote Shenzhen Spirit, vigorously cultivate the innovation culture, expand the investment on cultural reconstruction, improve the public cultural service system, build its own civic culture brand, and strengthen the protection on history cultural heritage. The "Certain Opinions" also pointed out that Shenzhen should built up more state-level creative industry parks, positively attract the well-known cultural enterprises, intermediary organizations as well as research training organization to locate their headquarters or centers of research and development, manufacture, purchase, and financial in Shenzhen, build the creativity design institutes together with Hong Kong, therefore find out a new pattern of culture industrial development under the policy of "one country, two systems." By actively participating in organizing a more international, specialized, market-oriented and standardized cultural fair with Hong Kong to work out an international platform for the cultural industry information, the product transaction, investment and financing serving based on the aid of Hong Kong's rich overseas market resources. It would also speed up the construction of "two cities, one capital and one base," positively participate in the world creativity city foundation activities, and make breakthroughs in the core sectors as design, animation, online game, TV and films, etc.[89]

Great importance should be attached to cultural talents. Fully developing and making use of the domestic and foreign human resources pools, allows more and more outstanding talents in theoretical study, literary and artistic creation, cultural science and technology, cultural management, cultural operation etc. to be introduced or cultivated into Shenzhen and help develop Shenzhen into a high grade cultural city.

The big platform for culture development should be constructed by the drive of innovation, opening-up and market, and also with strengthening cooperation home and abroad. In order to raise Shenzhen's international market share and make Chinese culture better understood by the world, the strategy of going out should be further implemented. A number of the widespread influential international cultural festivals, conventions and sports events should be held in Shenshen to expand Shenzhen's international popularity. The 26th World University Games in 2011 should be taken as the turning point, by taking advantages of sports events' wide international influence, the world would get a chance to see Shenzhen's city image and spirit, thus comprehensively promote Shenzhen's cultural power.

1.7.2.3 The New Historical Mission of Shenzhen Special Economic Zone

At the beginning of March 2008, when he participated in the first session of the 11th National People's Congress Conference, Premier Wen Jiabao pointed out, "Shenzhen Special Economic Zone must keep running. This does not lie in how many special policies would be granted, but Shenzhen special zone was a national flag."[90] At the end of March of the same year, Wang Yang, member of the Political Bureau of CPC Central Committee & Secretary of CPC Guangdong Committee, participated the seminar on Shenzhen and stressed that Shenzhen must keep on developing the spirit of exploitation and enterprising, with its "special" consciousness, deliberations and measures, take the lead in exploring the system pattern with Chinese characteristics, construct the model city with Chinese

89 Shenzhen Special Zone Daily, multi-media version, http://sztqb.sznews.com/html/2008-06/24/content_229399.htm.

90 Wen Jiabao's speech at the first session of the 11th National People's Congress conference, Nanfang Daily special report on 2008 NPC & CPPCC, March 10th, 2008, http://www.nfdaily.cn/special/2008specail/2008lh/lh_opin/content/2008-03/10/content_4344414.htm.

characteristics, fully demonstrate the brand-new style of the special economic zone and China's glorious future, further strengthen the influence, attraction and competitiveness of Chinese characteristic socialist system.[91] In the new period, shouldering the new historical mission, Shenzhen was destined to try again for China's reform, and explore the way to transit the pure and evolution-like economy to the Omni-directional synthesis coordinated reforms which would effortlessly involve the economy, politics, social and cultural aspects of the country.

In the new historical period, Shenzhen Special Economic Zone must stand at the frontier of China's reform and opening-up, continue to be a national flag by further freeing the mind and stimulating the courage and wisdom to overcome difficulties, make the reform cover all the visual, economical, cultural and social areas, play an exemplary role for the all-around reform, and strive to be the pacesetter of China's Reform again.

Therefore, in June 2008, "Certain Opinions of the Chinese Communist Party Shenzhen Municipal Party Committee and Shenzhen People's Government about to Construct the Chinese Characteristic Socialism Demonstration City though Insisting Reform and Opening-up policy and Impetus Scientific Progress Diligently" (hereafter refers to as "Certain Opinions") was passed through the four session of 10th Conference of Chinese Communist Party Shenzhen Municipal Party Committee after undergoing many large-scale discussions and modifications within Shenzhen Municipal Party Committee until a public announcement was made. In that period of time, certain arrangements had been made in the following nine aspects: (1) lead the national radiation in the development of socialist democratic politics; (2) develop the cooperation between Shenzhen and Hong Kong and construct the international urban city; (3) promote the structural reform as well as the innovations; (4) establish the modern industry system and construct the innovation city; (5) build a harmonious society; (6) build a model city for civilization; (7) boost the cultural soft strength; (8) innovate the talents training system and mechanism.; and (9) be regarded as "Shenzhen's reform road map." The "Certain Opinions" had been the programmatic document to guide the reform and opening-up as well as the scientific progress.

Together with "Certain Opinions", the recently released "The Reform Summary of Shenzhen in the near Future (the draft)" (hereafter refers to as "Reform Summary") was another important document to instruct Shenzhen reform in political system, administration system, economic system and social arena for the next three years. The "Reform Summary" includes 19 main reform tasks, such as the democracy development within the party, the

---

91 Xinhua net, http://news.xinhuanet.com/local/2008-04/01/content_7895940.htm.

direct election in some district level deputy, the adjustment and supposes of the Political Consultative Conference sector group, exploration the independent system of a new judicial power, the leading cadre of the party reporting property, recommendation of chief leaders of area and department, volunteering and chosen by public election, reply publicly before the ticket, separation powers of the administration, transformation of government function, deepening organizational reform in public utilities supervision, educational system reform, health organizational reform and culture organizational reform. Among the 19 main reform tasks, the political restructure everything seem new and fresh. Especially the "Reform Summary" emphasized the multi-election on district head, expanded the quantity of candidates for the deputy positions, required the candidates to carry on public speaking, reply and elected the district head as well as deputy head by the National People's Congress of the same level, in which accumulated experience for the future multi-election on the position of mayor. These actions meant that Shenzhen had already moved an important step forward against China's democracy exploration.

In December 2008, the State Council deliberated and passed "Pearl River Delta Reform and Development Program (2008~2020)," which authorized Shenzhen to National Synthetically Reform Testing District. On May 6, 2009, the most attention-attracted "Comprehensive Reform of Shenzhen Overall Program" had been approved by the State Council, which clarified the key points of promoting Shenzhen's reform and opening-up, the main direction of realizing the new round of development, and six aspects for making breakthrough in Shenzhen's reform: (1) deepening reform of the administrative system, taking the lead to complete the collective services government with the core of transforming the government function, modifying the big divisional management system and advancing the urban administration regionalization and the management system reform; (2) taking the lead to establish and improve a socialist market economy by strengthening the economic system reform; (3) positively advancing the reform in social arena and accelerate the pace of building an harmonious socialist society; (4) perfect independent innovation system and mechanism and accelerate the speed of constructing a national innovation pilot; (5) innovating comprehensive opening-up and region cooperation system mechanism in the key point of close cooperation between Shenzhen and Hong Kong; and (6) build resource managing model with the environment friendly system and mechanism, accelerate the pace of developing a national ecological demonstration city. Officially approved by the State Council, the "Comprehensive Reform of Shenzhen Overall Program" indicated that Shenzhen, a city had once created Chinese economic miracles, would advance the reform and opening-up in a broader scope and higher standards, be the leader in making breakthroughs in some key fields and links, promote Shenzhen to become the forerunner in deepening reform and opening-up as well as recreating new superiority of the system mechanism, thus making Shenzhen step forward in the reform and opening-up.

In July 2009, the carefully worked-out "Institutional Restructuring Plan of Shenzhen Municipal People's Government" had been approved by the Editorial Board, the Provincial Party Committee and Provincial Government. Shenzhen Municipal Government implemented the reform against big department integration since August 2009, taking one month and eight days, being completed at the beginning of September. On the basis of exploration against function unification among big departments and under the requirement of mutual restrict and coordination among the decision-making rights, conducted rights and supervisory rights, this deep and all-encompassing government institution reform reduced 15 government service departments, simplified 1/3 of the organizations, and set up 31 government departments, including seven committees, 18 execution bureaus and six offices, much lower than the organization quota 40, which is required by the Central Government for big cities.

The government institution reform was the core of deepening reform of the administrative system, and important to implementing the comprehensive reform. Based on a series of explorations to the government functions transformation, started from the reality of urban government directly serving the enterprises and residents, together with strengthening the market regulation, the Shenzhen Municipal Government paid more attention to the market supervision, the social management and the public services. It comprehensively went over the department functions, largely reduced the market access threshold, vigorously reduced the administration examinations and approval items, earnestly reduced government's micromanagement, and proposed specific requirements on the function transformation to various departments. As China's first Special Economic Zone, Shenzhen, which once acted as the forerunner in the economical battlefield and obtained magnificent victory for the last few years, was again at the forefront in the reform of administrative systems? Shenzhen was looking forward to acting as a demonstration for the urban government institution reform, and exploring the ways for the reform of administrative systems through bold innovation and relentless pursuit of breakthroughs in the organization reforms.

Standing at the frontier of China's reform and opening up, Shenzhen, was once again striving to be the vanguard of China's reform.

2 History of Zhuhai Special Economic Zone: Tough Exploration on the High Standards of Harmonious Development

Zhuhai Special Economic Zone was one of the two earliest built Special Economic Zones of China's reform and opening up (the other one was Shenzhen Special Economic Zone, which was previously represented in Section 1), earlier than Shantou and Xiamen Special Economic Zones in the planning and construction.[92] Thanks to superior policy conditions and great efforts, the economic and social conditions of the Zhuhai Special Economic Zone were greatly changed since its official foundation on August 1984 (Figure 2-0-1). As the window of China's socio-economic transformation, together with other local SEZ, Zhuhai Economic Zone contributed profound significance to China's economic system reform, social transformation and emancipation of the mind.

Although Zhuhai Special Economic Zone was less competitive than Shenzhen and most other cities around the Pearl River Delta (refers to the narrow sense of the Small Pearl River Delta[93]) in an economic factor, the open conditions of Hong Kong, etc., made it lower in development speed and supporting efforts than Shenzhen at the start stage.[94] By exploring its suitable development direction on the basis of drawing upon Shenzhen's experience, Zhuhai had gradually embarked on the hard but meaningful exploratory path on the pursuit of harmonious and high-level development. By looking only at the effect of

---

92 *Opening issue of China Special Economic Zone Yearbook, 1983,* Hong Kong China Special Economic Zone Yearbook editorial department, Hong Kong China Special Economic Zone Yearbook Press, 1983 edition, Page 145, 235, 265, 315; Wu Jianmin, *Guangdong literature material 78 album: memories of zhuhai special economic zone founded for five years,* Guangdong People Press, 1998 edition, page 75.

93 The narrow sense of Guangdong Pearl River Delta or "Small Pearl River Delta" generally referred to the Pearl River Delta region except Hong Kong and Macao, covering seven cities: Shenzhen, Zhuhai, Huizhou, Dongguan, Zhongshan, Guangzhou and Foshan. The Customarily called "Greater Pearl River Delta" still included Hong Kong, Macao, Jiangmen, as well as a small part of Zhaoqing and Qingyuan. However, after CEPA ("Mainland and Hong Kong Closer Economic Partnership Arrangement") was signed in 2003, appeared "Pan-Pearl River Delta", which was reference to the Pan-PRD regional cooperation, including nine provinces and regions as Fujian, Jiangxi, Hunan, Guangdong, Guangxi, Hainan, Sichuan, Guizhou, Yunnan and Hong Kong and Macao Special Administrative Region (referred to as "9 +2").

94 Wu Jianmin, Guangdong Literature Material 78 Albums: memories of zhuhai special economic zone founded for five years, Guangdong People Press, 1998 edition, Page 98~99.

economic growth rate, Zhuhai had been exceeded by many of the "Little Pearl River Delta" cities in the last decades, and what's more, its growth momentum was also less than the Shanghai Pudong New Area and Tianjin Binhai New Area, the two of which were established later. However, the speed of Zhuhai's development was still significantly higher than the national average. More rare and unique was that Zhuhai had taken on several bold and lasting practices in the aspects of high grade economic development, high quality of urban construction and harmonious social development, all of which, to a certain extent, played an and innovative role in building of the special economic zone.

We tried to narrate and discuss these local events and courses on the macro background of space and time, thus to help people better understand the origin and the influence Zhuhai has played in the process of the reform and opening up, as well as the development of Chinese special economic zones.

Figure 2-0-1 A recent bird's eye view of Zhuhai Special Economic Zone

Source: Zhuhai audio-visual nets, *Today's Zhuhai.*

2.1 The Unique Spatial Background of Zhuhai Special Economic Zone's Foundation

Though the Zhuhai region in ancient times was only a group of remote islands which scattered around the Pearl River estuary, it was rising rapidly in modern history, and fortunately got the glory of the first group of Mainland's Special Economic Zone in the contemporary era. Zhuhai's great change was not only affected by its macro geographic location, but also by its unique historical process and humanistic evolution. The following sections will briefly review some of the histories which closely relate with the contemporary Zhuhai: it has been at the rim of the Inland Civilization for a long time, and had access to the west only after Macau's rise; it deigned to edify the western civilization of Hong Kong in the modern history, and even tried to set up a so called "special economic zone" in the late Qing Dynasty, but fall as a silent border town before the reform and opening up. These histories might help us further understand the advantages, constraints and characteristics of Zhuhai Special Economic Zone.[95]

2.1.1 Geographical Features and Humanities Brief on Zhuhai SEZ

At the beginning of the establishment of Zhuhai Special Economic Zone, only 6.81 square kilometers could enjoy the treatment of Special Economic Zone, and soon gradually expand to the whole Zhuhai City. Located in the Guangdong coastal area in southeast China, Zhuhai was at the estuary of the Pearl River, which was very important to Guangdong Province (see Figure 2-1-1). The Pearl River runs into the sea in the south, and the east and west coastlines have long been occupied by the western counties because of its important economic and strategic position, which gradually developed Hong Kong and Macau by each side. Thirty years ago, at the beginning of the reform and opening up, the pioneers chose Zhuhai, geographically close to Macau as the special economic zone, just as they chose Shenzhen based on its geographical advantage to Hong Kong.

Figure 2-1-1 Zhuhai's location in the Pearl River Delta (left) & Zhuhai administrative figure

Resources. Adapted from nine map nets, etc, "Zhuhai Map", http://9ditu.com/m/zhuhai.htm.

In the geographical sector, present Zhuhai is composed of land and numerous islands. Located in the north latitude 21°48′~22°27′, east longitude 113°03′~114°19′,[96] governing

---

95 The related historical documents could be found in *Zhuhai history review*, edited by Zhuhai Public Record Office, and *Zhuhai History*, edit by Chinese people's political consultative conference literature material research council, Zhuhai committee.

96 Edited by Commission of Zhuhai Local History: ***Zhuhai Local History***, Zhuhai Press, 2001, p1

Xiangzhou, Doumen, Golden Bay areas. The land area of 1,687.8 square kilometers, slightly smaller than its neighbor Shenzhen as well as Zhongshan, was the smallest municipal city of Guangdong Province in terms of land area. Besides the island, the mainland part at the west side of the broad Zhujiangkou Bay (also known as Lingding Yang) included the low hills as well as the Delta plain, which was developed by sediment deposition. As the main body of Zhuhai, many rivers crossed this piece of land, which makes transportation quite inconvenient. There were eight sea entries for the north, east and west Pearl River, and within the range of Pearl River, there were five entries for the north and west river. (Figure 2-1-1). Covering 5,965.2 square kilometers, the Pearl River had 146 islands, which spread outside Zhujiangkou and islands of Hong Kong, facing the South China Sea. The island was mostly composed by small massifs of 100 meters high.[97] The scenery is exquisite, but the water source is scarce, with few people living in the immediate area. Besides being adjacent to Macao, the present Zhuhai is neighbor to Jiangmen by land, meeting Zhongshan in north, with waterways crossing Zhujiangkou and connecting Hong Kong and Shenzhen to the northeast, and connecting Guangzhou's Nansha area to the north, approximately 140 kilometers away from the Guangzhou urban district.

In the history of the establishment, the mainland of Zhuhai, together with Zhongshan city, was named Xiangshan County for a long time in the ancient times. To commemorate Sun Yat-sen, the father of the Republic of China, who was born in the area, the name had been changed to Zhongshan County. In 1953, to consolidate the frontier, the southern region of Zhongshan County and many coastlands, which used to affiliate to the nearby counties had been disintegrated and formed Zhuhai County. The biggest change in Zhuhai's establishment history began in 1979. In order to expand the connection with Hong Kong and Macao, in this year, together with Shenzhen, Zhuhai County upgraded to a provincial city. In 1980, as the important step of China's opening up, again, Zhuhai and Shenzhen founded (known as the pilot at that time) the first group of China's special economic zones.

The so-called "joining Macao by land" meant that "mini Macao" was completely surrounded by Zhuhai, both by land and water. With a direct connection between the core part of Zhuhai and major islands of Macao, Zhuhai obtained an important political position, but did not yet gain adequate driving forces for economic development from Macao, due to its lower level of influence than Hong Kong. Zhuhai's economic development mainly relies on Hong Kong. Although Zhuhai is only 36 sea miles (about 66 miles) away from major areas of Hong Kong, it is more remote than other regions of the Pearl River Delta in the

---

97 Edited by Commission of Zhuhai Local History: ***Zhuhai Local History***, Zhuhai Press, 2001, p1

area of land delivery of major bulk cargos. In the early days of Special Economic Zone (SEZ), there was no Humen Bridge at the Pearl River mouth. So people went to Hong Kong then had to pass through Shenzhen and Dong Guan, making a detour by Guangdong and Shun De, and then cross Zhong Shan, spending more than one day's drive and crossing several rivers with no bridge. Now Zhuhai is more distant from Hong Kong by road than that between Hong Kong and Guangdong (about 200 miles). Only after the establishment of the bridge connecting Hong Kong, Macao, Shenzhen and Zhuhai, could the regional advantage have the possibility to be improved. Besides Hong Kong and Macao, Zhuhai has the most inconvenient transportation to Guangzhou in small Pearl River Delta region in terms of its most important economic and social links with Guangzhou and interior regions. With road between Zhuhai and Guangdong be cut by several rivers which flow to the ocean and little water transportation (with no big port at the time), Zhuhai was a remote place, particularly at the beginning of reform and opening up. Zhuhai now is planned to be a core city and transportation hub in the west bank of Pearl River in the future. However, there are many different points of view on its developing to be an economic center, a livable city or other patterns.

The regional advantage of Zhuhai Special Economic Zone was mainly because of its unique geographic conditions. One of the advantages Zhuhai has is its land border with Macau and water border with Hong Kong.[98] However, in economic terms, the regional advantages of Zhuhai were much weaker than Shenzhen. As one important target of setting up SEZ here, the political significance of neighboring Macao is more embodied in its regional characters. In the early days of running experimental SEZ, designers, by no means, hoped that its economy could equal that of Shenzhen or even that it could be developed into an important economic city. However, the actual development of Zhuhai exceeded original anticipation because of the enormous vitality of reform and opening up. It provided a precious experience for reform and opening up. It could be said that Zhuhai's development politically fulfilled its targets of safeguarding the return of Macao and practicing "one country, two systems."

In terms of social and economic aspects, Zhuhai developed to be a garden city and tourist city with an outstanding cultural environment from a remote county of agriculture and fishery before opening up. The registered population and permanent residence of Zhuhai in 1979 was only 360.7 thousand (including the population of Doumen County in

---

98 Wu Jianmin, Five Years Remembrances of establishing Zhuhai Special Economic Zone, 78th volume of Guangdong History Data, Guang dong People's press, 1998 edition, P.25.

1983), and reached 1.0265 million in 2009.[99] With the prominent character of a sparse population in a vast territory,[100] Zhuhai had the smallest land area and smallest population in Guangdong Province, equal to two thirds of that of neighboring Zhongshan County with a very close area. In 2009, the permanent residents of Zhuhai totaled about 1.4912 million, smaller than that of other prefecture-level cities in Guangdong Province. The margin between permanent residents and registered population was 500 thousand, which referred to the number of non-permanent residents who lived in Zhuhai for over one year. Experience showed that the 500 thousand residents occupied about a better half of the migrant workers. With such a small number of migrant workers, the economic intensity of Zhuhai then remained at a very low level. Statistical economic data also shows that its economic aggregate was the smallest in the Pearl River Delta, but its outputs per capital ranked fourth among the seven cities in small Pearl River Delta regions,[101] which proved that the quality and value of its economic entity were not bad.

Zhuhai's small population and low economic intensity had a bearing on at least three factors. Firstly, large areas of newly deposited land were not suited for economic development. Most plain land of Zhuhai was formed from the ocean by sediment deposition of the Pearl River, and some were even the result of sedimentation and reclamation works over several decades. Among them, some land could not be planted because they were not yet mellow soil. The construction of industrial park and built up areas spent more on piling due to the lacking of firm foundation in most areas. Secondly, Zhuhai had no special advantage in undertaking internal and external economy due to its remote location. As mentioned above, Zhuhai had the most inconvenient communication with both Hong Kong and Guangzhou in the small Pearl River Delta regions. After opening up, Hong Kong was the most major investment source of Pearl River Delta. In recent years, oversea investments became more and more important, but Zhuhai's traffic conditions, with inadequate port and railways, were not good enough. Thirdly, the economic development pattern of Zhuhai is different from that of other cities in Guangdong Province. With a strict requirement of choosing the type and grade of investment of high-tech industry, Zhuhai refused numerous labor intensive and polluting enterprises for the long-term protection of the environment. Taking the advantages of preferential terms of SEZ, Zhuhai attracted many high value added enterprise, but the industrial system, with complete facilities and

99 Zhuhai Statistic Bureau, Investigation Team of State Statistic Bureau in Zhuhai, Statistic Bulletin of National Economy and Social Development of Zhuhai in 2009, 19th, March, 2009.

100 Zhuhai Statistic Bureau, Statistical Yearbook of Zhuhai (2009), China National Statistical Publishing House, 2009.

101 Zhuhai Statistic Bureau, Statistical Yearbook of Zhuhai (2009), China National Statistical Publishing House, 2009.

scale economies, did not take shape due to insufficient economic agglomeration and development strength.

In terms of the climate and environment, Zhuhai had sub-tropical maritime climate with flowers in all four seasons, rich species and no snow in winter.[102] As a remote terminal of undertaking Chinese mainland civilization, it's hard to develop its society and economy. Benefiting from western civilization on the other side of the ocean, Zhuhai played a relatively important role in modern Chinese history. The Pearl River Delta is located around the Tropic of Cancer. Like Taiwan and some regions of India, it now is one of the several regions with rapid economic development around north-south Tropic of Cancer. Compared to the North Temperate Zone, which had the vast majority of economic developed areas of the world, the sub-tropical zone around the Tropic of Cancer had only desert-like North Africa and Australia and mountain forest in Southeast Asia and South America with few inhabitants. The only economically prosperous regions in sub-tropical zone were the places that could be gradually developed in to an effective and open coastal society. Besides the basic comfortable climates, and the form of opening had relations with their unique historic pathway.

2.1.2 Unique History of the SEZ: From Remote Terminal to Forefront of Opening Up

2.1.2.1 From Terminal Point of Land Civilization to Starting Point of Ocean Civilization

The status of Chinese coastal areas in Chinese civilization undertook a slow process of going from low to high level. Zhuhai region had always been a sea island out of the Pearl River mouth until Tang Dynasty with small inhabitable areas, insufficient fresh water, inconvenient transportation and unchanging population.[103] In the light of archaeological finds, people already lived in the gulf with fresh water four thousand years ago, mainly lived on hunting, fishing and gathering.[104] Giant rock paintings left 3000 years ago still could be seen in Gaolan Island where Zhuhai built a deep-sea port.[105] According to the research of ancient scholars, these first settlers belonged to "Baiyue" ethnic group, which is called "liren" by later settled Han ethnic group, as the inland inhabitants of Guangdong

---

102 Zhuhai Archives edited, Looking back to the history of Zhuhai, Zhuhai Press, 2005 Perface, P, 1.

103 Local chronicles committee of Zhuhai, Guangdong province, *City Annual of Zhuhai*, Zhuhai Press, 2001, P.1; Zhuhai Archives edited, Looking back to the history of Zhuhai, Zhuhai Press, 2005, P.7.

104 Zhuhai Archives edited, *Looking back to the history of Zhuhai*, Zhuhai Press, 2005, P.3.

105 Local chronicles committee of Zhuhai, Guangdong province, *City Annual of Zhuhai*, Zhuhai Press, 2001, P.37.

Province.[106] The First Emperor of China, Qin Shihuang designated Yangyue areas as Nanhai County and set up Fanyu County in the area of Pearl River mouth after his unification of Nanling regions, starting up the administrative management. However, there was no administrative institution in Zhuhai then.[107]

The flourishing Central Plain Civilization after the spring and autumn period, like ancient Greek civilization at the same time, was developed in temperate regions around latitude 40 degrees north with a moderate climate, but worse than sub-tropical environment (although the earliest ancient civilization probably originated from the Euphrates and Tigris in about latitude 30 degrees north). Recent academic research shows that huge climate changes in Chinese history were often caused the migration of ancient people.[108] Long periods of freezing weather invariably deteriorated northern pastures, and made northern nomadic people move to the south to the Agriculture-Pasture Transition Zone. Therefore, northern Han ethnic group was forced to immigrate to the south in the consequence of agricultural degradation and social crisis, which were the reasons for Zhuhai's several huge immigrations. The earliest Han ethnic group in the Pearl River Delta was also forced to move, rather than voluntary immigrate. Several hundred years after the Qin and Han Dynasty, the climate of China "turned out to be very cold for a quite while as the third century became the fourth century," causing a decrease of grain outputs and great social turmoil.[109] The remaining rebels of the Luxun uprising escaped to remote islands out of the Pearl River mouth, which were far away from East Jin Dynasty and lived together with Baiyue ethnic groups after their failure.[110]

Until the Tang Dynasty, some sea islands of the Pearl River Delta turned out to be alluvial plain and Zhuhai regions began to get a certain standing thanks to both domestic factors and the beginning of oversea influence. At that time, Xiangshan Island, the biggest

---

106 Committee of Cultural and Historical Data of Zhuhai in Chinese people's political consultative conference, *Historical Organization System of Zhuhai Administration,*1990, P.1; huhai Archives edited, Looking back to the history of Zhuhai, Zhuhai Press, 2005, Preface, P. 1; Liu Shuyong edit, "A Brief History of Hong Kong", Joint Publishing company (Hong Kong), 1998, P. 3.

107 Huang Qichen, General History of Macao, Guangdong Education Press, 1999, P. 19; Zhuhai Archives edited, *Looking back to the history of Zhuhai*, Zhuhai Press, 2001, P. 1.

108 Wangzhen, Zhang Peiyuan and Zhou Qingbo, *the Influences of Climate change upon China's Social Development, -on relations between land and human beings, Geographic Journal,* 1996, fourth issue, P. 329-339

109 Wang Zhen, Li Huaqun, Kong Xiangde and Zhang Peiyuan, *History of the Influence of climate Warming upon Chinese Agriculture,* Progress in Natural Science, 2005, 6th issue, p. 706-713. Zhuhai Archives edited, *Looking Back to the History of Zhuhai,* Zhuhai Press, 2005, P. 4.

110 Jian Bozan edited, Out Line History of China, first volume, People's Press, 1983, P. 341-345; "A Brief History of Hong Kong", Joint Publishing company (Hong Kong), 1998, P.6

island of Zhuhai Sea Islands, undertook rapid development in its economy because of the salt boiling industry. It was said that the Mountain produced abundantly famous tea and orchids, which "can be smelled five kilometers away."[111] Southern Song Dynasty named this county after the mountain (now is called Zhongshan County, and diverge Zhuhai County after the founding of PRC) and created "Xiangshan culture," which is famous and widely accepted by both Chinese and western cultures. The population and economy gathered in the northern coastal area later developed to today's Zhongshan town. While the developed ports and economy in eastern and southern area of Phoenix Mountain, a branch of Xiangshan, developed into the county town and urban districts of Zhuhai respectively after reform and opening up.

Oversea contacts played a more important role in promoting Zhuhai's development. In Tang Dynasty, China's connection with the outside world made great progress. As the most important gateway to conduct oversea contacts, [112] Guangdong already became the administrative and traffic center of the Pearl River Delta with quite prosperous foreign trades. The export-oriented economy has a long history here. Tunmen of Hong Kong, an out port of Guangdong Province, was located in the air line of going to Southeastern Asia, Iran and Arabic regions. Zhuhai region also attracted more and more Han ethnic groups here because of the foreign trade activities.[113]

However, Zhuhai then made more contributions to domestic economy system than export-oriented economy. Ancient China did not pay much attention to overseas relations and often took it as an ornament for the "Central Empire with vast territory and abundant resources," different from today's China. China's oversea relations carried weight only after the overturn of strength between China and western countries in the Ming and Qing Dynasty. Zhuhai's prosperity in Tang Dynasty benefited from the positive and passive spread of interior society and economy to southern coastal areas. Take the famous Huang Chao uprising at the end of Tang Dynasty, for example. The rest of the rebels escaped to Da Island, Sanzao Island, etc after their failure.[114] This kind of southward migration of interior civilization reached a climax in Song Dynasty, and then gradually gave the leading role to overseas relations, until now.

---

111 Zhuhai Archives edited, *Looking back to the history of Zhuhai,* Zhuhai Press, 2005, P.13.

112 Jian Bozan edited, Out Line History of China, first volume, People's Press, 1983, P. 525.

113 Liu Shuyong edit, "A Brief History of Hong Kong", Joint Publishing company (Hong Kong), 1998, P.6; Jian Bozan edited, Out Line History of China, first volume, People's Press, 1983, P. 525.; Zhuhai Archives edited, *Looking back to the history of Zhuhai*, Zhuhai Press, 2005, P.4.

114 Zhuhai Archives edited, *Looking back to the history of Zhuhai*, Zhuhai Press, 2005, P.4.

Alluvial plain of the Pearl River Delta constantly expanded in Song Dynasty, and economic status of the Zhuhai area was promoted by the diffusion of inland population. Taking the advantage of Haidao County's local natural resources, its economic development then mainly relied on the primary industry rather than secondary and tertiary industry. However, it became improper to focus on minerals and agriculture when Zhuhai decided to develop export-oriented economy in the early days of reform and opening up.

Active spreading of inland economy to Zhuhai was strengthened in the southern Song Dynasty, and the passive diffusion of inland society peaked, betokening the decline after ancient inland civilization has reached its peak. It is another cold period of China. To avoid war, Han ethnic groups endured untold suffering on their trip to Zhuhai by Zhujixiang, Nanxiong, the passageway of Guangdong for immigrants from time to time.[115] On the evening of Southern Song Dynasty, northern Mongolian power reached the southern end of China. Southern Song Dynasty historically ceased to exist in Zhuhai, rather than in numerous coastal ends of Mainland China.

> At the end of the Southern Song Dynasty, the largest sea warfare in ancient Chinese history broke out. In 1279, Mongolian troops marched south and fought against the Southern Song Dynasty imperial family by the Doumen cliff of Zhuhai. Millions of soldiers and civilians and over three thousand warships were involved. One hundred thousand dead bodies floated in the ocean after the war. Zhang Shijie fought to the death and was buried on Huangyang Hill in Doumen. Lu Xiufu jumped into the sea with the prince. Over two hundred thousand soldiers and civilians of Southern Song Dynasty settled down in Zhuhai after their failure.[116]

This narration briefly describes the battles that broke out in Zhuhai and nearby regions in those two years.[117] During this period, Wen Tianxiang, General of Southern Song Dynasty, wrote his famous quotation "No one can live forever. Let me but leave a loyal heart shining in the pages of history." Thus, as an ordinary end of inland agricultural civilization, Zhuhai became the falling signal of the civilization.

Which direction should we go, what kind of social pattern should China adopt for a better development? Today China is still are looking for the answer for these unfulfilled

---

115 Wangzhen, Zhang Peiyuan and Zhou Qingbo, *the Influences of Climate change upon China's Social Development, -on relations between land and humanbeings, Geographic Journal*, 1996, fourth issue, P. 329-339; Zhuhai Archives edited, Looking back to the history of Zhuhai, Zhuhai Press, 2005, Perface P.4.

116 Zhuhai Archives edited, Looking back to the history of Zhuhai, Zhuhai Press, 2005, Perface P.3.

117 Zhuhai Archives edited, Looking back to the history of Zhuhai, Zhuhai Press, 2005, P.133~134; Jian Bozan edited, Outline History of China, second volume, People's Press, 1983, P. 117.

wishes of Wen Tianxiang. Lessening complacency and conformism, learning from western civilization and reform and opening up became China's important aspects in searching for the answer. Coincidentally, Zhuhai became a major stage for a new Chinese development pattern, implying reasonable factors. Southern coastal regions of China have the tradition of oversea contact, and Pearl River Delta became the most superior place due to the limited navigation capacity of ancient China and its location.

The end of the land was just the beginning of the ocean. Soon after Southern Song Dynasty, western civilization spread to China through Zhuhai in the Ming Dynasty. At that time, the agricultural civilization seemed to be overburdened, and more and more people (include Zhuhai inhabitants) went to the South Pacific to make a living, becoming a constant economic pathway lasting until the last century. However, the contacts between Chinese and overseas countries, especially western countries, became more and more important. Zheng He's seven voyages (not aimed to Europe and America) seem to be a momentary recovery of the prosperous agricultural civilization, and a central empire's political action of showing off, which should not be overvalued. Beliefs and following science and technology transferred from Europe through Zhuhai and trade activities were more meaningful. Soon after the last three inventions of the Four Great Inventions, namely, paper, printing, the compass and the gunpowder, China gradually relied on western science and technologies.[118]

In the Ming Dynasty, Macao, in Zhuhai regions then governed by Xiangshan County, was rented by Portugal. Catholic Portugal and Spain give support to Prince Enrique and Columbus to find the new continent with great zeal for spreading the gospel and the salvation of mankind, but their trade and colonial expansion also contained the mercantilist interests and greed of the royal.[119]

It was generally acknowledged that the Portuguese obtained the rental rights to Macao in 1553 (but Macao was China's territory until the late Qing Dynasty).[120] Since then, the Pearl River Delta, where Macao and Guangzhou were located, played a more important role in China's oversea relations, and the history of Macao made the Zhuhai region play a

---

118 Jian Bozan edited, Out Line History of China, second volume, People's Press, 1983, P. 258

119 [Britan] Adam Smith, The Wealth of Nations, translated by Tang Risong, Huaxia Publishing House, 2005, P. 402-408; [American]Burns and Ralph, History of the World Civilization, translated by Luo Jingguo, Commercial Press Ltd, 1987, second Volume, P.223; Mander, the Real Source of Great Powers, China Election and Management website http://www.chinaelections.org/newsinfo.asp?newsid=148267,11th, May, 2009.

120 Jian Bozan edited, Out Line History of China, second volume, People's Press, 1983, P. 257; Huang Qichen, General History of Macao, Guangdong Education Press, 1999, P. 29-31.

more and more important role in the following historical process of China.

2.1.2.2 Connecting Macao by Land

The following development of the Zhuhai region went hand in hand with Macao. It had always been one of the most important objective factors, which endowed Zhuhai with a unique position before Hong Kong was founded as a port in modern history.

Three lonely island of Macao stood in the ocean in ancient times, and were governed by Xiangshan County as other Zhuhai regions. Before the Ming Dynasty, sediment deposition of Pearl River Delta enlarged the aforementioned Xiangshan Island, connecting it to the continent on the north, and starting to join the most northern island of Macao on the south (refers to Macao Island, see photo 2-1-1).[121] The path crossing the ocean was a long and narrow sandbar, and turned out to be an over 200 meters long stone road leftover from the residence of the Portuguese, changing the north island to Macao peninsula, and became the most important and prosperous region of Macao because of its connection with the mainland.[122]

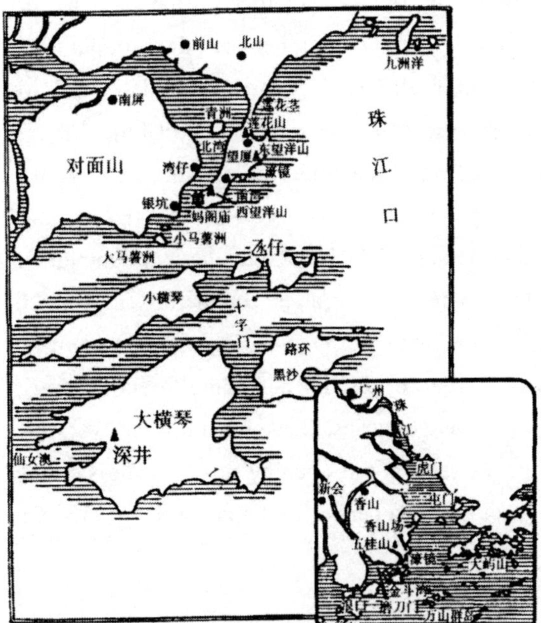

Figure 2-1-2 Sketch Map of Ancient Macao

Resources: Huang Qichen, General History of Macao, Guangdong education Press, Guangdong, 1999, P.3.

---

121 Huang Qichen, General History of Macao, Guangdong Education Press, 1999, P. 1.

122 Huang Qichen, General History of Macao, Guangdong Education Press, 1999, P. 1-2

Hence, Macao became an important gateway connecting China and western countries, developing rapidly from a small fishing village with only hundreds of inhabitants to a port with ten of thousands of inhabitants over decades.[123] Its subsequent population fluctuated between thousands to ten thousands, but only hundreds of Portuguese by birth and most were Chinese. With a thriving trade business, Macao became one important east-west trade transshipment port because of the revitalization of Chinese agricultural economy and the coming of western peoples in the Ming Dynasty.[124] However, the Ming Dynasty continued the ancient national policy of physiocracy, and even closed Quanzhou and Ningbo ports before Portuguese entered Macao, instead promoting trades in Macao and Pearl River Delta, thanks to the only open port-Guangzhou port.[125]

Zhuhai area made great progress because of the prosperity of Macao in the Ming Dynasty. In Ming Wanli (AD 1573 - 1620), there were more than fifty villages.[126] As the thriving of the trade and explosion of the population in this region, the Ming Dynasty felt more and more anxious about the failure of the "Sea Forbidding Policy,"(a policy against all sea trading or related activities) thus Qianshan Zhai was set up near Macao to strengthen the sea defense in 1621,[127] another military Zhai after Xiangshan Zhai. It controlled the passageway to the mainland between the mountain and the sea, playing the role of defending "Japanese Pirates," as people said. Traditionally, the "Japanese Pirates" referred to the pirates from Japan, Korea and China, but research in recent years showed that a lot of pirates were maritime traders who fight against the "Sea Forbidding Policy."[128]

Since then, Zhuhai served a dual and paradoxical function. First, it served as an important window for connecting foreign countries. This function had made great contributions to China in the late Qing Dynasty and early days of reform and opening up. The other function was as front fortress for defending foreign countries, or even cutting the communication with foreign countries. This function always worked in the late Qing Dynasty and early days of reform and opening up. As the symbol of dual function, the gate of Macao could be closed as a barrier, and open as a door. (See photo 2-1-3).

---

123 Huang Qichen, General History of Macao, Guangdong Education Press, 1999, P. 9

124 Huang Qichen, General History of Macao, Guangdong Education Press, 1999, P. 49-53.

125 Huang Qichen, General History of Macao, Guangdong Education Press, 1999, P. 53-55.

126 Zhuhai Archives edited, Looking Back to the History of Zhuhai, Zhuhai Press, 2005, P.4.

127 Zhuhai Archives edited, Looking Back to the History of Zhuhai, Zhuhai Press, 2005, P.14.

128 Japanese Pirate, http://baike.baidu.com/view/14434.html, 2008 年; Huang Qichen, General History of Macao, Guangdong Education Press, 1999, P. 53-54.

Figure 2-1-3 Zhuhai ancient gate with a dual function

Resources: Zhuhai audio and visual web, Today's Zhuhai, http://www.zhtv.com/hd/2005tequ/pic/history/pages/pic004.htm

In the Qing Dynasty, the status of Macao as a transshipment port of international trade was on the wane, a result of further "Sea Forbidden Policy" of Qing government, chasing Portuguese away by the Japanese, the economic recession of Portugal and the rising of Britain and other countries.[129] The trade of Macao gradually developed by attaching to Hong Kong after it was founded as a port in the late Qing Dynasty, and its population reached one hundred thousand before the Anti-Japanese War.[130] Accordingly, Zhuhai's status slid downward as Macao, with the sea defense as its main task and sprung up after Hong Kong was founded as a port for connecting Hong Kong and foreign countries.

2.1.2.3 "Connecting Hong Kong and Its Opening Spirit"

The development of Macao was mainly the outcome of European economic development pattern with the character of mercantilism in the 16th century. This economic development pattern, represented by Spain and Portugal, laid stress on foreign trade and robbery of gold and silver to sustain their national military strength and satisfy the luxurious demand of the noble in the consequence of a corrupt and swelling government caused by catholic ceasaropapism. They mainly relied on the advanced sailing technologies and military power to become a strong country. However, Hong Kong was the war trophy

129 Huang Qichen, General History of Macao, Guangdong Education Press, 1999, P. 177-185.

130 Zhuhai Archives edited, Looking back to the history of Zhuhai, Zhuhai Press, 2005, P.10.

of the European market economy in the 19th century. The open economy, represented by Great Britain and the U.S.A., manifested the spirit of Christianity after the Protestant Reformation, advocated freedom and limited the power of the king, and attempted to develop economy and technology in line with objective laws. Although real free market economy had severe defects, it had done great contribution in the bumpy road of enriching the country and peoples. The ancient empire of the Far East that had always been self-sufficient was encroached upon by eastern invaders 300 years after the coming of the Portuguese in the late Qing Dynasty. In the following 100 years, China achieved a quicker development in its economy, technology and national strength after the establishment of the market mechanism and reform and opening up, undergoing many difficulties and postpones upon dealing with the relations between military power, technology, system and faith. Shen Zhen and Zhuhai are the first areas opening to the outside.

The opening of Hong Kong made the earliest fatal shock of the market economy to China's natural economy. Great Britain understood the importance of Hong Kong at an earlier time. In 1833, an ambitious speech from the British lower house mentioned: "upon canceling the limitation of foreign trade, if direct relations could not be established between the empire and other countries, it would be a desirable strategy to set up a foreign trade center in China's coastal islands or peninsulas to get over the control of Chinese authorities."[131] In 1841, Britain occupied Hong Kong by the unjustifiable First Opium War, making it and the Pearl River Delta a focus of contacts and conflicts between China and Western countries. Moreover, Treaty of Nanking in 1842 opened another five ports, booming the development of Shanghai and making its economy exceed that of Hong Kong. Hong Kong's economy again surpassed Shanghai before reform and opening up and contributed a great deal to Pearl River Delta's reform and opening up.

After the opening of Hong Kong as a port, Macao quickly lagged behind Hong Kong. It was caused the fact that the development of east side of Pearl River always took the lead of west side, insinuating that today's Zhuhai is not located in the best area. Zhuhai had always been unwilling to admit or even ignore this truth, causing over development. However, modern Zhuhai did not stay on the ground as Macao. Its standing was enlarged from the dual function of economic window to the outside world and political defending fortress to breed a new role given by Hong Kong. However, Macao's influence on Zhuhai was strengthening. Macao was rented by the Portuguese for over 300 years, but it had always been Chinese territory with Chinese customs. Taking the advantages from Chinese

131 Liu Shuyong edit, "A Brief History of Hong Kong", Joint Publishing company (Hong Kong), 1998, P16.

setbacks and chaos after the Opium War, Portuguese urged Qing to sign the Sino-Portugal Commercial Treaty after continuous efforts. With a small amount of economic benefits by assisting Chinese customs to collect the revenue of opium, Portugal obtained permanent residential administrative power in Macao.[132] But Macao was not ceded or handed to another owner. Macao has always been a part of China's sovereignty and territory which became a unique region due to the administration of Portuguese, a kind of destroying China's sovereign rights.[133] The change of Macao's status actually reinforced Zhuhai's function as a window and fortress. For example, the nearby Qianshan Zhai strengthened its defense, becoming Lin Zexu and other peoples' front for fighting against western invaders.[134]

However, Zhuhai's outstanding role in Chinese modern history since this period went hand in hand with Hong Kong, Shanghai or even the whole nation rather than its closest neighbor, Macao. It also has relations with its opening spirit bred over hundred years in this region.

Firstly, the historical spirit of culture became an important foundation for Zhuhai peoples' rising. Huang Xiaodong made the following statement:

> Zhuhai, Zhongshan and Macao all belong to Xiangshan County with the same ties of blood, kindred history and culture. They all belong to the ecological community of Xiangshan culture. The culture of the Zhuhai areas is an important part of Xiangshan culture. Xiangshan culture went through four phases: the bud phase in Tang and Song Dynasty; accumulative phase in Ming and Qing Dynasty; ripening phase; and development phase. It is outcome of the combination of "two mountains" and "two oceans" culture. The two mountains refer to south and north side of the mountain, while two oceans mean south and west Pacific. Under the synergy of multi culture, Zhuhai people obtain the cultural characters of attaching more importance on humanities and education, with very distinct oceanic characteristics. Their courage of exploration, mechanism, opening to the outside and tolerance embody the blue civilization traits of "coming from the ocean, heading for the ocean."[135]

Descendants of Central Plain people who crossed Nanling in the Tang and Song Dynasty already intended to change some conventional traditions, and some people even

132 Huang Qichen, General History of Macao, Guangdong Education Press, 1999, P. 278-303; Zhuhai Archives edited, *Looking back to the history of Zhuhai*, Zhuhai Press, 2005, P.17-18

133 Huang Qichen, General History of Macao, Guangdong Education Press, 1999, P. 302-303.

134 Zhuhai Archives edited, *Looking back to the history of Zhuhai*, Zhuhai Press, 2005, P.15.

135 Zhuhai Archives edited, *Looking back to the history of Zhuhai*, Zhuhai Press, 2005, Preface, P.5.

went to the south pacific. The communication with western civilization over hundreds years changed the culture and beliefs of the Zhuhai people. The real launch of this change happened after Britain occupied Hong Kong in 1841. Two important names should be mentioned here. One is Rong Hong, who sped up China's Western Learning. In 1828, Rong Hong was born in Zhuhai. He went to Macao to start his primary school when he was very young, hoping to do business abroad after growing up. He moved to Hong Kong with his school soon after the opening of Hong Kong as a port, and then went to the U.S.A. with a schoolmaster. He graduated from Yale University in 1854, becoming the first Chinese overseas student who graduated from an American college.[136] Soon after, he devoted himself to saving the country by enterprise of Westernization Movement, and then started to save the country by education, sending 120 children to study in America, including 23 Zhuhai children who later became important people of China. In his later years, he was devoted to saving the country by engaging in politics and supporting Sun Yat-sen, which is the other important name to be mentioned. Sun Yat-sen was from Cuiting Village in Zhongshan County, which is close to Zhuhai. He attended a primary school in Honolulu, Hawaii, learned medicine when he was young, and believed in Christianity. Zhuhai was the main area where he made great contributions to people's democratic revolution.[137]

A large number of influential Zhuhai people suddenly appeared on the stage of China's economy, politics and culture. People may be surprised to find that the rising of Zhuhai and Pearl River Delta was indeed influenced by its unique converged endowment of Chinese and Western cultures. These influences spread to its economy, politics and cultural believes, and brought some benefits to modern reform and opening up. In economic aspects, "Zhuhai merchants created numerous firsts: the first cement plant, the first Chinese Merchant Newspaper, the first department store, the first insurance company, the first machinery printing factory, the first self-built railway, the first steam locomotive made in China, etc."[138] Although these pioneering works were not done in Zhuhai, they were developed by Zhuhai people in Shanghai and other places.

Secondly, Zhuhai then was one of the forefronts in promoting China's modernization by revolution and opening up. Its ocean culture spurred after long accumulation and manifested an important role in China's revolution in many important regions.

Neighboring Hong Kong, the open and pioneering Zhuhai people were easier to

---

136 Zhuhai Archives edited, *Looking back to the history of Zhuhai*, Zhuhai Press, 2005, P.96.

137 Li Changqing, *the Revolution of 1911 in Zhuhai* ommittee of Cultural and Historical Data of Zhuhai in Chinese people's political consultative conference, *History of Zhuhai Volume 10,* Printed in2005, p. 6-8

138 Zhuhai Archives edited, *Looking back to the history of Zhuhai*, Zhuhai Press, 2005, Preface P.7-8.

benefit from the western civilization spread from Hong Kong and many people went to Shanghai after rising. Huang Xiaodong also has a bright viewpoint:

> It could be said that the modern history of China is the history of the Guangdong people. While the modern history of Guangdong started from Zhuhai, with favorable opportunity and geographic position, Zhuhai got rid of the old and took in the fresh and firstly enlightened the benighted with Western Learning, becoming an important promoter for China's modernization.[139]

From the experiences of many notable Zhuhai people with pioneering spirit, we can see that this kind of spirit not only comes from the openness of Zhuhai, but also benefits from choosing a favorable place to develop rather than only pay attention to local development. So it is with Rong Hong and Sun Yat-sen (his hometown is next to Zhuhai). We, more often than not, see these characteristics in Zhuhai people. For example, Liang Tingshu, famous entrepreneur and officer advocated Westernization Movement in Rong Hong period, studied in Hong Kong when he was young and went to Shanghai later. Xurun, notable businessman also based in Shanghai. Tang Shaoyi, whose father did business in Shanghai, was sent to America to study by Rong Hong, and became a official in Tianjin after returning home, and later the first prime minister of The Republic of China.

2.1.2.4 "Special Administrative Region" in the Later Qing Dynasty and its Outstanding Political Function

After a great period of historical growth, Zhuhai's economic and political functions were greatly upgraded in the late Qing Dynasty and early Republic period with unique opportunities of the times. The improvement of its economic status was mainly because of early reform, the last new policy of the Qing government. The authorities then encouraged overseas Chinese and entrepreneurs of Hong Kong and Macao to invest in interior areas. In 1908, Wu Yuzheng, an overseas Chinese businessman, Wangshen, a businessman of Macao and other people proposed to establish trading port in Xiangzhou urban districts.[140] After decades' sedimentation accumulation, it has already formed a fishing village, which connected Macao and Xiangshan County, only 10 kilometers away from Macao.[141] Guangdong Province immediately gave permission for its open and bold

---

139 Zhuhai Archives edited, *Looking back to the history of Zhuhai*, Zhuhai Press, 2005, Preface P.2

140 Zhuhai Archives edited, Looking back to the history of Zhuhai, Zhuhai Press, 2005, P.21.

141 Guan Rongguang, the Industry and Commerce of Xiangzhou Before Liberation, see editorial group of Zhuhai CPPCC, Literature and History of Zhuhai, volume 3, 1984, P. 45.

plan to build up "tax free commercial port in 60 years," which was a great event of reform and opening up then (see photo 2-1-4):

Figure 2-1-4 Xiangzhou soon after open as a port (around 1910)
Resources, Zhuhai audio and visual web, Today's Zhuhai, http://www.zhtv.com/hd/2005tequ/pic/history/pages/pic003.htm.

The commercial port used the form of Shanghai commercial shops for reference in building business streets. At the beginning, they built 28 two-storied buildings, 20 buildings with six stories and 8 buildings with three stories and two three-storied buildings four meters apart from each other, in a neat north to south pattern. There were over ten streets then, which became very lively when after night fell. Hailed as "Zhongshan Downtown Street," it attracted businessmen from Hong Kong, Macao, Siyi and other places to invest in the area and fishermen of the South China Sea to settle down in the area in succession. In the second year of Xuantong (1910), there were 1600 shops in total, 20 meter-wide roads and two docks shipping to Guangdong, Hong Kong and Macao. Among them, there were relatively big shops such as "Zhongxing Textile Company," famous stores such as "Xie Chang," "Kang Zheng," "Yong Lilong," etc. Both overseas and domestic journalists vied to report on prosperity. In the third year of Xuantong (1911), there were about 200 shops including grain shops, oil shops, grocery stores and pawnshops. Qing authority announced Xiangzhou as a free port and tax-free region. However, a six-hour fire burned thousands of shops into ashes in the end of the same year. Moreover, different ideas on tax-free commercial port were heard in the government and foreign customs commissioner of Gongbei interfered, making investors transfer their capitals. Xiangzhou Commercial port went downhill since then.[142]

The bold announcement of Xiangzhou as free port and tax-free area of Qing authority on the brink of collapse shows that its vigor of reform and opening up at least exceeded that

142 Zhuhai Archives edited, *Looking back to the history of Zhuhai*, Zhuhai Press, 2005, P.22.

of modern reform and opening up. It was a pity that the reform in the late Qing Dynasty was not intensive and comprehensive and too late to succeed. According to other documents, Xiangzhou commercial port did not completely collapse and still gave services to a limited local economy.[143]

In terms of development pattern, "Rong Hong already proposed, 'with cheap Chinese material and labors, machines made in China would be cheaper than ones produced in Europe and America.' It should be the initial idea of 'three plus one' and Export Processing Zone."[144] It's a pity that the conditions then were not mature.

In the period of Late Qing and Early Republic of China, Zhuhai not only promoted its economic status, but also played an outstanding role in the political reform of China. Thanks to its connection with western countries, especially with Hong Kong and Macao, Zhuhai and the Pearl River Delta became an important bridge tower and window for overthrowing the government of Qing Dynasty and contacting overseas patriotic forces. This region was neither the political center nor the economic center, but further developed to be the base of new political forces.

2.1.3 The Condition Before Reform and Opening Up

The center of political strength moved north after the success of northern expedition started from the Pearl River Delta in the early days of Republic of China. The role of Zhuhai as bridge tower came to an end in victory. In addition to the strengthening of Shanghai's position as economic center, the Pearl River Delta again gradually turned to be a remote area of China's politics and economy.

But Zhuhai continued its momentum in previous periods and its remaining local economy and politics made some progresses. Xiangzhou Commercial Port's position as an economic center went downward due to losing the qualification of tax-free "special zone," which "a variety of industries sprung up and Xiangzhou town took shape" in the early 1920s.[145] In the early Republic of China, "Sun Yat-sen planned to build Xiangzhou into a third-class fishing port," "reflecting that fishery played an important role in Xiangzhou's economy."[146] Although it made some progress under the management of Tang Shaoyi, the first prime minister of the Republic of China when KMT came to power, its economy and politics stagnated and declined as the consequence of war-torn chaos and Japanese

143 Editorial group of Zhuhai CPPCC, Literature and History of Zhuhai, volume 3, 1984, P. 44-52

144 Zhuhai Archives edited, *Looking back to the history of Zhuhai*, Zhuhai Press, 2005, Preface P.9.

145 Editorial group of Zhuhai CPPCC, Literature and History of Zhuhai, volume 3, 1984, P. 44

146 Editorial group of Zhuhai CPPCC, Literature and History of Zhuhai, volume 3, 1984, P. 49.

occupation."[147] After the victory of Anti-Japanese War, "Xiangzhou recovered its economy, but was then accompanied by drug dealing and smuggling."[148]

After the founding of the People's Republic of China, Zhuhai turned out to be an important border town to defend Hong Kong and Macao and KMT remainders from overseas hostile forces. Its military role was strengthened, but its economic role remained in an appurtenant position. Fu Gaoyi, an overseas scholar with a great understanding of Guangdong, held the viewpoint that "the spiritual center of the communist revolution has already left Guangdong and other coastal areas to interior areas of China. China closed its door to the capitalist world after 1949, and paid all attention to domestic development with no more relations with outsiders. Communist leaders adopted the same political structure, policy, and movement to Guangdong as other provinces."[149]

However, it was just in this period that Zhuhai obtained independent administrative system, marking the improvement of its political status. The main reasons are as follows: In the early days of PRC, China faced frequent military harassments from Macao authorities and threats of British naval craft in Hong Kong after the break out of Korean War, so Zhuhai's defense became more important.[150] In addition, the task of consolidating the defense became more difficult because the problem of fishery for export: "the population of this region reached 130 thousand in 1953, while fisherman accounted for 30 thousand. Although smaller a group than farmers, but their sphere of activities were so broad and their political influences so great that they far exceeded that of farmers who engaged in agriculture, forestry and sideline. In particular, the flowing fishermen shares 80 percent of fishermen, they travel between the Mainland, Hong Kong and Macao, even to South Pacific and Taiwan with larger influences and more complicated situations."[151] Therefore, the work for flowing fishermen to accept the policy became a great event of the national defense. It was also a need of political military to develop fishery industry.

For this reason, it was necessary to uniformly manage the numerous islands belonging to different counties. The military organization defending these islands was set up in Tang

---

147 Zhuhai Archives edited, Looking back to the history of Zhuhai, Zhuhai Press, 2005, P.62; Editorial group of Zhuhai CPPCC, Literature and History of Zhuhai, volume 3, 1984, P. 44.

148 Editorial group of Zhuhai CPPCC, Literature and History of Zhuhai, volume 3, 1984, P. 44.

149 [U.S.A]Fu Gaoyi, Taking the first step, Guangdong in reform, Ling kefeng, Ding anhua translate, Guangdong People's Press, 1991, P.4.

150 Committee of Cultural and Historical Data of Zhuhai in Chinese people's political consultative conference, Historical OrganizationSystem of Zhuhai Administration, the History of Zhuhai, volume 9, 1990, P.6.

151 Committee of Cultural and Historical Data of Zhuhai in Chinese people's political consultative conference, Historical OrganizationSystem of Zhuhai Administration, the History of Zhuhai, volume 9, 1990, P.8.

Jiawan and Zhuhai in 1950, and promoted to division grade in 1950.[152] In January 1951, over one hundred islands of Zhongshan, Bao'an and Dongguan County formed the county level or regimental grade administration "Islands Administration of Guangdong Provincial People's Government, Zhuhai Branch." In 1952, it was turned into the fisherman region of Zhongshan County, and the district government was also located in Tang Jiacun.[153]

As relative people remember, the proposal of founding an independent county-level administration in Zhuhai was probably brought up by Ye Jianying, the first secretary of South China Sub-Bureau of CPC Central Committee and Chairman of Guangdong Provincial People's Government.[154] The independent Zhuhai County was officially founded in May 1953. The county town was located in Tang Jiawan, the important military base, rather than Xiangzhou, the economic center of the county, showing that economy was not the top priority then. As a leader said, "Although Zhuha has more peasants than fisher folks, Zhuhai should mainly develop its maritime economy and fishery industry. Otherwise, it seems to be meaningless to found this county."[155] While the key of how to do the works of fisherman was to win their support and assure them not to harm the new regime. As Zeng Wen, the first secretary of county party committee, emphasized, "KMT, Macao and Hong Kong authorities are fighting for this force, and their political and economic influence can not be underestimated."[156]

Therefore, the target of fighting for these then external oriented fisherman was changing them to be internal oriented, politically and economically, contrasting present day's development guiding policy. Eighty percent of the flowing fisherman traveled between Hong Kong and Macao had to abandon the outgoing economic benefits. The guiding principles of Zhuhai's founding therefore were "consolidating the ocean border defense, striving for fisherman to support PRC and developing fishery and agriculture."[157] However, consolidating the defense and developing economy contradict with each other

---

152 Committee of Cultural and Historical Data of Zhuhai in Chinese people's political consultative conference, Historical OrganizationSystem of Zhuhai Administration, the History of Zhuhai, volume 9, 1990, P. 5.

153 Zhuhai Archives edited, *Looking Back to the History of Zhuhai*, Zhuhai Press, 2005, P. 5.

154 Committee of Cultural and Historical Data of Zhuhai in Chinese people's political consultative conference, Historical OrganizationSystem of Zhuhai Administration, the History of Zhuhai, volume 9, 1990, P. 9-10

155 Committee of Cultural and Historical Data of Zhuhai in Chinese people's political consultative conference, Historical OrganizationSystem of Zhuhai Administration, the History of Zhuhai, volume 9, 1990, P. 8-9

156 Zhuhai Archives edited, *Looking Back to the History of Zhuhai*, Zhuhai Press, 2005, P.235-236; Committee of Cultural and Historical Data of Zhuhai in Chinese people's political consultative conference, Historical Organization System of Zhuhai Administration, the History of Zhuhai, volume 9, 1990, P. 9.

157 Zhuhai Archives edited, *Looking back to the history of Zhuhai*, Zhuhai Press, 2005, Preface P.11.

due to the situation and policies at that time. Therefore, Zhuhai, Guangdong or even many coastal areas have endured economic satisfies for the country, and turned to be rimland of national economic development.

Overseas scholar Fu Gaoyi believed that "during the 1960s and early 70s, China not only laid stress on investing in the interior areas, but also became politically introverted and exclusive. All the over-westernized and capitalized people or people with foreign ties were doubted. Everybody fight for self-preservation. Guangdong Province topped all provinces as the object of criticizing, and was more thoroughly distorted by the policy of isolation."[158]

The problem of Zhuhai, however, lies more in its rigid running system of the economy formed in planned economy, which is different from that of market economy. China's planned economy temporarily and partly attained its planned goals at the expense of low efficiency, insufficient enthusiasm for labor and other serious problems. Thanks to its special location of closing to Hong Kong, Guangdong was not completely closed down in its economy. The surviving Guangzhou Commodity Fair was the example. Out of political or economic purpose, some flexible economic mode is allowed in this remote economic area, or even to name the early trial of opening some areas:

> In 1957, Chen Yun proposed to establish professional bases for the production of export commodities. Guangdong already set up a series of bases during the late 1950s and 60s. The so-called export production base was absolutely the export market, especially the farm and factory, which provided products for Hong Kong. However, this plan became obsolete in 1969. Until 1971 and 1972, scores of export production bases were established again for the carrying out of new system of purchasing contracts for export production. These bases perfectly finished the export task and convinced the Beijing officer who was in charge of economic plans to expand and solidify the specialization of these bases. Ministry of Foreign Trade appointed Foshan area to set up the first "unified export production base" in 1973. For the purpose of obtaining more foreign exchanges, Beijing shall guarantee that export production is more attractive to the local.[159]

Although Zhuhai is the closest place to Macao, it failed to be a major pioneering area of opening up due to its military role, and its economy even fell behind to the level of a remote country or fishing village. However, the factors of a rigid planned economy were not much and relieved the burden and obstacles for its reform and opening up later. It was

158 [U.S.A]Fu Gaoyi, Taking the first step, Guangdong in reform, Ling kefeng, Ding anhua translate, Guangdong People's Press, 1991, P.4.

159 [U.S.A]Fu Gaoyi, Taking the first step, Guangdong in reform, Ling kefeng, Ding anhua translate, Guangdong People's Press, 1991, P.363.

one reason that more achievements were made in the remote and unimportant Pearl River Delta rather than in the very important Yangtze River Delta in early reform and opening up of China.

2.2 Primary Experimental Period of Zhuhai SEZ: Cautious Exploration and Hard Breakthrough

Zhuhai once had a special position in the history of economy and politics and played a role in the development of Pearl River Delta, even the whole nation, but became remote, abandoned and silent farming and fishing village. Its openness to advanced culture and innovative spirit had been long stifled. Some described Zhuhai at that time as the following:

Xiangzhou, the county center of Zhuhai, was like a remote fishing village. This was not a malicious belittling, but a portrait of its economic trail. Some people said Zhuhai was a place with one street, one granary, one factory and one restaurant. At that time, the transportation between Zhuhai and Guangzhou was bad, with narrow and uneven roads. People needed to pass four piers, which was really inconvenient. There was no direct shipping between Zhuhai and Hong Kong. The only way was to take boat in Macau.[160]

It could not maintain a rural life with small country and population like ancient times. It was not only because of a very low life standard, with 149 yuan income per capita in the village in 1978 when reform and opening up just started, but also the big disparity between Zhuhai and Hong Kong and Macau that were connected both by land and sea.[161] During the recent decades, many people in the area illegally migrated to Hong Kong and Macau and the tide became high again. In 1978, the numbers of farmers and fishermen in Zhuhai (not including Doumen County which was not combined into Zhuhai) was less than in 1953, which decreased from about 100,000 and more than 30,000 to 80,000 and 30,000.[162]

The reform and opening up that started in 1978 brought hope to the people who began to reflect deeply. A former Vice Governor of Guangdong Province said, "We must appreciate the Cultural Reform, without which may we never take this fundamental reform.

---

160 WU, Jianmin: ***History of Guangdong. Volume.78: 5 Years Memory for Zhuhai SAR***, Guangdong Renmin Press, Edition of 1998, P22.

161 WU, Jianmin: ***History of Guangdong. Volume.78: 5 Years Memory for Zhuhai SAR***, Guangdong Renmin Press, Edition of 1998, P22.

162 WU, Jianmin: ***History of Guangdong. Volume.78: 5 Years Memory for Zhuhai SAR***, Guangdong Renmin Press, Edition of 1998, P22.

The Cultural Reform made us realize the weakness of the old system."[163]

Therefore, if China wants to implement the policy of reform and opening up, it must put down burden and self-adulation, learn and explore modestly and break the resistance bravely. To appoint a small scale of special area (SEZ) for experiment and exploration was not only cautious and scientific, but also was apt to reduce resistance and to take bold attempt. We can say that during that period, the Central Government's attempt to set up SEZ was important measure for an active, stable and step-by-step reform. However, the exploration in the small SEZ was more difficult than expected. Because of the concept of the idea and the confusion on which method was better, people often made difficult choices between braveness and cautions, between insistency and waiver, which left a lot of experience, lessons and unsolved issues to the descendents.

2.2.1 Attempt to Establish an Export Base and the Upgrade to the Prefecture-Level City of Zhuhai

2.2.1.1 The Development of Opening Policies and the Establishment of Export Base and Quasi Prefecture-Level City of Zhuhai

There was a gradual exploring and accelerating procedure at the beginning of the reform and opening up of Zhuhai, while the idea of the Central for reform and opening up was also gradual developing. The change of the Central was earlier than that of Zhuhai. Reform and opening up was a top-down procedure.

Several changes on the concept of the Central Government became the driving forces for the development of Zhuhai at different levels at the beginning period of its reform and opening up. The earliest change was under the old planned economic system, the opening mode of establishing productive base proposed by Chen Yun in 1957 (mentioned above) developed from partially to overall. After 1977, an important development strategy of introducing advanced foreign equipment and technology and realizing modernization of China through opening up became consensus of the major Chinese leaders.

Introduction of foreign equipment and technology needed foreign exchange. To create foreign exchange by developing export production base was also a key measure. Due to the huge potential capacity of taking advantage of Hong Kong and Macau, a pile of export production bases succeeded in early 1970s. Except for the tentative plan to establishing ten Daqing (a major oil production base) and coal export industry to earn foreign currency, to

163 [American] FU, Gaoyi: ***Walk Firstly—Guangdong in the Reform***, Translated by LING Kefeng and DING Anhua, Guandong Renmin Press, Edition of 1991, P43.

increase exportation to Hong Kong and Macau from the most convenient area of Pearl River Delta became one part of the plan of the Central.

In order to establish this kind of export base, in March of 1978, officials from the National Planning Commission and Foreign Trade Ministry arrived at Guangdong and, together with the provincial government, researched the "establishment of food bases" at Bao'an and Zhuhai, which were nearest to Hong Kong and Macau.[164] Under the macro situation of that time, the export bases were soon upgraded.

"After ten years of chaos, among the policy makers and the theorists, there generally is an eagerness for winning back the lost time."[165] In 1978, national leaders like Deng Xiaoping and some high level study missions frequently visited foreign countries to check the possibilities of promoting the development by opening up. In the second period of June, Vice Prime Minister Gu Mu reported the situation after the inspection to Western European countries with a large delegate. "Ye Jianying, Nie Rongzhen and Li Xiannian indicated that it was time for making decisions and to take measures." Hua Guofeng believed that "Japan implemented modernization for only 13 years, while Germany and Denmark started ten more years. We can catch up with them." Deng Xiaoping heard Gu Mu's report separately and said, "The business with foreigners should be of large scale, say 50 billion yuan. We need to make use of the capitalist risk and catch up with the situation. Be brave and walk big steps. Do not only discuss opportunities. When you see the opportunity, start immediately. Start hundreds of programs from tomorrow."[166]

Not long before that, another economic and trading delegate, composed of officials from National Planning Commission and Foreign Trade Ministry, "made inspections in Hong Kong and Macau from April 10th to May 6th, 1978. They visited many factories, farms, harbors, construction projects, markets for agricultural products and other stores and also discussed with relevant enterprises and departments."[167] When they came back, the idea for export bases in Bao'an and Zhuhai was greatly upgraded. The "construction plan" they drafted became the starting point of the great change in Shenzhen and Zhuhai. Its eight major proposals were:

---

164 WU, Jianmin: ***History of Guangdong. Volume.78: 5 Years Memory for Zhuhai SAR***, Guangdong Renmin Press, Edition of 1998, P18.

165 XIAO, Donglian: ***Proposal and Depute of National Economic Adjustment in 1979—Documentary for Turning Point Volume One, Extensive Reading on the History of CPC***, Issue 10, P4-10.

166 XIAO, Donglian: ***Proposal and Depute of National Economic Adjustment in 1979—Documentary for Turning Point Volume One, Extensive Reading on the History of CPC***, Issue 10, P4-10.

167 WU, Jianmin: ***History of Guangdong. Volume.78: 5 Years Memory for Zhuhai SAR***, Guangdong Renmin Press, Edition of 1998, P17.

1. Suggest upgrading Bao'an and Zhuhai from counties to provincially administered municipalities (equal to prefectural Party Committee).

2. Gradually changing their agriculture from "grain as mainstay" to "majoring in the exportation of food."

3. Actively develop construction materials industry and processing industry. Based on the local conditions and the need of the markets of Hong Kong and Macau, establish small and medium factories by planning. Do not frequently put the construction into big scale.

4. Develop tourism and improve commerce, service industry and recreation projects. Attract Hong Kong and Macau residents to spend holidays here.

5. Have the government appropriate 50 million yuan to the investment of the facilities for these two cities, with a total investment of 150 million yuan in three years.

6. Offer corps of engineers for the infrastructure.

7. Bao'an and Zhuhai were planned to be small and medium cities. For example, the population of Bao'an may reach 500,000, while Zhuhai reached 200,000.

8. Offer preferential policies support to Bao'an and Zhuhai after the establishment of prefecture-level cities.[168]

These aspects were larger in exploration compared with normal exportation bases. The planned economic and population indicators also asked for swift development. For example, "by 1980, foreign exchange income for these two counties should reach 200 million USD, increasing twofold from 1977. In 1982, the amount should reach 500 million USD, increasing by seven times than in 1977."[169] These requests were too high for Zhuhai to fulfill. However, compared with the eagerness of the plan for the whole country, it was not ahead of its time. Its assumed special polices were more interesting and was beyond the scope for pure opening up with some spirits of reform:

1. Under the unified arrangement, these two cities may directly contact trading organizations stationed in Hong Kong and Macau and have direct power of approval for export of commodities acquisitions and the import of materials and equipment for the construction of the bases.

2. Establish special stores for guests entering China, which were under the charge of trading organizations stationed in Hong Kong and Macau and were regarded as the exportation to Hong Kong and Macau.

---

168 WU, Jianmin: ***History of Guangdong. Volume.78: 5 Years Memory for Zhuhai SAR***, Guangdong Renmin Press, Edition of 1998, P18-19.

169 WU, Jianmin: ***History of Guangdong. Volume.78: 5 Years Memory for Zhuhai SAR***, Guangdong Renmin Press, Edition of 1998, P18.

3. Trading organizations support these two cities with materials and equipment. The expense could be deducted from the foreign exchange earned by export. The goods mentioned above were exempt from taxation.

4. In order to accelerate the construction of the bases, expect for pay back of the loan, tax income and benefit of these two cities had no need to submit to the Central within three years. Foreign exchange for exporting sand and stone was given to the local government.

5. Simplify the check-in procedures for Hong Kong and Macau compatriots, overseas Chinese and foreigners who came for holidays. Make use of computer and shorten the check-in time.

6. Resume the small trading business along the frontier and allow boarder villagers and fishermen to be kept for flexible arrangement.

7. Raw and subsidiary materials, spare parts and equipment for the processing supplied materials were exempt from taxation.

8. The income from processing should be independently accounted. From then on, foreign exchange mortgage also needed independent accounts, which was convenient for the supervision of the banks and direct pay back of the loan. Fifteen percent of the foreign exchange from processing industry was left to the enterprises, fifteen percent of it was under charge of the local government and seventy percent of it should be submitted to the Central.[170]

All these assumptions "should be regarded as a breakthrough in the planning of the policies and measures for the opening up before the 3rd Plenary of the 11th CPC Congress. It made a useful exploration, both for the whole deployment of reform and opening up after the 3rd Plenary Session and the experiment of SAR pilots."[171]

In October 1978, the "Reform Commission" of Guangdong Province handed in the report named "Tentative Plan for Export Trading Bases and Municipal Infrastructure of Bao'an and Zhuhai" to the State Council, saying "the Provincial Committee decided to build these two counties as medium-sized cities equaling to prefecture-level cities," which upgraded its scale again.[172] In order to avoid the conflicts brought by administrative changes, the Plan only mentioned that the two cities were under dual leadership, both

---

170 WU, Jianmin: ***History of Guangdong. Volume.78: 5 Years Memory for Zhuhai SAR***, Guangdong Renmin Press, Edition of 1998, P19-20.

171 WU, Jianmin: ***History of Guangdong. Volume.78: 5 Years Memory for Zhuhai SAR***, Guangdong Renmin Press, Edition of 1998, P20.

172 WU, Jianmin: ***History of Guangdong. Volume.78: 5 Years Memory for Zhuhai SAR***, Guangdong Renmin Press, Edition of 1998, P21.

provincial and municipal, but actually they wished to be provincial municipalities. In February 1979, the State Council approved this plan partially without the agreement oft prefecture-level cities, but issued "Three Build-up" for wider opening up. It proposed to build up an exportation bases with industry and agriculture highly combined, a place of tourism attractive for Hong Kong and Macau compatriots and a boarder city of new style.[173] These were the suggestions of the delegate to Hong Kong and Macau in 1978 mentioned above. In the past, the idea of Duan Yun, Deputy Dean of National Planning Commission, was to "deal with SAR specially for its special area and situation, to break old institutional frame and offer independent indicators."[174]

Maybe this was one of the earliest occasions for high officials proposing "Special Administrative Region," which demonstrated the attention on these two cities from the Central and admitted the necessity of partial reform. However, at the beginning of the establishment of the city of Zhuhai, its concrete development was faced with many obstacles. At least, one of the reasons was that the economic reform of the nation was not greatly promoted.

In January 1979, the Provincial Committee of Guangdong formally issued "Decisions on Establishing the Cities of Shenzhen and Zhuhai" and appointed Wu Jianmin to be the Municipal Party Secretary, which was approved by the State Council in March.[175] He strongly felt that the start of the reform of the "fishing village" was "faced with lots of difficulties." It demonstrated the deep brand for natural economy of China and also reflected that during the wartime, military communism deeply infected ideology and consciousness of the cadres (See Figure 2-2-1).[176] Zhuhai was not as lucky as Shenzhen when the Central approved, in early 1979, the "Shekou Industrial Park of Hong Kong Merchants Bureau" as a "special zone" that was proposed by Yuang Geng, Executive Vice Chairman of Hong Kong Merchants Bureau. In the summer of 1979, this industrial park, independent from the development of Shenzhen, started its big-scale construction, which offered it biggest promotion "outside the development plan" of Shenzhen. During the same period, policies for the reform and opening up of Zhuhai started to reveal and it was

---

173 Communist Party History Research Center of Zhuhai Committee of CPC: ***Great Events of Communist Party History of Zhuhai 1924~1990***, Edition of 1991, P56.

174 WU, Jianmin: ***History of Guangdong. Volume.78: 5 Years Memory for Zhuhai SAR***, Guangdong Renmin Press, Edition of 1998, P26.

175 Communist Party History Research Center of Zhuhai Committee of CPC: ***Great Events of Communist Party History of Zhuhai 1924~1990***, Edition of 1991, P56.

176 WU, Jianmin: ***History of Guangdong. Volume.78: 5 Years Memory for Zhuhai SAR***, Guangdong Renmin Press, Edition of 1998, P31.

difficult for a wide opening.

Figure 2-2-1 Xiang Zhou—Center of Zhuhai when it was just built up[177]

2.2.1.2 The Difficult Start of Zhuhai: Resume Small Trade Along the Boarder and the First Private Foreign Company in Mainland China

The start of Zhuhai was difficult and the work was gradually unfolding in the exploration. During that period, except for the research on the development plans and urgently stopping illegal migration of its people to Hong Kong and Macau, big issues done by Zhuhai itself on economy were to mainly deal with the rubbish problem of Macau and the resume of small trading business along the boarder.

The resume and opening of the small trading business was part of the plan of the construction of Zhuhai (see Figure 2-2-2). Many places of Macau were divided from Zhuhai by small river-wide gulfs. Every day, "many fishermen stopped by the gulfs and sold fish, bought rice, watered and bought necessities for fishing." In the 1950s, "a group of people of Wan Chai, Hong Kong who got the Certificate of Small Trading Business on the Boarder took fresh flowers every day and sold them in Macau," and "with the money earned, they bought distiller's grains and brought them back to Wan Chai to feed pigs." "Relying on this business, there was a prosperous view here." Later, "only the foreign trade department of the nation owned the authority for exportation of fresh flowers and the preferential policies for the frontier small trading business were revoked." Instead of Wan

177 Resource: *Zhuhai Daily*, http://www.zhtv.com/hd/2005tequ/pic/history/pages/pic001.htm.

Chai, suppliers from Taiwan and Japan dominated the fresh flowers market of Macau.[178] After discussions, leaders of Zhuhai decided to resume this policy first to improve the production and livelihood of rural areas. In April 1979, "the frontier small trading business fully resumed and the rural areas were full of joy." "After eight months, foreign exchange earned only by fresh flower business reached 523,000 HKD by primary accounting."[179]

Figure 2-2-2 Frontier Small Trading Business of Fresh Flowers in Zhuhai[180]

The first foreign enterprise at the beginning of reform and opening up, Xiang Zhou Textile Factory was established in Zhuhai and it became one example for the reform and opening up of China. However, this project was not brought in by Zhuhai itself, but by "up-to-down introduction and grafting." In May 1978, before the opening of Shenzhen and Zhuhai, "Mr. Cao Guangbiao, a businessman of Hong Kong, visited Beijing and discussed the possibility of investing and establishing a (textile) factory in an area of Guangdong Province, which must be close to Macau, with China Textile Import and Export Company (CHINATEX)." Hereafter, CHINATEX appointed Guangdong Foreign Trade Bureau to realize the introduction of this project and finally located it in Zhuhai.[181]

Xiang Zhou Textile Factory became the first private company invested by foreign

178 WU, Jianmin: ***History of Guangdong. Volume.78: 5 Years Memory for Zhuhai SAR***, Guangdong Renmin Press, Edition of 1998, P39.

179 WU, Jianmin: ***History of Guangdong. Volume.78: 5 Years Memory for Zhuhai SAR***, Guangdong Renmin Press, Edition of 1998, P41.

180 Resource: ***Zhuhai Daily***, http://www.zhtv.com/hd/2005tequ/pic/history/pages/pic001.htm.

181 WU, Jianmin: ***History of Guangdong. Volume.78: 5 Years Memory for Zhuhai SAR***, Guangdong Renmin Press, Edition of 1998, P155.

capital since 1949. Cao Guangbiao was called the "first pioneer to taste crabs" because of his investment of several million USD and the creation of processing industry and compensation trade.[182] For it was an up-to-down promotion, the agreement for this textile factory, from its planning, approval and sign to establishment, from Beijing, Guangzhou to Zhuhai, did not come across any barriers and the speed was too fast to be expected. It was signed in August 1978 and the construction of the factory started in November. In August 1979, 6000 m^2 of factory was built up with all equipment fixed. The tests start in September and it formally started to produce in November.[183] The opening ceremony of Xiang Zhou Textile Factory was held not long after the establishment of Zhuhai SAR. More than 500 companies and journalists at home and abroad and guests from more than ten countries attended the ceremony. They called the establishment of the factory "head program" of the reform and opening up and the first pilot of the SAR in China.[184]

After it started to produce, many contradictions were revealed because of the management, the supply of raw materials from Macau and the heavy burden to carry out the agreement. Some of the contradictions even aroused reports and investigation of *Renmin Daily* and the Foreign Trade Ministry. After all, this was the first experiment of the reform and opening up. After suspending production for rectification and the reform of economic management institution, Xiang Zhou Textile Factory later made big progress. Appearance of this kind of foreign invested corporations was the partial experiment of China breaking through the traditional planned economy. There was micro opening on economy and it was meaningful for emancipating the mind and the development of the market economy.

2.2.1.3 Different Opinions on the Direction of the Development

During this period, the development idea of Zhuhai had come across three sudden and important changing points: a fishing county with boarder forces as main task and economy relying on fishing after October 1, 1949; an export base with food exportation as mainstay, which was changed from "with grains production as mainstay" of 1978; and the planning of "three establishments" of industrial and agricultural development, tourism and cities of

182 Anonymous writer: ***Cao Guangbiao, Overseas Chinese of Ning Bo***, http://www.ocao.ningbo.gov.cn/004/005/5730.html, 2002/3/5.

183 WU, Jianmin: ***History of Guangdong. Volume.78: 5 Years Memory for Zhuhai SAR***, Guangdong Renmin Press, Edition of 1998, P60.

184 WU, Jianmin: ***History of Guangdong. Volume.78: 5 Years Memory for Zhuhai SAR***, Guangdong Renmin Press, Edition of 1998, P61.

1979. Zhuhai was not clear about its plan for development in the future. Although Guangdong Province implemented "three establishments" of the State Council, both in Shenzhen and Zhuhai, for their development within three to five years, there was an illustration about it:

It was a must to develop agriculture, change the status of the agricultural production, develop farm and sideline products and seafood by making use of the local advantages, establish bases for exportation, enlarge the community collective economy, increase people's income, improve people's life standard and motivate the activity of the people. On this basis, people should actively develop processing industry, assembling industry and constructive materials industry and build up tourist districts and urban areas.[185]

This emphasized to develop agriculture first and then industry. This kind of tone might be concerned with the rectification on the "economic increase by leaps and bounds following the way of foreign countries" and the industry. Therefore, it aroused disputes on the developing orientation in Zhuhai with the main stream insisting on establishing cities on the basis of industry, which believed Zhuhai should make full use of the economic and technologic conditions of Hong Kong and Macau to develop urban area and economy, and should not "leave the fundamental guidance of economic activity."[186] Actually, during its first year as a prefecture-level city, Zhuhai made efforts in all aspects—fishing and agriculture, processing industry (processing, assembling and introduction of technology), tourism, and general planning for the city and infrastructures. The State Council then continuously proposed the plans of "exportation SAR," "economic SAR" and "integrated SAR," which upgraded processing industry to a core position. However, the development of processing industry in Zhuhai was still limited (there is detail illustration in the next chapter).

As soon as Zhuhai started to establish the prefecture-level city, it concentrated on the future planning. "From May 1979, after one year's preparation, measures, investigation and then research, drafting and inviting groups of experts for discussion and seminars and amending," the first general plan for city construction among the four SAR was carried out in 1981. It proposed a general orientation to "establish a coastal garden city" with a far-reaching plan that Zhuhai "would play an important role in the economic development

185 WU, Jianmin: ***History of Guangdong. Volume.78: 5 Years Memory for Zhuhai SAR***, Guangdong Renmin Press, Edition of 1998, P45.

186 WU, Jianmin: ***History of Guangdong. Volume.78: 5 Years Memory for Zhuhai SAR***, Guangdong Renmin Press, Edition of 1998, P46-47.

in Southern China in the future."[187] It could be noticed that Zhuhai concentrated on environmental protection and harmonious development and had a high positioning for itself. During that period, Zhuhai started planning to set up one harbor: Jiuzhou could connect with Hong Kong and other places.

The early planning and infrastructure development of Zhuhai could be regarded scientific and reasonable. Thereafter, it started to purchase goals beyond its capability and the contradiction between local benefit and overall situation. This will be discussed in Chapter Four.

2.2.2 Primary Exploration of the Pilot of SAR

2.2.2.1 Establishment of Zhuhai Special Administrative Economic Zone

As mentioned in the previous section, the wave of opening up in 1978 made Guangdong Province bravely propose to establish export bases and prefecture-level cities in Zhuhai and Bao'an. In 1979, Zhuhai was upgraded to provincial municipality of Guangdong and faced with more precious development opportunity than was mentioned above. This year was extremely important for the reform and opening up. At that time, China stopped "economic increase by leaps and bounds following the way of foreign countries," implemented measures of "adjustment, reform, rectification and improvement" and took more solid and bold steps on the way of economic development and reform and opening up.

In April 1979, Xi Zhongxun, Provincial Secretary and Governor of Guangdong, reported to Deng Xiaoping about the acceleration of economic development and reform and opening up in Guangdong. Deng Xiaoping greatly supported this idea and addressed Shenzhen and Zhuhai as the Special Administrative Regions. However, he said that under the background of economic rectification all over the country, the Central Government could not offer Guangdong with supporting capital and asked Guangdong and its SAR to "blaze a new trail."[188] Not long after, the Central dispatched Secretary of Secretariat of the Central Committee of the CPC and Vice Prime Minister Gu Mu, who took charge for the SAR much later, and others to research and investigate in SAR.

In July, the Central officially proposed to establish "Export SAR," which became the historical changing point of Zhuhai. In the "Two Reports Approved by the Central and the

---

187 WU, Jianmin: ***History of Guangdong. Volume.78: 5 Years Memory for Zhuhai SAR***, Guangdong Renmin Press, Edition of 1998, P50-51.

188 RU Qing, ***Liang Guangda, Being the Governor In Zhuhai for 16 Years***, China Economic Press, Edition of 2001, P19.

State Council and Forwarded to Principal Committee of Guangdong and Fujian On Implementing Special Policies and Flexible Measures in Economic Activities Abroad," it said that "about the export SAR, Shenzhen and Zhuhai can be two pilots. When the experience is gained, we think about establishing SAR in Shantou and Xiamen." This offered Guangdong Province, especially Shenzhen and Zhuhai, preferential policies in trading, finance, planning, materials and price and the new economic institution and flexible measures were implemented.[189] Actually, the name of "SAR" had been "spread like a fairy tale in people's consciousness in their economic life."[190] Guangdong Province also hoped to treat the whole province, at least the Pearl River Delta, as SAR and even turn the goal of reform to market economy.

Not long after 1979, the proposal of "Export SAR" had been greatly changed. "This name had no obvious difference with similar foreign trade zones, free trade zones or export processing zones."[191] Wu Nansheng suggested to call it "special economic zone" when he reported to the Central in Beijing in December 1979.[192] In March 1980, Gu Mu arrived at Guangzhou to hold the conference on foreign trade and SAR of Guangdong and Fujian, which was a milestone in the preparation of the SAR. In the conference, the nature of SAR, experimental methods and the affairs that needed to be noted were discussed and "Summary of Conference in Guangdong and Fujian" was carried out.[193] The name of "Export SAR" was officially changed to "Economic SAR," which was a name with more comprehensive meaning and more Chinese characteristics.[194] On May 16th of the same year, when the Central of CPC and the State Council approved the "Summary of Conference in Guangdong and Fujian" (that can be called the document about the Economic SAR), they formally affirmed the proposal of "Economic SAR." In the "Summary," it asked that, based on the financial and material capability of Guangdong and Fujian, Guangdong should firstly concentrate on the construction of Shenzhen and then

189 Main Editor: FANG Weizhong, ***Great Economic Issues of PRC (1949~1980)***, China Social Science Press, Edition of 1984, P630.

190 WU, Jianmin: ***History of Guangdong. Volume. 78: 5 Years Memory for Zhuhai SAR***, Guangdong Renmin Press, Edition of 1998, P75.

191 RU Qing, ***Liang Guangda, Being the Governor In Zhuhai for 16 Years***, China Economic Press, Edition of 2001, P19-20.

192 WU, Daoshan: The First CPC Secretary of Shenzhen: SAR Must Blaze A New Trail, China News, http://www.chinanews.com.cn/2000-09-01/26/44209.html, 2000/09/01.

193 WU, Jianmin: ***History of Guangdong. Volume.78: 5 Years Memory for Zhuhai SAR***, Guangdong Renmin Press, Edition of 1998, P96-99.

194 RU Qing, ***Liang Guangda, Being the Governor In Zhuhai for 16 Years***, China Economic Press, Edition of 2001, P20.

Zhuhai. Plans and preparations for establishing Shantou and Xiamen as SAR could be drawn first and then implemented gradually.[195]

On August 26, 1980, the Standing Committee of the 5th National People's Congress of PRC officially approved "Regulations on Economic SAR of Guangdong Province" that was carried out by the State Council and agreed to experiment to set up economic SAR in Zhuhai. The "Regulations" was "only about 2000 words, but from its draft to 13 amendments and the approval, it took one year, which was weighted word by word."[196] It was regulated in the 1st Article of the 1st Chapter of the "Regulations" that the goal of the SAR was "in order to develop economic cooperation and technical exchanges with foreign countries and to improve the socialist modernization, Shenzhen, Zhuhai and Shantou of Guangdong Province separately divide parts of their districts to set up economic SAR.[197] It emphasized on encouraging preferential policies for foreign investment and management institutions, different from the traditional Chinese institutions. It offered a legal basis for enlarging opening up and deepening reform for the SAR and laid foundation for the opening up of economic society and the spread of the reform of the second and the third industries from the SAR to the whole country.

The pilot of economic SAR greatly improved the liberation of people's mind, contributed to the instruction of market economy and played an important role in the reform of many aspects. Because of these, the SAR suffered from pressures and obstacles in the beginning years. Until 1984, Deng Xiaoping affirmed the measures of establishing SAR during his tour in South China, the resistance of setting up of SAR was cut down. Until his second visit to south China in 1992, the idea of implementing market economy was totally affirmed. Zhuhai, from 1979, started a brand new historical period, but each step of its development was full of difficulties. Especially during the first period of the pilot of SAR, the economic base of Zhuhai was weak. The policies of opening up and reform were neither completed nor perfected. People's minds were not open enough. These caused Zhuhai to suffer from three years' primary period full of difficulties.

2.2.2.2 Adjacent to Macau but Without Advantages

Zhuhai was located in a special area that was a subtle position in Pearl River Delta

195 RU Qing, ***Liang Guangda, Being the Governor In Zhuhai for 16 Years***, China Economic Press, Edition of 2001, P21.

196 WU, Daoshan: The First CPC Secretary of Shenzhen: SAR Must Blaze A New Trail, China News, http://www.chinanews.com.cn/2000-09-01/26/44209.html, 2000/09/01.

197 Hong Kong ***China Economic SAR Annual*** Editorial Department: First Issue of China Economic SAR Annual of 1983, Hong Kong China Economic SAR Annual Press, Edition of 1983, P46.

including Hong Kong and Macau. This greatly influenced the economic development and position of Zhuhai. The economic radiation capability of Macau and its institutional advantages were less than Hong Kong. The economic relation between Zhuhai and Hong Kong could only be solved by waterway. Compared with Shenzhen, Zhuhai had congenital shortcomings for its development. However, Zhuhai was adjacent to Macau and had the privilege to be open to Macau. Could this advantage support the development of Zhuhai?

Macau, like the cities in Pearl River Delta Zhuhai, Hong Kong and Shenzhen, was a small fishing village several hundreds years ago. The position of international trading center of Macau was replaced by Hong Kong and it gradually went downhill. In 1944, "Portuguese officers in Macau started to rely on the gambling industry. From 1970s, with the appearance of new hydrofoil boats and air-cushion vehicles, the trip from Hong Kong to Macau was reduced from four hours to one. Then the tourism and casino of Macau was gradually thriving. It became the casino city of the Asia-Pacific area."[198]

When Zhuhai was built up as a special administrative zone, Macau was a tiny city. After several times of reclaiming land from the sea, its land area increased from more than ten square kilometers to more than twenty square kilometers. Macau had the same political position as Hong Kong. If people never went to Hong Kong or Macau, they might think there was no big difference in the economic development between Hong Kong and Macau. Therefore, people who had ever visited Macau often said that "Macau was actually very small" and realized Macau could not catch up with the economic development of Hong Kong.

The economy of Macau existed between Hong Kong and the Mainland. Its economic development was mainly positioned to avoid the advantages of Hong Kong and the Mainland and to seek the aspects they missed or the mutual complementary opportunities with them. The special position and complementary role of Macau in the relations among Hong Kong, Macau and Pearl River Delta had great impacts on the economic development and positioning of Zhuhai. Zhuhai could not play the lead in the big district but it needed to find developing space in the environment with both advantages and disadvantages, in which difficulties took the major part. In addition, according to the moral norms of the Zhuhai people and laws of the Mainland, Zhuhai was not allowed to borrow the experience of Macau to develop casinos. Common research believed that Macau was, in reality, no great help to Zhuhai. Actually, much of the investment to Zhuhai originated from Hong

198 [American] FU Gaoyi: Go First—Guangdong in the Reform, translated by LING Kefeng and DING Anhua, Guangdong Renmin Press, Edition of 1991, P166.

Kong. The opening up of Zhuhai should be oriented in Hong Kong, although it was comparatively far away. This made the development of Zhuhai SAR seemed slower and more difficult than that of Shenzhen. However, compared with Shantou and Xiamen, those were further away from Hong Kong. Zhuhai had obvious advantages for the primary opening up.

2.2.2.3 Disputes of the Reasonable Scope of SAR

Before the combination with Doumen County in 1983, the area of Zhuhai was only about 600 square kilometers, which was comparatively small with other cities nearby. As prefecture level city, its downtown was small. At the beginning, the SAR was set up in a small and unimportant area in Zhuhai, which was about 6.81 square kilometers. What was the relationship between the comparatively small Zhuhai and its SAR? What was their reasonable size? These were important issues having great impact on the development.

On the scope of a reasonable size of SAR in Zhuhai, it took a long way, full of disputes. Someone briefly introduced it like this:

The indications and documents for an SAR were ready. The following question was how to operate and implement. At that time, it was asked that in the SAR, there could not be resident households and it must be divided from people in order to manage it. Therefore, remote beaches and abandoned coastal hills in Zhuhai were found with about 6.8 square kilometers. People reflected wondered how SAR could be set up in such a small area with dozens of mud and sand building up factories. It cost a lot only to lay the base. Many comrades asked to enlarge the area of the SAR. Some municipal officials said that 3.6 square kilometers' SAR in the world could be called big. Why did Zhuhai need a large area? They persuaded not to enlarge the area for the SAR. However, limited by the regulation of the SAR, one street was divided into several sections. One side was under the management of the SAR, but it was not SAR on the other side, which was truly uncomfortable.[199]

Actually, this key issue was more complicated than expected.

No. 50 Document in July of 1979 carried out by the State Council, which firstly mentioned the SAR, named the SAR as "Export SAR," proposing to set up "pilots" in parts of Shenzhen and Zhuhai and also said to "implement special policies and flexible measures for foreign economic activities. This is a new task and is lacking of experience in each aspect, especially the foreign economic activities, which we know less about."

---

199 Edited mainly by ZHOU Shulian and LU Guoying: A Good SAR of Zhuhai, Central Communist Party Press, Edition of 1996, P14.

The following sayings were the definition for the scope of Zhuhai SAR from Wu Jianmin, first Secretary of Municipal Committee of Zhuhai.

After "research on the situations of SAR all over the world and the domestic SAR," Zhuhai believed that to set up this kind of professional SAR often needed advanced position and the construction scope increased from small to large, then to a district. The district was to be used as a whole to speed up the capital turnover and accumulation (the suggestion given by the UN Industrial Development Organization for the countries those tried to set up SAR also insisted on this principal). Therefore, it was better to establish SAR in depopulated zone and concentrate on "basic construction as a start."[200] By borrowing experience from foreign countries, Zhuhai positioned its guidance as: "(1) rely on harbors, customs and other places with developed transportation; (2) start from a small area and do not be greedy for big area; (3) avoid SAR accepting too many of the original rural population; (4) facilities and buildings cannot be arranged to be set up in the SAR, but try its hardest to build them up outside the SAR to avoid taking too much of the land of SAR."[201] "On the basis of rounds of discussions, investigation on the spot and multi plans, an area of SAR with 6.74 square kilometers was established in the east, the middle and the west.

At that time it was neglected that the foreign SARs were not only located in good positions, but also had developed economy. Depopulated zones were also close to the prosperous districts, which gave easy use of the living services, basic facilities and economic links to the SARs. Therefore, its construction scale could increase "from small to big" and develop to SAR with high density in a small area. At that time, the conditions in China were contrary. The development of the SAR could start from extensive economic zone with low density.

In December 1979, Wu Nansheng inspected Zhuhai and still insisted on borrowing experience from abroad. He believed that although there were only three pieces of district for the SAR, "the small pieces would grow up." At that time, Wu Nansheng had different opinions on Shenzhen. In the same month, he suggested to change "Export SAR" into "Economic SAR" because "our SAR does not only develop industry, but it also develops agriculture, scientific research, commerce and trading, tourism, apartments and cultural

---

200 WU, Jianmin: ***History of Guangdong. Volume.78: 5 Years Memory for Zhuhai SAR***, Guangdong Renmin Press, Edition of 1998, P91.

201 WU, Jianmin: ***History of Guangdong. Volume.78: 5 Years Memory for Zhuhai SAR***, Guangdong Renmin Press, Edition of 1998, P93-94.

causes."[202] He started to think about enlarging the area for the SAR.

One key meeting for the decision of the size of the SAR was a meeting held in Guangzhou by Gu Mu, which was about the foreign trade and SAR of Guangdong and Fujian in March of 1980. Duan Yun from the National Planning Commission "issued one new opinion, demonstrating that it was not a must to avoid the original counties to set up SAR." He said that it was better to set up SAR by making use of the original conditions of the county. There was no need to draw a piece of new area and to enclose it. This way needed more money."[203] Under the background of adjusting and reducing basic facilities cost, Gu Mu believed that "to establish SAR in Guangdong, no matter two or three, the key point was to build up Shenzhen well. It was not to cancel Zhuhai. If you have the capability, just do it. "We do not give up Zhuhai. It is a comparatively small area. Our strategy is to develop from small to big, from low level to high."[204]

It seemed that there were two types of guidance for Zhuhai. The position of Zhuhai became a second line SAR depending mainly on its own exploration. The minutes of this meeting formed the important "Economic SAR" documents.

Wu Jianmin believed that leaders of Zhuhai thought they had already mastered inquires of the foreign merchants and the policies should be obeyed. "They researched on the distribution again." In July 1980, an SAR of 6.81 square kilometers was formed, which was approved by the SEZ Management Commission of Guangdong and the Economic Management Office of the State Council later.[205] "The area of Shenzhen SEZ was harshly beyond our expectation, which was about 327.5 square kilometers. It may be the biggest SAR in the world. In the past, we said to start from small ones, but suddenly it leap to the biggest. It was too difficult to make sense of the interior situation. At that time, Zhuhai did not regret and there was no need to."

It was felt that Zhuhai neither knew the development trend of Shenzhen at the beginning, nor realized the change of the mind of the Central Government. However, at that time, Wu Jianmin must have noticed the great adjustment of changing single "Export SAR"

---

202 LU Di: Wu Nansheng Thought Back the Difficult Start of Reform and Opening Up: If Someone must be killed, kill me. Nanfang Daily, web edition, http://www.nfdaily.cn/bignews/content/2008-04/07/content_4370536.htm, April 7th 2008.

203 WU, Jianmin: ***History of Guangdong. Volume.78: 5 Years Memory for Zhuhai SAR***, Guangdong Renmin Press, Edition of 1998, P97.

204 WU, Jianmin: ***History of Guangdong. Volume.78: 5 Years Memory for Zhuhai SAR***, Guangdong Renmin Press, Edition of 1998, P98-99

205 WU, Jianmin: ***History of Guangdong. Volume.78: 5 Years Memory for Zhuhai SAR***, Guangdong Renmin Press, Edition of 1998, P100-101.

into comprehensive “Economic SAR” in the documents of the Economic SAR.

Li Changqing took charge of the comprehensive planning of the preparation for the SAR. When he memorized these, he emphasized the procedures for Zhuhai to define the size of its SAR after this change.

At the beginning of June 1980, Xi Zhongxun, Secretary of Guangdong Provincial Committee, said in Zhuhai: “Zhuhai (as a whole) was an SAR. That which part starts first was only an issue of distribution and procedure.”[206] In the same month, “the standing committee of the municipal government held several meetings to discuss the size of the economic SAR of Zhuhai.” Li Changqing issued three plans: “the first was in accordance with the opinion of Secretary Xi Zhongxun, the administrative district of Zhuhai was defined as the scope of the SAR.” The other two plans also defined that districts including Xiangzhou, downtown with the best conditions, should make full use of the existing base.[207]

The commissioners of the Standing Committee of municipal government had rounds of discussion on these three plans. The attendees delivered their own opinions from different points of view. Officials taking charge of the rural construction issued that Haibin Park was the entertainment venue for its people. He did not agree to subsume it to the scope of the SAR. Officials taking charge of tourism were against classifying Shijingshan Tourism Center into the SAR. They believed it must be divided from the drain to the south of Jida. The governors of Xiangzhou District were opposed to incorporating Xiangzhou, Jida or Qianshan into the SAR. Leaders of Gongbei District were also against including Weiji and Beiling into the SAR.

Most of the commissioners of the Standing Committee neglected the three plans proposed by Li Changqing. Secretary Wu Jianmin summed it up in the following:

The size of the SAR should grow from small to large and increase gradually. In accordance with most of your opinions, we drew the coastal areas as SAR.

Therefore, Li Changqing had to agree with the majority in accordance with the organizational principle of the CPC. On July 8th, Wu Jianmin held the Standing Committee meeting again and after discussions, with all the plenary, the 6.81 square kilometers area was defined as the SAR.[208]

---

206 Cultural and Historical Materials Department of CPPCC Zhuhai Committee: ***Culture and History of Zhuhai*** Volume 15, Cultural and Historical Materials Department of CPPCC Zhuhai Committee, Edition of 2005, P85.

207 Cultural and Historical Materials Department of CPPCC Zhuhai Committee: ***Culture and History of Zhuhai*** Volume 15, Cultural and Historical Materials Department of CPPCC Zhuhai Committee, Edition of 2005, P86.

208 Cultural and Historical Materials Department of CPPCC Zhuhai Committee: ***Culture and History of Zhuhai*** Volume 15, Cultural and Historical Materials Department of CPPCC Zhuhai Committee, Edition of 2005, P87.

These different attendees had various memories about the definition of the area of the SAR. It seemed like situations in *Rashomon*, the Japanese philosophy movie. Based on different concepts and understandings, it could be understood that they had different narrations of the history. The modern historical research has developed into a cautious attitude to recover historical accuracy. We hope that readers do not think the conclusion here is wholly correct. Although it might be very hard for descendents to clearly see the reality of the definition of the plans of SAR, we could believe that Zhuhai had realized the change of the Central's mind, which seemed that the idea of the leaders were not unified at that time and the officials of Zhuhai had a unified point of view. We could generally feel that Zhuhai might think the SAR would be a separate zone with an undefined future and it was not regarded as the most important position for the development of Zhuhai.

Hereafter, the State Council held SAR Working Conference in May and June of 1981. The document summarized was the third most important one following the documents on "Export SAR" of 1979 and on the "Economic SAR" of 1980. The documents could be described as being about a "comprehensive economic SAR," which definitely required that Zhuhai develop integrated economic SAR.[209] This was another great upgrade for the development model of the SAR and the officials of Zhuhai further realized the importance of the SAR. Soon after that, Guangdong Province upgraded Shenzhen to sub-provincial city, on the same level with Guangzhou. At the same time, "officials of Zhuhai discussed the issue of the scope of the SAR." Comrades who worked in the SAR were afraid if the scope of it was too big, the work would be very difficult;" while "the municipal officials thought the scope was too small."[210] The interior of the SAR was lacking in powerful reform and opening up policies, which would greatly promote the development. "Given to the limitation of financial and material capability and the management level of the cadres, Zhuhai took the construction strategy to develop from small to big—a gradual procedure."[211] Cadres outside the SAR found that they could hardly enjoy the privileges of the SAR and "had a widespread discussion that aroused high tide of public opinions."[212] From then on, the small scope of the SAR restrained the development of Zhuhai, who

---

209 Communist Party History Research Center of Zhuhai Committee of CPC: ***Great Events of Communist Party History of Zhuhai 1924~1990***, Edition of 1991, P11.

210 WU, Jianmin: ***History of Guangdong. Volume.78: 5 Years Memory for Zhuhai SAR***, Guangdong Renmin Press, Edition of 1998, P174.

211 Editor SU Ru: Chinese SAR On Its Way Up, China Finance and Economy Press, Edition of 1983, P212.

212 WU, Jianmin: ***History of Guangdong. Volume.78: 5 Years Memory for Zhuhai SAR***, Guangdong Renmin Press, Edition of 1998, P174.

started to constantly ask for enlarging the scope of the SAR. Based on some reasons, the Central Government did not approve its inquiry. In April 1983 when Gu Mu inspected Zhuhai, he still said it would be very difficult:

As far as the scope of the SAR is concerned, why can Shenzhen have a large one? This decision was the last resort. Until now, there were many problems which could not be solved and which are complicated. On this issue, we are not regretful. For other SARs, the size cannot be large. As for the idea to enlarge it, I did not agree at all. Why do we need to launch the "second satellite?" If we just need an experiment, one is enough. If Xiamen wants to be an SAR as a whole, it is easy to set up one entrance to manage the interior part. It is convenient, but we did not like to do this. To enlarge the scope to the whole island, the Central Government must re-think the establishment of the SAR. I think the plan of subsuming Xiangzhou in the SAR cannot be considered at all. If all the SARs act like this, how can we continue the work?[213]

After the provincial officials assisted with communication, Gu Mu agreed to appropriately enlarge the scope of the SAR in the following day. He asked that Zhuhai should "submit the plan researching to slightly adjust the size of the SAR but without subsuming Xiangzhou inside." Therefore, a plan to enlarge the size of the SAR to 15.16 square kilometers was carried out over night. It only combined two separate pieces of areas in the east into one and enlarged it (see Figure 2-2-3).[214] In the same year, Doumen County merged into Zhuhai as a municipality county.

The scope of the SAR was larger than before, but it was still difficult to distribute. Many projects were introduced and tied together. Light industry, textile, chemical industry, tourism and sideline industries were all located in this area. Each of them asked for one square kilometer for the factory, because there was not enough space. The cadres of the SAR started again to ask for enlarging the size. It was not long after Deng Xiaoping's visit to Zhuhai and voice for reform and opening up was high. Therefore the municipal committee submitted report to the Central again. Finally the State Council approved to enlarge the SAR to 121 square kilometers. The documents issued by the SAR Office of the State Council were scientific and the boundary line was flexible.[215]

---

213 WU, Jianmin: ***History of Guangdong. Volume.78: 5 Years Memory for Zhuhai SAR***, Guangdong Renmin Press, Edition of 1998, P183-184.

214 WU, Jianmin: ***History of Guangdong. Volume.78: 5 Years Memory for Zhuhai SAR***, Guangdong Renmin Press, Edition of 1998, P185-186.

215 Edited mainly by ZHOU Shulian and LU Guoying: A Good SAR of Zhuhai, Central Communist Party Press, Edition of 1996, P14-15.

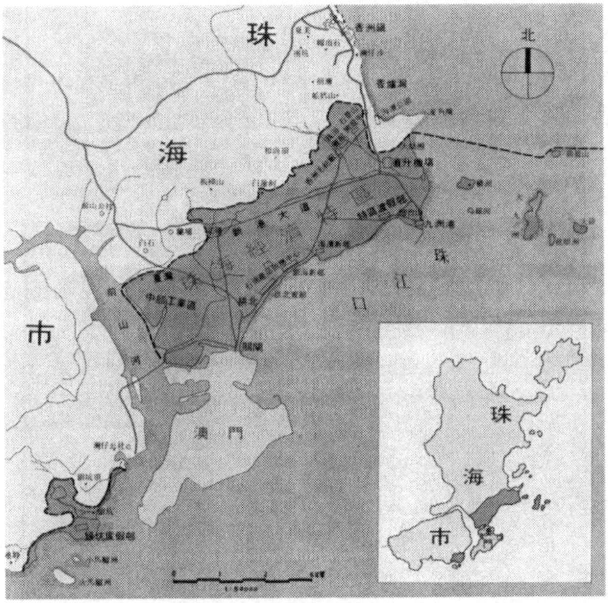

Figure 2-2-3 The size of the economic SAR of Zhuhai increased from 6.81 to 15.16 square kilometers in 1983

Note: Doumen County is not included in this map, which was just merged into Zhuhai then. (It was located to the west of Zhuhai. See Figure 2-1-1)[216]

The second inquiry to enlarge the size of the SAR mentioned here was formally submitted to the State Council in 1987 and was approved in 1988.[217] At that time, the scope of the SAR, except for Doumen County, was enlarged to all major parts of Zhuhai, including the major downtown. Xiangzhou had better facilities and economic conditions. In 1990, the typical description of the plan of Zhuhai was: "Zhuhai administrated its economic SAR in Xiangzhou District and Doumen County. The area of the SAR is 121 square kilometers with a population of 140,000 people. Xiangzhou District was 654 square kilometers (the SAR was inside the administrative scope of Xiangzhou) with 203,000 people. Doumen was 612 square kilometers with 283,000 people."[218] At that time, in order to establish the west coastal area into a future transportation hub (air harbor of Sanzao), a new polar of economy, and to enhance the development of Pingsha in the west, the area of

216 Resource: Hong Kong ***China Economic SAR Annual*** Editorial Department: First Issue of China Economic SAR Annual of 1983, Hong Kong China Economic SAR Annual Press, Edition of 1983, P220.

217 RU Qing, ***Liang Guangda, Being the Governor In Zhuhai for 16 Years***, China Economic Press, Edition of 2001, P21.

218 Policy Research Department of Zhuhai Municipal Committee: Ten Years of Zhuhai SAR, Guangdong Science and Technology Press, Edition of 1990, P4.

Hongqi Overseas Chinese Farm and Wanshan Islands in the east. Zhuhai set up four management districts in succession, which had economic management authority on the level of the county, including Wanshan, Sanzao, Pingsha and Hongqi. They hoped to obtain more development conditions familiar with the SAR.

Hereafter, Zhuhai municipal government reported to the State Council asking to enlarge the scope to the whole western part, including Doumen and two overseas Chinese farms with an area of 600 square kilometers, which could enjoy the privilege of the SAR. It was handed in according to the procedure and was approved by the State Council. Foreign-funded enterprises in the western part majoring in exportation could enjoy the preferential policies of the SAR. It actually spread the preferential policies all over Zhuhai.[219]

Under the background of that time, the steps of Zhuhai seemed to be cautious and it often thought back and forth about the new indication from the Central. However, it explored hard but bravely for the experience of setting up SAR and created the basic condition for the reform and opening up. Zhuhai together with Shenzhen brought great encouragement to the reform and opening-up of the mainland at the beginning period.

2.3 The Economic Development of Zhuhai Special Economic Zone (SEZ)

Zhuhai was established as a city and trial SEZ because of the reform and opening up policy. It also witnessed significant and profound changes in its economic and social aspects thanks to the reform and opening-up policy and the emancipation of mind. Zhuhai's experience and pitfalls in its 30 years' development was a treasure for China in transformation and development.

The development strategy of Zhuhai SEZ deeply affected its economic development, which can be roughly divided into four phases: The SEZ had undergone a difficult exploratory time in the beginning period of preparation and establishment since 1979. It initially experimented with the market mechanism and explored for a development path of a comprehensive SEZ. It was in economic take-off phase after 1984. The market economy was boldly promoted, the strategy of "giving priority to industry and comprehensively develop agriculture and fisheries animal husbandry, tourism, business trade and others" was

---

219 Edited mainly by ZHOU Shulian and LU Guoying: A Good SAR of Zhuhai, Central Communist Party Press, Edition of 1996, P14-15.

energetically advocated, and strategy of "focusing on export-oriented economy" was brought into practice. It went through a phase from hyper growth to tortuously slow developing process after 1990. The market mechanism was fully established with strong government guidance and the strategy of "taking high and new technology as the leader" and vigorously improving infrastructure was established and implemented. It had entered into a phase of adjustment and further development since 2000. The unsound industrial foundation was replenished and the economic development witnessed a rapid growth after twists and turns.[220]

2.3.1 Exploratory Phase of Developing a Comprehensive SEZ in the Early Days (1980~1983)

With a weak industrial foundation, Zhuhai, at first, had been dominated by agriculture and fishery for a long time. "There were only 28 industrial enterprises when it was established as a county in 1953." Before it was established as a city in 1978, there were 135 industrial enterprises in all, with an output value of 38, or 68 million yuan."[221] In those years, Zhuhai had been mainly attempting to weaken the traditional obstacles and exploring for the way of development. If we talk about reform and opening-up respectively, Zhuhai seemed to be focusing strongly on opening-up at the beginning, while the reform of market mechanism was gradually strengthened.

2.3.1.1 Initial Formation of Economic Development Pattern

As mentioned in the previous chapter, Zhuhai's economic development direction underwent several significant changes before and after it was established as a city and trial SEZ. Before it was established as a trial SEZ, the direction was focusing on fishery for consolidating frontier defense after the founding of PRC, and "give priority to food" later. Until 1978, it changed to "give priority to operating non-staple food for export" because of the attempt at establishing it to be an open export base, but soon it "actively developed building materials and processing industry." In 1979, the State Council required Zhuhai to achieve "three build," which refers to building Zhuhai to be a base for producing export commodities, foreign tourists area and a new border city after it was established as a city. However, the provincial government demanded that Shenzhen and Zhuhai first develop

220 Please see the primary data of this period on Zhuhai official websites, and refer to relative treatises and academic papers on Zhuhai. For instance:

221 Wu Jianmin, *Five Years Remembrances of establishing Zhuhai Special Economic Zone, 78th volume of Guangdong Historical Accounts of Past Events,* Guang dong People's press, 1998 edition, P. 59-60.

agriculture rather than processing industry, which aroused argument on development direction. According to Wu Jianmin's memories, the mainstream was adhering to developing the city based on industry.[222]

The actual development of Zhuhai was very difficult. The reasons include the obstacles of traditional values and planning system and the backward economic foundation. The economic development breakthrough was hard to form. In the first year of establishing as a city, Zhuhai made many attempts, especially in fishery and agriculture, processing industry and tourist industry.

Zhuhai experienced three transitions from "Special Export Zone," "Special Economic Zone" to "Comprehensive Special Economic Zone" after the proposal of establishing a trial special zone. The third was put forward at a very important Special Zone working conference of two provinces held by the State Council in 1981 when the SEZ development was in hard times. The conference reviewed its experience and pitfalls during the past two years after it was established as a trial special zone, and focused on solving the basic issues of the system and industry direction in its development. Principal central leaders supported to give "privilege" to special zone which increased the possibility for special zone to reform and opening-up, as well as testing market economy. Gumu said, "Comrades of the two provinces unequivocally said that they were not satisfied with the State Council and various departments' implementation of the No.50 document. In many documents, the State Council and Departments plus 'Guangdong and Fujian Province are no exception' If anything is no exception, what else is there to talk about except special policy and flexible measure?"[223]

On the development direction of special zone, the central authorities affirmed its important role in China's reform and opening up. As Gumu said, "It is important to allow the two princes to take the first step and get the experience of the economic management system reform as the vanguard, while the special zone should lead the way."[224] On the economic guiding direction, central authorities made a new and clearer formulation in the Minutes of the Meeting, and the document on comprehensive Special Economic Zone which was issued in July: "the planning and building of special zone shall be adjusted to

---

222 Wu Jianmin, Five Years Remembrances of establishing Zhuhai Special Economic Zone, 78th volume of Guangdong Historical Accounts of Past Events, Guang dong People's press, 1998 edition, P. 46-47.

223 Wu Jianmin, Five Years Remembrances of establishing Zhuhai Special Economic Zone, 78th volume of Guangdong Historical Accounts of Past Events, Guang dong People's press, 1998 edition, P.147.

224 Wu Jianmin, Five Years Remembrances of establishing Zhuhai Special Economic Zone, 78th volume of Guangdong Historical Accounts of Past Events, Guang dong People's press, 1998 edition, P.148.

local conditions and be pragmatic with different emphasis. Shenzhen and Zhuhai should be built to be comprehensive special zone operating various industries, such as agriculture, industry, animal husbandry, commerce, housing, tourism, etc. Xiamen and Shantou Special Zone should mainly develop processing exports, as well as tourism and other industries."[225] This statement defined Zhuhai SEZ as a comprehensive special zone and made a higher and more comprehensive requirement for it, becoming the key policy in guiding its development.

However, the implementation of its development direction was still in deep waters with no idea of how to breakthrough. On the major development direction at that time, accessible comments now are mainly subsequent viewpoints:

> On this issue, there had been many arguments. Zhuhai also went through many twists and turns. Shenzhen made it at one stroke. Shenzhen was the focus of central authority then. Wang Zhen, Deputy Prime Minister, led more than twenty departments, which is a strong power, to develop the Special Zone in Shenzhen. However, Zhuhai was too small to be valued. So Zhuhai government officers invited experts and scholars here to hold seminars and conferences by which modestly listened to their opinions. Another opinion is to establish a comprehensive special zone including industry, agriculture, fishery and sidelines. As the debate continued, the opinion of setting up a special zone characterized by tourism was gradually accepted by most people, forming the viewpoint of giving priority to tourism. Therefore, Shijingshan Tourist Center was built, as well as Zhuhai Hotel and Gongbei Hotel. However, Zhuhai still is unfrequented with nothing special to attract visitors. Once is enough, twice is too much, third time is so boring. Comrade Gu Mu once got angry when he was visiting Jiuzhou port. He said that he would not come if only to see such things.[226]

This brief summary may be overly simple and clear. Zhuhai indeed took the advantage of tourism and real estate industry for their high efficiency and rapid profits to promote the construction and accumulation of the city when every industry and sector needed to be improved on the condition of lacking funds and poor foundation. It seemed to be like Shenzhen, which vigorously developed real estate industry at the beginning, but the principal leaders of the Zhuhai government probably took it as a way to kick-start the economy. They still paid attention to the industry and comprehensive development in their conception, and wrote these ideas into some important local document. Meanwhile, the

---

225 Wu Jianmin, Five Years Remembrances of establishing Zhuhai Special Economic Zone, 78th volume of Guangdong Historical Accounts of Past Events, Guang dong People's press, 1998 edition, P.149-150.

226 Zhou Shulian and Lu Guoying edited, *Great Zhuhai Special Economic Zone,* Central Party School Press, 1996 edition, P. 17

provincial government also advised to promote economy through tourism.[227] However, the phenomena of inadequate development of industry indeed existed in Zhuhai, which was maybe caused by insufficient emancipation of the mind, obstacles of economic management system, as well as the difficult environment.

The hardest phase to understand is probably the beginning period of establishing Zhuhai as a trial SEZ. There were many different interpretations on this phase due to huge traditional resistance, vague conception, and different viewpoints at different times. About the importance of the early days, the previous text introduced a lot.

As mentioned, the area of Zhuhai SEZ finally expanded in 1983, which added favorable conditions for reform and opening up. However, the government administration system still seriously hindered the opening up and development then:

> After the establishment of the SEZ management committee, it surprisingly became an institution incompatible with Municipal Committee and People's Government. They were locked in a fierce fight, blocking each other. They argued with each other on the distribution of fiscal levy every year. The finance then was only tens of millions with no more money to do construction. Some comrades would call names once the investment for SEZ was less. The Municipal Committee and People's Government had no right to manage, while the comrades of SEZ complained that Municipal Committee took no count of them, making the Municipal Committee feel unjustly treated. The SEZ did not allow the Municipal Committee to take parts and many policies could not be applied to the city, making it was hard to deal with. The SEZ investment was only twenty to thirty million, which wasn't even enough to build roads. After several years, the SEZ had no great enterprise with only tens of million output values. There was nothing to look at except Xian Zhou woolen mill when higher authorities came to visit. The mill then was very backward and was basically a manual operation. The secretary of municipal committee and mayor felt embarrassed to report to Central Authorities due to its poverty. Shenzhen was thriving then, while Zhuhai was floundering. The cadres became more and more anxious, complaining and criticizing each other. Some comrades of the Municipal Committee and People's Government had an idea of developing another special zone to run counter to the SEZ. Guided by such a conception, numerous factory buildings were built. Many jokes and contradictions were unfortunately made due to the unevenness of institutions and mechanism.[228]

---

227 Wu Jianmin, Five Years Remembrances of establishing Zhuhai Special Economic Zone, 78th volume of Guangdong Historical Accounts of Past Events, Guang dong People's press, 1998 edition, P.133-153.

228 Zhou Shulian and Lu Guoying edited, *Great Zhuhai Special Economic Zone,* Central Party School Press, 1996 edition, P. 15-16

At the end of 1983, the principal leaders of Municipal Committee and People's Government finally decided to address the contradictions between management institutions. Liang Guangda, the new mayor, canceled the reduplicated institutions soon after he assumed office. SEZ was directly led by the municipal committee and People's Government. The mayor held a concurrent post as the director of SEZ Management Committee, while other deputy mayors held concurrent posts as Deputy Director of SEZ Management Committee, effectively keeping down the endless haggling and shifts of responsibility and interferences. Therefore, the SEZ became a key priority of Zhuhai, and the relations between the two institutions became reasonable. "Only a few people developed SEZ at first, but now it was developed by all cadres of the city and the crowd together, showing vigorous vitality for development."[229]

2.3.1.2 Initial Reform and Opening Up and Quick Economic Start Up

Although Zhuhai SEZ went through numerous difficulties and hindrances in the beginning period of opening up and development, it got precious opportunity to take the first step on the road of opening up and reform, compared to the interior provinces, and achieved preliminary economic development. Taking its development between 1979 and 1983, for example, its economy showed significant changes, which had not been seen for decades (see Figure 2-3-1). The proportion of three industries changed from 1979's 38.6:30.6:30.8 to 1983's 31.7:35.1:33.2.[230] Although its economic aggregate was still not large due to its weak economic foundation, Zhuhai made many ground-breaking moves in the difficult exploration process which became historical treasures of China's reform and opening up.

Besides its favorable location, the most important advantage for Zhuhai's economic development is that it took the first step to open up and do market reform, while the preferential policies for opening up and reform are the key factors to promoting and safeguarding those practices. Zhuhai SEZ "is an area of carrying out special economic policy and special economic management system under the jurisdiction of the national sovereignty. Zhuhai People's Government could flexibly deal with problems which are not under the unified management of the Central Authorities according to relative laws, regulation and policies, as well as practical local conditions."[231]

---

229 Zhou Shulian and Lu Guoying edited, *Great Zhuhai Special Economic Zone*, Central Party School Press, 1996 edition, P. 17

230 Zhuhai Statistics Bureau, Zhuhai Statistical Yearbook of 2009, China Statistics Press, 2009, page 106.

231 *Ten Years of Zhuhai Special Economic Zone*, edited by Policy Research Office of CPC Zhuhai Committee, Zhuhai Science and Technology Press, 1990, p. 4.

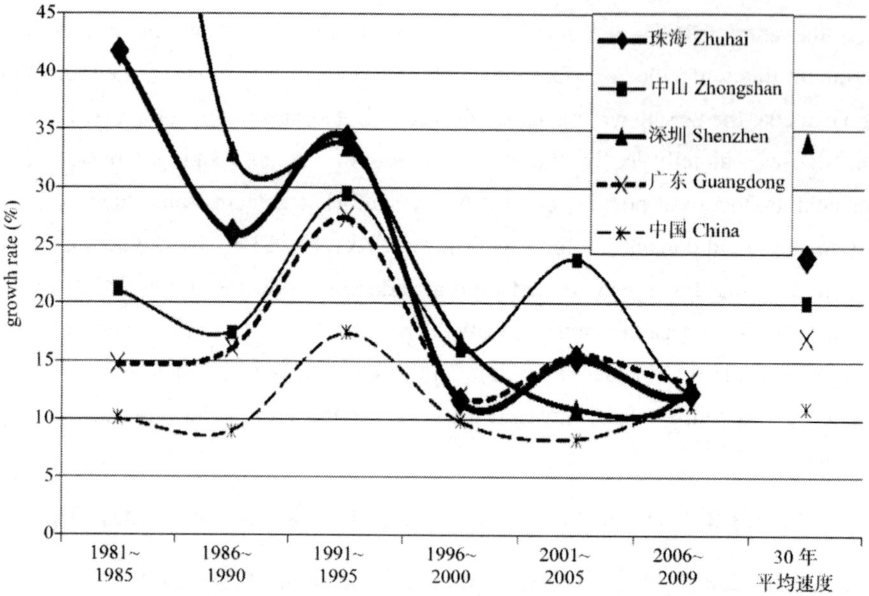

Figure 2-3-1 Five years' average growth rate of the secondary industry in Zhuhai and other areas as well as the whole country、Chart of 30 years' average growth rate between 1980 and 2009

Resources: Statistic yearbook of China and other areas, as well as statistics bulletin of recent years.

These preferential policies were of great interest for foreign investors, though there were many hindrances and coordination difficulties with complex procedures of investment invitation. At that time, the process of reform was just starting, and new enterprises were established with the public ownership as the dominant, so it was hard to match up with foreign market economy very well. However, the increasing importance of various forms of economy greatly promoted the economic mechanism reform and economic development.

Typical enterprises of Zhuhai in this industrial development phase were frequently visited by the Central Government leaders. Xiangzhou Woolen Mill (mentioned in the previous chapter) and Wanzai Huasheng Tape Factory were more representative. The latter was a model of the biggest leading industry, the electronic industry of Zhuhai. It rapidly expanded and upgraded from a small processing firm, finding out a road to success. The factory was a collective enterprise, which was founded at the end of 1985, by using 2.1 million USD of self raised funds and bank loans since 1982. 38.07 million various tapes were produced in 1985. The total exports ratio raised from one-third in 1984 to two-thirds in 1985, with an increase of 66.7% for foreign exchange earning.[232]

---

232 *Economy and Finance of Zhuhai Special Economic Zone*, written and edited by Guguang, Zhongshan University Press and Wuhan University Press,1988, P.75.

Tourist industry was the first industry that gained momentum in Zhuhai. Its representative was Shijingshan Tourist Center (mentioned above), which was located in the main city. Zhuhai Tourist Department preserved the management right and did not put it into the scope of SEZ at first. It was the first tourist enterprise which was founded by foreign investment in Zhuhai, and also the first foreign owned tourism enterprise within the Mainland. Its contract was singed with a Hong Kong investor in September 1979, when the SEZ was not yet founded. It was established in December 1980 and opened for business in January 1981, with a thriving business for a while.[233] In 1982, it was named the Advanced Unit of the national tourism. In 1984, it ranked in advanced units of the national social spiritual civilization. The success of Shijingshan Tourist Center in the early days also benefited from the opening up and reform of operating and management. However, it gradually went down after rapid development in the beginning period because its customers were only Hong Kong and Macao tourists with a limited market.

Affected by comparative superiority law, the enterprises of Zhuhai were mostly, at first, small labor-intensive firms operating in "three plus one."[234] Most of them were joint ventures or private companies, but they were mainly in the clothing of public ownership such as collective enterprise or state-owned enterprise. Those enterprises were backward technology projects that foreign countries hoped to move to less developed areas, but they often were advanced technology projects, at least appropriate projects for Zhuhai. However, the Central authorities requested to introduce advanced technologies that were advanced overseas. The development conditions were not mature yet. Those advance technology projects overseas were mostly too advanced for Zhuhai. However, Zhuhai gradually got the tendency to develop more advanced technology projects beyond its realistic conditions. Wu Jianmin, the first leader of SEZ expressed a typical opinion like this: "some introduced projects intending to transfer the old equipment, some attempted to transfer heavy labor intensive or polluting companies to open areas." We, of course, should reject the redirected behavior of dropping the heavy load of 'equipment renewal' when we introduce foreign projects in the process of developing our SEZ."[235] The tendency of super high-level of Zhuhai economy was not obvious due to the simple and crude conditions. The economic efficiency of

233 *Yearbook of China's Special Economic Zone*, edited by Hong Kong Yearbook Editorial Department, Hong Kong Yearbook of Special Economic Zone Publishing, 1983, p. 244.

234 *Economy and Finance of Zhuhai Special Economic Zone*, written and edited by Guguang, Zhongshan University Press and Wuhan University Press,1988, P.75.

235 Wu Jianmin, *Five Years Remembrances of establishing Zhuhai Special Economic Zone*, 78th volume of Guangdong Historical Accounts of Past Events, Guang dong People's press, 1998 edition, P.100.

Zhuhai SEZ was quite low. Increasing economic efficiency and opening up to international markets required the reform of economic mechanism. Zhuhai encountered big resistance in this aspect. "In 1979, smuggling was once prevalent in Hailufeng area of Guangdong, and the whole country called for a stop of developing SEZ," while Guangdong Municipal leaders and Gu Mu and other Central Government leaders struggled to protect the SEZ.[236] It's surprising that the Central Document on SEZ of 1980 boldly affirmed that the SEZ mainly practice market regulation. Zhuhai and Guangdong Province gradually did many reforms in the price, public finance, planning and other aspects. However, the arguments toward SEZ in political and academic circles did not stop. Some even took market economy as capitalism, while the leaders of SEZ and Guangdong Province still adhered to stepping forward.

2.3.2 Giving Priority to Industry and High-Speed Development of Export-Oriented Economy (1984~1990)

After five years' difficult starting up, Zhuhai had achieved preliminary results in the construction of infrastructures, economic opening, market reform, management mechanism adjustment and other aspects, though slower than Shenzhen. The affirmation of Deng Xiaoping when he made his southern tour 1984 greatly encouraged the deepening of the reform and devolution of powers. With less constraints and bold promotion of new municipal leaders, the economy and society began a rapid development.

2.3.2.1 Den Xiaoping's Affirmation to the SEZ During His Tour in Southern China

The development of SEZ persisted for four years in the voice of support and opposition from all walks of life, while Deng Xiaoping, as the chief architect of the reform and opening up policy, did not take a clear stand towards SEZ. During January and February of 1984, Deng Xiaoping finally visited Shenzhen, Zhuhai and Xiamen, three of the four SEZs. This visit turned out to be a crucial event towards the destiny of trial SEZ.

Deng Xiaoping finished his visit in Shenzhen in late January and headed to Zhuhai. Wu Jianmin, the first secretary of Zhuhai Municipal Committee who was going to retire, was responsible for the reception. Deng Xiaoping stayed for three days in the Zhongshan Hot Spring Hotel. In the morning of January 29, 1984, Den Xiaoping made an inspection tour with Wu Jianmin in a car.[237] From Wu Jianmin's reception record of that day, we can roughly

---

236 Ruqing, *Sixteen Years of Liang Guangda in Zhuhai*, China Economic Publishing House, 2001, P. 42-46.

237 Wu Jianmin, *Five Years Remembrances of establishing Zhuhai Special Economic Zone*, 78th volume of Guangdong Historical Accounts of Past Events, Guang dong People's press, 1998 edition, P. 277-279.

understand some status of the development of Zhuhai and Deng's attitude towards Zhuhai:

> Comrade Deng and I got on another car. I knew that I would probably get no chance to systematically report to him on the way, so I unfolded a small map and introduced some situations off and on in a hurry:
>
> I knew that Deng is hard of hearing, so I spoke close to his ears. He seemed to be absorbed, so I continued to say, "Since the carrying out of the opening up policy in full scale and the establishment of SEZ, Zhuhai, taking the advantage conditions of being close to Hong Kong and Macao, introduced numerous processing projects which equipped the commune and brigade enterprises, invigorated rural economy and stabilized the border. The industrial and agricultural reached nearly two hundred million last year, plus that of Domen County, it would be nearly five hundred million."
>
> We rode in the car for about an hour and then turned. After a turnoff, the car slowly entered into the woolen mill. The guests got off and visited this firstly imported factory of Zhuhai. We had seen all procedures include wool sourcing, mixing, combing, mule spinning, and plying yarn, part forming and packing. The factory director briefly introduced every single procedure with his hands moving in the air.
>
> At noon, Deng Xiaoping and followers had a lunch in Zhuhai Hotel. Zhang Qianling (Director of Zhuhai Hotel, noted by editor) came over, and whispered to Deng's ear, "Would you please write an inscription as a remembrance?"
>
> The aged man looked up, slowly pondered, "Oh, what should I write?"
>
> Hearing that, I knew that Xiaoping would like to write an inscription. I caught my breath and quickly said, "Anything such as your judgment to Zhuhai SEZ—"
>
> The aged man nodded, then stood up, and walked to a prepared writing desk with Chinese art paper, brush pen and ink by side.
>
> The aged man stroked boldly and vigorously. His calligraphy was forceful. He wrote seven characters, stating,
>
> "Zhuhai SEZ is great" and signed his name. The crowds immediately applauded. That was another affirmation of Deng Xiaoping towards the policy of establishing SEZ four to five years after the decision. It was also an inspection conclusion of the development of Zhuhai SEZ.
>
> When we returned to the lunch table, Zhang Qianling asked me, "Would you drink some Mao-tai?" I asked for Deng's opinion, he nodded. The aged man was indeed very pleased.[238]

This is the first time that Deng Xiaoping wrote a public judgment for China's SEZ. It was of significant importance for Zhuhai SEZ, as well as China's reform and opening up. Deng Xiaoping did not speak most of the time when he visited Shenzhen. His inscription of

238 Wu Jianmin, *Five Years Remembrances of establishing Zhuhai Special Economic Zone*, 78th volume of Guangdong Historical Accounts of Past Events, Guang dong People's press, 1998 edition, P. 279-284.

"January 26, 1984" for Shenzhen was written at Shenzhen's invitation later in Guangzhou. We do not know why Den Xiaoping first wrote for Zhuhai SEZ. The inscription he wrote for Zhuhai cannot be more concise, but emphasized "great," reflecting his high affirmation and support to the development of SEZ. The inscription he wrote for Shenzhen later was more specific with the word "correct." For Xiamen, his inscription became relatively concise again: "Develop SEZ faster and better." This inscription was also for all Special Economic Zones, giving people more hope to develop Special Economic Zones. The behaviors of Den Xiaoping at least reflected his cautiousness as the chief architect. Although he did not answer that SEZ is social or capitalist, his words carried great weight and authority. Since then, he repeatedly emphasized the importance of developing Special Economic Zones on different occasions. His words provided an important driving force and safeguard for SEZ to further emancipate the mind and experiment in the early difficult days of the reform and opening up.

Zhuhai reformed its personnel system, labor distribution system and other aspects, strengthen the development strategy of giving priority to industry, and started more frequent activities of introducing foreign capital and establishing domestic connections just in 1984.[239] This sudden increase of economic development momentum was closely related to new Zhuhai Municipal leaders besides the foundation laid by Deng Xiaoping.

2.3.2.2 Strengthen the Development Strategy of Giving Priority to Industry

Zhuhai's development had been connected with Liang Guangda since 1984. He had held the post of Mayor or Secretary or other important posts of Zhuhai People's Government or Municipal Committee for 16 years in succession. Almost all the prosperities and setbacks that Zhuhai went through were related to him. His influence to Zhuhai could even be found in today's Zhuhai. The provincial government leaders proposed to appoint him as the Acting Mayor of Zhuhai and asked him to take a look at Shenzhen before assuming the office when Wu Jianmin, the first Secretary of Zhuhai Municipal Committee, was going to leave his post in 1983. "Liang Guangda was a standing committee member of Foshan (Guangdong Province) Prefectural Party Committee, Deputy Commissioner and Director of Public Finance and Trade Office before he assumed office in Zhuhai. Nanhai became one of the richest counties when he was Secretary of Nanhai Municipal Committee.

---

239 *Economy and Finance of Zhuhai Special Economic Zone*, written and edited by Guguang, Zhongshan University Press and Wuhan University Press,1988, P.73-74. *20-Year Chronology of Zhuhai*, edited by Zhuhai Historical Archive, printed in 2000, P. 24-30

His nickname 'bold man' was given by the Guangdong people in this period."[240] After Liang Guangda assumed his office in Zhuhai, the leading group of Zhuhai government had compared with Shenzhen and held various activities to communicate and extensively ask for advice and suggestions on the development of Zhuhai since September 1983. The discussion continued until the southern tour of Deng Xiaoping in February 1984 and new secretary FangBao assumed office. Different thoughts were gradually unified to be: "over the past four years, we failed to take full advantage of the good policies. The positivity of broad cadres and the mass was not fully mobilized. The ideological emancipation was insufficient with heavy fetters of left thoughts. The development guideline was not clear. The system of the government restrained from each other. Some people could only make high-sounding talks but no one would like to take the responsibilities. The lack of creativity and pioneering spirits, doing things step by step and the thought of 'waiting up, depending on and asking for' were relatively conspicuous."[241]

The further emancipation of the mind enhanced peoples' pioneering awareness. Zhuhai Municipal Government smoothed the management system of the SEZ and stood up to the dissatisfaction from the Provincial Government at the end of 1983. At the beginning of 1984, Zhuhai again affirmed the strategy of focusing on industry and comprehensive development of all sectors, and boldly brought it to practice. Fang Bao was transferred from Deputy Secretary of Shenzhen Municipal Committee to Secretary of Zhuhai Municipal Committee. He vigorously trumpeted the renewal of Zhuhai's development strategy after he came here. He issued an article titled "Positively Develop and Speed Up" in *People's Daily* on January 28, 1985. In the article, he put forward that Zhuhai would do five aspects of work in the future: "(1) Further get rid of the 'Left' thoughts influence. (2) Deepen the economic management reform and continue to increase liberty of enterprises. (3) Continue to make efforts to reform the system, promote the construction of infrastructure projects, and create favorable investment environment. (4) Actively do a good job of introducing foreign new technologies and running joint ventures with domestic provinces and cities. Vigorously develop industry of the SEZ with an emphasis of introducing technology and knowledge intensive industries. And (5) positively solve the problem of talents."[242] Under such background that was deeply influenced by conservative ideology, Liang Guangda boldly promoted opening up and economic activities, looking for a way out

---

240 Ruqing, *Sixteen Years of Liang Guangda in Zhuhai*, China Economic Publishing House, 2001, P. 26-27.

241 Ruqing, *Sixteen Years of Liang Guangda in Zhuhai*, China Economic Publishing House, 2001, P. 31.

242 Ruqing, *Sixteen Years of Liang Guangda in Zhuhai*, China Economic Publishing House, 2001, P. 32.

for the financially embarrassing SEZ. "If the constructors of the SEZ walked in the right way, sat steadily in the right position, if it was beneficial to the development of Zhuhai SEZ and not against the spirits of Central Authority and State Council document, Liang Guangda dared to do anything: "(I) shook hands with capitalists, drank with capitalist, and also had a meal with them by the same table... (We) not only drew funds for development, but also introduced advance technologies, equipments and management experiences. We got a lot of outside information."[243] Over the past several years, Zhuhai strongly promoted reform and opening up, and boldly expanded pilot units for market economy in the SEZ.

Since 1984, Zhuhai's activities of opening up increased significantly, as well as the coalition activities with the Mainland. The image and economy of Zhuhai witnessed a dramatic increase. As the strengthening of development emphasis, more and more oversea investors came here to discuss business, inspect industrial projects and negotiate commercial cooperation. The starting projects increased rapidly. The quick changes before and after this year could be seen in Memorabilia of Zhuhai.[244]

2.3.3 The Development of Export-Oriented Economy

In August 1985, Deng Xiaoping put forward an important viewpoint of SEZ when he met the delegation of Japanese Komeito Party: "Our Special Economic Zones are switching from internal-oriented to export-oriented economy. We just started up without enough great products to export. As long as Shenzhen does not finish this transformation, it could not pass the exam and prove that its economy is healthy. However, I have heard that a little progress was made in this aspect."[245]

In line with this requirement, the development strategy of Zhuhai city was adjusted from focusing on industry to focusing on export-oriented economy. The city government formulated industrial strategic guidelines as "Four Combination" and "Four Priority": "the 'Four Combination' is the combination of introducing foreign capital and establishing domestic connections and developing by ourselves, the combination of export-oriented economy, substituting economy and self-sufficient economy, the combination of the strength of city, county, district, village and town, the combination of large, medium-sized and small projects." "The 'Four Priority' is the giving priority to introducing foreign capital, export-oriented economy, the strength of the city and giving priority to medium-sized and

---

243 Ruqing, *Sixteen Years of Liang Guangda in Zhuhai*, China Economic Publishing House, 2001, P. 35.

244 *20-Year Chronology of Zhuhai*, edited by Zhuhai Historical Archive, 2000, P. 25-33.

245 Deng Xiaoping, Deng Xiaoping anthology, third volume, People's Publishing House,1993, P. 133.

small projects."[246]

This guideline focused on introducing foreign investment, export-oriented economy and gave priority to developing small and medium-sized enterprises, but did not mention former advocated technology- intensive enterprises. This guideline was more appropriate for Zhuhai. However it continued the former economic model with an emphasis on developing state-owned enterprises and slowing down the development of township enterprises. During those years, Zhuhai developed rapidly and its economy took off.

In 1988, Zhuhai further put forward "Five Transform": "(1) Transform merely relying on the preferential policies granted by the state in the past to taking full advantage of preferential policies, moreover, relying on our accumulated power and advantage to develop export oriented economy. (2) Transform from labor-intensive processing industry focused in the past to technology-intensive industries focused and attaching importance to basic industries. (3) Transform from relying on extension-expanded reproduction in the past to focusing on both connotations expanded reproduction and extension expanded reproduction. (4) Transform from domestic market focused in the past to exploring international market and gradually focusing on international market. (5) Transform from mainly using domestic funds in the past to using both domestic funds and foreign capital and positively looking for foreign capital with a variety forms and measures, and primarily utilizing foreign capitals as soon as possible."[247]

At that time, Zhuhai attached the utmost importance to export-oriented economy, but again the industry focused on technology-intensive economy. The thinking excelled that of before. This could be seen from the outstanding performance after 1992.

The society and economy of Zhuhai developed rapidly in the phase of 1984~1990 (see Figure 2-3-1, 2-3-2). "The foundation laid several years after the establishment of trial SEZ inserted the soar away wing for Zhuhai industry. Patches of modern industrial areas suddenly appeared and numerous industrial enterprises mushroomed. In 1989, the gross industrial output value of the city reached 24.7 billion yuan (constant price of 1980, hereinafter inclusive), forty times that of 1979. There were 765 industrial enterprises in the whole city with 3.301 billion gross industrial outputs, an increase of 23.6 times that of 1979. If calculated by heavy and light industry, the gross output value of light industry was 2.617 billion yuan with 22.5 times increase and the gross output value of heavy industry was 0.684 billion with 30 times increase. By

246 *Economy and Finance of Zhuhai Special Economic Zone*, written and edited by Guguang, Zhongshan University Press and Wuhan University Press, 1988, P.68.

247 *Ten Years of Zhuhai Special Economic Zone*, edited by Policy Research Office of CPC Zhuhai Committee, Zhuhai Science and Technology Press, 1990, p. 52.

economic character, the industrial output value under the ownership of all the people reached 1.263 billion yuan, 13.5 times that of 1979. The industrial output under collective ownership was 0.655 billion yuan with a 12.9 times increase. The output value of foreign invested industry and other economic types of ownership reached 1.102 billion yuan. The industry of village level and below had also made relatively rapid growth, with 0.281 billion outputs."[248]

On the development characteristics, Zhuhai "formed a relative complete industrial system including electricity, food manufacture, textile industry, light chemical industry, light-duty machinery, building materials, etc. (Zhuhai) established modern functional zones for technology-intensive industry, preliminarily forming the industrial structure based on export-oriented economy."(Zhuhai) took industrial group as the engine to drive the development of the city's industry."[249] The agriculture of Zhuhai also "endeavored to change to be export-oriented." "Barren Mountain basically disappeared and the forestation rate reached 99.2%. Forest coverage rate increased to be 31% from 19.2%."[250] The proportion of three industries was upgraded from 31.7: 35.1: 33.2 in 1983 to 14.4: 43.6: 42.0 in 1990.[251]

Figure 2-3-2 Xiangzhou, downtown of Zhuhai city in 1990

Resourcing: Photo by Li Zhiju, *Zhuhai City*, edited by Policy Research Office of Zhuhai municipal committee, China City Press, 1994, P.12 in preface.

---

248 *Ten Years of Zhuhai Special Economic Zone*, edited by Policy Research Office of CPC Zhuhai Committee, Zhuhai Science and Technology Press, 1990, p. 6.

249 *Ten Years of Zhuhai Special Economic Zone*, edited by Policy Research Office of CPC Zhuhai Committee, Zhuhai Science and Technology Press, 1990, p. 7-8.

250 *Ten Years of Zhuhai Special Economic Zone*, edited by Policy Research Office of CPC Zhuhai Committee, Zhuhai Science and Technology Press, 1990, p. 11.

251 Zhuhai Statistics Bureau, Zhuhai Statistical Yearbook of 2009, China Statistics Press, 2009, page 106.

Zhuhai elected ten great events in ten years when it celebrate its 10th anniversary of the city in 1988. They are as follows: "(1) The success of Zhuhai SEZ experiment, and its investment environment attracted thousands of investors here. (2) Garden seaside new city began to take shape and the tourism was prosperous. (3) The first farmer holiday village in the mainland was set up by the Lake of White Cane (4) The structure of export oriented lead by industry was basically formed. (5) Zhuhai took the lead in reforming labor system in the province and the whole country. (6) Education investment was steadily increasing with an obvious growth rate. (7) Huangmei Beer won the Asian highest quality award (8) Communication network was extended in all directions. (9) Financing grew rapidly. (10) Internal and external promoting activities and the culture flourished."[252] Until 1990, Zhuhai SEZ had made impressive results during 11 years' development and continued to keep a good momentum for further development.

2.3.4 Advanced Development Led by High and New Technology (1991~2000)

2.3.4.1 Establishing the Guideline of Focusing on High and New Technologies

In the 1990s, development trend of the world's "New Economy" was gradually changing to be a knowledge economy. Pursuing for high-level development of the national economy, Zhuhai made an important and very advanced strategic decision to "focusing on the development of high and new industries, making great efforts to adjust industrial structure, and establishing export-oriented economy based on high and new technology." Zhuhai gave up "three plus one" processing industries which were more in accordance with Zhuhai's comparative superiorities and attached an importance to developing high and new technology industries with adequate conditions. Its main aim was to develop Zhuhai to be a modern coastal garden city with advanced technologies, prosperous economy and rich cultures in 15 years.

Deng Xiaoping again made an inspection visit to Zhuhai SEZ in January 1992. He visited high-tech enterprises of the SEZ three times in seven days. He laid stress on the viewpoint that "science and technology are the primary productive forces." Deng Xiaoping's southern tour greatly encouraged the development of market economy in the whole country. Many areas, with better or poor conditions, rapidly turned to develop high and new technologies that top the economic structure.

In line with Den Xiaoping's remarks during his inspection tour of southern China,

252 *20-Year Chronology of Zhuhai*, edited by Zhuhai Historical Archive, 2000, P.80.

Zhuhai began to establish complete market system with a relative strong guidance of the government. Deng's emphasis of technology deeply impressed Liang Guangda. In order to speed up the development of high and new technology industries, Zhuhai successively issued a series of policies and measures, such as the resolution on promoting economic development through technological progress, the resolution on rewarding people who made outstanding contribution in technological progress, etc.[253]

In March 1992, Liang Guangda held a grand conference to rewarding people who made outstanding contributions in technological progress. At the conference, he said: "Welcome all the learned people who study overseas, talented oversea Chinese experts, as well as experts, scholars and professors from any country to work, teach and settle down in Zhuhai. Welcome concerned domestic units and technicians to bring in scientific achievements to develop and produce together, or transfer, or invest, or run cooperative joint ventures with technologies."[254] The behavior of generously rewarding technicians was the first case in China Mainland, causing quite a stir in press circles. Zhuhai persisted on doing this practice for many years and would be followed by major cities in Pearl River Delta.

In June 1994, General Secretary Jiang Zemin visited Zhuhai and said, "My first feeling is that Zhuhai has made earthshaking changes after just two day's visit. You already realized one important viewpoint. You had given up 'Three plus one' as introducing target since 1991, and laid stress on developing high and new technologies. This strategy was correct."[255]

2.3.4.2 Development of High-tech Industries and the Lagging Industrialization

In 1988, The State Science and Technology Commission started up "Torch Program" to promote the development of high and new technological industries. In the same year, the development direction of Zhuhai already tilted to high technological industries. Zhuhai started to speed up its development of high technological industries. Until 1992, its high and new technological industries had taken shape. Zhuhai established the economic developing strategy of focusing on high and new technologies in this year. The high and new technological industry made a rapid growth in the beginning and middle period. Ruqing recalled like this:

---

253 Liang Guangda and Huang Longyun, chief editor, The Development Road of Zhuhai During the New Century, Guangdong People's Publishing House, 1998, P. 216.

254 Ruqing, *Sixteen Years of Liang Guangda in Zhuhai*, China Economic Publishing House, 2001, P. 88-89.

255 Ruqing, *Sixteen Years of Liang Guangda in Zhuhai*, China Economic Publishing House, 2001, P. 83.

> As other Special Economic Zones did, Zhuhai also introduced numerous "Three plus one" projects on a ground scale in the beginning period.
>
> After Deng Xiaoping made a tour to Zhuhai in 1992, they made a prompt decision and adjusted the economic structure in time.
>
> Zhuhai decided to depend on science and technological progress and established a structural system led by high and new technological industry, based on advanced industries and braced by high level socialized tertiary industry.
>
> The connotation of high-tech economic zone was added to formerly determined city position of modern coastal garden city.
>
> Zhuhai made urban comprehensive development planning of seizing the commanding height and developing modern economic zone, completely ridded itself from former status of wondering at low level productivity.[256]

Zhuhai's advanced development focusing on high and new technological industries was continually strengthened into the 1990s until Liang Guangda retired in the late 1990s. The high and new technological industries then became leading industry of Zhuhai. Meanwhile, Zhuhai municipal government strictly limited the development of labor-intensive and polluting industries and gave up "three plus one" processing enterprises. Strong interference of the government promoted the industrial structure to a high level, making a higher leap forward before the realization of industrialization. In the same period, Zhuhai invested its limited funds to advanced infrastructure construction and finite funds for the second industry (see specific introduction in the next chapter). The primary and intermediate industrialization for economic foundation were ignored to a great extent, which decreased the growth rate of other industries, gradually slowing down the industrialization progress and causing an imbalanced industrial structure (see Figure 2-3-1). After several years, the development of high and new technological industries slowed down and talents flew out due to inadequate general conditions.

According to the theory of comparative superiority in economics, high-tech enterprises are knowledge-intensive and technology intensive economic entities, which top the high-grade development of international industrial structure. They need to be developed in the place of industrial agglomeration with good conditions even in developed countries. There was a certain comparative advantage to developing high- tech industries in China because of its large population, but obvious shortages did exist. Many regions which rushed up in a crowd to develop high-tech industry did not have mature conditions. Vast economic realities and theories convinced that regional economic development should be directed by

---

256 Ruqing, *Sixteen Years of Liang Guangda in Zhuhai*, China Economic Publishing House, 2001, P. 92.

its comparative superiority. China's catching up strategy and leaping forward of foreign investment by giving support to regions with comparative disadvantage would not achieve planned effects. More haste, less speed. Actually, most of the vast Chinese high-tech enterprises were in the downstream of industrial chain that focused on capital and labors. As a result, many regions had low efficiency in leaping forward but at a high cost. They developed as before in line with their comparative advantage.

International high-tech industries tend to swarm in cities that have good development software and hardware such as talents, finance, living conditions etc, with a strengthening specialization and polarization. Chinese high-tech industry also should be developed in appropriate areas, so all the national high-tech industry parks were located in provincial capitals or cities that have good industrial or technological conditions. Guangdong Province accounted for six among the 53 national high-tech development zones, and all of them were located in Pearl River Delta areas. They are: Guangzhou high-tech industry development zone, Shenzhen high-tech industry development zone, Zhuhai high-tech industry development zone, Foshan high-tech industry development zone, Huizhou high-tech industry development zone, and Zhongshan torch high-tech industry development zone. Zhuhai were not prominent with many challenges. Tan Zhengxun analyzed the downturn of Zhuhai's high-tech industries in 2007:

> The last twenty years of 20th century is an era of international industrial migration. Numerous multinational corporations transferred their labor-intensive industries into China and other developing countries in this era. Taking this opportunity in time, Guangzhou and Shenzhen accepted a lot of labor-intensive industries through OEM (Original Equipment Manufacture), realized industrialization and accumulated original capital for the optimization and upgrading of industries and the development of high-tech industries. In recent years, Guangzhou, Shenzhen and other cities timely adjusted their industrial strategy and vigorously developed technology-enabled and profitable high-tech industries. Zhuhai failed to make city development and industry development strategy in line with situations. Its strategic orientation was modified several times, nearly letting this opportunity slip. Therefore Zhuhai did not accumulate essential original capital for industry optimization and upgrading. Its economic efficiency was totally different from that of Shenzhen and Guangdong by accepting transferred international industry through OEM in different periods. The competition between intermediate suppliers was not so intense and the profit margin was larger when Shenzhen and Guangzhou took outsourcing OEM orders in the late 20th century. However, as international labor-intensive industries transferred to developing countries and areas represented by Vietnam and interior areas, the competition for OEM orders became more and more intense with a reducing profit

margin because these countries and areas had cheaper lands and labors than that of costal cities. (This is main external reason for Zhuhai's reduction of the value-added rate and return on sales of high-tech industries year by year). What's more important is that Guangdong, Shenzhen and other cities had formed relative complete industrial agglomeration and chains with high value-added rate because of technology spillovers and their hard working over the past twenty years. In conclusion, Guangzhou and Shenzhen already stepped into post-industrialization, and their high-tech industry was also in a phase of independent innovation, while Zhuhai was realizing industrialization, and its high-tech industry was in a phase of digestion and assimilation.[257]

Over ten years, Zhuhai went through the early rapid development and increasing internal and external difficulties later. Compared to surrounding and other relative or similar cities and regions, its process of industrialization gradually slowed down (see Figure 2-3-1). China's SEZ research center of Shenzhen College analyzed "it could be said that Zhuhai's industries and economy went through the most difficult time between 1994 and 1999. Deficit-ridden enterprises of industrial enterprises above designated size annually made for a total loss of 1.02 billion yuan on average, while the profitable enterprises annually made only a total profit of 0.71 billion yuan on average. Zhuhai's industry made Zhuhai waste the 1990s."[258] In 1999, Zhuhai's GDP and GDP per capita ranked 10th and 8th large respectively among 12 cities in the Peal River Delta, falling back from front rank.[259]

The advantages of SEZ and preferential standing had been gradually weakened since China transferred in full swing to market economy in 1992. However, Zhuhai developed its society and economy in spite of these difficulties. It began to reform the social insurance system and housing system, and basically completed the operational mechanism for market economy. Between 1996 and 2000, "Zhuhai's GDP increased by 10.7% on an annual basis in the environment of Asian Financial Crisis and changing macroeconomic situation." Foreign trade economy increased in difficulties. The amount of foreign direct investment actually used over the past five years came to 3.47 billion USD, and exports reached 14.62

---

257 Tan Zhengxun, *Study on the core competitiveness of Zhuhai's high-tech industry—in Guangdong based comparative perspectives,* Science and Technology Management Research, No.5 (2007), P.97-98, 103.

258 Chen Hongquan, ZhongJian, History review of Zhuhais' reform and opening up, major achievements and lessons, Chinese SEZ Forum in 2008: Proceedings of the Conference for Commemorating the 30th anniversary of reform and opening, 2008.

259 Ma Yuedong, YanXiaopei, 20 years' rational thinking of city development in Zhuhai's reform and opening, economic-geography, No.1, 2004, P.67-71,90.

billion USD, with an annual growth of 8.2% and 10.6% respectively."[260] In 2000, its GDP increased 79.6 times among which the primary, secondary and tertiary industry increased 47.6, 180.4 and 117.5 times respectively, while the GDP per capita only increased 24.0 times than that of 1979. The proportion of the primary, secondary and tertiary industry upgraded from 38.6, 30.6, 30.8 to 4.3, 52.2, 43.5.[261] What's more valuable is that Zhuhai perfectly completed the political task of greeting Macao for its return, realizing one of the key goals for establishing Zhuhai SEZ twenty years before.

2.3.5 Replenishing Industrialization, Economic Achievements and Challenges (2001~2009)

2.3.5.1 Explore New Development Pattern in Introspection

The government and academics realized many difficulties and problems of Zhuhai after its slowing down in most time of 1990s. Guangdong Provincial SEZ seminar held an opinion that "Chinese economic development was still in the tone of industrialization. The SEZ had not become the technological center of China. Only if we focused on industry could the high-tech industry have a carrier. Zhuhai city drew relatively more foreign investments and established many industrial enterprises, but did not establish internationally competitive manufacturing sectors and enter into the phase of massive technological innovation. Speeding up industrial economic development and quickly establishing modern industry system are the engine and motility of SEZ economic growth. This conception has to be firmly established.[262] As Liang Guangda retired at the turn of the century, new leaders of Zhuhai municipal government reflected on the development patterns little by little."

While the conclusion of Zhuhai government working report of 2001 may represent a typical opinion, it did a further inspection on the problems and shortages of the manufacturing sector. It commented that the quality of manufacturing sectors were lower in general comparing with advanced regions. The report laid stress on many issues that may retard future development:

> (1) Relatively low level of industrial technology. With a weak technological innovation power, most enterprises were just processing companies, and hard to shake off

260 Fang Xuan, *Report on the Work of Zhuhai Municipal Government*, 2001.

261 Zhuhai Statistics Bureau, Zhuhai Statistical Yearbook of 2009, China Statistics Press, 2009.

262 Luo Musheng, Zhou Shuwei, and Zhang Haibo, Thoughts on the Development Strategy of Zhuhai Special Economic Zone, Economy of Special Economic Zone, No.10, 1999, P. 9-13.

the circle of "import, fall behind, die out, import again." They could only be a processing company. The development and application level of key technology obviously lagged behind international advanced level. Enterprise informatization just started up.

(2) Inadequate industrial supererogation. China had certain international competitiveness in labor-intensive sectors, but had nearly no competitive power in capital and technology intensive industries comparing to the USA, Japan, German and other developed countries, or even to Malaysia, Indonesia and other developing countries. In general, Zhuhai's manufacturing was at low level of term processing, and most were in the ultimate end of international vertical division of labor and at a disadvantage in international trade.

(3) Insufficient industrial systemization. With defective labor division system, low industrial concentration and overly small size under the Minimum Efficient Scale, numerous small and medium sized enterprises failed to enter into the industrial chain of large enterprises and their labor productivity had a big gap with that of developed countries and advanced developing countries. Quite a number of enterprises developed at low level of resource utilization efficiency. Therefore, the ecological environment pressure was relatively great and problems of sustainable development were outstanding.

The question of low industry level, weak innovation power, small scale of using foreign capital, short of influential large enterprises, and inadequate abilities for sustainable development existed in Zhuhai's manufacturing. There was a lot of work to do before establishing an advanced manufacturing base. The development of high-tech industry did not achieve planned goals."[263]

Zhuhai began to realize the problems brought by the advanced development of focusing on high and new technologies, but its development strategy changed a little.

2.3.6 Gradual Adjustment of Development Patter, and the Speed-Up of Economic Development

In the early years of the 21st century, Zhuhai tried to gradually change its economic development pattern and the speed of its economy development. In 2002, "gratifying future of industry laid before Zhuhai. Key enterprises such as Canon, Flextronics, Mitsumi, and Gree expanded investment or upgraded, and numerous small and medium sized enterprises grew rapidly. Open economy boomed. The amount of direct contracted foreign investment utilized reached 1.32 billion USD, with an increase of 87.7%. The paid-in foreign direct investment was 0.698 billion USD, with an increase of 34%. The exports totaled 5.2 billion USD, increased by 37.4%. New achievements were made in opening up

---

263 Fang Xuan, *Report on the Work of Zhuhai Municipal Government*, 2001.

to the domestic."[264]

In recent years, Zhuhai's understanding of its problems in development became profound. Subtle changes could be found in the conclusion of Zhuhai's government work reports. In the report of 2003, "the progress of industrialization was relatively slow. The power of technological innovation and subsidiary industries was not strong. The economic aggregate was not big, economic development of different regions were imbalanced. The town and village economy was weak. The development of private economy lagged behind, while the allocations of state-owned enterprises needed to be upgraded. The infrastructures were not matching with each other. The airport and seaport did not give their full play. The former comparative advantages had been weakened. The overall competitiveness and development potential need to be enhanced."[265] In the report of 2005, it did a more public and profound analysis on its shortages: "The economic aggregate was still relatively small. Its growth speed was slower than that of the advanced cities in Pearl River Delta. The quality and efficiency of its economic development remained low. The economic structure needs to be improved. The fiscal capability was relatively weak. The task of handling inherited problems was arduous. The unbalanced development made many people's lives quite difficult. Economic and social development was facing the systematic obstacles. The task of further reforms in difficult areas was heavy. Loop holes existed in social management and public services. The ability and quality of many public servants needed to be improved, as well as their work style."[266]

During this period, "taking this new opportunity of international industrial migration and making full use of its comparative advantages, Zhuhai sped up the progress of heavy industry according to the changes of the internal and external consumer markets." The proportion of heavy industry outputs caught up and exceeded that of light industry. In early 2003, the ratio of heavy and light industry outputs reached 58:42, taking the lead in entering into heavy industry focused phase among cities in western Pearl River Delta,"[267] Its external environments were significantly improved. "Economic globalization and the acceleration of structural adjustment and industrial migration, 'Great Pearl River Delta' and 'Pan-Pearl River Delta' strengthened regional cooperation, the building of railways,

264 Wang Shunsheng, *Report on the Work of Zhuhai Municipal Government*, 2003.

265 Wang Shunsheng, *Report on the Work of Zhuhai Municipal Government*, 2003.

266 Wang Shunsheng, *Report on the Work of Zhuhai Municipal Government*, 2004.

267 Wang Liwen, ZhangRenshou, Thoughts on Promoting Zhuhai's Industrial Competitiveness, Guangdong Economy, No.10, 2004, p. 23, 24, 35.

ports, highways and other big transport infrastructural projects were started"[268] These became precious opportunities for Zhuhai's development.

Zhuhai gradually changed its development target to making up a lesson for promoting industrialization. The development thinking tended to emphasize industrialization and speed to a higher degree. It said to "adhere to giving priority to development, promoting industrialization, urbanization and informatization with all the strength, as soon as possible, as good as possible. Focusing on the industrial development, building of transport infrastructure, development of a new city, cooperation with Hong Kong and Macao, and work related to agriculture, rural areas and farmers."[269] In 2005, it urgently emphasized that "the key to speeding up Zhuhai's economic development lies in the promotion of new type industrialization," and stated that "(we) have to thoroughly understand the importance and urgency of speeding up industrial development and take the promotion of new types of industrialization as the principal line for the city's economic works. Depending on industrial development, we flourish the service industry and nurture agriculture, shifting the emphasis of economic works to industrial development."[270]

Zhuhai made further changes and intensification especially in industrial development mode. It was generally emphasized that "making our best efforts to develop industry, adjust and improve the structure, as well as enhancing industrial strength and competition". On the path "persist on developing industry vigorously with no relief," "unswervingly take the new-type industrialized road and attach the highest importance to the development of industry in current economic works, further enhancing macro-guide and improving micro-service." About industrial structure, it continued the past pattern to "vigorously develop high and new technological industry." However, it put forward that (Zhuhai) should "bring large enterprises and large projects into play in the industrial development" for covering the shortage of high-tech industry. (Zhuhai) also needs to complete the foundation of industrialization and extend industrial chain and "make great efforts to support the development of small and medium-sized enterprises, and encourage them to manufacture accessory products for large leading enterprises." (Zhuhai) chose electricity and communication facilities manufacturing, electric equipment and machinery, medicine and medical devices as three major pillars, and hoped to "size new opportunities of upgrading provincial industrial structure to heavy industry oriented structure, give full play

---

268 Wang Shunsheng, *Report on the Work of Zhuhai Municipal Government*, 2004.

269 Wang Shunsheng, *Report on the Work of Zhuhai Municipal Government*, 2004.

270 Wang Shunsheng, *Report on the Work of Zhuhai Municipal Government*, 2005.

to Zhuhai's comparative advantages to develop heavy industry and try its best to make a breakthrough in developing petrochemical industry, energy, equipment industry and other industries in major harbor industrial zone."[271]

In this period, Zhuhai finally witnessed a small climax of economic recovery and relatively rapid growth. During the tenth five-years (2001~2005), under the condition of giving top priority to development and better external macro-environment, "local GDP annually increased by 13.8% and the revenue increased by 15% on average. The gross industrial outputs of 2005 amounted to twice that of the ninth five- years. The tendency of heavy and advanced industry is clear. Outputs of high-tech industry accounted for 38% of the gross industrial outputs, with an increase of 12.5 percent than that of the late ninth five-years. The scale of using foreign investment and trade obviously expanded, "breakthrough progress has been made in major projects."[272] Pan-Pearl River Delta cooperation made progress at the end of 2003. On the first day of 2004, Closer Economic Partnership Arrangement (CEPA) was formally introduced, strengthening its economic relations with Hong Kong and Macao.

In December 2003, a brand new economic model of "one country, two systems" laid a foundation for Zhuhai-Macao Cross Boundary Industrial Zone, which set a model for "one country, two systems" as an institutional innovation and express that the economic reform and opening up were intensified. The mini SEZ connected Zhuhai Park with 0.29 square kilometers and Macao Park with 0.11 square kilometers by a special checkpoint. The preferential policy of "bonded area plus taxes rebate of export processing zones plus special customs clearance run in 24 hours" (simply three-in-one) was carried out in the area.[273] The first intention was to weaken the impact of canceling the textiles and clothing quota system to Macao and prevent Macao's local clothing enterprises from migrating to the north and affecting local employment in 2005.[274] It "maintained rapid growth momentum" after December 2006.[275] Until 2010, the scale remained very small, but changed the target to be "setting up a new platform for Hong Kong and Macao's service industry and high-tech industrial cooperation" for the industrial transformation and upgrading.[276]

---

271 Wang Shunsheng, *Report on the Work of Zhuhai Municipal Government*, 2004.

272 Wang Shunsheng, *Report on the Work of Zhuhai Municipal Government*, 2006.

273 http://www.zhftz.gov.cn/cn/pages/news.jsp?category.categoryId=24&categoryId=44&newsId=488, 28th, October, 2008

274 Yangmi, Zhuhai-Macao Cross Boundary Industrial Zone: New Brilliant Spot of Regional Economic Cooperation, International Economic Cooperation, No.6, 2005, P, 22-25.

275 http://www.zhftz.gov.cn/cn/pages/news.jsp?category.categoryId=12&categoryId=227&newsId=326, 23th, July, 2008.

276 Weimeng, Zhuhan amend its plan to promote the transformation of Zhuhai-Macao Cross Boundary Industrial Zone, China Daily Website. http://www.chinadaily.com.cn/dfpd/guangdong/2010-05-21/content_342893.html, 21st, May, 2010.

2.3.6.1 Current Development, Economic Achievements and Problems

After several years' recovery and relatively fast growth, Zhuhai maintained a good momentum and developed quickly. Meanwhile, the crisis consciousness of the government was gradually enhanced, and the introspection of development path became more clear and profound: "Small economic aggregate and insufficient industrial development still were the most basic conflicts that impeded the economic and social development of Zhuhai. The issues of inadequate economic structure and unbalanced development were still outstanding. Most industries were at the low level of industrial value-added chain with insufficient innovation. The general economic develop did not get over extensive development model with low quality and efficiency. The social and economic development was faced with systematic and mechanistic obstacles. Tasks of further reform in difficult areas were still heavy. In several years ahead, the tasks of solving conflicts and dealing with problems left over by history would be arduous."[277]

In recent years, Zhuhai "maintained a rapid development in its economic development, as well as the economic quality." The effect of implementing the strategy of "relying on industry to develop the city" was obvious. Between 2004 and 2006, the gross industrial outputs realized the span from 100 billion RMB to 200 billion RMB. The tertiary industry steadily developed. Tourism, real estate, vehicle, communication, culture, and education formed the consumption hot spots.[278]

In 2007, Zhuhai's industrial development showed the feature of coordinative and rapid development: "the pillar industries contributed a lot, the industrialization of industrial economy and industrial clusters' development was enhanced. Enterprises in major economic type maintained relative rapid growth, the state holding enterprises, corporate enterprises, and enterprises invested by foreigners or investors from Hong Kong, Macao and Taiwan witnessed the quickest growth." "The tendency of heavy industry-focused became obvious, with an increase of its proportion. Industrial economy of all districts flourished, the functional zone and industrial parks became important growth points for industrial economy. Industrial development of high-tech industries sped up, with a raise of its proportion. Enterprises over 100 million output value per a year continued to expand, and became the main force of industrial growth. The efficiency and quality of the industrial economy maintained a relatively high level, and the overall efficiency index for industrial

277 Wang Shunsheng, *Report on the Work of Zhuhai Municipal Government*, 2006.

278 Zhong Shijian, *Report on the Work of Zhuhai Municipal Government*, 2007.

enterprises broke a new record."[279]

In 2008, the global financial crisis greatly struck Zhuhai. Its economy dropped sharply and productive difficulties of enterprises appeared out of nowhere due to their high degree of trade dependence on international market. However, a steady growth was maintained, with an increase of 8.95% in its GDP.[280] Sustainable growth of the port economy encouraged the government to put forward the petrochemical industry-focused strategy of "depending on the port economy to build up the city for the first time."[281]

In 2009, the impacts of the global financial crisis to Zhuhai's economy manifested. According to Zhuhai's statistical bulletin of 2009, its GDP only increased by 6.6%. The main problems of its economy was that "structural conflicts of economic growth was still a outstanding issue, the investment structure was unreasonable, the proportion of private economy remained low, the capability of innovation was not strong, and enterprises had relative weak ability to withstand risks confronting with financial crisis."[282]

In recent years, great events that may influence the future of Zhuhai came one after another: (1) Guangdong Province made great efforts to promote the upgrading of the industrial structure and industrial migration in Pearl River Delta area, which brought not only difficulties to the realization of basic industrialization, but also opportunities to the development of heavy chemical industry. (2) In January 2009, the State Council enacted the "Outline for the Reform and Development of the Pearl River Delta (2008~2020)", which granted Guangdong a better policy. (3) After many years' feasibility studies and changes, the gigantic Hong Kong and Macao - Zhuhai Bridge was launched at the end of 2009 (see more detail in Chapter Four). (4) Untapped Hengqin Island (next to Macao), which had been planned for nearly 20 years, was picked out to conduct secret programming by Wen Jiabao in 2005. Hengqin Island development project finally appeared in 2009. The State Council authorized Macao to set up new Macao University in the island and excise administrative management in the area. The overall development plan of Hengqin upgraded Hengqin to be the third national new development area, following Shanghai Pudong, Tianjin Binhai development area. This special region of SEZ was taken as a demonstration

279 Zhuhai Statistic Bureau, The Pillar Sectors hold up Zhuhai's industry, http://www.stats-zh.gov.cn/o_tjfx/ofx_ztfx/200802/20080203038l8.htm,2008.

280 Zhuhai Statistic Bureau, Investigation Team of State Statistic Bureau in Zhuhai, Statistic Bulletin of National Economy and Social Development of Zhuhai in 2008, 18th, March, 2009; Zhuhai Statistic Bureau, Statistical Yearbook of Zhuhai (2009), China National Statistical Publishing House, 2009.

281 Zhong Shijian, *Report on the Work of Zhuhai Municipal Government*, 2008.

282 Zhuhai Statistic Bureau, Investigation Team of State Statistic Bureau in Zhuhai, Statistic Bulletin of National Economy and Social Development of Zhuhai in 2008, 19th, March, 2009

region of exploring new cooperative mode between Guangdong, Hong Kong and Macao under the policy of "one country, two systems." It became another important experimental field of the second round of "Early and Pilot Implementation" reforms since 1992, and new platform for industrial upgrading of Zhuhai and west bank of the Pearl River. Hengqin Island became the hottest place in the whole country, for a time, and it was even compared to Shekou development zone (Shenzhen Province) thirty years ago. However, its opening up did not make many substantial progresses. Without intrinsic factors and external conditions, it's hard to make a radical change simply relying on a relatively weak Macao or institutional innovation. The "Land Lease" of Hengqin indeed means a lot to the political institutional innovation of a more prosperous and confident China.

In 2009, Zhuhai's local GDP reached 103.769 billion yuan. The three industries contributed for 1.4%, 18.2% and 80.4% to the economic growth, and their proportion was changed to 2.8, 51.7, 45.5. The added value of private economy reached 26.172 billion yuan, with an increase of 10.2%, sharing 25.2% of the GDP. The GDP per capita reached 69.8 thousand yuan, about 10,218 USD at average rate."[283] On the whole, Zhuhai's current economic development is on a bright road with challenges and opportunities.

Zhuhai Special Economic Zone has passed 30 years. It achieved great and profound changes in its economy and society. The main achievements are as follows:

(1) The achievements of reform and opening up are impressive and its economy and society developed rapidly (see Figure 2-3-1). According to the latest comparable statistical data, the GDP of 2008 increased 225.7 times that of 1979. The primary industry, secondary industry and tertiary industry increase 69.3, 571.2, 305.2 times respectively. GDP per capita only increased 55.5 times. The ratio of the three industries upgraded from 38.6: 30.6: 30.8 to 2.9: 54.7: 42.4.[284] The economic scale was greatly expanded with an improved structure. Its economic output values ranked 8th among the nine cities of Pearl River Delta, while the GDP per capita ranked fourth, a slightly decrease than that of previous several years, but obvious improvement than that of ten years before.

(2) Foreign economic ties developed rapidly, especially with Hong Kong and Macao.

(3) The infrastructure became quiet well and developed quickly.

(4) People's living conditions greatly improved with a good living environment, as well as social takings.

---

283 Zhuhai Statistic Bureau, Investigation Team of State Statistic Bureau in Zhuhai, Statistic Bulletin of National Economy and Social Development of Zhuhai in 2008, 19th, March, 2009

284 Zhuhai Statistic Bureau, Statistical Yearbook of Zhuhai (2009), China National Statistical Publishing House, 2009. P. 106.

Many inevitable problems or issues that could have been abated appeared in its development:

(1) Vigor of reform and opening up was often inadequate. The emancipation of the mind was insufficient. Defectiveness existed in institutional innovation. The system was not perfect, negative influences of human factors were relatively great.

(2) Incomplete knowledge of industrialization, swinging development direction, inadequate industrial foundation, small economic aggregate, and industrial structure at low level.

(3) The construction of infrastructure was relatively precocious, bringing big obstacles to economic development.

Zhuhai always emphasized the harmonious development of society and economy. There would be many important challenges and opportunities in its future development. Specific discussions will be made in next chapters.

2.4 Exploration on Harmonious Development of Social Economy in Zhuhai

Zhuhai Special Economic Zone has experienced twists and turns in four stages of economic development, which closely related to, not only the objective conditions of Zhuhai, but also its social goals and development concepts. In order to promote high-reaching economic development, Zhuhai has implemented, for a long period of time, the exceeding development. When improving the economy, Zhuhai attached great importance to environment construction on the pursuit of the harmonious development between man and nature. The road towards economy and social harmony and scientific development may be filled with difficulties and setbacks, Zhuhai should thus should highly avoided blindness in seeking high speed and goals in development.[285]

2.4.1 Exceeding Development in Infrastructure

Modern and open economy should be based on the applicable transportation facilities. As been discussed earlier, Zhuhai, was in a poor transportation condition when its administrative area was set. "Zhuhai is located on the crossing area of the south bank of the Pearl River Delta and the mouth of Xijiang River's branches. Land transportation is

285 Reference to "16 Years-During Liang Guangda's Tenure of Office" by Ruqing,(China's Economy Press,2001), essays in relevant academic journals on construction of Zhuhai, and official websites, i.e. http://www.zhzgj.gov.cn

blocked by the river. The original roads are at a low grade, with thin density and a lot of crossings. Transportation in Zhuhai is extremely backward. The most important outbound road of Guangzhou-Zhuhai Highway was at the third or fourth level connecting several ferries. The connection with outside world was extremely inconvenient."[286]

At an increasingly high demand on infrastructures, Zhuhai's successive leaders attached great importance to infrastructure development. Especially after the mid-1980s, one wave of large-scale infrastructure construction came after another. In 1988, Zhuhai set the slogan of "great port, great industry, great development and great prosperity." The so-called "Destiny Project," due to the advanced awareness of the optimistic judgment on Zhuhai's status, was on a strong planning of developing ports, airports, railways, highways and other infrastructures so as to model Zhuhai as a transport hub by land, sea, and air.[287] In 20 years, most of the temptations have caused much controversy and showed some of the negative effects caused by exceeding development.

During the sixth–"Five-Year Plan" period, "two important sea and river ports, the Jiuzhou Port and Qianshan Port, became important channels for outbound transportation. In highway construction, Zhuhai has completed the construction and improvement of the main roads in the city as well as Zhuhai Highway and some major bridges. All highways in Zhuhai met the construction standard of the first level."[288] These projects were mostly developed on the requirement of economic development and played a very beneficial supporting role.

In 1991, it started to construct Gaolan Port, the large-scaled deep-water port in southernmost China. The construction of deep-water port cost large sums of money, but with slow efficiency and low utilization. Until the 21st century, a major turning point turned out in Gaolan Port. It became the exclusive hub port in the Pearl River Delta. Economic zones near Gaolan Port have gradually become a leading role and crucial bases for the development of heavy industry. "Within the area, there were 10 wharfs with the capacity of over 10,000 tons and a series of wharfs under 10,000 tons of capacity, 14 under construction, the largest of which was a 30-ton crude oil dock."[289] Gaolan Port Economic Zone showed such strong development momentum in recent years that the

286 Edited by Party History Research Center of CPC Zhuhai Municiple Committee, "Establishment and Development of China's SEZ-Volume of Zhuhai", Chinese Communist Party History Press, 1996, p33

287 Reference to "16 Years-During Liang Guangda's Tenure of Office" by Ruqing, China's Economy Press, 2001, p194

288 Edited by Party History Research Center of CPC Zhuhai Municiple Committee, "Establishment and Development of China's SEZ-Volume of Zhuhai", Chinese Communist Party History Press, 1996, p34

289 Advertising materials: *Zhuhai Gaolan Port Economic Zone*, 2007, p9

government stated for the first time, in 2008, the strategy of "building up the city by constructing the port"[290] to develop the heavy chemical industry, which has been more realistic than the exceeding plan of developing infrastructure, but still needed to proceed cautiously. Neither the large-scale construction of the railway nor the expansions of the harbor were necessarily in good implementation.

The most controversial point lied in the construction of the Zhuhai airport. The first flight took off on June 30, 1995 from Zhuhai airport, which was designed to hold craft landing of 100,000 times, with the passenger throughput of 12 million people and annual cargo throughput of 600,000 tons. But development is not satisfactory. The actual number of cargo and passenger in 2003 were 10.7 thousand tons and 605,000 people. Zhuhai airport had been equipped with the world's leading navigation systems, landing systems, air traffic control systems, emergency handling systems and other modern facilities. It positioned itself as the modern air traffic hub of western Pearl River Delta region towards outside world. But its most important function lied in its role of the holding place for China International Aviation and Aerospace Exposition, which was held every other year since 1998.

In such a low utilization and huge debt, Zhuhai airport became a major burden on economic development in Zhuhai, triggering a wide long-lasting debate (Figure 2-4-1). "Zhuhai airport was at the highest level in domestic and international class airport, the investment, some said, was to be 8 billion yuan, some said 12 billion yuan. The amount of the investment was staggering, the exact number was seen as an enigma. A public uproar was aroused when the debt of 1.7 billion yuan was revealed. Investment in Zhuhai airport, which regarded as the government action, was said to have three decision-making errors."[291] Fortunately, in August 2005, the Hong Kong airport, after a long negotiation, finally took over the Zhuhai Airport, which made its revival possible.

On December 16, 2000, the Guangzhou branch of China's Xinhua News Agency published an article named "No Longer Seeing Itself as a Big City." It said that the development in Zhuhai's western areas, which was once very popular, has been inactive for many years. It aroused a thoughtful insight to see through the strand of the 20 billion construction funds on Lingdingyang Bridge project, connecting four cities on the west and east banks on the Pearl River, and also the low utilization of the Zhuhai Airport.

290 Zhong Shijian: *Zhuhai Municipal Government Report*, 2008

291 He Xuelin: *To See Decision-making Failure Through Zhuhai Airport Event*, Decision-making Consultation, October, 2001, p24-25

Figure 2-4-1 Zhuhai Airport

Source: Google Earth http://www.williamlong.info/google/archives/316.html, April 20, 2007

By the end of 2009, Zhuhai-Hong Kong -Macao Bridge, which went through nearly 30 years of ups and downs, finally began construction. Major publicities described the huge benefits from its future, such as "to bring new pattern of economic interaction and new impetus to the three regions' development, to reduce the worried concern on geographic limitations of the Hong Kong, which was thought to be marginalized in the rapid development of mainland China." Zhuhai also relied on its location to eliminate the marginalization of its own.[292] However, these benefits may not be able to achieve while the risk has long been under cautions:

> However, soon after the implementation of reform and opening up in the mainland, Hong Kong businessman Wu Yingxiang offered advice in 1983 to construct the Lingdingyang Bridge, linking Hong Kong and Zhuhai. The bridge can bring huge opportunities for development on an occasion when many enterprises in the mainland are waiting to be restored. However, the idea could only be set by the Central Government after years of rivals of multiple groups. Dragged on for twenty-five years, major obstacles were finally removed away, and the "Y-shaped" design of the formation of the three cities

292 Editorial: *Say No to Turing Zhuhai-Hong Kong -Macao Bridge into White Elephant*, HK Sing Tao News, Feb. 29th, 2008

of Hong Kong, Zhuhai and Macaw would be in shape in a few years. During this period of time, the rapid development of Guangdong Province, especially Shenzhen, lessened the logistics reliance on Hong Kong. When the "Double-Y" plan to connect Shenzhen was voted down, it was conceived to build a bridge to connect Shenzhen and Zhongshan for logistics needs in the western part of Guangdong Province. Thus the cost of building the bridge to connect Hong Kong, Zhuhai and Macaw soared to over 30 billion RMB. People doubled the willingness of drivers to pay several hundred yuan per trip across the bridge which, if not, could turn the bridge into a big white elephant.[293]

The construction of advanced infrastructures in Zhuhai had close relations to the high-expected economy and strategic priority in the Pearl River region and further areas (Figure 2-4-2). By 2004, Zhuhai was still expected to "become regional center of the Pearl River Delta and further develop into one pole of the three metropolitan poles, as the Macao-Zhuhai, Guangzhou-Foshan, and Hong Kong-Shenzhen metropolitan circles."[294] Later, Guangdong Province got rid of the proposal while Zhuhai made continuous efforts to make it real. Even though the expectation itself was beyond Zhuhai's capability, the future it drew for the city had probably more good than harm. In 2009, the State Council published *Reform and Development Plan for the Pearl River Delta (2008~2020)* for turning

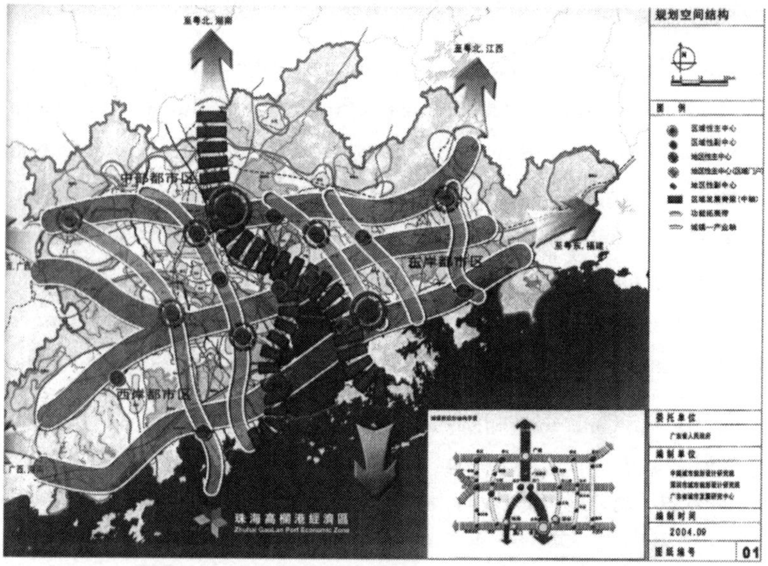

Figure 2-4-2 Zhuhai's Regional Role in the Plan

Source: Investment promotional material: ***Zhuhai Gaolan Port Economic Zone***, 2007, P4

293 Editorial: *Say No to Turing Zhuhai-Hong Kong -Macao Bridge into White Elephant*, Feb, 29th, 2008

294 http://www.southcn.com/NEWS/dishi/zhuhai/ttxw/200404080390.htm

Zhuhai into the core city of the west bank of Zhujiang River, a transportation hub and a modern regional city. The current strength of Zhuhai was weaker than Zhongshan and Jiangmen. It was crucial to distinguish short-term from long-term plans, and practical plan from unpractical ones.

2.4.2 Harmonious Development of Human and Environment

From the initial period of setting up the city, Zhuhai has strived to develop itself into a modern coastal garden city. Nowadays, it is a rare city exposed to the modern economy, while maintaining good ecological environment.

Zhuhai has long explored the long-term harmonious development of economy and environment. Sometimes, it was worthy to make economic sacrifices for the noble ideal. Zhuhai "stipulated urban environmental protection planning and urban landscape planning which provides' Eight Forbidden,' for instance, it is not allowed to build projects with high chimneys or any other pollutants. The exceeding environment protection, to a certain degree, affected the pace of development in Zhuhai because of setting threshold to many traditional projects."[295] What has been paid finally obtained high return." Zhuhai scored remarkable achievements in ecological environment construction. In 1998, it won "International Award For Best Practices to Improve the Environment" by the UN, and in 2000, was nominated by the State Environmental Protection Administration as a "National Ecological Demonstration Area," being one of the most comfortable cities for living."[296]

Zhuhai indeed took a step, or even a few steps, ahead in the construction of ecological city. But it also led to the slow-down in the city's industrialization process as well as the lack of stamina in lasting urban development. In recent years, some phenomena, such as the economic slump, market downturn and staff turnover, appeared in the implementation of the policy of controlling environment and population development, waiting for the exploration and adjustment in the coordination of scientific concept of economic and social development.

Compared with other areas, Zhuhai put a greater emphasis on social harmony and spirit in the long-term development. It often stressed the coordination of material with spiritual development, and actively carried out united front work, which laid a long-term

---

295 Chen Hongquan, Zhong Jian: *Historical Retrospect, Achievements and Experience of Reforms and Opening-up In Zhuhai, 2008 China's Economic Zone Forum: Symposiums Commemorating the 30th Anniversary of Reform and Opening up*, 2008

296 Ma Yuedong, Yan Xiaopei: *Rational Thinking On the Zhuhai's Development In the 20 Years of Reform and Opening-up, Economic Geography, 2004, No.1, p67-71, p90*

preparation for the smooth return of Macao. In 1999, Zhuhai successfully made its contribution in the return of Macao. "On December 20, 200,000 cadres and the masses took to the streets, orderly arranging in 8,800 meters of the queue, bidding a warm farewell to The PLA Macao Garrison stationed in Macao to fulfill defense task"[297] (Figure 2-4-3). Years of development of Zhuhai SEZ won favorable impressions from the Macao compatriots on the mainland, as well as a lot of the goodwill from the international community. It has completed successfully the political mission endowed upon Zhuhai.

Figure 2-4-3 1999 Macao people bidding farewell to Macao troops in Zhuhai

Source: Archives of Zhuhai City Code: Events OF Zhuhai IN 20 Years (1979~1999), Zhuhai City Archives, 2000, color pages p15

2.4.3 Future of Zhuhai SEZ: Developing Under Crisis and Opportunity

Through the ancient and modern times, to the tortuous development of the SEZ,

---

297 Compiled by the Communist Party History Research Center: *Spiritual Civilization Construction of China's SEZ(Volume of Zhuhai)*, Party History Press, 2001, p327

Zhuhai had unique features in its development process. It caused the people of Zhihai to think deeply. These evaluations were diversified. Different parties would have different views on the future of Zhuhai. Zhuhai Municipal Government thought that:

> Zhuhai had two favorable conditions to achieve scientific development. First, the SEZ brand. Zhuhai Special Economic Zone as the "experimental field" of reform and opening-up, it formed a dynamic innovation system, which embodied the concept of "bold vision and courage, daring to try and be pioneers," to establish the image of Zhuhai. Second, it had great geographical advantages. Near to Macau, facing the Pacific Ocean, backed by the Pearl River Delta, connecting the western Guangdong with the southwest, Zhuhai took the best of the location. Third, it had great environment advantages. Zhuhai had beautiful natural scenery and city style, suitable for living. Fourth, the area had development space superiority. Zhuhai had abundant resources such as seaports, airports, ports, coastline, islands, fresh water and so on. Compared with the increasing scarcity of land resources in the Pearl River Delta region, Zhuhai provided the crucial space for a new round of development. Zhihai was duty-bound to properly handle the relationship between economy and environment, to achieve win-win in economic development and environment protection, and to break a new path to scientific development. Seizing the opportunity and playing to its strengths, Zhuhai was fully able to meet the high expectations. [298]

However, many people had many different of worries concerning Zhuhai. For example, weak economic basis in Zhuhai, industrialization remaining to be completed, significantly lagging behind to other cities in the Pearl River Delta, weak previous leading role in high-tech industry, which caused worry on the future prosperity of the software industry. Restraints also appeared in relations between economic goals and environmental ones. Zhuhai was shrouded in the shadow of the neighboring Shenzhen with dominant advantages. Government sank into deep pessimism and deficient in aggressive courage. Zhuhai greatly benefited from the original preferential policies, but in recent years, these privileges were gradually disappearing. In 2008, after tax integration, "the last preferential policies will be canceled, no longer pinning hope on preferential tax policies." Some enterprises settled in Shenzhen valued the effect of the industrial gathering. "Its urban competitiveness, including environmental, industrial gathering, location advantage, resources, government efficiency and other aspects, were still attractive to enterprises."[299] In these aspects, Zhuhai may have more newly aroused disadvantages than previous

---

298 http://www.zhuhai.gov.cn/xxfw/zhdt/zwyw/200803/t20080311_41254.html

299 Zhang Yuanyuan: Tax Integration: How to recreate advantages in Shenzhen, Securities Times, copied on http://finance.jrj.com.cn/news/2007-03-24/000002088959.html

advantages. Zhuhai was bound to deeply think on how to create new advantages.

On the development of infrastructure, some agreed with the government to adhere to the ideals of high quality, while others deplored the exceeding development of the past and held uncertainty about the future. Several issues were proposed by a CPPCC member: (1) Zhuhai did not find its own role, instead letting people wait for hope, but wait in disappointment; (2) We should have thorough thinking on the advantages and disadvantages over Zhuhai, not to make it look like a "tailor's shop," checking in changing; (3) The existence of populations division, the division between newcomers and the natives, etc. will severely affect the harmonious development of Zhuhai; (4) The work-style of government needed to be improved by following the principle of people-oriented, improving the quality of civil servants, and fully enhancing the initiative of civil servants."[300]

Zhuhai should learn lessons from the past, being pragmatic and gaining ease in city construction. "According to a sample survey of some investors in Zhuhai, organized by South China Small And Medium-sized Enterprises Union, 98% of the investors in the past two years no longer complained about the hard investment environment in Zhuhai, and began to worry more about the soft environment, particularly administrative intervention system by the government."[301] Many CPPCC members had similar views.

For quite a long time, the institutional friction was reducing Zhuhai's energy. System innovation could not adapt to the intensity of competition. The courage in self-reform, innovation and taking the lead were reduced. In terms of administrative management system, Zhuhai was following suit of some advanced cities instead of adopting self-innovation. In the administrative system reform, an overall framework was missing, and objectives and specific plans were out of reach. Without a strong organization to organize and implement, deep-seated reform was merely a remote legend. Therefore, economic development and potential to further development were in restraint, which lead to Zhuhai miss many development opportunities. With the disappearance of preferential policies for SEZ, and the weakening of geographical advantage, previous advantages Zhuhai once owned were gradually disappearing. The impression that Zhuhai SEZ gave was not that "special" any longer.[302]

Zhuhai administrative reform in the SAR may be a choice for the city to recreate a new advantage while fading from the specialty. It was confronted with certain resistant force and depended on the principles and paces of the Central Government.

---

300 Edited by Executive Office of Zhuhai CPPCC: *Compilation of The Second Meeting of The Sixth Plenary Session Zhuhai CPPCC, Executive Office of Zhuhai CPPCC*, 2005, p140

301 Edited by Executive Office of Zhuhai CPPCC: *Collections of CPPCC Members' Proposals* (Feb. 1999—Feb. 2004), Executive Office of Zhuhai CPPCC, 2004, p121

302 Zhuhai Committee of the Jiu San Society: *Suggestions on Strengthening Administrative Management System Innovation*, Zhuhai Committee of the Jiu San Society,2006

In the recent two years, several big events occurred, especially in the conditions of the Zhuhai SEZ development: the State Council promulgated the "Plan for Reform and Development in the Pearl River Delta Area (2008~2020)," which endowed Guangdong Province and Zhuhai the opportunity to restart. It was still unknown whether the State Council believed "General Development Plan for Hengqin" could lead to a profound Zhuhai-Macao cooperation. The construction of Zhuhai-Hong Kong-Macau Bridge expanded the possibility for the economic development of Zhuhai. Government and academia in recent years have increasingly attached importance to Zhuhai's living environment and hoped that it developed various entertainment industries, playing the backyard role of Macao's Casino industry and even develop various business, convention, tourism and other service industries as a competitor of its neighboring Macao. In dealing with the relationship with Macao and fostering strengths, Zhuhai needed to be cautious with how to deal with the major issues of the corruption factors showing the trend of steep rise in cultural and spiritual aspects.

It remained to be unknown in many aspects of Zhuhai's future, which was being affected by many aspects. It seemed to repeat its history. Glory and tranquility were difficult to remain unchanged. The ideal may not always be able to reconcile with reality. Risks and opportunities coexisted in the future. Zhuhai would continue to develop. Whether it could hit the road to realize fast, good and harmonious development, it depended not only on its own spirit and courage to explore, but also on the opportunity endowed by changing internal and external environment.

3 History of Shantou Special Economic Zone: the Rise of Shantou, the Pearl of East Guangdong

Known as "The Gateway Through the Dawang Mountain and the Fortress of South China," Shantou set off to become a commercial port in the early 1960s, and gradually became one of the most important commercial cities in southern Guangdong. However, lasting prosperity was not easily attained, but the Shantou people's strong existence of business tradition brought forth its modernization. Before the reform and opening-up, Shantou was a place where there were "rough roads, no electricity or telephone." On one winter day in early 1981, the first generation of the SEZ citizens, with a gust of the infinite pioneering passion and courage, started the arduous construction work of the SEZ using shabby, primitive tools. In the 30 years since then, Shantou has made a qualitative change from a remote and backward town into an all-embracing modern coastal city.

In the initial period when human and financial resources were extremely scarce, the constructers of SEZ who carried forward the aggressive spirit completed the infrastructure construction in the export-processing zone in very short time. The SEZ building entered a rapid development stage, thus forcing the SEZ construction process to enter into a rapid development stage on the basis of such a solid developmental foundation. Through two adjustments, the scope of the SEZ extended from 1.6 square kilometers of Longhu area to the whole Shantou city, with a total area of 234 square kilometers. Hardware and software facilities have been greatly improved. Integrated economic systems have been established. The positive outlook of the city and its citizens strengthened. Economic and social progress has been made in all aspects of development. However, some of the potential crisis was brewing as the SEZ stepped into steady development. In the middle of 1990s, unprecedented economic development difficulties struck Shantou. The Southeast Asian financial crisis severely hit Shantou, which depended greatly on the import and export trade. In addition, the deterioration of social credit and the explosion of the local financial crisis greatly hampered the development of social productivity. When Shantou faced these setbacks, the municipal government unveiled the "Two Rectification." Through one round of the consolidation and governance of market and social order, Shantou took the lead to establish a formal credit system, and realized the economic recovery in 2002. In 2006, the East Guangdong Conference was held in Shantou, which precluded the second development wave of local economy. Provincial government issued a series of policies to foster and promote the development of east Guangdong, proposing an overall development of "three years to lay the foundation, five years to make major changes, and ten years to realize great development." Through these efforts, in 2008, Shantou's economic growthexceeded the provincial average for the first time since 1999. The goal of the first stage of using the "three years to lay the foundation" plan had been realized. Hard-working and enterprising local people plunged into the construction of Shantou to realize "great change and great development" in the new historical period, as when originally constructing the SEZ.

Practices of the previous 30 years proved the importance of emancipation of the mind and the innovation of ideas. Construction must be based on actual conditions, obeying economic law, and giving full play to regional advantages. However, the economic decline in the late 20th century caused further thinking: With the full commencement of the construction in market economic system, an overall change was made in the formal system, while in the informal system, the core values adapting to the market economy were still missing, and the social reputation mechanism to meet the requirement market economy remained to be formed.

Although bringing short-term prosperity to the regional economy, s variety of speculative and abnormal profit-making behaviors caused long-term "system cost" to the Chaozhou-Shantou area's economic development, which may take a long time to compensate, and make social and economic decline inevitable. Shantou's rocky economic development illustrated that, in the economic transformation period, in order to realize institutional balance and obtain the benefits of the new system, not only was a formal system for market economy establishment and improvement inevitable, but also depended on effective changes of informal system adapting to the modern market economic system.

3.1 Shantou Before the Establishment of SEZ

Shantou once had unique cultural and historical traditions and was once "a commercial port with 100 years of history and trading with many countries." However, during the 12 years of the Japanese invasion and frequent civil wars, Shantou's economy and livelihood of the people kept worsening. After the liberation, Shantou's economy recovered for a while, but under the influence of the "leftist" ideology, economic development was very slow, and the people were left living in extreme poverty.

3.1.1 Economic Development in Modern Shantou

3.1.1.1 The Opening of Shantou as a Commercial Port

As a famous port city, the trading tradition has existed in Shantou for a long time. As early as the 1800s, there have been merchant boats anchoring in the Laoma Palace area. After 1821, due to frequent trading, some merchants ran businesses, such as selling rice, firewood, medicinal herbs, repairing ship, and so on. In 1854, Fujian merchants and local businessmen established "Zhongshan Guildhall" as the trading market for five businesses of shipping, medicine, food, matches, and collecting and the Shantou market began to take shape. Currently, the operating activities have flourished and various traders do trade centered in Shanhai, active in the Chaoshan Plain, shuttled in ports such as the Laiwu, Dahao, Haimen, and Shenquan and other ports across Asia, handling a large quantity of materials.[303]

At the same time, through maritime trade, foreigners began to realize the unique business value of Shantou. Community theorist Friedrich Engels thought Shantou was "the only city with a little business value" besides Shanghai, Guangzhou and other three ports.[304] During the reign of Jiaqing in the Qing Dynasty, foreign vessels already shuttled back and forth around Nan'ao Island in the Chaozhou-Shantou area for mooring purpose as well as landing on the island. In the early 1840s, foreign businessmen built houses, bridges and roads on the island. Illegal trafficking of opium and slaves, mainly from Asian countries, emerged during this period and developed rapidly during the two Opium Wars. The Chaoshan area, by virtue of favorable harbor conditions, a large population, good market and the tradition of engaging in maritime trade, aroused the interests of businessmen from the United States and Britain.[305]

Based on the information mentioned above, the British, French and Americans raised the aggressive requirement to the Qing government to open up trading ports along the Chaozhou-Shantou area in the Second Opium War, which was the antecedent of modern inception in Shantou. At first, their further requirement of providing additional ports was refused by the Qing government; however, at the threat of military escalation, the Qing government gradually softened its attitude. Before the Anglo-French invasion force's attack

---

303 Chen Pian: *History of Shantou SEZ*, referring to *History of China's SEZ*, Guangdong Economy Press, 2001, p250

304 Engels: *Russian's Success in Fareast*, referring to *Collections of K. Marx and F. Engels*, edited by Compilation and Translation Bureau of the CPC Central Committee, People's Press, 1972, Second Volume, p38

305 Yao Xianhao: *Documents of China's Foreign Trade in Modern China*, Volume One, Zhonghua Book Company, Edition of 1962, p454-456

on Dagu forts, the Qing government agreed to "open two additional trading ports in Fujian and Guangdong provinces."[306] As Dagu forts fell to occupation of the Anglo-French invasion force, and the troops advancing at the gate of Tianjin brought the Qing government to its knees. The "Treaty of Tianjin" was signed with the United States, Britain and France representatives on June 18th, 26th, and 27th 1858, respectively. Provisions on opening two additional trading ports were also included in the three Treaties.

On December 9th of the ninth year since Emperor Xianfeng took throne in Qing Dynasty (which was January 1, 1860 in accordance with the A D Chronology), Chaozhou was opened to the U.S. as trading port as scheduled. The new port was opened in Shantou (Shantou was known as a coastal village under Chenghai County at that time). The specific trading fair was located in Shantou as well (later generally referred to as "Chaohaiguan"), which symbolized the beginning of the inception of Shantou opening as a port.[307]

Figure 3-1-1 Chaohaiguang in 1930

Resources: History of Shantou

3.1.1.2 Development of National Economy in Shantou Area

After World War I, the emersion of economic recovery of Western countries brought the opportunity for national economic development in the Chaozhou-Shantou area. From the 1920s to 1930s, with great improvements in transportation and communications conditions, the development of modern industry and the increasing investment from overseas Chinese, Shantou reached its peak in commercial trading development. Early commercial streets included Xingjie Street, Shunchang Street and gradually to Zhenbang Street, Huai'an Street, Yi'an Street, and expanding to the Pinglu area. There were also commercial districts with

306 China History Association: *China's Modern History Documents: The Second Opium War*, Shanhai People's Press, 1978, p298

307 Chen Pian: *History of Shantou SEZ*, referring to *History of China's SEZ*, Guangdong Economy Press, 2001, p250

distinctive features: the bustling commercial center of Zhenbang with foreign goods, silk and cloth as its main business; the teahouses and restaurants on Huai'an Street; Yi'an Street for furniture; Zhiping Road as the only way leading to the wharf, occupied by many hostels. In the initial period, commercial wholesales and retail outlets were managed together, and later, with business prosperity, the gradually separated into "the wholesalers" (engaged in the wholesale and distribution), "middle businessmen" (small-scale wholesale for retailing) and "retailers" (detailing with retails), formulating a large business network. The Oriental Jews of the area said the Shantou Chaozhou merchants made remarkable contributions to the economic prosperity of the early Shantou. In 1932, Chinese Indonesians (who were born in Mei County) Li Bohuan, Li Yaozog, Li Yuanbo, Li Jingbo jointly built a 7-story building, the tallest building in the city at that time. In the building, the first and second floor was occupied by the Nansheng Company (Chaozhou's most famous department store), the third and fourth floor was the central restaurant, and the Central Hotel occupied the fifth to the seventh floors. Subsequently, a number of clothing stores, gold shops, restaurants and teahouses were gathered around the small park, making it the city's main shopping center. Apart from the park business network, two major commercial networks "Si'an-Bangyong" network (Yong'an, Yonghe, Yongtai, Yongxing and Shengping Streets) were also formed in the city also formed the "Four-Ann Zhenbang" (Wing, Yonghe, Wing Tai, Wing Hing Street and Shing Ping Street). In 1933, the city had 3,441 business houses with total trading volume of about 692.2 million yuan, ranking seventh only after Shanghai, Tianjin, Dalian, Hankou, Jiaozhou, and Guangzhou. In 1935, the number of ships arriving in Shantou Port totaled 4,531, showing a busy "commercial port of 100 years of history and having trade with many countries."

In 1937, the breakout of the Marco Polo Bridge Incident brought negative influence on the business activities in Shantou, leading to the deterioration in economic conditions. When the Japanese occupied Shantou, the control of the business and trade fell into the hands of Japan, so many businesses moved, and almost all shops shut down. The market was in a complete depression. Succumbing to the Japanese, some shops re-opened, But being exploited by the Japanese authorities and some Japanese firms, the future of these businesses was bleak. Abnormal development existed in opium dens, casinos, pawn shops, liquor houses and so on. Japanese blockade of the roads led to scarcity in daily supplies and high food prices. Unscrupulous merchants hoarded supplies and profiteered; so many people lived in an extremely tragic situation. During this time, Shantou's economy was seriously damaged, and maritime transportation ran aground. Shantou became a dead port and entered the darkest chapter in its history.

Figure 3-1-2 former site of Nansheng Company located in the park

Resources: http://www.0754map.com/home/Article.aspx?c=4bbdcec2-067c-492d-a9ca-0cd7b355c89b&g=00473005-7748-4b5b-b99e-2c0b2e263b30

In 1945, after the victory in the anti-Japanese War, due to the sluggish domestic industrial and agricultural production, the damaged transportation routes in the Chaozhou-Shantou area had not been repaired. With the inconvenient traffic conditions and low purchasing power, business's economic recovery was rather difficult. The Civil War launched by the Kuomintang government led to the continuing decline of Shantou's economy. During the 12 war-torn years when Shantou was trapped in internal and external troubles the once bustling commercial port has been completely changed. The entire national economic system has completely collapsed.

3.1.1.3 Economy of Shantou Before the Reform and Opening-Up

After the founding of New China, Shantou's market economy experienced a quick recovery. In 1950, private businesses registered in the city amounted to over 5,000, with about 8,000 vendors. The city's private businesses, which took the majority of market share, accounted for 82.6% of wholesale turnover, and 95.1% of retail turnover. In 1951, the Shantou Municipal Government began to make adjustments, reorganize and transform into the private sectors. A number of new food stores, stationery shops, grocery stores, cloth stores and hotels took the place of old liquor houses, hotels, goldsmiths and foreign goods shop. At the same time, the government has also vigorously supported the development of state-owned businesses. In 1952, the state-owned companies had taken control of the main business of production and consumption in wholesale market, covering most of the food, salt, sugar, cotton, daily necessities and kerosene. In the three-year period of economic recovery, these measures played a positive role in ensuring people's living standard.[308]

However, development was soon destroyed by incorrect polices in the "Great Leap Forward" period. The over-emphasis on public ownership led to inappropriate demands in transferring Shantou from a "consuming city" to "productive city," which greatly limited commercial development. The fast production under the slogan of "large in size and collective in nature" in rural areas did not enhance productivity, letting enable it to "catch up with America." On the contrary, it made the fragile rural economy even worse. From 1960 to 1962, during the economic recovery period, the government began to correct the mistakes made in the "Great Leap" and the market began to improve. By 1964, supplies in the market had been relatively abundant. Unfortunately, it did not last long. In the next 10 years during the "Cultural Revolution," under the influence of "leftist" ideology, control of commercial activities in Shantou reached an incredible degree. Vendors were not allowed into state-owned food vendor stalls and were labeled as "black-hearted traders," "abandoning agriculture for business," and "tail of capitalism." These practices violated economic law, imposing obstacles for urban and rural commodity exchanges, and inhibited the development of the market. The result was that more and more commodities could only be purchased by stamps, more and more people lived in extreme poverty, and the national economy was on the brink of incapacitation.[309]

3.2 The Establishment of Shantou SEZ (1979~1984)

Without the convention of the Third Plenary Session of the 11th Central Committee, without the original plan for "export processing zones," without instructions of "being aggressive to be the pioneer," there would be no SEZ in Shantou.

3.2.1 The Birth of SEZ

3.2.1.1 The Origin of Shantou SEZ

In December 1978, the Communist Party of China held the Third Plenary Session of the 11th Central Committee, which shifted the focus of the party's work to socialist

---

308 Chen Pian: *History of Shantou SEZ*, referring to *History of China's SEZ*, Guangdong Economy Press, p254

309 Chen Liming: *History of Chaozhou-Shantou Area*, Guangdong Tourism Press, p195-196

modernization, and proposed to "conduct reform on the economic management system and method, to positively develop economic development on the basis of self-reliance, equality and mutual benefit with all countries in the world, and to adopt advanced technology and equipment."[310] In the end of January 1979, the party secretary Wu Nansheng of CPC Guangdong Provincial Committee led a working group to Shantou to convey "The Third Plenary Session spirit," and conducted studies and lead discussions with the working group members on how to boost the economy in Shantou. From February 12th to 19th, leaders at three levels were gathered together in Shantou. Wu conveyed the expectations and requirements from the Central Government on Guangdong Province, and from the Guangdong Province on Shantou. All people present at the meeting were greatly inspired, participating in the lively discussion.

Wu spent two months in Shantou, taking part in the large meeting of the Standing Committee of Shantou and meeting of cadres at three levels of county and municipal levels, grasping a deep understanding of the backward situation in Shantou. He began to propose ideas on how to help Shantou solve the current difficulties of dense population, poor resources, and shortage of funds, and to catch up with city at the same level. In the discussion with regional leaders, Wu took ideas from Taiwan, which was in a very similar situation to Shantou, establishing export-processing zones to drive the economic development of the city, the province and even the country. He shared his ideas with leaders in Shantou, to which they immediately agreed.

On February 21, Wu sent a telegram of over 1,000 words to the provincial committee, in which pointed out that:"As one of China's major ports before the liberation, Shantou had the cargo throughput of over six million tons per year, and up to 350 thousand passengers. With such abundant labor, great productive potential, and other favorable conditions for foreign trade and processing, as long as Shantou conscientiously implemented the policies, mobilized internal and external positive factors, at the same time broke the limits, and delegated certain powers to encourage them get into action, it would take three to five years for the region to improve production, living standards and other aspects that had been long time in passive situation."[311]

At the end of February, Comrade Wu again made a proposal at the meeting held by Provincial Standing Committee: To get the approval from Central Government to take the lead in setting up a trial export processing zone in Shantou. Since Shantou was geographical

---

310 *Report on the Third Plenary Session of the Eleventh Central Committee*, December 22nd, 1978

311 Lu Qiu: *How Did SEZ "Fight Its Way Out (Part One)—Interview With Wu Nansheng*, South Daily, April 7th,2008.

far away from the capital city, it had little effect on the overall situation, even if the result was unsuccessful. His idea gained unanimous approval of the members of Standing Committee, who also proposed to not only set a trial zone in Shantou, but also in Zhuhai and Shenzhen, adjacent to Hong Kong and Macao.

In mid-April 1979, the Central Government convened meetings to discuss economic development issues. Xi Zhongxun, the first secretary of the Guangdong Provincial Committee and governor talked about his idea on the reform and opening up of Guangdong Province, and asked the Central Government to endow the opportunity on Guangdong Province so that the province could fully use favorable conditions, delimit a certain area in Shantou to practice independent management as foreign investment destination for overseas Chinese investors from Hong Kong and Macao and foreign investors, and conduct production according to international market needs. It was named the "Trade Cooperation Zone." This proposal immediately won approval from Deng Xiaoping and other central leaders and named it the "SEZ." On July 15, 1979, when the CPC Central Committee and State Council approved the "Report on Exerting Guangdong Favorable Conditions, Expanding Foreign Trade and Accelerating Economic Development," the proposal gained formal confirmation. Guangdong Province was thus authorized to implement special policies and flexible measures in foreign economic activities. It first experimented in the pilot export zones of Shenzhen and Zhuhai and considered the similar trial in Shantou and Xiamen when gaining experiences. On November 23rd, Gu Mu visited Shantou again to further investigate the establishment of the SEZ. In mid-December, at the briefing held in Beijing, Gu Mu comrades raised the requirements of the economic work on Guangdong and Fujian Provinces: make them one step ahead of other provinces in the adjustment of the national economy and reform through the construction of the SEZ, as well as utilizing foreign investment.[312]

On March 30, 1980, a working conference was held in Guangdong and Fujian Provinces, which resolved the following: the SEZ absorbed foreign funds and funds from overseas Chinese for construction; improved infrastructures such as water, electricity, roads, communication, etc.; and engaged in some projects with less investment, quick turnover and great effect. In this meeting, "export SEZ" was changed to "economic SEZ."

On 26 August,1980, the 15th Meeting of the Fifth NPC Standing Committee approved to establish four special economic zones, including Shenzhen, Zhuhai, Shantou, and Xiamen, and published the "Regulations of PRC Special Economic Zone in Guangdong Province,"

---

312 Du Jingguo: Arduous Rising—Ten Pioneering Years in Shantou SEZ, Shantou University Press, 1996, p4-12

marking the birth of the SEZ and special policies going through legal procedures.

3.2.1.2 Preparation Work for Pilot SEZ

On January 22, 1980, the establishment of "Shantou Special Economic Zone Preparation Group" marked the launch of choice of location, exploration, planning, etc. preparatory work. Through careful research arguments, the northwest corner of Longhu Village was decided, with an area of 1.6 square kilometers of sand dunes area as the site for an export-processing zone. It was close to the water plant and power plant, which enabled it easily supply water and electricity. It was also close to the coast, thus easy for the construction of facilitate of ports, terminals and other infrastructure. It was also near to the Shantou urban area, port, and airport, making it easy for economic and trade exchanges. Production and service facilities could also rely on the old urban area. Good geological location and conditions made it conducive for construction. Integrating all the factors, Wu Nansheng, Sectary of the CPC Guangdong Provincial Committee, agreed with other comrades in charge of Shantou on the choice of the area as the location of Shantou SEZ.

From May 27th to June 14th, 1981, the State Council held SEZ working meetings of Guangdong Fujian in Beijing. On July 19th, the CPC Central Committee and the State Council issued "Document [1981] 27," approving and transmitting "Minutes of SEZ Working Meetings of Guangdong Fujian," which noted that SEZs in China were economic zones, not political zones. Its specialty lied in the implementation of national economic policies and special economic management systems. SEZ banks were allowed to use all money deposited as loans. The revenue of Shantou and Xiamen should be turned over to the government and decided on the reduction after the government's audit. In the principle of "adapting to local conditions, laying stress on practical results, and making focused development," Shantou SEZ should give priority to the development of export-oriented processing industries and at the same time develop tourism and other industries", and utilize foreign capital to transform the old enterprise for the purpose of exports, which can enjoy preferential treatment in imports of production materials and paying income tax.

On August 29, 1981 in Guangdong Province, the Shantou Special Economic Zone Office of the Commission was established, which was responsible for the preparatory work of Shantou SEZ. On November 14, it was officially renamed the Management Commission of Shantou Special Economic Zone with Liu Feng as the director, who was also the member of the Standing Committee, and Deputy Secretary of the Standing Committee of the CPC Prefectural Committee of Shantou. This marked the formal construction of

Shantou Special Economic Zone.[313]

Figure 3-2-1 Building of Management Commission of Shantou Special Economic Zone

Resources: http://www.shantou.gov.cn/tpst/index.asp

3.2.2 Longhu Export Processing Zone

The establishment of the Administration Committee of Shantou Special Economic Zone in 1981 marked the official start of construction of Shantou SEZ. In the winter of 1981, the first generation of the SEZ constructors brought simple tools such as hoes, poles, sand shovels with them, wading barefoot through Longhu Gou, a 20-meter-wide, knee-deep ditch, arrived at the barren sand dune and began the arduous construction of the SEZ. At that time, the Central Government issued the policy without capital support. Considering the geographic location, weak infrastructure, financial constraints and other factors, leaders of the SEZ made every effort to rely on Shantou's own accumulation to realize development and expand reproduction through improving investment environment and forming productive capacity. Without blind accumulation, they adopted realistic principles of "developing one area and then constructing the area, putting fund into one industry and then gaining the benefits from the area," which integrated three factors of the speed, scale and benefits of the basic construction.[314]

313 CPC Shantou Party History Research Center: *Establishment and Development of China's SEZ—Volume of Shantou*, Party History Press, 1996, p29-38

314 CPC Shantou Party History Research Center: *Establishment and Development of China's SEZ—Volume of Shantou*, Party History Press, 1996, p38-39

3.2.2.1 Plan for Longhu Export Processing Zone

After the location of Shantou SEZ was confirmed, it was the crucial task of the SEZ Preparation Office to carry out the construction of export processing zone on the 1.6 square kilometers area under the conditions of limited funds and equipment supplies. In order to make practical plans, a number of meetings were held by the Office to collect opinions from all sides. Relevant personnel were sent to Shenzhen and Zhuhai to study the experience of planning and construction the SEZ. By the end of 1981, with the assistance of Beijing Iron and Steel Design and Research Institute, the SEZ Office completed the "Plan for Longhu Export Processing Zone." It focused on the 1.6 square kilometer area as the export processing zone, setting up ports, agricultural areas, and developing tourism industry, to coordinate, service and promote construction of the processing zone.

First of all, the fundamental task, according to the plan, lied in the 1.6 square kilometer area of the Longhu export-processing zone. Considering the situation of limited funds, the area was divided into five sections for industrial development. The development of the first area, an area of 0.2 square kilometers, was launched in March 1982 as the administration area. The development of the second area, an area of 0.24 square kilometers, was launched in 1984. The introduction of the industries in the early period chose labor-intensive light industries with light energy consumption, less pollution, and greater income, and at the same time, to make full use of the old town, set up some parts-assembly processing industries, such as light industry, textiles, electronics, instruments, daily necessities, clothing, food, crafts, etc. In addition, industries of higher technical performance, such as small machinery, precision machinery, metal, machinery and other products were also developed.

The second task was the opening of the 1.7 square kilometer area, covering from the southern tip of Longhu processing zones, extending to the coastline, as the port area. The planned construction in the port area included the construction of terminals for passengers and cargos, warehouses, packaging site, a small amount of processing enterprises and other supporting facilities, for the purpose of transportation and storage of import and export goods. On December 7, 1982, the Shantou SEZ and Ministry of Machine-Building Industry set up the Joint Shipping Co., operating the SEZ passenger transport, cargo transport, warehouses and other related business. At the initial period, one 500-ton-berth wharf was set up, and later two 3000-5000-ton-berth wharves.

The third task was developing the low-lying area of about 10 square kilometers along the coastline into an agricultural development area. The joint company of agricultural development was established to introduce improved crop and advanced technology and fertilizers, grow vegetables, fruits and other crops and develop aquaculture and animal husbandry. Products were mainly for export and supply of the processing zone, port area and the whole Shantou area.

The fourth task was developing tourism in the SEZ. Construction of the tourism industry was essential in order to attract foreign investment. Scenic areas, such as Panshi Scenic Spots, Mayu Island and suburban Dahao Albatron rocks were repaired and constructed. Zhongshan Park was expanded and the new park in the south area was built.

While starting a number of new projects, Shantou took advantage of the solid foundation of the old industries to transform the old enterprises. Thanks to the special policies and preferential conditions, through the introduction of foreign capital, updates were made in factory plants, technical equipment and technology. Twenty enterprises, which were promising businesses and had sound management systems and organizational structures, initially conducted transformation by using foreign funds. The transformation of these old enterprises drove the development of other companies and promoted the economic development and prosperity of Shantou.[315]

3.2.2.2 Infrastructure Construction

Processing zones were located close to the old town, thus the constructors made full use of this geographical advantage, enjoying the use of port, electricity supply, water supply, as well as schools and dormitory for workers, etc., constructing a small environment of its own. On the tranquil, modest land, a number of infrastructure projects were set up:

(A) Road and Bridge

On October 1, 1980, the major road connecting Shantou Special Economic Zone to the urban areas—Jinsha Road—was under construction. It was a concrete structure measuring a length of 2.27 km and 40 meters wide, and was supposed to open to traffic in March the following year. On June 15, 1982, Yingbin Road, the first road, and Yingbin Bridge, the first bridge, leading to Longhu zone was opened to traffic. By the end of that year, roads in Longhu export processing zones had commenced construction.

(B) Water and Electricity

On September 1982, the water pipeline connecting Dongdun Water Plant to Longhu

---

315 CPC Shantou Party History Research Center: *Establishment and Development of China's SEZ—Volume of Shantou*, Party History Press, 1996, p39-43

zone completed construction. At the length of 2 km, with daily water supply of 20 thousand tons, the construction of the pipeline cost 1.01 million yuan. By 1983, the length of the water pipeline built was up to 3.4 km, meeting the water demand in the Longhu area. In 1981, 80 thousand yuan were invested into setting up a 10 KV power supply line (known as Dongte Line) from the 110 KV Dongdun transformer substations as the initial temporary power supply facilities. In May 1985, after Longhu substation was put into operation, Honglianchi substation, Dongdun substation and Longhu substation formed the looped-in power supply mode, which marked the start of the power supply undertaking of the Shantou SEZ.

(C) Postal and Telecommunications Construction

In May 1983, the SEZ invested 85,000 yuan into the construction of 100 communication cable lines connecting Shantou Posts and Telecommunications Building to the Longhu area, which was at the length of 6.2 km, completed in June of the same year. In November 1983, the municipal government issued a requirement of a prompt start in telex business connecting Shantou to Hong Kong, based on the needs of foreign-run enterprises. In 1983, the installation of 48 automatic telephones were set up in the SEZ, and a HJ 905 (200) crossbar automatic telephone exchanger was installed in the Longhu Hotel. In 1984, Public Utility Companies in the completion of telecommunications cable design work, preceded with the preparatory work for program-controlled telephone exchangers.

(D) Sewage Facilities

Shantou sewage system construction was carried out in conjunction with road construction. From 1981 to 1989, two sewage systems were built in SEZ, one for Longhu area, the other for the outer area. Length of rainwater drain connection and sewage drain connection reached 71,310 m and 91,332 m, respectively.

(E) Construction of Factory Buildings

According to the needs of customers, from September 1982, factory buildings were under construction in batches every year. On August 13, 1983, the first factory building was completed, marking the beginning of foreign enterprises opening factories in the SEZ. Three factory buildings were built in 1984. On June 21, 1983, the 400-ton "Shantou" freighter made its virgin voyage to Hong Kong, opening up water routes from the SEZ to Hong Kong. In November 1984, the "Longhu" luxury liner, a joint=operated ship, also arrived in Hong Kong.

Constructions in Longhu area started in March 1982, with a total investment of 4.004 million yuan. In two years, by the end of April 1984, roads, electricity and water supply, etc. infrastructures connecting Longhu to the downtown were completed. The first of the five areas, which covered an area of 0.2 square kilometers, realized basic construction in terms of infrastructure. A total area of 46,000 square meters for factories, hotels, restaurants, shopping malls, dormitories, and clinics was finished. The total length of 11 roads reached 170,000 square meters and a variety of pipelines of more than 15,000 meters.[316]

3.2.2.3 Encouraging Overseas Chinese to Draw Foreign Fund

Shantou is one of the most famous hometowns of overseas Chinese. According to statistics, the total number of overseas Chinese and Chinese in Hong Kong and Macao whose hometown was Chaozhou was over 800 million. These people were scattered in more than 50 countries. Some of the overseas compatriots made extraordinary achievements in the business field. In Southeast Asia, the Philippine Chinese, accounting for 1% of the total population, owned 35% of the country's retail sales. Indonesian Chinese, accounting for 2% of the total population in Indonesia, controlled 70% of the country's capital. Indonesian Chinese controlled 20 of the 25 largest companies. Thailand Chinese, accounting for 10% of the total population, had 90% of the country's industrial and commercial capital. Outside Southeast Asia, overseas Chinese may not cope with the Chinese in Southeast Asia in the financial resources, but among them, there were a large number of talented people in the field of science, technology, culture, education and medicine, having became the backbone of the local community.

Overseas Chinese are eager to see the revitalization and prosperity of the motherland.

In November 1980, Thailand Chia Tai Group set up the first foreign-funded enterprises in the Shantou SEZ.

Hong Kong Cheung Kong Holdings Chairman Li Ka-shing invested 100 million U.S. dollars for the establishment of the Shantou University. He said, "The establishment of Shantou University is the greatest happiness of my life."

On September 6, 1984, Shantou Management Commission engaged 21 famous people in Hong Kong, enlacing Chuang Shih Ping as the first batch of consultants of Shantou Advisory Committee. In early October, the Hong Kong consultants were invited to Shantou. Consultants were concerned with accelerating the construction of Shantou Special Economic Zone and developing its economy. Mr. Chuang Shih Ping said, "It's important to improve the investment environment and conditions in SEZ. We should improve the credibility of the SEZ, so that investors are willing to come." Mr. Ni Shaojie, Justice of the

---

316 CPC Shantou Party History Research Center: *Establishment and Development of China's SEZ—Volume of Shantou*, Party History Press, 1996, p45-47

Peace of Hong Kong Industry, said, "Geographically, Shantou does not have favorable conditions like Shenzhen and Zhuhai, but we have millions of overseas Chinese, Hong Kong and Macao compatriots, who love their home, who would be willing to contribute to the construction of their hometown. We generous Chaozhou people should bring bright prospect for the future of our hometown. Why not construct an international airport like in Xiamen? It's time to roll up our sleeves and get some things done. I would like to take the initial step." Hong Kong Jiahua Plastic Products Co. Ltd. President, Mr. Xu Wei said: "It's more useful that the advertisers make profitable investments, making the investors return with a smile. Many people from Chaozhou and Shantou were operating small and medium enterprises in Hong Kong. They need to be motivated to launch factories in their hometown."[317]

Hong Kong Advisory Commission held a monthly meeting in Hong Kong, making persistent efforts for the construction of Shantou SEZ. Fully playing their role of owing high social status at home and abroad and contacting a wide range of people, consultants provided information about investors, introducing projects and raising funds. They used every single occasion to promote the construction conditions of Shantou, and used preferential policies to attract foreign investment to Shantou. They have made careful studies in development plans, strategic goals, industry structure and other issues. The deep-water port of Shantou, sea-crossing bridge, Guangzhou-Meizhou-Shantou railway, highways and power plants, condensed their efforts.

3.2.3 Breaking the Limit of Export Processing Zone

In its early stages, SEZ was initially met with suspicion, even denial, but gradually gained understanding and acceptance. In this process, it also confirmed its position through constant practices. Once the SEZ had been established, the question of how to realize further development remained. At first, only export processing zones could be established. As economic construction expanded, export processing established merely to attract foreign funds constrained the development of the SEZ. Thus, the SEZ constructors began to realize the necessity of breaking through the limitations of the export processing zones, and developed a comprehensive SEZ integrating the development of agriculture, industry, commerce, transport, services and other industries.

First, introducing investment from abroad and establishing lateral ties with enterprises at home.

---

317 Chen Pian: *History of Shantou SEZ*, referring to *History of China's SEZ*, Guangdong Economy Press, 2001, p266

In the initial trial period of SEZ, the Central Government and the State Council pointed out that the SEZ should establish an export-oriented economy based on industries and combine trade with industry. The SEZ was the place for information, technology, capital and advanced management experience. The strengthened economic integration, with the mainland enterprises, could exert the influence of the SEZ on the mainland.[318]

On December 10, 1984, the Shantou Municipal government and SEZ Administration Committee held a joint meeting, focusing on how to combine SEZ's special policy and foreign advantage with the mainland's advantage in resources, capital and technology by researching the economic ties between Shantou and Chaozhou in order to drive overall economic development of the SEZ and the mainland. The "Interim Provisions on Joint Enterprise in Shantou SEZ" stipulated that joint enterprises enjoyed the same preferential policies for their own businesses as the SEZ-owned enterprise. Production equipment, transportation equipment, office supplies and the raw materials, and spare parts for export productions could be purchased from the duty-free international market after getting approval. Joint enterprises exporting products or the mainland primary products processed with more than 20% value added exporting could enjoy the preferential treatment of SEZ-produced products. Joint enterprises in the SEZ paid corporate income tax at the rate of 15%. In addition, joint enterprises in Shantou SEZ could receive preferential treatment in land use fees, housing rental and purchase costs, foreign exchange payment, etc.[319] In order to enhance the attractiveness of foreign investment, Shantou Administration Committee had also taken a series of measures for "attracting, keeping and benefiting" from foreign investment. Through a series of efforts, Shantou SEZ made great achievements in attracting foreign investment. In November 1980, Shantou Special Economic Zone Development Corporation and Hong Kong Chia Tai International Investment Corporation jointly set up a carpet factory in Shantou, which became the first Sino-foreign cooperative enterprise. Shantou Special Economic Zone Administration Committee and the International Petrochemical (Group) Co., Ltd. signed the project agreement to establish a joint venture petrochemical company in Guang'ao Wan Bay. Then, Fen Cheng Industrial Co., Ltd., Yi Xing Industrial Co., Ltd., Hua Yi Industrial Factory, Shan Rong Furniture factory, Jin Long Clothing Co., Ltd., Longhu Shopping Centre Co., Ltd., and a number of three-capital enterprises entered Shantou. On August 12, 1983, Liu Feng, the director of the Shantou

---

318 *Notice of the State Council on Approving and Transmitting Minutes of SEZ Working Meeting*, Feb.7th, 1986

319 Chen Pian: *History of Shantou SEZ*, referring to *History of China's SEZ*, Guangdong Economy Press, 2001, p273-274

SEZ Administrative Committee led a delegation to attract foreign investment in Hong Kong. In June 1984, the Liaison Department of Shantou SEZ in Hong Kong was established. On August 7, 1984, the construction of 3000-ton-class container dock was launched in Shantou. By the end of 1984, 18 foreign companies had set up export processing enterprises in Shantou SEZ.[320]

Second, changes in SEZ agriculture.

In the SEZ world history, there is no precedent in initially developing agriculture. Shantou set the precedent. In December 1981, among the first batch of state-owned enterprises in the SEZ, Shantou SEZ Agricultural Development Joint Enterprise was on the list. Why did Shantou SEZ set the precedent in agriculture?

Chaoshan Plain has always been known as a base for agriculture and aquaculture. With superior natural environment, mild climate, abundant sunshine and rainfall and fertile land, it was a natural greenhouse. Dotted with reservoirs, ponds and ditches, the coastline stretched far, with broad deep water fishing grounds. The unique natural conditions made the Chaoshan Plain productive in biological resources. Tasty fruits, vegetables and aquatic products were abundant in all four seasons and many of these products have long been known throughout the country and the world. With agriculture being such an important position in economy, it was appropriate for the SEZ to give priority to agriculture.

To develop agriculture in SEZ, the pattern of state-owned farms could not be adopted. China's traditional agricultural system was a typical "separation in production and sales" mode. Under this mode, industrial and agricultural sectors were in charge of production while trade departments operated sales, the foreign-trade department was responsible for export, while the commercial department was responsible for domestic sales. Agricultural Development Corporation, determined to break this pattern, created a new road throughout production, sales and multiple developments. After much thought and discussion, they cleared the company's operating principles: integrated management in agriculture, forestry, animal husbandry, and fisheries; coordinated industry, commerce and agriculture; and coordinated domestic and foreign trade. Different from state-owned farms, it was not simply a food base for the SEZ. As an enterprise under the direct leadership of the SEZ Management Committee, it enjoyed favorable treatment, the rights of import and export, parts of personnel power and economic independence. The main task and business scope of the company was to introduce the world's modern agricultural technologies (seeds and planting), as well as advanced agricultural equipment, foreign capital, scientific management

320 Chen Pian: *History of Shantou SEZ*, referring to *History of China's SEZ*, Guangdong Economy Press, 2001, p262

of agriculture, so as to serve for an agricultural modernization of the Chaozhou-Shantou area, and realize the prosperity of rural economy. For effective operation, it should break from the tedious executive approach and adopt various forms of economic integration, in order to promote agricultural modernization in Chaozhou-Shantou area. Under the guidance of this new idea, a piece of land was left out between two fishponds for three-dimensional cultivation and breeding. Pavilions, seafood restaurants, game restaurants as well as tourism agriculture were on their way toward development. This new mode was undoubtedly a challenge to the traditional agricultural mode, and a great change indeed.[321]

Practices proved the rightness of advanced agriculture mode at the initial developing period of Shantou SEZ. In its continuous exploration, the SEZ agriculture system played the leading role. With the vast rural area as the hinterland, the SEZ made efforts to achieve "three services and three benefits": provide service for the Chaozhou-Shantou agricultural modernization, for scientific farming and for the Chaozhou-Shantou agricultural economic development; and seek the combination of ecological, social and economic benefits. The practices and experiences drew broad concern at home and abroad.

3.3 Ast Development of Shantou SEZ (1985~1995)

In November 1984, the economic SEZ of Shantou was enlarged to 52.6 square kilometers and it started to develop from a processing industry export district to integrated economic zone. In November 1991, its area was enlarged for the second time and Shantou gained the prerequisites for integrated development as a multi-functioned city. It entered a new phase.

3.3.1 Two Adjustments in the SEZ

3.3.1.1 The First Enlargement of the SEZ

In order to catch up with the need of reform and opening up, on November 29, 1984 No.167 Document of the State Councilofficially approved the adjustment of the scope of Shantou SEZ. Longhu District was enlarged from 1.6 square kilometers to 22.6 square kilometers, plus the Guang'ao District, which was located to the south of Shantou downtown and east of Dahao Peninsular with 30 square kilometers, the area of Shantou economic SEZ was enlarged to 52.6 square kilometers.

After the enlargement of Longhu District, it connected with Shantou at the west, with

321 Du Jingguo, Arduous Rising—The Years of Pioneering in Shantou SEZ, Shantou University Press, p71

Xiapeng County at the north, with Shantou Gulf at the south and east. Longhu and Chenghai County were divided by the Xinlv River. The land in this area was flat, which was beneficial to the rural construction planning. Xinlv River could be the water source for the SEZ. In Shantou Gulf, deep-water harbor could be built up. Most of its land was low yielding agricultural land. Making use of this kind of land for the construction of the SEZ was suitable for Chaozhou-Shantou area that held a large population in a comparatively small area.

Shantou SEZ, after the first enlargement, gained wider development space. It started to convert from an export processing SEZ to an integrated district majoring in industry with agricultural exports, commerce, finance, transportation, tourism and real estate developing together. Its recent development focused on Longhu, which was close to the downtown and had a certain foundation. At the same time, it gradually created the conditions and strove to introduce and develop large projects in Guangdong-Macau circle.[322]

3.3.1.2 The Second Enlargement of the SEZ

Under the encouragement of Deng Xiaoping's South Tour Speeches and direct concern from the Central leaders like Jiang Zemin and Li Peng following the enlargement of the SEZ to 52.6 square kilometers by the State Council, on April 6, 1991, No. 20th Document of the State Council approved that Shantou SEZ could be enlarged to the whole city from 52.6 to 234 square kilometers including Chaoyang, Chenghai and Nan'ao, which would be larger than Zhuhai and Xiamen. By then, the wish of the Shantou people to merge the whole city into SEZ was finally realized, offering Shantou with a perfect environment for creating new advantages to develop the SEZ.

At the same time of the enlargement of the SEZ, the Central Government adjusted the administrative districts of Shantou.

First, the Central Government adjusted the administrative districts of Shantou. On September 14, 1991, the State Council approved the report submitted by the Ministry of Civil Affairs and agreed to adjust its six administrative districts—Anping, Tongping, Gongyuan, Jinsha, Dahao and the rural area into four—Longhu, Jinyuan, Shengping and Dahao. After the adjustment, to the need of the export-oriented economic development, the government reduced and merged the original administrative organizations, trying to reduce unnecessary SEZ organizations, levels and staff. Four newly-built districts had 100 less Party and administrative organizations than before. A primary administrative management institution matching the economic operations of the SEZ was established.

---

322 CHEN Pian: *History of Shantou SEZ*, see *Brief History of Chinese SEZ*, Guangdong Economy Press, P269, 270.

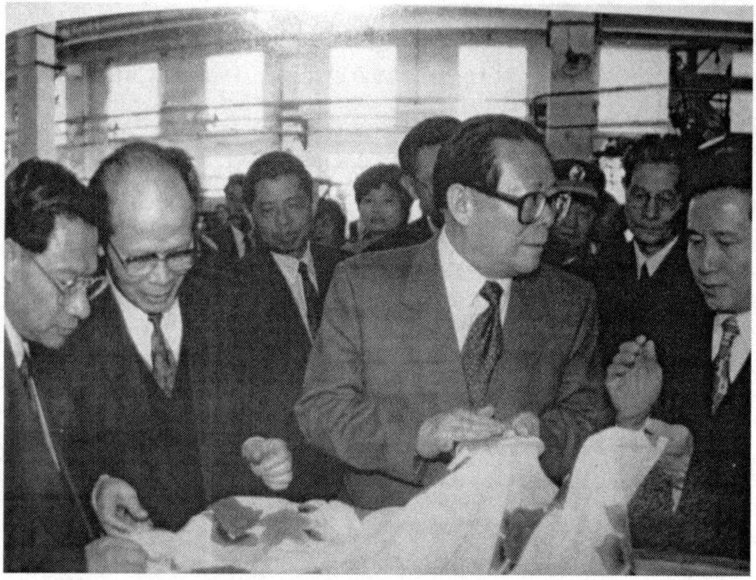

Figure 3-3-1 December 29, 1995 Secretary General Jiang Zemin inspected in Jingwei Group of Shantou (Photo by SUN Rixuan)[323]

Figure 3-3-2 October 11, 1991 Prime Minister Li Peng inspected in Dongsha Community of Shantou (Photo by Shantou Rural Construction and Development Corporation)[324]

323 Resource: Party History Research Department of Shantou Municipal Committee of the PCP: The Establishment and Development of Chinese SEZ—Shantou, CPC History Press, Edition of 1996.

324 Resource: Party History Research Department of Shantou Municipal Committee of the PCP: The Establishment and Development of Chinese SEZ—Shantou, CPC History Press, Edition of 1996.

Second, change the administrative divisions of Chaozhou-Shantou area. In December of 1992, the State Council approved to adjust the administrative divisions of Chaozhou-Shantou area. The eight counties and one city (county-level city) under the management of Shantou in the past were adjusted into three big administrative divisions—Shantou, Chaozhou and Jieyang. After the adjustment, Shantou exercised jurisdiction over three counties (city)—Chaoyang, Chenghai and Nan'ao and five divisions under jurisdictions of the city.[325]

After the enlargement of Shantou SEZ, its population grew from 57,300 to 856,400 including 578,600 non-farm population, which reached a population scale of a large city. At the same time, the economic position of Shantou at home and abroad was updated. Its GDP per capita reached 3,490 yuan RMB, close to the comparatively well-off level that was proposed as the second strategic goal by the Central (GDP 800USD per capita. It was about 4,000RMB accounting for the exchange rate at that time.)[326]

3.3.2 Deepening the Reform and Enlarging the Opening Up

3.3.2.1 Setting up the Shantou Bonded Area

In order to improve and continuously occupying the highest position of opening up under the new structure of China's opening up, the Shantou Municipal Party Committee and the government decided to set up a bonded area to push the export-oriented economy of Shantou to a higher level. The bonded area was the highest-level open district at present and was the SEZ inside the SEZ. Some free harbor policies were implemented there. On January 11, 1993, with the approval of the State Council, Shantou Bonded Area was formally set up and became one of the thirteen bonded areas of China. On December 22nd of the same year, the bonded area passed the examination of the General Administration for Customs on its supervision installations and stated to work.

The bonded area of Shantou SEZ, located in southeast of Dahao Peninsular of South Shantou, was a closed integrated open area under the jurisdiction of Customs. It was 2.34 square kilometers, with Houjiang Gulf of South China Sea to the east, Hukong Mountain of Xitou Village to the west, Guang'ao Deep-water Gulf to the south and Guang'ao Xitou Village to the north. It was surrounded by mountains and the sea and having good gulf and geographic conditions, which were easy to implement with a closed-end management policy. It was faced with major international shipping lines of

325 Party History Research Department of Shantou Municipal Committee of the PCP: The Establishment and Development of Chinese SEZ—Shantou, CPC History Press, Edition of 1996, P150-151.

326 CHEN Pian: *History of Shantou SEZ*, see *Brief History of Chinese SEZ*, Guangdong Economy Press, P269, 271.

the West Pacific Ocean and was 179 nautical miles from Hong Kong and 180 nautical miles from Kaohsiung of Taiwan. Shantou Bonded Area had a good investment environment with developed communications and transportations from an integrated sea-land-air support. Shantou Harbor worked with more than 160 harbors of more than 40 countries and districts, all with major harbors in China. A thirty-thousand-ton cargo ship could directly park in Guang'ao Deep-water Harbor that was 500 meters far from the wharf of bonded area on land, with expressways connecting Guangzhou and Shenzhen in the south, national highway 324 linked Xiamen in the east, and with Guangzhou-Chaozhou-Shantou Railway starting in Shantou and connecting the Beijing-Kowloon Railway in Longchuan County. In aviation, there had been more than forty lines, domestic or international. In the bonded area, the "five getting through, one getting even" project had been completed, with the green area accounting for 36.5% of its area and more than 420,000 square meters' factory, storage, freight yard and office buildings for both sale and leasing.

The development of the bonded area, strictly following the spirit of the State Council on establishing the bonded area in Shantou SEZ, made full use of the harbor advantages of Shantou to comprehensively develop transit trade, storage and transportation, along with the processing industries serving the exportation together with finance, information and insurance. After several years' striving, the bonded area could be established as an integrated district with international trade as the leading operation and with storage and transportation, export processing industry finance and information as the base operation. At the same time, the third industry was set up as the major industry of the bonded area. The bonded area and Shantou High-tech Industrial Park worked in conjunction with each other and would surely promote the adjustment of the industrial structure of Shantou and its update to speed up the modern construction of Shantou. Since the birth of the bonded area of Shantou SEZ, it has attracted the attention of guests and businessmen at home and abroad, becoming the new focus of investment.[327]

3.3.2.2 The Establishment of Shantou High-Tech Park

Modern developed countries build up high-tech industries as the mainstay of the economic development. Whether Shantou could develop groups of high-tech industries would be the key to accelerating and the realization of modernization. The 6th Congress of CPC Shantou Committee proposed that Shantou must consider the high-tech park as one of

327 http://www.stftz.gov.cn

the three open districts of the development. Early at the High-tech Industry Working Conference on June 15, 1991, Shantou Committee of CPC proposed the plan to establish a high-tech district. In April 1992, the municipal government decided to establish the Shantou High-tech industrial district as an integrated base for researching, developing, testing, producing and operating high technologies and high-tech products. A leading organization was established for the operation works. In July 1993, Guangdong Provincial Government approved Shantou High-tech industrial development district as a provincial level district. In October of the same year, the east part of the district started its construction, entering the real construction period.[328]

In September 1997, Mayor of Shantou issued the governmental command, offering the High-tech District Committee municipal level management authority. The area of the entire district was about four square kilometers. The east part of the District was located between Longhu and Jinyuan in the center of Shantou, covering one square kilometer. It was close to the deep-water terminal and international pier to the south, next to No. 324 National Express to the east, eight kilometers away from Shantou Airport and two kilometers away from the major railway station To start, the east section was divided into three parts—integrated, industrial and living. The west section was located to the southwest of Shantou University at the foot of Sangpu Mountain, covering three square kilometers. It linked the estuary of Shantou Harbor to the east and Chaoshan International Airport to the west, with a flexible transportation by sea, land and air. Otherwise, there were two technical parks built in Dahao and Hepu districts in the south part of Shantou, covering 1.8 square kilometers. In 2002, they were listed in the preferential investment districts, enjoying the same preferential policies as the high technological district.

Shantou, in accordance with the strategic goal of "realizing industrialization of high technology, promoting its economy, setting up the developing district a cultivated, beautiful, fully functioned high technological district with obvious industrial series and capability in international competition," developed electronic information technology, integration of optics, machinery and electronics, new materials, fine chemicals, new energy, energy-efficient technology, biotechnology and other high technologies that could accelerate the change of traditional industry and could earn foreign currency as its key developing areas. At the same time, Shantou set up three strategic industrial series: the first included electronics, precision instruments and automatic machinery; the second included ocean chemistry and biotechnology; the third included information industry, energy, raw materials and other

328 http://www.swatow.gov.cn

energy-efficient industries.

3.4 Infrustruction for the Development of Shantou SEZ (1996~2000)

In the middle of the 1990s, the economic development of Shantou came across unprecedented difficulties. Firstly, foreign trade of Shantou was badly hurt in the financial crisis of Southeast Asia, which directly impacted its economic and social development. The lost of social credit and the local financial crisis greatly tarnished the image and credit of Shantou, which badly influenced the development of social productivity. The economy of Shantou that was once prosperous went into a very dark period.

3.4.1 The Influence of the Southeast Asia Financial Crisis

On July 2, 1997, Thailand announced their change from a fixed exchange rate and the implementation of a floating exchange rate, which aroused financial crisis all through Southeast Asia. On the same day, the exchange rate between the Baht and USD reduced 17%. Foreign currency and other aspects of the financial market were completely in chaos. The economy of Shantou was highly foreign-oriented. Since the reform and opening up, more than 90% of the investment used by the city came from Asian countries and districts. 85% of its production was directly exported to Asian countries and regions or transported via these countries and regions. more than 95% of the "foreign-funded enterprises" and "three-plus-one enterprises" were brought from Asian countries and regions.[329]Shantou had trading relations with all Asian countries and regions. The Asian financial crisis directly impacted the economic and social development of Shantou.

3.4.1.1 Challenges Faced by Export Industry

Southeast Asia was one of the most important export markets for Shantou. After the financial crisis, the export volume to Southeast Asia sharply declined. Most of the production stopped exportation to this market. For orders, the clients asked to reduce prices, which was unacceptable for the exportation companies and for the new orders, most of them asked only for replenishment. For example, Shantou Native and Livestock Product Import & Export Company exported feather dusters, hemp ropes and fragrant powder to

---

329 WANG Liangyuan: *Influence of Asian Financial Crisis on Shantou and Its Countermeasures*, *Economy of the SEZ*, July 25th 1998, P55.

Southeast Asia. Since January and February of 1998, the tradition business nearly stopped. This company lost 8.03 million USD. In January of 1998, the export volume of Shantou Machinery Import & Export Company that regarded Southeast Asia as main market reduced 50% than that of the same period in 1997. The export volume of traditional export product (marine products) from this company to Indonesia reduced from 700,000 USD in 1996 to 200,000 USD in 1997. In the first quarter of 1998, this business was bogged down. There was even no one order for the goods.[330]

Devaluation of the currencies of Southeast Asia led to a great decline of the price over the export goods and their price competitive capability increased, becoming powerful competitors for the similar goods made in China, except for a part of high-tech products, which suffered from little challenges in their technological advantages. Many of the export goods from Shantou, which were once a priority, came across various influences. Among the major export goods of Shantou, textile, toys, shoes and hats were competitors with Southeast Asia for the international market. Many of the distributors asked for a discount for the original orders, which led to the situation that the original contracts could not be continued and the exporters of Shantou faced difficulties.

With the development of the financial crisis in European and American markets and because of trade protectionism, anti-dumping cases, especially those against Chinese producers, were issued frequently. This had a negative impact on the exportation of bulky goods. Although the quantity and amount of money concerned with Shantou were not large, its exploration in European and American markets had difficult taking a step forward because of the trade protectionism.

Influenced by these factors, foreign trade of Shantou continued to decline from 1998 to 2000.

3.4.1.2 Severe Situation of Employing Foreign Investment

Generally speaking, for the newly approved foreign investment projects, capital from foreign investors would gradually arrive after one to two years after signing the contract. Although the real utilization ratio of foreign capital of Shantou reached 1.011 billion USD at its peak in 1997, the approved projects with direct foreign investment and the amount of money of contracts using foreign capital sharply declined, compared with the previous year. The situation became even worse in February 1998, when nearly no new projects with

330 LI Shenggao: *Influence From Asian Financial Crisis On Shantou Foreign Trade and Countermeasures, Foreign Trade Practice*, June of 1998, P37,38.

direct foreign investment were approved.

Foreign capital arriving at Shantou mostly came from Hong Kong, Southeast Asia, Japan, Korea and Taiwan. The Asian financial crisis exacerbated the capital deficiency for "foreign-funded" and "three-plus-one" enterprises from these above countries and regions, which made it difficult to continue the upgrade and transference of existing projects and the reducing of capability to increase capital. The devaluation of currency and collapse of the stock market greatly reduced the capital of well-known overseas Chinese consortium that invested in Shantou. The reduction of their economic strength influenced the procedure for their investment.

In addition, the financial crisis of Asia reduced confidence of investors from Europe, America and Japan to invest in Asian countries and regions. In order to change the situation, countries under crisis implemented new measures to attract investment and competed with China in introducing foreign investment. Comparatively, there were shortcomings in Shantou in optimizing investment environment and enhancing preferential policies to foreign investors, which also created obstacles for introducing foreign investment.

With the deepening impact from Asian financial crisis, the speed of Shantou economic development slowed and the market lacked basic needs. At the same time, deep economic and social problems occurred, hidden behind the deepening of reform, and the change in society and its development were appealed.

3.4.2 Credit Crisis

Trading was a traditional advantage of Shantou. Since its opening in modern times, the prosperous commercial activities in Shantou once greatly promoted the development of the productive forces and the accumulation of its credits. "Be honest to others and be rooted in honesty" gradually made up the principle for the Chaozhou-Shantou people to realize their careers. The historical accumulation, cultural storage and credit conditions laid a good foundation for the long-term economic and social development of the Chaozhou-Shantou area.

At the beginning of the establishment of Shantou SEZ, depending on the preferential policies from the country and the hard work and intelligence of its people, Shantou developed rapidly. However, with the economic institution changing from a planning economy to market economy, and with the economic growth mode changing from extensive to intensive, in some places of Shantou some people still remained poor. They gradually forgot the commercial principle to "keep honest" in dealing business and some even took the criminal route. This finally led to the credit lost in some places.

3.4.2.1 Credit Lost

Chaozhou-Shantou area that was once called "Zoulu on the Beach"(Zoulu was used in reference to places with prosperous economy and culture), which once created splendid commercial culture, ran ahead in the reform and opening up and set up the credit concept in the construction of the SEZ. In the 1990s, the economic and social orders fell into chaos, which destroyed its credits over products, market, economy, the credit of the entire society, and even morality. It badly hurt the image and credit among foreign investors, which are elaborated in the following sections.

3.4.2.1.1 Tax Fraud and Evasion Badly Destroyed the Credit for the Chaozhou-Shantou Area

The Asian financial crisis brought serious negative impact to the economy of China. In order to resume foreign trade and to promote the continuous growth of the national economy, and at the same time to implement positive financial policies and enlarge the domestic need, Chinese government greatly upgraded the export tax rebate rate in 1998. To some, the high tax rebate attracted the illegal idea of misappropriation of state property. During one period, tricking tax rebate from the state became popular and continued for a while. From the establishment of the "three-no" policy for fake companies to issue false value added tax (VAT) invoices, from counterfeiting "Export Declarations Form" of the customs, "Export Verification" of Foreign Exchange Bureau to money laundering, the criminals offered "package service" to cheat tax rebate. This kind of crime affected more than ten provinces and spread to more than half of China. It brought negative impact to the national market economic order. Nineteen provinces and cities issued documents asking their own enterprises to stop working with those of Chaozhou-Shantou area. Enterprises having business with those of Chao-Shan area doubted and their relationships grew uneasy. The business came back to the original "number crunching" status. Serious tax rebate crimes led Chaozhou-Shantou area to the lowest level of the credit.

3.4.2.1.2 Counterfeiting and Selling Fake Goods Made in Chao-Shan Area Face a Serious Credit Crisis

At the beginning of the reform and opening up, Xiashan Town in Chaoyang City was once one of two biggest distribution centers for smuggling goods into China. The case for seizing pirated video compact disc (VCD) producing lines there was once a main media news focus, both at home and abroad. At the start of 2000, in the joint actions against counterfeit products, counterfeiting dens of tobacco were found in bonded area of Shantou, which aroused the focus of the media and society. Because of counterfeiting and selling fake products, goods made in the Chao-Shan area were banned by the domestic market. Business centers of some cities even hang up plates saying "no Chao-Shan goods here" to make a clean break with goods from the Chao-Shan area. Not only were the goods regarded as corrupt, but also the personality and moral standard of businessmen from Chao-Shan area were doubted. They were regarded as "swindlers."

3.4.2.1.3 "Mark Six" Gambling Crashed the Folk Custom

To meet some people's dream to make a fortune over night, some Chao-Shan people introduced Mark Six, a lottery betting from Hong Kong, and changed it into various ways of gambling. High speculative rate and "Mystery Report" issued by illegal bankers cheated many innocent people who knew nothing about the reality of gambling. The prosperity of underground gambling, like drugs, seriously crashed the folk custom of the Chao-Shan area. In some places, farmers did not go farming; students did not go to school; shops were closed and workers did not go to work. Men and women, young and old, instead, went to Mark Six. Because of gambling, many people gave up farming and working, which led to land abandonment and even bankruptcy and heavy debt. Social cultural credit and folk custom suffered from gambling, which severely hurt the productive forces.

3.4.2.1.4 Malicious Debt Evasion Caused the Economy to Fall into a Vicious Circle

Some of the enterprises gave up the concept of "keeping contract and credit." They evaded debt on purpose and did not timely pay back loans. Some even said shamelessly: "If I knew I needed to pay back the loan, I would not have borrowed." Some key projects made use of foreign investment. However, the promises violated objective law and relevant policies of the state. They could not be carried out, which led to credit loss among foreign investors. In some areas, serious debt evasion began to cause local financial risks and critical financial crisis.

3.4.2.1.5 Incorrect Working Style of the Party and Political Ethics and the Negligence of the People

As the Chinese saying goes: "the train runs fast behind a fast engine"; only if the local government devoted themselves to public issues and served its people whole-heartedly, could the local construction and development go well. In 1990s, some people criticized that in Chao-Shan area, things were neither easy, nor impossible. Some Party officials' corruption and bad working style were obvious problems. In some of the government agencies, the working style was incorrect and was inefficient, which seriously hurt the environment of the investment. There were four difficulties in some of the industries and organizations: it was difficult to gain entrance, to see a gentle face, to hear pleasant words and to solve the problems there. Staff and law enforcement officers made use of their authority to ask for a kickback, which seriously impacted the positive attitude of the foreign businessmen, overseas Chinese, Hong Kong, Macau and Taiwan people to invest in Shantou. The bad working style and negligence made it difficult to mobilize the people. The image of the Party and the government was tarnished. As a window of China open to the world, Shantou could not play its role of an SEZ.[331]

3.4.2.2 Local Financial Crisis

After Shantou entered the 9th Five-Year Plan period, an obvious division turned up in 1998. In the two years since 1998, although the Asian financial crisis, smuggling, counterfeiting, dilution of SEZ preferential policies and other negative factors of economic development, which slowed down the speed of the economic growth of Shantou, it kept a fast growth rate of 15%. In the following two years after 1998, the economic development speed of Shantou slowed down too fast to keep balanced.

The fuse of the sharp decline for the economy of Shantou may be the wave of concentrated withdrawal in the Shantou Commercial Bank in July 1999. A series of financial corruption cases brought by this wave threw Shantou to the edge of economic collapse.

On July 1, 1997, approved by People's Bank of China, 13 credit unions were merged and formed Commercial Bank of Shantou with a total property of 8 billion RMB, with more than 50 outlets and special background from government. This greatly improved the state of Shantou's financial industry. However, the payment crisis started in 1998 and the wave of concentrated withdrawals exploded in 1999, which caused this local commercial bank be at a standstill. In 2001, People's Bank of China asked Commercial Bank of Shantou to stop business for rectification. Huge debt made the reorganization a failure.[332] In 2004, Commercial Bank of Shantou claimed bankruptcy because it could not pay back

331 XIE Mingjia: *Credit: Lifeline For Modernization—Practice of Shantou and the Construction of Social Credit in China*, Renmin Press, P177-178.

332 Finance SINA: Shantou First Project Against Corruption Revealed Case of Commercial Bank of Shantou, http://finance.sina.com.cn/roll/20031114/1735520046.shtml.

1.5 billion RMB to the private depositors nor recover a debt of 4 billion RMB.

The influence of Commercial Bank of Shantou bankruptcy case was no less serious than a local financial crisis. Finance was blood of economy. Many owners of the enterprises complained that: "the tax could not be rebated while money in the bank could not be withdrawn. It is a problem to pay for the cost. How can we expand the reproduction?"

The whole economic development of Shantou suffered, resulting in credit lost. It was recorded that there were 454 enterprises moved from Shantou, which equaled the accumulated amount for the past five years. During the 9th Five-Year Plan period, the economic growth speed of Shantou reduced year by year. The growth rate of GDP declined from 16.04% in 1996 to 7.3% in 2000, which was below the average level of the whole country and Guangdong Province. In 2000, the GDP per capita of Shantou only accounted for 80% of the average amount of Guangdong Province, which equaled to the level in 1991 and was the lowest point for that decade. In 2001, a negative growth rate occurred, which was the first time in the past 18 years. It was the only prefecture-level city with negative GDP growth rate in the entire province.

Shantou, once famous for its "abundance of buildings and boats abroad and a one hundred years' old business center" went to the fatal edge in the waves brought by credit lost.

3.5 Rise from Difficulties and Obtained Advantages (2001~2009)

In order to resume the prosperity of Shantou, its municipal government, based on the policy of "rectification on the market order and social order" issued by the principal committee and government in the impromptu meeting, started "life projects of the new century" all over the city. This made use of various measures to rebuild credit and the image of Shantou in the new century. After a round of serious modifications over the market and society, Shantou went from a city with credit lost, to setting up a standard credit system all over the nation. 2002 saw Shantou's economic recovery.

3.5.1 Rebuild Credit and Image

On January 17, 2000, State Administration of Taxation issued "Notice on Enhancing Management over the Tax Rebate of Chao-Shan Area of Guangdong Province," listing four cities of eastern Guangdong as "cities with problems." There were 19 provinces and cities that issued notices asking their local enterprises not to do business with enterprises of

Chao-Shan area. In the light of serious tax fraud problems in Chao-Shan area, in August 2000, the Central Committee of CPC and the State Council dispatched working teams with more than 300 officers to investigate the tax fraud cases at Chaoyang and Puning of Guangdong. Tax fraud had become a serious problem all over the country, impacting the economic orders of the whole country. If serious and efficient rectification could not be carried out and the new credit system and city image of Shantou could not be set up, the national economy and order would be badly destroyed and the benefit of the nation, enterprises and people would be injured. It may also worsen the investment environment and the achievement of reform and opening up and the establishment of SEZ may disappear.

3.5.1.1 Decision to Rectify Market Economic Order

The chaotic situation of market economic order in the middle and late 1990s aroused the attention of the Central Committee, the State Council, the Provincial Committee and the government. In order to solve the problems of economic and social orders, from February 26 to 27, 2001, Guangdong Provincial Committee and government held an on-site meeting. Li Changchun, Member of the Central Committee Politburo and Guangdong Provincial Party Secretary, held the meeting, mainly proposing to rectify the economic and social orders in Shantou and the east part of Guangdong (hereinafter referred to as "Two Rectifications"). It asked Shantou and the east part of Guangdong to concentrate power and time on enhanced measures to rectify market orders and strived to efficiently contain serious problems within one year. Then after several years' effort, a comparatively standardized order of the market and the society should be set up.[333]

This meeting was of great importance, held at the critical moment for Shantou's economic and social development. It not only disposed the task of rectification on the economic and social orders, but also combined "Two Rectification" and the rebuilt of credit, pointing out the direction for the development of Shantou and east part of Guangdong. It marked Shantou's entrance into a new period of modernization construction.

3.5.1.2 Implement of the "Two Rectification"

After the Provincial Committee and government issued the decisions to rectify the market and social orders at the meeting in Shantou, the Municipal Committee and government

333 HUANG Jinxiong, SU Weidian, HONG Yuehao: *Documentary Of Credit Establishment In Shantou, Shantou Daily*, May 13th 2002.

clarified their attitude and strong will to carry out all details for the rational decisions. They started "life projects of the new century," making all efforts to rebuild credit and the image of Shantou.

3.5.1.2.1 Deep Reflection, Active Mobilization and Programming

As soon as the on-site meeting held by Guangdong Provincial Committee and government finished, Shantou Municipal Committee held several meetings to unify ideas and the mind of the whole city and erase negative attitudes of some cadres. At the mobilization meeting of "Two Rectification," with more than 100,000 attendees, Deputy Secretary of the Municipal Committee and Mayor, Li Chunhong, faced with the reality, proposed to implement rectification on market and social orders within a half year and promised for the rectification. He said, "We have made the greatest determination, won't hide our mistakes by beautiful words but do real work and made solid achievement."[334] In order to guarantee the rectification action and the effects of all measures of the "hard-strike battle," Shantou Municipal Committee and government set up leading teams and organizations for rectifying market and social orders. They studied "Plans For Rectification Action Of Market And Social Orders," defying the guidance idea, general goal, key points, procedures and measures of the task. At the same time, six specialized teams were established to fight against defrauding export tax rebates, counterfeiting and debt evasion, investigate cases of economic and principle violations, clean up the stock of inventory of assets and rectify bidding of the construction market. The detail working schedules for each team were also carried out respectively.

3.5.1.2.2 Hard Strike on Various Crimes

By using an iron fist, striking on various crimes were the breakthrough to removing on the blemishes of the economic and social orders and rectify the situation.

First of all, special battles fighting against defrauding tax rebates, smuggling and arbitraging foreign exchange started all over the whole city, striking hard on counterfeit VAT receipts and defrauded export tax rebates. Second, joint actions against counterfeiting products were seriously implemented. Third, steps were taken to rectify financial order, start specific action against debt evasion, strive to recover overdue loans, investigate illegal business activities of the financial institutions and punish financial "borers." Meanwhile,

---

334 Li Chunhong: *Speech On The Mobilization Meeting Of Rectification Over Market and Social Orders of Shantou*, March 22nd 2001. See XIE Mingjia: *Credit: Lifeline For Modernization—Practice of Shantou and the Construction of Social Credit in China*, Renmin Press, P456.

rectify activities of the market players and ban the enterprises without capital, site and equipment and the businesses without a license; check enterprises and brokers' cheating on the accounts and income and offering false credit statements; rectify bidding of construction market, check unfair competition and try to maintain a fair competitive market order; remediate social orders and maintain social and political stability; strike hard on robbery and activities that negatively impacted social stability, such as violent crime, vicious hooligans, triad organizations and other criminal offenses; fight against gambling hidden behind Mark Six.

3.5.1.3 Comprehensive Promotion of the Construction of Social Credit System

Credit is an essential part of society. Without credit, one cannot buy a home and businesses could not continue. Where there is no credit, there is no order. Without order, market economy cannot properly develop. Policy makers of Shantou deeply realized this point. Although the "Two Rectification" achieved stage progress, a short period of rectification could not give a fundamental solution to the problems. To let social economy develop healthily, society must rely on perfect social credit system. Therefore, the Municipal Committee and government started to embarks on promoting the construction of social credit system.

3.5.1.3.1 Spread Ethic Education of Honesty and Trustworthiness

Officials of Shantou Municipal Committee and government publicized consciousness, concept and ethic of credit all over the city, enhanced the credit concept, made use of the function of media, explained law and principles by using true cases, educated cadres and people with law and credit and aroused people's focus on credit. On May 29, 2001, representatives of all walks of life in Shantou held a signing ceremony of "Credit Declaration." On June 13 of the same year, more than 200 entrepreneurs from Chaoyang Liangzhen Textile and Garments Association initiated "glory with credit, shame without credit." In January of 2002, to the request of "Implement Outline of Civic Morality Construction," Shantou Spiritual Civilization Construction Committee issued "Shantou Civic Credit Convention," regulating personal accomplishment, credit among people and the compulsory and a promise to the family and society.[335]

335 XIE Mingjia: *Credit: Lifeline For Modernization—Practice of Shantou and the Construction of Social Credit in China*, Renmin Press, P396.

3.5.1.3.2 Government Goes Ahead in the Construction of Credit

Local government is the major player promoting the construction of a regional credit system. Credit of the government not only played a role of guidance and sample for the whole society, but it also was the foundation and source of credit for the whole society. Especially under the "powerful government" institution in China, for all people, a government with credit is responsible and reliable. Therefore, seeking for solutions to the credit problems via administrative institution reform was the permanent cure. Since 2001, surrounding credit system construction, Shantou had taken series of measures to actively deepen reform of administrative institution. The major measures included: implement reforms of administrative examination and approval system, improve efficiency and strengthen accountability; carry out financial institution reform and implement transparent financial management; enhance management over specialized capital; deepen reform of personnel management and lay a good human resource foundation for the credit system construction.[336]

3.5.1.3.3 Deepen Reform of State-Owned Enterprises and Make Full Use of Their Major Players' Function in the Credit System Construction

Enterprises were major players both in the market and the credit system construction. Deepening the reform of the enterprises was of great help to regulate their economic behavior and to promote their capability of operation management and self-control, laying a good foundation to set up a credit system. Shantou regarded modern enterprise institution construction as one of the key tasks in deepening the reform. A group of key enterprises were guided to implement a shareholding system reform: Their goal was to release and activate some enterprises by cooperation, reorganization, merger, property transfer, dissolution and bankruptcy; at the same time of reform, strengthen management of the state property and take care of authorized operation of the state property; and cultivate and support a pile of enterprises and groups to be head of their industry and improve the core competitive capability of the enterprises. In order to speed up the development of private enterprises, the government actively guided the private enterprises to correct the development concept, to insist on acquiring wealth legally, to develop industrial projects by making use of the capital accumulated and to legitimately enlarge the business scope. The government made

---

336 XIE Mingjia: *Credit: Lifeline For Modernization—Practice of Shantou and the Construction of Social Credit in China*, Renmin Press, P280-284.

good efforts to perfect the social security system concerned with insurances of unemployment, pension, medical, employment injury and maternity.

3.5.1.3.4 Perfect Constrain, Punish and Supervision System Over Social Credit by Using New Technology and Measures

The cost for losing credit was low. That's why the problem of credit lost was so serious. Therefore, to establish constrain, punish and supervision system over credit lost and to increase cost for losing credit became an important part of the establishment of credit system.

On April 1, 2002, Shantou started to run the Credit Network. It regulated that if enterprises making business in Shantou who participated in illegal activities (smuggling, arbitrage foreign exchange, counterfeiting, tax evasion, contract fraud) and with the situation of revoking business license and a large penalty would be recorded in the Bad Behavior Record Management System. At the same time, it as necessary to clear up credit-lost industries, make the access system strict and get rid of enterprises existing in name only and those who had serious law-violating behaviors; make full use of chambers and associations, educate, supervise and constrain enterprises consciously keep credit. In addition, set up efficient credit and public supervision systems over the whole society. Corruption was born easily among authority without supervision. In recent years, Shantou made continuous efforts to set up an efficient supervision system. Meanwhile, the Municipal Government opened a report phone and mailbox for the "Two Rectifications," General and Mayor hotlines and a direct line to People's Representative. Different levels of the government were open to supervision from related departments and people by debriefing, letters and Reception Day.[337]

3.5.1.3.5 Complete Law System, Strict Law Enforcement and Regulate Enforcement Procedures

Perfect legislation was the foundation for a perfect legal community. However in China, in the procedure of constructing a socialist market economy, problems of inadequate law and legal services still existed. Under the situation lacking of upper law and practice experience, Shantou, based on guaranteeing legislative procedures to obey related law and regulative spirit, actively explored, bravely practiced and made stage progress on the

337 XIE Mingjia: *Credit: Lifeline For Modernization—Practice of Shantou and the Construction of Social Credit in China*, Renmin Press, P288, P289.

legislation of credit. By the end of April 2002, Shantou carried out several provisions including: Enterprises Credit Information Publish Management Regulation (Trial), Enterprises Credit Information Collection Management Regulation, Enterprises Credit Grades Provisional Regulation, Civic Credit Convention, Civil Service Credit Rule, Interim Measures on Management of Social Credit Information Network and Regulation for Practitioners of Social Information Service. From this, they continued the research and plan for credit legislation in accordance with the authority given by the National People's Congress.

All laws and regulations depended on strict enforcement, without which, laws became only a mere scrap of paper. Therefore, while Shantou enhanced enforcement, the government also took measures to punish credit-losing behaviors. After one month of rectification, Shantou erased unstable factors, promoted the self-construction of the enforcement practitioners and laid a foundation for enhancing law enforcement supervision.[338]

3.5.2 Economic Resurgence

After a round of rectification of market and social orders, Shantou starting from a city of credit lost, but established a comparatively regulatory credit system all through the country and made steps to rebuild the credit. Shantou bottomed out from economic depression in 2002, catching up with the average growth rate of the nation in 2003 and the speed of economic growth accelerated year by year. This change demonstrated that credit is the lifeline for economic development and also the foundation of socialist market economic development.

In November of 2006, State Administration of Taxation published "Notice on Publishing Regulations on Transfer by Letters of the Export Taxation" and defined to stop enforcement of "Notice on Strictly Enhance Import and Export Taxation in Chao-Shan Area of Guangdong Province" (State Taxation Letter [2000] No.51 No. 51 Document in short). The release of taxation encouraged people and the prosperity of Shantou finally returned. The stop of No.51 Document greatly promoted the economic development of Shantou.

3.5.2.1 Adjustment of the Districts

In March of 2003, in order to increase development advantages of Shantou in the new period, to accelerate the procedures of industrialization, urbanization and modernization, to

---

338 XIE Mingjia: *Credit: Lifeline For Modernization—Practice of Shantou and the Construction of Social Credit in China*, Renmin Press, P296-299..

enlarge its development space, to build Shantou from a trading city into an industrial city of east Guangdong Province and to realize the general goal of a moderately prosperous society, based on the "Approval of the Administrative Districts' Adjustment of Shantou Guangdong" by Guangdong Provincial Committee and government, Shantou adjusted its administrative districts: Longhu, Jinyuan, Shengping, Dahao, Hepu and the other two cities held in trust, Chaoyang and Chenghai, were adjusted into Jinping, Longhu, Chenghai, Haojiang, Chaoyang and Chaonan. In the past, Chaoyang and Chenghai were county level cities and were controlled by the Province with independent approval authority, but it was also hosted by Shantou. Therefore unreasonable factors and management chaos turned up easily. After this adjustment, two cities were changed into districts, which was helpful to solving the conflict. At the same time, it enlarged the economic and cultural radiation of Shantou, enlightening its central position in the east part of Guangdong. It was also of great help to merge the resources to accelerate the modernization of the east part of Guangdong. After the adjustment, the area of Shantou was more than five times larger than before.

Jinyuan and Shengping were combined into Jinping District, which created conditions for the planning of the whole western part of the city. Shantou Municipal Government had appropriated 290 mu of land to prepare for the establishment of Shantou University and Technological Park in the west. This would promote the development of the industry and the high tech industry and then to promote the economic development of Shantou in the whole.

3.5.2.2 Formation of a New Economic Development Idea

The adjustment of the administrative districts had been done, but the following questions were raised: How to realize the space optimization of the city and to form reasonable city layers structure? How to cultivate the function of the city to make use of its capability to gather and transfer capital and population? How to improve its integrated competitive capability? Around this series of questions, in April of 2003, after more than ten departments' three-month research, Shantou Municipal Committee and the government carried out "Principle Idea and Framework of Economic Society Development" after the adjustment of its administrative districts: with development as mainstream, with improvement of integrated competitive capability of the regional center city as core, implement "stand with credit, strengthen with industry, invigorate with opening, prosper with science and technology, manage with laws" and sustainable strategy for the development; make use of two advantages—extravert economy and private economy to promote industrialization, industrialization of agriculture and the urbanization; and establish Shantou an economic powerful city in Guangdong. The main points of the Framework were as follows:

3.5.2.2.1 Establish the New Path of Industrialization and Set Up a Powerful Industrial City

To accelerate the new style industrialization was the basis of promoting urbanization and was also a strategic development focus in order to accelerate a powerful city in the east part of Guangdong after the adjustment of the administrative districts. The general requests were: rally around one "general goal," develop "three bases," establish "three kinds of districts (parks)," enhance "eight pillar industries" and take good care of "a group of key enterprises."

The three bases were: textile and garments base with Chaoyang and Chaonan as the center; handcraft and toy base with Chenghai as mainstay; and heavy industrial base with Guang'ao (Lin'gang) as the core.

Eight pillar industries were: electronic information, textile and garment, chemical and plastic, handcraft and toy, food and pharmaceutics, machinery, videos, print and packages.

Three kinds of districts (parks) were: in accordance with the present situation of the industrial structure of the city and the prospect of the future, plan and set up industrial parks or districts in levels and reasonable structure. That was: three prefectural districts [high tech district (east part), high tech district (west part), Lin'gang industrial district (Guang'ao)], six district level, nine sub-district (central town) industrial parks and twelve industrial districts with their own specialty.

A group of key enterprises were: request to enhance the leadership, policy support and capital investment; ensure key projects finish early and start to run, which could be the highlight of a powerful industrialized city. For the projects with more than 10 million RMB, on the basis of tracking service, enlarge the preferential policies to improve the capability to attract investment of Shantou.

3.5.2.2.2 Promote Urbanization and Accelerate Modernization

The general goal was to establish an economically powerful city and strive to be a sub-central city of Guangdong. In the aspect of city space, with downtown of Shantou as center, Chaoyang, Chaonan and Chenghai Districts as sub-core, set up a city with several towns with a strip structure along the coast, which was a new develop structure of the city. On the basis of optimizing city space, it was necessary to perfect the function disposition of city and town and the timing of the development, check and sort out land resources, optimize disposition of construction land, promote comparatively concentrated development of industrial, business and residential districts.

3.5.2.2.3 Accelerate the Development of Transportation Network and Enhance Integrated Functions of Regional Transportation

"Fast" was highlighted in the construction: two centers—logistics and passengers centers of Eastern Guangdong; three ensure: passage clear, convenient and safety; four standards: network supporting, completed functions, advanced equipment, efficient operation. Five "cans" need to be reached in 2010: people can drive to the express way within 30 minutes; can arrive at the airport within one hour; goods can arrive at the piers within one hour; can be dispatched within two hours and can reach any of the cities or towns in east part of Guangdong within one hour. By 2020, a modernized integrated transportation hub can be established and become modern regional centers for logistics and passengers.

3.5.2.2.4 Insist on Sustainable Development and Enhance Ecological Environment Construction in the City

Modernization of the city must be with comprehensive development as the core and final goal. Therefore it must obey the ecological sustainable development concept of "healthy, safe, vigorous and developing" to continuously promote the environment construction and ecology protection and to set up city ecological system with beautiful environment, man and nature existing with balance.

The general goal was by 2010 to obtain the following: the pollution and ecological destruction could be controlled and gradually improved; the environmental integrated index could be beyond 85; the environmental quality could reach the standard for related functions; the central city set up samples, enhance the achievement and continue to improve; and newly-established districts could reach all standard for a sample district. More than 80% of the towns would be built ecological areas. The whole city would be the national ecological city. Before 2020, a city ecological system could be set up with beautiful environment, man and nature existing with balance.

3.5.2.2.5 Speed Up Information Industry and Construct Modern Information Harbor

The general request was: optimize the policy environment for information industry, support the construction and reform of information network, encourage the development and usage of information resources, promote unconventional development of information industry, spread the utilization of information technology in national economy and different fields, accelerate information industrialization and production information-based, use information industry to promote industrialization, push urbanization and comprehensive development of the whole society and strive to realize the social productive forces developing exponentially, and concentrate on the development of information administration, Shantou Software Park and information industry in the enterprises.

3.5.3 New Development Opportunities

Since the reform and opening up, Guangdong was the leading province of the national economy, with its GDP the first among the provinces and municipalities. At present, although the overall economic strength of Guangdong kept its power, with the development of mainland cities, especially the development of Yangtze River Delta, the original advantages of Guangdong was at risk. In recent years, the "unbalance between east and west" turned up, especially the economy of the east part with Shantou. It might hinder the economy of Guangdong Province and finally became a burden for the rise of Pearl River Delta.

3.5.3.1 "Yuedong Meeting" Sounded the Horn of Shantou's Economic Development

In order to adapt the situation and offer aid to the economic development of Eastern Guangdong, in September of 2006, many high officials and heads of departments gathered in Shantou and held the meeting, called Yuedong Meeting, to accelerate the economic and social development of Eastern Guangdong. In the meeting, they discussed and approved "Guangdong Provincial Committee and Government's Suggestions on Accelerating Economic and Social Development of Eastern Guangdong," focusing on enhancing support of industrial disposition, infrastructural construction, finance and education, proposing the comprehensive planning to "lay the foundation within three years; make great change within five years; develop greatly within 10 years" and drawing anew blueprint for the development of Eastern Guangdong. At the same time, "Industrial Development and Key Projects Planning of Eastern Guangdong" with 270 billion RMB expectant investment, was officially published. In accordance with this planning, during the 11th Five-Year Plan period, Guangdong would build 390 projects in the east part (including Shantou, Chaozhou, Jieyang, Shanwei and Meizhou) concerned with industry, transportation, energy, water conservancy and agriculture and the total investment would reach 270 billion RMB. During the 11th Five-Year Plan period, the expected investment was 170 billion. On the basis of

"Specific Plan on Economic Development of East and West Part of Guangdong, Specific Plan on Industrialization of East and West Part of Guangdong" carried out by Provincial Committee and government and other supporting plans and measures to accelerate the development of east and west parts of Guangdong, Shantou was listed in the top five petrochemical bases of the whole province during the11th Five-Year Plan period. The request was issued to "enhance the regional central position of Shantou in east part of Guangdong; set up provincial-level logistic supporting center; develop industries near the harbors," which was a great step in the economic development of Shantou, and the important content for the coordinate development of the whole province.[339]

3.5.3.2 Realization of "Laying the Foundation Within Three Years"

In accordance with the general disposition of the Provincial Committee and government's "lay the foundation within three years; make great change within five years; develop greatly within 10 years," Shantou made efforts in three years to organize a group of key projects to lay a solid foundation for infrastructure, industrial development and social environment. In 2008, the economic development speed surpassed the average level of the whole province since 1999 and the stage goal to "lay foundation within three years" was realized.

3.5.3.2.1 Lay a Solid Foundation for Infrastructure

Accelerating infrastructure construction could let the investment directly effect economic development and could force the foundation for the long-term economic development. The projects of Shantou that were listed in "Industrial Development and Key Projects Planning of Eastern Guangdong" accounted for 173 with 121.08 billion RMB in investments. By the end of 2008, 27 projects were completed; 26 projects would be continued and 49 new projects would start during the 11th Five-Year Plan period; 59 projects were in the procedure; and the capital accumulated reached 17.289 billion RMB. Three major economic zones, harbors, transportation and energy were accelerated, which optimized the development environment of Shantou, encouraging confidence, people and investments.

In the aspect of harbor investment, at present, Guang'ao Harbor finished two piers of 50,000 tons and Haimen Harbor was building coal pier of 150,000 tons. A group of harbor projects from 50,000 tons to 100,000 tons were well prepared for the start. In the aspect of energy construction investment, one of the single largest capacity thermal power projects under construction was located in Huaneng Haimen Power Plant in the Haimen Gulf of

339 South Net: Industrial Development of Eastern Guangdong, http://www.southcn.com/news/gdnews/sz/yuedong/

Chaoyang District of Shantou. The development strategy had been changed from thermal power plant to a big energy base integrated with electricity, coal, road, harbor and transportation all together. However, six generators with millions of kilowatts, three piers of 150,000, 70,000 and 50,000 tons would be built. At the same time, construct railway to support harbors with more than 100 million tons of coal transferred.

At that time, Haimen Power Plant would become the largest coal pier in Eastern Guangdong and an important part for Shantou to establish a deep-water harbor of 1000 million tons. In the aspect of transportation, Nan'ao Bridge started from January of 2009 resolved the problem of transportation between Nan'ao Island and the mainland. It realized the connection between islands and cities. The bridge would combine the constructions of east part of the city and enlarge the space for the city, forming a new structure of regional economic development. In addition, fortification project in west part of Guang'ao District, Guang'ao Railway, Xiamen-Shenzhen Railway connect station in Shantou, electrification reform of Guangzhou-Meizhou-Shantou Railway, Su'ai Gulf Channel, transportation center for coal in east part of Guangdong, Shantou-Jieyang Express and other key projects all made progress during the preparation period. A group of environment protection projects, like sewage and rubbish treatment, were accelerated. Some main streets, entrance and exit reconstruction projects and projects of forestation, beautification and lighting had been put into use, which offered the city a brand-new look.

3.5.2.3.2 Compact the Base for the Industrial Development

At the end of 2008, an unexpected financial crisis occurred, which seriously impacted the world economy. However, the economy of Shantou developed in a contrarily. The stable and fast development resulted in a comparatively good industrial base. Most of the industries of Shantou relied on local private economy, which had powerful root and vitality. Most of these enterprises developed by their own accumulation and paid attention to creation and brand establishment, so their foundation was solid. Faced with the financial crisis, the economy of Shantou showed its capability against disasters. The toy industry in Chenghai was a typical representative. At present, Chenghai became the biggest base for producing and exporting toys around the country. In the face of international financial crisis, toy industry of Chenghai found a new opportunity and the turnover rose.

With the promotion of the "great industrial city" strategy, industrial economy of Shantou continuously developed and formed the eight pillar industries of electronic information, textile and garments, handcrafts and toys, chemistry and plastics, food and pharmaceutics, machinery, printing and package and video materials. Eighteen industries, of which included toys and gifts, handcrafts and sweater, package and printing, were granted as regional brands at the national level. To develop and strengthen a group of enterprises with a comparatively large scale laid a solid foundation for cultivating head industries with more than 5 billion and 10 billion RMB turnover each year.

In addition, Shantou municipal Committee and government carried out "Decisions on Accelerating Modern Industrial System" and proposed to speed up the construction of modern industrial system with integrated advantages of SEZ, harbors, convenient connection to Taiwan and a hometown for overseas Chinese and marine. By 2020, a new industrial system with high tech as the lead, advanced manufacturing and coastal industry as the mainstay, district economy as support would be formed with high concentration, distinctive characters and powerful competitive capability. The publishing of "Decisions" offered powerful support to set up a strong Shantou.

3.5.2.3.3 Compact Social Environment Base

"Ecological city" was the nickname for Shantou. In order to establish the most comfortable city for both living and working, Shantou made full efforts to set up a "gardening city of the nation." It collected 1.7 billion RMB for the municipal administration and the constructions of streets and 2.8 billion RMB for pollution reduction and sanitary work. It paid more than 500 million RMB within three years to the green construction and conservation. Gardening and green projects went on a new stage and the ecological environment was greatly improved. In order to upgrade the beautification level along the streets and to offer people a pleasant environment, Shantou concentrated on the major projects along Airport Express, Haibin Road and Zhongshan East Road with high starting point and high standard. According to the statistics, more than 900,000 trees and bushes were planted along these roads. Newly constructed or reformed green areas accounted for more than 640,000 square meters. These made the environment smooth and elegant. Lighting projects enhanced the nights of Shantou.

Shantou, with "promote development, benefit the livelihood of people" as theme for the implementation of ten projects, concentrating on solutions to increase income, employment, social guarantee, housing, education, environmental protection and social security and other major problems for the people. This transferred more economic achievement to peoples' lives and let more people enjoy the benefits of reform.[340]

---

340 ZHAO Lingwei: *Realization of the Stage Goal for Shantou to "Lay the Foundation within Three Years"*, *Shantou Daily*, June 17 2009, http://www.stdaily.com.cn/strbold/20090617/index.htm.

3.5.3.3 Opportunity and Challenge for Shantou—West Coastal Economic District

On May 14, 2009, the stand meeting of the State Council approved "Suggestions of the State Council Supporting Fujian to Accelerate Construction of the Economic District to the West Coast of Taiwan Channel." The construction of an economic district to the west of Taiwan Channel must promote a related area to develop quickly and become the fourth growth power following Yangtze River Delta, Pearl River Delta and Jing-Jin-Tang. Shantou was the central city of Eastern Guangdong, the SEZ closest to Taiwan of Guangdong Province and one of the places where Taiwan investment first arrived. Whether it could seize the historical opportunity to upgrade its position and function in the west coastal economic district to push the development of Eastern Guangdong was the urgent question that Shantou needed to explore.

The relationship between Shantou and Taiwan had a long history, exhibiting the characteristics of geographic neighborhood, close ties, similar culture and associated business. It was recorded in historical reference that since the opening of Shantou in 1861, there was direct shipping between Shantou and Budai Harbor, Anping Harbor, Jilong Harbor and Gaoxiong Harbor. Trading between Shantou and Taiwan developed fast. Businessmen and industrial practitioners from Taiwan came to Shantou and Chaozhou to invest and set up enterprises. After the reform and opening up, the industrial and trading relations between Shantou and Taiwan was further improved. Since the establishment of the first Taiwan company set up in Shantou in 1978, the number of Taiwan companies registered in Shantou accumulated to 550 with more than 1.6 billion USD investment, with the utilization of Taiwan investment reached 1.1 billion USD. However, in the west coast economic district, Shantou did not have advantages. First, no matter whether "three direct links (post, airlines and business)" or "mini three links ('Trial on Direct Marine Links Between Quemoy, Matsu, Penghu and Fujian Province')" was mentioned, Fujian Province had natural advantages. Xiamen, Quanzhou and Zhangzhou in Southern Fujian would be a direct beneficiary. Among the three cities of Eastern Guangdong, Chaozhou was located next to Fujian and was the closet place to Taiwan from Guangdong. If Guangdong enlarged the cooperation with Taiwan, Chaozhou would be the biggest beneficiary of geographic advantages.

Secondly, in terms of economic strength, the economic development levels of Zhangzhou and Shantou, central cities for Southern Fujian and Eastern Guandong, were greatly different. Therefore, if Shantou wanted to obtain the opportunities brought by the west coastal economic district, but not to be abandoned gradually, it must enhance the cooperation between Eastern Guangdong and Fujian, especially Xiamen, Quanzhou and Zhangzhou. Shantou proposed in its 11th Five-Year Plan period to accelerate merging into the west coast economic district and strengthen the integrated function of Shantou as an important harbor along the southeast coast of China. Huang Zhiguang, Secretary of Shantou Municipal Committee, demonstrated at several occasions that Shantou would actively devote itself to the construction of the west coast economic district, make Shantou enjoy preferential policies as extensive Pearl River Delta and SEZ and enjoy the preferential policies and measures from the west coastal economic district. If not, Shantou may lose chances for development and with the promotion of the west coast economic district, it may fall far behind Southern Fujian Delta, which rose fast. Therefore, the collapse of barriers between Taiwan and Mainland brought Shantou both challenges and opportunities.

3.6 Summary on the Instruction and Future Prospects of Shantou Special Economic Zone

During the past three decades, Shantou Special Economic Zone has gone through an extraordinary path of development, covering its establishment and expansion. With the continued reform and opening up within China, many of the original advantages of the Special Economic Zone gradually disappeared, which made Shantou's economic and social development face new challenges. In June 2009, after the implementation of "Reform and Development Plan (2008~2020) of Pearl River Delta in Guangdong," the Guangdong government and the Provincial Party Committee held a working conference in Shantou and issued the "Guidelines on Promoting the Big Change in Five Years of East Guangdong, given by CPC Guangdong Provincial Party Committee and People's Government of Guangdong Province," which strongly motivated the economic leap forward in Shantou. At the same time, Shantou seriously faced its own defects and problems, trying it best to create new advantages, thus achieve the rapid economic growth together with overall social progress.

3.6.1 The Achievements of Special Economic Zone

At the beginning of the establishment of Shantou Special Economic Zone, with very a cautious social environment, on the 1.6 square kilometers of land, the pioneers started from scratch, gained and learned experience while searching for a way to build the Special Economic Zone. With the great support of the Central Government, builders of the Special Economic Zone gradually grew despite many doubts, difficulties and a series of trials. After overcoming many difficulties in its development, the SAR has been enormous changed, mainly in the following aspects:

3.6.1.1 The Economic Strength has Markedly Increased

In 2009, the total GDP of Shantou was 103.573 billion yuan, 20,382 yuan per capita, respectively 95.98 and 55.69 times to the figure of 1980 (Figure 3-6-1, 3-6-2).[341] The industrial structure had been optimized and the proportion of three industries had been adjusted from 25: 34.1: 40.9 in 1980 to 5.27: 55.26: 39.46 in 2007. The primary industry had been continuously strengthened and enhanced, the traditional intensive and meticulous farming had been developed into a science, technology and export-oriented modern agriculture with high yield, quality and efficiency; the secondary industry also kept a rapid development—the ultrasonic electronics, textiles and clothing, plastic chemical, mechanical industry, food, medicine, toys and other backbone industries grew steadily while the high-tech industry rose; the tertiary industry enlarged from the traditional business sector, catering to transportation, telecommunications, finance, insurance, real estate, information consulting and other emerging industries, and the trend increasingly focused on socialization, specialization and modernization. Tourism, with the features of "sea, business, tidal and special" would have a promising future. The management of socio-economic was increasingly standardized and legalized; the economic operation mechanism stepped up with international standards.

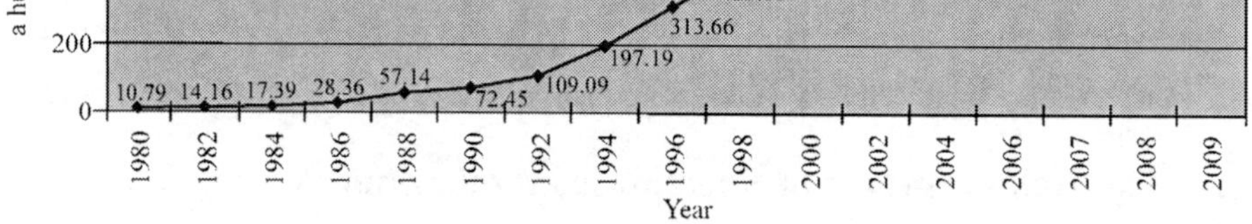

Figure 3-6-1 Trend on the GDP of Shantou Special Economic Zone

Source: data before 2005 was from *The Statistical Yearbook of Shantou and the Statistical Yearbook of China*; the data from 2006 to 2009 was from the *Statistics Bulletin on National Economy and Social Development of Shantou Special Economic Zone*, released by Shantou Bureau of Statistics.

341 Shantou Bureau of Statistics.*Statistics Bulletin on national economy and social development, 2009.*

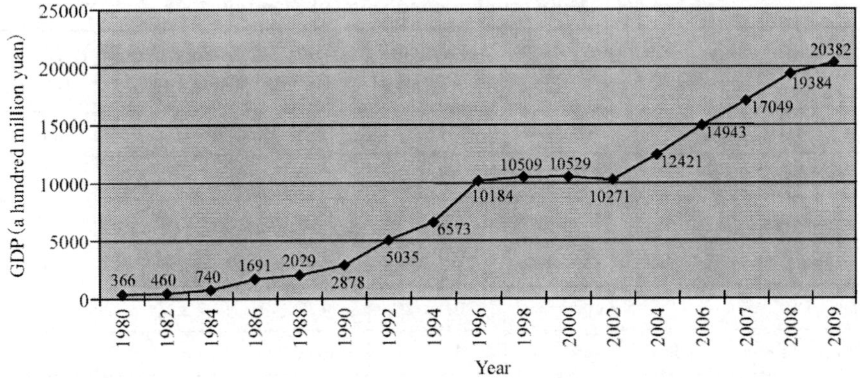

Figure 3-6-2 Trend on the per capita GDP of Shantou Special Economic Zone

Source: data before 2005 was from *The Statistical Yearbook of Shantou and the statistical Yearbook of China*; the data from 2006 to 2009 was from the *Statistics Bulletin on national economy and social development of Shantou Special economic zone, released by* Shantou Bureau of Statistics.

First, the industry's economic performance had been further enhanced, and its effects on economic growth had been further strengthened. Since set the goal of building an industry-oriented city, Shantou was dedicated to improving its capability of independent innovation, which greatly promoted the rapid growth of industrial production and the continuous optimization of industrial structure. In 2009, it had realized 53 billion yuan industrial added value, increasing 10.6%, and 37.717 billion yuan large-scale industrial added value, increasing 15.4%. Currently, there are 2,253 large-scale industries, 13 well-known trademarks of China (businesses), 10 famous Chinese brands, 188 provincial-level famous trademarks and 63 provincial-level famous brands. In 2009, the Guangdong government vigorously promoted the industrial restructuring, upgrading and cluster development, and the industry's independent innovation capability had been continually increased. 2009 saw the emergence of 24 new high-tech enterprises, seven provincial enterprise technology center, 3,692 authorized patents, and achieved high-tech product output value of 40.3 billion, a 18.5% increase over the previous year. The market competitiveness of the toy, clothing and other distinctive industries had been further enhanced. The Industrial Transference Park had been identified as Provincial Demonstration Garden, successfully bid 500 million yuan of the provincial supporting fund for industrial transference. The basic subsidiary facilities of the first Longing Industrial Transference Park phase had been completed.

Second, the development speed of the service industry is also accelerated. In 2009, the added value of tertiary industry went up 11.7% and contributed 43.1% to the whole economic

Table 3-6-1 Main economic indicator of Shantou, 2009

Index	Unit	Subtotal (absolute value)	Increasing rate (%)	Increasing rate of Guangdong (%)	Increasing rate of China (%)
GDP	100m yuan	1035.73	10.70	9.50	8.70
primary industry	100m yuan	54.63	3.20	4.90	4.20
secondary industry	100m yuan	572.38	10.80	8.70	9.50
tertiary-industry	100m yuan	408.72	11.70	11.00	8.90
Per Capita GDP	100m yuan	20382.00	9.50	8.4	
Added value of large scale industry	100m yuan	530.85	10.60	8.9	11
Total output value of large scale industry	100m yuan	1533.66	14.1		
Investment in fixed assets of the whole society	100m yuan	291.90	11.70	19.50	30.10
Investment in fixed assets of the cities and towns	100m yuan	225.23	11.80		30.50
# capital construction	100m yuan	106.34	21.80		44.30
Real estate exploitation	100m yuan	38.09	15.80		16.10
Total retail sales of consumer goods	100m yuan	672.59	18.20	16.30	15.50
Consumer price index	%		-1.70		-0.70
Total volume of imports and exports	100m USD	60.28	-4.30	-10.80	-13.90
# Total exports volume	100m USD	40.16	-7.10	-11.50	-16.00
Total imports volume	100m USD	20.12	1.90	-9.70	-11.20
Actual usage of foreign investment	100m USD	2.04	5.20		
Local Budgetary Financial Revenue	100m yuan	58.54	14.30	10.30	
Local Budgetary Financial Expenses	100m yuan	97.19	15.90	14.60	
deposit balances held at financial institution	100m yuan	1623.06	18.80	24.20	
# remaining of the urban and rural inhabitants' savings	100m yuan	1168.73	14.00		
Per capita disposable income of urban residents	Yuan	13651.00	8.80	12	9.8
Per capita expenditure of urban households of city centre	Yuan	11659.00	8.30	8.6	10.1
Per capita cash income of rural residents	Yuan	5260.00	7.70		8.5

Source: sorted by the respective data of *Statistics Bulletin on National Economy and Social Development of Shantou City, Guangdong Province and Bulletin on National Economy and Social Development of China*.

growth, a 20.9% increase from the previous year, of which the added value of modern service industry was 18.785 billion yuan, increasing 6.1%. The harbor handling capacity exceeded 30 million tons, and the handling capacity of Shantou Airport reached 1.267 million passengers, increasing 16.1%. Great encouragement had been given to the construction of the Coastal Eco-tourism Demonstration Area, and the total tourism income reached 7.429 billion yuan, an increase of 9.4% from the previous year. The financial institutions and foreign currency deposits reached 162.306 billion yuan, with the loan balance up to 57.047 billion yuan, respectively increased by 18.8% and 33.7%. The industries of building and real estate developed soundly. The construction of the National Quality Supervision and Inspection Center for Toys were undergoing smoothly. The development of the Game Fair, Food Fair, Literature Fair and other exhibition industry also accelerated.

Third, the modernization and industrialization of agricultural continued to increase. The total output value of agricultural reached 10.432 billion yuan, increasing 4.2%. The construction of distinctive agricultural products base and modern agricultural park had been promoted and Niutianyang modern agro-ecological demonstration zone had been identified as the "base of national agricultural products processing business." The construction on Taiwan farmers Pioneering Park has been started in Chaonan; the first phase of Chenghaixiadaimei and the Chaonanshangnan modern vegetables production demonstration area was completed. "Donghua Super Green" in Chaoshan became the first agricultural collective trademark of Shantou, developing the leading agricultural enterprises and cooperatives and jointly encouraging the increase farmers' income. The fishermen were encouraged to steadily change their work to other industries. Building of the national level Haimen Central Fishing Harbor progressed well. The building of DAHAO Primary Fishing Harbor has been started and the tentative plan of Yun`ao Central Fishing Harbor passed the review by Ministry of Agriculture.[342]

3.6.1.2 Continually Strengthened Economic Characteristics of Export-oriented Economy and Constantly Up-graded Level of Export-oriented Economy

Three out of five National Special Economic Zones was adjacent to Hong Kong, Macao and Taiwan. Although Shantou was not among the ones with a favorable geographical position, it had the unique advantage of being the hometown of many overseas Chinese and also one of the largest modern immigration ports. Currently, the

---

342 Cai Zongze: 《Shantou governmental work statement of 2009》, Feb 24th, Shantou governmental website http://www.shantou.gov.cn/common/view.asp?id=41745&lmdm=047100

number of overseas Chinese, Chinese merchant and Hong Kong and Macao compatriots was over 10 million, of which the Shantou membership were more than three million. The unique advantages of geographical convenience and harmonious human relations with overseas Chinese made Shantou have great potential in opening up.

3.6.1.2.1 The Abundant Overseas Human Resources was an Important Force for Promoting the Export-oriented Economic Development of Shantou

At the initial stage of the establishment of the Special Economic Zone, Shantou had implemented a series of policies regarding overseas Chinese affairs, which greatly stimulated the enthusiasm of the Chinese people, and attracted a large number of overseas compatriots to start their industries in Shantou. Meanwhile, the Shantou government specifically hired many financiers, industrialists, experts, scholars and leaders of Chao Group among the patriotic overseas Chinese as the consultants of the Special Economic Zone, aimed at obtaining more council to Shantou's development plan. In this period, the hometown economy of overseas Chinese mainly depended on overseas Chinese "donation" investments, of which the cultural and educational undertakings took the leading position.[343] After 1984, the investment type of overseas Chinese gradually transferred from the "donation" to "industrial." Shantou carried out more preferential policies to encourage the overseas Chinese to directly investe in the infrastructure, high tech industries, agricultural development projects and the tertiary industry. The overseas investments increased rapidly, and the investment structures also greatly improved. Since the reform and opening up, the cumulative amount of the four cites across Chaozhou-Shantou area received 9.918 billion yuan from Chaozhou Chinese and overseas Chinese and compatriots of Hong Kong and Macao, of which 4.918 billion was donated to Shantou, accounting for 50%.[344] Currently, more than 10,000 enterprises with a total industrial output value over 200 billion yuan are operated by overseas Chinese.[345] With the improved investment environment, a large number of powerful overseas enterprises, like Thailand Bangkok Bank, Thailand's China Tai Group, started their own business in

343 Xu Siliang, *The17th meeting for Shantou returned overseas Chinese and their relatives*, *Shantou Daily*, December 21st, 2007.

344 Huang Yingfa, Chen Jiayuan, *Album on Chaoshan historical cultural picutres of antique* volume 2, Page 379, released by the information department of Chaozhou, Jieyang, Shantou and Shanwei municipal Party committee, 2008.

345 Chenjian, *Enlightens from the visit of Shantou Friendly delegation to four southeast Asian countries, Shantou Daily*, November 3rd, 2008

Shantou. Especially in the last couple of years, the overseas Chinese investment has significantly accelerated its pace with international standards, and the third and fourth generation of Chao people started to actively participate in investing in Shantou. These generations are not only younger, but also have much more dynamic thoughts and richer knowledge and vision of the new economic era. In addition, groups of high-tech investment projects have access to Shantou.

3.6.1.2.2 Improved Investment Environment and Rapidly Increased Foreign Investment

From the "Fifteen National People's Congress," there was a temporary obstacle in Shantou's economic development–the investment environment deteriorated, altogether with the drop of foreign investment. However, under the leadership of the Municipal Party Committee and government, the united citizens rose and enacted a series of measures to improve the investment environment, which made the foreign investment achieve a satisfactory recovery of growth.

In 2010, Shantou was selected as one of the "200 Chinese Characteristically Charming Cities" for the past 60 years by the joint election of World Brand Organization, the U.S. Trade and Investment Chamber of Commerce, and the Global Cooperated Organization on building the harmonious society, which helped Shantou successfully attract more attention from the investment and trade bodies at home and abroad.

Following the strategy of attracting investment by business, emotion and overseas relationships, together with the improved investment environment and increased investment confidence, a growing number of national and regional entrepreneurs frequented Shantou to make inspections, hold trade talks, and invest in and build factories. According to the statistics from the municipal foreign trade and economic department, over the past 30 years of reform and opening up, more than 5,000 foreign-funded enterprises were invested in Shantou, and the actual used foreign capital was more than 70 billion USD. All these foreign-funded enterprises and the actual use of foreign capital were not only from the overseas Chao people, but also some multinational companies and large financial groups, including 13 Fortune 500 companies,[346] and the majority were businessmen from Hong Kong and Macau. With the deepening of the reform and opening-up policy and Hong Kong and Macao's return to Chinese

---

346 Chenshi, *Shantou attracted over 5,000 foreign enterprises in the past 30 years of reform and opening up, Shantou Evening*, December 17th, 2008

sovereignty, the Chao people living in Hong Kong and Macao got a more realistic and comprehensive understanding on their hometown, which sped up Shantou's trade and economic cooperation with Hong Kong and Macao. By the end of 2008, 4,762 of Hong Kong's direct investment projects had been approved by the Shantou government; the actually amount of Hong Kong's direct investments used equaled 5.68 billion USD.[347] All these statistics effectively demonstrated the close economic and trade cooperation between Shantou and Hong Kong. After the reunification, especially since the implementation of Closer Economic Partnership Agreement (CEPA,) the economic and trade cooperation between Shantou and Hong Kong changed from the simple trade and investment to all-round cooperation and exchange. Hong Kong's capital, technology and advanced management experience effectively sped up the process of Shantou's industrial modernization. In addition, Shantou realized the historical breakthrough in economic and trade cooperation with Taiwan. Great efforts were made to construct the main channel for Guangdong and Taiwan's direct traffic. In 2009, ahead of other cities in Guangdong, Shantou first achieved the direct sea freight to Taiwan, completed 106 direct voyages with 17,600 standard containers. Meanwhile, it also realized the charter shipping tourism to Taiwan, and the Shantou Tourism Corporation was appointed as one of the second batch of travel agents which had the authority to operate the mainland residents travelling to Taiwan, taking a leading role in building economic and trade cooperation test area between Guangdong and Taiwan.

The improved investment environment helped Shantou gain rapid development in attracting foreign investment. In 2009, the actual amount of direct foreign investment in Shantou was 204 million, a 5.2% increase from the previous year, which was the best score of the recent six years. In the same year, investors from Hong Kong, Taiwan, Australia, Thailand, Samoa and the United States come to Shantou to start their new projects, 31 foreign direct investment projects had been set up, among which 23 were foreign-owned enterprises, and the actual foreign investment amount was 140 million USD, an increase of 22%.[348]

3.6.1.2.3 Remarkable Development in Foreign Trade

Since the establishment of the Special Economic Zone, Shantou's import and export

347 Li Yiqing and Li Xiaoting, Trade between Hong Kong and Shantou was constantly enlarged, and Hong Kong became the biggest investment render, October 21th, 2009, http://www.pprd.org.cn/92/guangdong/200910/t20091021_68870.htm.

348 Cai Zongze, 2009 work statement of Shantou government, February 24th, 2010, web of Shantou government, http://www.shantou.gov.cn/common/view.asp?id=41745&lmdm=047100

trade developed significantly. The representative trade products are clothing, toys, furniture, textile yarn and etc, and the major trading partners are from the United States, Japan, the European Union, Hong Kong and the Association of Southeast Asian Nations (ASEAN). In July 2005, the ASEAN and China officially launched the process of tariff reduction, marked the China-ASEAN Free Trade Area, which entered into a comprehensive and substantial construction phase, providing a development space and opportunity for the trade between ASEAN and Shantou.

The outbreak of the global financial crisis greatly impacted the enterprises of eastern Guangdong Province and the exports continued to show negative growth. The negative impact of the financial crisis was highlighted in the first half of 2009. Except in February, the export value for each month hovered between 2-3 billion dollars. In the second half of 2009, by the co-work of the national macroeconomic policies and positive signs of internationaleconomic recovery as well as the small export base with the same period in the pervious year, the exports fell significantly over the first half, showing signs of recovery, and in September and November, the single month export growth rate showed a positive growth. December saw a substantial increase of 24.2% compared with the pervious year and a chain growth of 21.8%. According to Customs statistics, in 2009, the total import and export value of Shantou enterprises was 6.03 billion USD, a 4.3% decrease compared to 2008, but fell below the national and provincial level over the same period, showing a strong resistance to shocks. Especially for the private enterprises with a flexible operation mechanism, the export value amounted to 1.98 billion USD, increasing 0.2%, among which in December, the monthly export value was 200 million USD, a 36.4% increase, which was significantly better than the foreign-invested and state-owned enterprises. In addition, the export of some representative products like clothing, toys, agricultural products, furniture, and textiles and so on exemplified the growth trend.[349] In addition, the unfavorable situation against exports to the U.S. was reversed, and the exports to the ASEAN and the Middle Eastern countries grew against the trend. In 2009, the export value of Shantou to U.S. hit 790 million, increasing 1.2%. In December, it finally reversed the declining exports situation of the previous 11 months, and obtained 37.04 million USD in exports to the U.S., a 36.9% increase than the previous year. In the same period, due to the impact of the financial crisis and facing the rapidly shrinking demand from European and America markets, Shantou enterprises shifted their exports

349 Guangdong Custom's office, Shantou's exports raised slightly, and exports gradually re-thrived in 2009, January 21th, 2010, http://guangdong_sub.customs.gov.cn/publish/portal91/tab1461/module14682/info209300.htm

focus to ASEAN, achieving good results. In 2009, the imports and exports to ASEAN equaled 1.7 billion USD, 42.2% increase from the same period in 2008, of which the export value was 940 million USD, up 25.8%. Import value was 760 million USD, a substantial increase of 69.6% and achieved a surplus of 180 million USD, ranking second to Hong Kong. Exports to United Arab Emirates (UAE) was 1.5 billion USD, up 2.6%. Exports to Saudi Arabia equaled 978.9 billion UDS, up 25.3%. Exports to South Africa equaled 52.75 USD, increasing 7.2%. The export situation in the same period was significantly better than the exports to the traditional markets of the EU, Hong Kong, Japan, etc.[350]

3.6.1.3 People's Living Standards has been Further Improved

People's living standards had continually improved over the 30 years after the establishment of Special Economic Zone. In 2009, the personal disposable income of urban residents was 13,651 yuan, 41.36 times (Table 3-6-2) over the average level of Special Economic Zone in 1980. Farmer's per capita net income was 5,260 yuan (Table 3-6-3), 18.45 times over 1980's average level. The savings deposits of urban and rural residents equaled 116.873 billion yuan, while only 0.88 million in 1980. Although in recent years, Shantou fell behind the other cities in the area of urban residents' income. By comparing the historical data before the reform and opening up and after the establishment of the Special Economic Zone, the income level of urban and rural residents in Shantou was once much higher than the national average.

In addition, the consumption level of urban and rural residents has undergone tremendous changes, and the expense of education, entertainment, transportation, telecommunications and health care have increased. The living environment has further improved, with the government consistently promoting the transformative construction of the old downtown buildings, speeding up the process of building low-rent public housing, and effectively solving the living issues of the poor houseless families. In order to further improve the living conditions of rural residents, the forces to repair the dangerous buildings and to build the houses for the rural poor households with subsistence allowances has been strengthened.[351]

---

350 Shantou government, *Exports and imports to ASEAN had been greatly increased.* January 1st, 2010, http://www.shantou.gov.cn/common/view.asp?id=40597&lmdm=04k004

351 Shantou Bureau of Statistics, *statistics Bulletin on national economy and social development of Shantou Special economic zone.*

Table 3-6-2 Changes of Personal Disposable Income of Urban Residents in Shantou Special Economic Zone in Comparison With Other Cities **Unit: Yuan**

Category \ Year	1980	1990	1995	2000	2002	2004	2005	2006	2007	2008	2009
Shantou	330	1917	6132	8707	8740	9930	10630	10949	11716	12542	13651
Average level of the nation	476	1686	4283	6280	7703	9422	10493	11759	13786	15781	17175
Comparison with the nation's average level	-146	+231	+1849	+2427	+1037	+508	+137	-810	-2070		

Source: data before 2005 was from *The Statistical Yearbook of Shantou and the statistical Yearbook of China*; the other data was from the *Statistics Bulletin on national economy and social development of Shantou Special economic zone*

Table 3-6-3 Changes of farmer's per capita net income in Shantou Special Economic Zone and comparison with other cities **Unit: Yuan**

Category \ Year	1980	1990	1995	2000	2002	2004	2005	2006	2007	2008	2009
Shantou	285	1230	5445	4343	3894	4089	4321	4450	4604	4885	5260
Average level of the nation	178	571	1578	2253	2476	2936	3255	3587	4140	4761	5153
Comparison with the nation's average level	+107	+659	+3867	+2070	+1418	+1153	+1066	+863	+464		

Source: data before 2005 was from *The Statistical Yearbook of Shantou and the statistical Yearbook of China*; the other data was from the *Statistics Bulletin on national economy and social development of Shantou Special economic zones*.

In addition, the government was continuously improving the urban and rural social security system and enlarging the coverage of social insurance. The health services have been improved by strengthening the primary health care team, promoting the transformation of poor township hospitals and building the county health care institution. The combined rate of New Cooperative Medical Scheme (NCMS) Senate was over 98%. It will continually work on enhancing the public health service capabilities, strengthening the prevention and treatment of major diseases, and improving the capacity of early warning and prediction against the public health emergencies. The implementation of the pilot project, the basic drug system, was started, the transform and integration of the Central Emergency and outpatient center was promoted, and the reconstruction of the Municipal Public Health School relocation began. Meanwhile, building of urban and rural social relief system was promoted steadily, and the development of social welfare accelerated.

3.6.1.4 Perfection of Urban Functions and Environmental Quality

After the establishment of the Special Economic Zone, Shantou's urban infrastructure developed rapidly through large-scale investment in fixed assets. In 2009, the capital investment in fixed assets equaled 29.19 billion yuan, an 11.7% increase from the previous year. The town investment was 22.523 billion yuan, the investment of rural areas was 6.667 billion yuan, respectively increased by 11.8% and 11.4%.[352] Compared with the status before reform and opening up, both the breadth and depth of investment in fixed assets has gone through enormous changes (Figure 3-6-3, Figure 3-6-4).

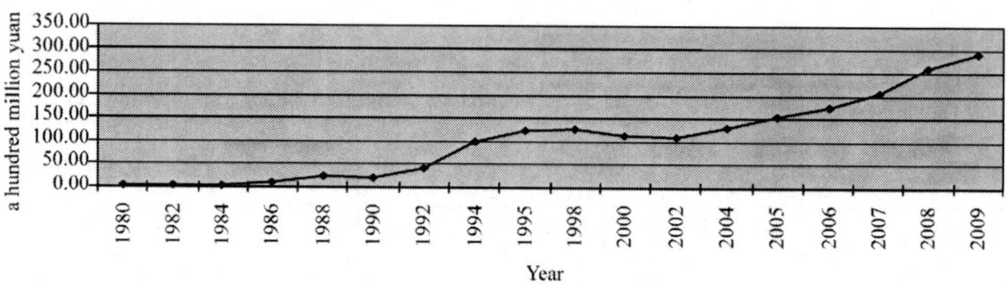

Figure 3-6-3 Trend of investment in fixed assets of Shantou Special Economic Zone

Source: data before 2006 was from *The Statistical Yearbook of Shantou and the Statistical Yearbook of China*; data after 2006 was from the *Statistics Bulletin on National Economy and Social Development of Shantou Special Economic Zone*

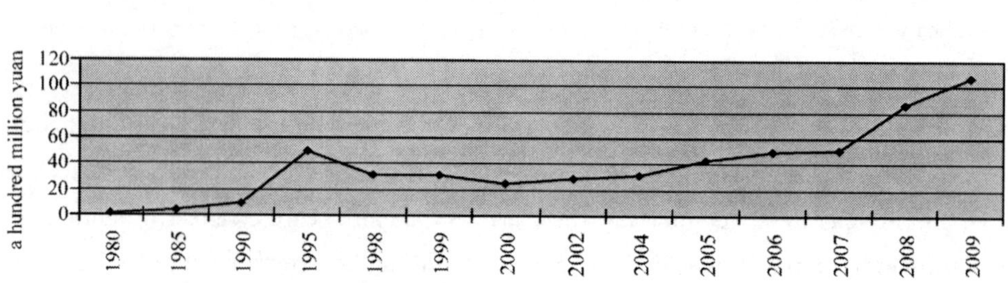

Figure 3-6-4 Trend of investment in infrastructure in Shantou Special Economic Zone

Source: data before 2006 was from *The Statistical Yearbook of Shantou and the Statistical Yearbook of China*; data after 2006 was from the *Statistics Bulletin on National Economy and Social Development of Shantou Special Economic Zone*

The construction of vital communication lines, like Guangzhou-Meizhou-Shantou

352 Shantou Bureau of Statistics, *Statistics Bulletin on national economy and social development of Shantou Special economic zone.*

Railway, Bay Bridge and the Shenzhen-Shantou expressway, greatly motivated the economic development of Shantou. An ocean liner of ten thousand tons, three air lines flying to more than 40 cities, the NO. 2 international submarine cables between Asia and Europe, America and Asia-Pacific, with the largest capacity in the world, landed in Shantou Special Economic Zone, all of which made Shantou become a very important mode of the international information highway. The seaport, airport and information harbor are at the heartand the railway, highway, bridge as the skeleton, the sea, land and air transportation network and modern information network has been initially formed. In 2009, the urban infrastructure construction moved to a new level. The building of the Shantou segment of the Shantou to Jieyang Expressway was started. The preliminary work of Shantou segment of Shantou to Jiexi, Jieyang to the Huilai, Chaozhou to Huizhou Expressway had been strongly promoting. The land acquisition work of the Shantou segment of Xiamen-Shenzhen Railway has been completed, and the feasibility study review of the contact line by Shantou Station had been passed.

Along with the continual expansion and promotion of new energy groups, transportation and municipal projects, the city function of Shantou steadily improved, and the living environment and quality of life in Shantou was also significantly perfected.

3.6.1.5 New Progress Made in Cultural and Ethical Construction and Other Social Undertakings

Since the reform and opening up, the complete educational system from the universities, secondary schools and primary schools to kindergarten and from general education, vocational education to adult education has been established in Shantou, which generally enhanced the quality of life in the Special Economic Zone. Shantou University was established, incorporating more than 2 billion Hong Kong dollars donation from Li Ka-shing into the national “211” project. The citizens’ quality and urban and rural civilization degree has constantly increased. The Science and Technology Museum, other museums, exhibition centers, Chaozhou arts centers, youth centers, women and children centers, veteran centers and other cultural facilities have been built up in secession. The public and corporate cultures have been widely carried out, and the cultural life of the masses has been increasingly enriched.

Chaoshan has its unique traditional culture and art, after the reform and opening up, all these cultural undertakings and industries, rich in regional characteristics has grown vigorously. The representatives of Chaoshan culture, Chao opera, Chaozhou music, Ying song and dance, and paper-cuts, have been brought into the first batch of the "national intangible cultural heritage" recommended projects list. In addition, great development has been made to the public utilities. The public health system has been constantly improved, the disease prevention and control center has been re-located, and the prevention and control capacity on SARS, avian flu, HIV/AIDS and other major infectious diseases has been strengthened. The coverage of new-type cooperative medical care in rural areas has been enlarged. Development of services for women and children, disabled, aged and charity was also gradually accelerated.

3.6.2 Problems and Reflections of the Construction of Shantou Special Economic Zone

Over nearly 30 years after the establishment of Shantou Special Economic Zone, it has achieved a number of remarkable results in all aspects, such as economic power, living standards and social development. However, together with the moving forward of China's reform and opening-up, the policy advantages of the Special Economic Zone have been gradually dismissed and, especially after China's accession to the World Trade Organization (WTO), the once unique policy advantage of Special Economic Zone disappeared. Comparing with the other devolved regions or cities in China, there still many problems exist in Shantou's economic and social development.

3.6.2.1 Economic Growth Lagged Behind Other Cities in Guangdong Province and Residents' Income was Comparatively Low

Among the five Special Economic Zones, the development of Shantou Special Economic Zone generally lagged behind. The overall economic position of Shantou ranked fairly low in Guangdong Province. Maoming in west Guangdong, which once fell far behind in groups of economic indicators, surpassed Shantou, the former leading city in East Guangdong. And even Qingyuan, Heyuan which was always regarded as a poor area, also became the province's latest highlights of economic growth because of the industrial transformation in the Pearl River Delta.

There is a certain gap in income and expenses level between Shantou and the whole province. Between 2000~2009, except in 2004 the income growth of Shantou residents lagged behind the provincial average level (Figure 3-6-5, 3-6-6). Regarding the absolute income, the gap between Shantou and the whole province in average income has enlarged from 1,054 yuan in 2000 to 7923.7 yuan in 2009.

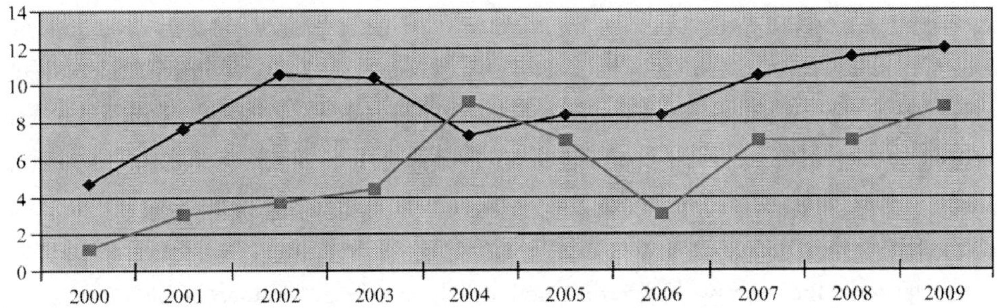

Figure 3-6-5 2000~2009 Comparison Between Shantou and the Whole Province in the Growth of Urban Residents' per Capita Disposable Income

Source: each years' *Statistics Bulletin on National Economy and Social Development of Guangdong Province and Statistics Bulletin on National Economy and Social Development of Shantou Special Economic Zone*

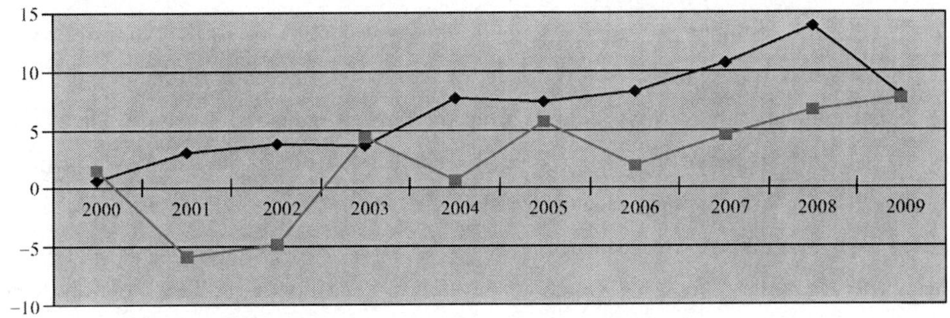

Figure 3-6-6 2000~2009 Comparison Between Shantou and the Whole Province in the Growth of Rural Residents' per Capita Disposable Income

Source: each year's Statistics Bulletin on national economy and social development of Guangdong province and Statistics Bulletin on national economy and social development of Shantou Special economic zone

3.6.2.2 The Weak Industry Base and the Further Optimization of Industrial Structure

Business has always been the traditional advantage of Shantou, however, based on the current situation, most of these historical business-oriented cities have developed into modern industrial cities through industrial restructuring and structural adjustment. In the recent years, Shantou's economic growth lagged behind the whole Guangdong province. A fundamental reason for this was a lack of industrial development and strong affect the opening up of the mainland and surrounding cities had on traditional commercial trade, while at the same time, the development of new service industry has been restricted by the slow developed industry.

Shantou was once unable to find a specific industrial orientation in the economic development, and the profit-oriented thinkingled it to the improper industry selection. For example, in the 1990s, particularly after Deng Xiaoping's 1992 southern tour speech, taking advantage of the rising fever of building the national development zone, Shantou focused on real estate industry, resulting in an upsurge in the construction of infrastructure, housing villas, high-rise commercial and residential buildings. By upholding the thoughts of developing the Special Economic Zone's economy via "regarding the real estate industry as the leader," the supply of housing and urban high-rise commercial and residential buildings was far more than the needs of residents. Due to the lagging industrial development, the majority's income was not enough to purchase the real estate, which resulted in a large number of unused buildings unused. The vacant housing not only caused the backlog of capital, but also caused an unfavorable impact to the economic development, which would have led to a local financial crisis.

All these phenomena proved that without industry support, the tertiary industry could not realize sound development.

Some scholars believe that, judging from the current industrial structure, Shantou is still in the early stages of industrialization. Its characteristics are the same as a primary industry that declines when the secondary industry develops rapidly. The industry focus has shifted from light industry to basic industries. The second industry occupies an important place, and the tertiary industry began to develop.[353] The major problems of industrial structure are as follows:

3.6.2.2.1 The Uncoordinated Industrial Structure And Unclear Characteristics and Benefits of Industrial Clusters

In 2009, the ratio of primary industry to GDP was 5.27%, secondary industry accounted for 55.26%, and the tertiary industry took 39.46%.[354] Judging from the output value structure of the three industries, the primary industry took a comparatively low proportion, while tertiary industry took a high share, but still needed to be further optimized. By the end of the "15th period," the employment structure of the three major industries was 31:35:34.[355] The employment proportion of the primary industry was relatively high, while

---

353 Chen Jianping and Liu Jianqi, *Study on the adjustment and optimization of Shantou's industrial structure during the period of the "11th Five-Year Plan"*, *Shantou university journal, January, 2006*, Page 63 to 65.

354 Shantou Bureau of Statistics, *Statistics Bulletin on national economy and social development of Shantou Special economic zone.*

355 Shantou Government, *The development plan of labor and social security in Shantou during the period of the "11th Five-Year Plan"*, November 19th, 2007, http://www.shantou.gov.cn/fwdt/fwdtA.asp?lmbm=sm0000&xjbm=SM1400.

the secondary industry and tertiary industry employment share was relatively low. In the industrial organizational structure, the quantity of large enterprises was comparatively low. Generally speaking, the small and medium sized enterprises still took an absolute advantage in numbers. The large leading enterprises were too few and there were great difficulties in stimulating the rapid economic growth, such as: low in overall industrialization level; lack of heavy industry, based on the small and low value-added traditional industries; products grade was lo;, the capacity of independent innovation was weak; lack of core technology and independent intellectual property rights; mainly relying on cheap labor, resource consumption, land use and preferential policies to accelerate its development.

3.6.2.2.2 Restricted Agricultural Development and Low Degree of Modernization

The agricultural development in Shantou was subject to the triple constraints of resources, markets and space. The overall quality of agriculture was not as high as could effectively support the steady growth of farmers' income.

With densely populated land, Shantou's agricultural resources, especially arable land resources, were very limited. The per capita arable land was only 0.14 acres, which means it was too hard to implement the large-scale agricultural operations. The agricultural and rural economic structure is still irrational, although the relatively profitable vegetable growing has formed a large industry, but the advantage of the other industries' development is still unable to participate. Little science and technology was contained in agricultural products, so the proportion of high-quality agricultural products is low, which requires further enhancement in the market competition. The export-oriented agriculture developed slowly and, in recent years, limited foreign capital has been applied to agriculture. The serious shortage in agricultural inputs affected the construction of agricultural infrastructure and the implementation of most production demonstration projects, except aquatic products. The organizational level of the agriculture was also low, and the processing, distribution and etc. social service system relatively lags behind, resulting in slow development of agricultural industrialization.[356]

3.6.2.2.3 Unsatisfied Industrial Economic Efficiency and Weak Industry Competitiveness

In comparison with the other relevant cities, there are some obvious deficiencies and

---

356 Shantou agricultural Bureau, *Plan for Shantou's agricultural development during the period of the "11th Five-Year Plan"*, November 10th, 2005, http://agri.shantou.gov.cn/layout/Class.asp?ClassID=28.

shortcomings in the development of Shantou's scaled-enterprises:

Firstly, the economic efficiency of enterprises is unsatisfied. According to the economic efficiency composite index of 40 above-designated-size industrial enterprises released by the National Bureau of Statistics in 2008, Shantou ranked number 35. The large-scale industrial realized added value of 22.053 billion yuan, contributed 61.3% to the whole city's industrial added value, much lower than neighboring Zhuhai and Xiamen, and 85.7% lower than the provincial average. The low proportion of scale industrial added value to the whole industrial added value directly affects the scale of tax revenue.

Secondly, the scale of industrial enterprises was relatively small. Among the 2107 above-designated-size industrial enterprises, the number of large enterprises was few, there are only 172 enterprises' output value exceed 100 million yuan, of which only seven with over 1 billion output value.

Thirdly, the industrial level is low. The traditional light industry took the leading position. The output value of traditional industries accounts for more than 85% of the total industrial output value. Moreover, the technical competence of traditional industrial was low, and the product grade and quality needed to be further improved. Lacking in core technology and independent intellectual property rights, the competiveness of industry was weak.

Thus, compared with the other developed cities, or even some big groups, no matter the firm size, efficiency, capability of independent innovation, or contribution to GDP or tax, the scale-enterprises in Shantou can be only regarded as small and medium enterprises. The low industrial development level and speed was seriously affecting the upgrade and optimization of Shantou's industrial structure.[357]

3.6.2.2.4 The Rapid Development of Tertiary Industry and the Irrational Structure

Fifteen years before the establishment of Shantou Special Economic Zone, due to the affect of constraints from the backwards transportation and traditional ideas, as well as the unitary industry structure, the development of tertiary industry was relatively slow, and its proportion of the entire industry was small. After entering into 1990s, with the gradually practice of all aspects of construction, the development of tertiary industry accelerated, especially in the sectors of business and real estate. However, concentrating only on commercial trade and neglecting the industries made the development of tertiary industry

---

357 Shantou government office, *Explanations on 'Measures of helping the above scaled enterprises to accelerate their development by Shantou People's Government'*, January 29th, 2008, http://www.dahuawang.com/ztxw/wxb/show.asp?no=455&type=3.

lack of a solid foundation and stamina.

Judging from the internal structure of the tertiary industry, the commodity industry developed rapidly, and accounted for a larger proportion. Specifically, the consumer goods market is very active. In 2009, the total retail sales of the social consumer goods was 67.259 billion yuan, an 18% increase.[358] In contrast, the development of producing services, personal services and new services was slow, only accounting for a small proportion, which could not meet the modern requirements. In particular, the producing services, including regional financial services, information consulting, modern transport and logistics, commercial exhibition, technology services and etc., had already become an important part of the modern economy, a leading force of economic growth and a pillar industry of many developed countries, playing an increasingly important role both in the development of world economy and the international competition. Shantou needed to be the center of eastern Guangdong and, in theory, should be the regional service center. After China's accession to the WTO, Shantou's economy melted into the wave of economic globalization, with a deeper level and the development of service producing also faced new opportunities and challenges.

3.6.2.3 Large Population Put Huge Pressure on Development of Economic Society

In 2009, the population of Shantou was 5.1073 million,5.0343 million of which were urban residents. The population density was 2,224 people per square kilometers,[359] ranking second among the five special economic zones, following Shenzhen. According to the latest statistics provided by Shantou Municipal Bureau of State Land and Resources, the cultivated land per capital of Shantou took only 11% of the national average standard and 34% of provincial average, both of which are far behind the 0.8 acre per capital—the warning line released by the United Nations Food and Agriculture Organization. Land resource scarcity has become more and more serious.[360]

Due to the intensive disparity between human and land, agricultural production's capability of absorbing labor force was limited. No matter if transferring within the region or of centralizing toward urban areas, how the secondary industry and the tertiary industry will absorb the large number of surplus labor in rural area has become an arduous task of population urbanization in Shantou. With a huge population base, although Shantou's birth

358 Cai Zongze, 2009 work statement of Shantou government, February 24th, 2010, web of Shantou government http://www.shantou.gov.cn/common/view.asp?id=41617&lmdm=043000

359 Shantou Bureau of Statistics, *Shantou National Economic and Social Development Communiqué*.

360 Xiao Tonglan, *Population Density of Shantou Reached 2,224 per sq.km*, *Shantou Metropolitan*, April 16th, 2008.

rate is reducing gradually in recent years, the population still maintains a relatively large increase. The rapid growth of labor force and economic recession brought about a great pressure for Shantou's employment market. The trend of unemployed population has grown younger and younger; especially among the female population.

3.6.2.4 Lack of Talent Resources

In the process of economic development, scientific and technological factors are crucially important, while the development of science and technology depends on talents. Although the introduction of technology is one of the main forces of economic development, the incorporation and constant innovation of the imported technology still relies on talent, otherwise the development would be unsustainable. Therefore, to train and retain talents is the core factor of economic development.

In the sector of talents training, the education level of the east Guangdong is superior to other regions of the province. It's a tradition in Chinese history teachers and the teaching career is respected by society. With a fairly good education, especially the fundamental education, every year, there are a number of students enrolled in the junior colleges and technical secondary school. However, since the continuous downturn of Chaozhou and Shantou, only a small number of graduates went back to their hometown. Moreover, even the Shantou-ese who graduated from the top schools were reluctant to go back, which caused a serious outflow of talent. Besides, there is a shortage of environment and facilities for the further development of talents. Especially, in the respect of adult education as well as vocational and technical education, the whole east Guangdong not only lags behind the Chu Chiang Delta, but also the west Guangdong and mountain areas.[361] To a certain extent, the insufficiency of the overall education environment has influenced Shantou's attraction towards talents. The insufficiency has also made existing talents unable to timely adjust their knowledge structure and the rate of updated knowledge lags behind the request of economy development.

From the aspect of the talent demand and supply structure, the demand of professionals exceeds supply in the fields of electronic communication, chemical textile and mechanical instrumentation, while in the fields of finance and accounting, as well as banking areas, there is a surplus of specialists. The imbalance between supply and demand of the talents'

---

361 Du Zhongnian: *Localization and Otherness of Economy Development under Globalization Circumstance—on the Basis of Comparison of Three Different Modes on Guangdong Economy Development*. Guangdong People's Publishing House, 2004, page 153.

levels and their majors has constrained the optimization and upgrade of Shantou's industrial structure and the changing of the economic growth pattern. In addition, the imbalance also makes it unfavorable for the development of the pillar industries, such as electronic information, textile and clothes, chemical plastic and mechanical equipment and so on.

In terms of the employment system, private enterprises in Shantou are developing very rapidly and are in need of talent. However, many enterprises, especially small and medium-sized enterprises, are still in the phase of family management, as they build management networks on the basis of kinship, lacking of courage and insight to employ advanced management professionals, which would result in surplus and a waste of talented people. Such a nepotistic employment management system cannot integrate with the modern enterprise management and increasingly impedes enterprises from bringing the management talents into full play, weakening the market adaptability and competitiveness, as well as restricting the development and expansion of the private economy.[362]

3.6.3 Future Development Plans

3.6.3.1 Significant Changes in Five Years and Remarkable Progress in Ten Years

Since the reform and opening up, Guangdong Province has been leading the national economy, but in recent years, an imbalance appeared between eastern and western parts of Guangdong. East Guangdong, represented by Shantou, has been in a standstill for a long time, which may become the weak point of Guangdong's economy, thus becoming the burden in the full rise of the Pearl River Delta.

With a good start of the implementation of the "Program of Action for Reform and Development in the Pearl River Delta (2008~2020)," Guangdong Provincial Party Committee and Provincial government made further arrangements to achieve a balanced regional development. On August 26, 2009, "Guidelines for East Guangdong to Make 'Significant Changes in Five Years'" was officially carried out so East Guangdong could embrace new opportunities for development.

The "Guidelines" states the guiding ideology, basic principles and major objectives for East Guangdong to make "significant changes in five years." It also points out that East Guangdong should increase its economic aggregate, development quality and ability for sustainable development. It is to actively blend into the Pearl River Delta to take part in the

---

362 Shantou Personnel Bureau: *the 11th Five-Year Plan for Talents in Shantou.* http://www.gdrst.gov.cn/info/Information.asp?type=rcgh&InfoID=20071109434750145б

construction of the Economic Zone on the west coast of the Taiwan Straits and to deepen its cooperation with Hong Kong, Taiwan, Macao and the ASEAN. It should step up the construction of key projects, accelerate the process of coordinated regional economy and optimize the structure of urban and rural development to achieve "a new level of economic strength, urban and rural development and people's living standards" by 2011.

Among the thirty-nine key projects promoted by the "Guidelines," seventeen are related to Shantou, and they are:

1. Economic Belt in Eastern Shantou
2. Shantou-Jieyang section of Shantou-Meizhou Expressway
3. Shantou-Jiexi Expressway
4. Denggang-Hongyang Expressway
5. Jiedong-Huilai Expressway
6. Guangdong Section of Xiamen-Shenzhen Railway
7. Electrification of the Longchuan-South Longhu Section of Guangzhou-Meizhou-Shantou Railway
8. Duplication of Shantou Section of Guangzhou-Meizhou-Shantou Railway
9. Nan'ao Bridge
10. Breakwater project in Guang'ao port area of Shantou Port
11. Construction of channels in Guang'ao port area of Shantou Port Phase
12. South passage way for 500,000v electricity from East Guangdong to the Pearl River Delta
13. Chaonan transmission and distribution project for 500,000v electricity
14. East Guangdong natural gas pipeline project
15. East Guangdong products pipeline project
16. Drainage project in Nanzonggan water logging area (including draining the 11.96-km-long waterway of Chaocheng Watergate of Dagang River and the lower reaches of Juding Watergate of Xigang River, rebuilding Chaocheng Watergate and reinforcing the 8.5-km-long bank by the standard of resisting 50-year flood)
17. Dawei project which is listed as one of the key provincial embanking projects

3.6.3.2 Integration to Hercynian Economic Zone

In 2010, the National Committee on Reform and Development listed Shantou as the key development zone of the national development priority zone in the "Plan of National Development Priority Zone (Draft for Deliberation)." According to the "Overall Plan of Tourism Development on West Side of Straits (Draft for Comment)," Shantou was listed as one of the core cities in the tourism zone on west side of Straits. Guangdong Department of Construction and the unit of the "Plan of Coordinated Development of Towns Cluster in the Eastern Guangdong" have identified Shantou (eastern Guangdong area) as an important part of development on the west side of the Straits.

Meanwhile, Shantou made effective progress by vigorously developing the plan of a national economic zone on the west side of the Straits. At present, Shantou gives its priority to transforming the Nan'ao Island into a demonstration zone to Taiwan by setting up industries, tourism and commercial market and the logistics supply base for fishermen. Now, this plan has headed into the provincial government for ratification. The direct flight to Taiwan has developed smoothly, and a convenient sea passage for economic, cultural and people-to-people exchange across the Taiwan Straits has been gradually built up. Development of major transportation hub in southeastern straits has also accelerated. The preferential policy for Taiwan self-catch aquatic products has already benefited Shantou and Chaozhou District. The import pilot projects for Taiwan self-catch aquatic products has been successfully launched. The rights of handling small-volume trade with Taiwan has been successively granted to the Taiwanese trading corporations of Chaoyang, Nan'ao and Zhuchi by the Department of Foreign Trade of Guangdong Province. The program of Chaoyang Haimen's small-volume trade with Taiwan has been approved by the Guangdong government. The process of the project application for establishing a micro Taiwanese commodity exchange market in Shantou has been accelerated. Along with China's Taiwan Affairs Office and Ministry of Agriculture's joint approval on the establishment of Taiwan agricultural innovation community in Chaonan, Shantou, Shantou government carried out "Several Policies on Encouraging and Supporting the Establishment of Taiwan Agricultural Innovation Community" in response, which approved to establish a Taiwan agricultural trade center and made every effort to advance the planning and building of an agricultural cooperation platform to conduct cooperation with Taiwan. The Shantou Tourist General has been authorized to organize the second set of trips to Taiwan by the China National Tourism Administration. Taking the winning bid for the third set of supportive funds for developing the industrial park of industry transfer demonstration project as a turning point, Shantou designed and built Taiwan Industrial Park in Nanshan District, located in the industrial belt, and is working to attract business and investment was in full swing.

In addition, Shantou will compete for more support from the Central Government and Guangdong Provincial Government to expand its economic and trade cooperation with Taiwan and take the lead in establishing Guangdong-Taiwan Economic and Trade Cooperation Test Site. It will also vigorously seek for Central Government's primary support for major infrastructures including port, railway, expressway, water conservancy facilities, communications and the arrangement of and investment in energy-related industrial projects of strategic importance, thus implementing the strategy of developing Shantou into a regional shipping hub. It will also work to extend the 28 specific measures, which were put forward last year by the State Administration of Quality Supervision, Inspection and Quarantine in supporting Fujian-Taiwan exchanges, seek Taiwan Affairs Office and the Ministry of Public Security to authorize Shantou port as the visa issuance office for Taiwan compatriots, work to launch pilot program of free convertibility between NTD (New Taiwan Dollar) and RMB, plan and build a Taiwan-oriented bonded logistics zone of petrochemical industry and attract more investment of Taiwanese petrochemical enterprises based on the existing Taiwan-oriented gathering and scattering system of natural gases in Haimen Port, accelerate the construction of a deep-water port and transform the Shantou bonded zone into a comprehensive zone as soon as possible, boost the integrated development of a bonded port in order to ensure the integration of resources and combination of functions and give full play to the favorable policies according to the special economic zone in order to accelerate the integration of Shantou with the Hercynian economic zone.

4 History of Xiamen SEZ: International Harbor City in Economic Development and Environmental Coordination

Resources: www.xm.gov.cn/zjxm/csmxp/20070830/t20070830_174038.htm

Established in 1980, Xiamen SEZ was one of the earliest of the four SEZs. At the beginning period of its establishment, it covered only 2.5 square kilometers of the Huli Industry Zone, and gradually extended to the whole island. It enjoyed preferential policies in taxation, foreign exchange, land use, investment protection, immigration and other areas. With the creation of an export-oriented economy as its development goal, Xiamen first implemented some free port policies and established the Taiwanese Investment Zone. In the first ten years of its high-speed development, Xiamen has gained noteworthy achievements.

Into the 1990s, Xiamen SEZ made establishing and perfecting the market economic system as the main objective. It initially established the socialist market economic system, completed market-oriented reforms in state-owned enterprises, taxation, finance, pricing, foreign trade and social security, while making great efforts to promote export-oriented economic development. Comprehensive economic strength has remarkably increased.

Entering into the 21st century, undergoing profound changes in the development environment, Xiamen SEZ maintained rapid development in order to realize full and sound progress in the socialist market economic system. In the new situation, Xiamen managed to maintain the advantages of special economic zones, and gradually highlighted the geographical advantages of Taiwan.

The location of Xiamen, adjacent to the Taiwan region, which has already achieved economic growth in 1980s, becoming one member of the so-called four "Asian Tigers" is the reason why Xiamen was able to become one of the first four economic zones established in the initial period of reform and opening up. Similarly with Shenzhen adjacent to Hong Kong, and Zhuhai adjacent to Macao, Shantou had the wealth of overseas resources, made full use its geographical advantage and bore the "window" function as the SEZ under the conditions of the planned economy. Therefore, the main consideration was to realize "overall development by promoting a certain area" and to play the role as "icebreaker" in cross-Straits relations by means of introducing capital, technology and advanced management in the Taiwan region through geographic advantage, people interaction and the emotional bond between Xiamen and Taiwan region. However, the wavering uncertainty of Taiwan authority's political and economic policies toward mainland China largely restricted the Xiamen SEZ to play a full role in economic development. In contrast, Hong Kong, adjacent to Shenzhen, took the low consideration of political factors in the investment policy, which enabled Shenzhen to make full use of its strength as an SEZ. After the return of Hong Kong, the process of integration between Hong Kong and mainland China accelerated. It could be concluded that Hong Kong played a vital role in promoting the development of Shenzhen SEZ. In contrast, Taiwan, which has been given high expectations, did not fully fulfill its task in promoting the development of the Xiamen SEZ. With the deepening of China's reform and opening up, the scope of SEZ developed from a small number of cities spreading to more cities from the eastern coastal areas to central and western inland regions. The continuous emergence of new economic zones and China's accession into the WTO has increasingly diluted the policy advantages owned by Xiamen as a special economic zone.

The development of Xiamen SEZ depends on the future. In 2009, the State Council issued the "Opinions on Supporting Fujian to Accelerate the Construction of the Economic Zone on West Bank of the Straits." Providing a rare opportunity to the future development of Xiamen SEZ may help it to achieve significant development.

4.1 Xiamen Before the Establishment of SEZ: Years Prior to 1980

Influenced by the domestic climate after the founding of the People's Republic of China, Xiamen's economic development level and economic base was relatively backward until the establishment of SEZ. With such background, the establishment and development of the Xiamen Special Economic Zone highlighted its vital role as the "experimental field" and "window" of reform and opening up. It also highlighted the historical significance of

China's special economic zones.

4.1.1 History of Xiamen

Xiamen has a long history. In ancient times, it was also called "Egret Island" because of the large egret inhabitance of the area.

In the Taikang Emperor's third year in the Jing Dynasty (282 A.D.), Tong'an County was designated as Jin'an County, later integrated into Nan'an County. In the Zhenyuan emperor's nineteenth year in the Tang Dynasty (803 A.D.), Datong County was designated southwest to Nan'an County, and promoted to Tong'an County during Five Dynasties and Later Tang Dynasty (933 A.D.) under the Quanzhou jurisdiction. In the Song Dynasty, it was under the jurisdiction of Qingyuan, Pinghai and Quanzhou. It belonged to Quanzhou in the Yuan and Ming Dynasty. "Xiamen City" was first set up in the Hongwu Emperor's twentieth year in Ming Dynasty (1387 A.D.), whose name meant "Gateway of the State," since when, Xiamen was thereafter included in historical archives. In the seventh year of the reign of Shunzhi Emperor of Qing Dynasty (1650) Zheng Chenggong stationed troops in Xiamen. In the twelfth year, set the state of Siming was established. In the nineteenth year of the reign of Kangxi Emperor of Qing Dynasty (1680) the state was repealed. In 1884, the Taiwan-Xiamen Military Defense Circuit was established. In 1728, Taiwan County was renamed Taiwan Circuit. In 1686, Quanzhou City set up the Military Defense Circuit. In 1727, the Xingquan Circuit was transferred from Quanzhou to Xiamen. In the twenty-ninth year of Guangxu Emperor in Qing Dynasty (1903), Gulangyu became the "International Settlement." In April of the first year of the Republic of China (1912), Jiaheli of Tong'an County, Kinmen and Daxiaodeng were combined into Siming County, and in September was renamed Siming City, but was soon repealed. In 1915, Jinmen and Daxiaodeng were separated and designated Kinmen County. In the same year the Nanlu Circuit was established (renamed in 1914 as Xiamen Circuit, but repealed in 1925).

In 1933, the "People's Revolutionary Government of the Republic of China" (the "Fujian People's Government") situated Xiamen City, but was soon cancelled. In 1934, Tong'an and Siming County were under the jurisdiction of the Fifth Administrative Inspecting District. In April 1935, seven islands, including Xiamen and Gulangyu composed Xiamen City. Heshan Special Zone took the place of Siyou County, together with Tongan County, under the jurisdiction of the Fourth Administrative Inspecting District. From May 1938 to September 1945, it fell into the control of the invaders. In October, Xiamen City was restored, covering four districts of Central (later changed to Siming), Kaiyuan, Gulangyu and Heshan. In September and October 1949, Tongan County and

Xiamen City were liberated. Tong'an County belonged to the fifth prefecture (changed to Quanzhou prefecture and Jinjiang prefecture in 1950). Xiamen became a provincially administered municipality. In October 1950, Xiamen set the five districts of Kaiyuan, Siming, Gulangyu, Xiagang (cancelled later) and Heshan. In 1953, Tong'an and Jimei were under the jurisdiction of Xiamen Municipality. In January 1958, Heshan district was cancelled and re-established as a suburb. In August, Tongan County was put under Xiamen from Jinjiang prefecture. In August 1966, Kaiyuan, Siming District change to Dongfeng and Xiangyang District, but reversed to original names in October 1979. In February 1970, Tong'an County was incorporated into Jinjiang prefecture (region); but in June 1973, it came back to the administration of Xiamen. In September of 1978, Xinglin District was built up. In 1987, Huli District was added and the rural district was named after Jimei District. Thus, the Xiamen City covered seven districts of Gulangyu, Siming, Kaiyuan, Xinglin, Huli, Jimei and Tong'an.

In May 2003, approved by the State Council, Xiamen made some adjustments in administrative division: first, integrating Siming District, Gulangyu District and Kaiyuan District into Siming District, and combining the original three districts under the jurisdiction of Siming administrative region; second, putting the Xinglin district offices and Xinglin County under the jurisdiction of Jimei District, renaming Xinglin District as Haicang District; third, establishing Xiang'an District, incorporating the five towns of Xindian, Xinwei, Maxiang, Neicuo and Dadeng under the Tong'an District before into the jurisdiction of Jimei District. In the new administrative division, Xiamen covered six districts of Siming, Huli, Jimei, Haicang, Tong'an and Xiang'an.[363]

4.1.2 Historical Starting Point of Xiamen SEZ

Before the establishment of the SEZ, Xiamen encountered many obstacles in its economic development, which was closely related to the social and historical conditions of the time. Figure 4-1-1 shows the real per-capita GDP of Xiamen from 1950 to 1980 and Figure 4-1-2 shows the corresponding growth rate. From 1950 to 1980, the real per-capita GDP growth in Xiamen fluctuated wildly, sometimes as high as 46.9% (in 1969), and sometimes as low as −37.2% (in 1961), with the average growth rate of 8.4%. As with all regions of the country during this period, the social and economic development of Xiamen was greatly influenced by the political climate, which focused on different areas, rather than on economic construction and social development. The violent fluctuations (with

363 www.xm.gov.cn/zjxm/xmgk/200708/t20070830_173888.htm

negative growth in 1954, 1961, 1962, 1963, 1967, 1968, 1973 and 1974) did not cease or reverse until 1975 when the economy was re-restored to the 1960 level (in 1960, real per-capita GDP was 343.2 yuan, in 1975 348.6 yuan). After the end of the "Cultural Revolution" and the destruction of the "Gang of Four" in 1976, the real per-capita GDP of Xiamen began sustained and stable growth.

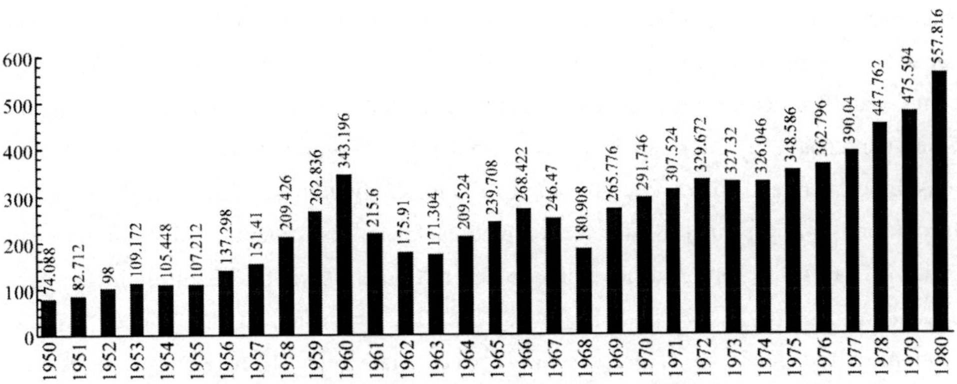

Figure 4-1-1 Real Per-capita GDP in Xiamen (1950~1980)
(1952 as the base year, household registered population, yuan/person)
Resources: Yearbook (2006) of Xiamen SEZ, China Statistics Press

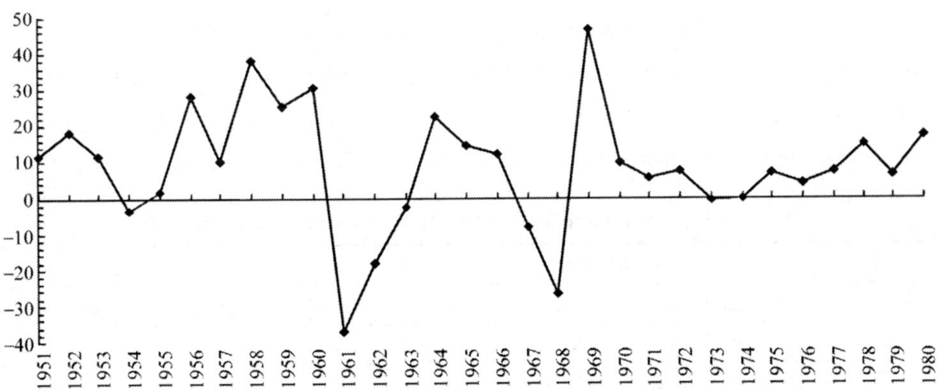

Figure 4-1-2 Real Per-capita GDP Growth Rate in Xiamen (1950~1980)
(1952 as the base year, household registered population, %)
Resources: Yearbook (2006) of Xiamen SEZ, China Statistics Press

Economic and social achievements before the establishment of SEZ were primarily completed in the "Fifth Five Year Plan" period (1976~1980). During this period, average annual growth rate of industrial and agricultural output value reached 11.2%, an average annual increase in real per-capita GDP growth of 10%, an average annual increase of collective investment in infrastructure of 28.2%, an average annual growth in port of 12.8%, in freight of 7.1%, in social commodities retail sales of 14.23%, in wage increase of 6.3%, and in net income of peasants per capita of 11.8%.[364]

During the "Fifth Five Year Plan" period, achievements were also achieved in urban infrastructure constructions. In the five years from 1976 to 1980, investment on infrastructure reached 310 million yuan, mainly in Xiamen's energy projects, water engineering and port construction. Three phases of expansion project of Xinling Power Plant were completed in 1980. Two sets of generators with 25,000 kilowatts of generating capacity were put into production. In 1979, the water diversion project of Beixi River was completed. The accomplishment of the expansion project of Lianban water plant greatly eased the tension in water supply with the annual water supply capacity of 30.02 million tons. Investment and construction began in 1976 for the first phase of the new Dongdu port. It took only one year in 1980 for its completion, for an investment of 21.9 million yuan. From 1976 to 1980, non-productive investment in Xiamen reached 82.22 million yuan at an annual increase of 26.6%. In 1980, it launched the expansion of the Xiamen Railway Station. By the end of 1979, direct ferries between Xiamen and Hong Kong were restored. In 1980, total business volume support increased to 3.09 million yuan, and the number of telephone exchanges was up to 4290.[365]

By 1980, Xiamen's GDP was 640.02 million yuan. Total industrial output value was 966.91 million yuan. The ratio of three industries was 21.6:57.8:20.6. Fiscal revenue reached 183.31 million yuan. Total volume of import and export foreign trade amounted to 140,270,000 USD, of which exports amounted to 140,270,000 USD. Total retail sales of social consumer goods reached 285.52 million yuan. Table 4-1-1 shows Xiamen's main

Table 4-1-1 Main Socio-economic Indicators of Xiamen in 1980

Serial	Main Indicator	Data
1	Xiamen's GDP at current prices	6.4002 million yuan
2	GDP per capita (household registered population)	685yuan
3	Total industrial output value	966.91 million yuan
4	Ratio of three industries	21.6:57.8:20.6
5	Total volume of import and export foreign trade	141.43 million USD
6	Total volume of export foreign trade	140.27 million USD
7	Total fiscal revenue	183.31 million yuan
8	Total retail sales of social consumer goods *	285.52 million yuan

Resources: Yearbook (2006) of Xiamen SEZ, China's Statistics Press
Note: adjusted on floor of economic census in 2004

364 Edited by Su Dongbin: ***History of China's SEZ***, Guangdong Economy Press, 2001, p313

365 Edited by Su Dongbin: ***History of China's SEZ***, Guangdong Economy Press, 2001, p313-314

socio-economic indicators in 1980. Data indicates that before the construction of the SEZ, economic development of Xiamen lagged behind and had a very weak economic base. However, compared with other special economic zones, the historical starting point and initial conditions of Xiamen SEZ was the best of the first four SEZs.

4.2 Early Construction of Xiamen SEZ (1981~1990)

The early construction of the Xiamen SEZ was conducted in the era of reform and opening up. Experiencing the period of what the Chinese refer to as "crossing the river by feeling the stones" (to move ahead steadily and pragmatically with economic reforms), Xiamen SEZ carried the special significance of "experimental field" as well as an "opening window." Xiamen SEZ fulfilled the mission, seized the historical opportunity for development, and made remarkable achievements and set a good example in reform and opening up.

4.2.1 The Establishment of Xiamen SEZ

On July 15, 1979, No. 50 Document, also known as the [1979] Document No. 50 was issued by the CPC Central Committee, namely "CPC Central Committee and State Council Approving and Transmitting Two Reports Concerning the Implementation of Special Policies and Flexible Measures in Foreign Economic Activities Raised by Guangdong Provincial and Fujian Provincial Committee," which was the first written document on the establishment of SEZ approved by the Central Committee. In the document, it agreed to practice special and flexible measures in the two provinces, and formally approve the setting up of a certain area as the pilot "SEZ for Export" in Shenzhen, Zhuhai, Shantou of Guangdong Province and Xiamen in Fujian Province.

On August 26, 1980, the Fifteenth Meeting of the Fifth National People's Congress approved "Regulations on SEZs in Guangdong Province" raised by the State Council, in which approved to set up SEZs in Shenzhen, Zhuhai, Shantou of Guangdong Province and Xiamen in Fujian Province. Thus far, the CPC Central Committee, the State Council and the NPC Standing Committee has essentially completed the decision-making process to set up SEZ and provided with legal and policy authorization for the establishment and development of special economic zones.

On October 7, 1980, the State Council decided to establish the Xiamen Special Economic Zone on an area of 2.5 square kilometers northwest of Xiamen Island. Under the leadership of Fujian Provincial Party Committee and Provincial Government, Xiamen Special Economic Zone Management Commission was set up on September 2, 1980, formally indicating the establishment of Xiamen Special Economic Zone. Xiamen Special Economic Zone Management Committee exercised unified administration, planning, development and management work on behalf of Xiamen Municipal Government. Under the Xiamen Municipal Government, there were construction companies, engineering companies, international trade and trust companies and labor service companies, responsible for helping businessmen invest in the SEZ, coordinating and processing businesses in banking, insurance, taxation, customs, border control, telecommunications and other agencies.

After careful preparation, the construction of the Xiamen Special Economic Zone officially started on October 15, 1981 in the Huli Industrial Zone. Since then, Xiamen Special Economic Zone opened a new chapter. In October 1980, the State Council approved 2.5 square kilometers for the construction of the export processing zones, 1.1 square kilometers for the first phase before October 1981, and by the end of 1983, completing the land acquisition and resettlement, "the capacity of supplying traffic, electricity, water, communication and drainage," and part of the construction in plant and related supporting facilities, with the total of 50.23 million yuan of infrastructure investment. At the same time, it actively introduced foreign investment. By the end of 1983, the SEZ had approved 24 "three-capital" enterprises (including nine industrial enterprises), with contractual investment reaching to 91,780,000 USD, with 37,150,000 USD of foreign investment, and the actual utilization of foreign investment only 7,850,000 USD. The first run foreign-funded enterprise was Yinhua Floor Tile Factory. The first foreign-funded enterprises put into operation were two electronics companies of Xiahua and Xiaxin. Unfortunately, most of the products were sold domestically.[366]

4.2.2 Early Development of Xiamen SEZ

4.2.2.1 Deng's Investigation for Efficient SEZ Development in Xiamen

Reform and Opening up has become an irreversible trend because of the Third Plenary Session of the Eleventh Central Committee's main focus on economic development. However, reform and opening-up is a steady process, and caution must be exercised. At that timeBefore the reform and opening up, the "left" ideology still faced serious limitations and could not be quickly stopped with the end of "Cultural Revolution." The vast territory of China made local history and actual conditions vary greatly. Therefore, reforms could not be conducted wholly and quickly. Thus, the SEZ became the trial

366 Edited by Su Dongbin: ***History of China's SEZ***, Guangdong Economy Press, 2001, p316-317

"window" and demonstration base for China's reform. In the historical conditions at the time, the establishment and development of special economic zones naturally led to controversy and criticism. As a "window," it could be closed at any time. Therefore the development of the SEZ called for firm support from the central level, which held true for the early development of the Xiamen SEZ. By 1984, after several years of construction, Xiamen SEZ gained some experience. At the same time, suspicion and accusations appeared inside and outside the Party.

From January 24 to February 17, 1984, Deng Xiaoping, Wang Zhen and Yang Shangkun visited Shenzhen, Zhuhai and Xiamen special economic zones. Comrade Deng Xiaoping tried to decide whether the development of special economic zones would be successful. After careful investigation, Deng expressed satisfaction with the achievements gained by the SEZ and was pleased to leave inscriptions for the three SEZs. Deng Xiaoping's inspection and inscription for the SEZ made a definitive conclusion to the debate on the issue related to special economic zones.

Figure 4-2-1 Deng Inspecting Xiamen SEZ

Resources: www.fj.xinhuanet.com/news/2004-08/03/content_2614438.htm

On February 9, 1984, Deng Xiaoping's inscription in Xiamen, "to develop the SEZ faster and better," demonstrated the Central Government's determination on the construction of the SEZ and the hopes and expectations of the rapid development of the SEZ, while at the same time affirming its development achievements in recent years and a series of new policies and new measures in the implementation of reform and opening up. Deng Xiaoping's inscription solidified the confidence and determination of cadres and masses to further improve reform and opening up. It had great practical and historical significance in mobilizing people's enthusiasm and creativity to accelerate the construction of Xiamen SEZ, as well as encouraging foreign investors to invest in Xiamen SEZ.

4.2.2.2 The Expansion of SEZ: The Implementation of Certain Policies on Freeport

On February 24, 1984, after Deng's inspection in the South, he discussed with several leaders in charge on how to further construct the SEZ and deepen the opening up of the city. Comrade Deng Xiaoping pointed out that "The guiding principle of establishing the SEZ was to open, instead of to control." He said, "The SEZ is a window, the window of technology, management, knowledge, as well as a window of the foreign policy." The area of Xiamen SEZ is too small. Let's make the whole Xiamen Island into a special economic zone... which will be able to bring up the surrounding area to make activate the economy of Fujian Province. Xiamen SEZ should not be called a free port, but some policies practiced in free ports can be implemented here."[367]

In order to put Comrade Xiaoping's idea into practice, from March 26 to April 6, 1984, the CPC Central Committee and State Council held a forum in Beijing, attended by leaders of related provinces, municipalities and departments in some coastal cities. After the meeting, the State Council issued "Minutes of Working on Some Coastal Cites" (hereinafter referred to as "Minutes"). It made a full affirmation of the achievements made by the SEZ over the years, at the same time, clarified economic focus and direction for development in the years following. The Minutes required all the SEZs should follow the principle of "to deal with special things with special methods; to deal with new things with new methods; to remain old stand with using new methods" and get rid of the current restraints not suitable for development of productive forces and reform the management system and the SEZ regulatory agencies. In the "Minutes," it also made the decision to continue opening up in 14 coastal cities and regions, which was approved and transited by the CPC Central Committee and State Council on April 30 of the same year.

Inspection by Deng Xiaoping and other central leaders, and their affirmation to

367 ***Selected Works of Deng Xiaoping*** (Volume Three), People's Press, 1993, p52

Xiamen's reform and opening up and economic construction was a great encouragement to the constructors of Xiamen SEZ. The transition and approval of the Minutes was a great motivator to the constructors of Xiamen SEZ. Fujian Provincial Committee and Provincial Government seized this favorable opportunity to accelerate the development of Xiamen Special Economic Zone. In order to better meet this requirement, on September 1, 1984, Fujian Provincial Committee and Provincial Government decided to integrate the Xiamen Special Economic Zone Management Committee into the Municipal People's Government of Xiamen, and have the latter play dual function as both the Xiamen Municipal People's Government Administration and SEZ Management Commission.

In order to better implement the "Minutes," and sum up the experiences learned in the construction of the SEZ in order to create a better future for the SEZ, from May 26 to June 1, 1985, the State Council held the first National Work Conference on SEZ in Shenzhen. The conference was held by Secretary of the Central Committee and State Councilor, Comrade Gu Mu. During several days of discussions, exchanges of ideas and visits, Gu Mu raised many new questions and carefully reviewed the positive and negative aspects of the past four years' work in SEZ. Based on the review and communication, the Special Economic Zones tried to identify their problems and fins adequate solutions. The conference was a comprehensive implementation of the "Minutes." It summed up and exchanged experiences, figured out the current situation, identified gaps and promoted the development of SEZ.

After the first national work conference on June 1985, the State Council officially approved the Xiamen Special Economic Zone to expand the scope of the region (bounded by the end of Gaoqi and Gaomei seawall) and Gulangyu Island (including the nearby small islands), an area of 131 square kilometers. At the same time, the municipal districts outside SEZ carried out related policies of 14 coastal open cities in economic activities. Tongan County followed related policies in economic developing zones.[368] Thus far, an all-dimensional opening pattern to the outside world has been form in the Xiamen SEZ. Free port policies that can be implemented in SEZ included:[369]

1. Under the guidance of state planning, Xiamen Special Economic Zone may give full play to the function of the market. The Central Government endowed the Xiamen Municipal Government considerable decision-making power in the utilization of foreign investment.

---

368 State Council: ***Ratification to Implementations of Xiamen SEZ***, No. [1985] 85 by the State Council

369 Luo Qinghe: **Introduction to Economics**, Compilation and Translation Press, 2001, p212

2. SEZ products are free of export customs duties. Production equipment and raw materials are free from imports customs duties, import and export product tax or value added tax (VAT). Tariffs of SEZ imported consumer goods and other market goods are in line with customs regulations before the completion of the management system.

3. Foreign goods, except for drugs and weapons, may be specified in the SEZ for storage, conversion, processing, labeling, re-exporting, etc under the strict supervision of local and customs, without paying tax or VAT.

4. Under the unified guidance of the State, SEZ has the right to import goods needed in the SEZ and export products made in the SEZ. Under the supervision of Customs, the SEZ may directly trade with Taiwan, and carry out entrepot trade and transit trade, may accept the commission of mainland enterprises, be the agent of the commodity import and export except commodities unified handled by the State.

5. Establish local financial institutions in accordance with relevant state regulations. Specialized banks are allowed to conduct foreign currency transactions for domestic residents. Approved by the State Council, it is legal to borrow money in foreign countries and issue bonds, stocks, stock trading. Approved by the People's Bank of China, foreign banks and overseas-funded banks may operate in the Xiamen SEZ.

4.2.2.3 Rise of Taiwanese Investment Zone: The Rapid Development of an Export-oriented Economy

Xiamen SEZ development was constrained largely by financial, technical and other factors. Until November 1987, the Taiwan authorities relaxed the limited restrictions on Taiwan compatriots to visit relatives in mainland China. Xiamen SEZ, one strait away from Taiwan and Kinmen, quickly became a hot spot for tourism, investment and trade from Taiwan. Xiamen special economic zone entered a new phase of investment-based, export-oriented economic development.

In order to further promote the rapid development of Xiamen, in April 1988, the State Council listed the city of Xiamen as one of China's six cities with independent economic management authority at the provincial level. Xiamen Special Economic Zone had more decision-making power in comparison with other regions, which created conditions for the SEZ to possibly establish management system compatible with an export-oriented economic development.

Since the Taiwan authorities relaxed restrictions on Taiwan compatriots investing in mainland China, the Taiwan businessmen played an increasingly important role in Xiamen SEZ development, and promoted businessmen from Hong Kong, Macao, overseas Chinese and foreign investors to invest in Xiamen. Xiamen Special Economic Zone gained rapid development in export-oriented economy, and its economic strength was also significantly enhanced. To further capitalize on this developing momentum, in May 1989, the State Council approved the Xiamen Special Economic Zone and Haicang, Xinglin regions under Xiamen Municipality as Taiwanese Investment Zone. After the second breakthrough of the expansion of Xiamen SEZ in 1984, the establishment of Taiwanese investment zone gained great significance. The establishment of Taiwan Investment Zone symbolized the second extension of the range of Xiamen SEZ from Xiamen Island to its suburbs, an area expanding from the original 131 square kilometers to 250 square kilometers.

After the early development of the Xiamen SEZ, the opening pattern had been formed—Xiamen Island and Gulangyu Island as the Special Economic Zone, the suburbs as Taiwanese Investment Zone and Tong'an County as economic open zones. Meanwhile, the direction for development of the Xiamen SEZ to further develop export-oriented economic and trade relations across the Taiwan Straits through the implementation of free port policies and promote economic development in China's southeast region had been established.

4.2.3 Rise of Xiamen SEZ

4.2.3.1 Construction Achievements in the Initial Period

Through a decade of development, the Xiamen SEZ made tremendous leaps in social and economic development and underwent enormous changes. It proved to the world that the practice of establishing SEZ was successful, and the general policy of reform and opening up was correct.

The first achievement was a rapid development in national economy. Figure 4-2-2 shows the real per capita GDP of each year from 1981 to 1990, with 1952 as the base year.

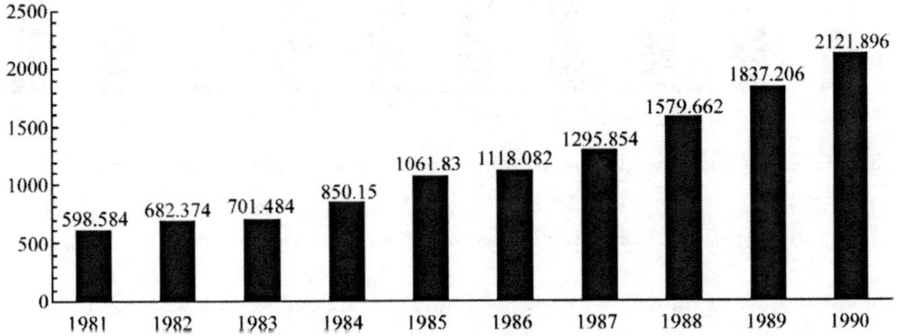

Figure 4-2-2 Real per Capita GDP from 1981 to 1990 (1952 as the base year, according to household registered residence, yuan per person)

Resources: Yearbook of Xiamen SEZ (1991), China's Statistics Press

Figure 4-2-3 shows the corresponding growth rate of real per capita GDP. Statistics showed that in the early decade of the construction of Xiamen SEZ, per capita real GDP growth remained stable. Real GDP per capita in 1990 was 3.54 times of that in 1981, at the average annual growth rate of 14.5%. Figure 4-2-4 shows the total fiscal revenue of each year from 1981 to 1990 calculated at the current price. In 1990, total revenue was 1.02982 billion yuan, 5.28 times than in 1981.

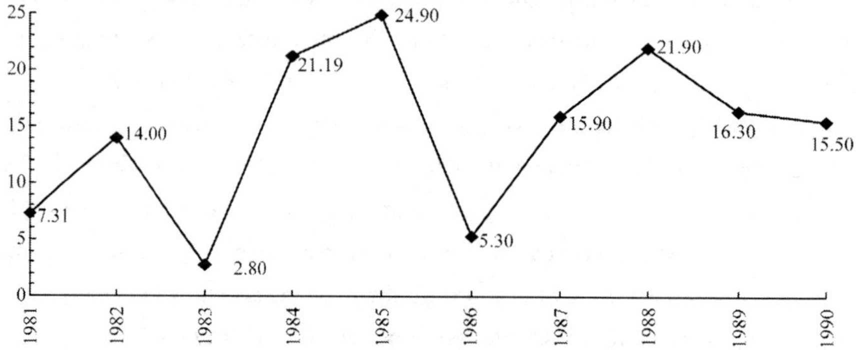

Figure 4-2-3 Real per Capita GDP from 1981 to 1990 (1952 as the base year, according to household registered residence, %)

Resources: Yearbook of Xiamen SEZ (1991), China's Statistics Press

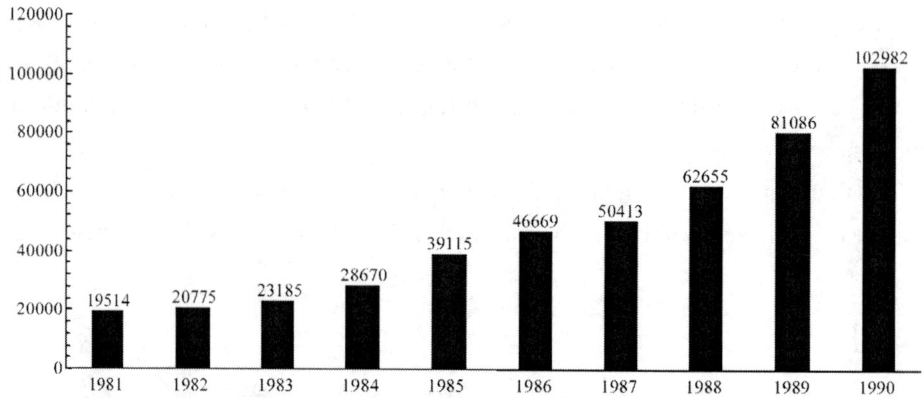

Figure 4-2-4 Total Fiscal Revenue from 1981 to 1990 (calculated at the current price, 10 thousand yuan)

Resources: Yearbook of Xiamen SEZ (1991), China's Statistics Press

The second achievement was the formation of an export-oriented economy. Figure 4-2-5 shows total volume of imports and exports and total exports from 1981 to 1990. In 1990, Xiamen's total imports and exports volume and exports volume were separately 7.62 times and 5.54 times of those in 1980. There was a higher degree of negative growth in

1986. In 1987, total imports and exports had not yet returned to the 1985 level. Since 1987, total imports and exports and total exports maintained steady growth. Figure 4-2-6 reflects contracted foreign capital and actual utilized foreign investment during 1983 to 1990. Figure 4-2-7 shows the corresponding growth rate. Although the contracted foreign capital and actual utilized foreign investment in 1990 were 5.75 times and 9.11 times of those in 1980, large fluctuations appeared during this period. The contracted foreign capital in 1986 and 1990, respectively, was at a negative growth rate of 88.6% and 36.9%, while the actual foreign investment in 1986, 1987 and 1990, was at a negative growth of 53.7%, 48.3% and 65.5%, respectively.

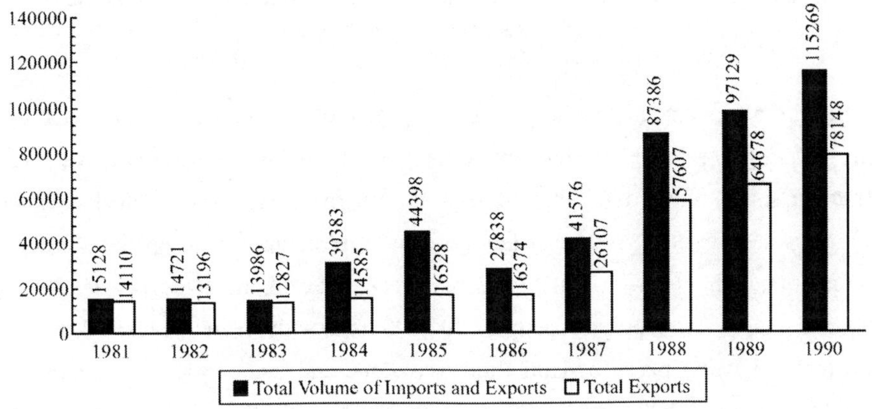

Figure 4-2-5 Total Volume of Imports and Exports and Total Exports from 1981 to 1990 (calculated at the current price, 10 thousand USD)

Resources: Yearbook of Xiamen SEZ (1991), China's Statistics Press

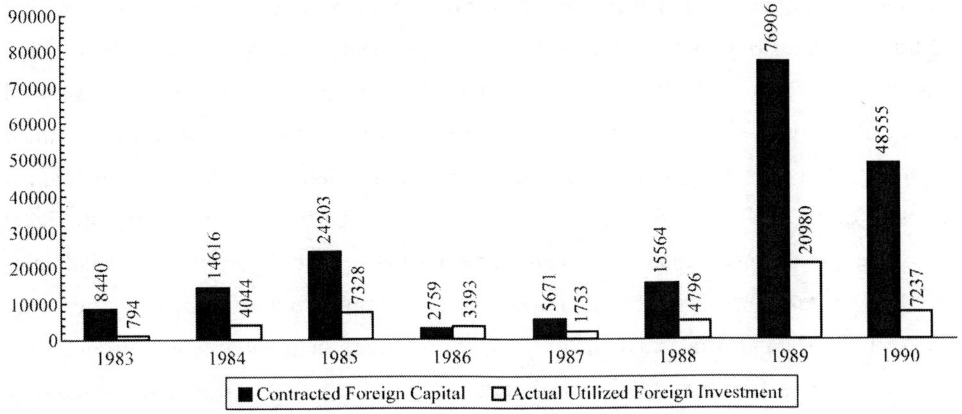

Figure 4-2-6 Contracted Foreign Capital and Actual Utilized Foreign Investment from 1983 to 1990 (nominal value, 10 thousand USD)

Resources: Yearbook of Xiamen SEZ (1991), China's Statistics Press

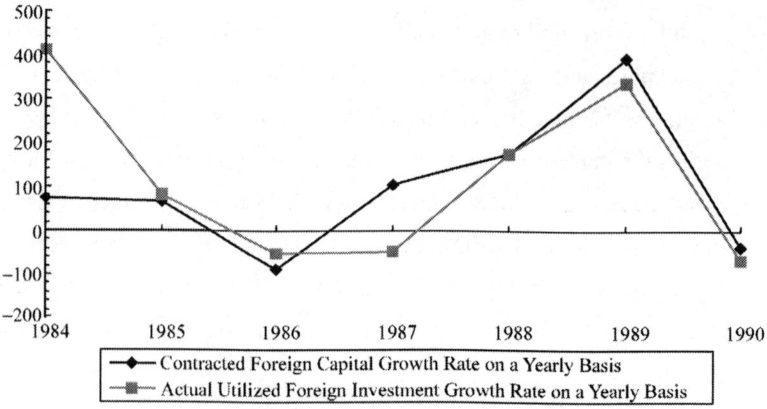

Figure 4-2-7 Contracted Foreign Capital and Actual Utilized Foreign Investment Growth Rate on a Yearly Basis (%)

Resources: Yearbook of Xiamen SEZ (1991), China's Statistics Press

The third achievement was the rapid development of urban infrastructure construction, initially forming a relatively sound investment environment. Cumulative investment of construction funds reached 8.748 billion yuan. International airports, docks, exchange telephones, water supplies, and other key projects were completed. It opened 40 domestic and international flights, with 200 flights per week, a telephone switchboard capacity of 43,000, and a tap water supply capacity of 301,000 tons, with an annual throughput of 5.29 million tons. The first phase of Huli Industrial Zone and eight residential quarters were built. An area of 15,170,000 square meters of various types of housing was completed. The city expanded from 14.16 square km to 42.5 square km.[370]

The fourth achievement was the consistently rising total industrial output valueand the three industries optimizing in structure. The tertiary industry increased significantly. Figure 4-2-8 shows industrial output value in each year from 1981 to 1990. The industrial output value in 1990 was 6.77 times that in 1981. Figure 4-2-9 shows investment in total fixed assets and the retail sales of consumer goods from 1981 to 1990. In that decade, Xiamen invested 8.742 billion yuan in fixed assets. In 1990, total fixed asset investment in Xiamen was 9.87 times of that in 1981. In 1986, there was a substantial negative growth. Total retail sales of consumer goods remained stable in that decade. In 1990, total retail sales were 8.57 times of that in 1981. Table 4-2-1 shows the proportion of three industries from 1981 to 1990. Data illustrates that the proportion of primary industry decreased from 26.5% in 1981, down to 10.6% in 1990 and an increasing of the proportion of tertiary industry from 21.9% in 1981, up to 44% in 1990.

370 Edited by Su Dongbin: ***History of China's SEZ***, Guangdong Economy Press, 2001, p336~337

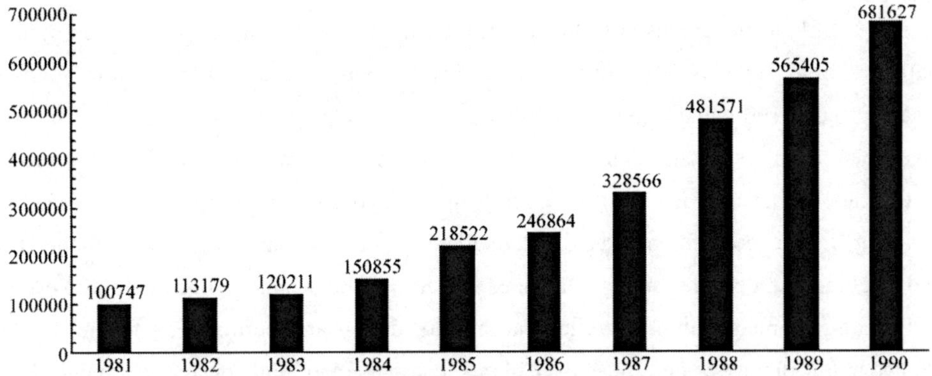

Figure 4-2-8 The Total Industrial Output Value (calculated at the price in 1980, 10 thousand yuan)

Resources: Yearbook of Xiamen SEZ (1991), China's Statistics Press

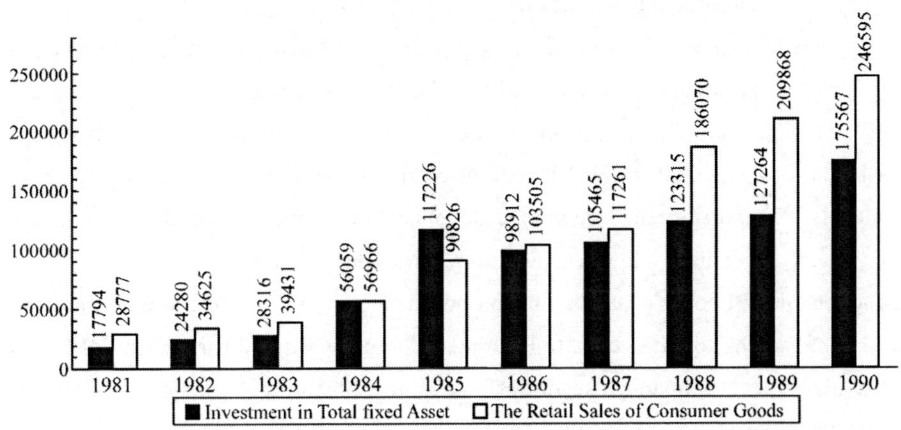

Figure 4-2-9 Investment in Total fixed Asset and the Retail Sales of Consumer Goods from 1981 to 1990 (10 thousand yuan)

Resources: Yearbook of Xiamen SEZ (1991), China's Statistics Press

Noted: investment in total fixed asset calculated at current price, the retail sales of consumer goods based on economic survey in 2004

Table 4-2-1 Proportion of Three Industries from 1981 to 1990 (%)

Year	Primary industry	Secondary industry	Tertiary industry
1981	26.5	51.6	21.9
1982	22.2	50.5	27.3
1983	21.3	49.7	29
1984	16.9	51.4	31.6
1985	14.7	50.2	35
1986	13.6	48.3	38.1
1987	13.4	47.8	38.8
1988	14.6	45.9	39.4
1989	11.8	45.8	42.4
1990	10.6	45.3	44

Resources: Yearbook of Xiamen SEZ (1991), China's Statistics Press

The fifth achievement was the improvement of urban construction. According to statistics, from 1980 to 1991, infrastructure investments reached 10.152 billion yuan, an area of 10,662,100 square meters building completed, equivalent to 12 times of the total investment in infrastructure than the first 31 years and 4.5 times the total housing area. In that decade, in accordance with the overall urban layout of the development of Xiamen, Xingang District, covering an area of 28.7 square kilometers, was developed, with the north end to Huli, south end to Binhu Road, east end to Fuzhou-Xiamen Highway and west end to Dongdu. Xiamen built an international airport, deep-water berths, the Channel Bridge, exchange telephones, water and power plants, coal-gas plant and sewage treatment plants, which greatly improved the city's transportation, communications, water, electricity, and gas supply and environmental protection.[371]

The sixth achievement was rapid development of the financial sector. In ten years, the city's financial departments provided funds for the introduction of more foreign investment and the development of an export-oriented economy in Xiamen SEZ. Before the establishment of the SEZ in 1979, Xiamen only had three banks and 46 branches. To meet the demands of export-oriented economic development, Xiamen Special Economic Zone restored Bank of China, Agricultural Bank, insurance companies, ICBC and China Construction Bank. People's Bank of China began to exercise the functions of the Central Bank in 1985, setting up Xiamen Life Insurance Company, the Industrial Bank of Xiamen, trust and investment companies, securities companies, urban credit cooperatives and other non-bank financial institutions, and actively introduced foreign banks, founding the first joint venture bank—Xiamen International Bank. The financial system, with a central bank for leadership, specialized banks as the main player and foreign joint venture banks and other non-bank financial institutions in coexistence were formed. The city's financial system was formed with multi-functional, multi-level and export-oriented features.

In 1991, Xiamen had 38 various financial institutions and 300 branches, which, compared with 1980, increased by 10.3 times and 5.16 times. There were five national banks, two insurance companies, six trust investment companies, eight urban credit cooperatives, eight foreign bank branches, four representative offices, one joint venture bank, one local financial institution, and one Securities Company. Financial employees reached nearly 5,000, 4.86 times that in 1980. Calculated according to the population at that time, an average of 3,733 people owned a financial institution.[372]

---

371 Edited by Su Dongbin: ***History of China's SEZ***, Guangdong Economy Press, 2001, p338

372 Su Dongbin: ***History of China's SEZ***, Guangdong Economy Press, 2001, p339

The seventh achievement existed in the realm of science and technology. Xiamen Special Economic Zone placed an emphasis on science and technology's role in promoting economic growth ever since its establishment. It made efforts to gradually combine technology improvement with SEZ economy to promote advancements in science and technology. In 1980, the city had over 7,000 science and technical personnel, and seven scientific research institutions. By the end of 1991, the number of various research and technology organizations reached 90, with sciences and technical personnel of more than 35,000. The Institute of Natural Science had 70 personnel with the membership of 1.4 million people. There were 95 technology intermediary and technical operating institutes. Relatively sound technical services and testing institutions covering patents, information, communication, standards, metrology, quality control, prevention, introduction, environmental, seismic etc were established. Xiamen SEZ established the Xiamen Torch Hi-tech Industrial Development Zone with its co-founder State Science and Technology Commission, and signed an agreement to found the Xiamen Branch of China Technology Development Center and the International Science and Technology Mall. From 1981 to 1991, the city arranged a variety of research and new product trial program equaling 2265, 967 of which gained achievements in scientific research, and 608 won awards for scientific and technological progress. Since the implementation of the "Patent Law" and "Technology Contract Law," the city delivered 364 patent applications, 173 patents granted by the State, 647 registrations of technology contracts and a contract value amount to 32,514,000 yuan. Promotion and application of scientific and technological achievements were soon converted into direct productivity. During the "Seventh Five-Year Plan" period, three fund input-output ratio from the Science and Technology Commission was 1:3:81, significantly higher than the input-output ratio of the fixed assets. In economic construction, scientific and technological content increased significantly. By 1991, the city's economic growth through scientific and technological progress factors accounted for 38%.[373]

The eighth achievement was the steady, continuing development, exchange and cooperation of Taiwan in education, culture and other causes. After nearly 10 years of efforts, the education of Xiamen Special Economic Zone also made significant progress, maintaining synchronization with the national economic development, forming a multi-level, multi-disciplinary, multi-channel education system in urban and rural areas adapted to social and economic development. In particular, due to Xiamen's unique history, geography and cultural conditions, Xiamen and Taiwan had a deep bond by blood,

373 Su Dongbin: ***History of China's SEZ***, Guangdong Economy Press, 2001, p339

geography and emotion. Culture in the southern Fujian region and local culture in Taiwan had the same strain. Since reform and opening-up, with the cross-strait relations being relieved from isolation to interaction, cultural exchanges with Taiwan have been expanding in the scope and involving exchanges in more and more areas, through more and more channels and forms, at increasingly higher levels.

4.2.3.2 Evaluation on Initial Rise

Although Xiamen SEZ made remarkable achievements in the early construction period, it had many shortcomings, especially in the irrational industrial structure and layout. At the beginning of its establishment, Xiamen SEZ3 planned to develop three types of industrial products: first, advanced technology and technological products, including electronics, small appliances, precision machinery and instruments; second, export products made by raw materials and semi-manufactured products, including wood, purple vine, herbs, sugar, fruit, leather, paper and tobacco, which were refined for the processing of new products; third, traditional best-selling products for processing, including knitting, garments, footwear, plastic products, home appliances, watches and handicrafts.[374] Among them, the first category was open for investment, conducive to long-term development of Xiamen SEZ, the second would help give full play to the advantages of local resources in Xiamen, while the third, acquiring for low investment but with quick payback, although not conducive to the upgrading and optimization of industrial structure, was quite attractive to foreign investors.

Because of its infancy stage, the relevant regulations were not sound, while the policies remained to be perfected. Investors held a hovering attitude. Therefore, foreign investment was scarce, especially in the second half of 1985. When China's overall economy was in adjustment, tightening up monetary policy and the infrastructure construction, coupled with the beginning of the special economic zone's lack of construction experience exposed many problems, proving an unsuitable environment for foreign investment. Many of the "three capital" enterprises ran poor business with huge losses and foreign exchange was difficult to balance. A sharp decline appeared in direct foreign investment in 1986,[375] and thus the choice of investors was not in strict accordance with the requirements of the rational distribution plan. Therefore, early projects into the Xiamen SEZ went to the third type, many of which, failed to match with the original industrial infrastructures in Xiamen

---

374 Su Dongbin: ***History of China's SEZ***, Guangdong Economy Press, 2001, p318

375 See date in Figure 4-3-6 and 4-3-7

or played the active role promoting industrial upgrading and optimization.

From the perspective of short-term economic growth, foreign-funded enterprises concentrated in labor-intensive projects in Xiamen City, adapted to the situation of abundant and cheap labor resources. But in long-term economic development, low technology content in foreign enterprise deviated from the original intention of using foreign investment to promote technological progress, and would inevitably bring negative effects to the economic development of Xiamen. From the long-term view, only the introduction of high-tech projects could truly promote the economic and social progress of Xiamen SEZ, and thus enhance the economic strength and its economic development potential.

4.3 The Overall Development of Xiamen Special Economic Zone: 1991~2000

In the 1990s, with Deng Xiaoping's important speech during his inspection tour to southern China in 1992 and the 14th National Congress of the CPC as significant symbols, China's economic reform began to enter a clarified track with a clear direction and goal and entered the preliminary stages of establishing a socialist market economic system. China's reform and opening up began a new chapter in history. However, in order to breakthrough the framework of the traditional planned economic system and meet the requirements of establishing the socialist market economic system, acceleration of reforms continued in the fields of State-owned enterprises, finance and taxation, banking, prices, foreign trade and social security. Xiamen Special Economic Zone had initially established the socialist market economic system in this period with the market-oriented reform at the core of all work and the reform and opening up being the driving force.

4.3.1 The Developing Course for the Establishment of Socialist Market Economic System in Xiamen Special Economic Zone

4.3.1.1 The General Secretary Jiang Zemin's Inspection in Xiamen Special Economic Zone: A Decade of Celebration and Highlights of Economy and Trade with Taiwan

1991 was the 10th anniversary of the establishment of Xiamen Special Economic Zone. On September 4, 1991, General Secretary Jiang Zemin wrote an inscription for the 10th anniversary of establishment of the Xiamen Special Economic Zone, saying, "Persist in reform and opening up and make every effort to establish a successful socialist special economic zone with Chinese characteristics." In order to further promote China's reform and opening-up policy and the brilliant achievements of the SEZ, Xiamen Municipal Committee and Government held several large-scale events to celebrate the success during the 10th anniversary of the establishment of the SEZ. Among those activities, the largest was the ceremony for celebrating the 10th anniversary of establishment of the Xiamen Special Zone on the afternoon of the December 18, 1991 at the Xiamen Central Stadium. General Secretary Jiang Zemin made a special trip to attend the ceremony and delivered an important speech.

On behalf of the Central Committee of the Party and the State Council, General Secretary Jiang Zemin pointed out in his speech in celebration that "ten years ago, we came to Xiamen where there were smaller cities, factories and a backward economy. However, today, we have witnessed a great change to this ancient city of Xiamen. Through opening to the outside world, was have attracted foreign business and investment from Hong Kong and Taiwan and brought in advanced technology and scientific management experience. Thousands of new businesses were set up; groups of high-rise buildings were built; commerce and trade flourished, which were helpful to initial forming of the industry-oriented, combining industry and trade and integrative development of the export-oriented economic pattern. Xiamen Special Economic Zone played an important role on the acceleration of economic development in the Southern Fujian. It also promoted cross-strait economic exchanges and made a positive contribution to the reunification of the motherland. Xiamen Special Economic Zone is located across the water from Taiwan, making it an important window for the economic and cultural exchanges. Xiamen Special Economic Zone should make full use of these advantages and actively promote the mutual understanding and exchanges between the compatriots across the Strait and warmly welcome Taiwan compatriots to participate in the construction of the Special Economic Zone and make contributions to the reunification of the motherland."[376]

The speech by General Secretary Jiang Zemin further affirmed the accuracy of the Central Committee of the Party's principle and policy on the construction of the Special Economic Zone. In addition, the speech spoke highly of the achievements from the ten years of construction of the Xiamen Special Economic Zone. The speech further pointed out the direction to put forward a higher requirement, which was a great encouragement for

---

376 Research on the History of Communist Party in Xiamen Municipal Government, *Establishment and Development of China's Special Economic Zones: Xiamen Volume*. Party History Press. 1996. P. 124-126.

the people in Xiamen and a very important guidance with far-reaching historical significance to the development of all business in Xiamen Special Economic Zone.

Figure 4-3-1 General Secretary Jiang Zemin's investigation in Xiamen Special Economic Zone

General Secretary Jiang Zemin visited Xiamen again on June 22, 1994. In the following two days, he investigated Xiamen Zone, Torch High-tech Industrial Development Zone, Qili Industrial Area, Haicang Investment Zone and Xinglin Investment Zone of Taiwan Businessmen. During the investigation period, General Secretary Jiang pointed out that the Special Economic Zone had entered a new stage of development, mainly through the deepening of reform and practicing good internal strength in order to upgrade the Special Economic Zone to a new level called "Increase in advantages of creativity, and climb a higher floor." Moreover, the special economic zone should keep its features, and continue to play a positive role as a window, trial zone and pioneer to the reform and opening across the country. He pointed out that Xiamen Special Zone should give its priority to Taiwan businessmen and investors in the process of developing economy and trade. These are the advantages and characteristics of Xiamen. Furthermore, it should enhance the guidance and strengthen macro-administration over all of Taiwan-funded enterprises, leading them to invest in the fields of basic industries, high-tech industries, high value-added industries and agriculture.[377]

During the investigation, General Secretary Jiang Zemin affirmed the great

377 Research on the History of Communist Party in Xiamen Municipal Government, *Establishment and Development of China's Special Economic Zones: Xiamen Volume*. Party History Press. 1996. P. 173.

achievements and historic contribution made by the economic zone. He concluded, specifically, the essential experience of the construction of the special zone. Once again, he fully affirmed its role as "window," "trial" and "vanguard" economic zone played in China's reform and opening up process. From the perspective of the strategic height in the construction of China's socialist modernization, he reaffirmed that the "central commitment to the development of special economic zones should remain unchanged, the central basic policy on the special economic zone should remain unchanged and the historical status and role played by the special economic zone should remain unchanged in the process of the country's reform and opening up and modernization." He also put emphasis to the "development of the special economic zone throughout the entire process of socialist modernization." This series of important speeches gave great inspiration and encouragement to the people in the SEZ. At the same time, General Secretary Jiang Zemin repeatedly stressed in the inspection process that the advantages and features of Xiamen should be reflected on the economic cooperation and trade with Taiwan, the role of which cannot be substituted by other special zones and will be more significant with the advance of the history.[378]

In order to highlight the important role played by Xiamen Special Economic Zone in the development of the cross-strait relations, following the establishment of Haicang and the Xinglin as Taiwanese investment zones in May 1989, the State Council also approved for the Jimei Taiwanese Investment Zone and Jimei jurisdiction, two towns in Jimei, in December 1992. The planning area was 78 square kilometers. Xiamen Special Economic Zone policy was carried out in Taiwan-funded enterprises in the special zone. Meanwhile, in order to truly protect the lawful rights of the Taiwan compatriots in Xiamen, it introduced the "Regulations on the Investment Security for the Taiwan Compatriots in Xiamen" after the local legislative right being granted by the National People's Congress, which endured the legitimate rights and interests of the Taiwan compatriots.

Since 1994, the Central Government has been determined to implement "Permit for Landing" for Taiwan compatriots who arrive directly at Xiamen Port. Moreover, on August 20, 1996, the "Shipping Management Method on Both Sides of the Taiwan Strait" promulgated by the Ministry of Communications of PRC was carried out. The Ministry of Communications decided to open Xiamen and Fuzhou as important areas for pilot ports for cross-straits direct transportation. This was an important measure and

---

378 Research on the History of Communist Party in Xiamen Municipal Government, *Establishment and Development of China's Special Economic Zones: Xiamen Volume*. Party History Press. 1996. P.174.

practical step of the mainland with the aim to realize the "three direct links," that is to say, a cross-strait links in mail, transport and trade. On September 10, 1998, by approval of the relevant authorities of the State Council, a small commodity trading market between Dadeng Island and Taiwan was set up in Xiamen. The market covered an area of one square kilometer. Residents in Fujian and compatriots in Taiwan and Jinmen Island could perform registration procedures and set up a booth to do business in the market with a valid identity certificate and approval from the Management Committee of trading market, which is the only small commodity trading market towards Taiwan approved by the State. To a certain extend, these measures reflected a powerful support given by the Central Government to Xiamen Special Economic Zone. Meanwhile, the measures could also accelerate the promotion of trade and economic co-operation between Xiamen Special Economic Zone and Taiwan.

4.3.1.2 Xiangyu Bonded Area: Accelerate the Implementation of Certain Freeport Policies

The State Council approved the establishment of Xiangyu bonded area in Xiamen on November 20, 1992. The first phase covered 0.6 square kilometers. Xiangyu bonded area was located in the northwest of Xiamen Special Economic Zone, adjacent to the Lake Industrial Area. It connected with the East Port in the west and Port Railway and Port Road in the east. It linked with Xiangyu Port and Xiamen Bridge in the south and north respectively. The planning area of Xiangyu bonded area covered 2 square kilometers. The first phase, which was 0.6 square kilometers, was accepted by the General Administration of Customs of P.R.C before its official operation on November 28, 1993.

To speed up the construction and development of Xiangyu Free Trade Zone, People's Congress of Xiamen City promulgated "Regulations of Xiamen and Xiangyu Bonded Area" on September 29, 1994. Xiangyu Bonded Area was a breakthrough for the implementation of certain freeport policies in Xiamen Special Economic Zone. It was the special economic zone that provided the most preferential policies and good investment environment for domestic and foreign investors. It was a bonded area that adopted the international practices and directly connected to international markets.

Foreign trade, transit trade and storage and transportation business were mainly developed within the bonded area. Meanwhile, it was allowed to set up a high value-added, low energy consumption and pollution-free commercial processing industry; it was also permitted to engage in finance, insurance, futures, commodities exhibition, retail and other businesses in a wide range of enterprise manufacturing and services.

The preferential policies implemented in bonded area were as follows:[379]

First was the Special Tax Policy. All of the machineries, equipments, construction materials, some vehicles and office supplies used in the import area and all of the imported raw materials, spare parts, components, fuel, packing materials, re-export goods for storage and processed export products in the bonded area were exempted from import and export licenses and granted duty-free or bonded.

The second was the Flexible Trade Policy. All types of enterprises established in the zone would be eligible to import and export business. They could operate on their own import and export trade and transit trade businesses in the zone. Non-import and non-export companies out of the zone could transact the second-line import and export customs procedures through the designated companies. To facilitate the import and export business, Chinese people in local enterprises in the zone could apply for multiple-entry endorsement to Hong Kong.

Third was the Preferential Tax Policy. All types of enterprises in the zone would be eligible for the relief from taxation within the reach of the policies and regulations. That is to say, the manufacturing enterprises with a term of more than 10 years were exempted from the enterprise income tax in the first two years counting from the profitable year. In addition, they were exempt from half income tax in the third year. Non-productive foreign-funded enterprises, whose investment from foreign businessmen was more than 5 million dollars and the operation period was over 10 years, were exempted from enterprise income tax in the first year, counting from the profitable year and a half in the next two years. Enterprises outside the zone were selling goods to enterprises within the zone and if they were treated as an export business, a tax rebate could be enjoyed. Goods entering the bonded areas from outside, except the other regulations of the State, should be exempt from value added tax, business tax and consumption tax.

Fourth was the Opening Financial Policy. Both Chinese and foreign financial institutions might apply to establish branches in the zone. Foreign exchange earnings of the enterprises in the zone might retain cash and be used as working capital. The net income from foreign-funded enterprises of Chinese enterprises could be exempted from foreign exchange within five years of their establishment and the amount would be retained. Foreign currency cash could flow in the zone. Enterprises in the zone might be approved to issue shares and bonds at home and abroad.

---

379 Research on the History of Communist Party in Xiamen Municipal Government, *Establishment and Development of China's Special Economic Zones: Xiamen Volume*. Party History Press. 1996. P.152-152.

4.3.1.3 Explore and Establish a Socialist Market Economic System and Promote the Development of Export-oriented Economy

Xiamen, as one of China's earliest special economic zones, was a pilot area of reform and opening up. Xiamen City was listed as a national comprehensive reform pilot city. Comprehensive reform focused on organizing and implementing the coastal economic development strategies and accelerated the development of export-oriented economies. Meanwhile, Xiamen City emphasized the deepening of enterprise reform and settled property relations. It established a market system, macro-system of indirect control system and smaller government. All of these comprehensive reforms were to establish a leading socialist market economic system. In this regard, the Xiamen Special Economic Zone has made many explorations and experimented bravely.

Social security system was an important part of the market economic system and Xiamen Special Economic Zone focused on this breakthrough to promote the full establishment of the socialist market economic system. Xiamen City was lined in the pilot cities to reform National Employee Medical Insurance System on June 27, 1996. Establishing Medical Insurance System of Employees was an important aspect to improving the social security system. As the Special Economic Zone, Xiamen became a pilot city of national social security reform. It fully demonstrated the "experimental field" effect of the special economic zone. At the same time, the establishment and improvement of Employee Medical Insurance System benefited the sustainable development of Xiamen Special Economic Zone in the market-oriented reforms. Xiamen City implemented the Minimum Living Security System of Urban and Rural on April 3, 1999. Security standards were 260 RMB for a single family per month and 235 RMB monthly for two-person households. Rural minimum living standard guarantee was 100 RMB for per person monthly. At that time, the security standards were the highest in the nation. Establishment of urban and rural minimum living security system was an important aspect to improving the socialist market economic system. The initiatives of Xiamen have highlighted the important role of the Special Economic Zone with the establishment and improvement of the socialist market economic system. The 26th Meeting of the Eleventh Standing Committee considered and adopted "Regulations on Basic Pension Insurance of Xiamen City," and "Regulations on Unemployment Insurance of Xiamen City" on June 21 and 23, 2000 in Xiamen. The formulation and implementation of these regulations further improved the social security system and actively promoted the old-age social security system. They improved the unemployment insurance system and promoted the legal process of social insurance of Xiamen. The social insurance system reform also made great progress.

Xiamen Special Economic Zone took the advantages of market-oriented reform to promote the state-owned enterprise reform and find the style of state-owned assets management under the market-oriented economy. It created a foreign-owned enterprise in Xiamen to transfer the overall property rights of breweries in Xiamen to foreign on February 23, 1998. It was a brave attempt, taking the advantages of multiple resources for economic development, to activate the state-owned assets. On March 31, 1999, Xiamen City recruited enterprise operators through national selection. The seven positions of opening selection included General Manager of Xiamen Engineering Machinery AG, Chief Accountant of the state-owned investment company and so on. Xiamen's open recruitment was a brave and active attempt to explore the way to "increase the value" of the state-owned assets under the socialist market economy and implement the reform of the state-owned enterprises and establish the modern enterprise system. Xiamen City began implementing the "Interim Measures on the Investigation of Loss of State Assets in Xiamen" on July 29, 1999. This was the first Chinese local government regulation, which investigated the issue involving the loss of state-owned assets. It could strengthen the management of state-owned assets and prevent loss of state-owned assets and improve the socialist market economic system. Xiamen Special Economic Zone made use of market mechanisms to attract foreign investment and to promote industrial upgrading and export-oriented economic.

Xiamen Taikoo Aircraft Engineering Company Limited held the opening ceremony on January 18, 1996. Xiamen Taikoo Aircraft Engineering Company Limited was a multinational associated enterprise set up jointly by six companies from China, the United Kingdom, Japan, Singapore and Hong Kong and so on. Aircraft Maintenance Center of Xiamen Taikoo Aircraft Engineering Company Limited was the leading project of the industrial area in Xiamen. It formed the capacity to overhaul and modify a Boeing 747 large passenger aircraft primarily. After the first phase of the project was complete, the Aircraft Maintenance Center could operate maintenance on two Boeing 747 aircraft at the same time. Led by the major project, British Lucas Aerospace, USA Allied Signal Aerospace Industries and General Electric Company also set up aircraft maintenance factories in the Center with the fuel, electrical, flight control system and turbine driven aircraft, the starter, hydraulic, etc. They formed the largest civil aircraft maintenance bases. Approved by the State Council, Xiamen Fuda Photographic Materials Co., Ltd. joined USA Eastman Kodak Company on March 26, 1998. They formed Xiamen Branch of Kodak (China) Co., Ltd. and the registered capital was 385 million. It was the largest Kodak

Production base in China. Kodak's investment in the Xiamen Special Economic Zone led to the development of related industries and optimize industrial structure and improve industrial competitiveness. It also helped to ensure sustained and stable growth of exports. The U.S. Dell Computer Company in Xiamen set up a "customer service center" in China on November 3, 1998. The center produced a full range of Dell products. China Customer Service Center in Xiamen was the second facility to provide production, sales, technical support and service in Asia Pacific.

4.3.2 The Overall Rise of the Xiamen Special Economic Zone

4.3.2.1 The Achievements of Emerging Xiamen Special Economic Zone

4.3.2.1.1 The Markedly Increasing of the Comprehensive Economic Strength

With the progressive development of the structure of socialist market economy, the comprehensive economic strength of Xiamen significantly enhanced from 1991 to 2000. The gross domestic product reached 50.187 billion yuan in 2000 (at the price of that year). In order to accurately present the achievement that Xiamen Special Economic Zone obtained over the last ten years, Figure 4-3-2 indicates the trend of increase in per capital GDP from 1991 to 2000. (1952 was the base year, approved by Household Registration). Figure 4-3-3 illustrates the corresponding chain growth rate. Statistically, the per capital GDP of Xiamen was 4.47 times in 2000 than in 1991. The corresponding chain growth rate is 18.43% over those ten years.

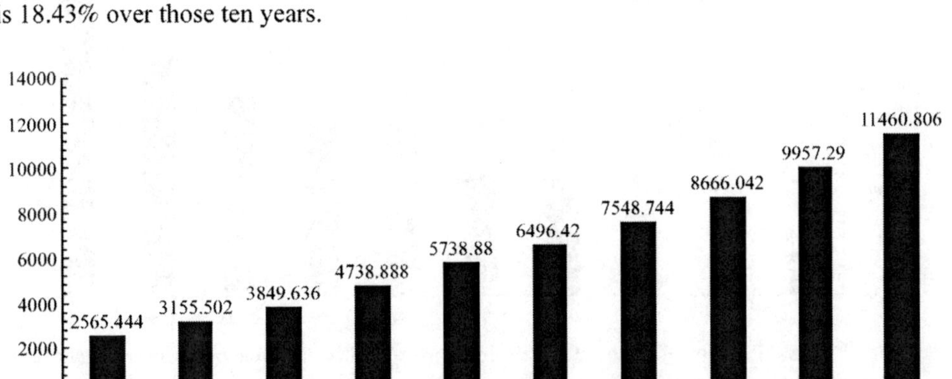

Figure 4-3-2 Per Capital of GDP in Xiamen from 1991~2000

Source information: Annual inspection in Xiamen Special economic zone (2001) China Statistical Press

With the rapid development of city economy and the improving overall economic efficiency of the enterprises, the financial income of the city increased substantially over those ten years, which contributed effectively to the financial revenue of Xiamen Special

Economic Zone, making finance continuously strengthen the economic development. At the same time, it also benefited a great deal from the establishment and improvement of the socialist economic system. Figure 4-3-4 indicates the overall financial revenue of Xiamen from 1991 to 2000 (at the price in 1991). The overall financial income of Xiamen city is 7.73 times in 2000 than in1991.

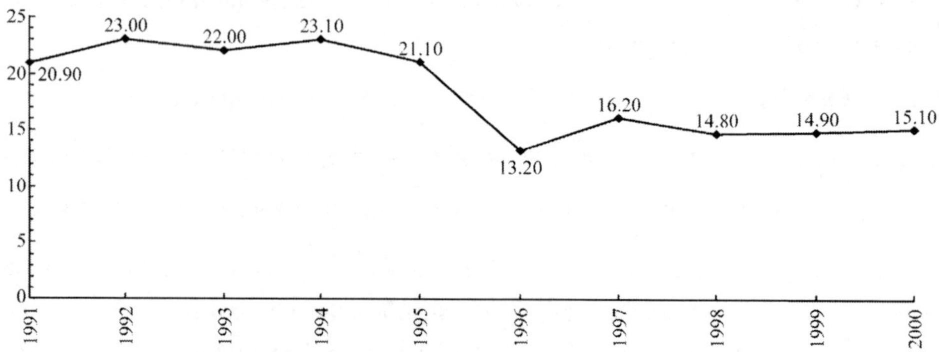

Figure 4-3-3 Real Per Capita GDP Growth Rate of Xiamen from 1991 to 2000 (Based on the growth rate of 1952, according to census register population)

Sources: Xiamen Special Economic Zone Yearbook Press, 2001 edition, Statistics Press

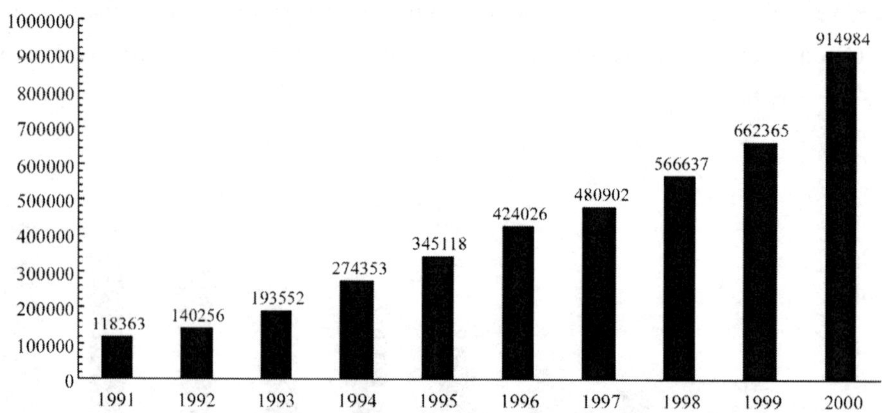

Figure 4-3-4 Fiscal Revenue of Xiamen from 1991~2000 (Calculated at current prices, ten thousand unit)

Resources: Xiamen Special Economic Zone Yearbook Press, 2001 Edition, Statistics Press

4.3.2.1.2 The Marked Increase in Industrial Economy's Comprehensive Strength and its Growing Role as the National Economy's Pillar Industry

Figure 4-3-5 shows the growing trend of gross industrial output value of Xiamen from 1991 to 2000 (calculated at current prices). Xiamen's national total value of industry in 2000 reached 77.636 billion yuan, 6.49 times from 1991. Industrial economy was a prominent driving force of the fast-growing economy of Xiamen. Industry generated 63.2% of all economic growth, directly bringing an 11.7% increase in economic growth.[380] In the meantime, the sustained growth of industrial economy of Xiamen was driven mainly by local backbone enterprises. 117 important industrial enterprises, which values are more than 100 million yuan, made industry production value of 52,639 billion yuan in 2000, accounting for 75.23% of the city's total industrial output.[381] Meanwhile, while industrial restructuring achieved initial success, more and more high-tech enterprises are displaying an important lead. Xiamen's industrial enterprises development are close in success to the industries of electronic, machinery and chemicals and active efforts, which also needed further adjustment in industrial structure. The output of these three industries accounted for around 60% of total production value.[382] With the rapid growth of enterprises, including Xiahua, Dell, Kodak, Xianglu, Tsann Kuen and other high-tech enterprises, the industrial structures of Xiamen upgrade continuously. The top five enterprises of total production value of Xiamen were all high-tech enterprises in 2000.[383] The overall economic benefit increased constantly in the process of economic growth over the past ten years. The aggregate index of industrial economic benefits 137.3%, made about 3,256 billion in profit, and realized profit tax amount of 6,658 billion yuan.[384]

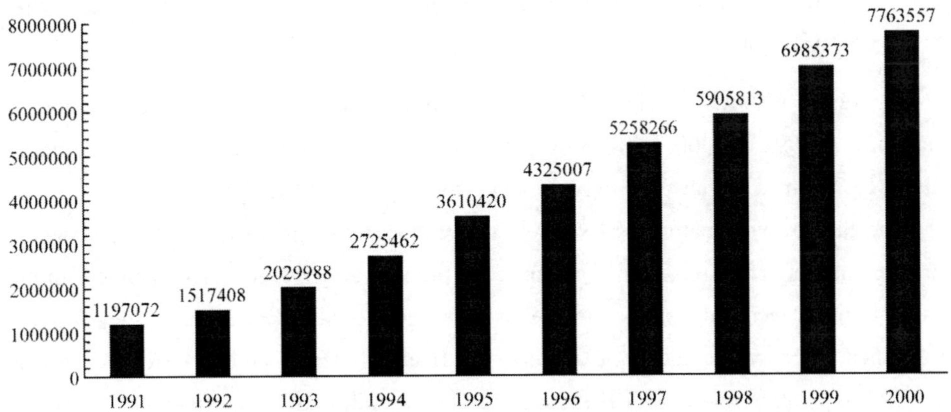

Figure 4-3-5 Total Industrial Output Value of Xiamen from 1991 to 2000

(Caculated at current prices and new range, ten thousand yuan)

Sources: Xiamen Special Economic Zone Yearbook, 2001 Edition, Statistics Press

380 *Xiamen Special Economic Zone Yearbook, (2001), Statistics Press, P37*

381 *Xiamen Special Economic Zone Yearbook, (2001), Statistics Press, P37*

382 *Xiamen Special Economic Zone Yearbook, (2001), Statistics Press, P37*

383 *Xiamen Special Economic Zone Yearbook, (2001), Statistics Press, P37*

384 *Xiamen Special Economic Zone Yearbook, (2001), Statistics Press, P37*

Table 4-3-1 shows the changing tendency of the three-class industry of Xiamen from 1991 to 2000. The number shows the economic growth of Xiamen mainly depending on the increase of secondary and tertiary industries. The proportion of secondary industry increased from 46.4% to 50.6%, while the tertiary proportion was relatively stable.

Table 4-3-1 Proportion of Three-Class Industry of Xiamen from 1991to 2000

Year	Primary Industry	Secondary Industry	Tertiary Industry
1991	9	46.4	44.6
1992	8.3	42.4	49.4
1993	7.1	44.3	48.6
1994	6.9	48	45.1
1995	6.3	51.1	42.6
1996	6.8	50	43.3
1997	5.9	48.9	45.2
1998	5.4	48.4	46.2
1999	4.8	49.7	45.5
2000	4.2	50.6	45.2

Sources: Xiamen Special Economic Zone Yearbook, 2001 Edition, Statistics Press.

4.3.2.1.3 The Swift Growth of Fixed Asset Investment and Total Retail Sales of Consumer Goodsinto the Main Drivers of National Economic Growth

Figure 4-3-6 shows fixed asset investment and total retail sales of consumer goods of Xiamen from 1991 to 2000. In the past ten years, investment in fixed assets totaled 120.224 billion, 13,75 times as many total investments from 1981 to 1991.[385]

The fast-growing nature of fixed asset investment strengthened the improvement of infrastructure construction, while urban construction underwent great changes andlife quality projects were put into use to greatly promote the industrial economy development of Xiamen. Meanwhile, the rapid increase of fixed asset investments also sped up the technical renovation of traditional industry, so the overall quality of Xiamen's enterprises have imporved significantly. Fixed asset investment also led to the vigorous development of the real estate market which had already become an important part of the national economy. In the process of establishing the market ecomic sturcture, business enterprises of Xiamen witnessed changes in the economic situation, increased reform strength, promoted the transformation of the operation system and adapted to market requirements, so as to

385 Xiamen's total investment amount to 8.742 billion from 1981 to 1990.

maintain good momentum of steady growth in overall commodities flow scale. The total retail scales of customer goods amounted to 14.766 billion yuan in 2000, five times as much as 1991. With the prosperity and stability of the consumer goods retail market, competition of market with different economy components will be more and more tight and non-public sections of economy developed fairly fast. The collective state-owned economy took 33.6% of the market share, individual privately owned economy took 48.75% of the market share, foreign investment and economies of Hong Kong, Macao and Taiwan took 5.11%, affiliation economy took 1.31% of the market share and other economies took 11.2%.[386] The competition between various economies promoted the prosperity and stability of the retail market.

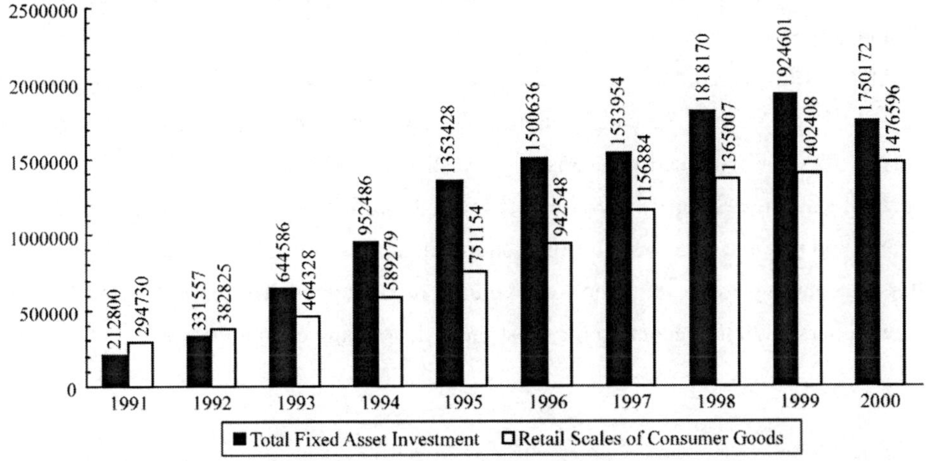

Figure 4-3-6 Total Fixed Asset Investment and Retail Scales of Consumer Goods in Xiamen (Calculated at current prices, ten-thousand yuan)

Sources: Xiamen Special Economic Zone Yearbook, 2000 Edition, Statistics Press.

Notes: Overall fixed asset investment caculated at current prices, retail sales of consumer goods adjusted according to the figures of 2004 economic census.

4.3.2.1.4 The Volume of Exports Revealss the Ceaselessly Expanding Trend

Figure 4-3-7 shows the change of total volume of imports and exports of Xiamen in 2000 (caculated at current prices). Affected by the Asian economic crisis, Xiamen's exports and imports showed negative growth until 1998, theamount of 1999 increased once more. The total volume of imports and exports were about 5.81 times and 5.11 times the number of 1991 respectively. Most of the growth of import and export business was due to Xiamen

386 Xiamen Special Economic Zone Yearbook, 2001 Edition, Statistics Press, P215-216.

Special Economic Zone's commitment to the reform and opening-up, seizing of opportunies, expanding the opening to the outside world, developing export-oriented economy and continuing to optimize the hard and soft environment of investment.

In this process, the structure of export commodities was optimized and the additional costs of export commodities had also been raised. Xiamen's export of electromechanical products amounted to 2.507 billion dollars, accounting for 42.64% of the total export volume. The export of high-tech product amounted to 8.680 million dollars, accounting for 14.76% of total export volume.[387] Further expansion of the scale and capacity of production of well-known domestic enterprises included: Dell, Tsann Kuen, Linde, Fuji, ABB, Xiahua, Xiaxin and Taeco. Enabling the electromechanical and high-tech products maintained a good export momentum, which took a leading role in the export development of Xiamen Special Economic Zone.

Along with the gradual establishment of socialism market economy, the reform of foreign trade of Xiamen Special Economic Zone had also made significant progress; the export of non-public-owned enterprises grew strongly. The total volume of imports and exports of state-owned enterprise amounted to 2.91 billion dollars, accounting for 29% of the total volume; the total volume of 3-endowment enterprises amounted to 6.61 billion dollars, accounting for 6.58%; the total volume of private enterprises amounted to 4.100 million dollars in 2000, becoming the most rapid developing economic type.[388]

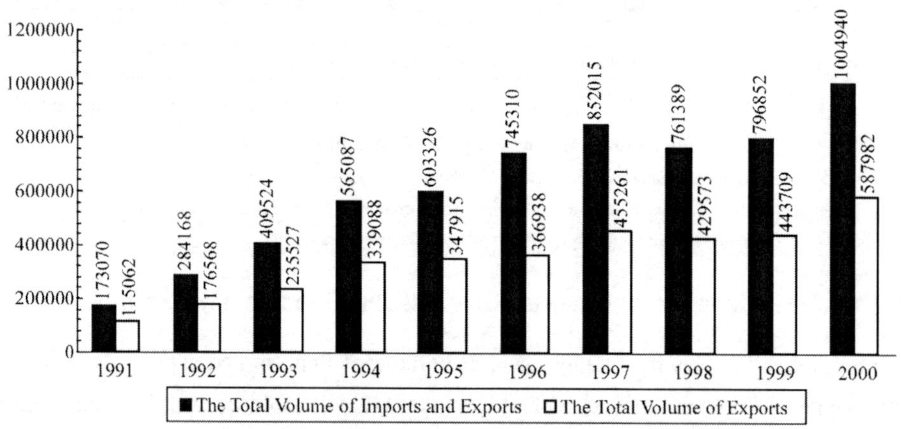

Figure 4-3-7 The Total Volume of Imports and Exports of Xiamen and The Total Volume of Exports (Calculated at current prices, ten thousand dollars)

Sources: Xiamen Special Economic Zone Yearbook, 2001 Edition, Statistics Press

387 Xiamen Special Economic Zone Yearbook, (2001), Statistics Press, P217.

388 Xiamen Special Economic Zone Yearbook, (2001), Statistics Press, P217.

4.3.2.1.5 Seek Development in Difficulties by Utilizing Foreign Capital

Figure 4-3-8 reveals the changing trend of contract and actual use of foreign capital of Xiamen from 1991 to 2000 (calculated at current prices). Figure 4-3-9 gives its correspondong growth rate. Xiamen's contract and actual use of foreign capital waved violently in the past decades. Commrade Deng Xiaoping's Southern Tour Speech and the Fourteenth Party Congress exerted beneficial effects on the contract and actual use of foreign capital of Xiamen, which increased substantially in 1992 and 1993 and presented negative growth in 1994.

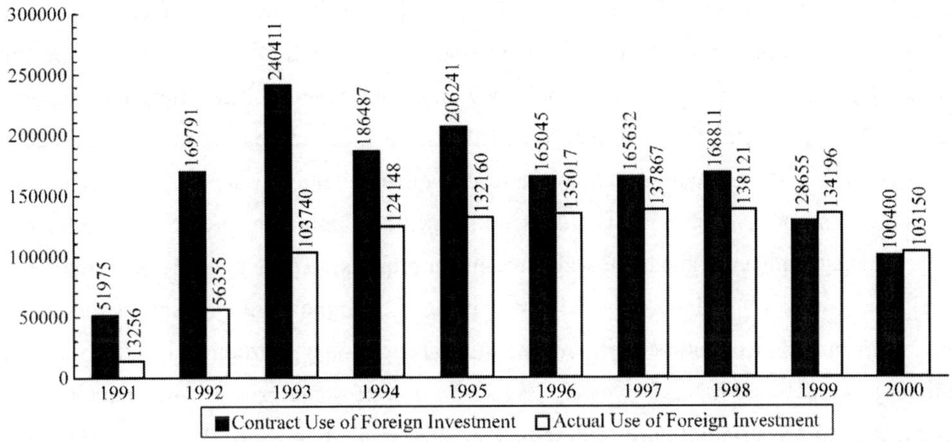

Figure 4-3-8 Contract Use of Foreign Investment and Actual Use of Foreign Investment of Xiamen from 1991~2000 (nominal, ten million dollar)

Sources: Xiamen Special Economic Zone Yearbook, 2001 Edition, Statistics Press

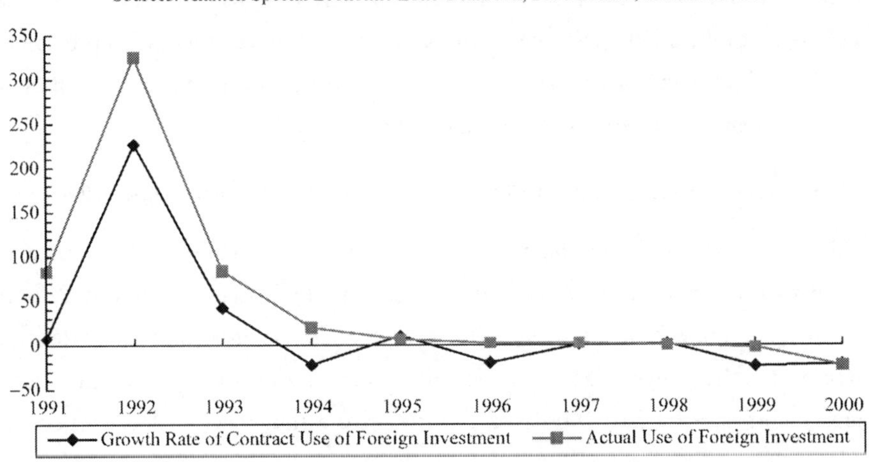

Figure 4-3-9 Growth Rate of Contract Use of Foreign Investment and Actual Use of Foreign Investment of Xiamen

Sources: Xiamen Special Economic Zone Yearbook, 2001 Edition, Statistics Press (%)

After the Asian financial crisis swept the South-East Asian countries, and some countries and regions of Asia, Xiamen Special Economic Zone faced the grim task of rearranging the international capital flow, because the foreign investment also showed a steady decline. The contract use of foreign capital in 2000 accounted for 41.77% of that of 1993, the actual use of foreign capital of 2000 nearly equal with that of 1993.

In the face of difficulties, Xiamen Special Economic Zone actively adopted measures, continued to improve fundamental construction of investment environment, focused on improving the weak environment of investment and actively solved problems for the foreign businesses, so as to attract investment while providing timely and efficient service. In 1997, Fujian International Fair for Investment and Trade had been approved by the state as the China International Fair for Investment and Trade, hosted by the State Economic and Trade Department, which was undertook by Fujian and Xiamen. The China International Fair for Investment and Trade further deepened Xiamen's influence of attracting investment, elevated Xiamen's reputation at home and abroad, maintained a steady development of investment attraction, shifted its focus to attracting high-tech program investments, multi-national companies and large-scale investment projects, so as to raise the performance of foreign investment.[389] Meanwhile, Xiamen Special Economic Zone gradually experiences the transformation from attracting investment to raising money, introducing technology and utilizing international market. A group of foreign invested enterprises, which have capital, technology and a bright future, are settled in this area, such as Kodak, Dell, Hamilton Sundstrand, Dejia Semiconductor, Balong Lithium Battery, ERC Zinc Nickel Batteries, GE Engine Maintainance Projects, Philips Lighting Electrical Applicances and so on. By the end of 2000, 24 of the 500 largest multi-national companies have invested 33 projects, with contract foreign investments amounted to 1.018 billion dollars in this area, each contract foreign investment amounted to 30.86 million dollars.[390]

4.3.2.1.6 Science and Education Obtain Considerable Development

The rise of Xiamen over the past ten years has been astonishing. Xiamen, very concerned with the role of technological progress in advancing economic development and social development, made great efforts to realize the growth from extensive to intensive by accelerating the development of science and technology. Xiamen had 147 high-tech enterprises by late 2000, accomplished 30 billion USD in production value,

389 Xiamen Special Economic Zone Yearbook, (2001), Statistics Press, P218.

390 Xiamen Special Economic Zone Yearbook, (2001), Statistics Press, P224.

organized and implemented four national class programs, nine state torch plans, six national spark programs fand our enterprises were named as technology innovation model enterprise. The main buildings of first phase of the project were Siming Software Park and Torch Software Park. The offical building of Beijing University Biological Park had been completed, Bridge and Road Technology Park and the first phase of Dell have been put into use and 70% of the Tsann Kuen Technology Park project had been completed.[391]

Xiamen was concerned with education development over the past decades. There were 912 ordinary schools and 3,196[392] school children. High growth in these three aspects have been achieved, with the ratio of the educational expenditure in the financial expenditure of the fudget increasing every year and the scale of school expanding continuously. In terms of the construction of a teacher's team, Xiamen persisted in standarizing teacher's continuing education and training and expanding the training channel to abroad. Teacher's social status, working conditions, salary, housing, medical treatment and other treatments were also improved. Meanwhile, the information construction of Xiamen's education made great progress. Xiamen Education and Research Network was upgraded to broadband Metropolitan Area Networkand most of middle schools and primary schools built campus networks which educational technique modernization. The Ministry of Education of China designated Xiamen as a computer education experimental zone of China.[393]

4.3.2.2 An Objective Appraisal of the Rise of Xiamen Special Economic Zone

Xiamen developed simutaneously with China from 1991 to 2000; it successfully build the system of socialist market economy. In the 1980s, the concept of Special Economic Zone of Deng Xiaoping aimed at ending the idea of closed-door policy and bringing economy construction to the center, so as to play a very positive role as a window. While in the 1990s, the historical mission of Special Economic Zone turned to explore how to build the systems of a socialist market economy. As the head of reform and developments of Special Economic Zone, Xiamen made significant developments during the process of establishing a system of a socialist market economy according to China's regualtions. However, in order to objectively present Xiamen's achievement of the past 20 years and its

391 Xiamen Special Economic Zone Yearbook, (2001), Statistics Press, P41.

392 Xiamen Special Economic Zone Yearbook, (2001), Statistics Press, P225.

393 Xiamen Special Economic Zone Yearbook, (2001), Statistics Press, P225.

position and level in China, Figures 4-3-10, 4-3-11, 4-3-12, 4-3-13 and 4-3-14 respectively give data of the per capita GNP, per capita disposable income of urban residents, local financial revenue, industrial enterprise production value and foreign direct investment of Xiamen and other cities. The other four Special Economic Zones include Shenzhen, Zhuhai, Shantou, Hainan and cities like Guangzhou, Ningbo, Shanghai and Suzhou have been chosen in order to make comparisons. The above cities and Special Economic Zones have been chosen because they reflected not only the differences between Special Economic Zones but also between the forefront cities.

Figure 4-3-10 shows the differences of per capita GNP between Xiamen and other cities. From the point of the result, the per capital GNP of Xiamen amounted to 38,021 yuan, ranking second, compared to other cities (provinces), 1724 yuan lower than Shenzhen. The per capita GNP is one of the keys to evaluating the overall level of economic development of a city. Therefore, Xiamen showed remarkable achievements in the ten years from 1991 to 2000.

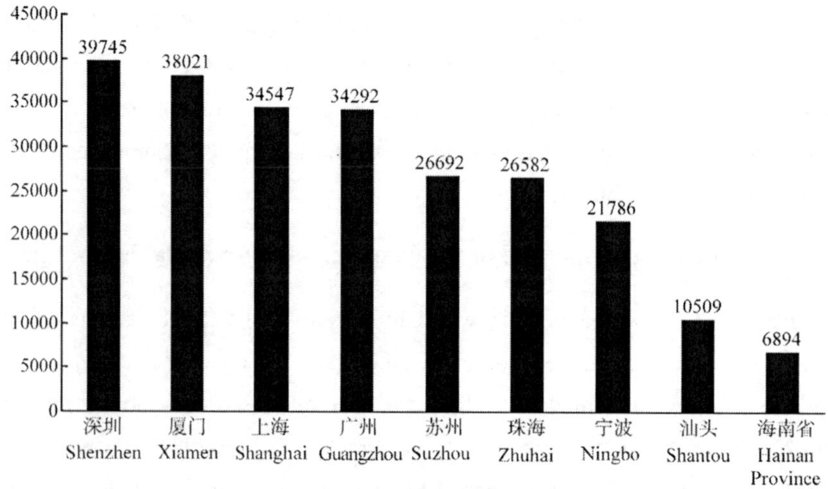

Figure 4-3-10 Comparison of Per Capita Of GNP Between Xiamen and Other Cities in 2000

Sources: China's Regional Economic Statistical Yearbook, 2001 Edition, China Financial and Economic Publishing House

Figure 4-3-11 shows the difference of urban family per capita disposable income between Xiamen and other cities. The per capita disposable income of Xiamen residents reached 10,261 yuan in 2000, ranking sixth behind Shenzhen, making up 47.45% of that of Shenzhen. It also indicates that, although per capita of GNP of Xiamen was relatively high, it did not translate into disposable income of city residents. Therefore, Xiamen Special Economic Zone should pay increased attention to improving the income of residents in the future.

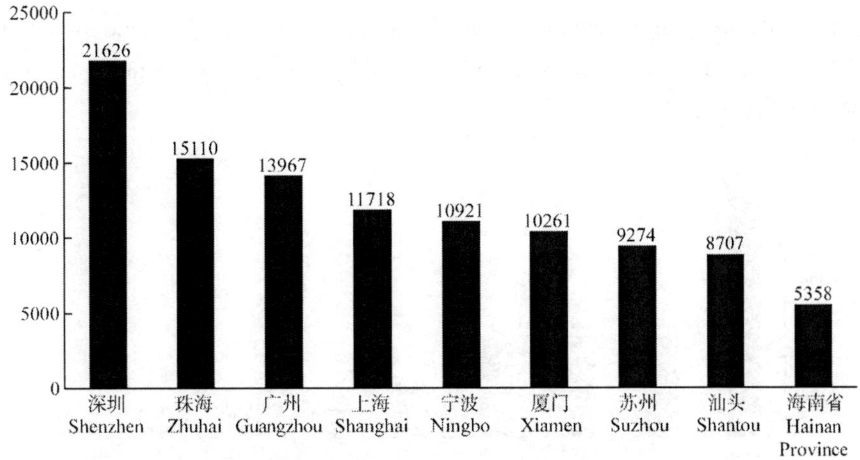

Figure 4-3-11 Comparison of Per Capita of Disposable Income of Urban residents between Xiamen and Other Cities in 2000

Sources: China's Regional Economic Statistical Yearbook, 2001 Edition, China's Financial and Economic Publishing House

Figure 4-3-12 gives the results of comparison of regional financial income between Xiamen and other cities. The regional financial income of Xiamen was 5.019 billion yuan in 2000, ranking sixth and accounting for 22.3% of total regional income of Shenzhen, showing Xiamen has great room for economic development.

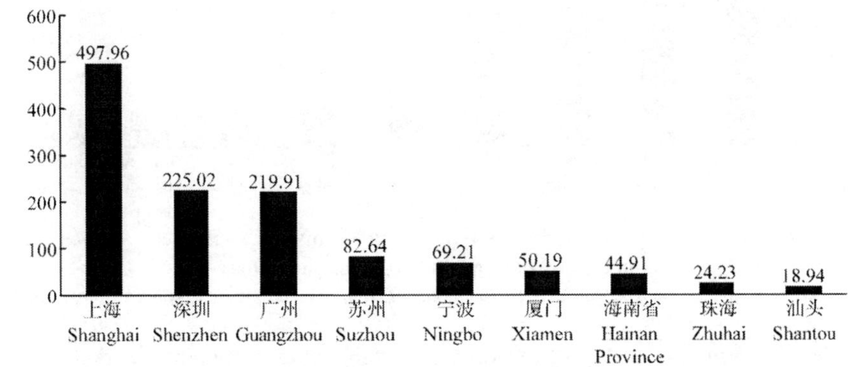

Figure 4-3-12 Comparison of Regional Financial Income Between Xiamen And Other Cities in 2000

Sources: China's Regional Economic Statistical Yearbook, 2001 Edition, China's Financial and Economic Publishing House

Figure 4-3-13 shows the comparison of industrial production value of enterprises above designated size between Xiamen and other cities in 2000. In terms of growth rate of industrial production value of enterprises above designated size, Xiamen ranked sixth just behind Shanghai, Guangzhou, Shenzhen, Suzhou and Ningbo. Figure 4-3-14 gives the comparison of direct foreign investment between Xiamen and other cities. The results indicate that Xiamen's utilization of direct direct investment ranked fifth behind Shanghai,

Guangzhou, Shenzhen and Suzhou. The gap between Xiamen and Suzhou only accounted for 35.77%, suggeting that Xiamen must proceed with the development in utilizing directforeign investment.

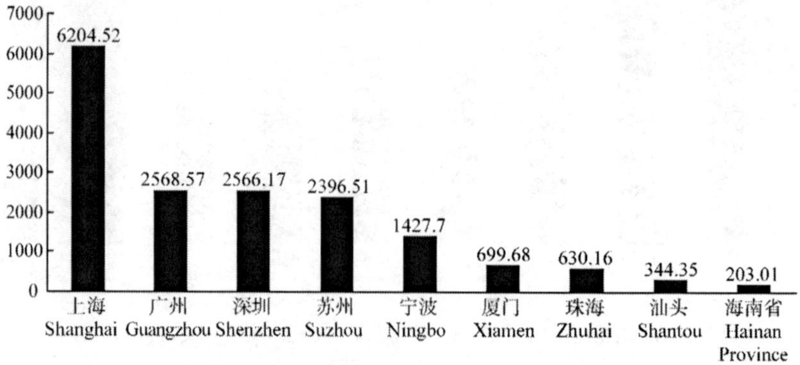

Figure 4-3-13 The Comparison of Production Value of Enterprises above Designated Size Between Xiamen and Other Cities (100 million yuan)

Sources: China's Regional Economic Statistical Yearbook, 2001 Edition, China Financial Economic Publishing House

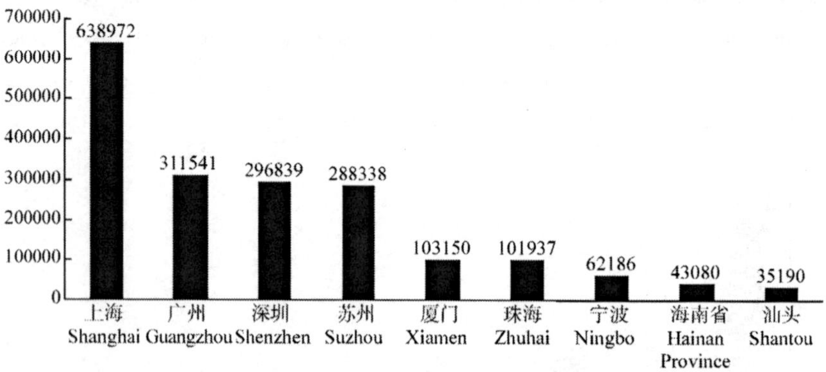

Figure 4-3-14 The Comparison of Foreign Direct Investment Between Xiamen And Other Cities in 2000 (10 thousand dollar)

Sources: China's Regional Economic Statistical Yearbook, 2001 Edition, China Financial Economic Publishing House

Under the principle that gives priority to establishing a socialist market economic system, the reform and development of Xiamen proceeded for ten years. Although Xiamen Special Economic Zone made great economic achievements, the establishment of a socialist market economy system was a long-term project that needed continuous research and effort. Xiamens still has a long way to go before establishing a relatively complete system of socialist market economy. The gap lies in five aspects:

First, although the pattern with public sector remains dominant and diverse sectors of the economy developing side by side has bascially taken shape in the Xiamen Special Ecnomic Zone, there is still a long way to go for state-owned enterprises to transforming operational systems and establish a modern enterprise system. The government still owns a large portion of Xiamen Special Economic Zone's economy. It cannot adapt well to the competition system in the condition of market economy. Meanwhile, the competitive factors that blocked the equal and well-ordered competition between state-owned economy and state-owned economy still exsisted; it cannot creat a system and policy environment that is good for various economies. The reorganization of cross-border, cross-sectoral and trans-regional assets, which is also restricted by many factors, might be harmful to establishing long-term and endogenetic economic motivation.

Secondly, although the system of commodity market and key material market had been initially established, the degree of economy commercialization was still not high. The market system had not played a fundamental role in the allocation of energy resources. It is difficult for market entities to compete in an equal, fair and orderly market environment. The market order needs to be further improved and completed and the legalization and standardization of the market activities must be strengthened further.

Thirdly, the implementation of the government's management system did not agree with the requirements of a socialist market economy. Since China's socialist market economy is transitted from planned economy, the government's intervention on the market could not be deiminished immediately, mainly showing improbabilityof seperating government asministration and enterprise management. The government's management needed to be standarized under the condition of a modern market economy, more legal and economic measures should be adopted instead of administrative measures, especially the reform of administrative examination and approval system. The standarization of the responsibility and function of the government of Xiamen Special Economic Zone needed to be further explored under the condition of market economy.

Fourthly, aimed at establishing a system of socialist market economy, a matched social security system policy should be established. Xiamen always paid great attention to the establishment and improvement of the social security system, but the regulation of management system, expansion of social security coverage and the maintainence and increasing of the social insurance funds still needed improvement. Furthermore, tax adjusting ability of personal income and property was too weak, efficient adjustment measures needed to be impelemted to reduce income differences.

Fifth, compared with the urban market reformation, the reform of rural economic system is relatively backward. More efforts need to be made in agricultural industrialization, rural management system innovation, grain circulation system, comprehensive reform, rural social service system and rural social security system establishment.

4.4 Xiamen Special Economic Zone in the New Century After 2001

The environment for the development of Xiamen Special Economic Zone underwent significant changes since the beginning of the 21st century. With China's accession to the WTO and the increasing trend of economic globalization, China's domestic market became increasingly international. Meanwhile, the strategic focus of national development moved towards inland areas, which showed the omni-dimensional and multi-level pattern of China's reform and opening up. Facing opportunities and challenges, Xiamen Special Economic Zone made accelerating development its theme to improve the socialist market system so that it could keep its advantage in the new situation.

4.4.1 Development Strategy of Xiamen Special Economic Zone in the New Century

In the new situation, Xiamen revolved around accelerating economic and social development. By way of restructuring and optimizing the industries driven by reform and opening up, advancement of science, technology and independent innovation, and starting from and aiming at rising living standards, Xiamen Special Economic Zone strove to realize people-centeredness and the Scientific Development Outlook, promote "three innovations,"[394] increase "three advantages"[395] and rise "five levels."[396] It aimed at realizing socialist modernization and giving better play to its role of driving force and as an exemplary special economic zone.[397]

In the new century, Xiamen Special Economic Zone faced new historic situations, such as the overall opening and improvement of the socialist market economy system and China's accession to the WTO. To seize the opportunities in such new situations, Xiamen Special Economic Zone worked out scientific development strategies. They are as follows:[398]

---

394 The "three innovations" are concept innovation, system innovation and technological innovation.

395 The "three advantages" are industrial advantage, location advantage and environmental advantage.

396 The "five levels" are economic intensification level, urbanization level, open level, living standards level and social civilization level.

397 Detailed statement about "three innovations", "three advantages" and "five levels", see the Outline of the Tenth Five-year Plan for Xiamen's Economic and Social Development.

398 This part is the extract from and summary of the *Outline of the Tenth Five-year Plan for Xiamen's Economic and Social Development*.

First, restructure economy, promote the optimization and upgrading of industries and improve the core competitiveness of industries. Xiamen Special Economic Zone should aim at becoming a center of high-tech industries targeting the international market by promoting high-tech industries, strengthening pillar industries (electronics industry, machine-building industry and chemical industry) and reforming characterized traditional industries. Efforts should be taken to commercialize high and innovative technologies, apply high-techs to industries, raise the scale and intensification of production and main products in order to make Xiamen an important part of the international industry and value chain and further improve its level of modernization. It should also try to become a regional center of international flights, tourism and business by promoting the information, logistics and tourism industries. Rural economy should also be optimized to increase industrialization and urbanization in rural areas.

Second, strengthen the construction of information infrastructure to promote the informationization of national economy and society. The construction of optical fiber transmission network, telecommunication supporting network and wireless access network should be quickened to form a basic physical network that could meet different needs. Xiamen should try to lift its construction of communication network and information exchange platform to an advanced national level. The information exchange with Taiwan is also to be strengthened to promote overall informationization of economy and the society.

Third, be more open to accelerating economic globalization. Xiamen is to successfully hold the "China Investment and Trade Fair," actively take part in international division of labor and coordination of work to perform its experimental and exemplary role as a special economic zone. Emphasizing attracting investment from multinational companies, it will continue to use foreign investment rationally and effectively. Three Taiwan-invested areas, i.e. Haicang, Xinglin and Jimei are to be well operated to attract more Taiwan companies, especially the top 100 companies, to invest in Xiamen. Because of this, the operation across the Taiwan Straits could be strengthened and the advantages complimented.

Fourth, promote scientific and technological innovation to build a competitive edge. A system-oriented market is to be built. The separation between scientific and technological innovation and the economic development is to be solved by way of making those market-targeting enterprises the leader of the scientific and technological innovation. The investment system should feature expansive participation, with government input as the guide, enterprise investment as the body and the social fund as other sources. Risk investment mechanism, insurance mechanism, tech credit mechanism and credit appraisal mechanism should be established and improved so that the capital market will become a powerful support for the development of science and technology.

Fifth, build "a city of education" and talents. The talent development strategy should give equal importance to talent training and introduction. All kinds of talents are needed in modernization, particularly high caliber personnel, which should be quickly trained or brought in. Education is to be taken as the priority of government and social investment to turn Xiamen into a city of advanced education and various talents.

Sixth, improve living standards and construct a socialist spiritual civilization. With rapid economic growth, the income of urban and rural residents should be increased by a large margin. An environment that is favorable to living and starting a business will be created by including non-public economies into social insurance system. Thus, various insurance systems, such as old-age, medical care, unemployment, work injury and maternity, will cover more people. Xiamen will also improve the management of social insurance funds to increase its efficiency. It will also improve the guarantee of subsistence allowances for urban and rural residents. Other social benefit undertakings, such as social welfare, social relief, preferential care, job placement and mutual aid should be expanded and more assistance should be given to groups with special needs.

Seventh, speed up the urbanization and raise the status of Xiamen. Emphasis should be given to make Xiamen a tropical, coastal city to shift its image and function from an island city into a modern and ecological gulf city, whose crowding and pulling effect will be enhanced. With an improved environment, man and nature will live more harmoniously with each other.

Eighth, protect the resources and the environment to improve sustainability. Comprehensive environmental protection is to be carried out by giving equal importance to pollution control and ecology protection to improve the environment and keep the natural balance. Xiamen is to become a preliminary ecological city.

Ninth, quicken system innovation to match the international society. In major parts, a socialist market economy should conform to international conventions and innovation should also be emphasized, so that the gradually improved system could act as a favorable environment for economic and social development. Fair market access is needed to break the barriers of administrative protection to productivity. In addition, non-public economies will be encouraged and guided under the principle of various economies developing together. These economies should compete fairly and develop mutually. In addition, the government should also adjust its functions. Administrative management reform is to be deepened and the role of regulations and plans is to be strengthened. With less direct administrative intervention and more economic and legal measures to regulate the economy, government action will be subject to the legal system.

4.4.2 Development of Xiamen Special Economic Zone in the New Century

4.4.2.1 Improving Socialist Economy Through Reform

Xiamen Special Economic Zone continued to adjust governmental function to improve the socialist market economy. With the foundation of Xiamen Investment Center on June 5, 2001, the job of attracting investments, which had been a purely government action, became a market behavior led by government and conducted by professionals. This exploration and shift of governmental functions was enlightening to regulating government in socialist economy. The natural combination of governmental guidance and the market's autonomous adjustment was beneficial to improving socialist economy. On November 13, 2003, the Mayor of Xiamen attended a meeting in Xike Town. The government of Tongan District agreed to pay 2 million yuan of liquidated damage to Gulong Group for the late delivery of industrial land. It was the first time in Xiamen history that a government paid an enterprise for its mistakes. This case showed that Xiamen government was able to regulate its own behaviors in accordance with the rules of market economy, demonstrating a big change in governmental functions and great progress in improving socialist market economy.

Xiamen Special Economic Zone strove to optimize the allocation of resources by cultivating a multi-dimensional market system. On June 25, 2002, Xiamen Land Transaction Market began operation. Since then, all the operational land for commodity housing would have to go through open tender, public listing or auction in the market. Thus, private transactions and "black case work" could be avoided to ensure the openness, fairness and impartiality of land transaction. Furthermore, buyers and sellers could search for one another themselves, which could save a lot of money and increase efficiency. In addition, in this market, people obtain information about the need and supply of land in Xiamen and the conditions of the land market and policies on investment in the land. The opening of this market was a key measure for Xiamen Special Economic Zone to improve trade transactions under the socialist market economy. On November 24, 2005, Xiamen started paid mining right transfers for the first time. Managers of fourteen already built mines signed agreements on paid mining right transfer with Xiamen Bureau of Land and Real Estate. Before that, the mining rights used to have to go through administrative approval and obtained without pay, which hindered the transparency and fairness of mineral resource allocation and the efficiency of its intensive utility. However, after the mining rights transfer, the mining right of newly built mines would all be gained through tender, listing or auction and that of the already built mines will be transferred through negotiation with pay or through auctions, listing or auction if the negotiation should fail. The shift from un-paid transfer to paid transfer is a significant revolution against the long-term administrative approval of mining rights.

Xiamen Special Economic Zone kept improving social insurance system to promote the development of socialist market economy. At the Eighth Session of the Twelfth Standing Committee of Fujian People's Congress on January 6, 2004, "Methods for Guarantee of Subsistence Allowances in Xiamen" was passed, which was the first in China to have included subsistence allowances for urban residents in legal system. This is the first local regulation that covered qualified people in cities, towns and villages in the guarantee of subsistence allowances. The specific stipulation of objects was: residents and villagers with the registration of Xiamen. By offering an official regulation, it ensured the basic life of urban and rural residents with a regulation and contributed to the stability of the society, the economic development and the improvement of the socialist market economy system. On July 23, 2004, Xiamen established a retirement insurance system for farmers, which was the first in Guangdong. At the Twenty-first Standing Conference of Xiamen Government, "Xiamen Basic Old-age Insurance for Farmers Expropriation of Land Tentative Measures" was passed. Part of the compensation farmers obtained for land expropriation would be put in their old-age insurance. This insurance was promoted by the government, guided by policies and subsidized by government finance and would be paralleled with that of urban residents. Institutionally guaranteeing the farmers who had lost their land, this was a good attempt in solving the conflict between urbanization and the rights of farmers who had lost their land during the process and a big improvement to socialist market economy system. On November 2, 2004, the Xiamen government promulgated "Tentative Measures for Basic Old-age Pension Insurance for Public Institution Staff and Workers in Xiamen," which would come into effect on July 1, 2004. Over 30,000 retired staff, of altogether 1,452 public institutions, began to enjoy the basic old-age insurance just like the staff of enterprises had done. On November 1, 2007, Xiamen released "Decision on Reforming and Developing Medical and Health Services and Solving the Problem of Difficult Access to See Doctors" and two supporting documents, marking China's first inclusive medical insurance, covering both urban and rural residents. On February 1, 2008, Xiamen started new community medical service network. Nineteen community medical service centers and twenty-one community public health centers began operation, and all these centers were under the control of four class-3 hospitals to offer preferential medical services to patients with insurance. In November 2009, college students studying in Xiamen were also included in the basic medical insurance system, in an attempt to avoid excluding any group.

4.4.2.2 Promoting the Economic Development Through High-tech Industries

Xiamen Special Economic Zone had always attached great importance to high-tech industries, through which it realized the upgrading of industrial structures and the shift from extensive economy to intensive economy. The Dell China Customer Center was established in Xiamen Special Economic Zone on May 10, 2001, which was the second integrated manufacturing facility in the Asia-Pacific region and the only manufacturing base in China. This base promoted the optimization and upgrading of industrial structure driven by information technology and advanced applicable technologies. It also boomed investment in electronic products, mainly represented by computer and peripheral devices, communication devices and internet devices. Xiamen thus became a key manufacturing and exporting base of national information products. On January 9, 2006, American Power Conversion (APC), the leading manufacturer of uninterruptible power began to operate its Xiamen factory in Torch Industrial Zone, becoming the first transnational enterprise investing in this zone, enhancing Xiamen's strength in manufacture and relevant industries. It indicated that Xiamen would attract more investments from famous transnational enterprises. On January 17, 2006, Chunghwa Picture Tubes and Xiamen Overseas Chinese Electronics respectively held signing ceremonies with Xiamen Torch High-tech Zone Administrative Committee, the investments totaling 3 billion yuan. The projects would go into production within two years, and by that time the factory will have become the largest manufacturing base of flat panel color TV. Xiamen Overseas Chinese Electronics is a key national high-tech enterprise and this project was the first after Chunghwa Picture Tubes *became its largest shareholder. This project was helpful in enhancing* the competitiveness of the electronic information industry of Xiamen Special Economic Zone and would manifest the pulling effect of high-tech industries for economic growth. On September 9, 2007, *AU Optronics* Corp., the world's third largest LCD manufacturer, settled in Torch Industrial Zone in Xiang'an.

With the constant development of high-tech industries, Xiamen got approval from the State Council to enlarge Torch Industrial Zone from 1 square km to 13.75 square km, including Torch Industrial Zone (Xiang'an), Tongji Park, Information & Optoelectronic Park, etc. The pattern of "one zone with lots parks" *took shape, with* one incubating base (Overseas Students Pioneer Park), three comprehensive parks (Torch Park, Torch Industrial Zone (Xiangan) and Tongji Park) and three professional parks (Software Park, Information and Optoelectronic Park and Peking University Biology Park). The three pillars were basically formed, that is, high-tech enterprises, transnational enterprises and key industries such as electronic information, Optoelectronic, electrical engineering software and bio-pharmaceutics. Over 1000 world-famous enterprises such as Dell, ABB, Lenovo, Panasonic, Tungaloy, Fuji Electric and FedEx have developed rapidly in Xiamen. Over twenty enterprises have an annual sales income of more than 100m yuan, including, Dell, Lenovo Mobile, ABB, Xiahua, Xiamen Xiasong, Panasonic, etc. Industrial value created by high-tech enterprises made up over 95% of the entire industrial zone. Torch High-tech Zone became an important part of Xiamen's economic growth and a window for opening up, which greatly helped foster the commercialization of high-tech industries and Xiamen's economic development. The State Council approved the construction of Haicang Bonded Port in Xiamen, with an area of 9.45 square km, which was the sixth bonded port approved after those in Shanghai, Tianjin, Shenzhen, Ningbo and Dalian and one of the most open specially supervised areas.

Xiamen Special Economic Zone had always paid attention to developing current competitive industries. On March 21, 2003, Taikoo (Xiamen) Aircraft Engineering Co. Ltd. opened its Taikoo third-phase hangar in Xiamen Aviation Industrial Town. After the previous two phases, the hangar could maintain nine large planes, becoming the largest airplane maintenance center in the Asia-pacific region. Taikoo attracted many transnational enterprises, such as GE and Boeing, bringing a rise in Xiamen Aviation industry. This industrial town majored in maintaining aircraft structure and minors in maintaining aircraft engines, aircraft electric equipment and other parts of aircrafts. On December 23, 2007, Singapore Technologies Engineering Ltd signed projects to maintain aircraft engines with Xiamen Aviation Industry Co., Ltd. and thus filled in the gap of aircraft engine maintenance in Xiamen.

While introducing advanced foreign technologies, Xiamen Special Economic Zone valued independent innovation. On November 23, 2001, with the approval of the Ministry of Science and Technology, nineteen projects in Xiamen, including electronics and information, new materials and application, biotechnology and new medicines, opto-mechatronics integration, new energy, high efficiency and energy saving, were listed in the 2001 National Torch Plan. These projects would greatly contribute to high-tech industries' advancement toward the international market, strengthening pillar industries and reforming and developing characterized traditional industries. It was also helpful in commercializing high and innovative technologies, applying high-tech into industries, raising the scale and intensification of production and recognizing main products so that Xiamen would become an important and more modernized part of the international industry chain. On June 4, 2007, JTEKT Steering Systems (Xiamen) Co., Ltd., the first domestic manufacturer of electric *steering* devices went into production in Haicang, with a desired industrial value of 1 billion yuan. In August 2009, Admiral Oversea Corporation, the world's largest monitor manufacturer, went into production. By now, Torch Industrial Zone (Xiang'an) has basically formed a high-tech industrial cluster of Optoelectronic *display*.

4.4.2.3 Promoting Relations with Taiwan Through Trade

Xiamen Special Economic Zone was well aware of its own advantages in promoting the relations with Taiwan and expanded areas of cooperation. It acted as a bridge between China's Mainland and Taiwan in terms of trade and information exchange, representing a great contribution to the mutual prosperity on both sides and national reunification.

On April 29, 2002, approved by the Ministry of Foreign Trade and Economic Cooperation, jointly sponsored by Xiamen Council for the Promotion of Trade and Taiwan Taichung World Trade Center, the first Taiwan Exhibition was held in Xiamen, with over 200 registered enterprises and 300 booths. With the increasingly open market in mainland China after its accession to the WTO, the consumer goods manufacturer in the Taiwan Islands and Jinmen were eager to enter this enormous market as soon as possible. This exhibition met the needs of Taiwan enterprises to seek for suitable sales channels in the mainland, making preparations for them to enter the mainland market. At the same time, it provided a platform for Taiwan-invested enterprises in the mainland to expand their market. Thus, the trade exchanges between the two sides would be expanded and deepened, boosting the "three links" and their mutual prosperity. The Ministry of Science and Technology authorized the construction of National Base for Scientific and Technological Cooperation and Exchanges with Taiwan, which was the first and only national base of its kind approved for Taiwan.

China Xiamen Machinery and Electronics Exhibition (CXMEE) was held in Xiamen every April 8 to 11, authorized by the Ministry of Commerce and jointly sponsored by and the Xiamen government. 2008 marked the twelfth year since its start. 715 enterprises attended the exhibition and the booths numbered 1,810, achieving the international standard, among which more than 500 were occupied by Taiwan enterprises. 27,815 businessmen from 39 countries and regions attended, including 4,352 from overseas, among which Taiwan businessmen totaled 2,242, still ranking the first in number.[399]

Cross-straits Tourism Exhibition is held in Xiamen every September 6 to 11, sponsored

399 Source: www.straitsfair.org.cn/About/about.html.

by National Tourism Administration and Fujian Government, undertaken by Fujian Tourism Administration and Xiamen Government and assisted by travel agencies in Taiwan, Hong Kong and Macao. Its goal is to boom the tourism industries, strengthen the exchanges and cooperation, and integrate tourism resources across the straits.

The trade across the straits involved finance and other fields other than the traditional manufacturing industry. On November 17, 2008, Xiamen Commercial Bank Taiwan became the first bank in mainland China that had Taiwan shareholding by Taiwan Fubon Financial Holding Co., Ltd. On December 17, 2008, Junlong Life Insurance Company jointly invested in Taiwan Life Insurance and Xiamen United Development (Group) Co., Ltd. opened in Xiamen, becoming the first corporate body involving Taiwan investment and the first insurance institution headquartered in Xiamen. On May 6, 2008, Xiamen Changgeng Hospital, by far the biggest hospital with Taiwan investment in the mainland, began to operate.

4.4.3 The Development of Xiamen Special Economic Zone in the New Century

4.4.3.1 The Achievements of Xiamen Special Economic Zone in the New Century

In the new historical conditions of the new century, Xiamen continued to play its exemplary role as a Special Economic Zone and has gained a number of achievements. They are as follows.

First, national economy continued to develop rapidly and comprehensive economic strength has been remarkably enhanced.

Second, industrial structure continued to be optimized and upgraded, becoming increasingly supportive to economic growth.

Third, key projects have successfully led the implementation of strategies. Construction of urban infrastructure was greatly intensified and the framework of central city began to take shape.

Fourth, continuing efforts were paid to Taiwan related affairs and Xiamen's role as a port continued to be enhanced.

Fifth, living quality and standards continued to improve.

Sixth, environmental protection made notable progress.

Seventh, rural development caught up and the work of "agriculture, rural areas and farmers" made remarkable achievements.

Eighth, reforms continued to deepen and the socialist market economy kept improving.

Ninth, socialist democracy, legal system and spiritual civilization continued progressing.

Figure 4-4-1 illustrates the GDP of Xiamen Special Economic Zone from 2001 to 2009 and Figure 4-4-2 gives the annual growth rate accordingly. Nominal GDP increased from 55.833 billion yuan in 2001 to 162.321 billion yuan in 2009, a rise of 191%. In the interim, the growth rate dropped noticeably due to the international financial crisis.

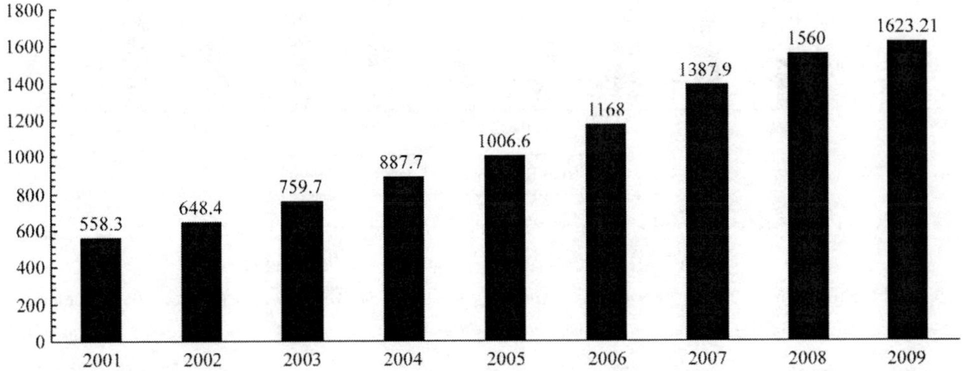

Figure 4-4-1 GDP of Xiamen Special Economic Zone from 2001 to 2009 (at current prices, 100m yuan)

Source: The figures from 2001 to 2008 are from *Xiamen Special Economic Zone Yearbook* (Volume 2002 to Volume 2009) and the figure of 2009 is from *2009 Xiamen Statistical Bulletin on National Economic and Social Development.*

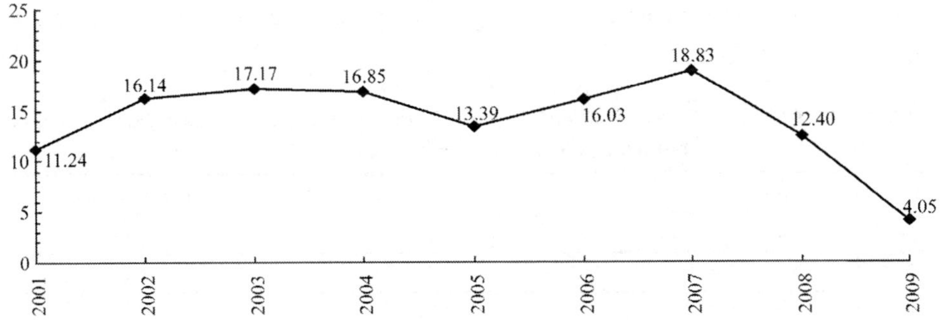

Figure 4-4-2 Annual growth rate of Xiamen Special Economic Zone from 2001 to 2009(at current prices, %)

Source: The figures from 2001 to 2008 are from Xiamen Special Economic Zone Yearbook (Volume 2002 to Volume 2009) and the figure of 2009 is from *2009 Xiamen Statistical Bulletin on National Economic and Social Development.*

Figure 4-4-3 shows the total and local revenue of Xiamen Special Economic Zone from 2001 to 2009, which respectively increased from 11.05 billion yuan and 6.531 billion yuan in 2001 to 45.141 billion yuan and 24.056 billion yuan in 2009, increasing by 309% and 268% respectively.

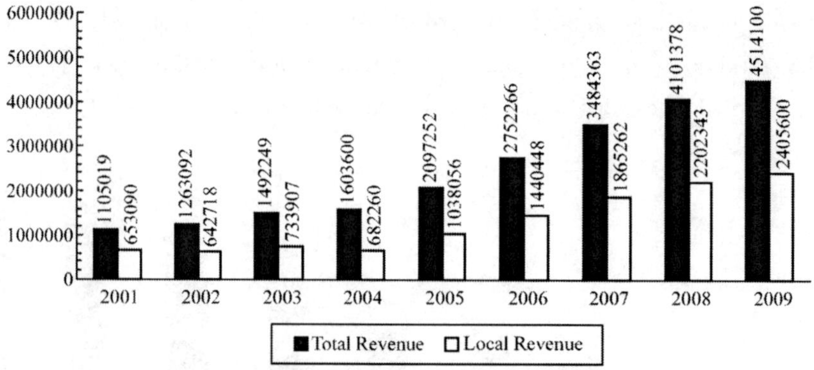

Figure 4-4-3 Total and Local Revenue of Xiamen Special Economic Zone from 2001 to 2009 (at current prices, 10,000 yuan)

Source: The figures from 2001 to 2008 are from *Xiamen Special Economic Zone Yearbook* (Volume 2002 to Volume 2009) and the figure of 2009 is from *2009 Xiamen Statistical Bulletin on National Economic and Social Development.*

Table 4-4-1 shows the changes in proportions of primary industry, secondary industry and tertiary industry of Xiamen Special Economic Zone from 2001 to 2009. The restructuring and change of mode of economic growth were a key component for Xiamen Special Economic Zone to achieve development. The proportions of primary industry and secondary industry in national economy kept dropping and that of tertiary industry rose steadily.

Table 4-4-1 Changes of Proportions of Primary Industry, Secondary Industry and Tertiary Industry of Xiamen from 2001 to 2009 (%)

Year	Primary industry	Secondary industry	Tertiary industry
2001	3.9	50.7	45.3
2002	3.4	53.1	43.4
2003	2.4	55.5	42.1
2004	2.3	55.8	42.0
2005	2.1	54.9	43.0
2006	1.6	53.9	44.5
2007	1.3	53.5	45.2
2008	1.4	52.4	46.2
2009	1.3	48.4	50.3

Source: The figures from 2001 to 2008 are from *Xiamen Special Economic Zone Yearbook* (Volume 2002 to Volume 2009) and the figure of 2009 is from *2009 Xiamen Statistical Bulletin on National Economic and Social Development.*

Figure 4-4-4 gives the per capita disposable income of urban residents and per capita net income of rural residents of Xiamen Special Economic Zone from 2001 to 2009, which respectively increased from 11,365 yuan and 4,425 yuan in 2001 to 26,131 yuan and 9,153 yuan in 2009, increasing by 130% and 109% respectively. The incomes of residents increased by a large margin, but compared with the increase of national economy and revenue, their increase rates were lower, which shows that despite the rapid economic growth, the distribution of national revenue did not favor residents.

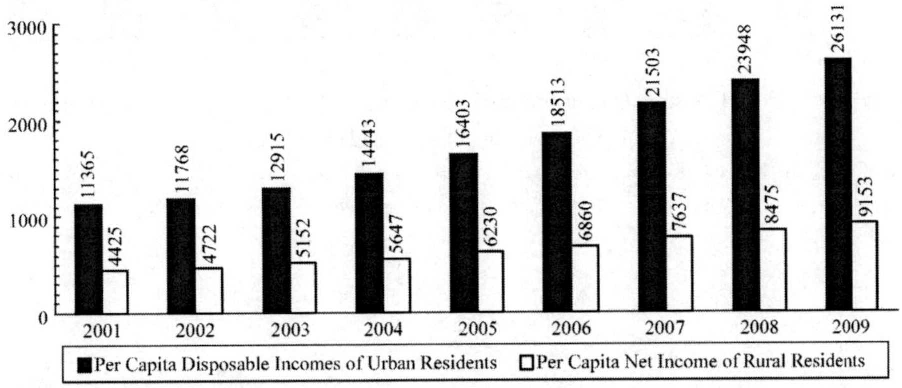

Figure 4-4-4 Per Capita Disposable Incomes of Urban Residents and Per Capita Net Income of Rural Residents of Xiamen Special Economic Zone from 2001 to 2009 (at current prices, yuan)

Source: The figures from 2001 to 2008 are from *Xiamen Special Economic Zone Yearbook* (Volume 2002 to Volume 2009) and the figure of 2009 is from *2009 Xiamen Statistical Bulletin on National Economic and Social Development*.

Note: The figure of 2006 per capita net income of rural residents has been subjected to agricultural census.

Figure 4-4-5 gives the total industrial output value of Xiamen Special Economic Zone from 2001 to 2009, which increased from 88.432 billion yuan in 2001 to 288.621 billion yuan in 2009, increasing by 226%. But due to the impact of the international financial crisis, the total industrial output value in 2009 fell sharply from 309.08 billion yuan in 2008 to 288.621 billion yuan, a decrease of 6.6%.

Figure 4-4-6 presents the total investment in fixed assets and the total retail sales of consumer goods of Xiamen Special Economic Zone from 2001 to 2009, which increased respectively from 19.189 billion yuan and 15.993 billion yuan in 2001 to 88.212 billion yuan and 48.862 billion yuan in 2009, increasing by 360% and 206% respectively. It can be seen that the increase of total retail sales of consumer goods is smaller than that of the total investment in fixed assets, so it somehow manifests that the economic growth of Xiamen Special Economic Zone mainly depended on investment. The investment fluctuation will impact the economic growth. For example, investment decreased in 2009 because of the international financial crisis.

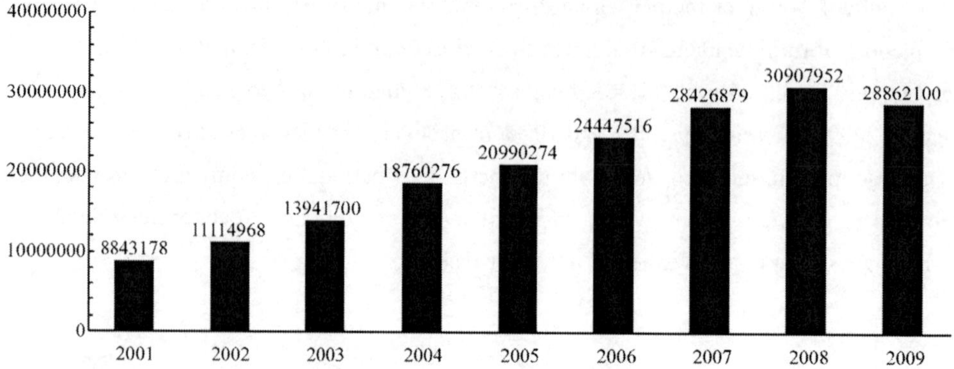

Figure 4-4-5 Total Industrial Output Value of Xiamen Special Economic Zone from 2001 to 2009 (at current prices, according to 1995 statistics, 10,000 yuan)

Source: The figures from 2001 to 2008 are from *Xiamen Special Economic Zone Yearbook* (Volume 2002 to Volume 2009) and the figure of 2009 is from *2009 Xiamen Statistical Bulletin on National Economic and Social Development.*

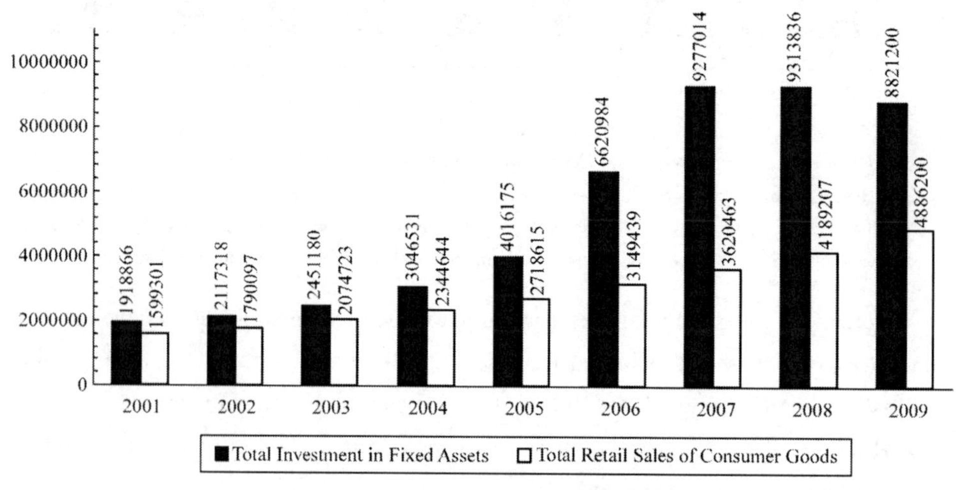

Figure 4-4-6 Total Investment in Fixed Assets and Total Retail Sales of Consumer Goods of Xiamen Special Economic Zone from 2001 to 2009 (at current prices, 10,000 yuan)

Source: The figures from 2001 to 2008 are from *Xiamen Special Economic Zone Yearbook* (Volume 2002 to Volume 2009) and the figure of 2009 is from *2009 Xiamen Statistical Bulletin on National Economic and Social Development.*

Figure 4-4-7 gives the total foreign trade volume and the total exports of Xiamen Special Economic Zone from 2001 to 2009. These figures reflect the trend of export-orientation of Xiamen Special Economic Zone in the new century. The total foreign trade volume and the total exports respectively increased from 11.07873 billion USD and 6.50492 billion USD in 2001 to 43.314 billion USD and 27.668 billion USD in 2009, increasing by 291% and

325% respectively. Total exports increased faster than total foreign trade volume, but both declined markedly in 2009 under the impact of the international financial crisis.

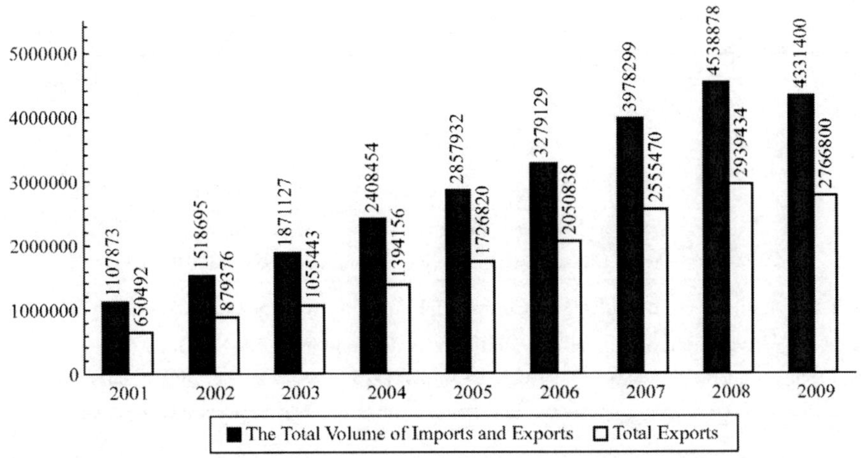

Figure 4-4-7 Total Foreign Trade Volume and Total Exports of Xiamen Special Economic Zone from 2001 to 2009 (at current prices, 10,000 US$)

Source: The figures from 2001 to 2008 are from *Xiamen Special Economic Zone Yearbook* (Volume 2002 to Volume 2009) and the figure of 2009 is from *2009 Xiamen Statistical Bulletin on National Economic and Social Development*.

Figure 4-4-8 shows the contractual foreign investment and the actual utilized foreign investment of Xiamen Special Economic Zone from 2001 to 2009 and Figure 4-4-9 shows the growth rates accordingly. Compared to the stable growth of foreign trade, Xiamen has

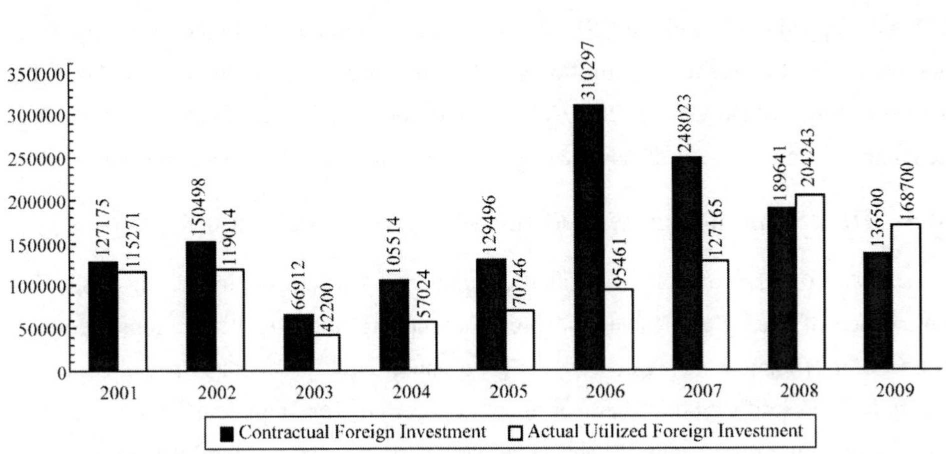

Figure 4-4-8 Contractual Foreign Investment and Actual Utilized Foreign Investment of Xiamen Special Economic Zone from 2001 to 2009 (10,000 USD)

Source: The figures from 2001 to 2008 are from *Xiamen Special Economic Zone Yearbook* (Volume 2002 to Volume 2009) and the figure of 2009 is from *2009 Xiamen Statistical Bulletin on National Economic and Social Development*.

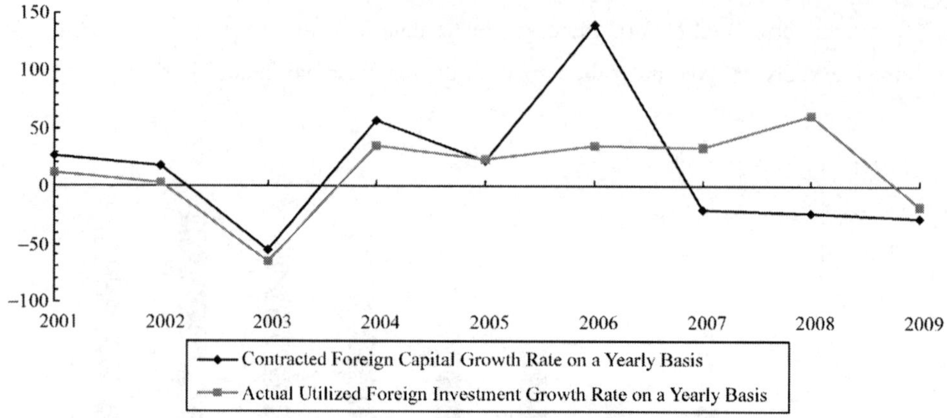

Figure 4-4-9 Annulus Growth Rate of Contractual Foreign Investment and Actual Utilized Foreign Investment of Xiamen Special Economic Zone from 2001 to 2009 (%)

Source: The figures from 2001 to 2008 are from *Xiamen Special Economic Zone Yearbook* (Volume 2002 to Volume 2009) and the figure of 2009 is from *2009 Xiamen Statistical Bulletin on National Economic and Social Development.*

undergone many fluctuations in contractual foreign investment and actual utilized foreign investment. The contractual foreign investment increased from 1271.75 million USD in 2001 to 1504.98 million USD in 2002, but declined to 669.12 million USD in 2003. In the following years it increased year by year to 3272 million USD in 2007.but dropped to 1896 million USD in 2008 and 1365 million in 2009 due to the global financial crisis, decreasing by 42% and 28% respectively. The actual utilized foreign investment has gone through the same situations. It increased from 1152.71 million USD in 2001 to 1190.14 million USD in 2002 and dropped to 422 million USD in 2003, a decrease of 64.5%. In the following years, it increased year by year to 1272 million USD in 2007 and 2042 million USD in 2008, but dropped to 1687 million USD in 2009. The sharp decline in 2003 and 2009 of both kinds of foreign investment were respectively the results of SARS and the international financial crisis.

4.4.4 Development Strategy of the West Coast Economic Zone

On May 6, 2009, the State Council promulgated "Several Opinions on Supporting Construction of West Coast Economic Zone" to support and promote the construction of West Coast Economic Zone, which offered great opportunity for Xiamen Special Economic Zone to realize significant development in the new period. The "Opinions" pointed out that with Taiwan to the east, Yangtz River Delta to the north and Pearl River Delta to the south, the location of West Coast Economic Zone carried a great deal of significance in coastal and regional economy. The economic development of West Coast Economic Zone was of great political and economic significance in achieving national reunification and improving coastal economic structure; Xiamen Special Economic Zone was vital in the development strategy of the whole West Coast region.

The "Opinions" stressed the importance of West Coast Economic Zone to trade relations with Taiwan. The measures to be taken are as follows:[400]

First, implement "Early and Pilot Implementation" policy to Taiwan. In communication and cooperation with Taiwan, such as in fields of trade, navigation, tourism, postal service, culture and education, more flexible and open policies and the Early and Pilot Implementation policy should be taken to gain more experience.

Second, to expand cross-straits trade cooperation. Various Taiwan-invested projects, as long as they are not banned by the Chinese government or do not involve national security risks, are allowed in the West Coast Economic Zone. It can first attempt to promote Taiwan's convenience in investment and market access for Taiwan service industry and additional land quota could be allowed in cooperation with Taiwan. Processing center of agricultural products to be exported to Taiwan will be set up. Other centers are also to be established to extend Taiwan agricultural technologies and new varieties and for Taiwan farmers to set up business. Cross-straits supervision and cooperation system in finance will also be actively promoted, in which Taiwan-invested financial institutions such as banks, insurance companies and securities will have priority in establishing branches or sharing stocks of financial enterprises in Fujian. It is encouraged to establish cross-straits investment funds.

Third, support cross-straits communication. Coastal airports and ports are the first option to realize direct links cross the straits. More tourists are encouraged to go to Taiwan via Fujian. Some measures will be taken for the convenience of the cross-straits communications, including issuing passports for Taiwan residents to go to mainland China and travel documents for mainland residents to go to Taiwan.

Forth, support the construction of platforms for cross-straits linkage. The Taiwan Investment Zone in Xiamen and Fujian will be expanded and a new Taiwan Investment Zone in Quanzhou will be established in the proper time. Major trade and cultural activities concerning Taiwan will continue to be supported.

To implement the "Opinions" by the State Council in promoting the development of the West Coast Economic Zone, related departments, Fujian Provincial Party Committee Fujian Provincial Government and related departments have announced detailed policies and measures, including *Ministry of Commerce, Opinion on Supporting Construction of*

---

400 Measures taken are quoted from the ninth part of State Council Several Opinions on Supporting Construction of *West Coast Economic Zone*.

West Coast Economic Zone, State Administration for Industry and Commerce Opinion on Further Supporting Construction of West Coast Economic Zone, State Administration of Surveying and Mapping Five Measures to Support Construction of West Coast Economic Zone, State Electricity Regulatory Commission Ten Measures to Support the Construction of West Coast Economic Zone, Fujian Provincial Government Signing Strategic Cooperation Agreement With Agricultural Bank of China to Promote Construction of Two Piloting Zones in West Coast Area, Ministry of Communications Taking Nine Measures to Promote Direct Sails Cross Straits, Both Sides Joining Hands to Tackle Crises and Taiwan Affairs Office of the State Council Announcing Eight New Favorable Measures for Taiwan, Ministry of Commerce and Taiwan Affairs Office of the State Council Circular on Mainland Enterprises Going to Taiwan to Invest or Set up Non-enterprise Legal Entities and Other Related Matters, Taiwan Affairs Office of the State Council Actively Supporting Early and Pilot Implementation in West Coast Economic Zone, Ministry of Personnel Opinion on Supporting the Construction of West Coast Economic Zone to Promote People Management in Fujian, Ministry of Information Industry and Fujian Government Cooperation Agreements on Accelerating Information Industry in West Coast Economic Zone, Implementation Plan for Gaining Talents Urgently Needed in Constructing West Coast Economic Zone, Fujian Outline of Constructing West Coast Economic Zone, Fujian Implementation Opinion on Sate Council Several Opinion on Fujian's Accelerating Construction of West Coast Economic Zone, Opinion on Supporting Strategic Arrangement of Fujian to Accelerate Construction of West Coast Economic Zone released by the Supreme Court, Opinion on Supporting Fujian to Accelerate Industrialization and informationization in West Coast Economic Zone printed by the Ministry of Industry and Information, Opinion on Supporting Fujian to Accelerate Construction of West Coast Economic Zone released by the Office of Legislative Affairs of the State Council, etc.

To implement the development of the West Coast Economic Zone, Xiamen Special Economic Zone passed "Xiamen Implementation Opinion on Accelerating West Coast Economic Zone Construction" decided by CPC Central Committee, State Council, Fujian Provincial CPC Committee and Provincial Government, making strategic arrangements for its leapfrog development.

The "Implementation Opinion" set development goals for Xiamen Special Economic Zone in the coming ten years.[401]

---

401 See Xiamen Implementation Opinion on Accelerating *West Coast Economic Zone Construction Decided by CPC Central Committee, State Council, Fujian Provincial CPC Committee and Provincial Government.*

First, by 2012, the per capita GDP will keep its top ranking among the fifteen municipalities at the deputy provincial level. Xiamen's role as an important port to communicate and cooperate with Taiwan will have been effectively played; the system featuring manufacturing connecting with service industry will have taken shape and an advanced manufacturing base and the accumulation areas of the most advantageous modern service industry will have come into being.

Second, by 2017, the per capita GDP will have surpassed 20,000 USD.

Third, Xiamen will strive to increase its total GDP to 700 billion yuan and the per capita GDP to or above that in Taiwan, forming a modern industrial system characterized by international advanced manufacturing industry and a modern service industry.

The "Implementation Opinion" underlines the significance of Xiamen Special Economic Zone in Taiwan affairs.[402] It suggests Xiamen giving full play to its geographical and human advantages, to become a model in blending the compatriots on both sides of the Taiwan Straits and in enhancing their communication and cooperation. Xiamen Special Economic Zone is to become a dock of cross-straits industries and to first establish pilot zones for cross-straits financing cooperation. Xiamen is expected to become a fort for communications cross the straits.

To achieve these goals, the "Implementation Opinion" points out that in the coming ten years,[403] Xiamen Special Economic Zone should strive to open its market, raise its export-oriented economic level and find the best development path as a free-trade zone. In addition, it should deepen the reform in economic system and social and governmental management system to alter its way of development and improve its independent innovation. It hopes to become an advanced manufacturing base and the most competitive city in modern service industry in the West Coast Economic Zone. It should also further integrate the construction inside and outside the island, coordinate the development in urban and rural areas and enhance its crowding and pulling function as a core city.

---

402 See Xiamen Implementation Opinion on Accelerating *West Coast Economic Zone Construction Decided by CPC Central Committee, State Council, Fujian Provincial CPC Committee and Provincial Government.*

403 See Xiamen Implementation Opinion on Accelerating *West Coast Economic Zone Construction Decided by CPC Central Committee, State Council, Fujian Provincial CPC Committee and Provincial Government.*

5 The History of Hainan Sez: the Great Opening-Up in Times of Uncertainty

China's largest special economic zone, Hainan Special Economic Zone, faced many obstaclesthroughout its development from an impoverished, backward remote border area into an international tourist island in 1988. Throughout the 20 years of development history, the most prominent featur was the full practice of advantages supported by "special" policies endowed by the Central Government, which gave Hainan the lead in China's opening up. Even though it was once trapped in various difficult situations due to over rapid development, fundamentally, its direction of development was in line with the road of "promoting reform by opening up, and promoting development by reform and opening up."

Hainan SEZ had a special geographical location and rich natural resources. Through the early "pre-SEZ period" and the strategy of "creating provincial SEZ," on April 26, 1988, Hainan entered into the era of development and construction of the "Great SEZ." In the initial ten years, Hainan experienced three major turning points in development. In the initial period after the establishment of Hainan Special Economic Zone, it took the lead in conducting national socialist market economic reforms. It established the new political system of "small government, big society," adopting the innovative development mode of "whole-area development" and "introducing investment from abroad and establishing lateral ties at home." Hainan launched the first large-scaled development and construction boom. Later, because of the "Yangpu Storm" and other major unexpected events, the development of the Hainan Special Economic Zone was hindered. In the three years after 1989, Hainan attempted to move forward from this predicament. In 1992, Deng Xiaoping's southern tour speech and the party's 14th National Congress brought Hainan into the second wave of "great opening, great reform and great construction." In 1993, under the country's policy to rectify the financial order, Hainan's economic situation rapidly declined once again. In 1995, due to the real estate bubble, Hainan was encountered with the "bubble economy." Once again, it bottomed out by establishing the strategy of "developing into a new industrial province with agricultural and tourist bases." The large-scaled construction of "intelligent island of information" and the construction of Yangpu Development Zone greatly promoted the overall economic development in Hainan.

Beginning in 1998, Hainan SEZ entered into the recovery period of economic growth. It pushed forward the construction of an "ecological province," stepping up in the development of large projects and the construction of the Yangpu Development Zone, as well as further improving the "small government, big society" system. The Tenth "Five-year Plan" period presented a rapid developing momentum in Hainan's economy, and continued to adhere to the strategy of "developing into new industrial province with agricultural and tourist bases," being successful in the implementation of the "healthy islands" strategy. During the Eleventh "Five-Year Plan" period, Hainan entered into a golden period of development. It put forward a development model of "developing into new industrial provinces with agricultural, tourist and marine bases", which was more in line with the features of Hainan.

Looking towards the future, Hainan SEZ adhered to the development model of "developing into new industrial province with agricultural, tourist and marine bases" and continued to develop the three "pillar industries," the economic development plan of "five strategies" and the functional design of "five districts," so as to build a "Free Trade Zone" and "international tourist island" at a national strategic level and provincial level.

5.1 Evaluation of Hainan's Economy before the Establishment of Hainan SEZ

As the second largest island in China, Hainan has mild climate and pleasant scenery, like a pearl in the South China Sea. Before the establishment of SEZ, poverty and backwardness were the greatest problems of the people of Hainan.

5.1.1 Geographic Conditions

Hainan Island is China's second largest island. Located in the South China Sea, it is frequently called the "South Sea Pearl." It is located east fo the Pacific Ocean, facing Malaysia and Indonesia across the South China Sea, neighboring with Vietnam across the northern Gulf in the west and close to Leizhou Peninsula of Guangdong in the north 18 sea miles across the Qiongzhou Strait. The province (including Hainan Island and Xisha, Zhongsha, Nansha Islands) covered the total area of 35,400 square kilometers (land area of 33,900 square kilometers), the sea area of about 2,000,000 square kilometers.[404] Hainan Island is China's largest tropical region, accounting for 42.5% of tropical land area, having

404 http://www.hainan.gov.cn/code/V3/zjhn.php

long summers, no winters and abundant rainfall. The average temperature is 22 to 26 degrees Celsius, with an average annual rainfall of 1639 mm. Forest coverage rate reached 35%. Suitable for agriculture, Hainan Island is an important production base for China's tropical and subtropical crops. The area of the land suitable for livestock farming reached 50 million mu.

Hainan Island is also rich in tourism resources. The sxotic scenery of the tropical rain forest, the magnificent coastal scenery, mountains and rivers, as well as a unique ethnic style, food and a variety of attractions in Hainan, make the province a fascinating tourist destination.

5.1.2 Historical Evolution

Hainan Island, known as "Qiong" and "Qiongzhou," gained its name from Qiong Mountain which, many locals say, "was formed by rocks as white as jade." Hainan had three ancient names: "Zhu Ya," "Dan Er" and "Qiong Tai," and was named "Hainan" for being isolated from the mainland in the period of Three Kingdoms.[405]

In April 1988, the National People's Congress approved the establishment of Hainan Province, with Haikou as the provincial capital. The newly-built Hainan Province was China's largest special economic zone, as well as China's 31st provincial-level administrative unit and 23rd province.[406] Hainan Province covered the jurisdiction of Hainan Island, Xisha, Nansha, Zhongsha Islands and the waters around, 19 cities and counties such as Haikou, Sanya, Tongshi etc. and county offices of Xisha, Nansha, and Zhongsha Islands. In 1950, the total population reached 2,468,200 in Hainan. In 1988, the total population reached 6,268,500, of which agricultural population took up 5,208,800.[407]

However, the socio-economic status in Hainan was relatively backward. The GDP of Hainan in 1978 was only 1.64 billion yuan, per capita GDP of 314 yuan. On the eve of the establishment of Hainan Province and SEZ in 1987, GDP growth was 5.73 billion yuan, 19.3% of growth over the previous year. GDP per capita was 939 yuan, 17.6% up over the previous year. The actual utilization of foreign capital was 9,110,000 USD. Total amount of imports and exports was 292,410,000 USD, of which the amount of exports took up 115,490,000 USD. (Table 5-1-1, Table 5-4-1, Table 5-4-2)

---

405 Chen Xiaoxing: ***Hainan—China's Largest SEZ***, Shanxi Tourism Press, 1988, p25

406 Chen Xiaoxing: ***Hainan—China's Largest SEZ***, Shanxi Tourism Press, 1988, p1-2

407 Data from ***Hainan Statistic Yearbook***

Table 5-1-1 GDP and Per Capita GDP of Hainan

Year	GDP (100 million yuan)	Primary Industry (100 million yuan)	Secondary Industry (100 million yuan)	Tertiary Industry (100 million yuan)	Per capita GDP (100 million yuan)
1978	16.4	8.72	3.65	4.03	314
1979	17.45	9.31	3.77	4.37	327
1980	19.33	10.8	3.61	4.92	354
1981	22.23	13.02	3.47	5.74	399
1982	28.86	17.25	4.04	7.57	510
1983	31.12	18.45	4.47	8.2	540
1984	37.18	20.48	6.68	10.02	636
1985	43.26	21.8	9.3	12.16	729
1986	48.03	24.05	9.92	14.06	798
1987	57.3	28.68	10.89	17.73	939
1988	77.13	38.59	14.15	24.39	1241
1989	91.4	42.85	18.25	30.3	1444
1990	102.49	46.02	20.12	36.35	1589
1991	120.51	50.22	24.65	45.64	1836
1992	181.71	54.13	38.34	89.24	2727
1993	258.08	77.73	66.29	114.06	3815
1994	330.95	107.55	83.66	139.74	4820
1995	364.17	130.86	78.64	154.67	5225
1996	389.53	143.54	81.32	164.67	5500
1997	409.86	151.28	82.68	175.9	5698
1998	438.92	164	90.63	184.29	6022
1999	471.23	176.42	94.95	199.86	6383
2000	518.48	196.56	102.45	219.47	6894
2001	566.72	201.79	132.01	232.92	7406
2002	624.89	228.95	146.09	249.85	8071
2003	691.69	251.35	171.92	268.42	8573
2004	790.12	287.3	201.17	301.65	9704
2005	903.6	301.1	228.91	373.59	10998
2006	1052.43	344.2	287.79	420.44	12654
2007	1223.28	361.07	364.26	497.95	14555
2008	1459.23	437.61	434.40	587.22	17175
2009	1646.60	461.93	443.43	741.24	19166

Resources: Yearly Hainan Statistic Yearbook, data of 2009 from Hainan Province Economic and Social Statistics Bulletin of 2009, website of Hainan Statistics Bureau www.hi.stats.gov.cn

Table 5-1-2 GDP Distribution of Industries in Hainan (Unit: 100 million yuan)

Year	Agriculture	Industry	Architecture	Transportation, post and telecommunication	Catering	Finance and insurance	Real estate	Other service industries
1982	17.25	3.07	0.97	0.94	3.06	0.81	0.48	2.28
1983	18.45	3.53	0.94	0.97	3.34	0.95	0.51	2.43
1984	20.48	4.7	1.98	1.29	4.01	1.44	0.53	2.75
1985	21.8	5.88	3.42	2.15	4.16	1.79	0.55	3.51
1986	24.05	6.67	3.25	2.57	4.59	2.03	0.65	4.22
1987	28.63	7.73	3.18	3.26	5.74	2.3	0.98	5.46
1988	38.46	10.04	4.16	4.07	8.66	3.25	1.17	7.18
1989	42.64	11.7	6.59	4.87	10.27	3.43	1.43	10.39
1990	45.71	13.17	7.03	6.21	11.41	3.96	1.65	13.28
1991	49.8	15.23	9.48	8.01	15.15	4.43	2.48	15.94
1992	53.59	20.97	17.29	11.35	29.56	6.12	20.57	25.46
1993	76.82	35.58	30.5	16.61	39.13	7.58	20.43	33.75
1994	106.12	44.57	38.76	21.93	48.36	8.05	17.2	46.99
1995	128.9	44.04	34.44	26.35	52.47	8.25	13.69	55.11
1996	141.15	49.2	32.32	29.91	55.23	8.35	11.28	62.24
1997	148.52	52.05	31.08	34.57	58.93	8.58	11.3	66.13
1998	156.05	59.1	32.32	43.76	61.9	8.78	12.91	67.31
1999	172.62	63.37	32.65	46.94	64.88	8.98	14.62	72.62
2000	192	70.46	33.51	52.45	70.3	9.27	16.62	82.2
2001	196.78	97.85	35.98	57.13	74.08	9.75	18.81	88.78
2002	222.89	111.42	37.46	61.97	78.65	10.08	21.45	98.82
2003	244.29	132.25	43.56	66.54	85.64	10.68	25.14	105.85
2004	278.76	151.56	54.04	77	96.5	11.56	30.64	119.6
2005	300.75	166.62	63.91	87.32	107.57	12.44	33.61	132.81
2006	323.48	217.55	70.31	96.69	122.18	13.76	34.41	153.47
2007	361.07	278.37	85.89	112.54	142.13	22.44	45.78	175.06
2008	437.61	321.1	113.22	127.04	172.63	26.74	57.31	203.50

Resource: Hainan Statistics Yearbook

The Third Plenary Session of the Eleventh Central Committee held in 1978 decided to shift the focus of national work to socialist modernization, which created a tremendous opportunity for Hainan's economic construction and development. In April 1979, upon listening to the report from Xi Zhongxun and Yang Shangkun—the leaders of the CPC Guangdong Provincial Committee, Deng Xiaoping, chief architect of China's reform and opening up, recommended that an area should be used for the construction of SEZ. That's the origin of the idea of establishing special economic zones.

5.2 Preparation and Birth of Hainan Special Economic Zone

Deng Xiaoping's broad visions determinately saught to create China's largest special economic zone. Concerned with the party and state leaders, the birth of Hainan SEZ was an arduous task to take on and preparations were in full swing. In 1988, the youngest province of China and the largest special economic zone, Hainan, celebrated its firstbirth day.

5.2.1 Early Preparations

After the Third Plenary Session, Hainan entered a new period of socialist construction. As the situation developed, the CPC Central Committee and State Council decided to accelerate the development and construction of Hainan Island.

5.2.1.1 Reflecting on Poverty and Backwardness

Hainan Island had long been the poorest area in the Guangdong Province and one of the most backward regions in China. Its economy was at the closed, semi-natural state. When China decided to reform, open up and modernize, it was necessary for Hainan to eliminate poverty. It had become the area's main concern, which required taking important measures.

On July 22, 1980, the State Council decided to accelerate the construction of Hainan Island in the "Minutes of Hainan Forum." It reflected the transferred focus from defense-oriented development to construction development, even though was limited to the idea of tropical crops and agriculture referring to the economic development issue. Particularly, the "Minutes" proposed Hainan's foreign economic activities follow suit with Shenzhen and Zhuhai's approach, which were given greater flexibility. It demonstrated that the Central Government had been considering opening Hainan Island. Although this was in fact not well implemented, it made necessary preparations for the future opening.[408]

5.2.2 Pre-SEZ Policy

In March 1983, the State Council convened to discuss issues of development and construction of Hainan Island. On April 1, 1983, the CPC Central Committee and State

---

408 Edited by Su Dongbin: ***History of China's SEZ***, Guangdong Economy Press, 2001, p398-399

Council approved the "Minutes on Speeding up the Development and Construction of Hainan Island Discussion," which pointed out the strategic importance of Hainan Island developing and building the resource-rich island to strengthen national unity, thus achieving the four modernizations and consolidate national defense on South China Sea. The Central Government decided to accelerate the development and construction of Hainan by the means of giving more flexibility in policy and positive support to labor, fund and materials. The leading party and governmentcenters of Guangdong and Hainan should improve the leadership in economic development, and mobilize the masses to strive for a new situation in Hainan. The Central Government also decided to expand the decision-making power of Hainan. In reference to Shenzhen and Zhuhai in external activities, it was to practice a variety of preferential policies to attract foreign investment, introduce advanced technology and equipment and develop tourism. The great measure of opening Hainan Island sparked their great historical leap from a long closed area to China's opening area, equivalent to special economic zones, in fact, a "pre-SEZ."[409]

5.2.3 The Strategic Vision to Build up Hainan SEZ

On February 24, 1984, Deng Xiaoping invited the central leaders to join in the meeting. He said, "When we build the SEZ, there is to be a clear guiding principle, that is to give out more freedom in its development."[410] He stressed that "we have to develop Hainan Island. It would be a great victory if we can develop Hainan's economy rapidly."[411] This showed Hainan Island's important role in Deng Xiaoping's opening-up strategy.

5.2.4 Accelerated Preparation of "Establishing a New Province and SEZ"

Under the guidance of Deng Xiaoping's strategic thinking, the Hainan Administrative Region leader, Lei Yu, and other major leaders seized this opportunity to lead the cadres and the masses of Hainan toward intellectual freedom and carry out foreign economic trade activities by using preferential policies. The development and construction was conducted in a large scale, unprecedented in the history of Hainan, creating the first "golden era."

On May 31, 1984, the Second Session of the Sixth National People's Congress adopted the State Council's proposal on the revocation of the Hainan Civil Administration, and the establishment of the People's Government of Hainan Administrative Region, and

---

409 Edited by Su Dongbin: ***History of China's SEZ***, Guangdong Economy Press, 2001, p400

410 http://news.xinhuanet.com/ziliao/2005-02/07/content_2558239.htm

411 CPC Document Compilation Commission: ***Selected Works of Deng Xiaoping(Volume 3)***, People's Publisher, 1993, p52

implementation special economic policies to further expand the self-decision power of Hainan. On August 21, 1986, Hainan Administrative Region was given the provincial-level administrative and economic management authority.[412]

On June 12, 1987, Deng Xiaoping met with Stefan Korosec, member of the Presidium of the Central Committee of the League of Communists of Yugoslavia. He said, "We are engaged in the construction of a larger SEZ, which is Hainan Special Economic Zone. Hainan Island and Taiwan are similar in territory. There are many resources, such as iron ore, petroleum gas, as well as rubber and other tropical and subtropical crops. Hainan Island did an extraordinary job in development."[413] Hainan celebrated its achievements and was pushed to the forefront of the wave of reform and opening up.[414]

5.2.5 The Birth of the Hainan Special Economic Zone

On September 26, 1987, the CPC Central Committee and State Council issued "Notification on the Establishment of Hainan Province and the Preparatory Work for Establishment" (the [1987] No.23 Document), in which was written: "Hainan Province will be given more decision-making power and preferential policies, making it China's largest special economic zone."[415] At the end of 1987, the preparatory group invited a group of experts from Chinese Academy of Social Research to Hainan for research purposes, who later wrote the "Report on Strategy Research of Hainan's Economic Development," in which put forward "Hainan mode," which stated that Hainan's economic rise relied on special policies and a new system. It proposed three strategic "edges:" the new economy, small government, big society and the overall transition. On April 13, 1988, the first session of the Seventh National People's Congress considered and passed the resolution on the establishment of Hainan Province and the Hainan Special Economic Zone. On April 26, 1988, Hainan completed the preparatory work for the establishment of the province. The birth of the first special economic province in China started a new chapter in the history of opening-up.[416]

---

412 Hainan Party's History Research Office: ***Establishment and Development of China's SEZ—Hainan Volume***, Party History Press, 1977, p9-11

413 CPC Document Compilation Commission: ***Selected Works of Deng Xiaoping(Volume 3)***, People's Publisher, 1993, p239

414 Edited by Su Dongbin: ***History of China's SEZ***, Guangdong Economy Press, 2001, p403

415 Edited by Su Dongbin: ***History of China's SEZ***, Guangdong Economy Press, 2001, p409

416 Hainan Party's History Research Office: ***Establishment and Development of China's SEZ—Hainan Volume***, Party History Press, 1977, p20-21

5.2.6 Initial Establishment of Hainan Special Economic Zone

Hainan successfully established the country's largest special economic zone on April 26, 1988 and entered a new historical period. In order to improve the economic environment of Hainan, the central and local government issued a number of regulations to encourage investment and accelerate the construction of Hainan.

Figure 5-2-1 The unveiling ceremony of Hainan provincial government held in 1988

Resources: http://hnrb.hinews.cn/html/2008-04/26/

On May 4, 1988, the State Council issued "Regulations on Encourage Investment in Construction of Hainan Island" ([1988] No. 26 of State Council),[417] which contained 23 regulations to implement more flexible economic policies in Hainan and grant Hainan Provincial People's Government more decision-making power.

---

417 http://www.hainan.gov.cn/data/news/2008/01/44714/

On August 1, 1988, the State Council issued a specific regulation of "Regulations on Accelerating Implementation of the State Council ([1988] No. 26 Document) in Hainan Special Economic Zone," which further accelerated the pace of development and construction of Hainan. On August 5, 1988, the Hainan provincial government issued "Tax Preference Method to Encourage Investment" (referred to as "twenty measures") developing specific measures on tax preference items, and making specific favorable preferences to incorporate income tax according to various industries.

From September 1 to 4, 1988, the first Hainan Province CPC Congress was held in Haikou. The congress proposed that, in order to form the SEZ mechanism and realize the goal of rapid economic development, a new order market economy needed to be quickly established, so as to exert the coordinating function of law of value, realize the coexistence of various economic sectors and establish a fully open market economy. Hainan was carved out of Guangdong Province to establish an independent province and was given more preferential policies and measures by the Central Government. These policies and measures embodied in the annual preferential loans and grants, expansion in the power of approval, expansion of the import and export quotas and right in licenses and self-financing in foreign trade, preferential tax rates, preferential financial policies, expansion in the land use right and personnel policy. The new system of "small government and big society" started operation, taking the lead in the reform of the administrative functions.

5.3 Exportation of the Early Development Stage Strategic Model of Hainan Special Economic Zone

Hainan Special Economic Zone was established as expected. In the preliminary establishment stage, Hainan constructed the socialist market economic system, "the small government and the big society" political system and a creative economic developmental model of "inviting investments from overseas and cooperating with inlands." Scholars and experts began to explore the developing model of Hainan.

5.3.1 Construction of Socialist Market Economy System

The 24th file declared by the State Council in 1988 states that: "The development of Hainan Province can be more flexible. According to the instruction in the macroscopic plan of our state, Hainan should construct a new systemic frame, which is good for regulating the market and the development of the commodity economy." After the construction of Hainan Special Economic Zone, according to the appeal of our country to build a new market regulating systemic frame, Hainan firstly carried out the socialist market economy system, which starts the reforms of the socialist market economy system throughout the country. In order to establish a new economic system, which is adjusted to the setup of Special Economic Zone and export-oriented economy, building a united and open market system is the most important aspect to optimizing the allocation of the resources.[418] Specific measures should be taken as follows: to transform the price system; to perfect the market system; to establish the finance market; to establish the labor market; to establish the market for exchanging property right, technology and information.Construction of the "Small Government and Big Society" Political System.

Under great support from the Central Government, Hainan constructed the new political system of "the small government and the big society." According to the summary of the forum, which was held in 1987, on Hainan Islands' further opening up to fasten the economic explorations and constructions of Hainan Province, Hainan Province, from its established, should conform to the demand of the reform of political system, insist on separating party affairs and political affairs, separating politics and enterprises, reducing the number of related institutions and making effort to establish economy entities. The setup of the political institutions should break through the institutional model of other provinces and autonomous regions, which should give more attention to capability and high efficiency, in order to realize the construction of "the small government and the big society."[419] After the 14th conference of the Communist Party of China, according to the "small government, big society" rules, Hainan pushed on the reform of the administrative managing system, transformation of the government functions based on the demand of the market economy, which reflected the features of "capability and high efficiency." It improved the rapid development of Hainan's economy and society, which was an important attempt to the reform of China's administrative managing system. To reduce government rights and government restrictions became the breaking point in the process of the transformation of the government function in Hainan. Hainan government emphasized management based on laws, developed the four aspects' functions of "providing service, guarantee, and regulation and taking part in it," which attributed to the establishment of the market economy system and provided the institutional guarantee to the opening up.

The transformation of the government function and the disciplinary and legal features of the government created a much better environment and conditions to the economic and

418 Chen Xiaoxing edited, *Hainan—the First Big Special Zone in China*, Shan' an Xi Travelogue Press, 1988, p34.

419 Chen Xiaoxing edited, *Hainan—the First Big Special Zone in China*, Shan' an Xi Travelogue Press, 1988, p34.

social development of Hainan. Peoples' living standard began to improve, and the spiritual civilization construction also made great progress. The new success of the economy appeared in Hainan, which also provided a solid foundation to Hainan's further development.[420]

5.3.2 "Inviting Investments from Overseas and Cooperating with Inlands"

In the early stage of the construction of Hainan Special Economic Zone, the Hainan government began to expand the scopes of the opening up, making use of the unique preferential policies of Hainan, and developing the creative developmental model of "inviting investments from overseas and cooperating with inlands." Therefore, the government of Hainan Province carried out a series of supporting measures to "planning wholly, exploring within a wide range, providing supplements comprehensively, and conducting in different separate periods," so as to attract foreign businessmen to make contracts with local governments, and lead the development and exploration of Hainan.

In the beginning of the establishment of Hainan Province, the leaders of the Province visited and invited political leaders and representatives from other countries and regions of the world to Hainan, to spread the geography, natural resources and unique preferential policies to them, which created conditions for Hainan to attract investments from overseas, and take part in the international economical cooperation. Hainan SEZ organized such activity in order to hold foreign trade talks in a fixed period, to invite investments, which achieved great progress. Meanwhile, the government also put forward a series of preferential policies to encourage the merchants at home and abroad to invest in Hainan economy. The "inviting investments from overseas and cooperating with inlands" policy provided the special economic zone with a large amount of capital, technology, material resources and talents, which greatly improved the exploratory construction and economic development.[421]

5.3.3 Discussion on the Developing Model of Hainan Special Economic Zone

After the establishment of the special economic zone, Hainan province was faced with

---

420 The third research department of the research office for the history of the Central Committee of the Communist Party of China edited, *the Opening and Reform of the Coastal Cities of China,* The History of Communist Party of China Press, 2007, p64-69

421 The third research department of the research office for the history of the Central Committee of the Communist Party of China edited, *the Opening and Reform of the Coastal Cities of China,* The History of Communist Party of China Press, 2007, p64-69

difficult problems, i.e., how to choose the most proper developing model and how to decide the developing strategy. This was vital to the construction of Hainan special economic zone.

During the process of creating Hainan Special Economic Zone, Mr. Deng Xiaoping and the Central Government designed its developing model. The developing model is reflected in Deng Xiaoping's talk in June 12, 1987 and the 24th and 26th files declared by the Central Government in 1987. The main content is as follows:

Hainan Special Economic Zone needs to carry out more flexible, more preferential polices, share more independency to conduct more economic activities, carry out other efficient measures aside from the special economic zone, such as opening up policy, and other favorable approaches which are widely used around the world that can also be applied in Hainan Province.

To construct Hainan Special Economic Zone, China needs a great amount of foreign investments, especially from Hong Kong and Macao, in order to gradually build the export-oriented economic structure with Hainan characteristics and develop the export-oriented economy with detailed plans.

The exploration and development of Hainan special economic zone cannot blindly copy the developing models of other areas. It should be based on the advantages of resources, and exploration and discovery of Hainan's own development road. Hainan should take the road of "exploring with wide range, exploring one area and harvesting from it at the same time."

The reform of Hainan Special Economic Zone can be more flexible. In the aspect of the economic system reform, under the instructions of the macroscopic planning of China, Hainan should establish a new systemic frame mainly used for regulating the market and goods for the commodity market development. With regards to the political system reform, Hainan should focus on separating political affairs and party affairs, separating politics and business, reducing the number of the institutions and making efforts to develop more economic entities. The design of the governmental institutions should also differ from that of other parts of China, to build less institutions in number but higher in efficiency and realize "the small government and the big society."[422]

In the one year before and after the construction of Hainan Province and the special economic zone, under the instructions of Mr. Deng Xiaoping on creating Hainan Special

---

422 Su Dongbin edited, *A Brief Introduction to the History of Chinese Special Economic Zones*, Guangdong Economy Press, 2001, p412-413.

Economic Zone, the leaders and theorists in Hainan began to explore the specific developing model of Hainan Special Economic Zone. Soon after the constructions of Hainan Province and Hainan Special Economic Zone, in May 1988, Hong Kong's *Wen Hui Daily* and people from Hainan who had visited Hong Kong held the "Discussion on the Developing Plans of Hainan" in Hong Kong to celebrate the foundation of Hainan Province. During the meeting, Mr. Xu Shijie and Mr. Liang Xiang made speeches in which they had specifically and systematically analyzed the opening up model, the economic systemic model, the administrative managing model of Hainan and the economic developing model. The theorists in Hainan also actively participated in the meeting. Through holding discussions and publishing articles, the theorists express their own minds and attributes to the design and choice of the developing model of Hainan Special Economic Zone.[423]

The one-year's discussions and research of experts and scholars in and outside of Hainan prepared the spiritual and theoretical basis for Hainan Special Economic Zone to choose the most proper development model for its own. From August to September 1988, "Two Conferences" were held in Hainan in succession, i.e., the First Conference of the People's Congress of Hainan, and the First Conference of Deputy of the Communist Party of China of Hainan. "Two Conferences" was the most important meeting held after the constructions of Hainan Province and Hainan Special Economic Zone. "Two Conferences" decided the developing model of Hainan Special Economic Zone as follows: to construct an opening to the outside system, as "free for talents in foreign affairs' communication, free for capitals and free for exporting and importing goods and materials" basic frame, as "attracting foreign businessmen to make contracts and comprehensively explore the industrial area" main form, as "attracting foreign capitals and developing export-oriented economy" main subject, in order to build Hainan as the large special economic zone which is more open and free, composed of several free trade ports, processing factories for exporting, economic exploring zones, and science and industrial parks; and make effort to build the second tariff area in Hainan to realize the pioneering trial zone "which is equal to the functions of several Hong Kong but made in inland"; to carry out a new economic system of the socialist market economy which is suitable for the export-oriented economic development in Hainan; to construct and perfect the political system of "the small government and the big society."[424]

---

423 Su Dongbin edited, *A Brief Introduction to the History of Chinese Special Economic Zones*, Guangdong Economy Press, 2001, p414-415.

424 Su Dongbin edited, *A Brief Introduction to the History of Chinese Special Economic Zones*, Guangdong Economy Press, 2001, p415-416.

5.3.4 The Decision of the Developing Strategy of Hainan Special Economic Zone

From August to September 1988, "Two Conferences" were held in Hainan in succession, i.e., the First Conference of the People's Congress of Hainan, and the First Conference of Deputy of the Communist Party of China of Hainan. The committee of Hainan Province and the government of the province have put forward the main object of the developing strategy of Hainan as followed: to maintain the policy that opening up and reform improved exploration; regulating the economy with the market; making an effort to develop the productivity; on the basis of attracting foreign capitals, technology and fasten the industrialism, to finally set up a comprehensively large special zone with the industry oriented and harmoniously developed industry, agriculture and trade sectors at the same time, with high developed commodity economy, with more advanced science and culture, with higher living standards; striving hard to make Hainan be listed in the ranks of more developed countries and regions in the southeast of Asia in no less than 20 years, with more than 2,000 USD per capita GNP. The future productivity structure of Hainan will be based on the port, as "the port city and cities with port basis" axis, as "the communication net" connecting point, to form five special economic zones with own unique features.

5.4 The Ebb and Flow of Hainan Special Economic Zone in the Last Decades

Hainan Special Economic Zone was a forerunner of China's reform and opening up. Since the date of establishment, Hainan created a development boom; it made significant achievements in the past ten years. Nevertheless, due to various reasons, such as a weak foundation, excessive economic growth and conflict between economic rationality and the greed of human nature, Hainan Special Economic Zone experienced many difficulties.

5.4.1 The Initial Construction Boom

During the first year of the establishment of Hainan Special Economic Zone, according to the development modes and strategies by first session of People's Congress of Hainan and Chinese Communist Party Hainan Province First Representative Assembly, Hainan created a construction boom. Its characteristics were the substantial inflows of investments in major development in port cities from merchants at home and abroad, for the construction of infrastructure and developing zone, then the investment extended to the whole Hainan.[425]

5.4.1.1 Infrastructure Construction

In order to attract more investors at home and abroad, Hainan focused on infrastructure construction and improvement of investment during its infancy. It mainly lied on the constructions of electricity, communications facilities, port, highway and airport. Infrastructure construction was the first construction boom of Hainan, and since then, the investment environment of Hainan improved rapidly.[426]

5.4.1.2 Establishing the Developing Zone

The early days of Hainan Special Economic Zone's establishment set the principle of "uniform planning, introducing foreign investment, plots of development and comprehensive composition" to strengthen the construction of the developing zone. According to this principle, all cities and counties established various developing zones to, as the Chinese saying goes, "attract bird by building nest" and created plots for a development boom. Hainan established 30 developing zones that were approved by State Council and provincial government. The developing zones that were established during the first construction boom were an experimental test of the development and construction mode of Hainan Special Economic Zone, the mode of their management-like plots, development and management provided a valuable experience for the construction of Hainan. Meanwhile, these developing zones became the main base for attracting investment, technology and advanced management and a new profit point.[427]

5.4.1.3 Confusions in Early Development

In the early days of the establishment of Hainan Special Economic Zone, Hainan began large-scale infrastructure construction and plot development by taking advantage of some special economic policies. The whole island developed rapidly, but soon Hainan lost its favorable international and home investment environments. Under the national rectification work and the Yangpu Event, the construction of developing zones suffered a

---

425 Su Dongbin edited. *A Brief Introduction to the History of Chinese Special Economic Zones*, Guangdong Economic Press, 2001, p423.

426 Su Dongbin edited. *A Brief Introduction to the History of Chinese Special Economic Zones*, Guangdong Economic Press, 2001, p423-426

427 Su Dongbin edited. *A Brief Introduction to the History of Chinese Special Economic Zones*, Guangdong Economic Press, 2001, p426-433.

disastrous decline, also bringing the nearly established Hainan Special Economic Zone numerous confusions.[428]

Deng Xiaoping gave the final word on the Yangpu Event, that "After knowing the situation, Hainan provincial committee's decision is correct. This is a golden chance and should not delay. Hainan provincial committee should make it clear to everyone, even those with different opinions and fulfill the procedures immediately." After that, the Yangpu Event died down. The 48-word written instructions of Deng Xiaoping are important to the people of Hainan.[429]

Figure 5-4-1 Deng Xiaoping and Hainan
Sources: http://hnrb.hinews,cn/html/2008-04/26/.

5.4.1.4 Development in the Confusion

Facing the negative effects and difficulties brought on by the Yangpu Event and national rectification work, Hainan struggled in the years following 1989.[430]

From August 23 to September 4, 1989, Hainan Provincial Committee held a large

---

428 Su Dongbin edited. *A Brief Introduction to the History of Chinese Special Economic Zones*, Guangdong Economic Press, 2001, p433

429 Su Dongbin edited. *A Brief Introduction to the History of Chinese Special Economic Zones*, Guangdong Economic Press, 2001, p437-438.

430 Su Dongbin edited. *A Brief Introduction to the History of Chinese Special Economic Zones*, Guangdong Economic Press, 2001, p438.

meeting in Haikou. The conference put forward that "The guideline of all the work of Hainan Special Economic Zone is the implementation of favorable policy of the Central Government, which lay a good foundation for future work." This principle was known as the "9 character policy" "using policy, laying foundation and fulfill implementation."

Some criticized the market economy in 1989. Under this background, Hainan Special Economic Zone shifted its strategy on market economy, proposing the guideline of "A variety of economy parts compete and develop jointly, advanced to treat all sorts of economy equally, pay attention to the development of non-public economy and mixed ownership economy."

After the Yangpu Event, the development mode of Yangpu that was proposed by Hainan Special Economic Zone won the approval of the Central Government and Deng Xiaoping, so the voice of dispute disappeared gradually. The development of Yangpu showed new life. Yangpu was considered as a key to open reform and opening up and a new situation of construction since 1989.

Hainan Special Economic Zone's efforts of "laying the foundation" in the reform and opening up achieved great significance in the past three years, particularly in the investment of the Yangpu Development Zone, which has taken a substantial step. However, it is probably difficult for Hainan to truly recreate a new phase of reform and opening up and walk out of the current economy, without the new changes in international and domestic situation.[431]

5.4.1.5 Getting Out of Trouble

In the second half of 1990, the new changes in international and domestic situations were conducive to China's reform and opening up; domestic situation was conducive to China's reform and opening up and modernization construction. First, the domestic environment improved. The Communist Party of China, with Jiang Zemin at the core of the third generation of collective leadership, summed up experience and lessons, promptly corrected erroneous trends of thought, vigorously promoted China's reform and opening up, in order to change the real market trend and slow the growth of production. Since September 1990, foreign investment in Hainan rose rapidly. Hainan ended the continuously decline of introducing investment and establishing lateral ties with enterprises at home and a good momentum exists in the construction of developing zones. After 1991, the

431 Su Dongbin edited. *A Brief Introduction to the History of Chinese Special Economic Zones*, Guangdong Economic Press, 2001, p447-449.

investment in Qiong from foreign and domestic businesses increased significantly; Hainan's economic construction marched into vigorous development.

Although three years' efforts of "laying the foundation" of Hainan was a passive choice, forced by the international and domestic situation, it laid a solid foundation for the second reform and opening up of Hainan.[432]

5.4.2 The Second Wave of Development

Two significant historical events occurred in China in 1992. One was the chief designer speech given by China's reforming and opening policy during a southern tour, and the other was The Communist Party of China's 14th National Congress decisions to set a reform target of establishing socialist market economic system and speed up the reform and opening policy. Those two historical events deeply affected the modern society of China, and give raise to the second tide of Chinese reform and opening policy.

This year was also a proud year in the history of reform and opening policy of Hainan. As pioneer of special economic zones, Hainan acted quickly, seized opportunities, and carried out new experiments of reform and opening up to meet the "spring" development.[433]

5.4.2.1 The "Broad Opening Up, Great Reform and Great Construction" Period

On April 14, 1992, the Hainan Province Governor, Liu Jianfeng, who was attending the 7th National People Congress Fifth Meeting spoke to the reporter of *Liaowang*, an official journal. The future of Hainan was moving toward great reform, broad opening up and great construction. On June 16, 1992, the Hainan government announced the "Communist Party of China, Government of Hainan's Views about Deepen Reform, Open Wider to the Outside World and Speed up the Pace of Construction" (hereinafter referred to as "Views"). Views proposed that Hainan would follow the spirit of Deng Xiaoping's speech and Political Bureau of the CPC Central Committee, suggested to speed up the implementation of basic thought and measures of reform and opening policy, exploration and construction.

In 1992, Hainan approved 4,700 sustainable enterprises, introducing investments from abroad and establishing lateral ties with enterprises at home, 1,830 foreign-funded enterprises, which equaled the total in the past 12 years. The Wholly Foreign Owned

---

432 Su Dongbin edited. *A Brief Introduction to the History of Chinese Special Economic Zones*, Guangdong Economic Press, 2001, p449-450.

433 Su Dongbin edited. *A Brief Introduction to the History of Chinese Special Economic Zones*, Guangdong Economic Press, 2001, p455.

Enterprise amounted to 1,221, associated enterprise amounted to 2,890, the amount of contracted foreign investment rose to 2.593 billion USD, exceeding 59 times the total sum of 12 years in Hainan. Hainan's actual use of direct foreign investment amounted to 531 million USD, foreign investment agreement amounted to 13.065 billion RMB and actual investment outside the province amounted to 1.953 billion RMB. During the current investment boom, investment from some big corporations and large enterprises entered Hainan, like Kumagai Gumi Hong Kong, Hong Kong Sun Hung Kai Group, Singapore Haw Par Group and East Japan Co, Ltd.

Table 5-4-1 Historical Investment in Hainan (10 Thousand/dollar)

Year	Actually utilized foreign capital	Borrowings from outside	Investment from overseas
1980	28		10
1981	109		109
1982	83		83
1983	438	200	192
1984	1784	313	1162
1985	2643	244	2095
1986	3259		3037
1987	911		893
1988	12,771	526	11,421
1989	16,097	5153	10,707
1990	18,982	8911	10,055
1991	22,232	4570	17,606
1992	53,160	8000	45,160
1993	128,584	23,800	104,784
1994	126,441	39,000	87,441
1995	145,501	40,000	105,501
1996	118,960	40,000	78,960
1997	112,134	41,000	71,134
1998	109,715	38,000	71,715
1999	84,149	35,700	48,449
2000	61,280	18,200	43,080
2001	57,291	10,600	46,691
2002	99,878	48,700	51,178
2003	61,782	3720	58,062
2004	66,998	2655	64,343
2005	70,711	2310	68,401
2006	79,259	4381	74,878
2007	112,499	498	112,001
2008 2009	128,468 94,300	131	128,337 93,800

Sources: Data originates calendar year "Statistical Yearbook of Hainan", data of 2009 come from Hainan province economy develops statistical bulletin 2009, Hainan Statistical Official Website www.hi.stats.gov.cn

Through the two years of "great reforms, great opening," Hainan's import and export trade rapidly developed, the total merchandise exports equaled 881 million USD in 1992, it increase 31.6% compared to that of 1955.[434] In 1993, the import and export trade maintained a good momentum of growth, annual total value of import and expert reached 2.569 million USD, a growth of 51.7% over 1992, the growth rate was less than that of 1992; the value of imports has increased 1.05 times. (See Table 5-4-2)

Table 5-4-2 Import-export Goods Total Amount in Hainan Province, Export Figures, Import Figures Growth Rate and Difference in Amount

Years	import-export goods total amount (10 thousand/dollar)	growth rate%	export figures	growth rate%	import figures	growth rate%	difference in amount
1987	29,241		11,545		17,696		-6151
1988	66,462	127.29	29,496	155.49	36,966	108.89	-7470
1989	109,620	64.94	36,082	22.33	73,538	98.93	-37,456
1990	93,697	-14.53	47,138	30.64	46,559	-36.69	579
1991	134,876	43.95	66,964	42.06	67,912	45.86	-948
1992	169,450	25.63	88,120	31.59	81,330	19.76	6790
1993	256,866	51.59	90,157	2.31	166,709	104.98	-76,552
1994	269,719	5.00	98,698	9.47	171,021	2.59	-72,323
1995	226,744	-15.93	83,000	-15.91	143,744	-15.95	-60,744
1996	228,667	0.85	84,132	1.36	144,535	0.55	-60,403
1997	194,901	-14.77	88,966	5.75	105,935	-26.71	-16,969
1998	190,913	-2.05	88,463	-0.57	102,450	-3.29	-13,987
1999	121,867	-36.17	74,860	-15.38	47,007	-54.12	27,853
2000	128,784	5.68	80,289	7.25	48,495	3.17	31,794
2001	176,238	36.85	80,094	-0.24	96,144	98.26	-16,050
2002	186,686	5.93	81,930	2.29	104,756	8.96	-22,826
2003	227,871	22.06	86,916	6.09	140,955	34.56	-54,039
2004	340,168	49.28	109,252	25.70	230,916	63.82	-121,664
2005	259,175	-23.81	102,254	-6.41	156,921	-32.04	-54,667
2006	397,358	9.81	145,456	34.53	251,902	-6.29	-106,446
2007	735,749	85.16	183,697	26.29	552,052	119.15	-368,355
2008	1,052,418	43.04	186,329	1.43	866,089	56.89	-679,760
2009	895,800	14.88	190,000	19.7	705,800	18.51	-515,800

434 *Hainan Yearbook*, 1992, Statistics Press.

The 35 key projects which were set into the eighth "5 Years' Plan" was started in Hainan economic zone, with a total investment of 157 million USD, most used in the construction of infrastructure and basic industries project. 15 projects were built in 1991 and three of them were finished in that year. The construction of the other 12 projects was fully expanded. In 1993, the start-up on the construction of many key projects became faster, such as Daguangba Hydropower Engineering Project, DongXian Highway, SanYa Phoenix Airport and so on. The spread of the construction of 35 key projects make a spectacular view for the development of Hainan, meanwhile, making a solid foundation for the modernization of Hainan.

The main characteristics of the construction of the economic area and reform in Hainan after 1993 can be concluded as following: first of all, reform is comprehensive and integrated. Secondly, focus on breakthroughs, being the first and overcome obstacles. Thirdly, be on the same step on reform and legislation, establish rules first and then to handle the affairs. Fourth, start from the government and reduce unnecessary power. Of course, this is very significant: Through various kinds of reforms, Hainan initially established a socialist economy market and provided a lot of valuable experience for the entire nation, region and other economic areas.[435]

5.4.2.2 Second Rapid Recession on Hainan

On June 24, 1993, to the arising problems of China's financial disorder, quickly growing on fixed assets, overheating on the development of estate, prominent inflation and so on, the Central Committee and the state council published a booked named "The Opinion of Present Economic Situation and Strengthen the Regulation in Order to Control and Change the Present Situation." With the increased control from the Central Committee, the economic situation of Hainan worsened.[436]

The causes for the worsening of Hainan's economy are reflected in the following: a serious slumped in import and export trade; the rapid decrease of the real estate market; reduction in foreign investment; an overall significant decline in the nation's economy. Hainan economic zones entered a new, slow growing period since 1994, with bitter consequences. Rational development of the economy and the people's passionate desires

---

435 Research Report of Chinese Academy of Social Sciences: *Experience of Hainan in the Establishing of Socialist Economic Economy*, Dec, 1992.

436 Su Dongbin edited. *A Brief Introduction to the History of Chinese Special Economic Zones*, Guangdong Economic Press, 2001, p470.

are reflected in the development of Hainan economic zones.[437]

5.4.3 Times of "Bubble Economy"

From 1995 to 1998, the development of Hainan's economy was standardized and mature. With a clear direction to move forward, the economic development entered a period of recovering growth.

5.4.3.1 The Industrial Developing Strategy of "One Province, Two Spots"

Since Hainan Province began to establish the large special economic zone, related industrial developing strategies were in constant discussion. For example, there were choices such as "Industry Dominant," "Trade for Thriving the Province," "Tertiary Industry Dominant," "Tourism Dominant," etc., for the dominant industry of Hainan Province. Those suggestions and arguments were beneficiary for the industrial development strategies of Hainan Province. However, Hainan at that time was extremely eager for some clear industrial developing strategies to activate general economic development.

On January 1, 1996, the Hainan Provincial Party committee of the Four Plenary Sessions summarized the experience and lessons learnt from the years of industrial development. The industrial development strategy of building Hainan into "One Province, Two Spots" during the period of the ninth "Five Year Plan," namely, the rising industrial province of China, the efficient tropical agricultural, and the vocational tourism, has been pointed out. Since the "One Province, Two Spots" was put forward, the industrial structure and principle of rising industry, tropical agriculture, and island tourism thriving together promoted the sustained, healthy and fast development of Hainan's economy for more than a decade.[438]

5.4.3.2 The Building of an "Information-Intelligent Island"

In April 1997, the Party Committee and the government of the province formally put forward the target to build Hainan into an "Information-Intelligent Island," and confirmed to make information industry the new economic growing spot. Efforts would be taken to make information industry the dominant and supporting industry of Hainan by the beginning of next century, to a thriving industrialization by informatization, and to realize the "great-leap-forward" development of Hainan's society and economy. In 1997, the

---

437 Su Dongbin edited. *A Brief Introduction to the History of Chinese Special Economic Zones*, Guangdong Economic Press, 2001, p470-472.

438 http://www.hainan.gov.cn/data/news/2008/04/50314/.

province began another series of building projects for information industry. The provincial government established a functional department, the Informatization Office, to be in charge of the informatized works, and tried to establish the related administrative, legal, technological and educational supporting systems, in order to create favorable conditions for the development of an information industry. With the help of those policies, the information industry of Hainan showed a positive developing trend. In April 1998, the first session of the People's Congress of Hainan province approved the "Government Work Report," which clearly pointed out that the building of Hainan's "Information-Intelligent Island" should be quickened.[439]

5.4.3.3 Actively Promoting Systematic Reformation

5.4.3.3.1 Systematic Reformation of Medical Insurance

On July 1, 1995, the Standing Committee of Hainan province issued 'The Regulations on the Medical Insurance for all Urban Employees of Hainan Special Economic Zone," which implemented the medical insurance system in a combination of personal accounts and social pooling for all urban employees in the form of social legislation. Hainan Province was the first to do so in the nation and the regulation for health insurance was the first provincial legislation to include all employees of both cities and towns. As the only pilot province in the nation to do healthcare reform, Hainan Special Economic Zone shouldered the responsibility of the "Experimental Field for Reformation," and was the first to test this exploration. Based on the pilot experience of areas like Hainan, by the end of 1998, the State Council issued the "Decision on the Establishment of Basic Medical Insurance System for Urban Workers," and the medical insurance system reformation for urban workers was quickly implemented throughout the country.[440]

5.4.3.3.2 Rural Social Pension Insurance

Since 1991, rural social pension insurance was piloted in the rural areas of cities or counties like Qionghai, etc. In November 1995, the provincial government published the "Regulations on the Rural Pension Insurance of Hainan Province." It specified that the rural pension insurance should hold to the voluntary principle, and implement the pooled funding, mainly by personal payment and collective allowance. It was implemented quickly among the nineteen cities in the province. In May 1996, the Department of Civil Affairs of Hainan

---

439 http://www.hainan.gov.cn/data/news/2008/04/50315/.

440 http://www.hainan.gov.cn/data/news/2008/04/50313/.

Province named Haikou the standardized management-modeling city to promote rural social pension insurance in the province. Up to the end of 1996, there were 2,506 (residents') committees in 307 villages and towns among 19 cities and counties promoting the project. There were 240,000 policyholders, and the fund of pension insurance was accumulated at 103,000,000 RMB, which was 61.2% more than that of 1995. In 1996, there were 7,577 people who received pension, together equaling 5,674,200 RMB. From 1997 on, the pilot of rural cooperative medical care in Hainan also made many improvements, and developed gradually. By 2000, it could be basically realized that every citizen could enjoy preliminary health care.[441]

5.4.3.3.3 Reformation of State-owned Assets Management

Hainan Special Economic Zone was the first in the nation to implement the system innovation of entrusted operation of state-owned assets. The entrusted operation of state-owned assets is a bold system innovation of the economic systematic reformation of Hainan Province. In May 1995, in order to improve the operational efficiency of the state-owned assets in corporations, and ensure a new, effective, property-relation-linked system of state-owned assets management as well as operation, the Standing Committee of the province issued and implemented the "Regulations on the State-owned Assets of Corporations in Hainan Special Economic Zone," the first in the country. According to the regulations, the state-owned assets management department could operate the state-owned assets of corporations by ways of "Entrusted Operation" and "Authorized Management." The first way was through the state-owned assets management departments entrusting the state-owned assets of corporate companies to other corporations to operate by way of bidding invitation, bidding negotiation and contracting, and the entrusted corporations shouldering the responsibilities of preserving and increasing the value. In May 1996, the state-owned assets of five corporations (including Southern Feed Mills of Hainan, Qiongzhou Hotel, and so on) were entrusted to operate, which indicated that the entrusted operation of state-owned assets of corporations had been realized.

5.4.3.3.4 The Establishment of the Oceanic Department of the Province

Hainan Province has the smallest land area, but possesses the biggest oceanic area in China. In order to fully utilize oceanic resources, on March 25, 1995, the departmental functional organization, the Oceanic Department of Hainan Province, was established. It

441 http://yjs.hainan.gov.cn/web/1997/main/08/8-63.htm.

was the first organization by the provincial government to manage the ocean in China. In February of the same year, by the approval of the Central Committee and the State Council, the organizational reforming plan of Hainan Province was confirmed. The Oceanic Bureau of Hainan Province was cancelled, and Oceanic Department of Hainan Province, which would be managed by the local government, was established. The establishment of the Oceanic Department marked the strengthening of the power of the provincial government to manage the ocean and islands authorized by the first session of the seventh meeting of the National People's Congress, and the beginning of a new period for Hainan to comprehensively manage the ocean and to develop oceanic economy.[442]

5.4.3.4 Opening Up and the Development of Tourism

5.4.3.4.1 Foreign Trade Reformation

Based on the "Releasing the Scope of Foreign Trade" in 1993, Hainan Special Economic Zone developed its foreign trade reformation. In February 1994, the provincial government released the "Notice on Further Releasing the Export and Import Trade of Corporations in the Province and the Related Problems," and implemented the second phase of systematic reformation of foreign trade, feathered by "The Release of the Subject of Foreign Trade." In 1994 and 1995, 46 and 49 corporations' operational rights of export and import were shifted and added, respectively. In March 1994, the "Chamber of Commerce of Export and Import of Hainan Province" was formed first among the countries' counterparts in the area to coordinate and self-regulate based on the tenet of "Coordinating, Servicing, Consulting, Displaying, Helping Mutually, and Cooperating," and acting as the bridge between the government and the corporations to promote the development of foreign trade. In order to adjust to the requirements of the zone to open up and change past problems that focused on the tediousness and ineffectiveness of the port, in March 1994, the province undertook a great reformation of the port's managing system and implemented new methods of port management to simplify the procedure according to the prevailing international practice.[443]

5.4.3.4.2 "Relaxing in Hainan"

In order to make Hainan a vocational tourist scenic spot, the policy of "One Province, Two Spots" of Hainan Special Economic Zone was implemented. In 1994, with the efforts

---

442 http://www.hainan.gov.cn/data/news/2008/04/50313/.

443 http://www.haikou.gov.cn/top/zcfgui/hnfg/katl.html.

of the province, the State Bureau of Tourism agreed to make Hainan the key area for China's vocational leisure tourism in 1996. In order to meet the activity of "China's vocational leisure tourism in Hainan," and improve the physical equipment level of the province's tourism reception, in the following two years, many tourism projects (like Sanya Yalong Bay National Resort District, Nanshan Cultural Tourism Zone, Haikou Wan Lvyuan, Holiday Beach, Wan Ning Xinglong Tropical Garden, Xinglong Overseas Chinese resort city, even the Chinese culture through the village, Fingers Village International Resort, etc) were quickened and the development wake of Hainan's tourism was formed.[444]

5.4.3.5 Agricultural Reform and Development

To continue improvement of the rural land system, and promote the circulation and concentration of landholding, the provincial government issued "Regulations on the second round of land contracting of Hainan Province" in October 1996, which further clarified the right to issue contracts, stabilize the right to contracts and liberalize the right to the management. Provincial People's Congress also promulgated the "Contract Management Ordinances of Hainan Province's Rural Collective Economy." Compared with the first contract, this round of contracts paid more attention to the concentration of contiguous land contracts, the reasonable flow the land, and allowed exchanges of land, which were excessively scattered and changed the contract correspondingly. Thus it prompted the relative concentration of land and the proper scale management. By the end of 1996, the province had an area of more than 30 thousand mu of land transfer. On this basis, in order to legalize the land management, the work of rural land registration and issuing in the province opened the curtain after it has been piloted successfully in Meitai, Lingao County in March 1998.[445]

5.4.3.6 Developing Yangpu By Driving Hainan's Economy

In 1995, the large-scale construction of Yangpu Development Zone had been begun. Investments in Yangpu had accumulated to more than 4 billion yuan, of which contained 3.6 billion yuan worth of investment in infrastructure construction. With the fields leveled to 18 square kilometers, and completing an 11.4 km long network of customs quarantine, Yangpu Developing Zone finished the main road in this region and the underground pipe network. Moreover, the power plant, with a capacity of 315.5 thousand kilowatts, and the

444 http://www.hainan.gov.cn/data/news/2008/04/50314/.

445 http://yjs.hainan.gov.cn/web/1997/main/06/6-06.htm.

provincial power grid collaborated for electricity generation. The three resident settlements include: Sandu, Guangdong and Xinyingwan. During Prime Minister Li Peng's visit on Hainan, February 11 to 15, 1996, he gave particular concern to the construction of the Yangpu Economic Development Zone. He emphasized that, under the support of the central and the local governments, through the developers and the joint efforts of the Yangpu Management Bureau, Yangpu Development Zone's infrastructure had made great progress, and the investment environment was improving. In the meantime, the conditions of large-scale development and construction were ready. He also wrote a dedication that said, "To drive the development of Yangpu by industry programs and to promote Hainan's Economy by Yangpu's development."[446]

5.4.4 The Achievements in the Last Ten Years

Recalling the developing route of Hainan Special Economic Zone from 1988, the founding of the Zone to 1998, the switch in developing focus from trade, industry and agriculture to tourism-led, to agriculture-led and then to establishing an "informational intellectualized island." The obstacles and accomplishments of Hainan's economic development in the past 10-years went through three stages: the first rise and fall occurred from 1988 to 1991, when Hainanjianxing was operated by the SAR, the implementation of a more open and flexible policy, economic development entered the "laying the foundation" period; the second occurred between 1992 and 1994, Deng Xiaoping's "Southern speech" hailed the extraordinary development of Hainan's economy and create a national economic growth; the third from 1995 to 1998, caused by the real estate bubble, Hainan entered the difficult economic growth period of the "bubble economy" and into the recovery period.[447]

5.4.4.1 The Strategy of "Thriving Hainan by Advancing Science and Education"

Hainan Special Economic Zone always accelerated the strategy of "thriving Hainan by advancing science and education." From 1993 to 1997, the province imported a number of outstanding scientific and technological personnel, continued to implement national and provincial "Torch Plan" and "Spark Program," made 371 major scientific and technological achievements, among which 157 won the national and provincial science and technology awards. It also concentrated tightly on economic construction, its multi-form and multi-level scientific generating and formed industrialization of scientific and technological

446 http://yjs.hainan.gov.cn/web/1999/main/jj_14.htm.

447 http://www.hainan.gov.cn/data/news/2008/04/50316/.

achievements. In January 1993, the State Council approved the Hainan International Science and Technology Industrial Park as the "National High-tech Industrial Development Zone", which became the source of scientific and technological enterprises in Hainan. In 1997, compared to 1992, the scientific and technological progress contributed to economic growth amounting to 37.6%, which increased by 9.2%.[448] In 1997, a technology worker (formerly South China Tropical Crops Research Institute, Provincial President Professor Huang Zongdao) was awarded the title of Academician of Chinese Academy of Science, which ended Hainan's history of no academician.

5.4.4.2 The Optimization of Industrial Structure

Hainan Economic Zone was predominantly an agricultural region, while other industrials, especially the secondary industry were backward. In 1987, the ratios of first, second and tertiary industries in Hainan's GDP were 50.05: 19.01: 30.94. The primary industry is accounted for more than one half, which the traditional agriculture-oriented economic pattern deemed very conspicuous. After two "ebb and flows" of the development of Hainan, the rapid development of real estate promoted the rapid development of the tertiary industry, and completed the substitution of the first industry's leading position in the national economy. In 1992, the third industrial structure evolved into a ratio of 29.79: 21.10: 49.11. 1987's "First, Third, Second" structure changed into a "Third, First, Second" structure, which indicated that Hainan had broken the traditional agriculture-led economic structure and realized a historic step toward the industrial structure. Since 1993, Hainan seized the opportunity to implement macro-control, speeding up industrial restructuring and the pace of industrial upgrading. From the reality of Hainan, the government defined the "one province, two places " strategy on industrial development, which was meant to develop high-efficiency tropical agriculture, new industries, the three major tourism and explore Hainan characteristics to industrial development. As a result, the third time of industrial structure changed turned to 30.12: 25.69: 44.20. By the end of 1998, Hainan continued to optimize the industrial structure of three, aside from the increasing proportion of primary industry, which is driven by the development of tropical high-efficiency agriculture. Establishment of the economic zone at the beginning of 1987 saw a GDP of 5.728 billion yuan, was established in 1998 with 44.213 billion yuan of GDP, excluding the bubble economy, and further solidifying the foundation of economic development. (See

---

448 Wang Xiaofeng: *Report on the Work of Government,* April 23, 1998, http://www.hq.xinhuanet.com/news/2003-01/17/content_152426.htm.

Figure 5-1-1, 5-1-2)

5.4.4.3 The Educational Reform

The gradual implementation of the Hainan Special Economic Zone policy of national development priorities of education, in-depth education reform, the implementation of the diversification of education, school forms, encouragement to set up private schools, the initial establishment of the socialist market economic system to adapt the basic framework of the education system and to rationalize the structure of education strengthened basic education. In 1987, there were 122.95 thousand students in the province, of which colleges and universities had 0.61 thousand, secondary schools had 33.3 thousand and primary schools had 89.04 thousand, with a rate of 72.26% of graduates entering primary school; there were 55.692 thousand full-time teachers. By 1998, Hainan achieved the goal of eliminating illiteracy. Higher education developed stably, and vocational and adult education had a greater development. The quality of education continued to increase. The number of school-aged students in the province was 154.03 thousand, of which there were 1.35 thousand in colleges and universities, secondary schools has 45.49 thousand students; there were 107.19 thousand primary school students; enrollment rate of primary school graduates was 83.8%; full-time teachers equaled 78,445. Compared with 1987, the number increased by 5.29%, 40.43%, 80.33% and 50.62%; compared with 1987, the second set of numbers increased by 25.28%, 121.31%, 36.6%, 20.38%, 15.97% and 40.86%. (See Table 5-4-3)

Table 5-4-3 Basic Education Situation of Hainan

Year	Student Enrollment(ten thousand)				Enrollment Rate of Middle School (%)	School-age Children Enrollment Rate (%)	Full-time Teachers			
	General Higher Education	General Secondary School	Middle School of General Secondary School	Primary School			General Higher Education	General Secondary School	Middle School of General Secondary School	Primary School
1987	0.61	33.3	32.57	89.04	72.26		1104	17964	16995	36624
1988	0.91	31.17	30.33	90.35	71.56		1222	18961	17868	37296
1989	0.95	27.42	26.42	91.89	72.78		1199	18853	17845	37451
1990	0.77	26.48	25.2	96.47	78.83		1215	19378	18034	39002
1991	0.76	26.16	24.76	101.05	80.7	98.8	1236	19378	17993	40656
1992	0.85	27.78	26.17	103.61	81.56	98.2	1146	19623	18209	41261
1993	1.02	29.28	24.71	106.73	81.6	99	1201	19390	17891	41682
1994	1.17	31.71	29.57	110.23	73.28	99	1280	19810	18125	42216
1995	1.2	34.16	31.71	111.75	74.13	99	1334	20674	18958	42583
1996	1.25	36.94	34.28	111.36	76.94	99	1379	22252	20294	43606
1997	1.28	39.65	36.75	109.08	79.31	99.39	1380	23635	21565	49470
1998	1.35	45.49	38.35	107.19	83.5	99.28	1362	27215	21970	49868

Source: Hainan Statistical Yearbook

5.5 The Development of Hainan Special Economic Zone from 1998 to 2009

After three consecutive years of economic downturn, Hainan Special Economic Zone achieved a recovery growth in 1998, with an increase of 8% in GDP. On April 13 of the same year, the 10th anniversary of the establishment of Hainan Province and Special Economic Zone was held in Hainan, where the then-Vice Premier, Li Lanqing, remarked highly on the great achievement during the decade and reiterated that the Central Government would not change its resolve in developing special economic zones, would not change its policy towards special economic zones, and the historical role and significance in national reform and opening up as well as modernization drive would not be changed.[449]

5.5.1 The Stage of Recovery Growth

5.5.1.1 Economic Recovery Growth

Hainan entered a period of recovery growth in 1998, after several years of slow growth in GDP, and achieved an 8% growth in GDP for the first time. In 1999, the national economy demonstrated a good momentum of steady, rapid and healthy development. The GDP of Hainan Province totaled 47.123 billion yuan, an increase of 8.6% over the previous year, and 1.5 points higher than the national growth. Though suffering from a catastrophic

Figure 5-5-1 The First Hongqi Automobile Produced by Faw Hainan Motor Co., Ltd. on May 14th, 1998.
Source: http://hnrb.hinews.cn/html/2008-04/26/.

449 http://www.hainan.gov.cn/data/news/2008/04/50316/.

flood in 2000, Hainan achieved a GDP of 51.848 billion yuan, an even higher increase of 8.8 percent over 1999, and 0.5 points higher than the national growth. These achievements demonstrated that Hainan Special Economic Zone had cast aside the negative influence of the bubble economy.[450]

5.5.1.2 Construction of the Ecological Province

In 1998, Hainan put forward the plan to develop itself into an ecological province. In September, Hainan Provincial Government set up the goal of developing itself into the first ecological province in China. In 1999, the Hainan Provincial People's Congress approved the strategy and objective for development. Hainan also gained approval from the State Environmental Protection Administration, thus becoming the first pilot city for building an ecological province. On July 30, 1999, the eighth session of the Second Provincial People's Congress deliberated and approved "Guidelines on Planning of Hainan's Development into An Ecological Province," which marked the beginning of developing Hainan into an ecological province. The guidelines spelled out the overall objective: a strong ecological economy in approximately 30 years; a human settlement with proper distribution and harmonious and exquisite ecological landscape; and a comprehensive economic competence among one of the strongest nationwide and a leading nationwide environment quality. The construction of the provincial city occurred in three phases: the recent term, the middle term and the long term.[451]

5.5.1.3 Development of Big Projects

In 1999, Hainan Round-the-Island Express Highway was fully open to traffic and Meilan Airport was open to navigation. Hainan also accelerated the construction of the Guangdong-Hainan Railway and the extension of the Lingshui-Sanya section of the Hainan Eastern Freeway. These efforts rewarded Hainan with improved transportation facilities. Hainan was also ready to launch some big programs and further improve its infrastructure. In 2000, Hainan built new exit sections at Yangpu, Changjiang, Baisha, Basuo and Jiusuo of Hainan Eastern Beltline Freeway and extended the Qionghai-Lingshui section of Hainan Eastern Freeway. Jiaji-Boao Highway and Haiwen Express Highway were also newly built. In these programs, the province and society at large made a fixed annual investment of 19.345 billion yuan, an increase of 1.7% over the previous year.[452]

---

450 http://www.hainan.gov.cn/data/news/2008/04/50318/.

451 http://yjs.hainan.gov.cn/web/2000/main4/4-13.htm.

452 http://www.hainan.gov.cn/data/news/2008/04/50318/.

5.5.1.4 Retrenched Structure

In May 1998, to implement the guiding principles of the Central Government on institutional reform and further improvement of the system of "small government, large society," Hainan Provincial Government decided to curtail the then-27 departments to 22. The restructuring of party and government institutions followed the overall arrangement of the Central Government and was fully carried out. The objectives were to transform governmental functions, to adjust organizations, to improve governmental functions in adjusting regional economy and supervision mechanism and to produce better troops and simpler administration so that an efficient, coordinated and standardized administrative system and a better system of public servants would be available. In the beginning of 2002, Hainan carried out the reform of party and government institutions on the city, county and village level.[453]

5.5.1.5 Yangpu Economic Development Zone

In August 1999, Hainan Provincial Government released "Preferential Policies towards Hainan Yangpu Economic Development Zone," which covered the latest preferential policies on investment, taxation, import and export and finance.[454] After referring to related documents on Yangpu issued by the State Council and the General Administration of Customs, the government came together and supplemented the existing policies. The new policies were the best that the government could offer to enterprises within its rights and on the basis of continuity.

5.5.1.6 The Adjustment of the Agricultural Economic Structure

From December 9 to 12, 1999, the Vice Premier Wen Jiabao visited Hainan and observed how local tropical crops were produced and sold. During the visit, he made three points on developing agriculture in Hainan: firstly, Hainan must press ahead with strategic adjustments in agriculture and rural economic structure; secondly, it must strengthen agricultural infrastructure and ecological environment construction; and thirdly, it must work hard to increase farmers' income. In 2000, Hainan made a positive move in promoting the strategic restructuring in rural economy. As a result, Hainan achieved 19.656 billion yuan added value of agriculture, an increase of 10.2% over the previous year.

---

453 http://www.hainan.gov.cn/data/news/2008/04/50318/.

454 http://yjs.hainan.gov.cn/web/2001/main/sx_01_20.htm.

Hainan also made stage achievement in reforming industrial enterprises. In 2000, the industrial added value amounted to 6.576 billion yuan. In the same year, after a thorough management of the tourism market, Hainan held many successful meetings, including the Fourth Island Sightseeing Policy Forum, where the number of visitors surpassed ten million.[455]

5.5.2 Rapid Development in the "Tenth Five-Year Plan" Period

On January 22, 2001, Hainan passed its guidelines of planning during the tenth "Five-Year Plan" period after discussion at the fourth session of the second Hainan Provincial People's Congress. According to the guidelines, during this period, Hainan made strategic economic restructuring and continued with its strategy of "one province, two bases" for industrial development. Hainan consolidated and uplifted the primary industry, accelerated the second industry, and fully boosted the tertiary industry. Meanwhile, it focused on developing marine resources and information industry. Hainan also stepped up efforts to cultivate new points of economic growth to develop its comprehensive economic strength. During the tenth "Five-year Plan" period, the first two years witnessed a continued steady recovery growth and the following three years witnessed rapid economic development.

From April 25 to 28, 2002, at the Fourth Hainan Provincial Congress of the Communist Party of China held in Haikou, four key tasks that focused on reform and opening up, restructuring, boosting domestic demand and optimizing environment were put forward. The Congress laid out four strategies, which included focusing on competitive industries, urbanization, rejuvenating Hainan through science and education and sustainable development. The congress also put forward the "Sixteen-Character Mentality" -- "south and north take the lead; east and west push forward; develop the periphery to support the interior", one of the many significant steps to press ahead with urbanization and to promote regional economic development.

Over the past five years, Hainan Special Economic Zone adhered to the strategy of "one province, two bases" to boost industries, took efforts to feature itself with a good environment, strong industries and a sound regime, and adopted the strategy of relying on big enterprises and significant programs to encourage development. These measures were rewarding in consolidating the basis of development. In addition, China won the fight against SARS, avian flu, drought, typhoons and other major natural disasters. China also

---

455 http://www.hainan.gov.cn/data/news/2008/04/50318/.

developed the "healthy island," the "longevity island" and the "infection-free area."

From 2000 to 2005, Hainan's GPD grew from 51.848 billion yuan to 90.36 billion yuan, its per capita GDP from 6,894 yuan to 10,998 yuan, cracking through the 10,000 yuan mark for the first time (refer to Figure 5-1-1).

5.5.2.1 Structural Optimization

In 1999, Hainan entered a period of slow economic recovery, but its economy grew faster than the national average. The following measures had been taken to optimize the economic structure. Firstly, Hainan optimized the ownership structure by preliminarily establishing the supervisory system of state owned assets in the period of the tenth "Five-year Plan." Hainan introduced large state owned enterprises to reform and restructuring Hainan's state owned enterprises (SOE); incorporated the Hainan Power Grid into China Southern Power Grid and launched the transmission and interconnection project for power grids in Hainan and the mainland; expanded investment in areas like energy and ports and integrated resources. Secondly, Hainan optimized the industrial structure by building distinctive industries so that emerging industries and competitive industries grew strong together. During the tenth "Five-year Plan" period, Hainan adjusted and optimized its industrial structure through the strategy of "introducing big enterprises and following large programs" by gaining investments from stock and promoting development in small increments. Thirdly, Hainan improved our social undertakings. During the tenth "Five-year Plan" period, Hainan provincial government spent a total of 726,000,000 yuan in capital construction and national debt occurred, covering science, education, culture, health, and sports undertakings. That was a great progress in developing social undertakings. Hainan decided to make education a priority and to fully implement the "planning of rural educational development in a decade." Hainan made new headway in the public health system and achieved the goal of "laying a foundation in *three years*, and accomplishing great changes in five *years" in the population and family planning work. As a result, we entered a phase of low fertility in population reproduction. New steps in construction of key cultural and sports facilities also had been completed.*[456]

5.5.2.2 Promoting Development through Opening up

Hainan's total foreign trade value and foreign direct investment increased sharply.

---

456 Wei Liucheng, *Report on the Guidelines of Planning During the "Eleventh Five-Year Plan" Period by Hainan Provincial Governor*, http://www.hainan.gov.cn/data/news/2006/03/8650/.

Boao Forum for Asia held in Hainan became a well-known and influential international conference. The project of *pilot* spots of open aviation attracted 14 foreign airlines to join in direct international flights to Hainan, opening 28 new international air routes. Hainan implemented the "Decision of the Hainan Provincial Party Committee of CPC on Several Issues Concerning Strengthening the Construction of Investment Environment" and carried out the activity of " The Year of Investment Environment Construction." As a result, Hainan properly handled a large series of long-standing investment errors and the government offices repaid a default on construction cost, worth over 100,000,000 yuan, thus basically resolving the history-made housing problem of the overseas Chinese. Hainan carried out the national project to facilitate customs clearance and greatly improved the efficiency and serviceability. Hainan implemented the "plan of interaction and cooperation between Hainan Special Economic Zone and metropolises" and took a proactive part in regional economic cooperation between the Pearl River Delta and the Yangtze River Delta. Economic exchanges and investment promotion on a large scale were made, which attracted a number of famous large enterprises, both at home and abroad, to invest in Hainan. A wave of development and construction took place in Hainan.[457]

5.5.2.3 The "Healthy Island" Strategy

From 2000 to 2005, the total area of natural reserve in Hainan expanded to 2.809 million hectares, and the area of natural forest reached 659,000 hectares. The newly increased forested area reached 185,000 hectares, with forest coverage of 55.5%. The land natural reserve accounted for 8.1% of the territory of Hainan in 2005, near the national average. Its biodiversity index ranked first in the country. Hainan made great efforts to prevent and control land degradation and desertification. In 2005, 20.4% of the degraded land regained its fertility; overall Hainan maintained a good environmental quality; the coastal waters mainly satisfied category 1 and category 2 standard in Sea Water Quality Standard; 86.4% of the monitored sea water satisfied the standard of water environment management, and the sea and beach remained intact. Hainan maintained an overall good environmental and air quality, which basically stood at the first national level.

Hainan took "no pollution, no damage to resources, and no redundant development at low level" as its principle to develop emerging industries. It guaranteed that while new programs were designed, launched and put into use, they were equipped with environmental

457 Wei Liucheng, *Report on the Guidelines of Planning During the "Eleventh Five-year Plan" Period by Hainan Provincial Governor*, http://www.hainan.gov.cn/data/news/2006/03/8650/.

protection facilities simultaneously. Hainan managed the industrial pollutant source along the Songtao Reservoir and Changhua River, closed and relocated a number of polluting enterprises, and investigated and punished some cases of damage to the ecological environment.

5.5.2.4 Institutional and Mechanical Optimization

In accordance with arrangements of the Central Government, the institutional reform at provincial, county and township had been completed, propelling the administrative system reform. The administrative examinations and approval system reform intensified, with 217 administrative licensing of provincial organizations items withdrawn and more effective examinations and approval methods promoted. The reform of the investment system deepened, and the approval or filing system applied to enterprise projects, which had been set up without government funds. The reform of the financial management system was promoted, creating a more complete treasury in a single account system, non-tax revenue management and government procurement system. The government administrative capability improved and new progress was achieved in transforming the government function. Great importance was attached to planning in order to exert its leading role in economic and social development. The government executive culture was advocated by implementing chief executive accountability, department leading accountability, leadership contact accountability of key project, the tracking and supervising system by provincial government determining and provincial leadership commenting. All these transformations intensified the executive mentality of the government and improved the administrative service efficiency.

5.5.2.5 Improvement of People's Living Standards

Basic allowance of laid-off workers from state-owned enterprises and pensions of retired workers in cities and towns was paid on time and in full. All urban residents entitled to basic living allowances were included in the Subsistence Allowance Program. The household enjoying the five guarantees in rural areas was supported by transferred local finance. The Hainan Provincial Party Committee and the provincial government, persisting in performing actual deeds for the people every year, invested 1.113 billion RMB to reconstruct rural power grids, increasing and renewing 4667 km of grids lines. The Rural Drinking Water Project had been implemented, providing safe drinking water for 1.3083 million people. 493,000 thatched sheds were restored and 147,000 methane tanks were built. Access to broadcasting in every village in the central region was accomplished. 514 million

RMB was utilized to adjust the standard wage in the county, increasing the wage of province's financial dependents to the level of "Hainan uniform standards with 70% floating" one year ahead of schedule.[458]

5.5.3 Golden Development in the Eleventh "Five-Year Plan" Period

Since 2006, Hainan entered a period of golden development, with its GDP exceeding 100 billion yuan and local financial revenue exceeding 10 billion yuan. Hainan realized this goal one year ahead of the plan. Its GDP reached 105.243 billion yuan, of which the primary industry totaled 34.42 billion yuan, the secondary industry 28.779 billion yuan, and the tertiary industry 42.044 billion yuan. Its per capita GDP reached 12,654 yuan. The fifth Hainan Congress of Party Representatives held in 2007 was a success, which put forward the slogan that "building Hainan on ecological protection, strengthening Hainan through opening up, and prospering Hainan through industrial development and solid work." The congress called on all Hainan people to "reconstruct awareness and to renew the spirit of Hainan Special Economic Zone," highlighting the specialty of Hainan SEZ. In 2007, its GDP reached 122.328 billion yuan, of which the primary industry totaled 36.107 billion yuan, the secondary industry 36.426 billion yuan, and the tertiary industry 49.795 billion yuan. Its per capita GDP reached 14,555 yuan. This growth symbolized that Hainan entered a new phase of steady, healthy and relatively rapid development. In 2008, Hainan proactively addressed the international financial crisis and maintained steady and fairly rapid economic development. Its per capita GDP surpassed 2,000 USD for the first time, reaching 17,175 yuan. Its GDP totaled 145.923 billion yuan, of which the primary industry totaled 43.761 billion yuan, the secondary industry 43.440 billion yuan, and the tertiary industry 58.722 billion yuan. Hainan's GDP in 2009 reached 164.660 billion yuan, of which the primary industry totaled 46.193 billion yuan, the secondary industry 44.343 billion yuan, and the tertiary industry 74.124 billion yuan. Its per capita GDP reached 19,166 yuan (refer to Figure 5-1-1).

5.5.3.1 Development Goal of "One Province and Three Bases"

During the tenth "Five-year Plan" period, Hainan adhered to the strategy of "one province, two bases" for industrial development, a strategy that benefited Hainan in guiding its industrial development, but also incurred many problems. As Chi Fulin pointed out in

---

458 Wei Liucheng, *Report on the Guidelines of Planning During the "Eleventh Five-year Plan" Period by Hainan Provincial Governor*, http://www.hainan.gov.cn/data/news/2006/03/8650/.

August 2005, the difficulty of developing "one province, two bases" was that Hainan focused only on industrial development and that developing emerging industries did not make Hainan a province strong in emerging industries. He also put forward the "one province, three bases" strategy and explained that "one province" referred to developing Hainan into a province of distinctive ecological civilization, and "three bases" referred to the South China Sea oil and gas resources exploitation base, the international holiday resort and the tropical green agriculture base. "One province, three bases" are distinctive in mainly three ways: firstly, full play was given to Hainan's prominence in development, and on that basis built a good development environment with Hainan characteristics and appeal; secondly, the strategy was in line and well-oriented with the scientific approach to development; thirdly, the strategy was clearly targeted and highly instructive on economic development. However, the goal of "one province, two bases" for development was an economic orientation based on the industrial orientation, unlike which, the goal of "one province, three bases" combined environmental protection and development of emerging industries, which highlighted Hainan's characteristics. It defined Hainan's direction of emerging industries as the processing industry that focused on South China Sea oil gas resources.[459]

5.5.3.2 Exploratory Planning of "Hainan City"

"The 2005~2020 Overall Planning of Hainan Urban and Rural Areas," approved by Hainan Provincial Government in April 2006, proposed that Hainan should be planned as a whole province and should be planned comprehensively as a whole geographical unit. Based on the characteristics of Hainan, this planning was implemented and coordinated with every department and county planning and industrial planning in specific locations to guide the complete urban and rural development. It can be regarded as an overall planning of Hainan and a comprehensive arrangement for the resource, industry, rural and urban development and facilities establishment. The planning mainly included the zone location and development goals, industry development planning, ecological resources and environmental planning, spatial development of urban and rural areas, major infrastructure planning and social service facilities planning, urban and rural space control, and immediate construction planning.[460]

---

459 Chi Fulin, *Setting the Goal of "OneProvince, Three Bases"—Suggestions on Orientation of Hainan's Economic Development Goal During the "Eleventh Five-Year Plan" Period*,

460 http://www.hainan.gov.cn/data/news/2008/04/50323/.

5.5.3.3 Yangpu Bonded Port Area

The Provincial Government declared on October 11, 2007 that the State Council approved the Yangpu Bonded Port Area on September 24, 2007. Therefore, Hainan embraced another significant development opportunity of "driving the Hainan economy by the development of Yangpu." Yangpu Bonded Port Area was the fourth bonded port area following Shanghai Yangshan Bonded Port Area, Tianjin East Bonded Port Area and Dalian Dayaowan Bonded Port Area. It was also the first in South China. According to the Yangpu Bonded Port Area construction planning approved by the State Council, the Yangpu Bonded Port Area was situated in the Yangpu Economic Zone in Hainan, covering an area of 9.2063 square kilometers, and was to be completed in three phases.[461]

5.5.4 Construction of Wenchang Space City

The new launch center in Wenchang, approved by the State Council and Military Commission of the CPC Central Committee in September 2007, covered an area of 20 square kilometers. On November 5, 2008, the project of a new generation of carrier rocket launch center and the local Economic and Social Development Forum were inaugurated in Wenchang, bringing together top specialists in space science and technology and senior management from world-class planning agencies to discuss the ways in which to build the launch center and promote the economic and social development in Hainan. On September 14, 2009, the construction of Wenchang launch center began and plans to be completed in 2013. It is believed that this project will set off a new upsurge of investment and tourism for Wenchang and Hainan. The first industries promoted by the aerospace industry in Wenchang were the real estate and tourism. The Task Force of Hainan Human Resources Development Institute led by Zhan Changzhi suggested in their report, "Research of Strategies for Adapting Wenchang and Hainan to the Development of Space Launch Bases," that Hainan and Wenchang should build a complete industrial chain of the launch center. They also indicated that the launch center will attract large international and private capital, improving the investment structure of Hainan. "Wenchang needs to recognize that this launch center effect could also be radiated to the whole province. At that time, Wenchang played a significant role in the economic development of Hainan and will change its position in the whole province's economic structure. The future Hainan will be divided into two major zones. The north zone, with its center in Wenchang, is composed of

461 http://www.hainan.gov.cn/data/news/2008/04/50325/.

education, scientific research and culture industries, while the south zone will be centered on Sanya, mainly the prosperous tourism. Hereafter tourists can enter Hainan Island not only from Sanya but also from Wenchang, improving the tourism framework of Hainan."[462] Rao Xueling and Xu Xin from Institute of Economic Management of Sanya College, Hainan University, figured out that the construction of a launch center would propel the development of tourism, high-tech industry, real estate, manufacturing, transportation, modern agriculture and education, and optimize the industrial structure.[463]

5.5.5 Achievements of Hainan Special Economic Zone Over the Past Two Decades

Over two decades has passed since the establishment of Hainan Province and Special Economic Zone, during which, both great achievements were made and daunting hardships were faced. People who came to Hainan in the early years of development have either accomplished great work or left Hainan for other causes. From the proposal of establishing the information island and the healthy island, from the development goal of "one province, two bases" to "one province, three bases," Hainan inherited a precious spirit of hard work and a solid foundation for the future development of Hainan Special Economic Zone.

5.5.5.1 Specialty of Hainan Special Economic Zone

As one of the special economic zones in coastal areas, Hainan Province has a land area, ten times of the total area of Shenzhen Special Economic Zone and other three SEZs. Hainan is rich in resources, but inferior in its ecological environment. Since the establishment of Hainan Province and Special Economic Zone over two decades ago, Hainan advanced bravely amid many obstacles and accomplished the change from the enclosed or semi-enclosed planned economy to the open socialist market economy.

Once the impoverished and backward island on the border, Hainan now is a characteristic special economic zone, full of national vitality. Over the past two decades, Hainan never deviated from its field in its development strategy. In the initial period of establishing Hainan Province and Special Economic Zone, mainly tropical economic crops and distinctive precious trees were cultivated. Agricultural development was planned on the basis of tapping and leveraging on a rich variety of tropical natural resources, marine resources, mineral resources and tourism resources. Hainan worked hard to strengthen

---

462 http://news.sina.com.cn/c/2009-09-18/040618674371.shtml.

463 http://www.chinareform.org.cn/cirdbbs/index.asp?boardid=25&page=.

infrastructure. Through these above efforts, an industrial structure with Hainan characteristics was established. Besides, the Central Government has all along granted Hainan with most special policies, vast authority and more preferential policies.

5.5.5.2 Forward Economic Development

Since the establishment of Hainan Province and Special Economic Zone over two decades ago, Hainan adhered to the policy of "one province, two bases" and "one province, three bases" for industrial development, and worked hard to implement the strategy of "introducing big enterprises and following large programs." Those measures helped achieved rapid economic growth. Hainan, a once isolated and backward island, is now in the forefront of reform and opening up and is the largest special economic zone in China.

From 1987 to 2009, Hainan's GDP grew from 5.73 billion yuan to 164.660 billion yuan and its per capita GDP from 939 yuan to 19,166 yuan. Its industrial added value increased from 773,000,000 yuan to 30.063 billion yuan and agricultural added value from 2.863 billion yuan to 46.193 billion yuan. Its added value of service industry increased from 1.774 billion yuan to 74.124 billion yuan[464] and its foreign trade value from 292,410,000 USD to 8.958 billion USD, including Sinopec Hainan Refinery (refer to Figure 5-1-1 and 5-4-2).[465] Hainan also maintained a leading ecological environment. These are all evidence of forward development achieved in Hainan Special Economic Zone.

5.5.5.3 Innovation of the Characteristic System

Over the twenty years after the Hainan Provincial Economic Zone was established, several reform breakthroughs, influential both at home and abroad, were achieved. Hainan was the first in the country to promote and construct the socialist market economy. Hainan was the leader in experimenting institutional reform of "small government, big society" at the provincial level; integrating road maintenance, road tolls and transportation management fees and other road fees into bunker surcharge; implementing parity of purchasing and selling food prices; piloting in transforming state-owned enterprises into stock companies and promoting comprehensive shareholding system reform; carrying out social pension, unemployment, work-related injury, and the medical insurance systems, and setting up the new framework of social security; reforming the bunker surcharge; reforming

---

464 Data in 2009 was the added value of the tertiary industry.

465 Source of data in 2009：http://www.hi.stats.gov.cn/tabid/185/InfoID/10898/Default.aspx.

business registration system; abolishing taxes on special agricultural products and eliminating agricultural tax one year earlier than other provinces; extending the basic public service to the grassroots level and rural areas, and gradually achieving equalization of basic public services within 10 to 15 years. Among those initiatives, some have been spread to the whole country and some continue to be the unique institutional advantages of Hainan Special Economic Zone.

5.6 Prospect of Hainan Special Economic Zone

In the new period, how would Hainan break the "frames" and constraints with its emphasis on the word "special," manage to loosen up in four respects, namely in possibility, way of thinking, bravery and action (as proposed by Du Qinglin[466]), and consistently hold on to the idea that "development is of overriding importance" and the fundamental criterion of Three Favorables: whether it promotes the growth of the productive forces in a socialist society, increases the overall strength of the socialist state and raises the people's living standards. Deng Xiaoping's guidance should always be kept in mind, that "without the spirit of taking adventures and running risks or courage and vigor, we cannot make a good and new way or carry out a new undertaking."[467] Then how is the prospect and fate of Hainan?

5.6.1 Strategies of Economic Development in the New Period

As pointed out by Professor Wang Yiwu from Hainan University in his essay "Strategies of Economic Development and Designs of Division Functions in Hainan Special Economic Zone," the "Five Strategies" of economic development in Hainan and the "Five Divisions" in designs of division functions are well integrated both with the choice of "one province and three places" in Hainan's regional development mode and with the structure of Hainan's Three Pillar Industries (the marine industry, the tropical crop and minimal processing industry, tropical marine ecotourism industry). Pieced together, these ideas and concepts turn into the "133551 Project": One Province and Three Places, Three Pillars, Five Strategies, Five Divisions, including building the One Free Trade Area. The regional development mode of One Province and Three Places, the industry structure collocation of Three Pillars, the economic development plan of Five Strategies, the division

466 *Hainan Daily*, March 8,[t] 1998 edition one.

467 Edited by Editorial Committee on Party Literature of the Central Committee of the CPC: *Selected Works of Deng Xiaoping*, Volume 3, People's Publishing House, 1993 edition, P 372.

function design of Five Divisions and the policy of the Free Trade Area should be earnestly carried out, and thus Hainan's economic prosperity is close at hand. Maximum achievement in Hainan's economic development can be naturally made with fewer efforts because the regional development mode, the economic development strategy, the industry structure collocation, the division function design and the more open policy of Free Trade Area, both matching the actual conditions of Hainan and following its development trend.

5.6.1.1 Five Strategies of Hainan's Economic Development

1. The strategy of developing an ecological-sound province. Hainan's future lies in economic development, guided by green GDP with its ecological and environmental quality kept among the nation's top. Hainan will feature a more and more garden-style tropical sea island, consisting mainly of the National Forest Garden, the Civilized and Ecological-sound Village, Ecological Reservations, Networking and Garden Towns. The world will be presented with a harmonious society, integrating the urban area with the rural area within the province, and eco-demonstration zone.

2. The strategy of competitive industries. To implement the strategy of competitive industries is a necessary and significant measure to accelerate Hainan's economic and social development. The competitive industries mainly includes: (1) marine and "blue" industries; (2) tropical crop agriculture and minimal processing industry; (3) business, exhibition, leisure and vocation tourism featuring the tropics, seashore and ecology.

3. The strategy of urbanization. To accelerate urbanization is an important task for Hainan to building a moderately prosperous society, the objective requirement for realizing modernization, and the inevitable trend for economic and social development. Building urbanization mainly includes: (1) scientific planning with clear priority, and putting forth effort in promoting the upgrading of small-town systems; (2) developing networks with strengthened functions and emphatically optimizing the economic structures of small towns' economy.

4. The strategy of prioritizing science and education. It is encouraged that capable scientific-research institutes and universities and colleges enter enterprises or cooperate with them in different ways, following the way of integrating production, education and researching, to solve the problem of weak and incomplete scientific, technological and educational systems. Innovation, competition and cooperation are encouraged. There should be a full series of incentives favorable to cultivating and utilizing talents to stabilize and attract them; it is encouraged that those who have studied abroad come to work here or serve for Hainan's economic and social development in appropriate ways.

5. The strategy of sustainable development. Based on the guideline of ecological rationality, diversity and permanence, the strategy of sustainable development encourages ideas and concepts and social and economic activities that contribute to preserving resources, the environment and ecology, to give the Hainan people an ecological system on the tropical sea island that will continue operate. This is the material base for realizing sustainable development. The strategy of sustainable development centers on the people and emphasizes satisfying the needs of the people to survive and fulfill and eliminating poverty as soon as possible. Emphasis is also put on the synchronicity, systematicity, relevance and consistency of economic, social and cultural development.

5.6.1.2 "Five Blocks" under Regional Division Function Design

According to the Five Strategies of Hainan's economic development, considering the allocation of Hainan's favorable resources, geographical location and administrative division, Hainan can be divided into the northern, southern, eastern, western and middle blocks, namely, centering around Haikou in the north, Sanya in the south, Qionghai in the east, Yangpu and Dongfang in the west and the Five Finger Mountain in the middle, respectively. The Five Blocks constitute the "Five Grips" of Hainan's economic and social development. Industrial structures should be established, which are appropriate to the competitive resources of a certain sector. The developmental pattern of "one trunk with two wings" is formed with the eastern, western and middle block as the trunk and the southern and northern block as the wings.[468]

5.6.2 Establishment of Hainan Free Trade Zone

Since over twenty years ago, when the Hainan province was established and the Special Economic Zone was set up, to open up more had been one of the main strategies during Hainan's development. On January 1, 2008, China's Modernization Strategy Research Panel and China's Modernization Research Center of the Chinese Academy of Science released the report "The 2008 Report on China's Modernization – A Research on International Modernization." The report proposed to establish the Free Trade Area on the Hainan Island and to improve cooperation and interaction between China and other Asian countries. The proposal to establish the Hainan Free Trade Area conformed to the features of the development of the Hainan Special Economic Zone and was also an inevitable

468 Wang Yiwu, *Economic Development Strategy and Regional Division Functional Design*, *Journal of Qiongzhou University*, 2008 edition 6.

choice for its development.

5.6.2.1 Possibility of Establishing Hainan Free Trade Zone

As pointed out by Chi Fulin, executive head of the Chinese (Hainan) Reform and Development Academy in his publication "The Development Trend of Free Trade Areas and the Future of Hainan," to open up much more is the goal and choice for Hainan to develop itself and establish the Special Economic Zone; Hainan depends on the Special Economic Zone to be more open. Also, twenty years after the establishment of the Special Economic Zone, to propose establishing the Free Trade Area is a significant matter for Hainan in the new period to further free itself from old ideas, revive the spirit characterizing the Special Economic Zone and design Hainan's developmental mode in the future. Based on the changed circumstances since twenty years ago, a series of new institutions and arrangements have been carried out to ensure the free circulation of commodities, capital and personnel, to make Hainan one of the most open international regions. He put forward that multiple practical measures should be taken, and the goal of striving to establish the Free Trade Area be practiced positively and pragmatically. The following specific measures could be taken: First, Industries are opened up in an all-around way with promoting the development of the international tourist island as its priority; second, the Yangpu Free Industrial Port Area should be developed faster, with the opportunity of building the Yangpu Bonded Port Area; third, opportunities are to be seized, efforts should be made to establish the Free Trade Area between Hainan and Taiwan; fourth, efforts should be made to turn Hainan into China's first environmental-protection special zone and an important ecological island in Asia, even in the world.

5.6.2.2 Significance of Establishing Hainan Free Trade Zone

He Chuanqi, director and researcher of China's Modernization Research Center of the Chinese Academy of Science proposes in his publication, "The Strategic Orientation of the Hainan Free Trade Zone" that to build the Hainan Free Trade Zone is necessary both for further implementing the Policy of Reform and Opening Up and for practicing the Strategy of Free Trade Zone and the Strategy of going international. The establishment of the Free Trade Zone will be a historic opportunity for Hainan's rapid development and bring a "second spring" for Hainan. The development of the Hainan Special Zone during the past twenty years also cultivated an environment with good policies for building the Hainan Free Trade Zone.

Professor Wang Yiwu from Hainan University revealed the importance for Hainan to build the Free Trade Zone in his essay "To Improve the Open Economy in an All-round Way and the Establishment of the Hainan "Free Trade Zone": first, Hainan's economic development is of vital importance to China's reform and opening up; second, Hainan is the best medium for China to connect with the international market; third, Hainan boasts the best basic conditions for building the Free Trade Zone; fourth, the South Sea is the advancing base for development and opening up; fifth, experience is gained and lessons drawn from having dealt with the special economic zone for twenty years.

5.6.3 Development of the International Tourist Island

5.6.3.1 Development of the International Tourist Island on the National Strategic Level

During his inspection tour at Hainan in April 2009, Premier Wen Jiabao demanded that building Hainan into an international tourist island should be taken as crucial and fundamental to further reform and opening up and to promote economic growth. On Dec. 31, 2009, "Some Proposals on Promoting the Establishment and Development of Hainan International Tourist Island from the State Council" [issued by the state (2009) Item 44] (hereunto referred to as "Proposals") was released, which elevated the establishment and development of Hainan international tourist island to be a national strategy. Since the province was established and the special economic zone was set up in 1988, Hainan has been faced with a second historic opportunity for development. According to "Proposals," during the past twenty years, Hainan has made remarkable achievements in its economic and social development. However, due to its late beginning of development and weak foundation, the overall economic and social development of Hainan still remains at a lower level, confronted with the formidable tasks of protecting the ecological environment, adjusting the economic structure and promoting the development of science. To give full play to Hainan's regional and resource advantages, building Hainan into an international tourist island and cultivating an internationally competitive tourist resort is significant for Hainan to accelerate the development of a modern service industry and facilitate the healthy and rapid economic and social development, which would set an important example for adjusting and optimizing economic structure and transforming the mode of development nationwide.

Nine proposals were put forward: (1) the guidelines, strategic orientation and goals of establishing and developing Hainan into an international tourist island; (2) strengthening ecological culture and improving the capability of sustainable development; (3) taking advantage of Hainan's unique characteristics and improving the overall management and service of tourism; (4) fully developing the modern service industry related to tourism; (5) vigorously developing modern tropical agriculture and accelerating the integration of the rural and urban areas; (6) strengthening infrastructure and improving the capability of service and protection; seventh, promoting social construction with improving people's lives as the priority and accelerating the formation of humanity and intellectual support; (8) making full use of local advantageous resources and developing intensively infant industries; (9) reinforcing organization and coordination and carrying out the protective measures.

5.6.3.2 Development of the International Tourist Island on the Provincial Level

After released by the State Council, the "Proposals" were actively studied and practiced by different sections of Hainan. At the Sixth Plenary Session of the Fifth Central Committee, Secretary of Hainan Provincial Committee of the Communist Party demanded that leading cadres at all levels should reinforce their learning, concentrate on studying the related documents from the State Council, improve their capability of understanding and flexibly and fully practicing the policies, properly handle the operation of all policies and do solid work with the focus on the actual effects.

The Hainan Development and Reform Committee put forth efforts in the following three aspects: (1) attaching importance to and dealing well with planning. Advanced development ideas should be introduced according to the requirement of internationalization, appropriateness and unique features. Plans on the establishment of the international tourist island and other subject plans should be made with the concern of all parties to ensure all projects can be conducted in good order with the direction of scientific plans. Active efforts should be made to connect to and communicate with related departments of the government and to get more major projects of our province listed among the State's "Twelfth Five Year Plan" and other subject plans of the ministries and commissions. (2) the policy of "Development of the West Regions" and other financing policies should be fully and well utilized and a series of major projects should be promoted with high standards and high quality. (3) Reforms should be further carried out and systems and mechanisms with Hainan features should be established.

2010 witnessed the beginning of the development of Hainan tourist island. At the Sixth Plenary Session of the Fifth Provincial Party Committee, it was proposed that a series of significant events and current affairs should take place in Hainan, including: first, holding the first Boao International Tourism Forum; second, practicing the tax rebate policy as soon as possible for international tourists who solely come to do shopping in China and leave and the policy of tax-free shopping for tourists who depart from the island; third, creating innovative products for tourists; fourth, initiating the preliminary work of a series of large-scale tourism programs and attracting investment; fifth, establishing the public tourism service system; sixth, setting up the platform for the investment and financing of developing tourism; seventh, planning and organizing publicity and promotion of high-quality tourism; eighth, reforming and improving the Hainan Joy Festival; ninth, accelerating the reform of the tourism management system; tenth, continuing the comprehensive improvement of the environment and the sanitary situations in urban and rural areas and striving to create a social environment that matches the international tourism island.[469]

469 http://hnrb.hinews.cn.

6 Shanghai Pudong New District Leader and Window of China's Reform and Opening Up

On April 18, 1990, Li Peng, the then-premier of the State Council announced to carry out policies of economic and technical development zone and some special zones in Pudong on behalf of The CPC Central Committee and the State Council, marking a new phase and historic period for China's opening up. In comparison to previous trial reform and opening in many cities, this was put into practive after reform and opening up had been practiced for ten years. China had since stepped into a new period of nation-wide and multi-directional opening up and anounced the irreversibility of China's reform and opening up to the world.

Globally, Shanghai is located in the most dynamic "Economic Corridor" in Asia, while Pudong is located in Shanghai with convenient geographic location, capacious surroundings and spacious radiation range, as well as a strong economic and cultural foundation. It may be said that the opening up of Pudong was implemented with "good timing, geographical convenience and good human relations."

The opening of Pudong was not only for its own development. It served as a carrier for Shanghai's establishment as a global financial trade and shipping center, and aimed to become the bridge between China and the world, giving service to Yangtze River Delta and the whole nation, as well as promoting their economic development. Twenty years have passed since the establishment of the Pudong SEZ. With the full support of the Central Government of Shanghai Municipal Government, Pudong New District, taking the advantage of the rising Chinese economy and intelligence and hardworking spirit of its people, made remarkable acheivements. In 2008, the GDP of Pudong New District was 32 times that of 1990. In 2009, there were 603 financial institutions and 135 transnational corporation headquarters in Pudong. The Shanghai Stock Exchange ranked the world's third largest in terms of its amount of transaction and financing, while the amount of transaction of Shanghai Futures Exchange topped the world. Both the container volume throughput of Yangshan Port and Wai Gaoqiao Port and cargo volume of Pudong International Airport ranked the world's third largest in 2009. Its functional zone as world economic center, financial center and shiping center took shape and its role as a leader and window for China's reform and opening up could not be changed.

However, it should also be noted that there was a wide gap between Pudong and other world financial shipping and economic centers. The above mentioned functions mostly relied on artificial support, but the level of radiation and cohesion capability remained inadequate as a finance shipping and economic center. Pudong was short of a mature and stable system which could promote its economic development, and government management level and efficiency of service still needed to be enhanced. There was a long way to go before giving services to the whole nation.

Pudong faced both challenges and opportunities in its further development. Only when Pudong turned its slogan of "serving the whole nation and facing to the world" into concrete actions could it develop further.

6.1 The General Situation of Pudong New District Before Development

Pudong New District is located on the east bank of the Huangpu River in the eastern part of Shanghai. The land is in a marginal fan-like pattern in the Yangtze River Delta, hence how it got its named. At the binding point of the T-structure, formed by the gold coastline of China and golden waterway of the Yangtze River, Pudong New District faces the Pacific, has the East China Sea on the east, borders Yangtze River to the north and is backed by the developed Yangtze River Delta with capacious neighbors and ideal geographic location. It is one major gateway for the world economy to the Chinese market and a bridge between China and the world. Pudong New District has a long history and is rich in natural and cultural resources.

Before exploitation, the economy of Pudong had always lagged behind Puxi. Although its area was roughly equivalent to that of Puxi, its population and GNP was only about one tenth of Shanghai, hence the saying "(People) want a bed in Puxi rather than a house in Pudong." There were many reasons for its lagging behind, but the principal reason was its poor transportation. The Huangpu River was wide and deep, making it an important wharf, but divided Shanghai between Pudong and Puxi. In addition, Shanghai City was not located near the sea and it was very hard to build bridges or bore tunnels due to limitation of technology and economic development.

As for the improvemnt of technology, the traffic bottleneck, which had restricted Pudong from developing, gradually disappeared and its geographic location and space advantages began to be revealed. Meanwhile, Shanghai, the metropolis of China with a long history and strong economy, technological and cultural power and developed transportation, backed Pudong with surpports in material, manpower and technological resources. Therefore, comparing to other cities in China, Pudong possesed incomparable strategic advantages in nature, economy and culture.

6.1.1 The General Situation of Pudong New District[470]

6.1.1.1 Geological Conditions

Pudong New District was located between 30.820 and 31.2322 degrees northern latitude, 121.2718 and 121.4843 degrees eastern longitude before Nanhui District was incorporated into Pudong New District in 2009, with an area of 533.45 square kilometers. Pudong New District was located next to the mouth of the Yangtze River in the east, bordered by Nanhui District and Minhang District in the south and faced Xuhui, Luwan, Huangpu, Hongkou, Yangpu, Baoshan district across the river in the west and north. The bank line of Yangtze River and Huangpu River in the district respectively was 46.43 km and 43.5 km. On April 24, 2009, the state council approved the "Request for Revoking the Organizational System of Nanhui District and Assigning it into Pudong New District" and agreed to revoke Nanhui District and assign it into Pudong New District. Since then, the area of Pudong New District reached 1210.41 square kilometers, with Hangzhou Bay in the south and facinf Ningbo, Zhejiang Province across the sea.

The stratum of Pudong New District was caused by an alluvial deposit of the Yangtze River. It was high-lying in the southeast and low-lying in the northwest. The ground was 3.5m to 4.5m high, and some places even higher than 5m, while the mean altitude was about 4m, the same as one part of the low flat Jianghai Plain. Pudong New District was characterized with a network of waters. There were over 9,400 riverways within its border, accounting for 10% to 12% of the whole area. The major eleven rivers were Huangpu River, Chuanyang River, Bailianjing, Gaoqiao Port, Pudong Canal, etc. The Huangpu River was 80 km long, 400 m wide and 7-9 m deep. Chuanyang River was 28.8 km long, 44-45 m wide and 3 m deep.[471] The entire primary Nanhui District was an alluvial plain 4-4.5 m above the sea level. Its coastal line was 59.5 km long and the major rivers were Daye River,

---

470 For vertical comparation, the information about Pudong New District in this section not include the Nanhui district unless specially state (on 24th, April, 2009, the state council approved the "Request for revoking the organizational system of Nanhui District and assigning it into Pudong New District" and agreed to revoke Nanhui district and assign it into Pudong New District.) hereinafter, Pudong New District includes original Nanhui disrict is called New Pudong or New Pudong New District. In this article, data of 2009 include original Nanhui district

471 Partial data are from *"Statistical Yearbook of Pudong New District, Shanghai"* China statistical publishing house, 1st edition, 2000, p.12.

Pudong Canal, Lema River and so on.

Located in the coastal zone with prevalent East Asian monsoons, both Pudong New District and original Nanhui District experienced maritime climate. It blew southeast wind in the summer and northwest wind in the winter. The area experienced four seasons with abundant rainfalls and light and moderate temperature. The primary characters of its climate were as follows: warm spring, hot summer, cool autumn and cold winter. Most rainfalls occured in the hot season.

6.1.1.2 The Beginning of Pudong New District and Administrative Division

Most areas of Pudong New District were formed relatively late, with a history of only about 1300 years. The sands carried upstream from the Yangtze River speded up their sedimentation because of the meeting of river and sea, and so enlarged the area of shoal lands and naturally promoted the coastal line to extend outward since the fourth century. In addition, coastal residents constantly embanked on the beach for their living and development, causing the coastal line to move east. In the six hundred years between the fourth century and the tenth century, the coastal line of Shanghai moved 20 km to the east. Some places of Pudong took shape just in this period and many early migrant villages appeared.

The history of Pudong New District (located in Chuansha County) can be traced back to Datong in the first year of the Liang Dynasty (535) in the period of the North and South Dynasty. Kunshan County, which belonged to Xinyi County, were set up at that time. The ancient Chuansha was the sea frontier opened up from wasteland by soldiers. It belonged to Huating County in the tenth year of Tang Tianbao (751) and subordinated to Nanhui and Shanghai County since the third year of Yongzheng (1725), Qing Dynasty. In the fifteenth year of Jiaqing (1810), the government separated it from Shanghai and Nanhui County and established it as Chuansha FuminDepartment. The department was changed into a county of Jiangsu Province during the Revolution of 1911. Twenty nine villages were separated from Nanhui to Chuansha in 1950. In 1958, Chuansha was marked out of Jiangsu Province and was under the Jurisdiction of Shanghai City. In 1961, all the countries of Pudong County, which existed for only two years, were marked into Chuansha, while the Gaomiao Region by the Huangpu River was incorporated into the Yangpu District. In 1984, Tangqiao, Lujiazui and Yangjing regions by the Huangpu River were again marked into Huangpu District, while Zhuojiadu to Yangsi Regions along the river were incorporated into Nanshi District. The area of the county in 1985 was twice that before the founding of PRC.

According to the official approval of the State Council, (State Letter [1992] No.145),

Shuansha County was revoked and Pudong New District was established on October 11, 1992. The administration area of Pudong New District included previous Chuansha County, Sanlin countryside of Shanghai County and some areas of original Huangpu, Nanshi and Yangpu District. In January 1993, Pudong New District was officially established. In March of the same year, original Xipu Road of Yangpu district, Zhoujiadu, Tangqiao, Nanmatou and Shanggang New Village Street, as well as the Sanlin countryside and Pudong Region of Huangpu District were officially marked into Pudong New District. With the approval of Shanghai Municipal People's Government, Pudong International Airport region of Nanhui County, with a area of 10.7 square kilometers, was incorporated into Pudong New District, increasing its legal land area from 522.75 square kilometers to 533.45 square kilometers. In 2003, the shoal out of People's Pond was marked into Pudong New District and its total area reached 569.57 square kilometres. Until the end of 2003, Pudong New District managed eleven streets and thirteen towns.[472] On April 24, 2009, the State Council replied to the "Request for Revoking the Organizational System of Nanhui District and Mark the Administrative Area of Nanhui into Pudong New District" and agreed to cancel Nanhui District and incorporate it into Pudong New District. After the adjustment, Pudong New District had an area of 1210.41 square kilometers with thirteen streets and twenty five towns.

6.1.2 The Economy of Pudong District before Development

6.1.2.1 The Economic and Social Survey of Pudong before Development

The Western colonialists launched the Opium Wars between 1840 and 1842. In August 1842, the United Kingdom forced the Qing Government to sign the Jiangning Treaty and opened Shanghai as one of the five treaty ports. A self-sufficient, natural economy predominated in Shanghai before 1900. During the forty years after its liberation, Pudong has made progress in its economy, but still lagged behind Puxi. Only one-half of Shanghai was, to some extent, developed.

In April, 1990, the CPC Central Committee and the State Council approved the development plan of Pudong, and gave official approval to the development programming of Pudong New District in June 1990. It can be said that Pudong had the largest land area of all Chinese coastal regions with great development potential before 1990. According to the statistics of 1990, Pudong New District had a population of 1.3394 million and its GDP, total investment in fixed assets, gross retail sales and per capita GDP were respectively

472 Resources, Administrative Division Website (http://www.xzqh.org/html/sh/0106.html)

6.024 billion yuan (current price), 1.415 billion yuan, 1.428 billion yuan, 4998 billion yuan which respectively accounted for 10.4%, 8.1%, 6.2% and 77.13% of Shanghai. About the composition of the GDP of Pudong New District in 1990, the primary industry, second industry and tertiary industry were 0.222 billion yuan, 4.589 billion yuan and 1.213 billion yuan, respectively, and accounted for 3.7%, 76.2% and 20.1% respectively of the GDP of Pudong New District. The proportion of the third industries were 4%, 65% and 31% respectively in the GDP of Shanghai. It was obvious that the second industry of Pudong New District accounted more than that of Shanghai, while its tertiary industry took less shares than the average level of Shanghai.[473]

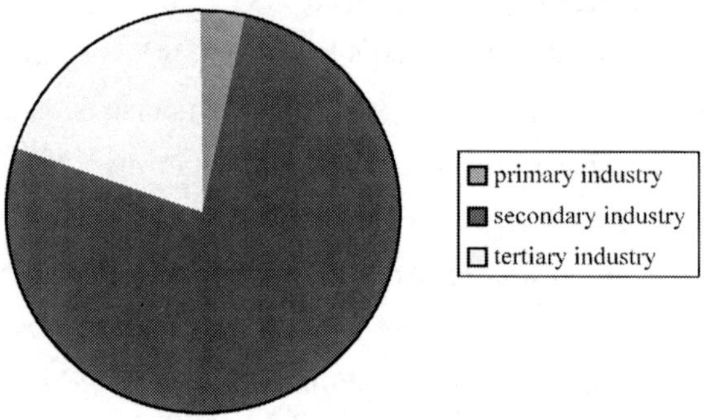

Figure Three industries of the GDP of Pudong New District in 1990

Resources: Statistical Yearbook of Pudong New District, Shanghai, China Statistic Press, 1994.

6.1.2.2 The Agriculture of Pudong before Development

The statistics of 1990 indicate that the land area of Pudong New District was 522.75 square kilometers (before 2000) and, the area of land under cultivation was 231.98 square kilometers, sharing 44% if the total land area of Pudong and 7.2% of Shanghai. Each rural population of Pudong New District had 0.74mu land under cultivation, on average, and each rural labor had 1.26mu land under cultivation, which were lower than the average levels of Shanghai with 1.16mu and 1.94mu. The output of the primary industry of Pudong New District was 0.22 billion yuan in 1990, sharing 3.7% of its GDP, less than the average level of Shanghai with 4%.

The agriculture of Pudong gave priority to animal husbandry and farm production before development. Its fishery and animal husbandry were relatively developed. The animal husbandry output accounted for 53% of the total agricultural output, well higher

473 Partial data resources, *Statistical Yearbook of Pudong New District, Shanghai"* China statistical publishing house, 1994; *Statistical Yearbook of Shanghai*, 1991

than that of farm production and the average level of Shanghai in 1990. One important characteristic of its agriculture was its obvious extraversion.[474] From the proportion of agricultural and sideline product exports in total commodity exports, the agriculture of Pudong New District was more export-oriented. The amount of agriculture and sideline products of Shanghai reached 0.661 billion USD in 1990, accounting for 12.5% of the total merchandise exports.

6.1.2.3 The Second Industry of Pudong before Development

The modern industry of Pudong grew after 1990. According to Chuansha Records, Shen Yuqing opened the first modern loomed towel factory in Chuansha, Pudong in 1900. During the 1920s and 1930s, the development of towel and textile industry put the clothing industry and embroidery industry in motion. Meanwhile, the modern brewing industry, food-processing industry and building industry also made a certain progress.

After the liberation of Shanghai, the state had invested and set up a batch of key enterprises, mainly on heavy industries along the Huangpu River in the 1950s and 1960s, forming the pillar industries of petrochemical industry, shipbuilding and repairing, metallurgy machinery, light industry and textile industry, etc. At the end of the 1970s, rural enterprises suddenly rose with the reform and opening up. After many years development since the liberation, the industries of Pudong New District possessed a confident foundation, but the industrial structure was unreasonable and inconsonant with its later positioning. Firstly, the heavy industries of Pudong District were relatively developed, accounting for 59% of the total outputs, higher than the average level of Shanghai with 48.15%, but the modern manufacturing and high-tech enterprises fell behind. Secondly, according to the strategic objectives of Shanghai's economic development, itsecured its role as the national economic trade and financial center, as well as the leader of the economies along the Yangtze River. Therefore, it was necessary to adjust its industrial structure to fit its target position.[475]

6.1.2.4 The Tertiary Industry of Pudong before Development

The tertiary industry of Pudong District greatly lagged behind, especially the modern service industry with sectors such as training, touring and information consultant. The

---

474 Chen Longting, Sun Zhongyi, Development Strategy and Programming Concept for Pudong New District's Export-oriented Agriculture, Shagnhai Agricultural Technology, 2nd, 1994.

475 Partial data resources, *Statistical Yearbook of Pudong New District, Shanghai"* China statistical publishing house,1994; *Statistical Yearbook of Shanghai*,1991

finance and insurance industry, the core of modern economy, were just beginning in Pudong District before its exploitation. There was no large financial institution in Pudong District before development, and most financial services were operated through financial institutions in Puxi District. At the end of 1990, the deposit outstanding and loan balance of the whole district was 3.7 billion yuan and 2.8 billion yuan, only a small percentage of that of Shanghai City.

In the tertiary industry of Pudong District, the commerce, catering and tertiary industry took more shares, but only operated in Pudong District with small radiation, and their quality and scale were far behind that of Puxi District.[476]

6.1.3 Development Advantages of Pudong District

6.1.3.1 Superior Geographic Location

Globally, Shanghai is located in the most dynamic "economic corridor" in Asia. The corridor started from Tokyo, through Seoul, to Shanghai, and down south to Taipei, Hongkong, Bangkok, Kuala and Lumpur, and ended at Singapore.[477]All cities in the corridor are dynamic regional economic centers and engines for driving regional development and hubs for connecting internally and externally, while Shanghai was located in the middle of the "economic corridor" of Asia. Domestically, the most developed region of China is the binding places between seas and rivers, while Shanghai is just located in the golden junction site of the "T-character." From a geographic point of view, Shanghai has the possibility to became the major city for the exchanges between China and the world, as well as the regional economic center in the area of Yangtze River. The development of Pudong itself is key for promoting Shanghai and fulfilling this unique function.

Pudong New District adjoins the downtown of Shanghai. Close to the Yangtze River and Huangpu River, it becomes an important gateway of the Yangtze River with favorable conditions for building a port and water transportation. The environment is preferable because of its flat terrain and upwind location. The average population density was low, with about 2,562 per square kilometers in Pudong New District before exploitation. The superior geographic conditions laid a good foundation for its development.

---

476 Data in the 4th part of this section Mao Wu, *Papers on the research of Pudong's economic development, industry department*, Shanghai Far East Press, 1st Edition,1997, P.1-25

477 Zhao Qizheng edited, New Century, New Pudong, Fudan University Press,1994, P. 3

6.1.3.2 Broad Geographical Space

The area of Pudong New District is 569.57 square kilometers, twice that of Shanghai old urban district with 149 square kilometers. Pudong New District is next to the sea and thus has growing tidal flat resources to prepare the land for development. Facing Puxi District across the Huangpu River and its location near the Yangtze River and ocean makes Pudong District suitable for developing export oriented economy with the world's resources in the background of globalization, and then to become the hub for exchanges between Chinese economy and the world's economy.

6.1.3.3 Favorable Conditions for Building Port

Port construction is very important to the development of Shanghai. In addition to the port at the east bank of Huangpu River, the WaiGaoqiao Port is 15 km west of the Wusong Mouth, and 25 km away from the downtown crossing Huangpu River. With a stable beach strand and 1.5 km from the shore, on average, with minus 10 meter depth, Pudong District possesses very good conditions for port construction.

6.1.3.4 A Relatively Well Founded Economy

The economy of Pudong New District has made considerable progress before exploitation, which laid the economic foundation for its later development. Comparing to agriculture and the tertiary industry, the second industry was relatively developed. In 1990, the third industries of Shanghai took share of 4%, 65%, and 31% in its GDP, respectively. The proportion of Pudong's second industry in its GDP was obviously higher than that of Shanghai. The character of extraversion of its economy was obvious. Either in introducing foreign investment or in foreign trade, Pudong New District had made some progress before its development, which laid foundations for later opening up.

6.1.3.5 Powerful Backing

Pudong District, one part of Shanghai, closely neighbors the downtown with a river in between. The development and opening of Pudong District is one part of the strategy of revitalizing Shanghai, and the strong economic, technological and cultural foundation of Shanghai provided Pudong with powerful backing. Shanghai used to be the biggest international financial center in the Far East and had a strong tradition of opening up. Between 1860 and 1930, Shanghai accounted for 68% of China's total exports, on average. Until 1947, there were 14 foreign banks, 128 state owned or private domestic banks, 13 trust and investment corporations and 79 bourses.

After the liberation, the economy of Shanghai also made definite progress. In 1990, its GDP reached 75.645 billion yuan; the primary industry, second industry and tertiary industry accounted for 4% 65% and 31%m, respectively. The second industry dominated the economy, the tertiary industry grew and Shanghai stepped into the middle term of industrialization.

Shanghai also had tremendous education and scientific research resources. In 1990, there were 1,053 science and technology institutions, divided into 300 scientific research units, 383 large and medium enterprises and 370 colleges and universities. The research funding of the same year reached 2.1 billion yuan, with 1,526 patent applications.

The economy of Shanghai had close international connections. In 1990, its total import and export commodities reached 7.431 billion USD, accounting for 47% of the GDP with 75.645 billion yuan (one dollar equals 4.7832 yuan). Besides economic connection, there were numerous overseas offices. Shanghai was also an important destination for foreign tourists.[478]

6.2 The Founding of Pudong New District

On April 18,1990, Li Peng, the then-Premier of the State Council, annouced to carry out policies for an economic and technical development zone and some special zones in Pudong on behalf of The CPC Central Committee and the State Council, marking a new phase and historic period for China's opening up.[479] The development and opening up of Pudong New District occured at the historic binding point of spreading the strategy of reform and opening up from south to north and east to west. It occured at the historic crucial time of all-around opening in the 1990s from the trial opening in the 1980s. The opening and development of Pudong showed China's resolution to reform and open-up to the world. Therefore, its opening and development had an important position and meaning in the national development strategy, opening a new page for China's reform and opening up. With a profound background, it was inevitable to open Pudong during the deepening of the reform and opening up. By 18 years' development, Pudong New District had made tremendous changes and become a renowned newlyopenned and modern city, with multiple

---

478 Partial data resources, *Statistical Yearbook of Pudong New District, Shanghai"* China statistical publishing house, 1994; *Statistical Yearbook of Shanghai*, 1991

479 People's Daily, 1st edition on April 19, 1990

functions in the world.

6.2.1 The Background of Establishing Pudong New District

6.2.1.1 The Reform and Opening up of China and the Development of Pudong

(a) The Deepening of Economic Restructuring Created Favorable Political Enviroment

The economic and political environment of China had been greatly changed after the reform and development in the 1980s, thus provided a favorable environmental and economic foundation for Pudong's development and opening up. China's reform adopted the thinking of gradual reformation, which was known as "crossing the river by feeling the stones," and most special economic zones, the experimental plots for exploring the reform, were set up in undeveloped southern locations with a low proportion of state owned economy. After many year's trial, it was required to deepen the reform. Pudong was located in relatively developed Shanghai, with high proportion of state owned economy. Its opening and development was the embodiment of this requirement. In short, the reform and development in the 1980s laid a solid foundation for Pudong's opening and development and created a very favorable environment and opportunity. As the economic restructuring deepened in China, the strategic center of reform and opening up gradually moved to relatively developed places in the Yangtze River areas, creating a valued opportunity for Pudong's development and opening up.

(b) The Development and Opening of Pudong was a Specific Reflection of the Regional Development Strategy for Opening up

The CPC Central Committee had made the guiding principle of opening up to first focus on opening coastal regions, then spreading to interior areas in the early 1980s (the early days of China's opening up). According to this guideline, the government divided opening regions into four levels: Special Economic Zone, Coastal and Open City, Coastal Open Economic Zones and Interior Areas.

The Special Economic Zone policy, with the character of testing and giving priority to the development of some regions, had some historic meaning at a fixed time, but it had its limits. Firstly, it would affect the impartiality and fairness of the market and eventually influence the effectiveness of resource allocation. It could not maintain sustainable development of the economy. Secondly, regional competitive advantages created by the policy would cause an imbalance between different regional economies and go against political stability. Therefore, the opening and development of Pudong was an important part of the strategy of transferring the center of opening up to the Yangtze River Delta from the Pearl River Delta.

In the process of transferring the center of opening up, Shanghai became the leader and center of opening up, with its unique geographic location, historical traditions and superiority in material, technology and talent resources. Therefore, Shanghai had the possibility of becoming the economic, trade and financial center of China, or even of the world, with the advantage of combining domestic and foreign markets. In the final analysis, the development and opening of Shagnhai was to change, inorder to become an economic center of the world, while all economic activities occurred in a certain space and Pudong District became the best choice for attracting the world's economic activities, thanks to its neighboring Shanghai downtown and the Bund where numerous financial institutions gathered before the founding of the PRC.[480]

(c) Specific Historical Background for the Timing of Pudong's Development and Opening up

In 1990, the CPC Central Committee decided to develop and open-up Pudong District. The timing of this had close relations to a specific political and economic environment. Many countries imposed economic sanctions on China after the political disturbance in 1989. Some that introduced investment began to withdraw from China and new investments were reluctant to flow to China due to political or economic reasons, as well as the doubt on the continuity of China's political and economic policies. The amount of foreign investment began to slow down.

It was essential to carry out corresponding measures to eliminate foreign doubts on the continuity of China's reform and opening up. Chinese leader Deng Xiaoping said, "The world now worries about our hesitation. We have to do something to show that the policy of our reform and opening up will not change, but further open."[481] Deng Xiaoping seized this historical opportunity, correctly assessed the situation and made the comprehensive decision to spread the reform and opening up to the Yangtze River Delta, to Shanghai, the economic center of China and to Pudong.[482] In early 1990, Deng Xiaoping visited Shagnhai and expressed his concern of the preparation of developing Pudong. He said to the central leaders after returning to Beijing, "I have already retired, but I have to ask you

---

480 Partial data of this part from Yao Xiye, Creating Glory-theory summary for Pudong's Opening up in Five Years, Shanghai Academy of Social Sciences, 1st edition,1995, P.7

481 Deng Xiaoping, *Deng Xiaoping Anthology* 3rd volume, People's Publishing House, first edition, 1993, P.313.

482 Zhao Qizheng, Logic of Pudong-the Opening of Pudong and Economic Globalization, Shanghai: The Joint Publishing Company Ltd., 2007, p. 8-9.

to pay more attention on the development of Pudong."[483] He also mentioned that if the government set Pudong as an Special Economic Zone in the early 1980s and had developed Pudong earlier "the influences would be huge. It is not only Pudong's problem, but a problem concerning the development of Shanghai, concerning the development of the Yangtze River Delta and Yangtze River areas." From the economic development strategy point of view, the opening and development of Pudong was a significant adjustment in balancing regional economic development. Politically, it showed China's resolution to unswervingly carrying out the reform and opening up to the world, with symbolic significance.

6.2.1.2 The Economic Development of Shanghai and Pudong's Opening up

With a superior geographic location and natural conditions, Shanghai quickly developed from a small fishing village to the biggest economic, trade and financial center of the Far East since its opening as an international trade port in 1843. After the founding of the PRC, the economy of Shanghai made some achievements, but had very severe problems. In general, Shanghai made great contributions in national economic development, but injured its self-development after the founding of PRC. Shanghai's economic development fell behind those of southern open cities in the 1980s, seriously restricting its further development. Under these conditions, Shanghai had to rethink its development target and function position and find a new development philosophy to guide its comprehensive reform and adjustment, as well as getting its economic development out of trouble and revitalizing Shanghai. Ultimately, Shanghai positioned its development targets on the international economic, trade and financial center, and chose Pudong as the carrier for the described centers. Thus, the development and opening of Pudong was not only a problem concerning expanding urban space and building a new city, but also an important measure to restructuring the economy and functions of Shanghai and revitalizing Shanghai, as well as driving the economic development and restructuring of the Yangtze River areas.[484]

6.2.2 The Founding of Pudong New District

Throughout history, many politicians have pondered over the development of Pudong, proposed far-reached assumptions and made numerous attempts, but the development of

483 Edited by CPC Shanghai working Committee for the Opening of Pudong New District and Management Committee of Pudong New District, Ten Years Development in Pudong, Shanghai Far East Press, 1st edition, 2000, P. 3

484 Data from *Statistical Yearbook of Pudong New District, Shanghai"* and *Statistical Yearbook of Shanghai* of relevant years unless specially state.

Pudong was only as aspiration, due to the economic and political limits at that time. The development of Pudong in its true sense started in the 1990s. Between April 15 and 18, 1990, Premier Lipeng paid a visit to Shanghai. On the fifth anniversary of Shanghai Volkswagen Automotive Company Ltd on April 18, he solemnly announced to the world that "the CPC Central Committee and the State Council recently decided to open the Pudong area and carry out policies of economic and technical development zone and some special zones in Pudong. This is another important layout for deepening reform and opening up. We welcome foreign enterprises and compatriots from Hong Kong and Macao, and overseas countrymen to invest in Pudong. We promise to provide preferential conditions for cooperation and improving investment environments."[485]

6.2.2.1 Assumptions and Practices of Pudong before the Founding of PRC

In early 20th century, Li Pingshu, Huang Yanpei and other local gentries of Pudong proposed the developing of Pudong by building a railway in Pudong. Sun Yat-sen later explicitly and systematically advanced the assumption of Pudong's development. He paid a visit to Shanghai and noticed the superior geographic location of Pudong. Sun Yat-sen described the grand blueprint of developing Pudong and imagined to build it into a large oriental port in his "General Plan for Founding a State" in 1919. Then, years after he put forward his expectation of building Pudong into a large oriental port, he drew up "Grand Shanghai Plan" and listed Pudong in the plan again.

Perceptive people of the Kuomintang Government of China (KMT) also noticed the problem of developing Pudong. KMT Shanghai Municipal Government put forward the proposal of building a grand port area in Pudong near the Wusong Mouth, building a new 30 square km town in southeastern region of Pudong to the south of the Huangpu River and building a new 60 square km town to the northeast and southeast of LuJiazui in the "Grand Shagnhai Plan" at that time. In 1945, KMT established the Urban Planning Commission with a special River Crossing Committee which was responsible for creating solutions for crossing the Huangpu River and resolving traffic problems for the development of Pudong.

6.2.2.2 Pudong Development Assumption between the Founding of the PRC and Third Plenary Session of the Eleventh Central Committee of the CPC

Shanghai was liberalized in May 1949. ChenYi, the first mayor of Shanghai, had

485 People's Daily, 1st edition on 19th, April, 1990

thought of developing Pudong, but had no time to give consideration to it because the most important thing for the new regime was to recover the economy and set up new political and economic orders when it was unstable. As the economy developed, experts in the Urban Planning Department of Shanghai Municipal Government raised the issue of developing Pudong many times after the founding of the PRC and formulated the blueprint of expanding downtown Shanghai to the east of the river in 1953, 1958 and 1963. However, all attempts failed due to the fact that realistic requirement of developing productions overwhelmed the long term interests of the city. Several years before Pudong's opening, Shanghai handed in one sixth of the national revenue to the treasury, but had no enough money for its urban construction. Therefore, the development of Pudong had not been effectively implemented and fell behind Puxi for several decades.

6.2.2.3 Pudong Development Assumption after the Third Plenary Session of the Eleventh Central Committee of the CPC

Shortly after the Third Plenary Session of the Eleventh Central Committee, the CPC Central Committee laid emphasis to economic construction and adopted the policy of reform and opening up, gradually stepping out of the semi-closed or closed state into the world again. As the emancipation of people's mind and the adjustment of development thinking began, as well as the demonstration effect of the reform and opening up in Shenzhen and other special economic zones, the passions to develop and open Pudong began to surface. Consequently, the opening of Pudong came up on the agenda and Shanghai began to think about the local strategy of redeveloping Shanghai.

In Feburary 1980, Infrastructure Situation and the internal briefing of Shanghai Municipal Construction Committee published the proposal of Chen Kunlong, engineer of Shanghai Planning Bureau, upon establishing a new downtown in Pudong. Research thinking of developing Pudong had made significant progress in mid-1980s. Some scholars put forward the idea of founding a special economic zone in Pudong and building Wai Gaoqiao port to be a free port zone from the position of system innovation. Research about Pudong's development began among the people, while the government was simultaneously studying and demonstrating the development of Pudong. On the strategic seminars for Shanghai's economic development held in September 1984, Shanghai Municipal Government and research group of redeveloping Shanghai from the State Council published the "Reporting Outline on the Economic Development Strategy of Shanghai" which described three plans: going down to the south, up to the north or to the east. Here, going to the east referred to developing Pudong and remolding the modern international metropolis.

The outline was officially approved by the State Council in Feburary 1985. The plans for developing Pudong in 1986tended to be very grand and Shanghai Municipal Government reported the Shanghai Urban Planning to the CPC Central Committee and the State Council on April 2, 1986 and reported the Shanghai Master Planning (revised version) to the CPC Central Committee and the State Council on July 22, 1986. The State Council approved the revised planning and again laid stress on building Shanghai to be one of the main economic, trade and financial centers in the Western Pacific. The official reply of the State Council fully affirmed the development direction of Shanghai and the assumption of spreading to the east and the development of Pudong.

To implement the important instructions of the State Council, Shanghai Municipal Government organized an united advisory group of domestic and foreign professionals for developing Pudong in June 1987. Entrusted by the Shanghai Municipal Government, Shanghai municipal committee of Jiu San Society, Tongji University and Shanghai Urban Planning Design Institute, consecutively submitted "General Plan of Developing Pudong New District," "Summing-up Report of the Development Pattern of Modern Pudong District," and "Outline for the Development of Economy, Science, Society and Culture of Pudong New Area." In the same year, Shanghai Planning Bureau worked out the Pudong New District Planning Outline (draft) and relevant preliminary plans on the base of the works of the advisory group.

Shanghai Municipal Peoples' Government held the "International Symposium for the Developing of Pudong New District" in Xijiao Guesthouse Hotel in Shanghai between May 2 and 4, 1988 and over 140 domestic and foreign experts attended this conference.[486] In the conference, over 40 experts also made excellent speeches and put forward many constructive proposals for Pudong's development. These suggestions played an active role in the research and development of Pudong. The conference at the end came up with the guideline of "combining old urban transformation and building a modern new district".[487]

After this conference, research occuring before its development sped up. Shanghai Municipal Government set up a leading group for the development of Pudong New District, headed by two deputy mayors (as group leader and deputy head). Zhu Rongji, then-mayor of Shanghai, made several on-the-spot investigations and held many on-site meetings in Pudong. On June 20, 1988, Zhu Rongji sent important information to American businessmen

---

486 Su Dongbin edit, *Brief History of China's Special Economic Zone*, Guangdong Economy Press, 2001, P. 524-525

487 Su Dongbin edit, *Brief History of China's Special Economic Zone*, Guangdong Economy Press, 2001, P. 524-525

in the seminar for industrial trade and economic development between China and the United States held in Beijing: "Shanghai will build the second Huangpu River Bridge and other projects in succession, further improving its transportation and communication facilities, and build Pudong New District into an economic trading center and export processing zone which will lay stress on introducing foreign investment with more preferential policies."

In September 1988, Jiang Zemin, Zhu Rongji, Wang Daohan and other Shanghai leaders made a special report to the Central Committee on the preparation for the opening of Pudong and obtained agreement in principle and a series of specific instructions from the Central Committee. After their return to Shanghai, they immediately organized the leading group and office for developing Pudong and assigned two deputy mayors as the group leader and deputy head. In early 1989, under the instruction of mayor Zhu Rongji, Shanghai Urban Planning Department listed the local planning for several key regions of Pudong into the work plans and necessarily accelerating the planning works for Pudong's development. In August of the same year, When Zhu Rongji made an inspection tour of the land and water conditions for building a grand oriental port, he pointed out that the first tasks were to develop Waigaoqiao regions and set up a new port and electric power plant, plus the Nanmatou Ningguo Road and other river-crossing projects. Once these projects were finished, the whole of Pudong would be revitalized.

On February 26, 1990, the Shanghai Municipal Party Committee and Municipal Peoples' Government handed in the "Request for Developing Pudong" to the CPC Central Committee and the State Council. On March 28 and April 8 of the same year, Vice Premire Yao Yilin, authorized by General Secretary Jiang Zemin and Premire Li Peng, came to Shagnhai with leaders of Special Economic Zone Office of the State Council, Planning Committee of the State, Ministry of Finance, Central Peoples' Bank, Ministry of Foreign Trade, Ministry of Commerce and Bank of China to study and evaluate the issue of opening Pudong. Six subgroups including special zone, investment, public finance, foreign trade, commerce and finance made detailed reports to relevant departments of the State Council since the afternoon of March 29. After five days worth of hard work, significant progresses were made in the assumption, policy design, fund-raising and other aspects. After an intensive study and exchange of views, comrades of the Central Committee from Beijing drafted the report outline of several questions on the development of Shanghai to CPC Central Committee and the State Council. Premier Li Peng held an executive meeting of the State Council to listen to Yao Yilin's special report on the development and opening of Pudong on April 10, after his return to Beijing and considered every question of the development and opening up. On April 12, the CPC Central Committee General Secretary Jiang Zemin held a meeting of the Political Bureau and agreed to the Development Planning of Pudong District handed by the State Council in principle.

Premier Li Peng made an inspection tour of Shagnhai between April 15 and 18, 1990. Li Peng inspected Pudong New District in the morning and listened to the working report of Shanghai City and assumption of developing Pudong in the afternoon of April 15. He made an important speech after hearing the report. He said, "Comrade Yi Lin made a report to the executive meeting of the State Council after his return to Beijing. We have discussed it in a meeting and also reported to the Politburo Standing Committee. We all agree the 'Developing Pudong and Opening up' in principle The CPC Central Committee and the State Council have a feeling that they should lay emphasis to the development of Shanghai. From Shanghai's point of view, it is necessary to develop Pudong because Puxi District is already filled to capacity. Which way shall we adopt in developing Pudong? Firstly we should take the advantages of Shanghai, which are the relatively well-off basic industries, relatively strong technological power, high management level and starting point. In addition, (Shanghai should) develop an export oriented economy and introduce foreign investment to the best of its ability and then share with overseas markets."[488]

After repeated arguments, the CPC Central Committee and the State Council officially made the decision of opening and developing Pudong on April 18, 1990. On the fifth anniversary of Shanghai Volkswagen Automotive Company Ltd on April 18, Premier Li Peng announced to carry out policies of the economic and technical development zone and some special zones in Pudong and emphasized that it was a significant arrangement of deepening the reform and opening up. Both the Central Committee and local places would give support to the development of Pudong. The development of Shanghai would promote the economic development of Shanghai and marked a new phase of China's reform and opening up.

6.2.3 The Strategic Positioning, Opinion and Significance of Opening Pudong

6.2.3.1 Strategic Positioning of Opening Pudong

There was foundational difference between the positioning of Pudong's opening up and other Special Economic Development in the 1980s.[489] Shenzhen, Zhuhai, Shantou and

488 Liberation Daily, 1st edition, 18th

489 Zhou Yupeng, Tracing back for the root and Looking forward- Writing New Chapter for Pudong's Development in the New Century, Pudong Development Report, 2001, P. 1-10

other special economic zones carried the character of experimentation and the basic thoughts of the reform in the late 1970s, which was "crossing the river by feeling the stones" with great exploration. It was known as firstly carrying out the reform in some experimental units, drawing lesions and experiences afterward, then popularizing it. Establishment of a special economic zone was just the first phase of experimentation, while Pudong's opening up was one part of nation-wide reform and opening up on the basis of drawing lessons from the past ten years. In April 1990, the CPC Central Committee and the State Council decided to open Pudong and listed it as the key place for China's reform and opening up for the following ten years. They hoped to find a new way of reforming large cities by opening Pudong, revitalizing the development of Shanghai and realizing the magnificent objective of "one leader, three centers," leading the economic upswing of the very developed Yangtze River area and the economic, trade and financial center.

Deng Xiaoping made brilliant expositions on the positioning of Pudong's opening up during his visit to Shanghai. He said, "Opening Pudong will have great influence. It is not only a question of Pudong, but a question of developing Shanghai, a question of developing the Yangtze River Delta and Yangtze River area based on Shanghai." The finance is the core of modern economy. It is very important. One correct move may win the game. Shanghai used to be a financial center, a place of freely exchanging currencies. China will firstly rely on Shanghai to obtain an international position in financing. It will take many years, and we shall do it from now on."[490]

From the exposition of Deng Xiaoping, it can be found that the target of opening Pudong was not simply building a new town or revitalizing Shanghai's economy, but recovering Shanghai's position as a financial and trade center in China, and even the world, and further motoring the economic development of the Yangtze River Delta and areas with its advantages in geographic location, talents, technology and culture, as well as the tradition of being an international economic, trade and financial center. Therefore, the opening of Pudong needed to start from the needs of further opening up and the socialist market economic development. The aim of building Shanghai to be one of the international economic, financial and trade centers embodied the great expectations of Deng Xiaoping and other Chinese leaders to promote Shanghai's development by opening Pudong. It was also the objective needs of economic development between late 20th century and the beginning of the 21st century since the reform that embodied their expectations.

According to the above strategic positioning of Pudong's opening up, Pudong was

---

490 Deng Xiaoping, *Deng Xiaoping Anthology* 3rd volume, People's Publishing House, 2004, P. 366-367.

to give priority to the development of its tertiary industry, centering on finance, trade and high-tech industries invested by multinational corporations, forging the urban functions of a modern international center pillared by the tertiary industry group, including finance and trade. It was a need to build a new town with modern economic urban functions in Pudong and promote Shanghai to be an international center which gave service to the whole country and prepared itself for the future. The development of Pudong should not only be the leader in economic construction, but also play the leading demonstration role in establishing the socialist market economy, constructing the socialist material and spiritual civilization, social comprehensive progress and other aspects. The Fourteenth Party Congress explicitly put forward the economic development strategy of taking the opening up of Pudong, with Shanghai as the leader, and building Shanghai to one of the international economic, financial and trade centers, as well as giving incentive to the economic upswing of the Yangtze River areas. In the 15 big reports, General Secretary Jiang Zemin again asked for a further improvement of the special economic zones and the Pudong New District. He said, "Be a leader in system innovation, industrial upgrading and opening up and play the demonstration, influential and leading role."

The development of Pudong was world-class. The short term development goal of the New District, at first, was to realized the urbanization in 100 square kilometers of rural areas before 2000. Miyazawa, former Japanese Prime Minister, called it the largest development in the world at the end of the 20th century. The massive development not only referred to project development and land development, but to comprehensive development for all-around social progress. The experience of many countries indicated that it was necessary to gear this kind of development to the word's economy. "Gearing" to the world refers to its world-class development scale rather than its location. The planning of development must conform to the world standard, the funds and intelligence could come from every corner of the world, the operational method must be geared toward international conventions and the target was to integrate itself to the development progress of the global economy, especially that of the Asia-Pacific economy. The so-called "gearing" to international conventions in its way of operating means utilizing both domestic and international resources and sharing both international and domestic markets. The development of Pudong shall firstly give impetus to the economic development of the Yangtze River areas, then conditionally realize its development to the world with its advantages in location, economy, human resource, culture and other aspects by learning from the world's experience and utilizing the world's lessons and funds.

6.2.3.2 The Strategic Thinking of Opening Pudong

The opening and development of Pudong, Shanghai was carried out in a large international city with the characteristics of an all-dimensional, multi-faceted and high starting point. The strategic position of Pudong New District was to forge the urban functions of a modern international center pillared by the tertiary industry groups, including finance and trade. Therefore, Pudong had to adopt an extraordinary development strategy. The economic development level of Pudong and its strategic positioning required diversified funding to meet the needs of rapid social and economic development. Pudong needed to formulate and elect a series of policies that conformed to the international conventions, making both domestic and overseas investors rapidly accommodate to the procedures and basically forecast their returns. Pudong also needed to deal the relations between building a new city and the transformation of the old town, increasing the land development benefits. The above mentioned five aspects were important strategic issues for Pudong's development and also the research targets and implementing bodies of Pudong's development. Based on the analysis of Pudong's domestic and international economic environments, Pudong put forward the concrete thoughts for its development. In short, they were "two linkages," "three going ahead," "four cards," "one centralization," and "two pieces of answer sheets."

In terms of "two linkage," Deng Xiaoping pointed out that the development of Pudong was not only the problem of Pudong, but also the problem of developing Shanghai, the problem of developing the Yangtze River Delta and areas on the base of Shanghai.[491] In the respect of the law of urban development, old Shanghai City severely restricted Shagnhai's development, due to high population density and its massive scale. Meanwhile, Pudong could evacuate partial population and industries of Puxi District with vast undeveloped lands, thus, giving impetus to the development of Pudong and restructuring of Puxi. From a social resource flow point of view, Pudong and Puxi had their own strength and weakness. The combination of the two districts was the benefit for playing the complementary advantages and promoting mutual economic development of both sides.

"Three going ahead" refers the strategy of firstly developing infrastructure, trade, finance and high-tech industrialization. The strategy of infrastructure focused on resolving the problems of river-crossing transportation, communication and source of energy in Pudong, as well as combining Pudong and Puxi Districts. The infrastructures of Pudong

491 Deng Xiaoping, *Deng Xiaoping Anthology* 3rd volume, People's Publishing House,1993, P. 366.

District were quite inadequate and some were even completely blank before the opening up. The infrastructure construction focused on city morphology in the early days and providing necessary conditions for attracting investments. In later stages, Pudong gave priority to function development, establishing a good capital circulation mechanism for self accumulation. As for giving priority to develop the financial center, Deng Xiaoping pointed out that finance is the core of modern economy and China firstly relies on Shanghai to obtain international position in financing.[492] He also said that China must develop its own advanced technology and have a place in the world's high tech area. To form the industrial structure of modern international metropolis, Pudong particularly must accept the challenges of knowledge economy and high technology, readjust and upgrade original industries, as well as adopt the strategy of industrial upgrading leaded by infrastructure, finance and trade and high-tech industries.

"Four Cards" means "Shanghai Brand," "Yangtze River Brand," "China Brand and "the World Brand." Pudong's development firstly relied on Shanghai, then the Yangtze River areas and even the support of the nation. In addition, Pudong needed to deepen its all-around opening up and gear itself to the world. Pudong's development was a major development facing the 21st century. With a high starting point and great difficulties, the significant project of building Pudong to be a modern international city needed a lot of investments. As for the investments, it was necessary to adopt the strategy of diversified funding.

As for the "one centralization," Pudong was to focus on the development of selected units and gradually develop the entire area. It is impossible to comprehensively launch the cross-century project with high starting point in one motion. Pudong was to adhere to the guideline of "exploitation, building, putting into production and yielding an effect" in the process of rolling development. General Secretary Jiang Zemin made important instructions that China should concentrate resources well.

For "Two pieces of answer sheets," Deng Xiaoping pointed out that Pudong, Shanghai and Shenzhen, Guangdong Province needed to answer the question of belonging to socialism rather than capitalism and become the model in both aspects.[493] On one hand, it was comprehensive national strength, but on the other hand, it was the spiritual civilization, giving equal importance to economic development in one respect and to the development of socialist culture and ideology in the other. It was an important principle Pudong was to

---

492 Deng Xiaoping, *Deng Xiaoping Anthology* 3rd volume, People's Publishing House,1 993, P. 366-367

493 Edited by CPC Shanghai working Committee for the Opening of Pudong New District and Management Committee of Pudong New District, Ten Years Development in Pudong, Shanghai Far East Press, 1st edition, 2000, P.8

follow in its development. The guiding ideology was to attach equal importance on social and economic development. Pudong was not only to develop projects and industries, but also promote an all-around social progress. It was necessary to coordinately develop its economy and society from the beginning and focus on the construction of social undertaking, social administration and spiritual civilization.

6.2.3.3 The Meaning of Opening Pudong

The opening and development of Pudong was the hope of several sessions of Shanghai Municipal Party Committee and People's Government and an important strategic decision made by the CPC Central Committee and the State Council in line with the overall arrangement of economic construction and China's reform and opening up in the 1990s. It was a significant measure made during a transition from a planned economy to a socialist market economy, marking a new phase for China's reform and opening up.

(a) The Development and Opening of Pudong Was a Symbol of China's Deepening Reform

Since the third plenary session of the Eleventh Central Committee, China's reform and opening up policy spread from rural areas to urban areas, from coastal regions to the interior areas, from the second industry to the tertiary industry, from a medium and small city to super huge city. China gradually found a socialist development road with Chinese characters. If the four SEZ, and following Hainan SEZ, set up in the early days of the reform and opening up were conducted in undeveloped areas or cities with small influence to national economic foundation and their main function were experimenting opening up and economic restructuring, the development and opening of Pudong in the 1990s was the beginning of all-round reform and opening up on the base of learning from the past. The development conducted in the large city with more bravery and more "Chinese character" was a milestone for China's gradual development in the coordination of regional reform and industrial opening up in the 1990s.

Pudong developed and opened at a breakthrough point of China's historical development. After many years' economic construction, China's economic development entered into a new phase. Many years' reform and the SEZ trial proved that the market economic system was the objective pattern for economic restructuring. The opening up made significant progress and an all-around opening up took shape. Pudong's development and opening up marked a new phase for China's course of reform and opening up, implying a new level reform and opening up oriented by market economy. Chinese leaders repeatedly announced, "The Central Committee and the State Council will unswervingly adhere to the policy of opening and developing Pudong, which is not only concerned the development of Shanghai, but is also a important symbol for China's reform and opening up."[494]

(b) The Influence of Pudong's Development to Shanghai, Yangtze River Area and National Economy

The development and opening of Pudong District not only helped Shanghai out of a former dull development state, but also created a new policy environment and space for Shanghai's development, giving great impetus for Shanghai's revitalization and economic upswing, as well as driving rapid economic development in the Yangtze River areas and the whole country. In 1992, when Deng Xiaoping made a tour to the southern part of China, he said in Shanghai that "tracing back, a big mistake of mine is not setting up an SEZ in Shanghai at the beginning, otherwise, there would be great differences in the Yangtze River Delta and Yangtze River areas or even the national reform and opening up."[495]

At the beginning of the 1990s, Shanghai faced dual challenges of domestic and international competition. The Shanghai Municipal Party Committee and Shanghai Municipal People's Government believed that Shanghai, as China's largest economic center and influential international city in the Western Pacific, with advantages in its location, industry, technology, human resources and other aspects in particular, was destined to develop to the top of the country in economic development and opening up. Therefore, the CPC Central Committee and the State Council decided to develop Pudong District and placed it as the key position in the following ten years' development, aiming to grasp this opportunity to comprehensively enhance the economic development of Shanghai with the opening of Pudong as the turning point. This was the ardent expectation of the CPC Central Committee and the State Council and the duty of Shanghai.

Actually, the meanings of opening Pudong go beyond Shanghai itself. The Central authorities repeatedly emphasized that it was not only for Shanghai, but also for the economic development of Jiangsu, Zhejiang and both sides of the Yangtze River. Therefore, the opening of Pudong was held great influence for Shanghai and the whole country.

6.3 Special Policies and Strategies in Developing the Pudong New Area

A special economic zone is the area where special policies are implemented, and is the

---

494 Edited by CPC Shanghai working Committee for the Opening of Pudong New District and Management Committee of Pudong New District, Ten Years Development in Pudong, Shanghai Far East Press, 1st edition,2000, P.8

495 Deng Xiaoping, *Deng Xiaoping Anthology* 3rd volume, People's Publishing House,1993, P. 376.

result of implementing special policies.[496] Though there was no "special zone" in the name of Pudong New Area, Pudong New Area actually enjoyed all the special policies of a special zone. In addition, Pudong also enjoyed some special policies that special zones do not. According to the properties of the special policies enjoyed by Pudong, there are three periods it can be divided into: the earlier period emphasizes the preferential policies of promoting regional development and adjusting to all areas; the middle period emphasizes the preferential policies aimed at the strategic locating of Pudong's development; the policies of the later period put forth efforts to give priority to Pudong to realize its comprehensive transformation of the society.

On the developing strategies, Pudong paid attention to shaping its function of a modernized international central city based on the tertiary industry such as finance, business and trade, etc. As a result, funds should be collected diversely, and a series of policy environment by international practice should be made and promoted, so that investors from home and abroad could become familiar with the procedures quickly in order to obtain a basic assessment to the investing return more easily; the relationship between the building of the new and the rebuilding of the old should be well managed, and try to rise the construction of the city to a new level by way of coordinating between east and west of Shanghai. The planning, developing and managing of the land should be dealt with adequately in order to give full attention to the benefit of land development. These are important strategic issues in developing Pudong, and also the object and implementing subject of the researches on Pudong's development strategy.

6.3.1 Special Policies of Pudong New Area

6.3.1.1 The Special Policies Implemented in the Early Developing and Opening up of Pudong New Area (1990~1995)[497]

Between 1990 and 1995, the preferential policies that the Central Government gave to the Pudong New Area were included in three documents: in 1990, "Approval on Issues of Developing and Opening up Pudong" (Central Committee No. [1990]100) from the Central Committee of the Communist Party of China and the State Council; on September 8, 1990, the "Ministry of Finance's Regulations on Reducing and Exempting the Corporate Income

---

496 Su Dongbin, *Theoretical Issues for China's Special Economic Zones Development*, Journals of ShenZhen University (Humanities and Social Science edition), 2001, 5.

497 This part will take reference to Huang Qifan, *On the policies, Strategies and Management of Pudong*, Shanghai People's Publishing House, 1sr Edition, 1995, P69-85.

Tax and Industrial and Commercial Tax to Encourage Foreign Investment of Pudong New Area" issued by the Ministry of Finance; in 1992, the "Notice Related Issues on Further Developing and Opening Up Pudong and Violating State-owned Large and Medium Enterprises of Shanghai" (State Document No. [1992] 5) from the State Council.[498] They can be divided as the preferential policies of economic development zone, the preferential policies of economic special zone and privately owned preferential policies, respectively, enjoyed by the Pudong New Area.

6.3.1.1.1 The Ten Preferential Policies of the Economic Development Zone

On April 18, 1990, Mr. Li Peng officially announced the development and opening up of Pudong at Shanghai to home and abroad on behalf of the Party Central Committee and the State Council. In June of the same year, the Central Government clarified another series of policies and strategies to support Pudong to fasten the construction of the infrastructure and improve the policy-system environment to attract foreign investment. Pudong New Area possessed all the preferential policies of economic development zone and some more advanced policies than a special zone, namely, the 10 preferential policies. In 1992, in order to further support the development of Pudong, improve the efficiency for Pudong to examine and approve projects, further increase the speed for the construction of infrastructure, and enlarge the fund-resources for developing Pudong, the State Council also gave the examining and approving authority of enlarging five categories of projects to Pudong New Area. Another five ways to collect funds were increased. The 10 preferential policies related to the economic development zone included five policies about income tax and another five about tax-exemption.

6.3.1.1.2 The Nine Preferential Policies of the Special Economic Zone

Preferential policies of special economic zones covered the economic development zones, that is to say, special zones could enjoy the 10 preferential policies of economic development zones mentioned above. In addition, special zones could also enjoy some special policies that economic development zones did not have, which mainly focused on Chinese enterprises' taxation, export channels, the scale of investment, credit indicators, foreign exchange retention, and so on. These special policies are shown in nine aspects, which ensured the equal position between Pudong New Area and the five early special

---

498 Xu Quanyong, *The Pushing Effect and Evolution Path of the Policies on the Developing and Opening Up of Pudong New Area*.(http://www.kalf.or.kr/new_kalf/data/datafile/07.pdf)

zones, like Shenzhen.

6.3.1.1.3 The Five Privately-owned Special Policies of Pudong New Area

Apart from the preferential policies of special zone, Pudong New Area also enjoyed its privately owned preferential policies that were not prevailingly implemented on development zones and special zones. There are mainly five aspects:

A. Foreign corporations were allowed to build the tertiary industry, like department stores and supermarkets, in Pudong New Area. This was a great breakthrough for the policy, which included at least five aspects. They are: giving foreign-funded commercial enterprises the right to retail, the right to import merchandise goods, the right of acquisition of exports, the right to foreign exchange swap and appropriate tariffs and corporate income tax reduction, and so on.

B. Foreign corporations were allowed to open financial organizations like banks, financial companies, and insurance companies in all parts of Shanghai. In parts of the special zones, there are also branches of foreign banks, but the managing areas were quite limited. Foreign banks in Xiamen Special Zone could not develop business in Fuzhou, or Fujian Province, whereas foreign banks in Shenzhen Special Economic Zone could not develop business in Guangzhou, or Guangdong Province. Foreign financial organizations in Shanghai could do business in the two banks of Huangpu River.

C. Stock Exchange Center could be set up at Shanghai, in order to examine and issue RMB and stock B by itself for the development of Pudong. This policy actually gave Shanghai the rights and benefits of developing a stock market and forming a fund-exchange center. Its economic effects and positive effects in promoting reformation were extraordinary.

D. In Waigaoqiao of Pudong New Area, the largest zone, namely the free trade zone, in China was set up. In this region, duty was free, license was free, the establishment of an international trade organization was allowed, international transit trade could be engaged, full profit of foreign exchange could be retained, all national currencies could be circulated and the trading center of production materials in the bonded zone was set up, and so on.

E. Enlarging Shanghai's authority to examine and approve projects in Pudong New Area in five categories: (a). Authorizing Shanghai to examine and approve the home and abroad investment to set up foreign trade companies that engage in transit trade in Waigaoqiao zone. This means the examining and approving of the companies' establishment, entrance, and the rights to do international trade. (b). Authorizing Shanghai to examine and approve the export and import operational rights for the property products of large and medium state-owned enterprises in Pudong New Area. (c). Enlarging Shanghai's examining and approving authority on the non-productive projects in Pudong New Area. (d). Enlarging Shanghai's examining and approving authority on the productive projects in Pudong New Area whose total investment is under 200 million RMB. (e). Authorizing Shanghai to release stocks and bonds within the approved amount range of the Central Government, and the specific releasing affairs could be decided on by Shanghai itself. At the same time, the released stocks all over China could be listed in Shanghai.

6.3.1.2 The Special Policies Realized in the Middle Period in Pudong (1995~2005)

The special policies enjoyed by Pudong New Area were not targeted specifically enough, and were suitable to all areas and corporations. Since 1995, the developing and opening up of Pudong has gone to the period that simultaneously develop the foundation and the function,which was also the second venture period of Pudong New Area. In order to support the construction of Shanghai as a international economic city and help Pudong to form its functions in finance, trade, etc, on June 20, 1995, the State Council issued the "Notice on Related Policies of Developing and Opening Up of Shanghai Pudong New Area During the Ninth Five-Year Plan," which equipped Pudong with a series of functional policies. The five policies the Central Government gave to Pudong New Area to better promote the functional development include: (a). With the approval of the Ministry of Foreign Trade and Economic Cooperation (MOFTEC), foreign trade companies by the export volume above 100 million USD, and self-production enterprises by the export volume above 20 million USD, could set up branches in Pudong New Area. The examining and approving rights were authorized to Shanghai; (b). It is allowed to select some representative countries and zones, and attempt to set up three or four Sino-foreign joint venture foreign trade enterprises. The specific plan will be prepared by Shanghai, and the operational sphere and volume will be checked and ratified by MOFTEC, and submitted to the State Council for examination and approval; (c). In the Waigaoqiao bonded zone, boned business activities could be conducted, with the exception of retailing, and gradually expanded to service trade; (d). Once agreed by the Central Government, RMB operation of the bank will be allowed to first pilot in Pudong, and the foreign banks in Pudong New Area will get priority; (e). With appropriate conditions and the approval of the People's Bank of China, foreign financial organizations registered in Lujiazui could set up branches in Puxi and Waigaoqiao boned zone, and also some foreign and Sino-foreign insurance organization in Pudong New Area.

On January 1, 1996, in order to implement the spirit of the "Notice on Related Policies of Developing and Opening Up of Shanghai Pudong New Area During the Ninth Five-Year Plan" (State Document No. [95] 61) issued by the State Council, the People's Bank of China printed and published the notice of "Interim Measures for Foreign Banks in China to Establish Branches," and decided to allow foreign banks, with appropriate conditions, in four cities like Shanghai to set up branches and the foreign-owned or joint venture banks with appropriate conditions to set up branches.

6.3.1.3 The Special Policies Implemented in the Middle and Later Period of Pudong New Area (2005-Present)

6.3.1.3.1 From Preferential Polices to Priority to Exploration

At the early period of Pudong's developing and opening up, the nation implemented the unbalanced regional development policy, which encouraged part of the region to obtain development and, after the advanced region developed to a certain degree, the nation turned to the strategy of balanced development. With the change of the nation's regional developing strategy, the policies to the special zone were changed from the preferential policies in the early period to the priority to explore. On June 20, 2005, the Standing Committee of the State Council officially approved to make Shanghai Pudong New Area the pilot for comprehensive reformation. Pudong New Area was the first experimental zone with comprehensive facilitated reformation. This dividing point marked great differences with the past in the developing mode, role and positioning of Pudong New Area. In the past, what made a special economic zone "special" mainly referred to better financial policies in comparison with other places. However, comprehensive facilitated reformation did not have any connection with financial subsidy or preference, that is to say, there was no preferential policy. The only special policy Pudong got was the "priority," which was the experimental right to do comprehensive facilitated reformation first. The comprehensive facilitated reformation of Pudong was at a national level, and was also the important strategic arrangement under the new situation. In April of 2009, the State council issued the "Suggestion of the State Council on Further Prompting Shanghai to quicken its Development of Modern Service Industry and Advanced Manufacturing to Construct Into an International Center and Transportation Center." In the document, further requirements are raised for the comprehensive facilitated reformation of Pudong New Area. The document pointed out that Pudong should further promote the comprehensive facilitated reformation to make Shanghai the most effective in executives, taking the lowest fees for executives, and make Shanghai the most developed in intermediary service.

6.3.1.3.2 The Comprehensive Facilitated Reformation of Pudong

Piloting comprehensive reformation in Pudong was not only an important historical opportunity for Pudong and Shanghai to realize new development, it was also an important strategic measure of the country to accumulate experience, comprehensively promote a new series of reformation and enlarge opening up. The comprehensive facilitated reformation piloting of Pudong was an important opportunity for China to enter a new phrase of reformation and opening up. After more than 20 years of reform and opening up, China had entered the key period of market economic system, and the reformation faced social contradiction of a deeper level and more complicate benefits relationship, so it was very important for consolidating the results of economic development and realizing sustainable development to systematically promote reformation. The comprehensive facilitated reformation piloting of Pudong would greatly effect the reformation and development of the country. By the comprehensive facilitated reformation, Pudong should build economic operational rules, setups and a system environment that are suitable to the requests of socialist market economy and are connected with international practice, showing its leading role as a prior reforming zone.

6.3.1.3.3 Endowing Larger Reforming Autonomy to Pudong

In order to shift the function of the government, put forth efforts to change the economic operational method, and coordinate with the Central Government's requirements for comprehensive reformation piloting in Pudong New Area, on June 6, 2008, "the First Meeting of the Leading Group to Promote the Comprehensive Facilitated Reformation Piloting Work" was held, and Shanghai planned to endow Pudong with larger reforming autonomy, independent reform rights and independent reform right by way of further de-centralizing the municipal government's power.[499] After the reformation, a series of powers such as planning, land management, examining and approving the investing projects, self-innovating, population management, price management, and cultural market management would be placed into Pudong. The authority to examine and approve types of encouraging and promising foreign investment projects was originally in the Shanghai Committee of Foreign Trade and Economic Cooperation. After the reformation, it would be endowed to Pudong, and other foreign-fund project related powers of examining and approving department in Shanghai would be established simultaneously.

---

499 http://news.xinhuanet.com/fortune/2008-06/06/content_8323016.htm.

6.3.1.3.4 Continue to Support the Construction of the Function of the Pudong New Area

While the preferential policies of the Pudong New Area weakened, the Central Government continued to intensify efforts in other ways to promote the construction of the function of Pudong New Area, especially give support to the construction of Shanghai International Financial Center. In order to further promote the construction of Shanghai's Financial Center, perfect the central bank decision and operating system, play the advantages of a line of the financial market, and improve the macroeconomic control level and efficiency of the central bank, approval was required by the Central Government to relevant departments to set up the Shanghai headquarters of the People's Bank of China.

In order to further promote the speed of the development of modern service industry in Shanghai and the Shanghai headquarters of advanced manufacturing, speeding up the construction of the International Financial Centre, International Shipping Center and the Modern International Metropolis was necessary. The state council issued "The Direction of the State Council about Further Advance the Reformation and Openness of the Yangtze River Delta Region and Economic and Social Development" and "The Opinion of the State Council on Promoting the Speed of the Development of Modern Service Industry of Shanghai and Advancing Manufacturing Construction International Financial Center and International Shipping Center" respectively in 2008 and 2009. The file further clarified the goals, the regional and national economic position and the specific measures of the further development of Shanghai. Pudong New Area was the core carrier of realizing the above development goals of Shanghai. The Central Government positioned the development of Shanghai's economy as Pudong Financial Center, Shipping Center Construction, Modern Service Industry and provided policy guarantee and strong backing to the development of Advanced Manufacturing Industry.

To further improve the energy of the function area of Pudong New Area, with the support and promotion of the Central Government and the Shanghai Municipal Government, a group of national, strategic, high-level, radiation equipment project settled in Pudong. China's Commercial Aircraft Co., LTD settled large plane project headquarters and production and research center in Pudong in 2009. In addition to the large plane project, wind power, nuclear power, solar energy and all projects of research and production settled in Pudong. Lingang Industrial Zone of Pudong New Area formally gathered Germany Siemens, Shanghai Electric and China Instrument Gas that are three leading wind power equipment manufacture enterprises, both at home and abroad, becoming China's largest wind power equipment production bases. Shanghai Electric Heavy Equipment, which was second to none in the nuclear power industry in China, also settled in Pudong.

To promote the construction of the Financial Center and Shanghai International Shipping Center, play advantages of the industrial system in Pudong, improve the economic level of Pudong and Shanghai, Yangtze River Delta and the national drive and radiation, the state council formally replied to Shanghai in "On the Instructions of Cancelling the Original Nanhui Administrative Organizational System in the Nanhui Area and Delimit Pudong New Area," agreed to cancel Shanghai Nanhui and merged the administrative area into Shanghai Pudong New Area. After merging into Pudong, itnot only meant an expansion of the land area, but was also more conducive to the integration of resources of Pudong and promotion of the construction function. New Pudong almost included Shanghai's financial, shipping, trade and all the core resources of the construction of all fields, optimizing financial, shipping, trade resources allocation, and further strengthened the construction of the status of the target of the Pudong New National Strategy.

6.3.2 Development Strategies for Pudong New Area

6.3.2.1 First Strategy for Infrastructure, Financial Trade and High Technology Industrialization

Shanghai Municipal Party Committee and government made "the three first" strategy for Pudong New Area according to its leading position, which was to develop the infrastructure, financial trade and high technology industrialization first and fund the construction by allocating 90 billion Y=yuan according to the proportion of the 4:3:3 during the eighth "Five-year Plan" period.

6.3.2.1.1 First Strategy for Infrastructure

The Development Strategies for Pudong New Area started with infrastructure. Until 2008, the total investment for infrastructure was nearly 220.93 billion yuan.[500] Infrastructure was not only the basic conditions for all economic activity, but also an important investment environment of the region.

Since the beginning of the development of Pudong New Area, from 1990 to 2008, the fixed assets investment for Pudong New Area reached 836.858 billion yuan, mainly focused on urban infrastructure construction. After 2000, the fixed assets investment for

500 Page56, *Statistical Year Book for Pudong New Area of Shanghai*, 2009, China Statistic Press.

Pudong New Area further increased and reached 561.89 billion yuan, which was more than the investment of first 10 years.[501]

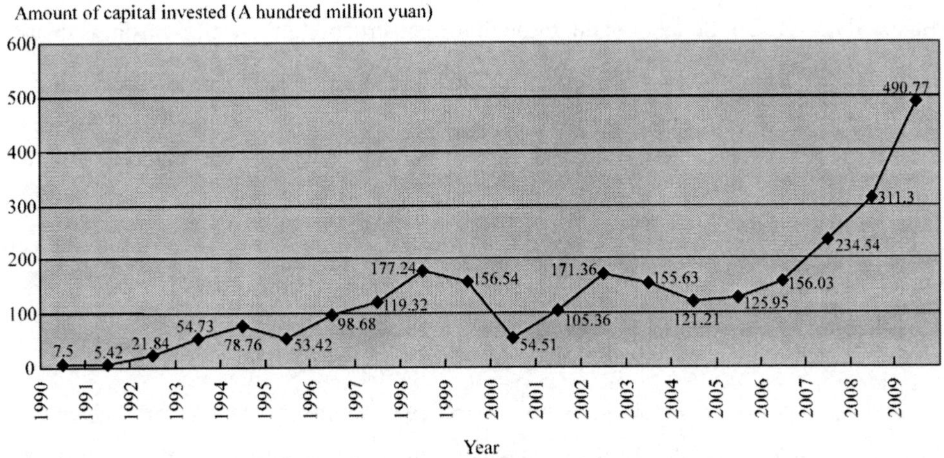

Figure 6-3-1 Amount of capital invested in urban infrastructure construction of Pudong New Area

Sources: Data from Statistical Year Book for Pudong New Area of Shanghai, China Statistic Press, 1993-2009, Website of Pudong New Area of Shanghai(http://www.pudong.gov.cn/website/html/shpd/XX200912/Info/Detail_298607.html).

Note: The data of Nanghui Area incorporated in Pudong New Area in 2009 is contained in the amount of capital invested in urban infrastructure construction of Pudong New Area.

6.3.2.1.2 First Strategy for Financial Trade

Finance was the core of modern economy. To boost Shanghai as the leading role of the Yangtze River Delta or Yangtze River Basin or as a platform to the outside world, financial industry should be developed first, and restore its status as an international financial center. Deng Xiaoping pointed out, "Finance is very important to the core of modern economy. If finance develops well, everything will thrive. Shanghai used to be a financial center, acting as a convertible currency place, and will be again Shanghai in the future. China's success in obtaining an international status in finance will first depend on Shanghai. The realization will take many years, but we need to start it now."[502]

The development of Pudong New Area was a process of development of financial and trade center, and also a process that boosted Shanghai as an international financial center. Since the turn of the century, the matrix for international central cities performing their urban function has already shifted from large scale industrial groups to the developed third

501 Page52, *Statistical Year Book for Pudong New Area of Shanghai*, 2009, China Statistic Press.

502 Page 366-367, Vol. 3, *Deng Xiaoping Anthology*, People's Publishing House, 1993.

industries such as finance, commerce and trade service. To develop the above-mentioned industries, on one hand, could create a solid financial environment, which would provide a new funding source for construction of Shanghai and lay the foundation for Shanghai to be a financial center. On the other hand, through the construction of a central business district, business center, carry out transit trade, would make Shanghai become a largest trade markets all over the country and one of the commodities distributing center in the Asia-pacific region. Therefore, financial trade of Pudong New Area was determined as one of the key industries to develop. Since the 16-year development of Pudong, Pudong Financial Industry experienced a change from weak to strong and has grown into the core industry of Shanghai, making an important contribution to the construction of the center.

6.3.2.1.3 First Strategy for High and New Technology Industry

Pudong paid great attention to giving full play to the comprehensive advantages, comparative advantage, and gradient advantage in order to form a more scientific and reasonable industrial structure. Currently, it has formed a unique emerging industry group across the city.

In developing Pudong financial trade and other modern service industries, at the same time, Pudong developed high-tech industry and made effort to promote manufacturing level. Since the implantation of "Focusing on Zhangjiang Strategy" by Shanghai Municipal Party Committee and Government in 1999, all kinds of resources unceasingly gathered in Zhanjiang, such as policy, industries, science, technology, talent, etc. According to an incomplete count, 3,606 enterprises entered the Yangtze Fiver Zone in 2006. The integrated circuit industry, led by Jingyuan, manufacturing in chip design dominated half of the domestic market share. With regard to the software industries, there were more than 200 enterprises entering Pudong software zone and software employees equaled more than 40.000. The park formed the most intensive biological medicine research and development innovation highlands in China; more than half of the enterprises in pharmaceutical sales that ranked in the top 20 entered Zhanjiang. For the cultural and creative industries, the output value of the online game industry, with Shengda and Jiulong as its leading enterprises in Zhangjiang Zone, accounted for over 70% of the whole country.[503] In 2009, high technology industry production of Pudong New area reached 176.718 billion yuan, accounting for 25.1% of industrial production of the new area of Shanghai. The total number of research and new technology enterprises was over 600,. The Research and

503 Fang Yuchan, Issue 6, *China's High-tech Zone*. 2007.

Development input ratio accounted for about 3% of gross domestic product (GDP). The applications for patent in total were nearly 14,645 pieces, which accounted for 36.7%.[504]

6.3.2.2 Strategic Steps for Development of Pudong New Area

In the beginning of the development of Pudong, the Pudong New Area covered an area of 544 square kilometers, most of which had not been exploited. The development of Pudong was a vast system engineering, which needed to be opened and developed step by step. According to the official count of the development of Pudong, the development of Pudong could be divided into three steps: pattern development (1990~1995), pattern development and function development (1995~the second half of 2004) and the comprehensive export-oriented construction, multi-function, modernization of the new stage in new area.

6.3.2.2.1 Pattern Development

The different stages of development and opening of Pudong had different goals. Since its start in the second half of 1995, the development of Pudong mainly focused on city pattern construction. The so-called pattern construction was pointed in the city infrastructure construction, of which included the main road, bridge, house, tree, river and lake.[505] Specifically, road construction included bridge roads, ground roads and the construction of an underground transportation; house construction included residential buildings, factory buildings, building construction, the reconstruction of the houses in the development of the new city construction, etc.; environmental construction included green park, green space, green space along the river and the green and nursery along the road. Because of the land in the development of Pudong New Area had not been previously developed, the first step in the development mission was the most important.

The internal mechanism promoting pattern development was the development mode of "land rolling," the external mechanism promoting pattern development was fiscal policy support to Pudong from the Central Government; the inside and outside linkage system promoting development of functional start was the large scale of the infrastructure construction and supernormal development of real estate industry. Net earnings for much of the land and the Central Government financial capital were injected into public infrastructure. The "land rolling" development mode drove the function development of

504 Data from *2010 Work Report of Government of Pudong New Area.*

505 Issue 4, Zhua Jiamjiang, *Practice and Exploration on Pattern, Industry and Function Development. Comprehensive Economy*. 2004.

Pudong New Area, including financial function and trade function formed by large-scale infrastructure construction and financing needs for real estate development and import demand, as well as city social function brought by the mass population concentration.[506]

6.3.2.2.2 Pattern Development and Function Development Carried Out Simultaneously

After 1995, the development and opening of Pudong simultaneously entered the period of pattern development and function development. After several years of pattern development, its infrastructure had improved greatly. Its further development was to focus on function development. During the ninth "Five-year Plan" period, Pudong infrastructure investment equaled about 59.5 billion yuan. High strength input quickened the urbanization process and the changing pace of the city. Investing heavily in pattern development such as infrastructure, Pudong also strengthened the function development at the same time. According to its overall goal of "face the world the 21 century and modernization" and "the promotion Shanghai, Pudong development, provide service throughout the country, and face the world," strategic outlook, which aimed to build Shanghai as one of the main economic, financial and trade centers and a modern international metropolis, the localization for function development of Pudong was: a) land function development with high technology and new technology industry group as the core; b) service function with finance and trade industry as the core; c) social function development supporting comprehensive, multi-functional urban economic development as the core. In this stage, the internal mechanism promoting development pattern shifted from the "land rolling" mode to "tax development" mode; the external mechanism promoting development pattern shifted from the Central Government's fiscal policy support to Pudong to functional policy support. The development of internal and external linkage mechanism was the function of high and new technology industry development. In this stage, the state council gave the Pudong New Area a series of new policies to speed up the function development. In September 1995, the Ministry of Foreign Trade approved that the foreign trade enterprise owned the right of import and export, with the annual export sum of over 100 million USD, self-operated enterprises with more than 20 million USD in the annual export and import sum, could set up subsidiaries in Pudong New Area. It was also allowed to choose the representative countries and regions in Pudong and set up three or four pilot Sino-foreign joint venture

---

506 Page 2-4, *Development Report of Pudong New Area* (1995~1996), Pudong Reform and Development Institute. Shanghai Academy of Social Science Press, 1996.

foreign trade enterprises. In addition, commercial and business activities with a bonded nature were allowed to be carried out in the Waigaoqiao free trade zone, except for retail business, and gradually expanded the service trade; the head office of the People's Bank of China approved parts of foreign banks to set up branch banks in Pudong and operate RMB business by the pilot. Through examination and approval by the People's Bank of China, foreign banks registered in Lujiazui could set up branch banks in Puxi and Waigaoqiao free trade zone, and set up branches and some foreign capital and Sino-foreign joint venture insurance institutions in the Pudong New area".[507] The central functional policy was the booster for Pudong functional development.

Along with the further development and opening of Pudong, the function of Pudong was becoming clearer. The guiding principle was presented in "Three Years Action for Economic Development of Pudong New Area": "the development and opening of the Pudong in the new stage and new century must continue to adhere to the development plan, revitalize Shanghai Pudong, serve the nation and face the world. It should focus on and serve the development of China, focus on and serve the goal for constructing Shanghai as the economic, financial, trade and shipping centers of the world, seize the opportunity of world expo, enhance the function of the area, and make efforts to construct Shanghai as the core functional areas of the 'four center.'"

During the eleventh "Five-year Plan" period, the Pudong New Area took four national development zones as the main carrier, advancing the function development and improving the comprehensive function city. By the end of 2009, more than 603 financial institutions gathered here in the Lujiazui financial and trade zone. The headquarters of the People's Bank of China in Shanghai, the Securities Regulatory Bureau, the Municipal Reassurance Company, the Shanghai Headquarters of Futures Margin Monitoring Center, Xinhua 08, Alipay, Unicom Pay and other functional institutions entered Pudong.

6.3.2.3.3 The Stage for Comprehensively Building an Export-oriented, Multi-functional, Modernized New Area

After 15 years of development, the Pudong New Area entered the stage for comprehensively building an export-oriented, multi-functional, modernized new district. In July 2004, Hu Jintao, the CPC Central Committee General Secretary, point out during a visit in Shanghai: "We shall continue to do well with regards to the development of Pudong's opening, in speeding up the system innovation, and constantly improving the

507 Quoted from *Pudong Logics*, Zhao Qizheng. Shanghai Sanlian Press. 2007, Page 67.

level of the export-oriented economy, and make efforts to achieve rapid development in a higher starting point." The eleventh "Five-Year Plan" put forward that the overall goal for Pudong economic and social development was: take the lead in accomplishing modernization by 2010; take the lead in creating a comprehensive well-off society; and take the lead toward the goal for comprehensively building an export-oriented, multi-function, modernized new area. The main symbols for achieving the above mentioned goals were five breakthroughs: (1) breakthrough would be accomplished in economy development, forming a economic scale and overall strength which would adapt to new levels of Shanghai's modern international metropolis; (2) breakthrough would be accomplished by constructing a harmonious society, forming a diverse, multi-level social service and security system and improving the people's living standards through a stability mechanism which would adapt to modernization, promote the all-around development of man as the core; (3) breakthrough would be accomplished through technological innovation, forming a internationally competitive technology innovation system; (4) breakthrough would be accomplished in system innovation and opening expansion, forming a relatively perfect system and relatively effective socialist market economy in accordance with international practices; (5) breakthrough would be accomplished in city construction and function improvement, forming a modern infrastructure system, city service system and harmonious ecological environment, both for humans and nature.

6.3.3 The Regional and Functional Planning of the Development of Pudong New Area

The regional planning of Pudong was based on Pudong New Area's guiding principle of "Developing Pudong, Prospering Shanghai, Serving the Country, Facing the World," associated with the actual situation, with reference to the successful experience of developing a new area at home and abroad. It also insisted on the idea of "Planning Goes First," and developing Pudong in an orderly fashion, trying to build Pudong New Area into a rational layout, where comprehensive traffic network goes first, complete infrastructure communication system developed and good export-oriented natural environment existed in the multifunctional and modern new area. The regional developing plan of Pudong always adhered to the strategic principle "Based on Puxi, Develop Pudong, Help Puxi by Pudong, and Develop Puxi and Pudong Simultaneously," which was made by the Shanghai Municipal Government to support the development of Pudong. The regional and functional planning of Pudong New Area was an important component to the whole regional and functional planning of Shanghai.

"Planning goes first." The developing Pudong shouldered the responsibility of prospering Shanghai. It was an important component to building Shanghai into an international economic, financial, trade and transportation center. In order to ensure the realization of the strategic goal of developing and opening up Pudong, the guiding principle of "Planning Goes First" was insisted upon throughout the process of developing and opening up. In the 1980s, which was the fermentation stage of developing Pudong, the planning research of developing Pudong has begun. In the preliminary stage of developing Pudong, based on the goal to build Pudong into an export-oriented, multifunctional, modern new city, under the frame of the whole planning of Shanghai, and adhering to the principle of "Planning First, Developing Next," the development plans of Pudong were made in accordance with high standards and high quality. A functional frame of a modern international metropolis from points and lines was made, and then spread to a flat structure.

According to the above planning ideas, Pudong changed its city planning mode in the past as "pursuing the scale only" to based on Pudong as the center, with an open type of layout planning, and forming comprehensive sub-zones with their own emphasis and independence. They are: Lujiazui Finance and Trade Zone, Jinqiao Export Processing Zone, Waigaoqiao Free Trade Zone, Zhangjiang Hi-Tech Park, Sun Qiaonong Business District, Sanlin Expo Functional Area, and Chuansha Functional Area. The planning of Pudong New Area insisted on the close connection of industrial development and functional development of sub-zones. The functional development of sub-zones was associated with industrial development, which made the developing zones important bases of finance, trade, modern manufacturing, hi-tech industry, modern agriculture and other modern service industries of Shanghai. At the preliminary period of Pudong's developing and opening up, the zones that put most emphasis were Lujiazui Finance and Trade Zone, Jinqiao Export Processing Zone, Waigaoqiao Free Trade Zone and Zhangjiang Hi-Tech Park. Later, based on the strategic positioning and actual demand for development, some other development zones were established.

Since Pudong's developing and opening up, the substance of the development was closely connected with the axis of YangGao Road. Waigaoqiao Free Trade Zone, Jinqiao Export Processing Zone, and Lujiazui Finance and Trade Zone were all along the YangGao Road. Only Zhangjiang Hi-Tech Park was located 5 kilometers away from YangGao Road. Because of the construction of Pudong International Airport, the development layout of Pudong New Area was changed. According to "The Municipal Overall Planning of Shanghai," adhering to the principle of regional development planning and optimizing space layout, Pudong New Area cleared its developing layout and functional position of the new developing period in the eleventh "Five-year Plan."[508]

The developing layout could be generalized as "One Axis, Three Zones." "One Axis" refers to the east-west directional developing axis from Hongqiao Airport to Pudong International Airport, which was ensured by the overall planning of Shanghai. The eastern period was the Junior Lujiazui of Pudong New Area, Century Avenue and Pudong International Airport. Taking the "One Axis" as the linage was necessary to develop Puxi and Pudong simultaneously, regarding the "One Axis as the pivot and spreading to the south and the north. The future development trend of Pudong New Area was revealed. It was the embodiment of Pudong's modernized city's landscape and corridor of modern service industry. The three zones were: the comprehensive developing zone along the Huangpu River based on Lujiazui Finance and Trade Zone, relying on the comprehensive development of the two banks of Huangpu River, and emphasizing the development of finance, insurance, professional service, business and trade, tourism, exhibiting industry and eco-living functions, and showing the prosperity of the central city and modern serving function; the middle development zone was headed by the nation-level developing zone of "One River, Three Bridges," which focused on developing hi-tech industries and productive service industries, and showed the industrial capacity and research innovative function; the developing zone along the river and the sea, relying on Waigaoqiao port zone and Pudong International Airport, focused on air and sea industries, like modern logistics, and municipal tourism, modern agriculture, and showed the function and developing potential of modern logistics.

Six functional zones were fixed in a functional layout. They were dominated by functional development, promoted the integrated development of functional zones, improved the comprehensive function of the city, so the six functional zones could be planned and built. They were the functional zones of Lujiazui, Zhagnjiang, Jinqiao, Waigaoqiao, Sanlin Expo and Chuansha.

6.3.4 The Developing Strategies of Sub-zones in Pudong New Area

The development of sub-zones in Pudong was an innovation. There are two important innovations: the first, it realized the unity of form development and industrial development. In other words, with the premise of getting a good overall city plan, and then divide the land into different zones later on, based on the competitive advantage of the region to enhance its regional function, which was to define the main developing industry in a certain

508 http://www.pudong.gov.cn/website/understandPudong/infoContent.jsp?sj_dir=PUDSWFZGH&pardir=understandPudong#link1

zone, and make it the gathering place of one or several industries; the second, business developing mode was used in the specific development of the sub-zones, with the guidance of the government, businesses and corporations were to complete the infrastructure construction of the land according to the commercialized principle, and also to manage the lands which were formally developed.

6.3.4.1 The Combination of Form Development and Function Development

The development of the sub-zones of Pudong New Area was a regional development strategy in combination with form development and function or industrial development. By the strategic idea of "Developing Pudong, Prospering Shanghai, Serving the Country, Facing the World," Pudong New Area formulated the idea to build Pudong into a first-class export-oriented, multifunctional, modernized new area, and to lay a foundation to build Shanghai into an international economic, financial and trade center. To fulfill the above tasks, there was no doubt that Pudong New Area should do superior regional and industrial planning in accordance with the given objectives and strategies. The developing ideas for Pudong New Area was in accordance with the requirements to build a world first-class export oriented, multifunctional, modernized new area, forming a city frame of a modern metropolis from points and lines firstly, then spreading to flat structure, later to focus on four defined sub-zones with clear functions. The four sub-zones were: Waigaoqiao Trade Free Zone with comprehensive free trade functions; Lujiazui Finance and Trade Zone with the tertiary industrial functions such as finance and trade; Jinqiao Export Processing Zone with capital and technology intensive export processing function; and Zhangjiang Hi-Tech Park with developing function of the hi-tech industry. The regional layout of the four zones was put on the central zone of all functional regions with the overall planning frame of Pudong New Area. The aim was, by spreading the development of the main sub-zones was to finally realize the development of the whole Pudong New Area. After that, based on the new situation, Pudong New Area planned the Shanghai Sunqiao Modern Agricultural Zone and Sanlin Expo Functional Zone in 1994 and 1995, respectively. The former was the first comprehensive modern agricultural development zone in China, and the latter took exhibition industry, tourism and modern living as the dominant function, with the area of 80.11 square kilometers, Pudong's part of Expo pavilions were also in this zone. Pudong New Area had realized the unity of municipal form planning goal or municipal development and industrial or functional developing goals in the planning of the city.

6.3.4.2 The Detailed Method for the Realization of the Sub-zones of Pudong New Area

The developing method for the Pudong New Area was a unique innovation. It was abandoned from the very beginning, but the government invested and took charge for all costs, and took on a new way of building companies to obtain commercial development, making the government responsible for the macro-control. Generally speaking, it took about 100,000,000 USD in investment of the infrastructure for each square kilometer of land.[509] The developing of Pudong New Area was carried out on a piece of finely planned land, where the population was condensed and the level of people's income was relatively high. On the other hand, the original goal of the development was comparatively high, and the pre-existing infrastructures were far behind its level. Thus, the development needed a large amount of investment to construct the infrastructures, including facilities of aviation, subways, tunnels, big bridges, communication facilities, etc., which would surely make the cost of investment comparatively high. In responding to this situation, neither the Central Government, the government of Shanghai and the Pudong New Area could afford such a great investment. The financial income of the Pudong New Area in 1993 was merely 1.2 billion yuan, therefore it was not able to afford such a large investment. Instead, the government of the Pudong New Area invented a new way of "drawing capital with the land, promoting the value of the land with the capital, and again, drawing more capital with the land, and through this way pushing forward a land development of a larger scale," through the method of "development by rolling."

The government organized the developing company of each sub-zone, and made the land the capital investment to the developing companies of important sub-zones. Firstly, the government estimated the amount of the capital of land assignment, making the amount the capital basis for the investment to companies of important sub-zones. When the land value rose, companies would receive dividends according to the proportion of investment by the government. The capital offered by the government was in fact "hollow," which was a check that could not be cashed until the contracts of land assignment became valid and the capital became "concrete." After receiving the check for the capitals, which was made on a shared basis from the capitals of the land assignment by the government, the developing companies of the important zones applied to the Land Administrative Department for the right to use the land. After signing the contract, the companies were handed the check,

509 Zhao Qizheng, *The Logic of Pudong*, Joint Publishing Co., Shanghai, 2007, P197.

which was derived from the government, to the land administrative department as the capital for the land assignment. At the same time, the sub-zone development company officially gained the right to use the land. Land Administration Department would remit the land acquisition check to the financial department. This kind of development strategy was vividly called "finance idling, land runs concretely." From this kind of operation, the investment of government for the sub-zone development company was the cash investment, and this investment would immediately be used for paying the land grant fee by the sub-zone development company, which meant that the government invested without paying anything to the sub-zone development company and the development company paid nothing for the land grant fee.

Compared with land assignment, developing from "finance idling, land runs concretely" has many advantages; the former would cause the obscurity of company property and the disorder of cost accounting, and the assigned land could not be made over, rented and mortgaged onerously. The latter made it clear that the government was in the main position and was helpful to complete the modern company managing system. Also, the developed land could go into the secondary land market. At the beginning of the development, Pudong New Area established the top four companies, including Lujiazui, Jinqiao, Waigaoqiao and Zhangjiang. As the main body of the organizer of the new area, these companies assigned land blocks and explore them by their function, then go into the secondary land market and use the earning from land assigning to invest in new land. This process would continue until the sub-zone was finished.

The sub-zone development was the main form of land development in Pudong New Area. As calculated, when the system of "finance idling, land runs concretely" is almost finished in 2011, Pudong New Area would have received 88.6 km^2 of land, which would make up nearly 80% of the total assignment land area in that period. The government invested 6.1 billion RMB, which made the development companies invest more than 20 billion RMB of land cooperation development. Meanwhile, the development companies received more than 12 billion RMB income for the land assignment and attracted more than 800 real estate companies from home and abroad, and a total of 40 billion RMB in real estate developing capital created favorable conditions for the development of Pudong New Area.

6.4 Social and Economic Development of Pudong New Area

Since the Party Central Committee and the State Department proclaimed the development and opening up of Pudong to the world on April 18, 1990, Pudong had 20 years worth of experience in which to make its historical emergence. The emergence of Pudong not only had a great effect on the rapid development of Shanghai and the Yangtze River Delta, but was also viewed internationally as one of the major events in the process of China's reform and opening up. Compared with the former situation before the development and opening up of Pudong, it changed dramatically. Currently, an outwardly-oriented, multi-functional, modernized new city is shown to the world. Pudong's development and the development and opening up was not only about economy, but more of a comprehensive social progress.

6.4.1 The Overall View of the Social and Economic Development of Pudong New Area

6.4.1.1 In the Rapid and Continuous Growth of Economy, the Comprehensive Economic Power Has Reached a New Level

After the development and opening up of Pudong New Area, its economic and social development achieved great progress. The continuous increase in economy made the Pudong New Area another growth pole in the Shanghai and Yangtze River area. The GDP of Pudong New Area increased about 52 times, from 6.024 billion yuan in 1990 to 315.099 billion yuan in 2008. The increase rate of which has been over 18% per year in the past 20 years, which was much higher than that of Shanghai. The ratio of Pudong's GDP to Shanghai's GDP also raised from 10% in 1990, to 23% in 2008. Moreover, Pudong has reasonably progressed with other economic fields. For instance, the total fixed investment and total volume of retail sales of Pudong were 1.415 billion yuan and 1.428 billion yuan respectively in 1990, and increased 62-fold and 37-fold, to 87.268 billion yuan and 52.689 billion yuan in 2008, which accounted for 8% and 6% in the past to 18% and 12% in 2008 of Shanghai's corresponding fields. During the tenth "Five-Year Plan" period, the total social fixed investment of Pudong New Area reached 295.1 billion yuan, which accounted for almost half of the fixed investment since the development and opening up of the area. The fiscal solvency of Pudong New Area was also much stronger. The fiscal income was 104.244 billion yuan which was 93 times more than that of 1993, and was 13% of that of Shanghai.[510, 511]

---

510 Resources: Shanghai Pudong New Area Statistical Yearbook, China Statistical Press, 2010; Shanghai Statistical Yearbook, China Statistical Press, 2010.

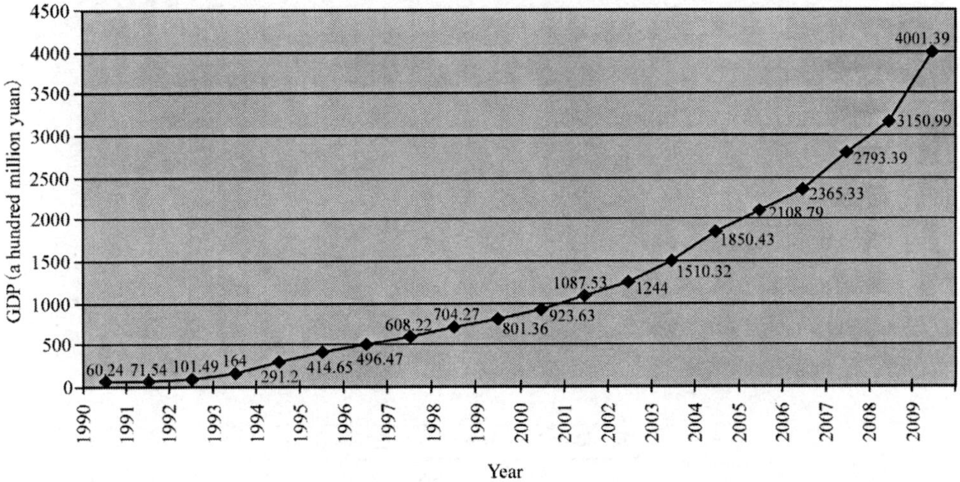

Figure 6-4-1 GDP in each year of Pudong New Area

Resources: Pudong Statistical Yearbook (China Statistics Press), Shanghai Pudong New Area People's government 2009 Statistical monthly (http://www.pudong.gov.cn/website/html/shpd/XX200912/Info/Detail_298609.htm)

Note: GDP in 2009 of Pudong New Area consists of the statistics of former Nanhui district.

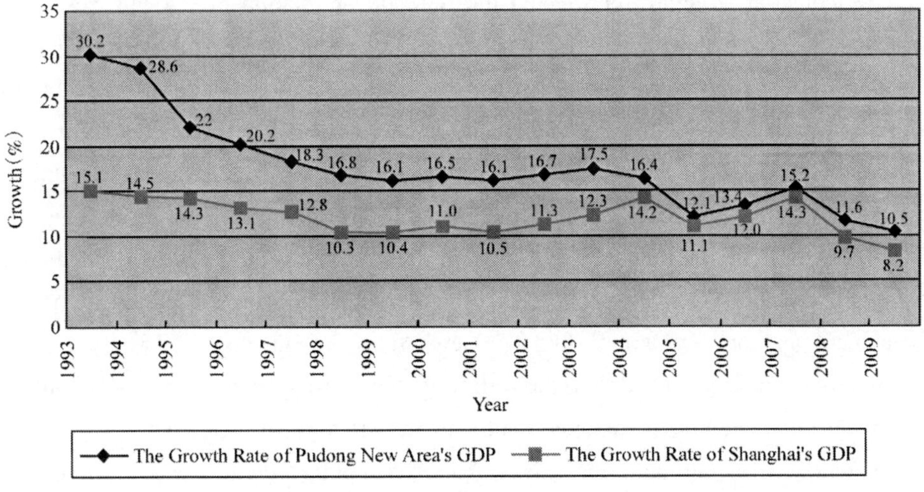

Figure 6-4-2 The ratio of Pudong New Area's GDP to Shanghai's GDP

Resources: Pudong New Area Statistical Yearbook, China Statistical Press, 2009; Shanghai Statistical Yearbook, China Statistical Press, 2009; 2009 Statistics Bulletin of the National Socio-economic Development of Shanghai; 2009 Shanghai Pudong New Area People's Government Bulletin.

Note: GDP in 2009 of Pudong New Area consists of the statistics of former Nanhui district.

511 The development and opening up of Pudong started in 1990, but the Pudong Management Committee was found in 1993.

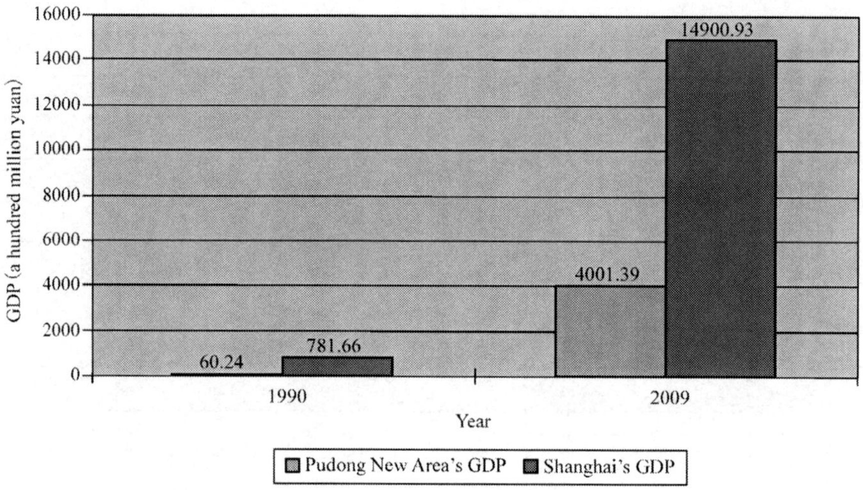

Figure 6-4-3 The ratio of Pudong New Area's GDP to Shanghai's GDP in 1990 and 2009

Resources: Pudong New Area Statistical Yearbook, China Statistical Press, 2009; Shanghai Statistical Yearbook, China Statistical Press, 2009; 2009 Statistics Bulletin of the National Socio-economic Development of Shanghai; 2009 Shanghai Pudong New Area People's Government Bulletin.

Note: GDP in 2009 of Pudong New Area consists of the statistics of former Nanhui district.

The industrial structure represented the function orientation of Pudong New Area. Shanghai, Pudong's development and opening up had features of a well-rounded, multi-domain and high starting point; it shouldered the important mission of promoting Shanghai to become one of the international economic, financial and trade center and boosting the economy of the Yangtze River. All of these factors determined that Pudong New Area should vigorously develop the modern service industry in its development strategy and focus on the functions of a modern international central city by depending on the tertiary industry, such as finance and trade. Compared with the period before the development and opening up of Pudong New Area, the quantity of tertiary industry increased tremendously. In addition, the shift in Pudong tertiary industry not only could be seen in the quantity, but, more importantly, in its structure or ratio. After 20 years of development and opening up, Pudong New Area's economic structure basically resembled its function orientation. Tertiary industry, mainly consisting of modern service industry, increased rapidly, about 141 times, from 1.213 billion yuan in 1990 to 171.486 billion yuan in 2008 and its ratio to GDP rose from 20% in 1990 to 54.4% in 2008. Contrarily, the ratio of primary and secondary industry GDP decreased from 3.7% and 76.2% respectively in 1990 to 0.2% and 45.4% in 2008.[512]

512 Resources: Shanghai Pudong New Area Statistical Yearbook, China Statistical Press, 2009

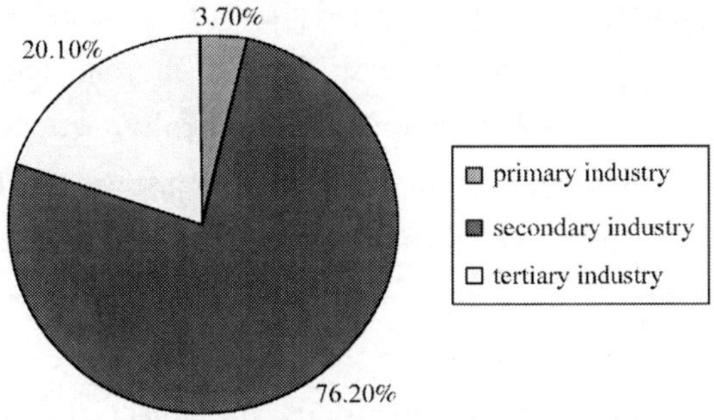

Figure 6-4-4 1990 Industrial proportion of GDP of Pudong New Area

Resources: Shanghai Pudong New Area Statistical Yearbook, China Statistical Press, 2009

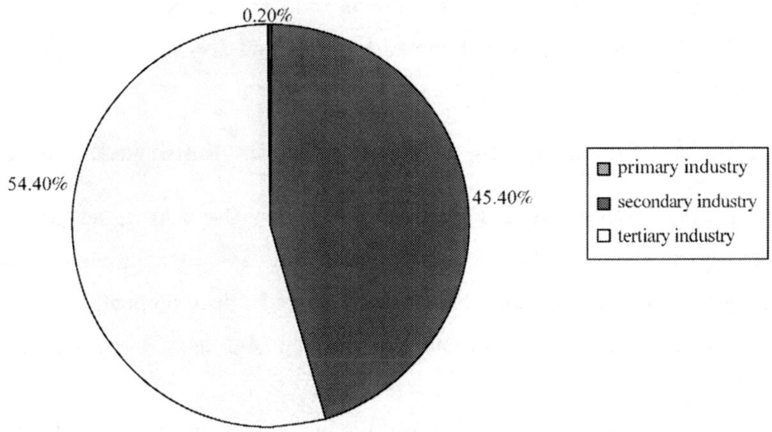

Figure 6-4-5 2008 Industrial proportion of GDP of Pudong New Area

Resources: Shanghai Pudong New Area Statistical Yearbook, China Statistical Press, 2009

Accompanying industrial structure change, Pudong also achieved industrial upgrading. Modern manufacturing rose. In the early period of the development of Pudong, the five industries, petrochemical industry, ferrous metal smelting industry, rolling processing industry, textiles and transportation equipment manufacturing and building materials accounted for 63.58% of the total industrial output value among which steel, petrochemical industry and textiles were the dominant. According to the Rostovian take-off model, the industry form and production level of Pudong New Area, at that time, was still at a pre-industrial stage. However, so far, the dominating industries are motor manufacturing, electronic information products and complete set of equipment manufacturing what corresponded to the transformation from "age of high mass consumption" to "stage of increase of standard of living" of the Rostow's Theory. The ratio of light industry to heavy industry adjusted from 1:1.45 in 1996 to 1:4.28 in 2008, which indicated Pudong's rapidly shift from the age of primary products to the end phase of traditional industrialization. Ever since the development and opening up, both domestically and internationally, Pudong promoted the development of both traditional and modern service industries like finance, trade, convention and exhibition, tourism and modern logistics, which set the foundation for making Shanghai the center of international economy, finance, trade and shipping. Before the development and opening up, Pudong's service industry was rather underdeveloped, mainly consisting of traditional industries like business, trade, catering services and entertainment, whereas modern service industries, like financial and insurance services, convention and exhibition, tourism and modern logistics were almost nonexistent. Nevertheless, after many years, Pudong's modern service industry significantly progressed. For example, tertiary industry,[513] whose core is modern service industry accounted for more than 22% of GDP, other than finance, logistics and convention and exhibition are mostly notable.

6.4.1.2 Constant Strengthening of Modern Urban Comprehensive Functions

Ever since the development and opening up of Pudong New Area, the strategy of zone development, coupled with industrial development, was always implemented in order to better Pudong's comprehensive functions. Pudong, since its development, depended on four national development zones to promote the development and strengthening of urban functions.

The implementation of "Focusing on Finance" strategy was accelerated. China Foreign Exchange Trade System, Shanghai Head Office of the People's Bank of China, Shanghai Securities Regulatory Bureau, China Financial Future Exchange and other vital functional financial organizations successively settled in Pudong. In 2009, there were 603 Chinese and foreign funded financial institutions and 17 foreign banks, which accounted for about half of the nation's banks, while the total assets of which accounted for 80% of the nation's overall foreign banks. Moreover, the environment for financial development became better. For instance, the building of Lu Jiazui financial city accelerated, the Shanghai Court of Financial Arbitration was founded and the widening of the financial city and the two-story pedestrian corridor was planned and started. The strategy of "Focusing on Zhangjiang" was continuously deepened and innovation capital gathered. For example, in 2007, about 510 million yuan government guided funding attracted 7.1 billion yuan venture investments and propelled 20 projects, belonging to 19 companies, to start the trial

513 Resources: Shanghai Pudong New Area Statistical Yearbook, China Statistical Press, 2009

of intellectual property pledge financing. In addition, innovative achievements were more and more notable. In 2009, high-tech industry's output value, with an increase of 9.0%, reached 176.718 billion yuan, which accounted for 25.1% of the total output value of Pudong New Area. Investment in the Research and development was supposed to account for about 3% of the gross product. The number of patent applications equaled 14.645 thousand, while among them, inventive patent possessed 36.7%.[514]

6.4.1.3 Improvement Level of the Outward-Oriented Economy

Pudong New Area exerted its first-move advantage since its opening up, providing strong investment and trade, both domestically and internationally, and improved the level of the outward-oriented economy. Compared with the situation in 1993, Pudong New Area's outward-oriented economy occupied a more important role in Shanghai's economy. Foreign trade of exports and imports increased 48 times, from 2.592 billion USD in 1993 to 138.989 billion USD in 2009, which correspondingly accounted for 20% in 1993 to 50% in 2009 of Shanghai's foreign trade. On the aspect of attracting foreign investment, Pudong New Area accomplished a great task. By the end of 2007, Pudong had 10.914 thousand registered foreign companies capital, of which totaled 22.8 billion USD. Especially during the tenth "Five-Year Plan" period, Pudong New Area absorbed seven thousand direct foreign investment projects that occupied 40% of the city's sum. Additionally, the level of investment attraction improved and "Headquarter Economy" massively gathered. By the end of 2009, the number of identified multinational corporations' headquarters was 135, which accounted for over half of the city's total amount. In 2009, contractual foreign

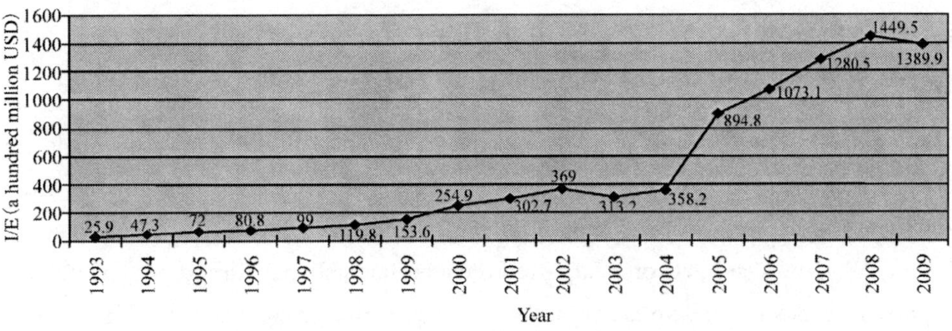

Figure 6-4-6 Volume of Imports and Exports of Pudong New Area

Resources: Shanghai Pudong New Area Statistical Yearbook, China Statistical Press, 1994~2009; 2009 Bulletin of Shanghai Pudong New Area People's Government

514 Resources: 2009 Shanghai Pudong New Area People's Government Bulletin

investment reached 5.529 billion USD, occupying 42% of the city's sum, and within which contractual foreign investment on tertiary industry possessed 80%, and companies' proportion of increase of capital reached 80%. Funds actually provided equaled 3.908 billion UDS, accounting for 36% of the municipal sum.[515, 516]

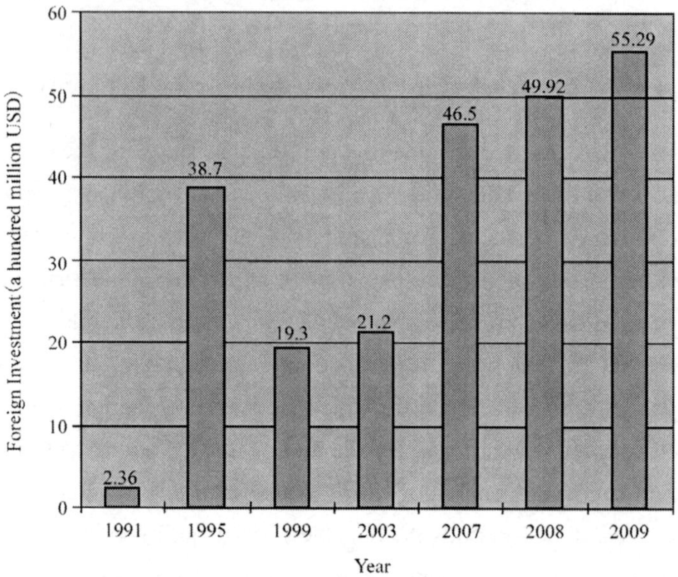

Figure 6-4-7 The Major Years of Pudong Foreign Investment Contracts

Resources: Shanghai Pudong New Area Statistical Yearbook, China Statistical Press, 1993~2009; 2009 Bulletin of Shanghai Pudong New Area People's Government, No.1 2010; (http://www.pudong.gov.cn/website/html/shpd/201001/list/list_0.htm)

6.4.1.4 The Initial Shape of the Modern Urban Pattern

Pudong New Area had an underdeveloped infrastructure before the development and opening up. After its opening up, Pudong kept intense and large scale investments in city construction and the amount of infrastructural investment reached 220.934 billion yuan in 2008. Infrastructural system, based on "three harbors" and "four networks," aimed at functionality, hubs and networks improved. Pudong International Airport became the only airport in the nation with two runways. Wai Gaoqiao port zone completed its fifth period of

---

515 2009 Statistics Bulletin of the National Socio-economic Development of Shanghai; 2009 Shanghai Pudong New Area People's Government Bulletin

516 Resources: Pudong Statistical Yearbook, China Statistical Press, 2007; Pudong New Area Governmental Work Report; (http://www.pudong.gov.cn/attach/infoattach/2008-06-0594097/2008-06-05620.doc#)

construction, while Fuxing east road tunnel, Dalian road tunnel, Lupu bridge and other cross-river projects were completed and open to traffic and urban rail transit construction was accelerated and the road network in the New Area became more and more developed. Urban environment also improved. In 2008, landscape area covered 89.2384 million square meters. The ratio of urban green area was over 37%, public green area per capita was 24.25 square meters. Consequently, Pudong successfully won the name of National Garden City, Sanitary City, National Advanced Areas of Accessible Facilities, and it passed the check and acceptance of National Model of Environmental Protection. In addition, Jiu Duansha was classified as a National Wetland Nature Reserve. To propel the construction of the New Area airport, rail transit network and road system for the Expo significant zones, Pudong New Area increased its investment in infrastructure in 2008 to 31.13 billion yuan for the year, which increased 32.7% each year, while in 2009, the investment was 49.077 billion yuan with a increase of 33% each year. 2008 and 2009 had finished the Expo infrastructural fixed asset investment of 2.333 billion yuan and 2.1 billion yuan respectively.[517]

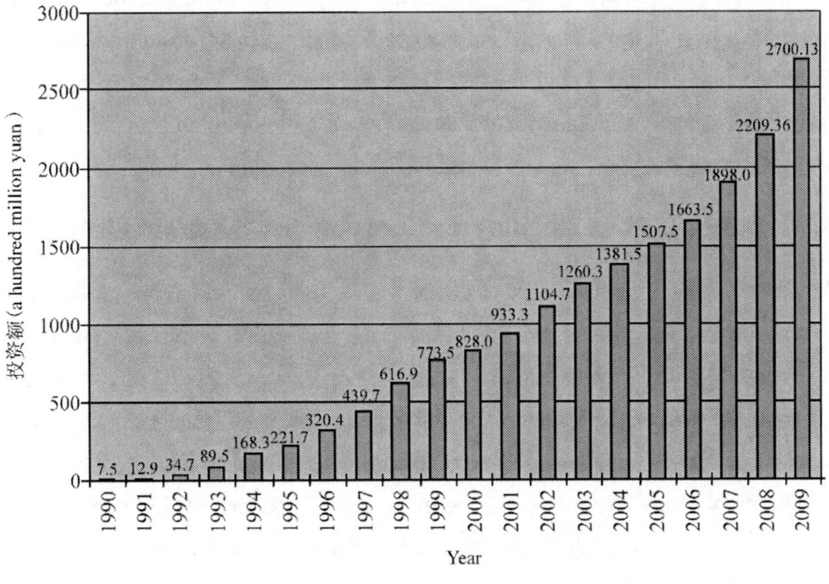

Figure 6-4-8 The Cumulative Investment infrastructure of Pudong New Area

Resources: Shanghai Pudong New Area Statistical Yearbook, China Statistical Press, 1994~2009;
2009 Pudong New Area Total Investment in Fixed Assets;
(http://www.pudong.gov.cn/website/html/shpd/XX200912/Info/Detail_298607.htm

517 Resources: Pudong New Area Statistical Yearbook, China Statistical Press, 2009; 2009 Pudong New Area Total Investment in Fixed Assets;(http://www.pudong.gov.cn/website/html/shpd/XX200912/Info/Detail_298607.htm)

6.4.2 Financial Development of Pudong New Area

6.4.2.1 Financial Product Development and Pudong's Development and Opening up

One of the vital strategical goals of Pudong's development and opening up was to regain Shanghai's status as an international center. Before opening up, Pudong's financial and insurance service was at the beginning phase, so to develop Pudong's financial industry and to build Pudong into a gathering place for financial institutions and financial dealings was a great challenge. Before the opening up of Pudong, Deng Xiaoping had said, "finance was very important and was the core of modern economy. Once we got the finance taken care of, then other businesses would be easier to be developed. Shanghai used to be a financial center and a place for free currency exchange, and would still be in the future. China, if it was going to gain the international status of a financial industry, should firstly depend on Shanghai. Although that could be the goal for a long time, but actions should be taken now."[518] In October 1992, Jiang Zemin proclaimed in the report at the 14th Party Congress that Pudong should be the leader opening up cities alongside the Yangtze River, build Shanghai as one of the centers of international economy, finance and trade and bringing a boost in the economy of the Yangtze River Delta and the entire Yangtze River. This, in fact, consolidated the strategically goal for the development of Pudong and Shanghai, which was also the first time the Party's Congress focused on a city's economic development.

6.4.2.2 Strategic Plan for Building the Core Functional Zone of Financial Center

The formation of a global financial center has its own specific geographical, economic, political and cultural background, but one of the common features is that they are all gathering places of financial institutions, client headquarters or operation center of financial institutions. Learning from the path of the formation of global major financial centers, firstly, headquarters or regional headquarters of financial service institutions gathered in a place, then followed by core institutions of global corporations. The gathering of financial institutions would provide the convenience for financial dealings, information flow among financial institutions, clients and other institutions and the formation of a powerful price of financial products.

Basically, the fate of an international financial center is determined by to what extent financial business and institutions gathered, because the more they gathered, the more likely the center would win in the future. So far, European financial experts still insist that

518 Resources: Selected Works of Deng Xiaoping, chapter 3, People's Publishing House, 1993, Page 366.

the gathering effect of a financial center mainly be seen at the increase of efficiency in trans-regional payment and financial resource allocation. Because the efficiency of a unitary financial center is similar to the efficiency of adding a unitary currency, when doing transactions, regions only deal with a unitary financial center. Therefore, banking and financial centers perform the functions of exchange medium and trans-regional store of value.

China is a developing country and, compared with developed countries, has an imperfect financial market, a low degree of marketisation and an underdeveloped modern financial industry, so it is difficult to build an influential global financial center within a short time if depended solely on the market. Considering the situation, the government, on one hand, could actively cultivate the financial market and attach more importance to the role of market in the financial resource allocation, but on the other hand, the imbalanced employed development strategy, which indicated taking the first-move advantage of places that were more suitable for financial centers construction as well as providing more support to these places.

For the sake of the building of Pudong's core functional zones of the financial center, the Central Committee took on many supportive policies. At the beginning phase of Pudong's development and opening up, four state-owned commercial banks established branches in Pudong, which created a unique picture in the nation of "two branches per bank in one city," which was Shanghai. During the ninth and tenth "Five-Year Plan," the Central Committee gave Pudong partly functional financial opening up policies. These policies included, the permission of foreign investment in financial industry, the permission of foreign financial institutions to run Reminbi business in Pudong, the permission of Pudong and Shenzhen to firstly experiment offshore banking business, and the permission of Shanghai Future Exchange to innovate new kinds of business. All these measures, taken by the Central Committee, expanded Pudong's scale of opening up and infused new blood into Pudong's financial industrial construction. Shanghai and Pudong New Area also strived to create a positive environment for Pudong's development of financial functions, in terms of hardware, encouraging banks and insurance corporations to accelerate their infrastructural constructions, like buildings and communication facilities, in respect of software, providing "Early and Pilot Implementation" policies with the right to experiment with new institutions, like creating new financial tools.

Another way was to attract financial institutions to settle in Pudong. In 1995, invited by Pudong New Area Management Committee, People's Bank of China found its branch in Lu Jiazui, under the influence of which Fuji Bank, HSBC, Citibank and Winterthur Swiss Insurance subsequently settled in Pudong. After Shanghai Stock Exchange's settlement in Pudong in 1997, Pudong's financial industry was boosted and followed by a lot more stock industries and companies, especially after the enforcement of the "Securities Law." On August 10, 2005, the Shanghai headquarter of the People's Bank of China officially established and would be settled in the central zone of Lu Jiazui, Pudong, while doing business at the branch building No. 181 in Lu Jiazui in the early period. By 2009, Pudong had 603 financial institutions that accounted for 80% of Shanghai's sum.[519] Among these institutions, there are famous transnational financial institutions such as Citibank, HSBC, SCB, Lloyds as well as significant Chinese funded financial institutions like ICBC, Bank of China, China Construction Bank, China Development Bank, Bank of Communications, Pudong Development Bank, Pacific Life Insurance Company and Orient Securities. Pudong has more than 20 headquarter-level business centers, like Credit Reference Center of People's Bank of China, China Construction Bank Credit Card Center, Bank of Communications Data Processing Center and new types of financial institutions, such as index company, money brokerage service and motor financial company. In the field of emerging financial industry, 15 foreign funded equity investment management companies were permitted to be registered, and the top 10 global private equities like Blackstone, Tessm, Apax Partners, one after another settled in Pudong. Construction of Lujiazui Financial City, Shanghai Shipyard and Shanghai Center accelerated. In May 2007, the definition of "Lujiazui Financial City" firstly emerged in the "11th Five-Year Plan of Financial Core Functional Areas Development of Pudong New Area in Shanghai." "National Strategy, Focusing on Shanghai and Pudong implementation" had been the official orientation of Lujiazui Financial City, and through a plan of widening eastward, small Lujiazui functional area will be enlarged from 1.7 km^2 to 28 km^2.

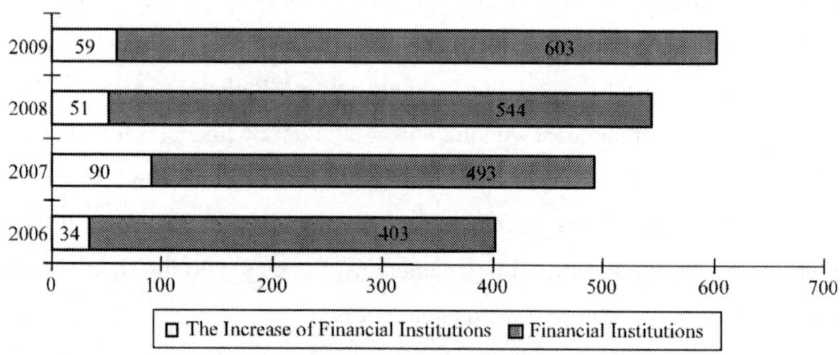

Figure 6-4-9 The Increase of Financial Institutions in Pudong New Area

Resources: *Shanghai Pudong New Area People's Government Bulletin*, No.1 2010; (http://www.pudong.gov.cn/website/html/shpd/201001/list/list_0.htm)

519 Resources: http://www.pudong.gov.cn/attach/infoattach/2008-06-0594097/2008-06-05620.doc#三

Table 6-4-1 Gathering of Financial Institutions in Pudong New Area, 2009

Type of Institutions	Degree of Gathering
Foreign Legal Person Bank	● 17 Foreign Legal Person Bank that accounts for about half of the nation's whose capital accounts for about 80% of the nation's. ● Nan Yang Commercial Bank settled in Pudong, SMBC and Calyon finished legal-personalization.
Asset Management Institutions	● 28 fund management companies which compose about half of the nation whose management fund property scale is approximately 900 billion yuan that composes 36% of the nation. ● The settlement of BNY Mellon Western Fund Management, Anderson Fund and Aviva has been actively promoted. ● Ping An Insurance Company and other four insurance asset management companies manage 1000 billion worth of asset which accounts for 43% of the nation's asset of insurance industry.
Securities and Direct Investment Enterprises	● Guotai Junan Securities, Shenyin Wanguo Securities, BOCI and Guoyuan Securities successively found direct investment companies in Pudong.
Functional and Subsidiary Institutions	● Securities Regulatory Bureau settled in Pudong, City Guarantee Company, CFMMC Shanghai headquarter, Xinhua 08, Alipay, Unicom Pay and so functional institutions have successively been found.

Resources: Shanghai Pudong New Area People's Government Bulletin, No.1 2010;
(http://www.pudong.gov.cn/website/html/shpd/201001/list/list_0.htm)

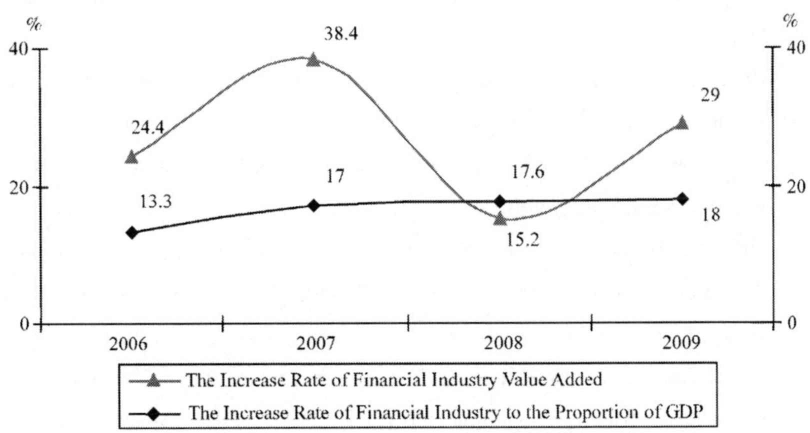

Figure 6-4-10 The Increase Rate of Financial Industry Value Added and its Ratio to the GDP of Pudong New Area

Resources: Shanghai Pudong New Area People's Government Bulletin, No.1 2010;
(http://www.pudong.gov.cn/website/html/shpd/201001/list/list_0.htm)

6.4.2.3 Improved Financial System of Pudong

Since the development and opening up, Pudong attached great importance to the construction of a financial market system and took advantage of the "Early and Pilot

Implementation" policy to create a positive market environment to attract national financial exchange to Pudong and make Pudong a major place for financial capital exchange. Pudong gathered, thus far, national and municipal financial elements market, which was the most integrated in the nation, including stock, futures, financial derivatives, and property right, and it owns multi-level market. In addition, the volume of the market is still widening. To be specific, these stock exchanges consisted of Shanghai Stock Exchange, Shanghai Futures Exchange, Shanghai Financial Futures Exchange, Shanghai United Assets and Equity Exchange, Shanghai Diamond Exchange and Shanghai White Platinum and Silver Exchange. All the exchanges mentioned above employed the aim of "Base on Shanghai, Serve the Nation, Face the World," and spared no effort in exploring operation regulatory and function development that contributed a great deal to building Shanghai onto an international financial center.

In 2009, Shanghai's Initial Public Offering (IPO) value and stock exchange value surpassed London and became number three in the world. In the meantime, Shanghai Stock Exchange's market value of shares was 2704.78 billion USD, and the value of stock exchange was 5061.98 billion USD, which surpassed Tokyo Stock Exchange, London Stock Exchange, HKSE, SSE and became the world's third biggest stock exchange after NYSE and NASDAQ.[520]

Meanwhile, Shanghai Futures Exchange's turnover had reached 435 million shares in 2009, with an increase of 210% each year and ranked the first in the world.

On April 8, 2009, the stock index futures were officially initiated in China Financial Futures Exchange which was a vital institutional innovation of capital market system and was compatible to national economic development. Stock index futures market, on the one hand, was beneficial for the improvement of Pudong's financial market system and structure, the founding of a multi-level capital market system, and the service capability of Pudong financial center. On the other hand, was beneficial for accelerating the financial gathering of Pudong, attracting financial institutions, best minds, capital and information, and strengthening the competitiveness and influence of Pudong as a financial center.

6.4.3 Development of Industry and Service Sector of Pudong New Area

6.4.3.1 Industrial Development of Pudong New Area

6.4.3.1.1 Overall View of Pudong's Industrial Development

After 20 years of development, accompanying the rapid expansion of the industrial

520 Resources: http://news.hexun.com/2010-04-09/123278790.html?from=rss.

economic scale of Pudong New Area, there was also improvement in the industrial level and quality, depending on foreign investment as well as new technology. Compared with Shenzhen and Hainan, who were Special Zones that were founded earlier, Pudong New Area had some industrial foundation before the development. Moreover, the development and opening up gave it remarkable development. In 2008, the industrial output value of Pudong New Area was 564.922 billion yuan, which was about 32 times greater that in 1990. Pudong's remarkable development in industry mainly depended on investments both domestically and internationally, while the former primarily came from the eastward movement of enterprises belonging to the Central Committee, national departments and Shanghai Municipality.

With the industrial structural adjustment and optimization of Pudong New Area, the ratio of industry to GDP inevitably dropped. Basically, the development path of Pudong's manufacturing was compatible to the law of evolution of industry, and, based on existed manufacture, the level of internal structure improved greatly. The results could be seen in the following: (1). with the change in the ratio of light industry to heavy industry in accordance with the economic management, the ratio increased, and the percentage of processing industry and assembly industry, two kinds of heavy industry, increased exponentially; (2). early industries, like textiles and food, possessed a small percentage, whereas modern manufacture, like electronic information devices manufacture and transportation equipments manufacture, possessed a large percentage; (3). with the development of processing industry, the export of mechanical and electronic products increased, while export of raw materials dropped; (4). innovative economy like high-tech industry developed very quickly.[521]

Table 6-4-2 Gross Industrial Output and Structure of Main Years of Pudong New Area (Unit: 100 million yuan)

Category	*1990*	*2000*	*2004*	*2005*	*2006*	*2007*	*2008*
Total	176.85	1635.77	3519.71	4242.47	4758.76	5188.12	5649.22
Light Industry	72.08	514.58	764.94	825.40	878.66	952.26	1070.62
Heavy Industry	104.77	1111.19	2754.77	3417.07	3880.10	4235.86	4578.6
State-owned	110.18	275.85	358.04	550.18	573.84	662.21	679.71
Mass-owned	49.09	70.91	49.09	38.67	36.87	34.89	31.60
Foreign Investment	7.07	1012.34	2461.66	2632.70	2980.46	3001.98	3088.54
Others	10.51	266.67	650.92	1020.92	1167.59	1489.04	1849.37

Resources: Shanghai Pudong New Area Statistical Yearbook, China Statistical Press, 2009.

521 Resources: http://www.pudong.gov.cn/website/understandPudong/infoContent.jsp?sj_dir=2007zhjjl&ct_id=174361

6.4.3.1.2 Gradual Atrophy of Traditional Industry and Emerging of Modern Manufacture of Pudong

Ever since the development and opening up of Pudong, the total amount and structure of secondary industry changed dramatically. The ratio of modern manufacture to secondary industry increased greatly. Advanced manufacture was a type of manufacture that absorbed information technology, new material technology, automatics and modern management and interacted with modern service sector. In 1990, traditional industry, like oil processing, steel, textiles and transportation equipments, were the pillars of Pudong's industry. The ratio of these four industries to gross industrial output were respectively 17.04%, 14.05%, 11.1% and 9.93%, and the total ratio was 52.12%. Nonetheless, in 2009, high-tech industrial output value was 176.718 billion yuan, which contributed 25.1% to the gross industrial output value of the New Area.

6.4.3.1.3 Development of Industry Cluster

Essentially, industries in Pudong New Area were developed in clusters. So far, there are approximately a few industrial clusters as following: (1) The core manufacture development strip between the inner and outer rings in which the important industrial cluster was advanced manufacture and high-tech. Dominated by Zhangjiang High-Tech Park, there are three high-tech industrial bases of microelectronics and information industry (national), biological medicine and Chinese medicine industry (national), and optoelectronics (municipal); centering on Jinqiao Export Processing zone, the area formed two industrial bases of automobile and automobile components, and semiconductor equipments; based on Waigaoqiao Free Trade Zone, it formed modern manufacture industrial base of electronic information and shipbuilding. (2) The outer ring, assorted with manufacture development ring, which was based on core manufacture development strip and took advantage of Pudong Airport and formed a gathering place for international business process outsourcing. Based on national development zone, it formed six industrial bases that provided subsidiary manufacture, automobile and components in Caolu town and Jinqiao town; high-tech industry in Tang town, Heqing town and Zhangjiang town; precision electronic, logistic equipment, aviation equipment and component in Shangchuan town and Jichang town; microelectronic, petrochemical industry and shipping in Gaodong town, Gaoqiao town and Gaoxing town. (3) The inner ring urban industrial development cluster. Around the inner ring and alongside the river, this ring formed a special, remarkable and mature urban industrial cluster, including fashion, package, advertisement, diamond design and processing, art souvenirs manufacture, print and food processing.

6.4.3.2 Real Estate Development in Pudong New Area

Since the development and opening up, Pudong experienced a rapid development in real estate, which greatly contributed to Pudong New Area's urban construction, urbanization and growth of national economy. Investment in real estate increased quickly and possessed a continuously higher percentage of the fixed assets capital. In 1995, real estate investment in Pudong New Area was 1.826 billion yuan, while in 2008, the number was 27.997 billion yuan, which was 15.3 times the amount in 1995. A quick growth of the ratio of real estate investment to fixed assets capital could also be seen as 6.4% in 1995 to 32% in 2008. In addition, foreign investment possessed a high percentage of the total. For example, in 2008, the total investment in real estate in Pudong was 55.455 billion yuan, while 27.979 billion yuan, 50% of the total, of which was from foreign funds.

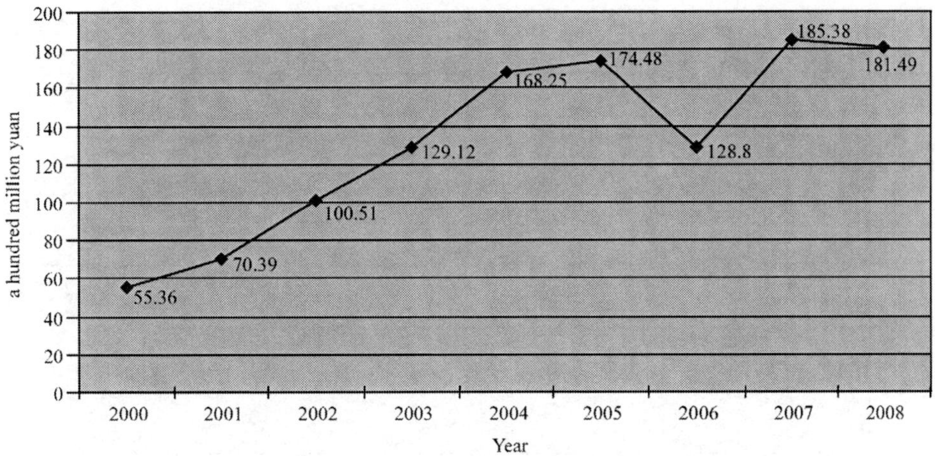

Figure 6-4-11 The Real Estate Industry of Pudong's GDP in Recent Years
Resources: Pudong New Area Statistical Yearbook, China Statistical Press, 2009

Along with the development of economy and the increase of the residents' income, people's demand for housing raised continuously, especially with the recent increase in national trade surplus, so as the foreign exchange reserve which resulted in excess liquidity. Due to lack of investment channel, much of capital flowed to real estate, so the price of housing was increased by the needs of actual housing and investment. In order to win political achievements, regional governments developed real estate and obtained income from land leasing fees. Objectively speaking, the development of real estate greatly contributed to Pudong's prosperity, especially in the early period, lack of money restrained infrastructural construction, but since it relied on land leasing, Pudong New Area government gain a great deal of money to, in turn, build infrastructure. However, since the land left to be developed became less, it was not sustainable enough to boost economy by land leasing and real estate, and was fragile to the influence of economic cycle and government macro-control policies. In the long run, Pudong's economy should depend more on modern service sectors, like finance and logistics and modern manufacture.

6.4.3.3 Development of Other Modern Service Sectors in Pudong New Area

6.4.3.3.1 Logistics Business in Pudong New Area

Ever since the development and opening up of Pudong, it has insisted on the strategy of "Finance and Trade First," and saw a sharp rise in trade. Total retail sales of consumer goods grew quickly from 36.7 times from the 1.428 billion yuan in 1990 to 52.689 billion yuan in 2008.[522] Business, based on the principle of "General Layout, Multi-level Arrangement,

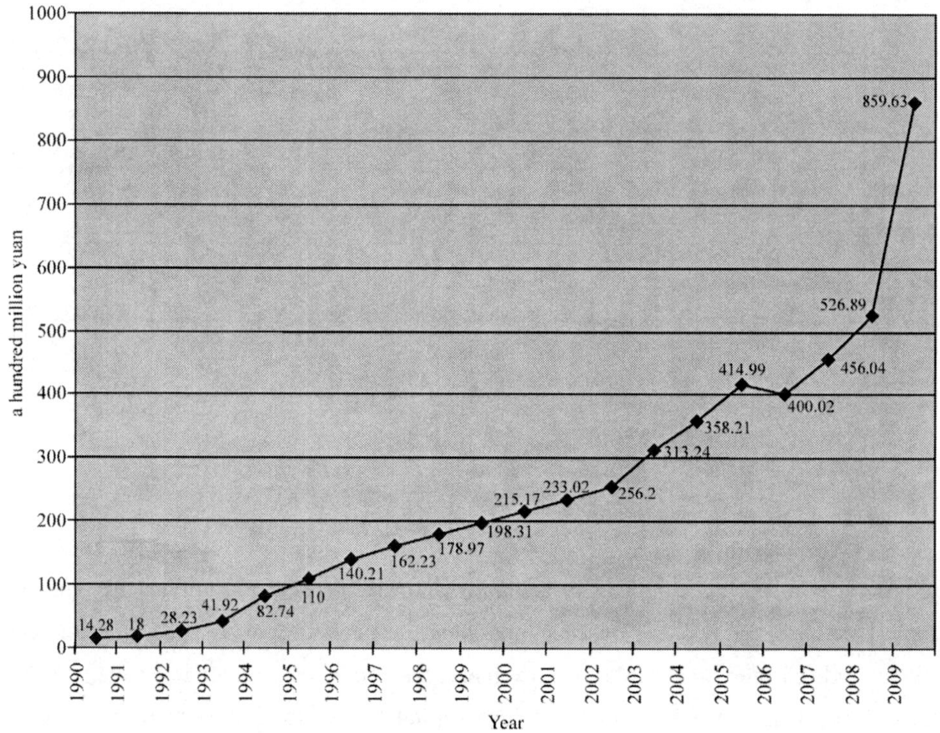

Figure 6-4-12 Retail Sales of Social Consumer Goods of Pudong New Area over the Years

Resources: Shanghai Pudong New Area Statistical Yearbook, China Statistical Press, 2009; Shanghai Pudong New Area People's Government Bulletin, No.1 2010; (http://www.pudong.gov.cn/website/html/shpd/201001/list/list_0.htm)

522 Resources: Pudong New Area Statistical Yearbook, China Statistical Press, 2009

Regional Orientation," saw a favorable development trend of a more reasonable layout and better structure, and developed three business circles in Pudong New Area: they were the urban business circle, community business circle and street-town business circle. Pudong central business zone was located in Lujiazui Financial Trade Zone, represented by the small Lujiazui area, New Shanghai Commercial City and Zhuyuan Commercial District, which was a core location of the Shanghai Central Business District and the "Four Centers" and was also the symbolic place with the function of cohesion and radiation since the development and opening up of Pudong. The business development of Pudong New Area Central Town relied on the respective advantages of geography, industry, transportation of each town to meet the demand of the multi-level, well-rounded, comprehensive and business service. The function of business development should also be able to show the functions of the image of urbanization, absorption of industrial radiation, the service to satisfy consumption, and lifting standards of living. In general, the main goal was to meet the needs of consumers of the mid-level and high-level, which were also compatible to a modern living environment, and meanwhile perform the main functions of a community business, which are services, recreation and education.

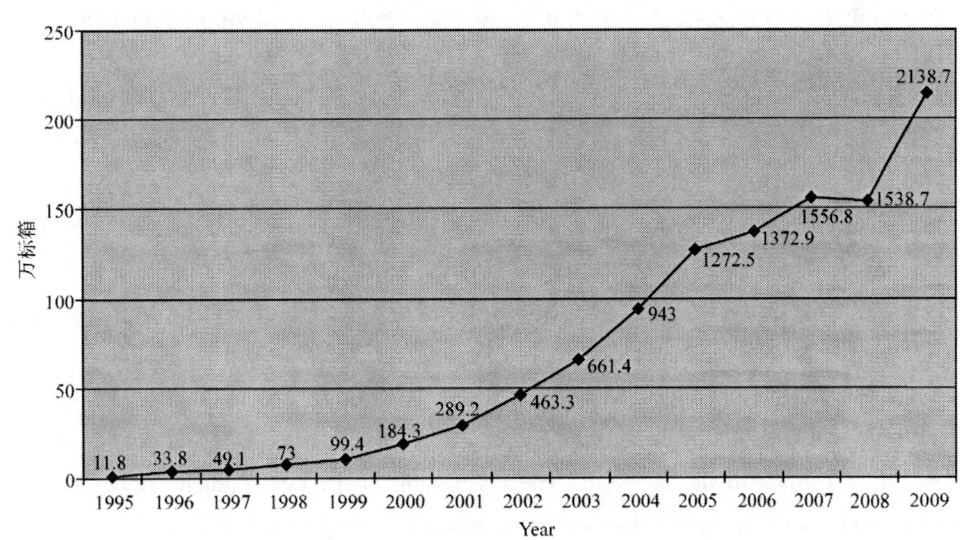

Figure 6-4-13 Container Throughput of Pudong New Area in Recent Years

Resources: Shanghai Pudong New Area Statistical Yearbook, China Statistical Press, 1996-2009; Shanghai Pudong New Area People's Government Bulletin, No.1 2010; (http://www.pudong.gov.cn/website/html/shpd/201001/list/list_0.htm)

Pudong's logistics experienced a boost since its development. During the tenth "Five-Year Plan" period, Pudong treated logistics as one of the four emerging industries that deserved special care and made many supportive policies. The favorable environment for Pudong New Area's logistics development had been gradually formed in a few years: the construction of infrastructure, information and policies had accomplished great achievements; the founding of four important logistics park had been actively propelled; and the settlement of ten global giant logistics enterprises, like UPS, Fedex, Deutsche Post and TNT and world's 20 shipping companies, include the A. P. Moller-Maersk, P&O, APL, OOCL. etc, constantly improved the level of Shanghai's logistics. Modern logistics contributed more and more to Pudong's economy. According to the relative industries of logistics, the growth rate increased year after year. Especially since 2000, the growth rate of logistics surpassed that of GDP and the ratio of logistics to GDP increased as well. In 2009, Yangshan Port and Waigaoqiao Port were supposed to achieve the container port throughput of 21 million tons, and 2.54 million tons of cargo throughputs for Pudong International Airport, which respectively accounted for about 85% of that of Shanghai.

6.4.3.3.2 Tourism, Convention and Exhibition Industry

To implement the strategy of making Shanghai the "Four Centers," Pudong New Area, as the leading role of Shanghai's reform and development, treated tourism and convention and exhibition as one of the vital industries, which showed a strong growth since Pudong's development. Annual meeting of Asian Development Bank, Asia-Pacific Economic Cooperation meeting and Shanghai International Industry Fair and other significant conventions and exhibitions had been successfully held in Shanghai that, to a large extent, showed the "brand effect" of Pudong's convention and exhibition industry. The scale of the industry had constantly expanded with a relatively high speed. The Expo planned to be held in Pudong Shanghai in 2010. According to experts, visitors might be over 70 million, but only the revenue of tickets, food, and souvenirs would be nine billion yuan. Moreover, the Expo will also promote the development of tourism, real estate, advertisement and business in Shanghai and peripheral cities. For the whole year, there will be approximately 105 exhibitions that will occupy 3.7 million square meters of exhibition area and obtain income of 6.5 billion yuan. In the meantime, the permission of the development of Disneyland would further promote the development of tourism of Pudong New Area.[523]

523 Shanghai Pudong New Area People's Government Bulletin, No.1 2010; (http://www.pudong.gov.cn/website/html/shpd/201001/list/list_0.htm)

Afterward

The idea of compiling and writing this book originated about seven years ago. Along with the deepening of China's reform and opening up and the general establishment of the market economy, Special Economic Zones (SEZs), the products of "special policies", have fulfilled its original role as "test fields" for the transition from a planned economy to a market economy. Meanwhile, its own function and its position in the transition society have also been inevitably changing.

The formation and growth of SEZs, as a structural breakthrough in China's structural transition, shows the development path of China's structural transition. Meanwhile, as "special policies", formed in the initial stage of reform and opening up in an attempt for structural transition, came to an end due to the institutional performance of reform, SEZs no longer purely played the role of "test fields" and "demonstration zones." As a profound mark in history, SEZs signified the beginning of a new era. As a far-reaching spiritual force, SEZs symbolized the awakening of a nation. With even a heavier responsibility to carry out more fundamental reforms, SEZs are bound to play their own part in the complete establishment of the market economy in China.

Considering that different SEZs were set up at different times, in different geographic areas, and with differentiated specific strategic orientations, this book studies each SEZ as an independent subject in each section to record each SEZ's unique development path.

Also, the book roughly arranges each SEZ in chronological order. For those that were established at the same time, i.e. Shenzhen, Zhuhai, Shantou, and Xiamen SEZs, Shenzhen SEZ is indisputably placed first, due to its very important role in China's structural transition. After Shenzhen are Zhuhai and Shantou, since these three cities are all located in Guangdong province. Pudong New Area of Shanghai is placed after Shenzhen, Zhuhai, Shantou, Xiamen and Hainan SEZs because it was established at a later time than the former five SEZs. In terms of administrative divisions, Pudong New Area is an independent district within the city of Shanghai, while the former five SEZs are all cities themselves. But of course, due to its special significance and regional effect, Pudong New Area occupies a preeminent position among the SEZs and development zones.

The publication of the first edition of this book marked the 30th anniversary of China's reform and opening up to the outside world. Therefore, we are well aware of the publication's significance, as the book is indeed a chronicle of China's structural transition during its transformation. However, the praise and affirmation the book received after publication still went beyond our expectation. In 2008, the year it was published, the Publicity Department of the Communist Party of China (PDCPC) designated the book as one of "the 35 books recording China's reform and opening up" to be recommended nationwide. In 2010, the National Planning Office of Philosophy and Social Science (NPOPSS) included the book in the "Translation Program for Chinese Academic Works" to be introduced worldwide. In 2011, the Guangdong Provincial Government awarded the book the first prize of "Excellent Works of Philosophy and Social Science." Meanwhile, Chinese and overseas scholars also thought highly of the book. We were grateful and proud of these achievements and, more importantly, they inspired us to continue our intellectual studies.

The second edition is revised on the basis of the first edition in 2008. We condensed the book from the original 800 thousand words to 450 thousand words, so as to be more refined and reader-friendly. In addition, historical facts and figures are now more abundant and accurate. We expanded the basic historical material indicating historical progress and time from December 30, 2008 to December 30, 2009. We re-sorted the major events of the SEZs and development zones in order to present their true history more accurately and we re-verified the sources of material so as to better conform to the academic norm.

It should be mentioned that the second edition adds a general introduction for each SEZ and development zone, which not only helps the reader to better grasp the historical development and characteristics of each SEZ and development zone, but also strengthens the validity of this book. The only disadvantage comes from the word limit for the translated version. We had to remove the two chapters of Binhai New Area of Tianjin and Chengdu-Chongqing National Urban and Rural Integrated Support Reform Pilot Area. These two areas, especially the latter, are not typical SEZs, but they are still an integral part of structural transition in China.

Tao Yitao
Shenzhen University
November 8, 2011

This book is the result of a co-publication agreement between Social Sciences Academic Press (China) and Paths International Limited (UK). This book is translated into English from the original《中国经济特区史论》with the financial support of the Chinese Fund for the Humanities and Social Sciences.

China's Economic Zones: Design, Implementation and Impact
Chief Editors: Tao Yitao & Lu Zhiguo
ISBN: 978-1-84464-102-4

Lightning Source UK Ltd.
Milton Keynes UK
UKOW010854050412

190214UK00004B/6/P

9 781844 641024